THE MEDIEVAL AND RENAISSANCE WORLD

GENERAL EDITOR: ESMOND WRIGHT

HAMLYN
London · New York
Sydney · Toronto

List of contributors
Walter Ullmann
Michael Angold
Barrie Dobson
G. R. Potter
Leonard Cowie
C. A. Burland
Geoffrey Hindley
J. C. Holt
J. B. Harrison
Robert Knecht
Anthony Bryer
Thomas Trautmann
L. K. Young
Michael Gough
J. H. Parry
V. J. Parry
J. R. Hale

Published by
The Hamlyn Publishing Group Limited
London · New York · Sydney · Toronto
Astronaut House, Hounslow Road, Feltham, Middlesex, England

Original text

Revised and updated 1979
This edition

ISBN 0 600 36328 7

Filmset in the United Kingdom by Tradespools Ltd., Frome, Somerset

Printed and bound in Spain
by Graficromo, S. A. – Córdoba

Part III
THE HIGH MIDDLE AGES
Page 110

SCLAUINIA
GIRMANIA
GALLIA
ROMA

Part I

THE AGE OF FEUDALISM

Introduction

'The western world', 'western ideals', 'the western way of life': these are common enough phrases in the political jargon of the twentieth century. Behind them lie three great historical developments: the industrial revolution of the eighteenth and nineteenth centuries which determined the economic growth of the west; the Renaissance and Reformation of the fifteenth and sixteenth centuries which established its frame of mind; and feudalism. To many this last may seem surprising, for 'feudal' and 'feudalism' have come to stand for outworn and moss-grown antiquity; for useless, even oppressive institutions. Yet the age of feudalism was not like this. It was constructive, not restrictive; it was the age in which western Europe was founded.

In the last years of the Roman Empire, in the fourth and fifth centuries AD, western Europe was simply part of a Mediterranean world which included the coast of North Africa, Egypt, Syria and Asia Minor and stretched to the mouth of the Danube and to the Caucasus. Its twin political centres were Rome and Constantinople. Its economic life was centred on North Africa, the eastern Mediterranean and the Bosporus. The western provinces, important though some of them were, lay near or on the fringe of a vast and cumbersome society. Gaul was less important than Greece, and Spain scarcely matched Syria. From the East the empire derived its thought, its art and finally, with the spread of Christianity, its religion.

By the end of the thirteenth century this world had undergone drastic change. Italy was still part of western Europe and provided an important strand of continuity with ancient Rome and the old Mediterranean civilizations. Likewise, Mediterranean trade was still vital to the European economy. However, the lands north of the Alps were now no longer peripheral. Indeed, many of the most characteristic features of western civilization were now to be found, not in Italy, but in Germany, England and the Netherlands and, most important of all, in France. Western Europe, as it is now understood, had taken shape.

This new Europe was not created at any one time or by any one circumstance. The unity of the Mediterranean world was broken by the settlement of Germanic tribes from across the Rhine and Danube in the western provinces of the empire in the fifth and sixth centuries and by the Arab conquest of the eastern and southern shores of the Mediterranean in the seventh century. Henceforth, the old Roman Empire was confined to a decreasing sphere of influence in the eastern Mediterranean. In the West imperial government was replaced by a number of tribal kingdoms, all of which were based on a mixture of Roman and Germanic civilization. The East was Greek in speech and Hellenistic in thought. The West was to a varying degree Latin in its language and intellectual inheritance from the Roman world.

These great movements of population and shifts in power created the basic political geography for the growth of western Europe. They did not of themselves create a thriving society. This was established slowly. One element in it was provided by the steady colonization of new land both within the old imperial provinces and in Germany and central Europe. Slowly at first, more quickly after AD 1000, the population increased and the standard of living improved. The pattern of rural settlement in villages and hamlets which had been established by 1300 has largely survived to our own day: modern villages are medieval villages. At the same time trade and wealth expanded northwards. Great new economic centres and trading links were established in the Rhineland, the Baltic, the fairs of Champagne and the valleys of the Seine, the Loire and the Scheldt. New staple items of trade, such as English wool, Flemish cloth and Baltic furs, rivalled the old luxury trade of the Mediterranean basin. The western provinces of the Roman Empire had been drained of precious metals by an adverse balance of trade with the East. The newly rich countries of northern and western Europe expressed their independence in their reliance on silver currencies of local manufacture rather than the gold which continued in use in the Mediterranean.

This was accompanied by the establishment of the states which have dominated the history of western Europe: Germany, France, England, the Spanish monarchies and the Baltic kingdoms. These new states established the conditions of stability necessary for economic expansion. They in turn fed upon this increasing wealth to support the burden of administration at home and aggression abroad. They were competitive and quarrelsome. The Spanish monarchies were founded on the ruins of the power of the Moors. The German kings and dukes pressed eastwards from their original centre of power on the Rhine over the Elbe to the Oder. From the Baltic states in the north Viking adventurers sailed west to Iceland, Greenland and finally to America. England, at first the prey of the Vikings and the Normans, subsequently turned to the conquest of the Welsh, the Irish and the Scots.

However, it was above all in the south that

this aggression was concentrated. Here was the lure of the old Mediterranean world. Here men's eyes turned to Rome as the centre of Christendom. Here, moreover, there were rich pickings: the luxury trade with the east and the wealth of Venice, Milan and the other towns of northern Italy. The kings of Germany, as Holy Roman emperors, waged numerous campaigns for the control of Italy. Norman adventurers arrived to found a well-organized, wealthy and aggressive kingdom in southern Italy and Sicily. Men from every province of western Europe came to the Mediterranean to visit the holy places and to fight in the Crusades.

This was also the first great age of European expansion. Within 100 years of Leif Ericsson's voyage to America Frankish and Norman knights were establishing their rule at Antioch and over the Euphrates at Edessa. Not all these efforts were successful. The Crusader states, in particular, did not last; but it was through this expansion that western Europe became conscious of its own identity.

The abundance of energy which went into this expansion was not all destructive. At the fringes it is now represented by the poverty-stricken archaeological remains of the Viking settlements on the west coast of Greenland and by the vacant walls of the crusader castles in Syria. However, in western Europe itself it established much of the framework of our life today. The age of feudalism has bequeathed to Europe languages, to a great degree national and political boundaries (and even the wars which have arisen over them), very frequently units of local government (the English counties or the German and Swiss provinces) and in many countries the framework of law. It has left not only its churches, but its dioceses and its parishes. It

has, moreover, left much that can be enjoyed. No later age has excelled the architecture of the great cathedral and monastic churches of the Romanesque and Gothic styles. Few later poets have matched the epic quality of the *Song of Roland*.

To some extent these are fossil remains. We no longer speak the language of Shakespeare, still less that of Chaucer. It may be argued that, if medieval institutions have survived, this is because they have been adjusted to our purposes; their origins no longer matter. Yet the real importance of the age of feudalism lies not so much in these survivals as in the scope which it gave to human endeavour. The lot of the medieval serf was hard, but he was not a slave. His condition was better and his energies better applied than those of the agrarian worker of the Roman Empire. The feudal baron often stood for anarchy and lawlessness, but it was men of this class who organized the colonization of new land, who founded ports and chartered towns, and who acted as the patrons and benefactors of the new monastic orders.

Our chief inheritance from this age is in feudalism itself. Feudal society was hierarchical. It attached specific functions to particular social grades: the priest prayed, the knight fought and the peasant ploughed. However, it also attached an idea of rights to this restrictive social doctrine, so that a knight, a priest and even a peasant might protest in defence of the rights associated with their status. Although the peasant rarely had the power or opportunity to do this openly or effectively, the knight or priest could act and frequently did so. That political activity which now seems so anarchical was the practical expression of an attempt to form a human society in which individuals might appeal to rights as well as perform functions. These rights were not yet viewed as individual, still less as natural, rights. They were regarded rather as property—as privileges which the holder might defend in a court of law or on the field of battle.

From feudal privileges to the modern idea of individual rights is a long road which has cost much thought and many lives. Nevertheless, the two concepts are linked and it is no accident that they both found their clearest expression in western Europe.

Above, Charlemagne's horsemen besieging a castle. Charlemagne imposed a central organization on his army for the first time and set up a training school for the knights at Aachen. Landesmuseum für Vorgeschichte, Halle.

Top, panel from the Franks Casket, a small whalebone box made in Northumbria, England, in about 700. It shows a combination of Latin and Germanic styles and also of Christian and pagan themes. British Museum, London.

On page 8, illumination from the Gospel of the Emperor Otto III, made in about 1000. It shows the four main states of Christendom – Germany, France, Rome and Slavonia – doing homage to the Emperor. Staatsbibliothek, Munich.

Chapter 1

From Charlemagne to the Feudal Age

The period between the fall of Rome and the coronation of Charlemagne in 800, which was also the golden age of Islam, is commonly called the dark age of European history. However, in the chaos that followed the collapse of the Roman Empire, Europe acquired an identity, discovering and developing a new form of social organization which enabled it to confront and later to conquer its enemies. This new social organization was feudalism, which came into being when France in the West and Byzantium in the East were both menaced by the seemingly irresistible Arab armies.

As the barbarians broke through the frontiers of the Roman Empire and swept over the countryside, Ammianus Marcellinus, the last great Roman historian, writing in the latter half of the fourth century AD, described how one could see 'women driven along by cracking whips, and stupified with fear, still heavy with their unborn children, which, before coming into the world, endured many horrors'. The fall of Rome brought tragedy and suffering to many people, and to others it brought despair and despondency. It was the end of the world they had known, and the future seemed hopeless. Yet Rome continued to influence Europe's development, and when the new age of feudalism came into being it inherited and preserved much of that ancient civilization.

The extinction of Roman power and the collapse of its political structure did not also result in the elimination of its culture or the disappearance of its way of life. Many generations before the Roman Empire came to an end, its ideas had been spread throughout its conquered provinces. When their political links with Rome were broken by the barbarian invasions, these distant countries resumed their separate existence, but the old influences remained embedded in their outlook and beliefs, and in their laws and institutions.

The legacy of ancient Rome was preserved for the western world in three main ways: the Byzantine Empire in the east, which maintained Roman tradition and influence for a thousand years after the fall of Rome itself; the medieval Catholic Church, centred in Rome, which preserved much of the language, laws and sense of unity of Rome; and the Holy Roman Empire, which was an attempt to revive the old Roman Empire in the West.

The Church and the barbarians

When the last emperor ceased to rule in Rome, its bishop remained, acquiring the title of pope and attaining the foremost place among the other bishops of the Church. Moreover, as the Roman imperial administration collapsed in the west before the barbarian invasions, the papacy was the most stable institution in Italy to survive and in many ways took the place of the old emperors. The English political philosopher, Thomas Hobbes, said in the seventeenth century, 'the papacy is none other than the ghost of the deceased Roman Empire, sitting crowned upon the grave thereof.' The pope inherited quite naturally from pagan Rome, the costume, ceremonies and administrative court which came to be associated with his office. He was not only the Christian leader and protector of religious orthodoxy but also a leaven of Roman civilization working within the barbarian mass which had overwhelmed western Europe.

In some of the conquered provinces the bishops similarly survived, and ecclesiastical organization was similar to the old imperial system. The regional dioceses corresponded to the empire's territorial divisions. The canon law of the Church was strongly influenced by Roman legal ideas. Latin remained the language of worship, scholarship, administration and diplomacy. Moreover, as Christianity continued to spread, the Roman influence reached regions the Romans had never ruled.

The most effective means by which the Church could spread and preserve its faith and civilized values was through the monastery. The real founder of western monasticism was St Benedict, who established the great Italian monastery of Monte Cassino and therein about 540 wrote his famous rule, which in the next three centuries was adopted by monks throughout Italy and most of western Europe.

The rule assigned a definite proportion of the monk's daily life to worship, meditation, study and manual labour. It contained all that was needful for the management of a self-sufficient religious community living on the produce of its land. Such was the essential character of Benedictine monasticism. Each monastery was independent, and if one were destroyed (as Monte Cassino was by the Lombards in 581) other survived and carried the essentials of western life through the worst times.

It was Benedictine monks, led by St Augustine of Canterbury, who went in 597 to evangelize the Anglo-Saxons in England. Shortly afterwards St Columbanus took a band of Irish monks to France, working first in Brittany and then in the Vosges district where he founded the great abbey at Luxeuil. In the first part of the eighth century St Boniface, a monk from Devon went to Germany and evangelized Bavaria, Hesse, Friesland, Thuringia and Franconia. Here he established many abbeys and nunneries, with schools attached which he staffed with monks and nuns from England. These were the institutions which, with their learning, teaching and copying of manuscripts, became the centres of civilization in western Europe.

The Germanic kingdoms

The Barbarians who invaded the northern provinces of the Roman Empire in the fourth and fifth centuries were Germanic peoples driven westwards by the Huns, a nomadic race which emerged from central Asia and penetrated into Europe and India. The Germans, unlike the Huns, settled permanently within the Empire, which by the early sixth century consisted of (apart from the Eastern Roman Empire) five great Germanic states.

The first of these to be formed was the Visigothic kingdom, centred upon Toulouse and including Spain, which was founded by Goths who crossed the Danube. The Ostrogothic kingdom was founded in Italy and Illyria by other Goths who crossed the Danube. Another Germanic tribe, the Vandals, crossed the Rhine and eventually established the Vandal kingdom by conquering the Roman provinces of North Africa.

The Germanic people who later played the most important part in the history of western Europe were the Franks, who crossed the Rhine into Gaul. Their ruler, Clovis, who was baptized at Reims in 506, gradually extended the Frankish kingdom until it stretched from the Rhine to the Pyrenees.

This Germanic division of the Roman Empire did not, however, remain long unchanged. Justinian, who became Byzantine

Left, Pepin the Short (714–68), the son of Charles Martel; he ousted the powerless Merovingian kings, and in return for assisting the papacy in Lombardy was anointed king in 751 by the pope. Propsteikirche, Petersberg bei Fulde.

Far left, late Roman bas-relief in terra cotta, showing a barbarian. Although well-armed, he is showing little hostility to the Romans, whose civilization the barbarian invaders were for the most part anxious to share. Musée de Saint-Germain, Paris.

Opposite, the tomb of a central European of about 700, presumably a military leader. Although the composition is based on a Christian model the style is entirely Scandinavian. Abbey of Saint-Gallen.

emperor in 527, wished to reassert imperial authority in the West. His brilliant general, Belisarius, crossed to Carthage, drove out the Vandals and regained for Justinian a large part of the former Roman possessions in North Africa. He then led an expedition to Italy and by 553 had expelled the Ostrogoths from the country. Soon after Justinian's death in 565, however, another Germanic people, the Lombards, moved into Italy and by 572 had conquered almost the whole north and Tuscany. The territory regained by Justinian in North Africa was also lost. In the seventh century it was conquered by the Arabs, who in the next century also overran Spain and destroyed the Visigothic kingdom.

The Frankish kingdom

Of the Germanic kingdoms established within the Roman Empire, only the Frankish kingdom remained, but under the Merovingian dynasty it might well have collapsed. The Franks followed more closely than their rivals the barbarian custom of dividing their kingdom, in the manner of a family estate, among a dead ruler's sons. The result was a series of family conflicts which gravely weakened the crown. Dagobert (629–39) was the last Merovingian king to wield effective power. After his death the three main regions of the Frankish territory—Neustria, Austrasia and Burgundy—asserted their right to be separate kingdoms, even when subject to one king.

In each of these divisions effective power was in the hands of the strongest nobleman, 'the mayor of the palace'. The great families struggled with each other for this position, while the later Merovingian kings, feeble nonentities, were largely kept in seclusion on their estates. Unity was at length restored by the mayor of Austrasia, Charles Martel, who by 719 had compelled the whole Frankish kingdom to acknowledge his supremacy.

Meanwhile, the Arabs, having conquered Spain, invaded southern Gaul. In response to an appeal for help from the Duke of Aquitaine, Charles Martel assembled a great Frankish army which met the Arabs under the walls of Poitiers in 732. The Arab horsemen dashed vainly against the close-locked lines of Frankish infantry, protected by mail-shirts and shields, and were overwhelmed. They retreated across the Pyrenees and did not renew the invasion. The victor received the name of Martel ('the Hammer'). The Franks regained their prestige and their leadership.

The Carolingians

Shortly before his death in 741, Charles Martel divided his power between his sons, Carloman and Pepin, but Carloman abdicated to become a monk in 747. Four years later, Pepin, known as 'the Short' because of his slight stature, banished to a monastery the last descendant of Clovis, the young Childeric III. He was then proclaimed king by the Frankish noblemen and became the founder of the Carolingian dynasty.

Unlike previous Frankish kings, however, Pepin became king not only by election but also with the blessing of the Church. He obtained from Pope Zacharias the decree that he who held the power should also have the name of king, and he was anointed by St Boniface. He was now king 'by the grace

of God' and 'the Lord's anointed' like David in the Old Testament.

Henceforward, there was a new connection between the papacy and the Carolingian monarchy. The papacy was now in danger of subjection to the Lombard kingdom, and when a Lombard army besieged Rome Pope Stephen II, after turning in vain to the Byzantine emperor for help, crossed the Alps to seek Pepin's assistance.

By two raids into Italy, Pepin forced the Lombards to withdraw their threat to Rome and to surrender their conquests from the empire. These territories, lying in the Romagna and the Marches, were not restored by Pepin to Byzantine rule but by the Donation of Quierzy in 756 were conferred on the pope as the legitimate representative of imperial power. This expedient crippled the Lombards, the most formidable rival of the Franks, but it also founded the papal states, independent of any temporal power, upon which great papal ambitions were later based.

At his death in 768 Pepin divided his kingdom between his sons, Carloman and Charles. But within three years Carloman was dead, and Charles the Great (as Charlemagne) easily secured recognition as sole king.

Contrary to the legendary portrait, Charlemagne was short and stout and did not have a 'flourishing beard'. He liked swimming and riding. Unassuming, he attached little importance to ceremony. He lived with several concubines by whom he had many children. Expressing himself easily and fond of the liberal arts, he was a particularly cultured sovereign for his time.

TSYRIAM SOBAL · ET CONVERTIT
IOAB · ET PERCUSSIT EDOM IN VAL
LE SALINARUM XII MILIA ·

Above, Charlemagne mourning for the death of his warriors in the background of this relief; his troops were campaigning, especially in Germany, for almost every year of his reign. Aachen Cathedral.

Above left, Charlemagne's horsemen, from a manuscript of the Golden Book of Charlemagne. *Continual expeditions, to Saxony, Bohemia, the Pyrenees and Italy, made Charlemagne and his knights feared throughout Europe. Abbey of Saint-Gallen.*

Opposite, Charlemagne being crowned emperor by the pope on Christmas Day 800; the coronation symbolized the alliance between the Frankish kingdom and the papacy and exacerbated the break between Rome and Constantinople.

He spoke Latin, understood Greek and earnestly received instruction from teachers of rhetoric, logic, astronomy and mathematics. He tried to learn to read, 'but his efforts met with little success because he had started too late', reported Eginhard, his chronicler. Though he did not allow churchmen to restrict the lusty behaviour of his vigorous private life, he was very pious and thought himself strictly bound to respect the Church's teaching.

Charlemagne was soon involved in Italian affairs. In 773 he crossed the Alps at Pope Hadrian's entreaty after Didier, the Lombard king, had captured some cities included in Pepin's Donation and had even menaced Rome. Having starved Pavia into surrender and sent Didier in captivity to a Frankish monastery, Charles annexed the whole of Lombard territory except Spoleto (which submitted to the Papacy) and Benevento. He declared himself king of the Lombards and took their famous iron crown, appointing his second son, Pepin, still a child, as his viceroy. Finally, he visited Hadrian in Rome and confirmed the Donation of Quierzy.

Charlemagne's empire

Charlemagne fought a long series of wars during his reign and made many conquests. He was prompted by both political considerations and personal ambition, but his wars had also a religious character. He sincerely wished to protect and extend Christendom. All these motives led him to attempt the conquest of Spain. Taking advantage of the continual civil wars of the Spanish Muslims, he led an army across the Pyrenees in 778; but he made little progress, and on his return his rear-guard was attacked and massacred by the Basques of Navarre, a disaster remembered in the famous *Song of Roland* of the twelfth century. Charlemagne, however, persevered in his Spanish policy, and in 811 his eldest son conquered the territory known as the Spanish March; this was the first Muslim province recovered for Christendom in Spain.

The fiercest and most constant of Charlemagne's wars was that against the Saxons; this too was a crusade against German heathenism as much as a campaign of conquest. The Saxons had changed little since their ancestors had invaded England in the late fifth and early sixth centuries. They were a fierce, warlike people devoted to their ancient gods. Year after year, from 772, Charlemagne led his forces against them, only to have them rise and overwhelm his garrisons as soon as he withdrew. He resorted to the wholesale decapitation of their leaders and the deportation of thousands of Saxons to the west to make way for Frankish colonists. The Saxons did not finally submit until 785.

Charlemagne's determination to unite all Germany under the Franks led him to seize the duchy of Bavaria in 788. The duke was compelled to become a monk, and his two sons and two daughters had also to abandon their luxurious palace in Ratisbon for Frankish abbeys. The Bavarians, in fact, gained from Charlemagne both good government and protection. When their country was invaded by the Avars, a heathen race akin to the Huns, who had settled on the middle Danube, he waged such ruthless campaigns against them that by 796 they had almost vanished as a people. Their vacant lands made possible German expansion northeastwards.

By the end of the eighth century Charlemagne had a vast realm stretching from the Elbe to beyond the Pyrenees and from the North Sea to central Italy. Once again most of western Europe was united under a single empire, ruled by a Christian sovereign who had enlarged the bounds of the Church by his conquests. The popes were well aware of the value of strengthening their links with the Carolingian dynasty and endowing it with the prestige of past tradition.

In the year 800 Charlemagne was in Rome, having marched into Italy to support Pope Leo III against his rebellious Roman subjects, and on Christmas Day, at the end of mass, while he still knelt before the shrine of St Peter, the pope rewarded him by placing a golden crown on his head and saluting him as 'Carolus Augustus, Emperor of the Romans'. The crowd shouted, 'God bless and save Carolus Augustus, crowned of God, the great and peace-bringing Emperor of the Romans', and the pope then fell at his feet to pay homage to him in the same manner as the bishops of Rome had formerly done to the Roman emperors at Constantinople.

The pope's action came at a favourable moment. In 797 the Empress Irene, widow of the Byzantine emperor Leo IV, had blinded and deposed her son, Constantine VI, and proclaimed herself sole ruler. Many doubted whether a woman could hold this position. Charlemagne considered marrying Irene, until she was ousted in 802 by Nicephorus I, who refused to recognize him. Charlemagne proceeded to attack Venice, the only remaining Byzantine dependency in northern Italy, but the lack of a fleet prevented him from carrying out any effective action. Events turned in his favour, however, when Nicephorus was killed fighting the Bulgarians, and in 814 Charlemagne obtained reluctant Byzantine recognition of his imperial title. Meanwhile, the Persians had welcomed Charlemagne's coronation as a blow to their Byzantine enemies, and Harun ar-Rashid, the caliph of Baghdad, sent courteous gifts to him.

The coronation of Charlemagne intensified the division between East and West. There were now two emperors, a Frank and a Byzantine. It also emphasized the religious differences between the two empires, for the pope saw in Charlemagne's coronation a mark of his hostility towards the Byzantine emperors who had supported the iconoclastic heresy which opposed the use of images in worship.

For contemporaries the coronation did not represent a new development. On the contrary, they believed that they had moved back 400 years to the time before the break-up of the Roman world when there had been peace and unity in western Europe. Charlemagne himself, however, seemed to regard his new title as only a personal distinction. In 806 he even decided to divide his lands among his sons according to the traditional Frankish manner, but this was not to be. When he died in 814, at the age of seventy-five, only one of his sons survived him.

Charlemagne ruled his territory as an autocrat with the assistance of his household

officers, who accompanied him wherever he went and were employed in various capacities in peace and war. For counsel he relied upon his trusted friends, both noblemen and ecclesiastics, whom he summoned to his presence either temporarily or permanently. However, as later events showed, in the end the government of the empire depended upon the wisdom and energy of the ruler alone.

Under Charlemagne local government continued on the old Frankish lines. On the marches or frontier districts, dukes or margraves ruled several counties, but elsewhere between 200 and 250 counts each governed a county, usually identical with a bishop's diocese, and were responsible for administrative, judicial and military matters. The link between them and the ruler was provided by envoys or *missi dominici*, whom the earlier Merovingians had first employed to perform particular duties in the provinces.

The ultimate guarantee of good government, however, depended upon the personality of the ruler. His presence alone in a locality could impose his decision on the counts and noblemen and ensure the preservation of order and justice. Consequently, Charlemagne led a life of continual journeying from one end to another of his vast realm. After 808, when illness confined him to Aachen, his capital, his decrees or directions revealed the continual spread of abuses.

The Carolingian renaissance

Charlemagne's empire did not last. Its government collapsed, its unity vanished and its prosperity declined. Its influence on the renewal of civilization in Europe was, however, more enduring. In alliance with the Church and encouraged by Charlemagne, there was a revival of learning and culture of sufficient importance to be termed the Carolingian renaissance.

Charlemagne's first concern was to improve the standard of education among the clergy, many of whom were very ignorant. He ordered the establishment in all the dioceses of his empire of elementary parochial schools and higher schools attached to abbeys or cathedrals for the training of the clergy of the future, and he even attempted to make parish priests undertake teaching. More books were written and monastic libraries enlarged.

Though it was rare for laymen to be educated, Charlemagne had a palace school in which his sons and young noblemen were taught. This school became an important intellectual centre. Charlemagne and his courtiers, despite their years, set an example

THE FRANKISH EMPIRE, ENGLAND AND THE EAST

Date	The Frankish Empire	England	Byzantium and Islam
600		Spread of Christianity	
	Dagobert I (628–39)		Death of Mohammed (632)
		St Augustine founds see of Canterbury (602)	
	Decline of the Merovingians		Arab conquest of Persia
		Edwin of Deira, king of Northumbria (617–33)	
	Pepin of Herstal: mayor of Austrasia (679); ruler of the Franks (687–714)	Synod of Whitby (664)	Constantine IV (668–85)
		Venerable Bede (*c.* 673–735)	
700	Charles Martel (715–41)	Aethelbald king of Mercia (716–57)	Arabs conquer Spain
	Pepin the Short (751–68) founds the Carolingian dynasty		Leo III the Isaurian (717–41)
		Offa king of Mercia (757–96)	Muslim army defeated at Poitiers (732)
	Charlemagne king of the Franks (768–814)	Offa defeats West Saxons (776)	Harun al Rashid (786–809)
	Charlemagne Emperor of the West (800)	First Viking raids	

Date	The Frankish Empire		England	Byzantium and Islam
800	Louis the Pious (814–40)		Egbert king of Wessex (802–39)	Arabs occupy Sicily
	Division of the Frankish Empire (843)		Egbert recognized as overlord of England (828)	Arabs in Rome (846)
				Basil I (867–86)
	France	**Germany**	Viking raids resumed (838)	Aghlabids in North Africa
			Danish kingdom at York (866)	
	Charles the Bald (843–77)	Louis the German (843–76)	Alfred the Great (871–900)	
	Vikings devastate large areas in France	Magyar invasions	Danelaw established (878)	
900	Rollo, first duke of Normandy (911)	Louis the Child (899–911), last Carolingian king in Germany	Athelstan king of England (925–39)	Expansion of Byzantium
		Henry the Fowler (919–36)	Edmund king of England (959–75)	Romanus I Lecapenus (919–44)
	Louis V (986–7), last Carolingian king in France	Otto the Great Holy Roman Emperor (936–73)	Aethelred the Unready (978–1016)	Caliphate of Cordoba
	Hugh Capet (987–96) founds the Capetian dynasty	Magyars defeated at Lechfeld (955)	New Viking raids on England (980)	
1000		Otto III (983–1002)		Fatimids in Egypt

by applying themselves to study. Lectures, discussions on all sorts of subjects and charades or riddles in verse became the fashion at court. Charlemagne himself delighted in theological discussion, and his favourite book was St Augustine's *City of God*.

The best of Charlemagne's teachers came from abroad. Peter of Pisa, the grammarian, and Paul the deacon, the historian of the Lombards, were from Italy, while Theodulf the Visigoth, the best writer of Latin verse of the day, was from Spain. The greatest of all was an Englishman, Alcuin, who came from the famous episcopal school at York. Alcuin prepared a more correct text of the Vulgate (or Latin Bible) and a revision of the Church services which has become the basis of the present-day Roman mass-book.

The dissolution of the Carolingian Empire

Charlemagne was succeeded by his son, Louis the Pious (814–840), who in 817 made his eldest son, Lothar, co-emperor with authority over Lothar's two younger brothers, who were allotted frontier kingdoms. In 823, however, Louis had another son, Charles (later named 'the Bald'), by his second wife, who was determined to secure an inheritance for her child. The result was a series of partition schemes and civil wars between different members of the royal house which continued after the death of Louis. Finally Lothar was defeated at the battle of Fontenoy in 841 by an alliance between his two surviving brothers, Louis the German and Charles the Bald, who united themselves by the famous Strasbourg Oaths, which, significantly for the future, were taken, not in Latin, but in the two languages spoken by the fighting troops, French and German. The two sides were obliged to make terms and in 843 concluded the Treaty of Verdun, which divided the Carolingian Empire into three parts.

Lothar received the title of emperor and a long tract of territory reaching from Italy to the North Sea, which included Rome and Aachen and the great trade route joining Friesland to the Po Valley. Charles obtained the western part and Louis the eastern; these roughly corresponded to modern France and Germany.

This division was not permanent. The middle kingdom, Lotharingia, soon became a prey to its neighbours. Part of it was secured by France and part by Germany; a considerable region round the Rhône became a separate kingdom, called Burgundy or Arles. The emperor retained only Italy, and after the deposition of the last Carolingian emperor, Charles the Fat, in 887 the country fell into disorder. Although several minor princes were crowned emperors and kings of Italy, the title was meaningless, and finally it disappeared. The imperial venture had failed. Three modern countries, France, Germany and Italy, had appeared.

The decay of the Frankish Empire exposed western Europe to attacks from fresh invaders—the Arabs in the south, the Magyars or Hungarians in the east and the Scandinavians in the north.

The Magyars, a mixed Finno-Turkish collection of nomadic tribes, moved over the the Carpathians from the banks of the Dnieper into the middle Danube basin in about the year 896. They soon spread terror among the neighbouring peoples by their raids in which they burnt villages and farms, killed the men and took away the women and cattle. Only fortified towns and castles escaped their attentions.

At first they advanced to the borders of Italy and then into Saxony and Bavaria. From 912 they penetrated still further, into Swabia, Thuringia, Lorraine and even Burgundy. Then they crossed the Alps and from 921 to 926 ravaged northern Italy and Tuscany. By the middle of the century, however, their power had declined, and in 955 they

Opposite, Louis the Pious receiving the ambassadors of the Emperor of the Eastern Empire after Charlemagne's death in 814. One of Charlemagne's greatest achievements was to win Byzantium's recognition that he had an equal claim to be the true successor of the Roman Empire.

were decisively defeated by Otto the Great, King of Germany, at the Battle of Lechfeld. Thereafter they ceased their invasions and took to a settled life in Hungary.

The attacks on western Europe by the Muslims (or Saracens as contemporary writers called them) developed in two ways. One was the invasion of Sicily and southern Italy, begun in 827 by the emirs of Tunisia. They captured Palermo in 831 and invaded the mainland six years later, capturing Bari in 840 and raiding Rome in 846.

The geography of Italy, however, made it difficult for them to advance inland. The Franks were able to check them, and in 871 the Emperor Louis II even regained Bari. The second form of Saracen attack was plundering raids on the southern coasts of France by pirates sailing from the ports of Muslim Spain. From the early years of the ninth century they sacked Nice, Marseilles and other places.

The Vikings

The most important invasions of the ninth and tenth centuries were made by the Vikings (or Danes or Northmen) who came from Scandinavia.

The reasons for their sudden outburst of hostile activity overseas are uncertain, but it was very likely the result of overpopulation. The forests and mountains of Scandinavia did not encourage the spreading of fresh settlements. Moreover, the geography of the region made its inhabitants a seafaring race, and it was natural that they should be attracted by the wealthy, undefended lands around them.

The Vikings sailed in long, narrow vessels, swiftly propelled by sails and oars. Each ship, with a leader and a band of about fifty men, acted as an independent unit. At first the Vikings made raiding expeditions, seizing plunder and abducting people to supply the wealthy Muslim kingdoms with goods and slaves. Later, however, they took to conquest and settlement.

The first Viking expeditions in the West seem to have taken place at the end of the eighth century. They attacked the southern coast of England in 787 and soon started to make incursions almost every summer; in 851 they began to settle there and by 875 they had formed their conquests into a district called the Danelaw. They extended their raids and conquests over the whole of northern Europe. They raided the greater part of Ireland and settled on the islands north of Scotland and in Iceland and Greenland. They sailed to the Netherlands, France and ports of Spain. They penetrated even further inland and in 881 destroyed Charlemagne's tomb at Aachen. Some entered the Mediterranean, eventually driving the Saracens from Sicily and establishing kingdoms both there and in southern Italy. Others explored the shores of the Baltic Sea, penetrated into Russia and even sailed along the Volga as far as the Caspian Sea and then down the Dnieper into the Black Sea and so to Constantinople. Yet others probably sailed across the Atlantic to the New England coast of North America.

The Viking raids on France were concentrated upon much of the same coastline that was being attacked by the Saracens. In 843 the Vikings wintered in France for the first time and captured Nantes. From 879 to 889 they devastated the countryside between the Loire and the Rhine. Resistance to them proved vain, and large numbers occupied the country as settlers.

In 885 and again in 911 one of their leaders, Rollo, threatened Paris. On the second occasion, Charles the Simple, a grandson of that Charles who after Charlemagne's death had received the western part of the Frankish Empire, entered into negotiations with the Norsemen. An interview took place in 911 at Saint-Clair-sur-Epte, on the road from Paris to Rouen. At this Charles ceded the basin of the lower Seine to the Norsemen, and Rollo became a Christian. This was the beginning of the dukedom of Normandy.

Above, the Empire of Charlemagne divided into three parts according to the Treaty of Verdun in 843. The western and eastern parts survived to form the core of the modern countries France and Germany, but the central kingdom, Lotharingia, was disputed for centuries.

Left, twelfth-century illustration of the stern of a small but highly flexible Viking ship. It has two steering oars and a primitive square sail. Bodleian Library, Oxford.

Opposite, The Emperor Charles the Bald (ruled 875–77); the feudal lords and soldiers are shown much closer to the emperor than are the clerics. The Bible from which the illustration was taken was one of the finest achievements of Carolingian art. Bibliothèque Nationale, Paris.

Chapter 2

Pope and Emperor

In the age of feudalism the Church exercised an extremely important influence in every country of Europe. Indeed, from the eleventh century, it was the driving force of medieval Christendom. Education and learning, art and culture, moral progress and economic development, the policies of rulers and the daily life of the people—all came under its sway. The Church alone was able to initiate the crusades. It had, however, faults, weaknesses and even vices, and Rome faced a powerful enemy in the person of the Holy Roman emperor, who threatened the papacy's independence. The conflict between popes and emperors dominated the history of western Europe from the eleventh to the thirteenth centuries and was waged mainly in Germany and Italy. The ultimate outcome was the decline both of the empire's political power and of the papacy's spiritual authority, as well as the rise of a new power —that of kings.

When, after the death of Charlemagne, the Carolingian Empire dissolved into a number of petty feudal dominions under rival rulers, the papacy suffered an equally severe and disastrous decline in its prestige and power. Successive popes failed to give the Church inspired leadership and good rule. Many of them were corrupt and incompetent, and some made themselves notorious by their evil and immoral lives. To many people it seemed as if the end of the papacy might be at hand.

In fact, the papacy did not recover from this dark period until late in the eleventh century. The most important figure in the revival was Hildebrand, who was the determined leader of the reforming party during the reign of several popes. He had a high view of the obligations of the clerical life and the standards which its members should observe in order that the people should accord them the respect due to their sacred office and the demands of their religious teaching. When Hildebrand became Pope Gregory VII in 1073, he set out to extend the temporal dominion of the papacy over the kings and kingdoms of the earth, a design in which he was only partially successful.

Nevertheless, papal control over the Church itself was firmly established. The Church became a monarchy, centralized in the Roman court or curia, which considered all important ecclesiastical questions in its deliberations. The pope made his deliberations known by 'bulls', so-called from the Latin *bulla*, the flattened sphere of lead affixed as a seal at the bottom of the parchment. As vicar of Christ, he had the sole power to grant absolution for the gravest sins, and he asserted his authority over the rest of the clergy.

The most important clergy in every country were the archbishops and bishops. Each governed a diocese, a district formed of groups of parishes. His own church was his cathedral, in which he had his *cathedra* or throne. The bishops had attained a high position in feudal society. They had palaces, lived in state and travelled with many servants; and, as well as being ecclesiastical officials, they were employed by monarchs as their ministers or ambassadors.

The increased power and activity of the papacy compelled it to resort to various means of raising money. The pope's income from his territory was inadequate for his needs, and he had to rely upon offerings and, above all, fees due on such occasions as appeals to the Roman curia, confirmations of privileges to abbeys or translations of bishops. This soon led to complaints of increasing corruption and extravagance in the papal court. Twelfth-century popes had to borrow money and employed Lombard bankers to manage their finances.

In addition, every diocese, cathedral and abbey possessed lands, chiefly gifts from devout laymen, and on these feudal payments had to be made to overlords. There were other sources of revenue as well. The Church possessed many manors or feudal estates, and from these it drew the revenue due from its tenants. The parochial clergy were maintained by tithes, the payment of a tenth part of all the produce of the lands.

The authority of the Church was expressed in the collection of ecclesiastical rules known as canon law, which had to be kept by both clergy and laity. Canon law was strongly influenced by ancient Roman law and, since feudal or manorial customs prevailed rather than universal, national civil laws, it was the most civilized of the age. It affected deeply the daily life of the people, since marriage, the care of children, the taking of oaths, usury, legitimacy and tithes were all covered by it. Its influence spread beyond the Church, and it played an important part in the shaping of medieval civilization.

The enforcement of canon law was effected by the ecclesiastical courts. The Church insisted that the clergy should be tried in these courts alone and that the severest penalty they could inflict on a cleric guilty of murder or other serious crime was to degrade him to the position of a layman again. Moreover, all lay people were subject to the jurisdiction of the ecclesiastical courts for breaches of canon law. Many offences received only minor punishments. A man might be fined for absence from church or a woman whipped on her bare back with a knotted length of hempen cord for doing her washing on a Sunday. For serious offences, such as heresy, the supreme penalty was excommunication, exclusion from membership of the Church. This was a grave punishment because secular rulers upheld the authority of the ecclesiastical courts. An excommunicated person might be outlawed or imprisoned or, if a heretic, burnt.

The life of the cloister

In the Middle Ages the highest form of religious devotion was to be found in the monastic life. The monks and nuns who chose this condition were seeking a more

Left, the monastery of Saint-Riquier, in France, in Carolingian times. As recipients of royal patronage the monasteries were already very wealthy, as well as centres of learning and administration.

Opposite top, St Benedict blessing Desiderius, one of his successors as abbot of Monte Cassino. The various Benedictine monasteries were bound together by a common adherence to the Rule of St Benedict rather than by any formal authority. Vatican Library, Rome.

Opposite bottom, a capital, dating from about 1095, from the Abbey church of Cluny, representing plainsong. Cluny was the inspiration for a powerful reform movement of Benedictine monasticism, which was felt all over Christendom. Abbey church, Cluny.

spiritual life than was usually possible in the everyday world. Christian monasticism began early in the fourth century in the desert of Egypt, where men began to live as hermits, occupying themselves in prayer and manual labour. From there it spread throughout Europe, and the first monks, such as those in Ireland, lived in communities of huts grouped together to form villages of their own.

The great epoch of western monasticism began, however, in the sixth century with St Benedict, the founder of the Benedictine rule. From the colour of their habit the Benedictines were known as the black monks, and they soon established themselves in many countries. Among their houses in England were such great abbeys as Westminster, Canterbury, Bury St Edmunds, Glastonbury and Peterborough.

The great virtues recommended in the rule of St Benedict were obedience to superiors and humility. The monks must not live as they themselves wished but as their abbot or prior ordered; the way in which they were to say their daily services was laid down precisely. The ruling idea of their life was seclusion. The monks were to live apart from the society of ordinary people so that they could attain virtue and holiness. Yet this did not mean that the monasteries had no effect upon the world. Everywhere they became powerful missionary agencies which saved Christianity from being completely overwhelmed by the continual advance of the pagan barbarians.

Indeed, for nearly a thousand years the monastic ideal dominated the Church in the West, influencing the form of its religion and providing it with its greatest strength and inspiration. Medieval religion became almost synonymous with monasticism.

With the passing of centuries, however, many Benedictine monasteries departed from the strict rule of their founder. They received large gifts of land, so that they became wealthy, and the monks led lax and comfortable lives. In the tenth, eleventh and twelfth centuries new and reformed orders were created to revive monasticism and to enable it to meet the new needs of the times. The first of these, and in many ways the model for the rest, was the Cluniac order. This came into being at the abbey of Cluny in Burgundy, founded in 910 by William the Pious, Duke of Aquitaine, who wanted the abbey to observe the Benedictine rule in its original strictness. Its reputation under its first two abbots. St Berno and St Odo, attracted men who wanted to take monasticism seriously, and an ever growing number of monastic houses followed its example.

Cluniac monasteries gave more time to worship and correspondingly less time to manual labour, but the greatest innovation was their relationship with each other. Whereas the Benedictine abbeys were independent, equal foundations, capable of survival in a Europe subjected to barbarian inroads, the Cluniac houses formed a disciplined, organized congregation, controlled from the abbey of Cluny itself, and so capable of united action in Christendom. Cluny alone was ruled by an abbot, and he visited the other houses, which were governed only by priors, to see that they obeyed the rules and followed the policy of the order. The Cluniac monasteries increased so rapidly in number that within 200 years of the founding of Cluny there were more than 2,000.

In the eleventh and twelfth centuries particularly, the Cluniacs exerted a decisive influence on the life of the Church. Its abbots and priors came from noble families and increasingly gained the confidence of popes and monarchs, yet themselves declining high office as archbishops or cardinals. The ideals largely inspired the reforms of Leo IX, who was pope from 1048 to 1054, and of Gregory VIII, who had himself been a monk at Cluny. Both these men insisted upon such measures as celibacy of the clergy and the repression of simony.

The Carthusian order, unlike the Cluniac and other orders, was not a reform of the Benedictine rule. It had more in common with the earlier hermits of the east and was a strictly contemplative order. Its founder was St Bruno, a canon of Cologne, who in 1084 built a monastery at the Grande Chartreuse in a wild tract of land in south-eastern France. Isolation and poverty were its principles. Its monks were vowed to silence, and each lived in his own cell within the monastery, where he prayed and studied

and met his brethren only at worship and for meals on feast days.

Many Carthusian monasteries were founded, especially in France. In England nine were established, known as 'charterhouses', the most famous being in London. The careful selection by the Carthusians of candidates for their order and their steady rejection of the world and its wealth ensured that, unlike other orders, they retained both their early zeal and their prestige throughout the Middle Ages.

Gradually, many of the monasteries of the Congregation of Cluny in turn became wealthy, possessing fine buildings and much treasure. In protest against such magnificence and growing laxity, the Cistercian order, the greatest of the new monastic orders, came into being. In 1098 Robert, prior of Molesme, a Cluniac monastery, and a group of his monks, who were troubled by its failings, left to establish a new house at Cîteaux, which was situated in a marshy forest not far from Dijon. There they sought to establish a form of Benedictinism stricter and more primitive than anything then existing. The new order owned most of its success to the second abbot of Cîteaux, Stephen Harding, an Englishman, and St Bernard of Clairvaux, the preacher of the Second Crusade, who became a Cistercian in 1113. Before the end of the twelfth century more than 500 Cistercian abbeys had been founded.

The constitution of the Cistercian order aimed at devising a system that was mid-way between the strict centralization of the Congregation of Cluny and the independent isolation of the Benedictine houses. Each new Cistercian abbey had a mother house, the abbot of which visited it annually, and the abbey in turn might become a mother house with dependent houses to supervise. Cîteaux itself was visited by the abbots of its four oldest dependent houses; and once a year all the abbots came together at Cîteaux in order to regulate and discuss the affairs of the order.

The Cistercians chose remote locations in the countryside for their monasteries. Their churches were not grandiose like those of the Cluniacs but were devoid of rich decoration, and their ornaments and vestments were not made from precious materials. Since their robes were made from undyed wool, they were often called the white monks. During the greater part of the year they ate only one meal a day; they never touched fish, meat, eggs or fat, and milk but rarely. They were expected to engage in manual labour but were assisted by lay brothers, who took the monastic vows of obedience, poverty and chastity, lived in the monastery and performed many of the

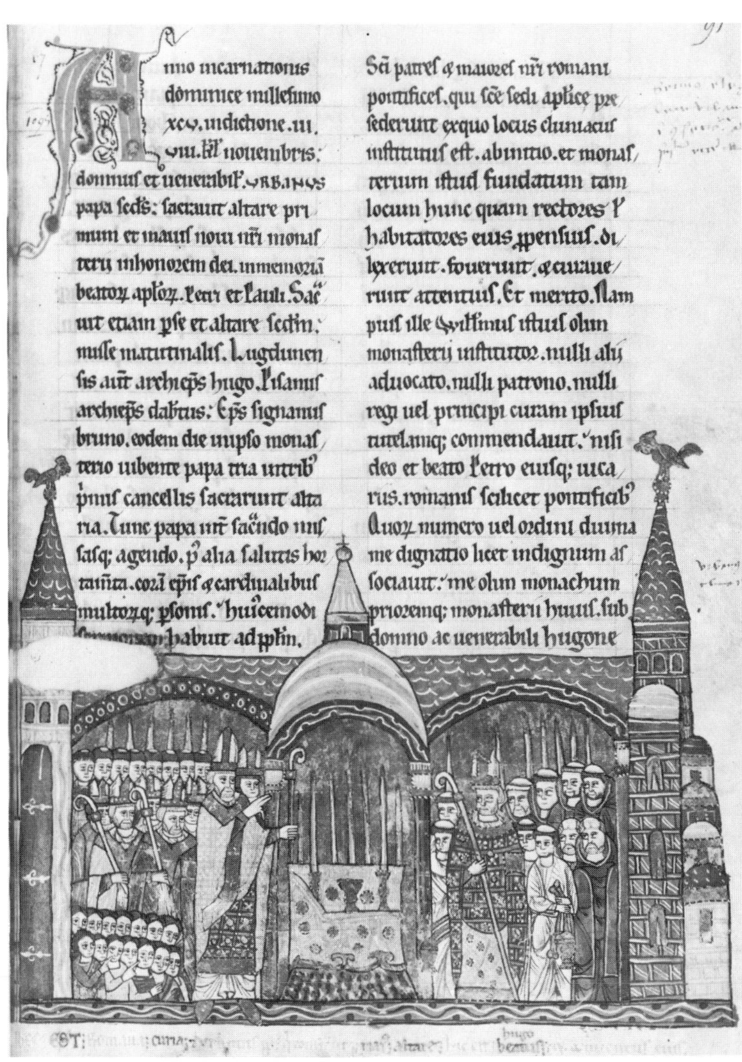

monastic tasks so that the monks could have time for worship, prayer and study.

More than 100 Cistercian houses were founded in England. The best known of these were the great abbeys, such as Fountains, Jervaulx and Rievaulx, in the Yorkshire dales. These were established in what was at first overgrown forest or barren wasteland. Fountains Abbey, for instance, was built on a site 'thick-set' with thorns, lying between the slopes of mountains and among rocks jutting out on both sides, fit rather to be the lair of wild beasts than the home of human beings. There, however, as at the other Yorkshire abbeys, the Cistercian monks and lay brothers cleared the land for large flocks of sheep, becoming in the thirteenth century the greatest wool-merchants in the kingdom. In other countries, too, they worked their 'granges' or farms with great efficiency and were agricultural pioneers.

The Benedictines, Cluniacs, Carthusians and Cistercians were the most important monastic orders in the Middle Ages, but there were others as well. Between the years 1020 and 1120 alone, no fewer than eight new orders were formed. Among these were the Augustinian Canons, who came into being late in the eleventh century. They were priests who lived together in communities according to a rule which they claimed was in conformity with the teaching of St Augustine of Hippo. In many ways they lived the same sort of life as ordinary monks, but their rule was flexible enough to allow them to undertake various tasks. Some of them took care of parishes and others supervised hospitals; St Bartholomew's and St Thomas's hospitals in London were both originally Augustinian houses. Another new order of canons were the Premonstratensians, founded in 1120 at Prémontré, near Laon, by St Norbert, who prescribed for them a rule which was strongly influenced by the austerity of the Cistercians.

The development of monasticism was shared by women. St Benedict himself and his sister, St Scholastica, had founded an order of Benedictine nuns, and the new orders also had houses for women. The duties of the nuns in respect of worship and prayer were the same as those of the monks, and they also performed needlework and other tasks. In general the nunneries were much less well endowed than the monasteries, but some of the old Benedictine foundations, particularly in Germany, were wealthy and confined their membership to women of noble rank. Medieval nunneries always suffered from the practice by families of sending unwanted daughters to them, especially those for whom dowries could not be found.

Above, Bernard of Clairvaux (1090–1153), shown here in a fifteenth-century illustration. One of the great medieval churchmen, he was a spiritual and theological leader, taking possession of the abbey of Clairvaux for the Cistercians in 1115. He is often called the second founder of the Cistercians.

Above left, the consecration of the third church at Cluny, which was dedicated to the ideal of reform. Cluny was free from lay supervision and even from the local bishop and was therefore able to pursue its aims unmolested. Bibliothèque Nationale, Paris.

Opposite, Offa, king of the central English kingdom of Mercia from 757 to 796, founded a fine monastery to the memory of St Alban, who had died in AD 303. Offa was an exceptionally powerful monarch, who organized the building of a large earthwork between his kingdom and Wales. British Library, London.

The faith of the middle ages

In every country in western Europe during the Middle Ages the faith taught by the Church played a supremely important part in the life of the people from the highest to the lowest. On Sundays and holy days they attended its services. These were still in Latin, which few people in an ordinary congregation understood, but they could all learn something in the church from the stained glass windows, the wall-paintings, the crucifix over the rood screen and the great doom, which was a prominent painting of the Last Judgement. There were also statues and images of the saints, whose prayers to God the people were taught to invoke.

Much of the religious life of the people in the Middle Ages rested upon the sacraments of the Church, which by the fourteenth century were generally accepted as being seven in number—baptism, confirmation, the eucharist, penance, extreme unction, holy orders and matrimony. Of these, it was the eucharist (or the mass) which meant most in the religious life of the people. Each celebration of the mass reenacted Christ's sacrifice on the cross: at it his body and blood were offered anew to appease God for man's sin.

Pilgrimages also had an important place in medieval religious life. It was an early custom for Christians to go to Jerusalem and visit the places consecrated by the presence of Christ, and Rome too was always a place of pilgrimage. Most common, however, were pilgrimages to shrines which contained the relics of a saint. Among the most famous centres of pilgrimage in Europe were Santiago de Compostela, traditionally supposed to be the place of burial of St James the Apostle, and Cologne, where the cathedral contained the shrine of the Magi. In England, the most popular shrines were the tombs of St Thomas Becket in Canterbury cathedral, St Alban in St Albans abbey, St Edward the Confessor in Westminster abbey and St Cuthbert in Durham cathedral. Few large churches were without some important relic, and even the poorest people could therefore make at least one pilgrimage in their lifetime.

In the eleventh and twelfth centuries church building on a vast scale took place in every country of western Europe. A French chronicler, Ralph Glaber, wrote, 'it was as if the world, casting off its old garments to renew its youth, set out to reclothe itself everywhere with a white mantle of churches.'

During this period the Romanesque type of architecture prevailed. Builders had now succeeded in equalling the skill of the ancient Romans in cutting and dressing stone. The chief features of Romanesque architecture were the stone-vaulted roof and the round-headed arch, both of which the builders borrowed from the Romans, and structural massiveness. The plan of the churches was usually a Latin cross, formed from the Roman basilica by the addition of transepts and an extended chancel. Early Romanesque decoration was simple, but later the round-headed arch was combined with richly carved columns and capitals and sculptured figures.

In England, before the eleventh century, the Anglo-Saxons had rarely used stone in building their churches. However, the Normans were skilled in the Romanesque style of architecture, and after the Norman Conquest in 1066 their craftsmanship soon began to make itself felt. Within a century they had rebuilt in stone almost all the cathedral churches and abbeys in England. They had also either founded or rebuilt a large number of parish churches in every part of the country. Undoubtedly one of the most striking examples of their church-building is the cathedral at Durham (c. 1093–1130), which stands out as a strong and massive symbol of skill and resolution.

Rome and the empire

Although the medieval Church adapted itself with remarkable ease to the feudal society of western Europe and influenced every aspect of the life of the age, it had, nevertheless, to struggle to assert its position. In the tenth century it was weak and under the control of the Roman nobility until in 963 Otto the Great asserted his right to nominate the pope. The reforming movement in the Church in the eleventh century demanded that control by secular rulers should cease. In 1059 Pope Nicholas II decreed that papal elections should rest with the cardinals. The chief opponents in the subsequent quarrel between emperor and pope were Henry IV and Gregory VII.

The German realm was the first Frankish country to recover from the disorder of the late ninth century. The revival of the German monarchy began with the election in 919 of Henry, Duke of Saxony, later nicknamed 'the Fowler', as the first non-Frankish King of the East Frankish kingdom. He was succeeded in 936 by his son, Otto I the Great. Both father and son set out to consolidate their rule in Germany. In particular, the eastern marches and forests between the Elbe and the Oder were made subject to the monarchy, and Bohemia also became a tributary state.

Having firmly established his power in Germany, Otto wished to follow in the footsteps of Charlemagne by having himself crowned as emperor and securing a special position as protector of the papacy. Events drew him into Italian politics. The peninsula was in a condition verging on anarchy through poverty and famine, the raids of Saracens and Hungarians, and the contentions of feudal princes and bogus emperors. In 951 Otto crossed the Alps with an army, defeated his rivals and became King of Italy. A request by him to the pope that he might be crowned in Rome was refused, but eleven years later his opportunity came in circumstances very similar to those of Charlemagne.

In 959 John XII, who had become pope because his father was the leader of the Roman nobility, appealed to Otto for help against the rulers of northern Italy. Otto

came, defeated the pope's enemies and arrived in Rome where he was crowned emperor in 962. The emperor also granted the pope the *Privilegium Ottonis* by which he assured the papacy of his protection but also insisted upon the emperor's right to confirm the election of the pope by the 'clergy and people of Rome', a right which had been conceded to the emperor Lothar I in 824. When Otto left Rome, John XII sought to regain his independence, but Otto returned and obtained his replacement by a layman, Leo VIII, who was made a bishop within two days and had to agree that no future pope was to be consecrated until he had taken an oath of loyalty to the emperor. On Otto's second departure from Rome, John again returned and secured Leo's deposition, but he died while Otto was on his way back. In 964 the Romans elected another pope, Benedict V. Otto starved the city into surrender and reinstated Leo. The emperor's triumph was complete.

Italy, however, had an unfortunate attraction for Otto's successors, Otto II (973–83) and Otto III (983–1002). Both sought to assert their authority over the peninsula with the result that they suffered frustration and disaster, while Germany fell again into disorder. Nevertheless, under the next three emperors, Henry II (1002–24), Conrad II (1024–39) and Henry III (1039–56), imperial power revived, and the empire reached the height of its strength and prosperity. The influence of the nobility was checked, the new kingdoms of Hungary, Poland and Bohemia paid homage to the emperor, and the kingdom of Burgundy (or Arles) was made part of the empire, so that Henry III possessed all Charlemagne's dominions except France. As a result of rivalry among the Roman nobility, there were by 1045 three rival popes, each claiming to be the rightful holder of the post. Henry III, who became known as the 'maker of popes', deposed all three and secured the election of a succession of German popes. However, imperial control of the papacy was not to last.

The arrival of the Normans

A new force had now appeared in Italy and a new factor had to be considered in the relations between the papacy and the empire. In 1016 the Normans had arrived in southern Italy as mercenaries at the invitation of one of the Lombard rulers. They soon realized that the feuds which distracted this part of the peninsula provided them with a good opportunity to conquer the country for themselves. By 1030 they had created a principality of their own in Naples and were engaged in extending its boundaries.

The Normans were ruthless conquerors, and tales of the atrocities they were committing in southern Italy reached Rome. Moved by the sufferings of the people, Pope Leo IX resolved to bring about the expulsion of the invaders. Having failed to obtain assistance from either Henry III or the Byzantine emperor, he himself led an expedition southwards, but his makeshift army was no match for the Normans. His isolated attack ended in his defeat and capture at Civitate in 1053. He was soon released, but he died in Rome the next year, bringing an important, reforming pontificate to a humiliating conclusion.

Before long, however, papal policy towards the Normans underwent a startling change. The death of Henry III was a fatal blow to imperial control of the papacy. His son, who was elected to succeed him as Henry IV, was only six years old, and his mother, the Empress Agnes of Poitou, was made regent. When Victor II, the last of Henry III's popes, died in 1057, the reformers in the Church succeeded in choosing as his successor one of their number, Cardinal Frederick of Lotharingia, who took the name of Stephen IX, and the regent weakly agreed to recognize him. The danger of this precedent was soon seen. Stephen died the next year and was followed by another reforming pope, Nicholas II, who decreed in 1059 that future popes were to be elected only by the cardinals.

This time the regent refused to accept such a clear challenge to imperial authority. To secure an ally the pope turned to the Normans. In 1059 he accepted their leader, Robert Guiscard, as his vassal. Robert promised to uphold the independence of the papacy, and the pope in return recognized his conquests and conferred on him the title of duke. This was further defiance of the emperor who claimed complete authority

Left, the Holy Roman Emperor Henry II (ruled 1002–24) and his wife Kunigunde, from a portal in Bamberg Cathedral. Henry was the last Saxon emperor, and his successor Conrad II founded the Salian dynasty. Bamberg Cathedral.

Opposite, the Madeleine church at Vézelay, Burgundy, one of the most remarkable examples of Romanesque architecture. Within the typical rounded arches are set finely carved tympana. Vézelay Cathedral.

over all Italy, including the right to dispose of lands and bestow titles. The open rupture between the papacy and the empire had already begun.

The revival of the Church

Actual hostilities came soon after the elevation of Hildebrand to the papacy as Gregory VII in 1073. As archdeacon of the Roman Church, he had already exercised great influence in the administration of the papacy, and his election by the cardinals was unanimous. He was bold and combative, practical and even unscrupulous in pursuing his aims. His brief sojourn at Cluny from 1047 to 1049 had strengthened his austere views about the obligations of clerical life and his resolve to free the Church from lay control.

Although Gregory was a determined reformer, the ideas he held were neither revolutionary nor original. Ecclesiastical reformers had already urged that certain measures must be taken for the good of the Church. One of these was the insistence that the clergy should not marry. This had been accepted by the Roman Church as far back as the fourth century but had not been rigorously enforced. Another was the abolition of simony, the buying and selling of ecclesiastical offices. These two desired reforms were connected with each other, since the sons of clergy were often provided with ecclesiastical preferment by their fathers. In a synod at Rome in 1074 Gregory condemned clerical marriage and simony and subsequently took energetic measures to bring them to an end. In this way, the clergy became detached from the laity, while at the same time the encouragement of auricular confession increased their power over them.

Ecclesiastical reformers also wanted the Church to be freed as much as possible from outside control. In 1075 Gregory issued the *Dictatus Papae*, a list of twenty-seven principles of papal policy. This included a condemnation of the practice of investiture by which the emperor and other lay princes claimed the right to invest a bishop-elect with the ring and staff of his office and to receive homage from him before his consecration. This practice had enabled the emperor to strengthen the position of the monarchy in relation to the hereditary nobility by choosing and controlling both the bishops and the wealth and jurisdiction attached to their sees. He was bound to resist its abolition strongly.

The result was the investiture controversy between Henry IV and Gregory VII. When Henry had grown to manhood, he ruled with vigour and soon showed himself to be ambitious, iron-willed and hot-tempered. He imposed his will upon the nobility and recovered the authority lost by the monarchy during the years of his minority until he had established himself firmly as lord of all Germany. He was not the man to accept Gregory's challenge unanswered.

In 1076 Henry sought to have Gregory deposed from the papacy as a criminal who had exceeded his powers. Gregory replied by excommunicating the emperor and releasing his subjects from obedience to him. Henry was deserted by the German princes and found himself isolated. He crossed the Alps in mid-winter, seeking forgiveness from the pope. He is said to have stood in the snow in the courtyard of Gregory's castle at Canossa in northern Italy for three January days and nights in 1077 before the pope absolved him from excommunication.

Canossa was not the end of the struggle. In 1080 Henry again defied Gregory and again declared him deposed. He invaded Italy and advanced on Rome, which he captured after a siege of three years. Gregory was forced to leave the city, never to return. He died soon afterwards, in 1085, and his last words were said to have been, 'I have loved justice and hated iniquity, and therefore I die in exile.'

In the end, the investiture controversy was settled through a compromise. By the Concordat of Worms (1122) Henry IV's son, Henry V (1106–25), and Pope Calixtus II agreed that elections to German, Italian and Burgundian bishoprics should be free, but made in the emperor's presence and therefore under his influence. Although the emperor would not now invest bishops with the ring and staff, symbolizing their spiritual office, he would still invest them with the sceptre, representing the temporal authority they exercised in his name. The conflict between popes and emperors continued, however, into the next century.

Chapter 3

The Origins of Feudalism

The deposition of the last western emperor in Rome by a barbarian ruler in AD 476 brought to an end the political system of the later Roman Empire but not its social structure which continued, though disintegrating, largely unchanged for another two centuries. The barbarian kings of the sixth and seventh centuries, the Visigoths in Spain and Ostrogoths in Italy, the Franks and the Germans adopted Roman titles and methods of government. Although independent in practice, they considered themselves as still under the suzerainty of the emperor who now ruled in Constantinople, which Justinian in the sixth century had made into a truly metropolitan city.

The great change in the social order of western Europe took place more than a century after the death of Justinian, in the eighth and ninth centuries. It came about as the cumulative result of the successive waves of invasion by Vandals, Lombards, Magyars and other nomadic peoples, the raiding and settlement by the Vikings, and the conquests of the Muslims. These finally destroyed the old social fabric of the Roman world and led to the creation of new institutions in its place.

The decline of trade

In the ancient Roman world the main artery of trade had been the Mediterranean linking East and West. At first, when barbarian kingdoms replaced the Roman Empire, commodities from the eastern and southern shores of the Mediterranean, such as gold, olive oil, silk and spices, continued to be used in western Europe, but gradually this trade declined until by the eighth and ninth centuries it had become only a fraction of what it had been earlier.

One reason for this was that in their ruined condition the barbarian kingdoms could no longer afford to pay for large amounts of imported goods from the East. Nor could they supply manufactures or luxuries to the Muslims, whose conquests in Central Asia and Africa had brought them vast new sources of silver and gold. The Muslims, however, did want raw materials, such as furs and timber, and, still more, slaves and eunuchs. Such trade as existed was in these, and the Vikings were pioneers in supplying the demands of the Muslims and engaging in commercial relations of this kind.

Another reason for the decline of commerce was the widespread insecurity of travel. The havoc wrought by invaders and the disintegration of the Carolingian Empire disrupted communications. The most important towns in northern Europe in the ninth and tenth centuries were Reims and Verdun, which were far removed from the coasts and thus out of reach of the Vikings and other pirates. However, even inland the decline of governmental authority made trading dangerous and expensive. 'Everywhere the country is infested with brigandage', wrote the Frankish historian, Nithard, in 841.

In such circumstances, the outlets for trade were restricted. There were markets, but they were mostly for local trade. Long-distance commerce was crippled by the

Above, the coronation of the Holy Roman Emperor Henry II, who was an important champion of reform in the Church, even though he insisted on the emperor's right to appoint bishops himself. Staatsbibliothek, Munich.

Opposite top, a seventeenth-century English illustration of the papacy's greatest moment of triumph against the emperor – when in 1077 the Emperor Henry IV was forced to wait for three days outside Canossa in the Alps for an audience with the pope.

Opposite centre, as an aftermath to Canossa, Henry set up an antipope and drove Gregory VIII to die in exile in Salerno in 1085. These events are described in this contemporary miniature.

Opposite bottom, Henry IV doing obeisance to Matilda, countess of Tuscany, to whom the castle at Canossa belonged, after humbling himself before the pope. On Matilda's death she left her lands to the Emperor Henry V.

absence of political stability. Hence European society became increasingly based upon a rural self-sufficiency which later found its expression in the forms of feudalism.

Feudalism was adopted by Europe as the form of social organization which enabled it to check and ultimately to conquer its invaders. It was an elaboration of a system already attempted in Persia which placed the well-armed horseman at a premium. Cavalry was the most powerful military weapon—but the high cost of maintaining it required a special social structure.

The basis of feudal society

In the course of the struggle with Islam, the Byzantine emperors evolved a military system in which hereditary landowners maintained the vitally important mounted warriors.

A similar development took place in western Europe. There the system was evolved as a result of the great battle at Poitiers in 732 between the Franks and Arabs. Although Frankish infantry defeated the Arab horsemen, Charles Martel was impressed by the mobility of his enemies and their use of an important new device, the stirrup, which enabled them to fight on horseback with sword or lance. He realized that, if the Muslim threat were to be checked permanently, it was essential that he should have such soldiers in his army. So he brought into being a class of armed horsemen or knights and for their maintenance granted them land taken from the Church.

In this way Charles Martel and his successors laid the foundations of feudalism during the eighth and ninth centuries. It was based upon the old Frankish ways of local government, which Charlemagne continued. Gradually the dukes, margraves and counts were endowed with land, in return for which they had to take an oath that they would faithfully serve their royal overlord and aid him with arms when required.

By the twelfth century this arrangement had spread to other parts of western Europe

and had become formalized and fully developed. The estates granted to the nobility had become heritable. The service they performed in return for these estates had been made more precise: the duty of knight-service. Each estates was valued at so many knights' fees, which represented the service due from the tenant-in-chief who held land directly from the king. For each knight's fee he had to bring to the royal army, when summoned, a fully-armed knight and maintain him there for a period usually limited by custom to forty or sixty days. He had other obligations, such as the payment of aids or fines to the king, but knight-service was the fundamental basis on which he held his lands. It expressed the essential military purpose of feudalism.

It was not easy for a tenant-in-chief to fulfil his knight-service. He was responsible for the steeds, equipment, training and permanent maintenance of the knights. This was expensive, and no medieval king of nobleman had enough money to pay them wages or allowances. Sometimes he might keep them in his own household, giving them food and board, clothing and equipment, but it was more common for him to allocate parts of his land as hereditary holdings to tenants of his own.

These tenants owed the same duty to their feudal lord as he did to the king. In particular, each had to be ready to serve as a knight under him or to provide so many knights to do so. Tenants in turn had their own sub-tenants who owed feudal obligations to them. These sub-tenants might again divide their holdings, and the process continue until some holdings were only the size of a single knight's fee. In this way a pyramid of feudal tenants was evolved with its apex in the king. The practice, however, presented a danger to the king and his tenants-in-chief, in that the allegiance of the sub-tenants was to their own immediate lord and not to his superior.

Around the military arrangements of feudalism there grew up a whole system of government and social order. The nobility, the king's tenants-in-chief, were often rich and powerful men possessing castles and vast estates, privileges and hunting rights. The king depended upon them, not only to protect him from his enemies, but also to assist him in matters of policy and administration.

The tenants-in-chief themselves possessed many rights of jurisdiction and government over their vassals. Thus, in many parts of Europe noblemen of the highest rank judged the more serious crimes, involving the death penalty, on their estates, while even the lesser lords held jursidiction over minor crimes.

The economic basis of feudalism was the manor. In its simplest form this consisted of one village with one lord, though a lord often possessed a number of manors. Part of the manorial estate was reserved for the lord and a small part of the rest was farmed by freeholders paying him rent, while the remainder was farmed by serfs, who formed most of the villagers. In return for their land, the serfs had to work two or three days weekly on the lord's land with extra days at seed-time and harvest, besides providing him with fowls, eggs, pigs and other produce.

In most manors the arable land was divided into three large fields, each divided into long narrow strips. The lord had about a third of these strips, the rest being held by the freeholders and serfs. Each man's strips were divided among the three fields and also

scattered about different parts of each field to ensure that he had a share of good and bad land alike. One of these fields was sown with winter wheat; a second with spring wheat, rye or barley; and the third left unsown and fallow. Each year a different field lay fallow so that there was some rotation of crops and the soil was not exhausted rapidly. In addition, hay was grown on the meadowland and cattle grazed on the waste land.

Such a system could support no more than subsistence farming. The manor normally produced little more food than was needed to support the village and the lord and his retainers; this rural economy would not have been able to sustain an effective feudalism without the marked increase in population which occurred in Europe during the eleventh century.

The increase was made possible by a number of developments which improved the productivity of the land. Among these were the replacement of oxen by horses for traction and the adoption of the three-field system of crop rotation. Perhaps the most important was the development of a new type of plough.

The original 'scratch-plough', consisted of a downward-pointing spike drawn by two oxen, first in one direction, then crosswise, over a square plot of land. This was gradually replaced by a heavier plough, which was much more effective and could be used even on heavy, damp soil. It had a coulter and ploughshare set to cut deep into the earth and a mould-board to turn the soil sideways and form a ridge and furrow so as to drain as well as turn the ground. Also, it was often set on wheels and drawn by a team of oxen and therefore ploughed a long strip rather than a square plot.

These innovations not only improved the productivity of the land but also demanded closely integrated social units in the countryside, since the team of oxen to draw the plough required communal ownership and the three-field system communal labour. So these developments themselves contributed to the growth of the manorial system.

However, the condition of the serfs remained unchanged by these developments. Since the average manor had from 900 to 3,000 acres to be farmed by perhaps two dozen families, their toil was incessant. The hardest work was at harvest-time when the grapes were crushed in France and Germany and the corn was cut in England. They had to suffer dangers and trials. The huntsmen ruined their poor crops, wild beasts killed their animals and even attacked their houses. Moreover, serfs were 'bound to the soil', which meant that they could not leave the manor without their lord's permission. Some, however, took to the forests which surrounded the villages and joined the bands of brigands and outlaws hiding there.

Charlemagne's successors

Among all the countries of western Europe, the growth of feudalism was most rapid and complete in the kingdom of the West Franks or France, which developed from the territory given by the Treaty of Verdun to Charles the Bald in 843. Its geographical position as the only country lying open to the Mediterranean, the Atlantic and the North Sea made her the centre of medieval culture and the typical medieval country. Here perfect feudalism was found. But its

Above, a ninth-century illumination of a prince being crowned by heaven; he is flanked by two churchmen, his advisers, but it is clear that his authority is primarily a secular and worldly one. Bibliothèque Nationale, Paris.

Top, an eleventh-century illumination of threshing and winnowing; the jobs of separating the grain from the chaff were still done by the same laborious processes known to neolithic times. British Library, London.

Left, a French sculpture of about 1100, showing a man with a scythe. The introduction of the scythe had recently made the task of reaping the crops far less arduous.

Opposite top, an ox-drawn plough. Ploughing was a job on which all members of a manor collaborated; in areas of heavy soil eight oxen might be needed, although horses were increasingly being used for this job by the thirteenth century. British Library, London.

Opposite bottom, thirteenth-century illustration of servants in a castle, drawing water from the well and carrying wine up from the cellar. This profusion of luxury and servants could only be brought about through the agricultural innovations of the early Middle Ages. British Library, London.

development was assisted also by the decadence of the French monarchy.

Charlemagne's successors in France proved to be very much like the puppet kings of the Merovingians. Because they were such weak rulers, power was seized by the dukes of Paris, Aquitaine, Brittany and other leading noblemen. France suffered particularly severely from the attacks of the Vikings. After the deposition of Charles the Fat in 887, the Carolingian kings reigned for a further century, but they were quite powerless to legislate. The line came to an end in 987 on the death of Louis V.

By now successive dukes of Paris had made their family the most powerful in France. They had, indeed, become to the later Carolingian kings what the mayors of the palace were to the Merovingians. When Louis V died, Duke Hugh Capet was able, largely through the support of Adalbero, Archbishop of Reims, and Gerbert, the future Pope Sylvester II, to secure election as King of France.

His accession to the throne brought to an end the last confused and troubled years of the enfeebled line of Pepin. His strength lay in the support of the Church and the possession of a royal domain grouped around the strong cities of Paris, Orléans and Laon, containing good fertile land and situated right in the centre of France through which ran important roads and trade routes. Moreover, a few months after his own accession Hugh was able to obtain the election of his son, Robert, as joint-king, which helped to establish the principle of hereditary succession to the throne. The Capetian dynasty continued to rule in France by direct descent until 1328.

The Capetians were not as rich and powerful as the dukes of Normandy and of Burgundy, the counts of Flanders and of Champagne and others among their leading vassals, who had more land and retainers than the crown itself. The kings did not attempt to govern the kingdom outside the royal domain, which was at first confined to a narrow strip of territory stretching approximately from Compiègne to Orléans and including Paris; it was surrounded by the territory of their formidable neighbours. It generally happened that the crown had the support of the Church, but not very much beyond this.

When Hugh Capet died in 996, his son, King Robert II the Pious, succeeded him on the throne without difficulty. He had married Bertha, the widow of the Count of Blois, but they were sufficiently closely related for the papacy to declare the marriage void. Constance, the daughter of the Count of Toulouse, was his next wife.

Such was the weakness of his position that he could not compel ready obedience even from the lesser nobility in his own domain. Yet he did succeed in regaining possession of several towns, and on his uncle's death he occupied Burgundy, though it cost him ten years of war to hold the province.

Robert's son and successor, who was crowned Henry I in 1031, had first of all to undertake a family war against his mother, Constance, who put his young brother, Robert, on the throne. The great vassals were ready to participate in this quarrel. The Count of Blois gave his support to Robert while his rivals, the Duke of Normandy, the Count of Anjou and the Count of Flanders, remained faithful to the king. Henry vanquished his brother, pardoned him and granted him the duchy of Burgundy,

The result of the contest was to weaken the French monarchy still further. Henry could not prevent the growth of Champagne, and in order to reward the Duke of Normandy, Robert the Devil, for his help in the war against the Count of Blois, he ceded him the French Vexin. When Robert the Devil was succeeded by the young Duke William the Bastard, Henry maintained the alliance with the future conqueror of England. It was Henry's help which enabled William in 1047 to inflict a decisive defeat at Val-ès-dunes, near Caen, upon his rebellious Norman vassals, and for a time the two men united against the ambitions of the Count of Anjou, Geoffrey Martel. Nonetheless, the military power and aggressive aims of Duke William alarmed his overlord and made him change his alliance. He now allied himself with Geoffrey against William, but two campaigns brought him humiliating defeats on Norman soil, and the war was still in progress when he died in 1060.

Philip I

Philip I was only eight when he succeeded his father, who had taken the precaution of crowning him the year before and arranging for his brother-in-law, Baldwin V, Count of Flanders, to act as his guardian and rule as regent.

The most important event of Philip's minority, one in which he took no part, was the Norman conquest of England. The Duke of Normandy now became King of England also, and his allegiance to the King of France became still more a mere formality; indeed, he was now the equal of the King of France.

When he came of age, therefore, Philip did not enter into a very powerful inheritance. He had, however, a shrewd and practical outlook on the situation. In this age of feudalism, political power depended upon the enforcement of the vassal's allegiance to his lord, and he saw that the power of the French monarchy must be based upon the royal domain.

Consequently Philip did what he could to extend the royal domain. Henry I had acquired the county of Sens in the absence of a direct heir. Philip annexed the neighbouring Gâtinars in 1068. This and other territorial additions made the royal domain markedly stronger during his reign.

At the moment, however, when Philip should have sought to exploit the crisis brought about in the Anglo-Norman kingdom by the dispute among William the Conqueror's sons over the succession to their father's heritage, he lapsed into a strange inertia which contrasted with the activity of the earlier years of his reign. According to the court-historian, Suger, Abbot of St Denis, he became 'enslaved to pleasure'.

He tired of his wife, Bertha, daughter of Count Florent of Holland, and in 1092 he abducted and bigamously married Bertrada, wife of Fulk le Rechin, Count of Anjou. Pope Urban ordered the dissolution of this marriage, and when Philip refused to obey he was excommunicated. At length he was absolved in 1104 on pretence of a separation. By then he had been in failing health for some years, and from 1100 he had associated his son, Louis, with the crown and had left the government to him. He feared that his illness was the punishment of God. He died in 1108 wearing the habit of a Benedictine monk, a practice which it was commonly believed at the time would gain a sinner salvation at the last.

A new age for the French monarchy

When Louis VI, having survived Bertrada's plots against his life, became King of France, the monarchy's position was still weak. Though the royal domain now extended as far as Bourges, it still formed but a small part of the country, and its barons continued to disobey the king's authority. The royal income was small, even when Philip supplemented it by drawing the revenues of vacant bishoprics and selling ecclesiastical appointments on a large scale. Finally, the crown lacked a seat of government and had few administrative officials.

Above, central and western Europe in about AD 1000. At this stage the French king's power was limited to a tiny area of royal domain, whereas Germany, like England, was a much more unified kingdom. Otto the Great had recently made north Italy part of the Empire.

Opposite, an early medieval knight. His sophisticated equipment, both the heavy chain-mail armour and the technological innovations such as stirrups and spurs, meant that a class of professional soldiers was required; to support this the system of feudalism was developed. Musée de Cluny.

Nevertheless, the Capetian monarchy had survived. Hugh Capet had made it a hereditary monarchy, which had given it a clear superiority over the German dynasties who quarrelled among themselves over a title which remained elective. The first Capetians had begun to extend the royal domain, which was to enable them to bring to an end the pretensions of their vassals. Philip I had started the centralization of government.

At the same time, the Capetians possessed other and more deep-seated advantages. They were the anointed kings of France, consecrated to their office in a manner accorded to none of the provincial nobility, and however difficult their relations with the papacy might be at times the bishops, who wanted peace and order in the land, were on their side. They were also the undoubted feudal overlords of the nobility, who became increasingly chary of flouting their supremacy openly, particularly when they found that their own vassals were prepared to take advantage of a weakening of the feudal tie. There was a growing reaction against the lawlessness and lack of authority of previous generations.

The Saxon dynasty

At the end of the ninth century Germany, like France, was in a state of advanced disintegration which the last Carolingians had not been able to check. The country was divided into four great duchies which corresponded to the territories of the old Germanic tribes. These were Swabia and Bavaria in the south, Franconia in the centre and Saxony in the north. Each of these duchies had its own different system of laws. The dukes claimed unrestricted authority over their states.

In 911 the death occurred at the age of seventeen of Louis the Child, who was the last of the German Carolingians, the last of the descendants of Charlemagne through Louis the German. Instead of offering the crown to Charles the Simple, King of the West Franks (in France), the leaders of the German tribes were persuaded by the Archbishop of Mainz to elect a king of their own who did not belong to the Carolingian family—Conrad, Duke of Franconia. Conrad, however, failed to establish the royal authority over the dukes.

When Conrad died in 918, it looked as if the realm were on the point of dissolution. On his death-bed, however, Conrad nominated to the kingdom his rival, Henry, Duke of Saxony. He seems to have realized that Henry was the only man capable of defeating the Magyars, whose raids into Germany were then at their worst. He therefore sent his brother with the crown and other regalia of the East Frankish kingdom to Henry.

Henry I was the first non-Frankish King of Germany, but he was subsequently elected by the Saxons and Franconians alone. He resolved to secure recognition from Swabia and Bavaria not only succeeded in doing so but also in 925 married his daughter to the Duke of Lotharingia and in 933 defeated the Magyars at Unstrut.

So great was the power and prestige gained by Henry I that after his death in 936 the election of his eldest son, Otto I, later to be known as 'the Great', to succeed him on the throne was undisputed. After he had been elected by the German nobility, Otto was anointed, crowned and enthroned by the Archbishop of Mainz in Charlemagne's palace church at Aachen. The ceremony expressed the new monarch's conception of himself as the successor of Charlemagne and as the supreme authority in Germany, recognized and sustained in his position by the Church.

As soon as he was crowned, Otto set out to assert his supremacy in Germany. His attempt aroused the dukes to rebellion, and from 938 to 941 he was engaged in their subjection, which he secured as a result of his own energy and determination as well as a lack of unity among his opponents. He was able virtually to abolish Franconia in 939 and make it permanently part of the royal domain, but the other dukedoms were too strong, and their continued existence was necessary for the defence of the frontiers of the kingdom. He contented himself, therefore, with replacing their existing dukes with men of his own family. By 947 he had given Bavaria to his brother, Swabia to his son and Lotharingia to his son-in-law, while the archbishoprics of Mainz and Cologne were in the hands of his nominees.

Even these members of his own family, however, were prepared to rebel against Otto. In 953 there was a widespread rising against him in Germany fomented by his own son, the Duke of Swabia, who was joined by the Duke of Lotharingia and the greater part of the leading noblemen of Bavaria. The rebellious dukes, however, were foolish enough to assist the Magyars when they made a fresh invasion of Germany in 954. The insurgents were deserted by their indignant supporters. Otto was able to subdue them. He deprived them of their dukedoms but spared their lives.

In 954 the Magyars had crossed the Rhine and raided Metz, Cambrai, Reims and Châlons. In the spring of the next year they swarmed into Bavaria and besieged Augsburg. The five German duchies rallied to Otto's support against them, and he mustered a strong force on the River Lech. There was a desperate struggle, and among those who died in battle was the recently-deposed Duke of Lotharingia, who had fought against Otto only the previous year. The Magyars were finally defeated and pursued beyond Vienna.

The victory at Lechfeld brought the Hungarian raids to a complete end. It gained Otto the title of 'the Great' and fame throughout Christendom.

The defeat of the Magyars displayed not only the military success of Otto but also the power and expansion which the German realm had achieved under him. Two months after his triumph at Lechfeld, he won another important victory on the Rechnitz over the Wends (or Slavs), who lived to the north and east of the Elbe, and against whom he had, throughout the internal troubles of his reign, been waging continuous warfare.

To consolidate his conquered territory, Otto relied not only on fortresses, garrisons and colonists but also on the power of Christianity. Between the years 946 and 948 he erected the missionary bishoprics of Aarhus, Schleswig, Riba, Havelberg, Brandenburg and Oldenburg and richly endowed them all. Further south, he compelled the Duke of Bohemia to submit to him but made no attempt to impose direct German rule on his territory.

The Holy Roman Empire

Because he enlarged his dominions to include Italy and was crowned by the pope in Rome in 962, Otto I is usually regarded as the founder of the Holy Roman Empire. To Otto and his contemporaries, his achievements in Italy represented a restoration of the empire of Charlemagne, the result of a deliberate effort to renew the western half of the old Roman Empire. Otto had sought to fulfil the dream of a Christendom united under a single ruler, a dream which was to haunt the medieval mind. But this ideal was not only incapable of achievement but also underminded all efforts to establish centralized rule over the German lands.

During Otto I's reign, however, that still lay in the future, as did also the conflict, between emperor and pope which did much to perpetuate both German and Italian disunity. Otto had saved Germany from foreign conquest, compelled its dukes to recognize him as their feudal overlord and re-established the empire in the West.

All this had been achieved in cooperation with the Church. He had been able to insist that the appointment to bishoprics within Germany must be in his hands, and he had secured virtual control of the appointment of popes and had compelled them to take an oath of loyalty to him. The emperor was in a stronger position in his relations with the pope than Charlemagne had been.

Chapter 4

Norman England and Capetian France

After the Battle of Hastings in 1066, William, Duke of Normandy and a vassal of the French crown, became King of England. The Norman conquest brought about important changes. Previously England had looked towards Scandinavia; now she was turned towards France. Within a hundred years Henry II had accumulated for England the immense Angevin Empire which spread across France from the Channel to northern Spain and from the Atlantic to the Massif Central. The fortunes of the two countries were now inevitably tied together. Norman noblemen had estates in both England and France, but the French could not forget their lost provinces.

Anglo-Saxon England

Despite the protection of the sea, Roman Britain had been no more secure than Gaul from the invasions of the Germanic peoples. The Angles (who were to give their name to the conquered island), Saxons and Jutes dispossessed the Celts in the fifth century and divided the country into their petty kingdoms. By the eighth century three of these kingdo[illegible]d become important—Northumb[illegible]ia and Wessex. During the reign [illegible]ing, Egbert (802–39), Wessex su[illegible] the rest, and from his dynasty ca[illegible] outstanding monarch, Alfred the G[illegible]7–900).

Originally t[illegible]uth of England had been converted by [illegible] Roman mission led by St Augustine, who came to Kent in 597, and the north and midlands by Celtic missionaries from Scotland, who were themselves the descendants of the first Christians in Britain during the time of the Roman occupation.

This meant that at first England was divided in her religious loyalties. But in 664 the Celtic Christians agreed at the Synod of Whitby to accept papal authority, and religious unity was established throughout the country. This meant that Britain, for the first time since the Anglo-Saxon invasions, became part of Christendom. Now she could share in the culture of the civilized world which the Roman Church preserved.

The union of the Celtic Church with the Roman Church was followed by a flourishing period for Christianity, especially in northern England. In 681 a monastery was founded at Jarrow in County Durham, and here for more than fifty years lived the Venerable Bede (*c*.673–735), one of the greatest scholars of the time. Among those inspired by Bede was St Boniface (680–754), the 'Apostle of Germany', Another great English centre of learning was the episcopal school at York, from which Charlemagne obtained Alcuin (*c*.735–804), who played such an important part in the Carolingian renaissance.

The Danish invasion brought a serious setback for Christianity in England, but after he had defeated them Alfred the Great set out to revive religion and learning. His work was continued by St Dunstan, who was Archbishop of Canterbury from 961 to 988 and was strongly influenced by the Cluniac revival. St Dunstan founded over forty new monasteries in England, including the great abbeys of Peterborough, Ely and Thorney, and sought as well to impose strict observance of the Benedictine rule upon all religious houses.

When the Danes began to raid England towards the end of the eighth century, the Anglo-Saxons were unable to resist them. To meet them they had the fyrd, a national army in which all freemen had to serve, and were armed with boar-spears and forks. They were no match for the Danish warriors with their coats of mail, battle-axes and skilled horsemanship.

The crisis was reached early in 871 when the Danes, who were now settling in England instead of raiding it, advanced southwards to conquer Wessex, which would enable them to dominate the country. There they were met by Alfred the Great and his army. The struggle between them was not concluded until 878, when the country was divided between English and Danes.

The Danish part of England was known as the Danelaw. It lay north of a line from the middle of the Thames to Chester and as far as the River Tees and Solway Firth. Although independent Danish occupation of the Danelaw did not last more than fifty years, the law administered in this territory remained different from the rest of England for many years after the Norman Conquest.

Alfred's successors were able to recover the Danelaw, but before the end of the tenth century Danish attacks on England began again, and these coincided with the reign of a weak king, Ethelred the Unready (978–1016).

When the Danes defeated him at the Battle of Maldon in 991, he attempted to buy them off with money raised by a new tax on land called the Danegeld. Nonetheless, the Danish invasions continued, and in 1002, during a truce, Ethelred treacherously ordered the massacre of many of the Danes in England on St Brice's Day (13 November). In revenge, Sweyn Forkbeard, King of Denmark, raided England in 1003 and in 1013 began a conquest of the country which was only interrupted by his death.

Above, Edgar, King of England (ruled 959–75), granting the charter to his New Minster at Winchester, which he founded to combat the corruption of the Old Minster. Edgar was an ardent proponent of monastic reform and friend of St Dunstan. British Library, London.

Opposite, The Holy Roman Emperor Otto I (ruled 936–73), and his family, kneeling before the Church. His coronation in 962 was seen as a restoration of the vision of Charlemagne, although the centre of political authority had shifted from northern France to Germany. Museo d'Arte Antica, Milan.

Canute and Edward the Confessor

On Ethelred's death, Sweyn's son, Canute, claimed the English throne, which he secured after a series of campaigns against Ethelred's son, Edmund Ironside.

Canute ruled Denmark and Norway as well as England. He therefore had, to delegate some of his authority in England, and he organized the kingdom into four earldoms. At the same time, he tried to unite Danes and English. The Earls of Northumbria and East Anglia were Danish while those of Mercia and Wessex were English.

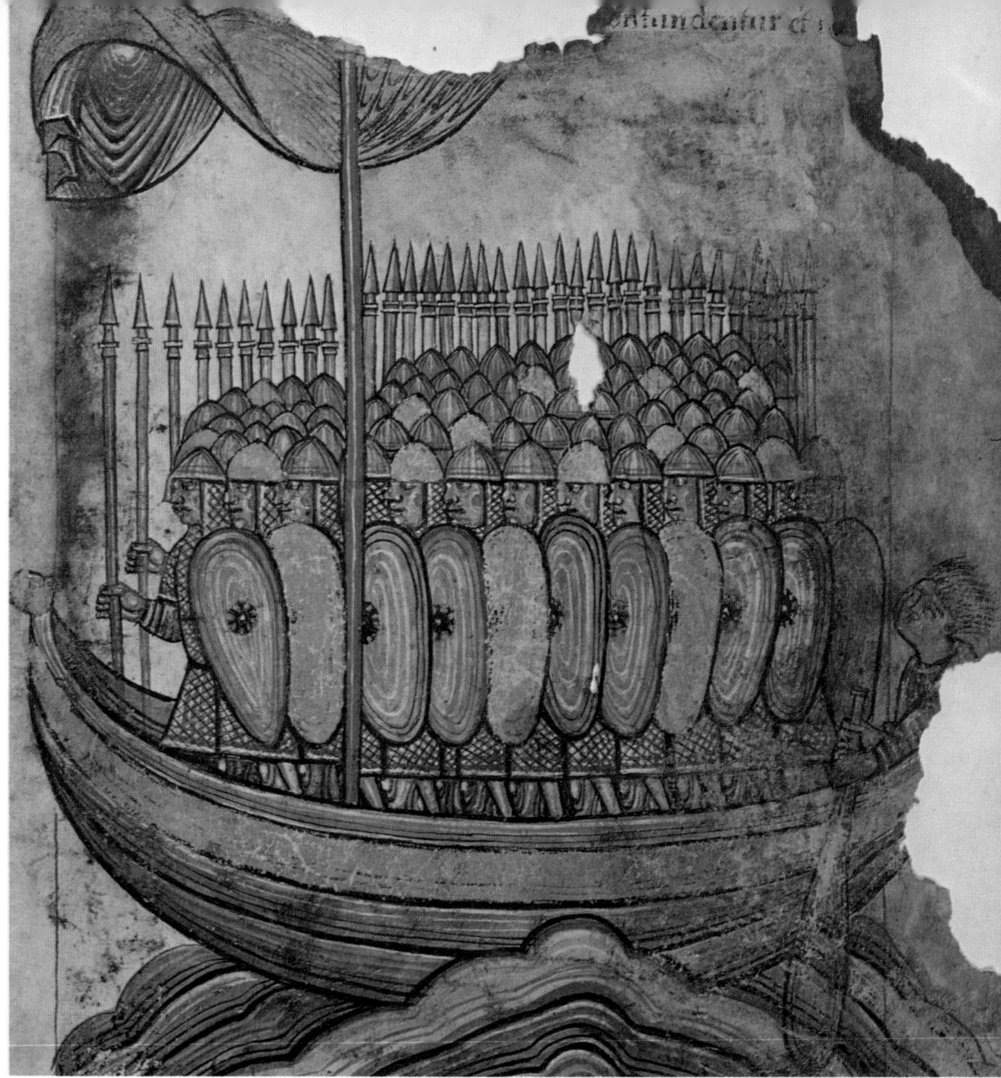

William the Conqueror

While the kingdom of England was weak and distracted, the duchy of Normandy was experiencing an unprecedented strength and unity under the rule of Duke William. Born in 1027, he was the illegitimate son of Robert the Devil and Arlette, the daughter of a tanner in Falaise. During the twenty years after he became Duke of Normandy in 1035, William made the ducal power greater than ever before. He let it be seen that the interests of the greater Norman families were closely linked with those of the duke; that if he could receive their support, they in their turn could rely upon his protection. So feudal service became regularly organized in Normandy. In wartime the duke could call upon the service of some 800 knights from his tenants-in-chief, while they themselves maintained another 1800.

The growing strength of Normandy during the reign of Duke William was also the result of an increasing religious revival in the province. New monasteries were founded, some by William or by members of his family. The most famous of these was the Abbey of Bec, consecrated in 1041, which was later to own considerable land in England, including Tooting Bec near London. In addition, the Norman Church was reorganized and reformed by a strong group of bishops who had the cooperation of the duke himself.

William wished to extend his power by conquering England. He claimed the English throne on the grounds of distant relationship to the Anglo-Saxon royal family. He also claimed that Edward the Confessor had recognized him as his successor and that in 1064 Harold, the head of the house of Godwin, after being shipwrecked on the Norman coast had taken an oath (in return for being allowed to go back to England) that he would help William to secure the English throne. However, when Edward died in 1066 Harold was chosen king by the Witan, although he was not of royal blood. He also re-enacted the laws and the customs of the English people.

When Canute died in 1053, Danish rule in England came to an end. His sons could not hold his dominions together, so his empire fell apart. The Witan, the Anglo-Saxon assembly of great landowners and bishops, chose Edward the Confessor, a son of Ethelred the Unready, as king.

Edward had spent the early part of his life at the ducal court of Normandy and had been influenced by these years of exile, but during his reign he did not introduce as many Normans into high places in England as has been sometimes supposed. It was not foreign favourites, but rather the absence of English unity, that really prepared the way for the Norman Conquest. Edward did not possess the character or ability to unite his kingdom, and his childlessness made the succession to the throne uncertain. He had a monkish temperament, and his piety impressed his subjects, who called him the Confessor; but he lacked long-standing personal support in England.

Edward had secured his election to the throne through the influence of Godwin (d.1035), whom Canute had made Earl of Wessex. Godwin induced Edward to marry his sister, to make him large grants of land and to confer earldoms on his sons, so that even after Godwin's death the family remained a power in the kingdom; but their greatness provoked strong resentment in other leading men.

To William this was a challenge which he could not ignore and he prepared to take an expedition to England. He gathered 800 ships and 5,000 men from many parts of Europe and with papal blessing invaded

England, landing on the coast of Sussex in the autumn of 1066. Harold had been compelled to march north to defeat an attempt at invasion by Harald Haardraade, King of Norway, but he returned to confront William with an army about the same size as that of the Normans but with fewer trained and well-armed men.

The two armies met outside Hastings. Harold's army was established on a hill behind a continuous line of shields, where they held firm against continuous Norman attacks until twice, deceived by feigned flights, the English foot-soldiers broke their line to give fight and were cut down by the Norman horsemen. Then the Norman archers, shooting high, subjected the English to a devastating hail of arrows. Harold was among those killed, and towards evening a final Norman charge was victorious.

William was crowned King of England in Westminster Abbey on Christmas Day 1066. However, it took him five years to complete his conquest, during which time the northern part of the country was laid waste. He was also forced to build and garrison castles in his endeavour to keep order among his rebellious subjects.

Norman feudalism

The Normans made England into a fully feudal state. William claimed to be the rightful successor to Edward as King of England, but he had also defeated the English in battle and so could claim possession of the whole country by right of conquest. He confiscated the estates of the English landowners, and from them he distributed land to his Norman followers, though he was careful not to give it to them outright. They had their land from him as his tenants, they had to take feudal oaths to him and become his immediate vassals. Moreover, through the Salisbury Oath of 1086, he prevented any weakening of the king's power by making all tenants swear to obey the king first and their feudal superior afterwards. This made English feudalism different from continental feudalism, in which the nobility were in a position to command the full allegiance of their followers.

William's feudal hold over England was firmly established in the Domesday Book, which contained the results of a survey of his landed property made in 1086. It described, county by county, all the land which was held either by the king in his own right or of him by his tenants-in-chief. It was a striking example of the thorough, efficient government which the Normans imposed upon their new kingdom across the Channel.

William also reformed the English Church and improved its efficiency. He replaced the Saxon bishops and abbots by more learned foreigners, including the saintly and scholarly Lanfranc, who had been prior of the Abbey of Bec and was made Archbishop

Above, Alan of Brittany swearing allegiance to William the Conqueror for the estates of the Saxon Earl of Mercia. William replaced all the old nobility but spread the estates of his barons out over the country so as to stop any of them winning supreme power in any single district. British Library, London.

Top left, a scene from the Bayeux Tapestry showing Harold enthroned as King of England. To his left is the Archbishop of Canterbury, Stigand; his worldliness was infamous and he was deposed by William the Conqueror. Bayeux Cathedral.

Above left, a scene from the Bayeux Tapestry, in which Harold is driven ashore on to the coast of Normandy by a storm in 1064. There he swore to support William's claim to the English throne. England was the richest country in Europe, and its throne was therefore eagerly contested. Bayeux Cathedral.

Opposite top, Norman knights in a longboat; the energy and military efficiency of the Normans made them feared throughout Europe, and they set up kingdoms as far apart as Sicily and England. Their militaristic organization of society brought about the introduction of a rigorous feudalism.

Opposite bottom, Canute granting a charter to the New Minster at Winchester with his wife Emma. Although ruler of an empire that included most of the lands bordering the North Sea, Canute spent much of his energy on integrating his Danish rule with English society. British Library, London.

of Canterbury in 1070. Several bishoprics were removed from villages to large and important towns—Norwich, for instance, replaced Elmham and Lincoln Dorchester-on-Thames. Cathedrals and churches were rebuilt in stone. The abbeys were made more effective centres of religion and learning and the first English Cluniac monastery was founded at Lewes in Sussex in 1077. Attempts were made to install a better-instructed parish clergy and to enforce celibacy upon them. The clergy were allowed their own synod to discuss ecclesiastical matters and also church courts to try both clerical and lay offenders according to canon law.

Because of William's known zeal for ecclesiastical reform, Pope Gregory VII had blessed the banner which he took on his expedition to England. However, William was equally determined to assert his rights as king over the English Church. He defied Gregory's decree and insisted upon investing his bishops. Moreover, he ordered that his consent was necessary for the recognition of papal authority and the enforcement of papal decrees in England, the publication of ecclesiastical laws by the church synods and the excommunication of a nobleman.

William Rufus

William I could not prevent his valiant and feckless eldest son, Robert, inheriting the duchy of Normandy, but he designated his second son, William II (nicknamed Rufus—the Red), to succeed him as king of England after his death, which occurred in 1087.

A powerful group of barons, who had their lands in both countries, disliked the division and rose against William in 1088, but he defeated them with the support of the rest, who preferred royal despotism to baronial anarchy. William himself was anxious to extend his rule to the other side of the Channel, and in 1096 he acquired Normandy on mortgage from Robert, who wanted money for the First Crusade.

Nevertheless, William soon became very unpopular in England. His favourite foreign minister was Ranulf Flambard (d.1128), whom he made Bishop of Durham. Flambard was a clever and ambitious man who did his best to enlarge the royal revenue. He enforced full payment of all feudal dues from the barons, particularly the profits of an estate passing to a minor or an heiress and the fines payable to the crown when an heir succeeded to an estate.

Flambard also soon brought William into serious conflict with the Church. He advised William to postpone appointments to vacant bishoprics and take the revenues for the crown. When Lanfranc died in 1089, the king did not appoint a new Archbishop of Canterbury until 1093, and then only because a grave illness made him fear imminent death. The new archbishop, Anselm, Abbot of Bec, resisted William and firmly upheld the rights of the Church and sought to protect its revenues. The climax of the dispute came when the pope sent over the pallium, symbol of papal confirmation of an archbishop's appointment. Anselm would not receive it from William but took it himself from the high altar of Canterbury Cathedral. William was so enraged that Anselm had to leave the country in 1097 and go to Rome.

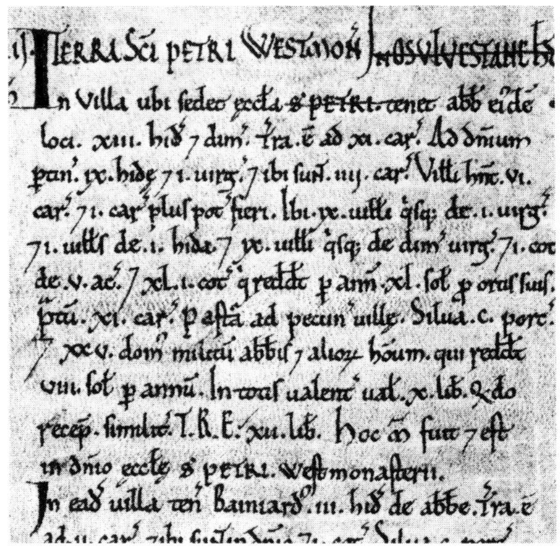

Henry I

William II's reign came to a sudden, violent end when he was killed in 1100 by an arrow while hunting in the New Forest in Hampshire. It was probably an accident, though he may possibly have been the victim of a conspiracy. He was succeeded by Henry I, the youngest son of William the Conqueror. Henry was nicknamed *Beauclerc* or 'the Scholar' because he could read and write. He had inherited his father's administrative ability, and while his brother had been impulsive and hot-tempered he was calm and persevering.

To gain support from the bishops and the barons, Henry issued a Coronation Charter in which he promised not to delay ecclesiastical appointments and not to exact feudal dues harshly. He also wished to have the good will of the native English, and so he married Edith, a daughter of the King of Scotland, who was descended on her mother's side from the royal house of Wessex. The only concession he made to the Normans was to rename her Matilda.

On the death of Rufus, Robert of Normandy returned from the crusades and resumed possession of his duchy. He also claimed the throne of England and in 1101, urged by Ranulf Flambard (who had been imprisoned by Henry but had escaped to Normandy), he invaded England in an attempt to dethrone Henry, who bought him off. Robert misgoverned in Normandy and attacked Henry's friends, who were barons in both England and the duchy. This presented Henry with an opportunity to intervene. In 1106 he invaded Normandy and conquered it; he pardoned Flambard but kept Robert a prisoner in England for the rest of his life.

At Henry's request, Anselm came back to England, but he was more than ever resolved to offer firm resistance to lay investitures. Although he had done homage for his archbishopric when first appointed by William II, he refused now to renew his homage to Henry or to consecrate any bishops who had been invested by him. When Henry refused to give way, he went into exile again in 1103. In 1107 he returned and reached a compromise with Henry. It was agreed that bishops were to receive their ring and pastoral staff from the pope but were to pay homage to the king for their landed estates before they were consecrated. Henry also agreed that each bishop should be elected freely by the clergy of the cathedral, but since this was done in the presence of the king in practice his wishes were obeyed.

Finally, Henry set out to strengthen and improve government in England. He organized the exchequer, a specialized committee of the Curia Regis to deal with the royal finances. Its officials, the barons of the exchequer, collected the dues, taxes and fines payable to the crown and kept a care-record of all payments and expenditure. This was the beginning of specialized departments of government in England.

Anarchy under Stephen

Henry I's only son, Prince William, was drowned in 1120 in the wreck of the *White Ship* on a voyage from Normandy to England. Prince William's twin-sister, Matilda, widow of the Emperor Henry V, had married Geoffrey, Count of Anjou, and Henry wanted her to succeed to the English throne. Geoffrey and Matilda would in time have controlled territory stretching from the Scottish border to the Loire, but the barons disliked the idea of female rule and feared that important posts in the state might go to Angevins. They chose as king Stephen, Count of Blois, the son of William I's daughter, Adela.

Although Stephen was a great lord in England and France and was brave and popular, he was imprudent and could not enforce his will over the whole country. There was constant civil war in England between his armies and the armies of Matilda. King David of Scotland crossed the border in support of Matilda and was defeated at the Battle of the Standard in 1138 by the army of the northern counties fighting under a standard of consecrated banners from the cathedrals of Durham, Ripon and York. The Scots, however, kept the counties of Cumberland, Westmorland and Northumberland until the next reign. Matilda invaded England in 1139, and Stephen was defeated two years later at the Battle of Lincoln. Shortly afterwards he regained power, although Matilda controlled parts of the West until she left the country in 1148.

Left, trial by battle; this was a common way for barons and knights to settle their disputes in the early feudal period in England. The Common Law of the Anglo-Saxon period was for the most part forgotten, and not until the late twelfth century did the king manage to restore his control of the judicial process. Public Record Office, London.

Opposite, a page from Domesday Book (1086) describing Westminster. In the main, the Domesday survey dealt with property in the form of land and manors; there is much less detail on the towns. British Library, London.

Such a situation produced a general lack of government and justice. The barons were able to assume too much power at their own will. They fought among themselves and pillaged the countryside. Stephen's reign showed the dangers of unregulated feudalism. If the king were not strong enough to impose his will on his great tenants-in-chief they could use their power to pursue their private feuds and undermine law and order.

Peace came at last because the barons grew afraid that France might capture their lands in Normandy while there was anarchy in England. The two hostile factions signed the Treaty of Wallingford in 1153, which provided that Stephen would be king for the rest of his life but that he would be succeeded by Matilda's son Henry by her second husband, Geoffrey of Anjou, who a year later, on Stephen's death, became king.

Henry II and the restoration of order

Henry II, the first of the Angevin or Plantagenet kings, ruled an extensive accumulation of territories. In addition to being King of England, he possessed more land in France than did the King of France himself. He inherited Normandy from his grandfather and Anjou, Maine and Touraine from his father. His wife, Eleanor, the divorced queen of Louis VII of France, brought him Poitou and Auvergne, and in 1159 he inherited Brittany from his brother, Geoffrey.

Henry displayed striking contrasts of character. He succumbed to furious outbursts of anger, was loose in his morals and keenly enjoyed sport; yet he was also religious and learned and had a sense of justice and considerable organizing powers. He was a restless, energetic man with a dominating personality who made his reign as much an epoch in English history as that of William the Conqueror.

His first intention was to restore order in England and regain the authority lost by the crown. The barons themselves were now mostly tired of warring and plundering and willingly cooperated in the restoration of peace. One after another, illegal baronial castles were destroyed and their foreign mercenary troops expelled from the kingdom. At the same time, royal castles and estates which had come into baronial possession were recovered for the crown. Private mints, set up by about a dozen bishops and barons during Stephen's reign, were closed and their coins replaced by royal coinage.

The crown was seriously weakened because it had to rely for its forces upon the barons, who might not always be loyal. Henry adopted two measures to provide himself with a more effective army.

Earlier English kings had levied a tax called scutage upon their ecclesiastical tenants-in-chief instead of requiring them to provide troops for the royal army. Henry allowed his barons to pay it as well and with this tax hired mercenary soldiers. They were more reliable than the baronial troops and served longer than the annual period required of a feudal force.

Later Henry, through the Assize of Arms in 1181, revived the fyrd, the old Anglo-Saxon army in which every freeman had served. He ordered all freemen to equip themselves with weapons and armour and to be ready to serve under the king when required. There were now two royal armies —a small, trained force to serve abroad and the fyrd to meet foreign invasion or baronial rebellion. In this way the military purpose of feudalism was largely destroyed.

Henry had to increase the royal income if he were to preserve his authority and hold his empire. Scutage gave him more money, and in 1170 he replaced most of the sheriffs by officers of the exchequer, since they were likely to be more efficient tax-collectors and could be more easily controlled by the crown than the sheriffs, who had nearly all been independent landowners.

Henry needed yet more money, partly because of the heavy cost of putting down a rebellion (1173–74) against him by his four sons, who were supported by their mother, Queen Eleanor, the kings of Scotland and France and a number of barons. One of his new sources of revenue was heavy fines, imposed through the Assize of the

Forest of 1184, on all who had taken game in the royal forests or broken the forest law in other ways. Another source of revenue was a new tax, the Saladin Tithe, levied in 1188 at first for the crusades. This marked the first taxation of personal movable property as opposed to land.

The barons in Stephen's reign had increased the powers of their feudal courts. Henry wanted to extend royal justice and to deprive the barons of much of the authority and profits their courts brought them. By the Assize of Clarendon in 1166, he ordered that when the royal judges held courts regularly in different parts of the country they were to be met in every county by twelve men from each division or hundred to present those accused in criminal cases. If a private individual sought redress in a civil case for some wrong he had suffered from another individual, in Normandy a 'trial by battle' was held between the two disputants. This had never been much liked in England and it became the practice to allow a second or 'petty jury' to try these cases. During Henry II's reign, 'trial by ordeal' continued in criminal cases, but in 1215 the Church ordered the clergy to cease to take part in it, and so the 'petty jury' was also adopted for these cases.

In 1155 Henry appointed a priest, Thomas à Becket, to be his chancellor or chief secretary. Becket was a friend of the king and hunted and feasted with him. He also became totally absorbed in the king's business and even supported him when he taxed the Church heavily. Then, in 1162, Henry appointed him Archbishop of Canterbury. Becket accepted the post reluctantly, realizing that sooner or later he would be drawn into conflict with the king.

Henry wished to have Becket as archbishop so that he could reduce the increased powers which the Church had gained by taking advantage of the crown's weakness during Stephen's reign. Becket was ardent and ambitious. Het set out to change himself from a splendid courtier to a perfect archbishop. He resigned from the chancellorship, adopted an austere way of life and proceeded to devote himself wholeheartedly to religious matters.

The crisis in the relations between Henry and Becket arose over the church courts. These courts alone could try a priest for any crime, but their heaviest penalty, even for murder, was to degrade him, that is to say to make him a layman again. It was common for men of bad character to become ordained to secure this protection, and more than a hundred murders were committed by priests in the early years of Henry's reign.

Henry therefore issued the Constitutions of Clarendon in 1164, which ordered that after a church court had degraded a guilty cleric it must hand the man over to a royal court to be punished. He claimed that William I had intended this when he recognized the authority of the church courts in England.

Becket rejected the arrangement. He insisted that it would mean that a cleric would be punished twice for the same offence. He fled to France and remained there for six years. Then king and archbishop agreed to a truce. Becket returned to England, but he was still determined to uphold his principles. He suspended the Archbishop of York and two other bishops who had supported the royal cause. When Henry heard of this, he uttered rash words which led four knights to murder the archbishop in his cathedral.

The murder caused deep indignation throughout Europe. In 1173 the pope made Becket a saint, and his tomb in Canterbury Cathedral became one of the most important centres of pilgrimage in Christendom. Henry did penance there in 1174 and was whipped by the monks of the cathedral. Moreover, he had to abandon his claim that degraded clerics should be punished by the royal courts.

Philip Augustus

Angevin England had known a great king in the person of Henry II. Now France also was to experience a decisive reign, that of Philip Augustus (1180–1223).

When he came to the throne at the age of fifteen, Philip Augustus was an energetic boy who was passionately fond of hunting. As he grew up, he retained that energy and also showed himself to be ambitious and politically astute. He was not to be an outstanding soldier, but he was always skilful and entirely unscrupulous as a diplomat. Indeed, he preferred intrigue to war.

At his accession, the royal domain was still of modest dimensions, flanked on one side by the possessions of his maternal uncle, the Count of Champagne, and on the other by the Anglo-Norman Empire, then at its height. Philip soon proved his independence and his desire for territorial gains. His first marriage, when he was still only fourteen, was with Isabella of Hainault, the last direct descendant of the Carolingians and a niece of the Count of Flanders. Her dowry was Artois; in 1185 by combined threats and diplomacy, he also obtained Amiens from the Count of Flanders. This brought the royal domain to the Channel and compelled the neighbouring counts to become his allies.

Philip could now safely turn his attention to his far more formidable Angevin rival.

Above, the Anglo-French Angevin Empire at its height, at the death of Henry II in 1189.

Above left, Philip II of France at his marriage with Isabella of Hainault in 1279. Bibliothèque Municipale, Boulogne.

Opposite left, the first four Norman kings of England, William the Conqueror, William II, Henry I and Stephen. British Library, London.

Opposite right, the death of Thomas à Becket. Becket's tomb was the most important shrine for pilgrims in medieval England until it was destroyed during Henry VIII's dissolution of the monasteries in the 1530s. British Library, London.

Just as his father, Louis VII, had assisted the revolt against King Henry II of England by Queen Eleanor and his four sons in 1173–4, so he now seized every chance of assisting the reckless quarrels of Henry's eldest surviving son, Richard, with his father. Henry died in 1189 and, cursing his sons, named Richard as his successor to the English throne.

Philip and Richard then set out in 1190 on the Third Crusade, but the two friends soon became mortal enemies. Soon after the capture of Acre, Philip went back to France. He said that he was ill, but he really wanted to plot against Richard's French possessions in his absence. Richard, for whom crusading was a dominating passion, advanced towards Jerusalem. He was unable to take the city and in the end he had to abandon the campaign. On his way home, he was shipwrecked on the Adriatic coast and fell into the hands of the Duke of Austria, with whom he had quarrelled during the Crusade. The duke handed him over to the Emperor Henry VI. Philip, who had by now made an alliance with Richard's treacherous brother, John, for the conquest of Normandy, tried to bribe the emperor to keep the King of England a prisoner. However, Richard's English subjects paid a heavy ransom, and after fifteen months he was set free in 1194.

Richard immediately opened a campaign in Normandy to win back the areas Philip had taken during his absence. He was a brilliant soldier, and within a few weeks he recovered numerous castles and towns. Philip fled before him, leaving behind his treasure and incriminating records of his negotiations with John. By the beginning of 1196, however, both sides were exhausted, and the Treaty of Loviers gave back to Richard most of Philip's conquests.

There followed, however, only a brief respite in the fighting between the two kings. Richard was determined to regain the rest of his territory. The starting-point for its recovery was to be his new castle of Château-Gaillard, which he built on the frontier of Normandy in the Seine Valley. It was constructed at great expense under his personal supervision and modelled on the crusading fortresses of the East. With its outworks, double walls and keep bristling with defences, it seemed impregnable.

When the war was renewed in 1198, the omens indeed, seemed, favourable for Richard. He made further gains from Philip, whose position was fast becoming precarious. During a truce in the war, however, Richard was killed by an arrow while besieging the castle of a rebellious vassal in 1199.

Richard died childless. He had designated his successor his younger brother, John who was accepted by England and Normandy; but many of the barons of Anjou, Maine and Touraine supported the rival claims of Prince Arthur, the posthumous son of John's elder brother, Geoffrey. Arthur was nearer in succession to the throne and, since he was only twelve years old, would allow the barons to enjoy more independence. Philip was once again ready to exploit the family differences of the Angevins. Since John needed his support, he could impose conditions in return for granting it. By the Treaty of Le Goulet in 1200 he accepted John as Richard's heir to all his French possessions and received his homage. John had to agree in return to pay a feudal relief of 20,000 marks and to cede important border districts of Normandy. Arthur was to rule Brittany as John's vassal, but he soon fell into John's hands, and he died at Rouen in 1203, perhaps murdered by his uncle.

King John was an able and energetic man. In England he gave special attention to the administration of justice. He made sure that the judges went round the country frequently to bring swift justice to the people and acted as a judge during his travels. At the same time, however, he had many inconsistencies in his character. He was unreliable, distrustful and irresponsible, sometimes generous but sometimes spitefully cruel.

John soon played into Philip's hands. He married in 1200 the fourteen-year-old Isabella, the daughter and heiress of the Count of Angoulême, who was betrothed to Hugh of Lusignan, a great vassal of Aquitaine. When the Lusignans protested, Philip summoned John to answer their charges at his court. On his refusal to appear, he declared him deprived of all his French lands and entered upon a campaign to enforce the judgement.

The Bretons rose in revolt against John at the news of the murder of Arthur. The barons of Maine defected from him. John lacked the nerve to defend Normandy and withdrew to England.

Before Philip could conquer the province, however, he had to capture Château-Gaillard. He directed the operations himself.

Eight months of siege from September 1203 to April 1204, were needed to overcome the brave resistance. The castle was blockaded so closely that the defenders suffered from famine and had to evacuate all the local inhabitants who had taken refuge within its walls. The French began their attack in February. A long artificial causeway enabled them to reach the corner-towers, one of which was mined and brought down. The first defensive wall was taken. The assailants resorted to an artifice to take the second; while an attack was mounted elsewhere, French soldiers crept secretly into a building on another part of the wall. The defences were turned. There remained the keep and its walls, which were fifteen feet thick, but these were breached by a siege engine. There followed savage hand-to-hand fighting in the passages and rooms of the castle until all the remaing 180 defenders were killed or captured.

By 1204 Philip possessed Normandy, Anjou, Maine and Brittany. John was left with only Gascony, which was the southern part of Aquitaine, and the Channel Islands.

Having added the Plantagenet lands to the royal domain, Philip now wished to expand northwards into Flanders, the centre of the cloth trade and the richest part of northern Europe. Here, however, he met continual opposition from John for whom the district was especially important, since the Flemish cloth-manufacturers obtained nearly all their wool from England. John's agents were well-supplied with money and won over the semi-independent Flemish cities, he also made an alliance with the Count of Flanders, based on their mutual trading interests.

Philip decided to take advantage of John's quarrel with the papacy and his own barons to invade England. As a preliminary step, he invaded Flanders by land and sea in 1213. The Count of Flanders appealed to his ally for help. An English fleet of 500 ships immediately sailed from Portsmouth, where it had assembled to guard against invasion. It caught the French fleet at anchor off Damme, the port of Bruges, quite unawares. The French knights were away plundering or besieging Ghent. Many of their 1,700 ships, richly laden with arms, provisions and other stores, were captured or destroyed, and the rest were later burnt by order of Philip.

Philip had to withdraw from Flanders and postpone the attack on England, while John planned to follow up his success by a double invasion of France in the summer of 1214. He gained Raymond, Count of Toulouse and the Emperor Otto IV as additional allies. After much delay, John himself led a diversionary attack on Poitou, but this came to an end when he failed to capture La Roche-aux-Moines and draw Philip southwards. The main attack, directed at northern France, was undertaken by Imperial, Flemish and English troops. Philip met this allied army in the marshy plain near the village of Bouvines between Lille and Tournai. Though greatly outnumbered, the French knights won the day and completely outclassed the enemy.

Bouvines was one of the decisive battles of the world. It placed Flanders under French control for about a century. It so weakened the position of the Emperor Otto IV in Germany that he had to yield his crown to his rival, Frederick II. It completely wrecked John's plans to recover the lost Angevin provinces and made the English barons so disenchanted with him that they revolted and compelled him to grant them the Magna Carta in 1215.

The kingdom of the Franks restored

A contemporary writer has recorded that when Philip Augustus was still a youth of seventeen a French baron asked him one day what he was thinking about. He answered that he was wondering if the time would come when God allowed him to restore the kingdom of the Franks to the great glory it had formerly enjoyed under the rule of Charlemagne.

Within France, Philip set out to achieve this aim by asserting his rights and authority under the feudal system. He insisted that

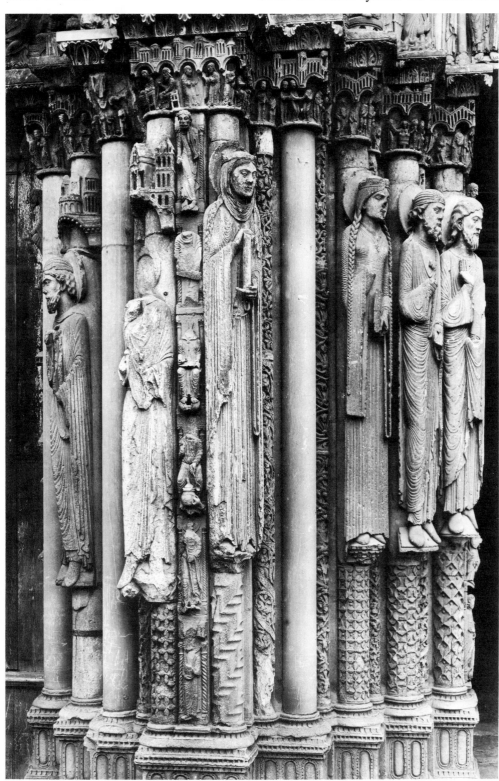

Left, the Royal Portal from Chartres Cathedral, built in about 1150. These elongated figures represent the kings of Judah; their sculpture is entirely blended in with the architectural demands of the pillars of which they form part. Chartres Cathedral.

Below, miniature by the thirteenth-century historian Matthew Paris showing the King of France, Philip II Augustus, unhorsed during the Battle of Bouvines in 1214. He nevertheless finished the battle as victor, and John of England lost all hope of recovering his French territories.

Opposite, the porch of the Alcazar, Granada, very similar in style to the Court of the Lions of the Alhambra. Moorish influence survived intact in this part of Spain until the sixteenth century.

even the greatest noblemen must respect the jurisdiction of the royal council and that its members should be present at its meetings whenever summoned by him. He was also able to introduce various innovations; the most important of these was that those who shared a divided inheritance should each hold their property directly from the crown, so that, for instance, the Count of Blois was the vassal of the king and not of his kinsman, the Count of Champagne. At the same time, he supported the towns against the claims of the nobility and sold them charters granting them rights of local government. With the money so obtained, Philip hired professional mercenary soldiers to form a royal army.

The growth of a strong, united France was accompanied by an important revival of French cultural activity and influence. Nowhere was this displayed more spectacularly than in the development of Gothic art. Now the great Gothic cathedrals were built. Notre Dame in Paris and Chartres were both substantially finished during Philip's reign, while Reims was begun in 1211 and Amiens in 1220.

Despite the considerable extension of royal power and national unity achieved by Philip Augustus in France, one part of the country remained distinct in many ways from the rest. Provence, the south of France, had always been more Roman than Frankish and had evolved a civilization of its own. Its towns were largely self-governing. Its serfs might obtain their freedom, and their sons could aspire to knighthood. Furthermore, it supported a class of troubadours, lyric poets who sang in the ancient Provençal language. They sang chiefly of chivalry and gallantry, which, however, was condemned by the Church as immoral and decadent.

Early in the twelfth century, there appeared in this part of France a heretical Christian sect, the Albigensians, who were called after the town of Albi, some fifty miles from Toulouse.

The twelfth century was a great age of heresy. Heretical doctrines spread from the Pyrenees to the Danube. There were many reasons for this. Towns were growing rapidly, commerce was spreading, wealth was increasing, and schools and universities were becoming more numerous. Clerical privileges and abuses were greatly resented by lay people; the Hildebrandine reformers had secured independence for the Church and had made the clergy into a disciplined class, but they had not been able to improve their quality or prevent them being corrupted by power. As merchants became wealthier, they became more educated and increasingly critical of the Church, finding ready hearers among the working classes of the towns.

Such an atmosphere encouraged the spread of opinions contrary to the orthodox doctrines of the medieval Church. The ideas of the heretics took various forms, and what is known of them cannot be taken as completely trustworthy as it comes mainly from their enemies.

The Albigensians seem however to be the most radical, ascetic and universal of all the groups of heretics. In other parts of Europe they were commonly known as the Cathari. The central belief of these heretics came from the Manichaeism which had challenged Christianity in the fourth century.

This was based on the conflict of light and darkness or God and matter, and it held that God had created only the world of the spirit, which was eternal, while Satan had created the corruptible material world. These beliefs gave the Cathari their name, which comes from the Greek word for 'pure'. The Cathari taught the need to live pure and apart from material things. They practised an extreme asceticism and rejected baptism and the other sacraments which made contact with material things.

The Albigensians became the most powerful of the Cathari. They spread among all

classes in the towns of southern France, where the growth of population had outstripped the Church's parochial organization. The austerity of the lives of the devoted Albigensian missionaries contrasted with the laxity of many of the clergy, and the people of Provence came to share their bitter hatred of the Church. Moreover, they found a princely protector, Raymond VI, Count of Toulouse, whose troubadours called him 'the greatest count on earth' and the equal of emperors and kings.

At first Pope Innocent II tried to convert the Albigensians. He sent Cistercian monks as missionaries among them and encouraged a Spaniard, St Dominic, to undertake a preaching tour of the country in 1205; but such efforts were unsuccessful. The crisis came in 1208 when the papal legate, Peter of Castelnau, was murdered at a crossing of the Rhône near Saint-Gilles. Count Raymond, suspected of complicity in the deed, was excommunicated but remained obdurate.

This event made Innocent decide upon a crusade against the Albigensians. He called upon Philip Augustus to confiscate the lands of the count as a heretic, but the king would not be deflected from his struggle with England and her allies.

Many barons of northern France were very ready to undertake such a holy war which would bring them a share of the wealth of Provence. A large force gathered at Lyons in 1209. Its leader was one of the best soldiers of the time, Count Simon de Montfort, the father of the Simon de Montfort who was to be so important in England during Henry III's reign. The campaign opened with the storming of the city of Béziers and the massacre of its inhabitants. 'Slay them all; God will know his own', ordered the legate, Arnold-Amalric. Carcassonne surrendered after a brief siege; Narbonne and other places were terrorized into immediate surrender. Some

Above, St Dominic attempting to win over the Albigensians in 1205 by means of a trial by fire. Such methods of persuasion were less successful than the military campaigns of 1209–29.

Above left, St Dominic (1170–1221), a Spanish canon who won fame for his preaching and in 1216 founded the Dominicans, an order of wandering friars dedicated to preaching and learning. Church of St Dominic the Great, Naples.

Opposite, Louis IX (ruled 1226–70), or St Louis, a sincere Christian who never failed in his religious duties, even on his journeys, he was considered an ideal monarch. Bibliothèque Nationale, Paris.

of the greater barons now returned home, but Simon de Montfort and the lesser barons were determined to dispossess the southern nobility and take their lands. They won a decisive victory at Muret in 1213.

After the death of Innocent III in 1216, the campaign became a war to incorporate Provence into France. This was eventually accomplished by the Treaty of Paris of 1229.

Pope Gregory IX established the Roman Inquisition in 1232 as an organization with special courts to seek out and try heretics, staffing it mainly with Dominican friars; the next year he charged it with the final extirpation of the Albigensians. The heretics were ruthlessly hunted down, brought to trial and burnt at the stake. The capture of the fortress of Montségur in 1244 deprived them of their last stronghold and brought their armed resistance to an end.

By the close of the century, no trace was left of the heresy, and the great new fortified Cathedral of Albi and the University of Toulouse marked the triumph of the crusade. The country was reduced to orthodoxy, but the distinctive Provençal culture had been destroyed.

A royal saint

When Louis VIII died in 1226 at the age of forty, his son, Louis IX, was only eleven years old. Until he came of age in 1234, his mother, Queen Blanche, the daughter of King Alfonso the Good of Castile and granddaughter of Henry II of England, acted as regent of France. She was a truly formidable woman, determined to preserve unimpaired for her son the power of the crown.

Queen Blanche had the members of the royal council and the people of the towns on her side and asserted herself successfully against the barons, sometimes by diplomacy sometimes by force of arms. There were several feudal revolts, but none seriously threatened the position of the monarchy. When the king's majority was proclaimed, she still held the greatest influence over her son and affairs of state. The monarchy was so strong that Louis was able to leave on a crusade in 1248; he only returned when she died in 1254.

Queen Blanche had brought up her son austerely and piously. His education had been almost monastic and very different from that of other princes of his time. Yet as King of France he became the symbol of medieval monarchy at its best, and after his death he was canonized with the universal approbation of western Christendom.

He had inherited great gifts of character from his family—the Castilian pride and intelligence of his mother, the courage of his father and the political sagacity of his grandfather, Philip Augustus.

He was a sincere and simple Christian. He would have liked to have lived as a monk and was prevented from relinquishing his crown to go into a monastery only by his strong sense of duty. His faith was absolute and unquestioning. He was a crusader not once but twice and showed himself a brave and chivalrous knight; indeed he died on a crusade. He practised his religion without ostentation or bigotry. Concern for the hardships of others produced in him a boundless charity. As he himself said, he was 'transfixed by pity for the unfortunate'. He distributed alms generously and tended even lepers with his own hands.

Yet, as was to be expected from the outlook of the times, St Louis' religion had its hard sides. He was inflexible towards all heretics, sceptics and blasphemers. He once ordered the burning of the lip and nose of an important citizen of Paris as a punishment for blasphemy. And he supported the organization of the Inquisition in France and its merciless persecution of the Albigensians.

St Louis believed that as King of France he had privileges which he had to maintain and duties which he had to exercise and that he had been placed on the throne by the will of God to promote justice and peace among his people and to uphold the cause of the Church and of the true faith.

It was, indeed, in the sphere of justice that St Louis most asserted himself. Like Henry II in England, he wished to extend royal justice and take away cases from the courts of the barons. It had long been possible in theory for people to appeal to the king against judgements imposed by these courts, but in practice delays and difficulties had generally prevented this being done.

To take royal justice to the people, St Louis appointed seneschals or magistrates to represent him in the provinces of France, to hear cases and to see that royal decrees were observed.

King Henry III of England wanted to recover the lands in France which his father, King John, had lost, but the expedition which he brought to France in 1242 was routed by St Louis. Louis could have expelled him completely from France and seized his lands. Under the Treaty of Paris in 1259, however, Louis allowed Henry to retain Gascony in return for doing homage to him for it and renouncing all claims to Normandy.

The reign of St Louis initiated a period of French predominance in Europe which was to endure for over five centuries. He himself made an important contribution towards its establishment. He gained throughout Europe a reputation for fairness and impartiality that soon brought him requests from many countries to act as an arbitrator in all sorts of political disputes. In one case he arbitrated between Henry III and the barons of England.

There were other ways in which his reign was important for France. The law and order which he promoted throughout the country favoured the growth of trade and prosperity. French markets and fairs flourished, dealing in goods which ranged from the spices and silks of the East to the dry,

Opposite, the Catholic Cathedral at Albi, in France, built in the 1280s to symbolize the victory of the Catholic crusade against the Albigensian heretics earlier in the century.

Opposite, a seal of Louis IX, showing the King's holiness and charity, as he admits blind beggars to a hospice. Archives Nationales, Paris.

salted fish of the North. The population was increasing, and wastelands and forests were being cleared for cultivation.

All this contributed towards the gradual evolution of feudalism into a freer system. At the same time as the king was making inroads into the power of the great vassals, at the other end of the social scale the serfs were beginning to better their position. Methods of cultivation were improving, and crops were getting bigger. Private baronial wars no longer destroyed the harvest. Many serfs were able to save enough money to purchase their freedom from their lord and become rent-paying tenants.

Poets and chroniclers

At the beginning of the twelfth century, most of the literature of France was in the form of songs, fables and romances which were usually sung or recited by travelling minstrels and story-tellers who went from town to town and from castle to castle.

Long remembered among these poets and minstrels were the troubadours of the south of France. The troubadours often sang their own ballads and lyrics in the castles of feudal princes or before the courts of love presided over by noble ladies. Full of imagery and movement, their poems spoke of love and battle and chivalry. Sometimes these troubadours were themselves noblemen or knights. Among them was Bertram de Born, who plundered and made war on his neighbours and then subjected them to dazzling and penetrating satire in his poems.

The troubadours were silenced when the Albigensian crusade destroyed the civilization of Provence, but the north of France also had its own poets and minstrels. Their epics and romances were mostly based upon old legends which told traditional tales of events lost in the mists of history. They also dealt with the romance of chivalry and preserved the stories of Charlemagne and the twelve noble Paladins of his court and of King Arthur and his Knights of the Round Table.

In the thirteenth century, however, poetry was supplemented by prose, especially in the form of chronicles and histories written by men who had witnessed the events they described. The first of these French historians was Geoffroi de Villehardouin, who took part in the Fourth Crusade and wrote the *Conquest of Constantinople*, describing the events from 1198 to 1207. This is his account of the spectacle of Constantinople as it appeared for the first time to the astonished eyes of the Christian noblemen:

They could not believe that there could be so wealthy a city in the world, when they saw these high walls and magnificent towers which enclosed it completely, and these rich palaces and lofty churches. . . . And be assured that there was none, however bold, whose heart did not tremble; and this was not surprising for no man had ever undertaken such a great enterprise since the world was created.

St Louis himself was interested in history and scholarship. While in the east, he had heard that the Muslim ruler of Egypt was making a collection of works by ancient writers, and 'he was afflicted', wrote Joinville, 'to perceive more wisdom in the sons of darkness than in the children of light.' He immediately began to collect manuscripts too, placing them in the royal chapel at Paris.

Left, Bernard de Ventadour, one of the best-known of the troubadours of Provence. These minstrels and poets were usually of noble rank and gloried in the chivalric ideal. Bibliothèque Nationale, Paris.

Opposite left, an early fourteenth-century manuscript of a song, Le Roman de Fauvel, *by Gervais du Bus. The court poets produced a genre of secular literature and art that had little in common with the religious work of the time. Bibliothèque Nationale, Paris.*

Opposite right, France after the Treaty of Paris in 1259, when the English king Henry III was allowed to retain his French lands in return for an act of homage to the King of France.

WESTERN EUROPE FROM THE ELEVENTH TO THE THIRTEENTH CENTURIES

Date	France	England	Germany	Italy
1000	Robert II the Pious (996–1031) Henry I (1031–60)	Canute (1016–35) Edward the Confessor, last Anglo-Saxon king (1042–66)	Henry II (1002–24) Conrad II (1024–39) Henry III (1039–56)	The Normans in Italy Benedict IX (1032–44)
1050	Philip I (1060–1108)	Battle of Hastings (1066) Norman conquest William the Conqueror (1066–87) William II (1087–1100)	Henry IV (1056–1106) Henry IV excommunicated (1076)	Investiture controversy Gregory VII (1073–85) Canossa (1077) Normans sack Rome (1084) Urban II (1088–99)
1100	Louis VI the Fat (1108–37) Louis VII (1137–80)	Henry I (1100–35) Stephen (1135–54) Matilda proclaimed queen (1141)	Henry V (1106–25) Concordat of Worms Conrad III (1138–52) founder of the Hohenstaufen dynasty	First Lateran Council (1123) Republican rising in Rome (1143)
1150	Marriage of Eleanor of Aquitaine and Henry Plantagenet (1152) Philip II Augustus (1180–1223)	Henry II Plantagenet (1154–89) Assize of Clarendon (1166) Murder of Thomas à Becket (1170) Richard I (1189–99)	Frederick I Barbarossa (1152–90) Henry VI (1190–7)	Frederick Barbarossa seizes Milan (1154) and Rome (1167) Alexander III (1159–81) Victor IV, Pascal III and Calixtus III anti-popes Peace of Constance (1183)
1200	French victory at Bouvines (1214) Accession of Louis IX Albigensian Crusade	John (1199–1216) Magna Carta (1215) Henry III (1216–72)	Otto IV (1198–1215) Frederick II (1215–50)	Frederick II invades the Papal States
1250	Treaty of Paris (1259) Death of Louis IX at Tunis (1270)	Battle of Lewes (1264) Edward I (1272–1307)	The Great Interregnum (1250–73)	Charles of Anjou ruler of Naples and Sicily (1266–85) Sicilian Vespers (1282)
1300				

Ο ΑΓΙΟϹ
ΠΕΤΡΟϹ
17.190.679

Part II

FRONTIERS OF CHRISTENDOM

Introduction

It is often taken for granted and sometimes, apparently, unrecognized that what is of most lasting value in western civilization was held in trust for a millenium by a power that was anything but 'western' in the accepted sense of the term. Indeed, the Byzantine Empire which died, not without honour and an hour of final grandeur, in 1453 was a composite state with the flexibility and self-confidence to adapt its heritage of Greco-Roman culture to the needs of a Levantine environment. That was the source of its often renewed vitality, and in its time represented the most fruitful synthesis that the world had seen of the divergent traditions of east and west.

Founded on the Bosporus in AD 330 on the site of the old Greek colony of Byzantium, Constantinople had three main advantages. Politically this new Rome was heir to the old city of the Caesars with its genius for orderly administration. Spiritually it was inspired by Christianity, a faith characteristically Semitic in its combination of sensitivity with a stern moral code. Finally, Constantinople was ideally situated both for the maintenance of contact with Europe and for the development of relations (often troubled but somehow profitable) with Asian neighbours. These the Roman of the old order may have respected as enemies, but not as fellow-citizens in Rome itself.

Greek gradually took the place of Latin as the language of the Byzantine court as well as of the provinces. Old Rome under the waning power of the western emperors and the growing authority of the Papacy became increasingly irrelevant except as a symbol of the ancient order in a barbarized Europe. Commercial and cultural ties with Asia became closer. All these factors altered the character of Byzantine autocracy.

As God's earthly representative, the emperor of Byzantium lived in appropriate material splendour. The Orthodox Church, as interpreter of the emperor's will, was usually a pliant instrument of state policy. Thus, in the hour of decision, with the Turk at the walls of Constantinople, the Church found submission to the young sultan. Mehmet II, politically more expedient than the acknowledgement of the authority of the pope at Rome. Indeed, although the Roman pontiff's triple crown symbolized spiritual rather than temporal power, he demanded a submission no less absolute.

It is true that Latin allies, the Venetians, manned the ramparts alongside the meagre Byzantine garrison during the last agonizing siege, but in the fifteenth century Venice was a Levantine rather than a true western power. Trade interests played the leading role in its wish to keep the old empire alive, and one may doubt whether the saving of Byzantium's collective soul was in the Venetian reckoning.

The rise of Islam rapidly changed the balance of power between Byzantium and its neighbours. Between 661 and 750, under the Umayyad caliphs of Damascus, the champions of the religion founded by Mohammed broke out from the Hejaz, occupied the whole coast of North Africa as far west as Morocco and then turned northwards into Spain. Another spearhead of the Muslim armies moved into Syria and Asia Minor with Constantinople as the ultimate objective. Had that city fallen to the Arabs in the siege of 717–18, the course of European history would have been altered. But it was there and in northern Spain, at the two extremities of Mediterranean Christendom, that Islam was first checked and then contained. Not for seven centuries were the last of the Moors expelled from Spain, and, after the same long interval, it was the Ottoman Turks, not the Arabs, who finally put an end to the Empire of Byzantium.

As time went on, the character of the Muslim caliphate changed. The new Abbasid dynasty at Baghdad gave due weight to Arab susceptibilities by sustaining Arabic as the official language in its territories and imposing Koranic law on public life. At the same time it allowed to established states like Persia a measure of local autonomy. Ultimate loyalty was to the caliph, a figure who became by degrees as politically and socially remote as a Byzantine emperor or a Persian king of kings. Under the Abbasids, Arab scholarship led the world, and in the tenth century a patriarch of Constantinople could declare without exaggeration: 'Two sovereignties—the Muslim and the Byzantine—surpass all sovereignty on earth, like two great lights in the firmament.'

The co-existence of these brilliant rivals was not peaceful, but their antagonism was enlightened by a genuine mutual respect. Eastern Asia Minor in those days was a no-man's-land disputed by Christian and Muslim frontiersmen who raided each other's territory more out of habit than necessity. This almost traditional state of affairs was, however, upset by an expansionist Byzantine emperor, Basil II, who annexed the uplands of eastern Anatolia and forced the native Armenians to accept Byzantine 'protection'. It was a sullen, cowed and uncooperative people that he left behind him, and within half a century Basil's frontier had been breached beyond repair by the Seljuk Turks under their warrior leader Alp Arslan.

From the earliest period of the Abbasid caliphate Turkish tribes had been moving southwestwards from their homeland in central Asia. Like the Mongols later, they were nomad herdsmen. Their natural mobility made them elusive enemies and hard to defeat, for they fought from the saddle as archers. The sons of Seljuk were among the most gifted of these warriors, and, as they embraced Islam with all the fanaticism of the newly converted, they were enrolled in the caliph's armies.

Here their freshness, military ability and endurance soon made them an independent political force in the Muslim world. Already, by 1055, their leader, Tughrul Bey, had conquered Persia and had been proclaimed sultan by the Abbasid caliph at Baghdad. However, although his nephew and successor, Alpaslan, carried out frequent harassing raids against Byzantine territory, his aim was not permanent conquest of Asia Minor but rather the neutralization of his right flank in a campaign southwards against the Fatimids of Egypt.

The outcome of the Battle of Manzikert in 1071, with the total defeat of the Byzantine forces and the capture of their emperor, Romanus Diogenes, was as fortuitous as it was deserved. Each side miscalculated the other's intentions, but Byzantium made the greater mistake by relying, in a hostile territory like Armenia, on a host of mercenaries, among whom were Turks whose loyalty could not stand the test of war against their fellow-countrymen. The subsequent advance of the Seljuks into Asia Minor and the establishment of the Sultanate of Rum provides a rare example of a conqueror's capacity to assimilate the conquered to its own culture without resort to brutality or coercion.

The change from Byzantine to Seljuk rule, from a Christian to a predominantly Muslim society, seems to have caused so little contemporary stir that it may be assumed to have been a relatively peaceful and painless process. The later struggle of the Byzantine Empire against the Ottoman Turks was, however, a more bitter affair.

The Byzantines were in constant touch with Persians, Arabs and Turks and, after their own fashion, understood and were understood by them. However, with India, China and the Far East, Byzantium had the most tenuous and indirect relations. It was only through trade in luxuries that any connection existed at all. Silk, a Chinese monopoly in the time of the Roman Empire, was manufactured during the Middle Ages at Byzantium and in Sicily, so that only the most delicate and costly work was imported from the Far East. However, spices to make meat more palatable, and purges to dissipate the ill effects of unhealthy eating were always in demand, and most of this trade was in Arab hands. The distances involved were vast and the hazards of travel such that it needed a unified political control in Asia to make trade between the two halves of the

Above, a mosaic from Catholicon Daphni, Greece, displaying Christ Pantocrator, the terrible judge of the world. This image constantly recurred throughout Eastern Christianity.

On page 48, eleventh-century Byzantine medallion of St Peter, from a church in Georgia. It is done in cloisonné enamel on gold and is a traditional image of the saint. Metropolitan Museum of Art, New York, gift of J. Pierpont Morgan, 1917.

world reasonably simple. Such control came with the establishment of the Mongol Empire, and, in particular, with the capture in 1258 of the Abbasid capital at Baghdad.

The Mongol Empire was at first a mushroom growth. Under their first great leader, Genghis Khan, the tribes united. In twenty-one years (between 1202 and 1222) they extended their power from their own homeland to the Yellow Sea in the east, and to the shores of the Black Sea in the west. As if that were not enough, within another twenty years the Golden Horde was master of Russia and, a little later in the century, was to make two attempts—both abortive it is true—at a sea-borne invasion of Japan. This group of restless nomad tribes was a curious people to inherit so great an extent of the earth's surface. That it could do so was due to internal discipline based on a sense of common national origin, familiarity in daily life with hardship and privation and superb skill in mobile warfare.

As the known enemies of the Muslim powers, the Mongols became the subject of much wishful thinking on the part of Christian Europe. Thus England and France could envisage a Mongol-crusader alliance, and Pope Innocent III actually suggested baptism to the Great Khan himself—a proposal that met with a dusty answer. Christians there certainly were among the Mongol tribes, but their capacity to influence events in favour of their separated brethren in the west was greatly over-estimated.

Although the Mongol Empire had no lasting influence on relations between Christendom and Islam, it did reopen direct mercantile contact between Europe, the Levant and the Far East. Italian merchants in particular were quick to seize this new opportunity to trade at the source, and such men as Marco Polo were able to bring to Europe first-hand accounts of the distant lands subject to the Great Khan. Priests too made the long and arduous journey, and in 1307 an Italian was enthroned as the first Archbishop of Peking.

The traffic was not all eastbound, and, towards the end of the thirteenth century, Rabban Sauma, a Nestorian monk from northern China, set out in the opposite direction, bound for Jerusalem on pilgrimage. He never attained his real goal, though he did reach England.

The decline of the Mongol Empire after the death of Timur in 1406, the fall of Constantinople in 1453 and the disappearance of Italian merchant posts on the Black Sea coast soon after meant the end of this vast trading area.

Chapter 5

The Byzantine Empire

What we now call the Byzantine Empire was regarded by its peoples as the continuing Roman Empire, its rulers following in unbroken sequence from the first Caesars. From Rome Byzantium inherited its political claim to rule the world, the origins of its pervasive bureaucracy and formidable military system, and even what passed for a Roman Senate. The reconquering of old Rome and the west was to be a recurring dream for eight centuries.

However, Byzantium differed from the empire of the past in two fundamental respects. First, it ruled only part of the Mediterranean world—the more prosperous and vigorous eastern half. Here great cities and an advanced economy flourished while urban life decayed in the west. Byzantium's neighbours and enemies were not illiterate barbarians such as overran the west, but Sassanian Persia and, later, the Muslim caliphate, which could only enhance Byzantine culture.

Secondly, when Constantine the Great inaugurated Constantinople as New Rome in AD 330, he adopted the most lively of the Eastern faiths, Christianity, giving his successors a unique position as regulators of Orthodoxy and 'equals of the apostles'. The liturgy of state was enacted in the slow ceremonies of the Sacred Palace. 'By such means', explained one emperor, 'we shadow the harmonious movement of God the Creator around the universe, while the imperial power is preserved in proportion and order.'

Justinian

The Emperor Justinian (527–65) established the outlook of the early Byzantine state. He is best remembered as a lawgiver and for his creation of a single astonishing building, the church of the Hagia Sophia. The jurist Tribonian's ponderous codification of Roman law and the emperor's own decrees were the foundation of the Byzantine legal system. They preserved a priceless Roman heritage which was not to be reintroduced to the west until the twelfth century.

Justinian built churches in all parts of his empire as an imperial obligation. But the Hagia Sophia in Constantinople was his singular experiment in imperial magnificence. A vast shallow dome is suspended over semi-domes, reaching down to a great pillared basilica, whose walls are encased in polychrome marbles.

The chariot races at the Hippodrome were the focal point of the life of the city's vast populace and charioteering came near to becoming a political system. The various teams, each with their earnest cheerleaders, even reflected the theological divisions of the empire. Here also the common people exercised their sole right: that of acclaiming the emperor with rhythmical greetings or, very occasionally, of lynching him (as was nearly the case with Justinian in 532).

Justinian's ambition was nothing less than the reconquest of the west. After securing the Persian frontier two brilliant generals Belisarius and Narses, reclaimed North Africa from the Vandals, all Italy from the Ostrogoths and even parts of Spain. It seemed as if the Roman Empire was a reality once more.

However, the cost to Byzantium of the interminable campaigns was enormous. All sources of manpower were exploited, including hired, semi-private armies and foreign auxiliaries. In any case, most of the conquered territories had been ravaged too long and their peoples proved apathetic towards the 'liberators'. Except for Greek southern Italy the recovered lands were lost for good within a century. Even contemporaries condemned Justinian for ruining the empire by his expensive victories.

Constantinople was by far the largest of all medieval European cities. Its sheer size never ceased to amaze visitors from western Europe and its display of wealth (especially in Christian relics) made it 'the city of the world's desire'.

Twelve miles of land and sea walls enclosed six arcaded forums, an aqueduct which fed the cisterns, scores of domed churches, palaces and monasteries, a covered bazaar and market gardens. Its streets were adorned with sculptures looted from the Hellenistic east.

It was an industrial centre. Prices, trading contracts and guilds were controlled by the prefect of the city. Silk was an imperial monopoly and the dyeing and weaving workshops were installed in part of the maze of courtyards, pavilions and offices which made up the Sacred Palace.

Trading ships from the Crimea, Beirut, Alexandria and Venice assembled in the Golden Horn. However, Byzantine merchants, faced with high tariffs and an inefficient credit system, tended to leave the transit trade of the capital to foreigners (Arabs and later Italians). Land was a safer investment.

At one time the population of Constantinople may have reached 1,000,000. Since the price of corn could double every fifty miles on the atrocious roads, feeding such numbers presented formidable problems. Before the Arab invasions corn was shipped from Egypt and Sicily. The Crimean cornfields also contributed, and cattle ranches and sheepruns were developed in Anatolia.

Even in a city such as Constantinople the country was not far away and many citizens were, in fact, farmers. Illuminated manuscripts of the 'Labours of the Months' show the vintage in September (when the Byzantine year began), coursing in October, ploughing with a heavy wooden two-ox plough in November, collecting firewood in December, opening the wine jars in January, feasting in February and harvesting with a sickle (the western scythe was not popular) in July. Oxen moving endlessly round the threshing floor, winnowing with beautiful wooden forks and milling by hand or by horizontal water-driven wheels, completed the annual cycle of rural life.

Oil and wine ran from rock-cut presses. Night fishermen lured the anchovies and mackerel of the Marmora and Black Seas into their nets by lamplight. Pastoralists took their herds and flocks to the upland summer grazing grounds in the Balkans and the central plateau of Anatolia, sometimes moving their encampments hundreds of miles in the year. Vlach shepherds came into Constantinople to sell their salty, white goats-milk cheese. Even town-dwellers retired to summer hill stations, away from the hot, plague-ridden cities.

Much has been made of the independence of the free communes of Byzantine peasants who, answerable only to the state, were the supposed backbone of the rather ineffectual provincial levies. In fact, they were never particularly free, though, even with the rise of great feudal landowners in the last centuries of the empire, they always enjoyed a greater independence than did their counterparts in western Europe.

The Byzantine Church

The 'Universal Empire' and the 'Universal Church' were coeval: the one represented the other. Conversion to Orthodoxy was the first step in submission to the imperial system, for the emperor was Christ's political representative on earth. Only through heresy were the minorities of the east able to establish their national separatism and escape the imperial tax collector. For Orthodox and heterodox alike their faith was a way of life and there was little distinction between religious and secular matters.

In the Eastern Churches authority rested on a consensus of the entire community of believers. These had been baptized in their thousands during the fourth and fifth centuries when Christianity was established as the state religion, until the terms 'Roman' (i.e. Greek) and 'Christian' (i.e. Orthodox) became practically synonymous.

The nature of Christ's divinity was defined in seven general councils of the faithful, represented by their bishops and state officials. The ecclesiastical hierarchies were

headed by five patriarchs: of Rome, Constantinople, Alexandria, Antioch and Jerusalem. But whereas the senior pope (or 'father') of Rome became the sole interpreter of faith and order in the Western Church, the Eastern Orthodox never lost the view that the Church was 'Universal' because it incorporated all Christians, worshipping in their own languages and styles. It is this diffuse eastern, as opposed to the centralized western, view of authority which lies at the heart of the schism which was slowly recognized to exist between the two halves of Christianity.

The differences were aggravated by mutual misunderstandings and mistrust after the crusaders met Byzantines face to face. From the elventh century the question of union of the two Churches was for the Papacy largely a matter of discipline, whereas for the Byzantine his very identity was at stake. Dogmatic distinctions were merely points of argument.

In the fourth century St Basil, the great pastoral theologian of the Orthodox Church, established a tradition of communal contemplative life. Soon almost every country district could look to a monastery, dispenser of the strongly-felt Byzantine virtue of philanthropy. Some monasteries gathered round important imperial foundations like the Holy Sepulchre on Cavalry, some round cult centres of a holy man, like that in Syria of St Symeon the stylite, but most arose from the spiritual needs of individuals and attracted local endowments later.

Byzantine monks were pious and partisan, and they took their violent political and theological struggles into the streets. While parish priests were usually married peasants, bishops had to be celibate and were therefore appointed from the ranks of the unmarried clergy and the monastic orders. Lands given to monasteries (often by pious widows) were inalienable. It has been estimated that by the last centuries of the

Above, the interior of the church of Hagia Sophia in Constantinople, showing the huge area enclosed by the central dome (100 feet in diameter) and its adjoining semi-domes. The Islamic banners are a later addition.

Top, the Byzantine Empress Theodora (died 548), wife of Justinian, depicted with her servants in a mosaic at Ravenna. She protected Justinian during the Nica riots of 532, when the traditional chariot-race rivalries seemed in danger of overthrowing the Emperor.

Above left, the Emperor Justinian I (ruled 527–65) in a mosaic in the Basilica of San Vitale at Ravenna. His restoration of the Roman Empire around the Mediterranean proved far less durable than his codification of Roman law. Basilica di San Vitale, Ravenna.

empire the monasteries owned one-third of the finest arable land. They were largely exempt from taxation and (through a persistent tradition of pacifism) reluctant to supply military manpower.

By the twelfth century the dramatic secular liturgy was being superseded in the cathedrals by the recitation of monastic devotions, as the hold of the monasteries over the Church tightened. During the last desperate centuries of Byzantium the spiritual life became increasingly attractive. While the Turk encircled Constantinople, the monastic retreats of Patmos, Bithynian Olympos, Athos and the Meteora flourished.

Byzantine learning

The University of Constantinople taught a course in ancient philosophy, rhetoric, natural sciences and theology. Its textbooks were largely compiled by Alexandrian schoolmasters in the first century AD, and set texts were chosen with little originality. Nonetheless, educated Byzantines (and the literacy rate was much higher than in the west) knew their Bible and spiritual handbooks, such as writings of St John of the Ladder, as well as their Plato. This combination of classical humanism and eastern mysticism is illustrated by both Byzantine scholarship and art, but it never developed, as in the Italian Renaissance, into a struggle between medieval scholasticism and a revival of the values of pagan antiquity.

In Byzantium humanism and Christianity were two facets of the same living tradition—no revival was needed. The clue to the continuity of this dual culture lies in a long adherence to the language and style of ancient Greece. The Fathers of the Church wrote in the same language as had the ancient philosophers. Even in the fourteenth century the emperor, John Kantakouzenos, could incorporate in his memoirs without any change of style Thucydides' description of the plague at Athens, when he was at a loss for words to describe the Black Death. Bishops, like Eustathios of Salonika, found nothing contradictory in writing a commentary on Homer as well as pastoral sermons.

Through the accidental survival of libraries almost every ancient Greek text known to us today comes through a Byzantine copyist—usually a monk. We glimpse the literature of classical Greece through the eyes of Byzantine scholars, with their comments and interpretations. It is true that they were rarely original, but here, as in so many fields, Byzantium preserved, interpreted and gave a new life to the past.

Heraclius

The cost of Justinian's reconquest of the west was borne by his successors. Justin II (565–78), overwhelmed by bureaucracy and harassed by religious dissent, lost Dara, the massive fortress city which held the Persian front, in 573. In turn his successor Tiberius II (578–82) lost Sirmium, the key to the Danube frontier, and Avars and Slavs poured into the Balkans. Maurice (582–602) was given a respite in the east by a pro-Byzantine usurper to the Persian throne, and was able to repair the breach in the Balkan frontier. However, here his army revolted, and, in the old Roman style, elected as emperor an illiterate officer called Phocas.

No Byzantine chronicler has a good word for Phocas. During his aimless rule (602–10) the Persians penetrated as far as Chalcedon, which faces Constantinople across the water.

In 610 Heraclius, a brilliant veteran general in North Africa, was persuaded to rid the empire of Phocas. His fleet sailed to Constantinople under the protection of an icon of the Mother of God, which it was claimed, 'had not been made by human hands'.

When Heraclius came to the throne the Balkans and most of Justinian's western conquests were passing swiftly into barbarian hands. However, his reign marks the beginning of Byzantium's imperial centuries—the central and most confident stage of the empire as an eastern power.

Heraclius was faced by simultaneous attacks on Constantinople by Avars from the north and Persians from the east. Damascus fell in 614, Jerusalem soon after and the True Cross, the most potent relic in Christendom, was carried away to Persian Ctesiphon. For a moment Heraclius considered transferring his capital from Constantinople to Carthage in North Africa. However, his restless and inventive genius initiated an even more remarkable and daring solution. He bought off the Avars, risked Slav attacks on the capital, and headed east to the source of the trouble, covering his troop movements with a powerful navy.

First he attempted to satisfy his own Eastern non-Greek subjects be devising a compromise formula of faith which bridged the gap between official Orthodoxy and their own beliefs. Then he took his eastern armies from Chalcedon to Ctesiphon—1,000 miles of conquest in six breathless years (622–28)—driving the Persians back from the Byzantine capital to their own and crushing their empire for good at Nineveh. The True Cross was brought to the Hagia Sophia amid scenes of high ceremony and great rejoicing. Heraclius' triumph was the last of the ancient world, the conclusion of the age-long rivalry between Rome and Persia.

From the end of the seventh century until the tenth century the Balkans were more or less lost to the empire—overrun by Slav settlers who were among the ancestors of the modern peoples of Yugoslavia and Greece. The Byzantines first tried evangelizing the Slavs in the ninth century, but gave them a Church which was instead to become a symbol of their national consciousness. They were then forced to subdue the Slavs in a war which did not end until 1018, leaving the empire exhausted and ready for revenge. In the east Heraclius' triumphs were even more short-lived. By 642, when he died, all the non-Greek provinces had fallen (often willingly) to a new and totally unpredictable enemy, the Arabs.

Heraclius left Byzantium an unmistakably eastern power. His successors led the empire into its great struggle with Islam, and with it Byzantium entered the Middle Ages.

Byzantium and Islam—the long rivalry

Nicolas Mysticus, patriarch of Constantinople (901–25) wrote,

Two sovereignties—the Muslim and the Byzantine—surpass all sovereignty on earth, like two great lights in the firmament. For

Above, an early seventh-century silver dish from Cyprus, showing David anointed by Samuel. The style still owes a great deal to classical traditions. Metropolitan Museum of Art, New York, gift of J. Pierpont Morgan, 1917.

Above left, the Backovo monastery, now in Bulgaria, founded in 1083 by two Byzantine generals. In the tenth and eleventh centuries, Byzantine influence in Eastern Europe and Russia was greatly extended by missionaries of the Orthodox Church.

Below, the ruined palace of Ctesiphon near Baghdad; it was the capital of Sassanid Persia from the third century AD but was abandoned when the Abbasids were established at Baghdad.

Opposite, the church of Hagia Sophia in Constantinople, built by the Emperor Justinian between 532 and 537. It was the largest church in the eastern Mediterranean, but after the Turks took Constantinople in 1453 it was turned into a mosque, and the minarets were added.

this one reason, if for no other, they ought to be partners and brethren. We ought not, because we are separated in our ways of life, our customs and worship, to be altogether divided.

Mysticus was the pupil of Photius who, as patriarch, had revealed that there were very considerable differences of outlook between the Eastern and Western Christians. By contrast the Byzantine Empire and Abbasid caliphate had a healthy mutual respect.

When Constantinople repulsed the great Arab attack of 717–18, the Byzantine and Muslim Empires entered a centuries-long rivalry which can be paralleled with that between Rome and Persia. Once again eastern Asia Minor was the major scene of conflict. For two centuries the struggle which was waged there turned the land into a desolate area of military garrisons.

Digenis, the hero of the Byzantine epic of the period, was part Saracen and part Byzantine. He belonged to a class of border barons who were matched on the Muslim side by the Ghazis, wielders of the scimitar of Islam. The Ghazis were the advance guard of the emirates which grew up round the periphery of the caliphate. They lived in the same sort of religio-military communalism as did the Templars and Hospitallers of the crusaders.

Yet men like the legendary Digenis and Muslim border emirs, such as Saif al Dawlap of Aleppo, had a certain mutual respect. They understood each other better than they did their nominal and distant rulers in Constantinople and Baghdad. This border chivalry came to an end when Byzantium conquered eastern Anatolia (and even parts of Syria) outright and then the Seljuk Turks, who lay on the fringes of the Muslim world, arrived on the new Byzantine borders in the eleventh century.

Byzantium won its long struggle with the caliphate in the late tenth and early eleventh centuries. Its elaborate defence system ran from castle to castle—from Erzurum to Edessa and Melitene. Victory was achieved by the ruthless Basil II at the expense of the people who lived between the caliphate and the empire—the Armenians.

The Armenians were mountain people, giving generals and even dynasties to the Byzantines but jealous of their distinctive Church and aristocratic, clan-based society. Their feudal chieftains resented the Byzantine bureaucrats. As part of his disastrous expansionist policy Basil II annexed the Armenian kingdoms, turning useful buffer states into restless vassals. For the Armenians Byzantium simply meant hectoring bishops and over-efficient tax collectors. They complained that Constantinople sent eunuchs to protect them and that, like cowardly shepherds, the Byzantines abandoned their Armenian flocks when the wolf came.

The Seljuks

The 'wolf' was a chieftain of one of the Turkic peoples who had passed through Abbasid hands, the Seljuk Alp Arslan. Within fifty years of the establishment of Basil II's Armenian frontier, the eastern defence system and the whole of central and eastern Anatolia, fell quite casually into Seljuk hands. At Manzikert in 1071 Alp Arslan captured the Byzantine emperor. By 1081 the Seljuks were in sight of Constantinople. The disaster was bad enough, but hardly surprising, for the Armenians had the Byzantine mercenaries slipped prudently away from the imperial army at Manzikert. The Seljuks were in no position to deal with determined resistance. Byzantium lay on the edge of their world. Only Byzantium was to blame when they made it instead their centre.

When the dust of conquest settled in 1081, it revealed a boundary between the Greek coastlands of Asia Minor and the central plateau which had been disguised for centuries by the common rule of the Roman and Byzantine Empires.

Nothing could alter that boundary for over a century, for it was the natural distinction between those who were Greek, and prepared to fight for Byzantium, and those who were not Greek and wished to escape the burden of an increasingly alien empire. Orthodoxy, symbol of the imperial oppressors, perished without a struggle in

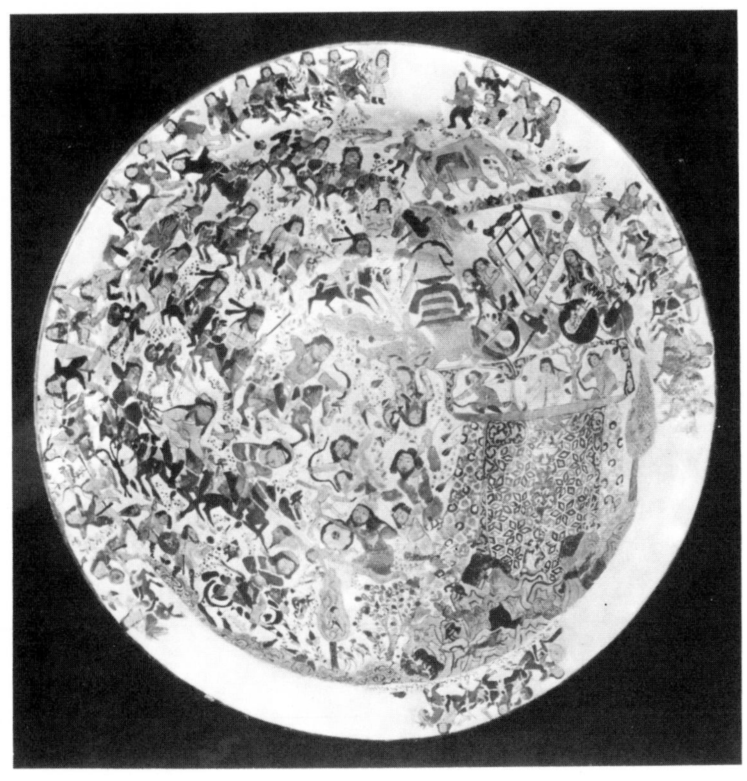

central Asia Minor and through no Muslim persecution. Here the inhabitants became ancestors of the modern Turks.

In these years Byzantium found its true identity. It was not a universal empire of different peoples and faiths all calling themselves 'Roman', but what amounted to a national state on the new western medieval model. At the same time Byzantium was losing just those characteristics which marked it out from other European Christian states. Byzantium became, slowly and haphazardly, feudalized.

Byzantine contemporaries hardly mention the disaster at Manzikert, which modern historians regard as one of the decisive battles in world history. In this the Byzantines were in some ways right, for they lost only a barren land of discontented subjects. Less than two centuries after Manzikert the Seljuk state of Rum in Asia Minor was crushed in the same Mongol onslaught from the east which extinguished the last trembling Abbasid caliph at Baghdad in 1258. Byzantium, as always, survived.

Decadence and renaissance

It is often assumed that a decline must precede a fall. The long-awaited fall of Constantinople in 1453 was preceded, for almost three centuries by the steady contraction of the Byzantine Empire until it comprised little more than the city itself. During this period Byzantium experienced one financial crisis after another and its commerce was almost entirely lost to Venice and Genoa. In addition, its emperors were increasingly forced to tour western courts to beg for help against the infidel—even, on two occasions (Lyons in 1274 and Florence in 1439) signing Acts of Reunion with the Roman Church in the hope of western support which rarely materialized. The meaning was only too clear: 'The future can only be worse', observed Pachymeres, 'In autumn there are no flowers; it is the season for dying.'

The autumn of the Byzantine Empire may have been a period of material decline, but it was hardly one of cultural decadence. These last centuries saw one of the most vigorous and impressive of all revivals of Byzantine civilization. For the last time the age-old empire triumphantly demonstrated that it had something to offer the contemporary world.

Outwardly Byzantium now looked very much like other western states. Great feudal lords controlled the surviving provinces of Thrace and the Morea (the Peloponnese), the old bureaucracy was less pervasive and the Church was politically prominent. The empire had narrowed to its cultural boundaries and now a few literary Byzantines began calling themselves 'Hellenes' (formerly a pejorative word indicating pagans), rather than 'Romans'.

In the Renaissance of contemporary Italy there was a revival of humanism and the values of classical antiquity but it could only be a self-conscious, even dilettante, movement compared with the Byzantine revival. Italians, such as Pius II or Pico della Mirandola, had to learn their Greek. Byzantine scholars had been brought up with the language of the ancients.

Fourteenth-century Byzantine civil servants, like Metochites or Choumnos, theologians like Gregory Palamas, scholars like Gregoras, and artists like Theophanes the Greek, all show a lively and individual approach to reinterpreting classical and Christian teaching and traditions.

Above, a Seljuk bronze bowl inlaid with silver, dating from the thirteenth century. The Seljuks had originated as tribesmen in Iran and were used as mercenaries by the Abbasids, until they conquered Baghdad in 1055. Cleveland Museum of Art; purchase from the JH Wade Fund.

Above left, a thirteenth-century bowl from Kashan, in Iran, commemorating a Seljuk victory. Freer Gallery of Art, Washington.

Below, an unusual bronze incense burner, made for the Seljuks in Iran or Iraq in 1181. Such intricate abstract designs are typical of Seljuk bronzework. Metropolitan Museum of Art, New York.

Opposite left, the dome of Malik Shah, at Isfahan, Iran, built in 1080, one of the finest examples of Seljuk architecture.

Opposite right, Nicephorus III Botaneiates, Emperor of Byzantium from 1078 to 1081. During his reign the Seljuks posed a serious threat to Constantinople itself, and he was forced to abdicate. Bibliothèque Nationale, Paris.

Frontier at the end of the reign of Justinian (565).

Frontier at the end of the reign of Basil II (1025).

The Greeks were able to look beyond their empire. The Cydones brothers translated St Thomas Aquinas, the Emperor Manuel II Palaeologos published his debates with a Muslim theologian. At the same time Byzantium endowed with its own particular quality the culture of two of its most brilliant offshoots: fourteenth-century Serbia and fifteenth-century Russia. Byzantine scholars, like Chrysoloras, taught in Italian universities.

In its last days Byzantium could still produce the wayward geniuses of Gemistos Plethon and Michael Trivolis. Plethon dreamed of setting up a neo-Platonic utopia in the Morea (a dream only, for he was a substantial feudal landowner there). In the late fifteenth century Trivolis was in turn, classical scholar in Venice and Florence, disciple of Savonarola, a monk on Athos and religious polemecist in Moscow (where he was the first to inform the Russians of the discovery of Cuba).

The crusaders

The fall of Constantinople to the crusaders in 1204 was simply the culmination of an internal process of disintegration, social, economic and political. The shock of the loss of their capital brought Byzantines to

Above, the Byzantine Empire between the reigns of Justinian and Basil II. Throughout the period it was based on its territories in Greece and Asia Minor.

Left, the church of Boiana, in Bulgaria, dating from the eleventh to the thirteenth centuries. The Bulgarian church had begun as autonomous from Byzantium but came under Constantinople's influence in the tenth century.

Opposite, Basil II (ruled 976–1025), who won the nickname 'Bulgar-slayer' for his conquest of Bulgaria in 1018. He asserted the power of the emperor over the landowners and brought the Byzantine Empire to its largest extent for almost 300 years. Biblioteca Marciana, Venice.

BYZANTIUM, PERSIA AND THE ARAB CONQUESTS AD 1000

Date	Byzantium	Persia	Islam	The West
200	Constantinople founded (330) Arcadius (395–408) Theodosius II (408–50)	Sassanid dynasty founded (226) Shapur I (241–72) Shapur II (309–79) Bahram V (420–40)		Valerian (253–60) Diocletian (284–305) Christianity adopted by Constantine (313) Division of Roman Empire (395) End of Western Roman Empire (476)
500	Justinian (527–65) Reconquest of Italy and North Africa	Khosrow I (531–79) Khosrow II (590–628)	Sassanid conquest of southern Arabia Birth of Mohammed (570)	Death of Clovis (511) Merovingians Gregory the Great (590–604)
600	Heraclius I (610–41) Defeat of the Persians Constantine IV (668–85)	Invasion of the Byzantine Empire (602–27) End of the Sassanids Arab conquest	The *hijrah* (622) Death of Mohammed (632) Muawiya caliphate (661) Umayyads of Damascus	Dagobert I (628–39) Pepin of Herstal (687–714)

Date	Byzantium	Persia	Islam	The West
700	Leo III the Isaurian (717–41) Arab advance checked The Iconoclasts	Persian revolt against the Umayyads Persian cultural influence on Islam	Conquest of Spain Islamic armies in Sind Muslims defeated at Poitiers (732) The Abbasids of Baghdad Harun al Rashid (786–809)	Charles Martel (715–41) Pepin the Short (751–68) Charlemagne (771–814)
800	Amorian dynasty Basil I (867–86) Macedonian dynasty	Taharid dynasty Growth of Shi'ite sect Saffarid dynasty	Arabs occupy Sicily invade Italy Aghlabids in North Africa	Expansion of Scandinavia Varangians in Russia Danish invasions of England
900	Expansion of the empire Romanus I Lecapenus (919–44) Nicephorus II Phocas (963–69) John I Zimisces (925–76)	Samanid dynasty Buyid dynasty Ghaznevid dynasty	Caliphate of Cordoba Fatimids in Egypt	Otto the Great (962–73) Hugh Capet (987–96)
1000				

their senses. Though Pope Innocent III never won his Universal Church, the short-lived Latin Empire was precarious from the start, and the crusading ideal was debased for ever.

Byzantium had, nonetheless, much to its credit. New life and a new confidence came to the surviving Greek provinces in Greece, western Anatolia and in the pocket empire of Trebizond (Trabzon), which bore notable fruit when Constantinople was restored to them in 1261. The Palaeologi, who ruled from then until 1453, were distinguished emperors, but they and their poverty were too well known in Europe and among the Turks. The empire had lost its mystery.

The Byzantines never really came to terms with the loss of their imperial role. In the last years of the fourteenth century a patriarch could still berate a grand prince of Moscow with the assertion that the emperor 'is not as other rulers are. . . . Yea, even if the Turks now encircle the government and residence of the emperor, he has still to this day the same appointment . . . as Emperor and Autocrat of the Romans—to wit of all Christians'.

Social conflict

Byzantium shared the social problems of most western countries, aggravated by the Black Death of 1347. The Zealots, who, created a commune in Salonika in 1342–50, in defiance of the great feudal lords and financiers, led the only 'Peasants' Revolt' in fourteenth-century Europe to achieve any measure of success. The Zealots were also concerned with the threat posed by the Balkan hegemony of Tsar Stephen Dushan of Serbia (1331–55). The empire was weakened by civil wars which broke out in 1341, 1354 and 1376, in which the feudal lords and the Church were unwilling or unable to defend their lands and the state could no longer hire adequate mercenaries.

In 1354 John VI Cantacuzene invited the Ottomans over the Gallipoli straits into Europe to fight Byzantium's war with Serbia. The expedient worked too well, for it gave birth to the Ottoman Empire as a European power and ensured that it would be the Turks, not the Serbs, who eventually took Constantinople.

The Ottoman threat

After the Seljuks had been crushed by the Mongols at Köse Dagh in 1243, Asia Minor disintegrated into a number of emirates. In the late thirteenth century Othman (Osman), the founder of the Ottoman (Osmanli) dynasty, created a border state in north-western Anatolia.

Because his was the only emirate in the front line against the Byzantine infidel, it attracted many Ghazi warriors. Ghazi emirates could thrive only on conquest and the Ottoman was the only one which could expand. The Ottomans were also willing to learn from the Byzantines and Italians, and Sultan Orkhan (1324–59) expanded his state not in Anatolia but in the Balkans. John V Palaeologos became the effective vassal of Sultan Murad I in 1373. Sultan Murad met his death on the field of Kossovo, where he destroyed the Serbian Empire in 1389.

Sultan Bayezid I (1389–1402), called 'The Thunderbolt', continued the Balkan conquests. He took the Bulgarian capital in 1393 and routed a western crusade at Nicopolis in 1396. He then turned to take control of the Anatolian emirates. However, he had not reckoned with Timur who, in 1402, defeated the Ottoman army at Ankara and captured Bayezid himself.

Byzantium was given its final respite. Timur restored all the old Anatolian emirates. The Ottomans retained little save their European conquests. Already they had been forced to employ Serbs and Bulgarians to run their state. The levy of Christian children into the administrative and military corps (especially as janissaries or elite soldiers) ensured regular transfusions of enthusiastic converts into the Ottoman system. Already the Ottomans had inherited the Serbian and Bulgarian ambition of making Constantinople the capital of a Balkan Empire. It was the Byzantines in 1354 and the Mongols in 1402 who created out of an Anatolian emirate a new European power, the Ottoman Empire.

Chapter 6

The Rise of Islam

The historic distinction between desert and fertile land is at its sharpest in the Arabian Peninsula. Driven by hunger and poverty, successive waves of the desert people of the heart of Arabia have moved outwards to raid the green lands of the Fertile Crescent. A network of family relationships linked the peoples who roamed the sparse pastures with their cousins who had become farmers on the fringes of the desert.

Some inland parts of the peninsula are by no means infertile. Small walled towns with shaded gardens marked the oases and the peninsula was crossed by great caravan routes. By Mohammed's day in the seventh century AD, Mecca and the western and central lands of the Hejaz had inherited control of the great route north to Syria. Mecca's trade then may have been worth 300,000 gold pounds a year.

The Arabs were traders and raiders. Mohammed's secular career reflects the old pattern. The Prophet started as a camel driver and contractor in a caravan company, later becoming a raider of the prosperous lands to the north and the west.

The Arabs are simply those who lived in Arabia. Their legendary ancestor was Shem and their first prophet was Abraham. They are the Jews of the early books of the Old Testament. Their language is the most important survival of the old Semitic tongue.

In the seventh century, when the economic centres had moved south from Petra and Palmyra to Mecca and Medina, three leading faiths can be distinguished among their numerous local cults. The first was a compound of animistic observances—the veneration of sacred trees, stones and wells—and the recognition of a supreme being, the Allah. These heathen had no concept of an afterlife. The Prophet, with his vivid preaching of a Heaven and a Hell, was utterly opposed to them, though he adapted their ancient pilgrimage to the sacred black meteorite which had fallen out of Heaven at Mecca.

Economically, perhaps even numerically, the Jews were the most important. They dominated the iron and armament trades. Beside the black stone at Mecca stood one of their holiest shrines, the Kaaba, Abraham's windowless house. The Prophet, uneasily recognizing his great theological debt to Judaism and the powerful attraction of the Kaaba, condemned the Jews

The Arab Christian tribes represented an eastern Christianity which stood closer to local beliefs than to the official dogmas of Rome and Constantinople. Christians shared with the Jews, and even the pagans, of Arabia the ancient and profound conviction that there was only one God and that He was indivisible. This belief became the cornerstone of Islam. The Trinitarian debates of the seven General Councils of the Church disturbed the Arab Christians. Their shameful exploitation by Byzantine officials alienated them even further from the west.

The armies of Islam could not have conquered the Middle East so rapidly if they had not been generally welcomed by local Christians. By the mid-seventh century the national minorities of the Levant—such as the Syrians and Egyptian Copts—had reawoken. Persia and Byzantium had fought themselves to a standstill. Arabia was restless. Its Jews, Christians and pagans were seeking a supreme god. For them Mohammed provided a definition of the Godhead. The subject peoples of the Byzantine East were seeking an identity. For them the Muslim armies brought at least a solution.

Allah is the One God

Mohammed was born in Mecca in about 570. He belonged to the leading tribe of the city, the Quraysh. His own family was respectable but not wealthy. The man himself is largely lost in the historic eastern interpretation of the role of a prophet, but, as with other visionaries, certain stages of development do seem clear enough.

Until his early forties Mohammed was an affluent, but apparently unremarkable trader of Mecca. Then in the year 610, while asleep in a cave, he had a vision of the archangel Gabriel. This left Mohammed with an overwhelming conviction that he had a mission to perform. This compulsion was strengthened in a series of religious experiences throughout the remainder of the Prophet's life. There are hints that he endured what Western mystics have described as 'the dark night of the soul', a period of self-doubt and torment.

During these obscure first years of his mission in Mecca, Mohammed's teaching of the One God found ready listeners. However, the materialist and conservative merchants of the city opposed his condemnation of local cults (with which he eventually compromised in a few but significant details) and mocked the new preacher for his concept of philanthropy on earth and divine judgement and a life hereafter.

Throughout the last twenty years of his life Mohammed recorded his moments of illumination when he was inspired by divine teaching. This he transmitted in the form of short verses which were gathered after his death to form the Koran, almost the earliest example of Arabic literature. The Koran

Above, the Koran was given to Mohammed by an angel in a cave on Mount Hira, according to this Arabic painting.

has something of the textual history of the Old Testament—to which it owes much. Several different versions circulated before an accepted text was reached. The earliest revelations are more purely religious, but the Prophet went on to develop a complete moral code.

The overriding message is of the unity of the One God, revealed through scripture to the uncomprehending Jews and Christians, who must be led back to the simplicity of the laws of Abraham. God is infinite and imminent, closer to a man than the vein of his neck. God is merciful and compassionate.

The Koran emphasizes the virtue of human charity and inspires a sense of social obligation which is felt by all Muslims and is reflected in their political institutions. Mosques are commonly embedded within a complex of schools, hospitals, baths, and charitable institutions whose upkeep is part of the duty of a Muslim.

Doomsday was forewarned in scenes of unexampled grandeur. The souls of the devout would be weighed in the balance and human injustice and oppression would lead to a Hell which Mohammed depicted in the vivid colours of a revivalist. Heaven, on the other hand, was a luxurious watered garden enhanced with every fleshy delight.

The Koran moves from passages of mundane condemnations of idolatry and immodesty and injunctions against the consumption of pork and wine to moments of high ecstasy and beauty:

God is the light of heaven and earth. It is lit from a blessed olive tree neither eastern nor western. Its oil would almost shine forth if no fire touched it. Light upon light; God guideth to His light whom He will.

The Muslim code

The duties of a Muslim became clear-cut in the years after the Prophet's death. He must conform to a moral code and be charitable.

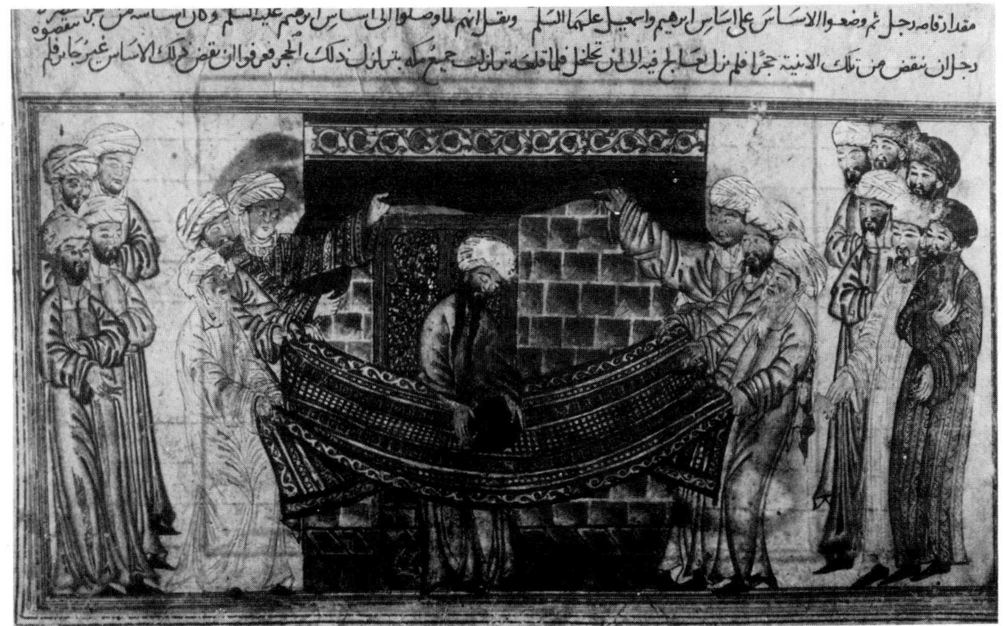

Above, the plan of the Kaaba is traced out on this Turkish pulpit tile. It is the duty of every believer to pay a pilgrimage to this shrine at least once in his lifetime.

Above left, the arcade of the Holy of Holies at Mecca, the central shrine of Islam. The Kaaba stands in the centre of a vast square, surrounded by this complex of colonnades.

Left, an incident from the life of Mohammed, according to an Arabic manuscript of the fourteenth century. Here Mohammed restores the sacred Black Stone to Mecca; it had been an important pagan shrine, and now its sanctuary, the Kaaba, became the most sacred place in Islam. Edinburgh University Library.

Opposite left, a painting of Mohammed being given a message by the angel Gabriel. Mohammed was often shown as faceless but with a burning halo.

Opposite top right, an ancient copy of the Koran, showing the exquisite calligraphy and abstract patterns that form the core of Islamic art. British Museum, London.

Opposite bottom right, a sixteenth-century Turkish ceramic tile decorated with a schematic plan of Medina. The main feature of the city is the house of the prophet, which was expanded into a mosque in the early years of the eighth century. Museum of Islamic Art, Cairo.

Five times a day he performs his religious exercises at the unforgettable summons of the muezzins who answer their cries from minaret to minaret:

God is most great. I testify that there is no God but Allah. I testify that Mohammed is God's Prophet. Come to prayer. Come to security. God is most great.

Through brilliant political insight Mohammed tempered his denunciation of idolatry and polytheism by retaining and transforming the most sacred of Arabian cults—that of the pilgrimage to the black stone and to the Kaaba in Mecca. Every devout Muslim performs the *hajj*, or pilgrimage, at least once in his life. He passes through a period of purification and visits the scenes of the Prophet's life.

Without the support of Mecca, the economic and political centre of Arabia, Mohammed could not hope to launch his faith. Mecca however, was unreceptive. Five years of teaching there gave him notoriety but few adherents. In 622 the Prophet fled to Mecca's lesser rival, Medina, 280 miles to the northeast, with his flock of some seventy-five of the first Muslims. The event called the *hijrah*, or 'emigration', is the turning-point in Islam, and from that year, 622, the Muslim calendar is dated.

Finding support in Medina Mohammed led expeditions of his followers south against Mecca. By the year six of the *hijrah* he had surrounded Mecca and an armistice was signed. As a result the nomads of the desert felt free to join the Prophet's standard. Only some Jewish tribes had misgivings and were massacred.

Mohammed entered Mecca in triumph for the pilgrimage of the year eight of the *hijrah*. In the remaining two years of his life he became master of the Hejaz. Submission to the Prophet's rule now preceded conversion to Allah's law. By the year ten of the *hijrah* (632), when Mohammed died, his armies had carried the green flags of Islam to the borders of the Byzantine Empire.

The holy war

The word Islam means 'submission' (to Allah'). For the Muslim the world is divided into the Land of Islam and the Land of War which had been created by the necessity of subduing the infidel. The early Muslim armies which challenged the Byzantine and Persian Empires combined a religious fervour with a military zeal which Mohammed had already described in his years at Medina as the Jihad or Holy War. The Jihad proved irresistible because Islam had emerged so early as a state as well as a faith. In fact it conquered as a state.

It is a myth that Muslim armies forced conversion at sword point. To the disaffected Christians of the Byzantine East they offered a semi-privileged status in return for recognition of Arab political supremacy. Sensing their cultural inferiority in the Mediterranean and in Persia, the Arabs were reluctant to share their faith with the peoples they conquered, for Islam was their sole and distinctive advantage, the mark of a conqueror.

Only later, when the Arab military aristocracy who had ridden out of the desert found that they had to rule as well as conquer, and so had to use the existing bureaucratic and commercial traditions of their new lands, did Muslims begin to mingle with their subjects. When that stage came, great numbers of their subjects became Muslim themselves through voluntary conversion. It meant the end of Arab supremacy in Islam.

Mohammed's successors were called caliphs, or deputies of the Prophet of God. They were also heirs to an empire which swiftly outgrew its origins in the Hejaz. As one conquest followed another—Damascus and Syria in 634, Alexandria and the Egyptian cornlands in 641—the caliphate became a glittering political prize. The Prophet left no sons, and disputes among his successors dictated Muslim politics for centuries to come.

Later Abbasid chroniclers have relegated the Umayyads, impious caliphs, to a sort of Muslim Dark Ages. In fact they were responsible for the first galloping expansion of Islam and for the creation of an empire out of the early state in the Hejaz. At Damascus, Muawiya, the fifth caliph, established a kind of dynastic monarchy to match those of the Byzantines and Persians. He and his successors ruled from Syria from 661 until 750, while Mecca itself gradually became a simple cult centre.

The speedy conquests of Islam very soon led to internal divisions. There were the puritan Kharijites and the procrastinating but tolerant Murjites. The most vigorous sect to oppose the orthodox Sunnis (who form the majority of the Muslim world) were the Shiites, the followers of Ali, the fourth caliph, whose entire family was killed by the Umayyads in 680. The Shiite sect was born in the civil wars between the fourth and fifth caliphs, but it was also a symptom of the growing unrest among non-Arab Muslims who fought in the armies of Islam as second-class citizens. The Shiites survive in great numbers today, especially in the eastern Islamic states.

Behind the differences lie a host of non-religious factors: social, economic and, above all, ethnic. The Arabs were becoming thin on the ground in their own empire and therefore clung tenaciously to their special privileges. Although the Umayyads removed the caliphate from Medina to Damascus they prolonged the Arab hold over the empire by institutional devices. Arabic became the official language; provincial governors were Arab; Koranic law was established; and a new coinage was adopted for the whole empire. The monograms stamped on the dirhems proclaimed the oneness of Allah and the universal mission of His faith.

For a century the Arabs were able to control the administration of the empire, but at the risk of compromise. Jews and Christians stood second in their religious and social hierarchy, paying a poll and land tax for the privilege, and escaping the burden of military service.

However, in established states, such as Sassanian Persia, the Arabs could only take over existing and long-perfected systems of

Above, painting from the Life of the Prophet *showing Mohammed and Abu Bakr on their way back from Medina to Mecca in 630, eight years after the original* hejira. *New York Public Library, Spencer Collection.*

Left, mosque built at the Ummayad capital at Damascus in about 710 AD by the Caliph Walid I, who was responsible for the Arab advance into Spain and India.

Opposite left, the ruined remains of the Blue Mosque at Tabriz in Iran, a fine example of Timurid architecture decorated with blue tiles. It is dated 1465.

Opposite right, the ceiling of the Dome of the Rock mosque in Jerusalem was completed in AD 691 and was a powerful symbol of the cultural confidence of Islam over Judaism and Christianity; Islam nevertheless tolerated these two religions, on account of their monotheism and their prophets.

government. Persian local feudalism survived. The old nobility clung to Zoroastrianism, but the local aristocracy became increasingly converted to Islam and thus renewed their power. From the Sassanians the Umayyad caliphs inherited a political symbolism and an imperial style.

The expansion of Islam

The first half century of Umayyad rule saw the greatest conquests of the still unified empire. In the west all the African coast up to Morocco was wrested from the Berbers by 710. Visigothic Spain was overrun by 713 in a three-year conquest. It took seven centuries for the Christians of Spain to recover the territories they had lost.

In the east the armies of Islam penetrated the Indus valley and Sind in 712. Two years later they were in Kashgar, on the fringes of the Chinese Empire.

There the conquest stopped. Later Islamic history has nothing to compare with these decades of expansion. In fact, the huge Muslim Empire began to contract within a century of the Prophet's death.

There is no doubt that one of the great turning-points in European and Islamic history is the Arab failure to take Constantinople by sea in the siege of 717–18. It proved to be more than seven centuries before a Muslim conqueror, Mehmet II, set foot in Constantinople.

Lesser encounters marked the bounds of Arab expansion in the east and west at this time. The Chinese drove the Arabs back to Ferghana in 715 and in 732 Charles Martel routed a small Muslim exploratory expedition at Poitiers, in the heart of France. The tide of conquest had turned early.

At Damascus the Umayyads had to create a culture and machinery of government to match their new empire. In administration the Arab military occupation was quickly superseded by local rule. From an early period the Islamic states ruled their national and religious minorities through their own courts and leaders.

In art and architecture the Umayyads adapted the existing Greco-Roman and oriental traditions as the Byzantines had done before them. Here, though, eastern forms were naturally dominant. The earliest important Islamic monument is the Dome of the Rock, a wooden cupola surmounting an octagon enclosing the site of Abraham's sacrifice (and the Prophet's ascension), which was built in Jerusalem in 691. In Damascus in 706 the Umayyads converted the fourth-century basilica of St John the Baptist (itself once the Temple of Jupiter) into one of the first congregational mosques.

The essentials of Islamic religious architecture became clear during the Umayyad

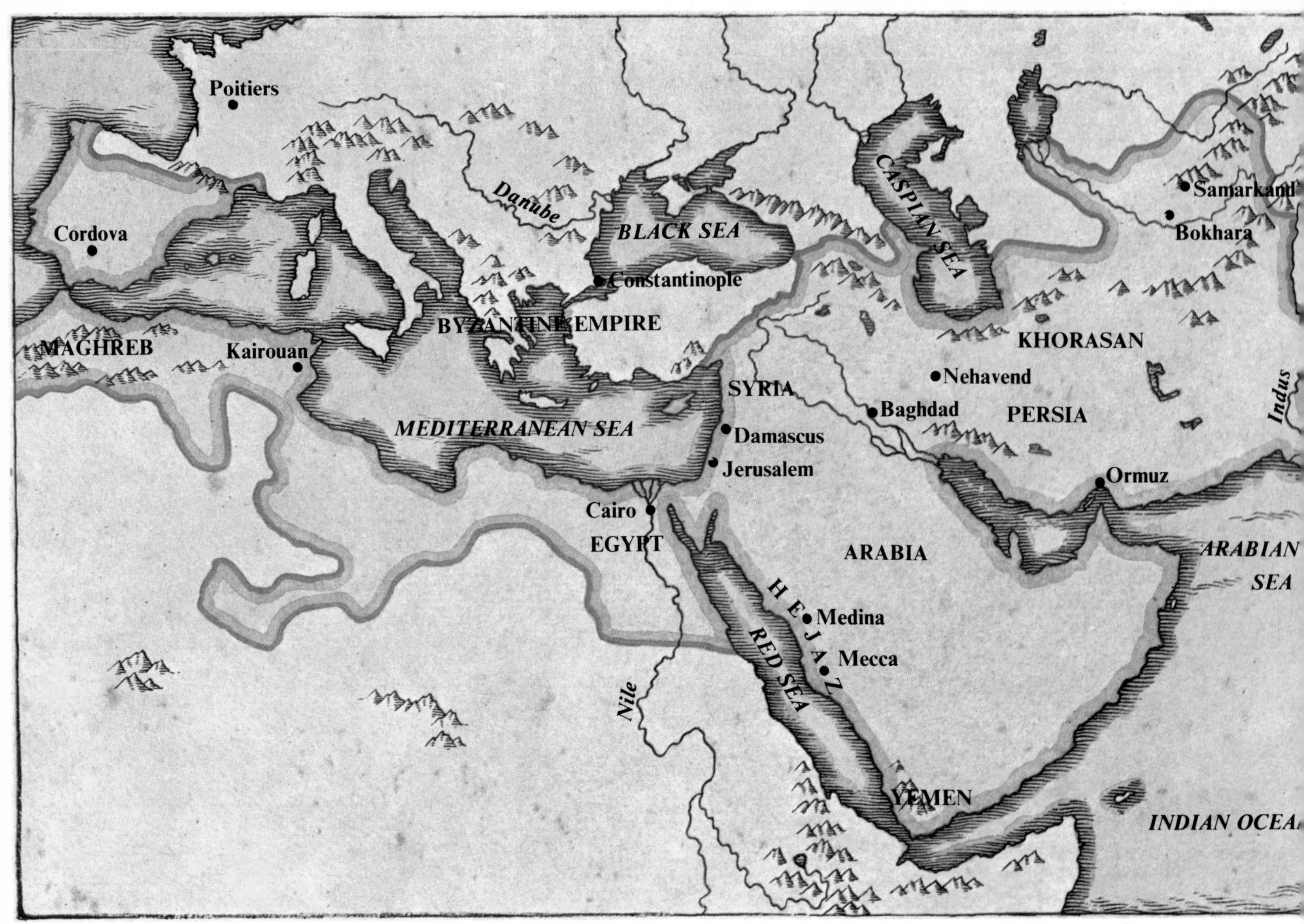

period, but its forms were derived from numerous local styles. Many of the great mosques of Islam are converted Christian churches, recognizable because the *mihrab* has to stand at an angle from the eastern apse, sometimes on the southern wall.

The power of the Umayyad caliphs was too closely restricted to Arab supremacy in the empire. Converts to Islam, especially in Persia, found that they did not enjoy the same legal and social privileges as their Arab conquerors. Unrest grew in the fourth decade of the eighth century and found leaders in the family of Abbas, the Prophet's uncle. In 750 Saffah, 'the shedder of blood' defeated Marwan II, the last Umayyad caliph and entered Damascus as the first ruler in a new dynasty, the Abbasid.

The Abbasids of Baghdad

The soundly based Abbasid claim to the caliphate was to be exploited by skilful propaganda of their agents, among them Abu Muslim, who had been leading what virtually amounted to a Persian revolt against the Umayyads since 746.

The resurgence of Persia and Mesopotamia under the banner of the new caliphate marks the passing of the initial impetus and control of Islam from Arab hands. As one caliph is said to have remarked: 'The Persians ruled for a thousand years and did not need us [Arabs] even for a day; we have been ruling for one or two centuries and cannot do without them for an hour.'

The new caliphate clearly satisfied a need among Arab converts. It held to the principle that public life should be regulated by Islam, but was fairly impartial about the heresies which divided the faithful. All Muslims could regard it as their state, and the old leaders of the lands which the Arabs had conquered could fashion its government according to their own patterns and ideas. It was in this way that the Abbasid caliphate was able to last until the Mongol sack of Baghdad in 1258, a period of some five centuries.

The outward symbol of the new regime was the transference of the capital from Damascus to the small Christian village of Baghdad in Mesopotamia. Here a succession of three brilliant caliphs devised a new administrative system and Baghdad entered upon a period of economic prosperity.

The administrative system owed much to the old Sassanian government of Persia, and, indeed, Persians now supplanted Arabs in the highest posts. The caliphate itself was soon hedged about by a palace ritual in which old Persian ceremonies were revived. The government fell increasingly into the hands of viziers or chief ministers, who established their own dynasties.

Ministries (*divans*) were set up for the army, finance, postal services and provincial administration. The postal system was particularly elaborate. Semaphore towers signalled from Morocco to Baghdad, desert lighthouses were built, and a regular carrier pigeon service was initiated. Local postmasters were used as intelligence agents.

It was, however, an essentially different government from that of the Umayyads. First, the caliphs, surrounded by traditional Persian luxury, became as remote as had the old Sassanians. The vigorous local aristocracies which now seized power in the provinces and which ran the ministries in Baghdad were bound to divide the empire into a loose confederation of warring states. The caliph himself became a sort of cult figure, a living relic to be placed on view on holy days.

This development was postponed until 809 by three great caliphs: al Mansur (754–75), his son al Mahdi (775–85), and Harun ar-Rashid, his grandson (786–809). Each surpassed his predecessor and the peak of achievement of the Abbasid caliphate came within half a century of its foundation.

Trade, both in the eastern Mediterranean and in the Indian Ocean, recovered. Arab dhows sailed from the Moluccas to Ormuz, and from Beirut to Almeria. Great urban centres grew up with their covered bazaars and merchant guilds. Arab translations from Greek and Syriac of the classical Greek and Roman texts of geography, natural history and the profane sciences gave the Muslim world a lead over Europe in scientific knowledge which was not lost until the fifteenth century.

The period of decay

Even during Harun ar-Rashid's magnificent reign, signs of disintegration were becoming apparent. Harun planned to divide his empire into eastern and western halves and it was only after the civil war which followed his death in 809 that it was nominally reunited under al Maman.

Persia and Khorosan were especially independent. From the early ninth century local dynasties there (the Tahirids, the Saffarids and then the Samanids) effectively dissociated the eastern half of the empire from Baghdad. Deprived of the revenues of its richest provinces the capital ceased to flourish and Harun ar-Rashid's palaces fell into elegant decay.

The old Arab military aristocracy was finally eliminated in the 830s. The caliphs and their viziers had to look to a new class to fight their wars and officer their armies. They were obliged to choose their most stubborn enemies to the east, the Turks.

Throughout the Abbasid period Turkic peoples passed into the Muslim armies to turn them eventually into their own war machine. The Turks were happy to leave theological niceties to the caliphs, but here the Abbasids faced another centrifugal tendency. Local heresies flourished in most provinces. Happily for the survival of the orthodox Sunni caliphate the Shiites were themselves divided. One Shiite group founded a state in the Yemen in 897, which was ruled by imams of the family of the Prophet until the middle of the twentieth century.

Abbasid governors showed a growing reluctance to retire from the provinces to which they had been assigned after their duties were over. Spain was an Umayyad outpost. The Aghlabids detached North Africa. In 831 they captured Palermo and their rule in Sicily until the Norman invasion of 1060 gave that island's culture much of its peculiar flavour. In 909 a Shiite group led by the Fatimids declared the end of Abbasid rule in Egypt. In 973 the Fatimids founded Cairo as a rival to Baghdad.

With Persia effectively lost to the rule of Baghdad and Egypt in rebellion under the Fatimids, the caliphate's real authority shrank to Mesopotamia. The later history of the Abbasids is one of a struggle with Egypt for the intervening lands of Syria. When there was a period of equilibrium, or weakness in Cairo and Baghdad, local lords in Syria and Palestine assumed practical independence. It was during one of these periods, in 1099, that the crusaders were able to capture part of the eastern Mediterranean coastal lands and Jerusalem. However, the precarious Latin outpost was endangered whenever either Mesopotamia or Egypt moved to attack the other.

There were other signs of decay. The status of women declined. Respectable women were now obliged to wear veils in

Above, a thirteenth-century miniature of an Arab caravan, painted in the style of Baghdad. Arab traders travelled throughout southern Asia and north Africa, enriching their own civilization.

Above left, a twelfth- or thirteenth-century illustration from Baghdad showing a pharmacist at work. Arab medicine was founded on a thorough knowledge of the workings of the body and on a wide experience of the efficacy of herbs. Metropolitan Museum of Art, New York.

Opposite, the extent of the Islamic empire in AD 750, little more than a hundred years after Mohammed's death.

THE DECLINE OF BYZANTIUM, THE TURKS AND ISLAM

Date	Byzantium	The Turks	Islam	The West
1000	Basil II (976–1025) Schism with Rome Byzantines defeated by Turks at Manzikert (1071)	Seljuk Turks in Asia Minor Alp Arslan (1063–72)	Almoravids in North Africa Taifas kingdoms in Spain	Normans invade England (1066) Gregory VII (1078–85) First Crusade
1100	Alexius I Comnenus (1081–1118) Manuel I Comnenus (1143–80)	Seljuk Empire collapses (1157) Zangid sultanate of Syria Sultanate of Rum Empire of Khorezm	Almohades in Spain and Morocco	Second Crusade Frederick Barbarossa (1152–90) Henry II Plantagenet (1154–89) Assassination of Thomas à Becket Third Crusade
1200	Crusaders capture Constantinople (1204) Latin Empire established Michael VIII Palaeologus (1259–82) Partial restoration of Byzantine Empire	Mongols defeat Seljuks of Rum (1243) Osman founds Ottoman Empire	Merinid dynasty in Morocco Mameluke rule begins in Egypt	Philip II Augustus (1180–1223) Fourth Crusade Albigensian Crusade Louis IX of France (1226–70)
1300	Andronicus II Palaeologus (1282–1332) Struggle against the Serbs John V Palaeologus (1341–91) Turkish encroachment	Turkish expansion in Asia Minor Murad I (1359–89) Orkhan (1326–59) Victories of Kossovo (1389) and Nicopolis (1396)	Burjite Mamelukes in Egypt	The Black Death in Europe Hundred Years' War Edward III of England (1327–77) Peasants' Revolt
1400	Decline of Byzantium Manuel II Palaeologus (1350–1425) Constantine XI Palaeologus (1448–53) Turks capture Constantinople (1453)	Bayezid I (1389–1402) Turks defeated by Timur (1402) Murad II (1421–51) Turkish conquests in South-western Europe Mehmet II (1451–81)	Wattasides in Morocco	Joan of Arc Medici family Leonardo da Vinci
1500				Discovery of America

public and the idea of the harem was evolved. Moreover, although many of the component peoples of Islam used the religious legitimacy and political self-effacement of the caliphate to establish their own local hegemony, many of the more downtrodden among the subject populations became restless. In the marshes of Mesopotamia the gipsy-like Jats, on the Persian Gulf the negro Zanjis and in Egypt the Copts (leading workers in the declining papyrus industry) all led local revolts against their masters.

The Umayyads of Spain

When the first Abbasid caliph defeated the last Umayyad in 750, he was not able entirely to obliterate the old dynasty. One member, Abd al-Rahman, escaped westwards. He reached Spain in 755.

Spain lay on the periphery of the Muslim world. Even during the period of the early caliphate it had shown its own separatism, for communications with Damascus were poor. Ostracized by the Abbasids, Abd al-Rahman founded, or rather re-founded, an Umayyad state which gave Spain its quite distinct Muslim culture. Abd al-Rahman himself had an impeccable Arab ancestry going back to the Quraysh of Mecca. Spain had largely been conquered by Berbers rather than Arabs.

The subject population was not entirely Christian and it included the largest Jewish minority in Europe. Thus there arose a lively interchange of Muslim, Christian and Jewish cultures. This gave medieval Spain a remarkably tolerant and enlightened character, which encouraged experiment in government and in art and learning.

Abd al-Rahman founded his capital at Corboda in 756. From Spain the widest Umayyad conquests even took in Provence and parts of Italy, but these were soon lost. In northern Spain a few pockets of Christian resistance survived. Slowly they expanded. The Christian reconquest of Spain took over seven centuries to complete. However, during a period of 300 years the Umayyads brought the country to a peak of political and economic achievement, and stimulated intellectual and artistic creativity.

Abd al-Rahman and his first successors encouraged agriculture and the planting of rice fields and orange groves. Spain became an important source for slaves and, later, armaments. An individual style of architecture developed—the horseshoe arch being its particular feature. Separated from the rest of the Muslim world, the Umayyads patronized Orthodox Muslim theologians.

However, their schools at Granada and Saragossa (lost to the Christians in 1230) were also concerned with ancient Greek learning. Averroës (1126–98) wrote, among other works, a commentary on Aristotle. Eventually the great library of Hakam II was to be burnt book by book; but during the early Middle Ages Western scholars had to go to Spain to discover, through Muslim intermediaries, the learning of the ancients.

Early in the eleventh century the Umayyads of Spain died out and the contracting Muslim state was divided into petty emirates. The Almavids and the Almohades retreated before the new kings of Leon and Castile. Semi-legendary crusaders such as El Cid (died 1099) conquered the central plateau. Toledo fell in 1085. Four centuries later the Christian kingdoms, united under Ferdinand and Isabella, drove out the last Moors.

Chapter 7

The Coming of the Mongols

Above, although some Christians believed the Mongols, who were religiously tolerant, to be led by Prester John, this contemporary French painting shows that legendary Christian monarch being killed in a battle with Genghis Khan. Bibliothèque Nationale, Paris.

Opposite left, the ninth-century Great Mosque at Kairouan, Tunisia, originally founded as a military outpost but soon becoming an important cultural centre under the Aghlabids. The minaret is the earliest example still surviving.

Opposite right, the fourteenth-century Court of the Lions in the Alhambra in Granada, southern Spain. Umayyad art in Spain was exceptionally delicate and was centred on the importance of the garden.

From time to time during the Middle Ages, Europeans were reminded how small their corner of the world was. Rumours would come out of the east of a land which stretched to the very edge of the earth. It was inhabited by centaurs—restless clans of herdsmen who lived on their horses. They shifted their black hide tents hundreds of miles in their annual quest for pastures. The men were squat and slit-eyed and they drank the sour milk of mares.

Every few centuries there was an upheaval. The clans united into hordes and sought the softer life of Mesopotamia or of northern China. Thus came the Seljuk Turks, mounted archers, within sight of Constantinople in the eleventh century: 'They worship the wind and live in the wilderness . . . they have no noses.'

The final and most devastating wave of conquerors from central Asia were the Mongols. Their empire was so vast, so sudden and so strange that it fitted into no known category. But twice it saved Byzantium by all but destroying its Turkish enemies in Anatolia—in 1243 by defeating the Seljuks at Köse Dagh and in 1402 by triumphantly carrying off the Ottoman sultan Bayezid from the battlefield of Ankara.

For Western Christians the Mongols gave hope of an ally to break the Muslim encirclement of the crusader state of Jerusalem. Tales of Nestorian Christians among the Mongol Khans inspired one of the most intriguing and persistent of western beliefs—that the Mongols were led by none other than Prester John, the legendary Christian king of some distant eastern country.

The Mongol homeland lies to the north-west of the Great Wall of China. To the west it is bounded by the High Altai mountains, to the south by the Gobi desert and to the north by Lake Baikal. Karakorum, the medieval capital, stood 200 miles west of modern Ulan Bator.

Temujin

The *Secret History of the Mongols* (in fact a collection of clan legends) describes how in about 1167 a Mongol tribe defeated the neighbouring Tartars. A Mongol leader called Yesugei captured a Tartar named Temujin-uge:

At the time Yesugei's wife, Ho'elun, was with child and beside the Onan river under the Deli'un-boldakh mountain she bore Temujin. When he was born, he was grasping a clot of blood in his right hand, in the shape of a knuckle-bone playing piece. It was because he was born at the time his father captured Temujin-uge that he was given the name Temujin.

When Temujin was eight, his father took him to find a wife. He met Dei-sechen who said:

This son of yours has bright eyes and a light in his face. Last night I dreamt that a falcon with the sun and the moon in its two claws flew to me and perched on my hand. Friend Yesugei, it is clear that your coming today with this child is the answer to my dreams. I have a daughter at home who is very young. Come with me and have a look at her.

The girl's name was Borte, and she was a year older than Temujin, who thought her very beautiful but was scared by Dei-sechen's boisterous dogs. Yesugei left his spare horse as a bride price.

Later Borte was kidnapped by the Merkits. Temujin, now a man, enlisted the Kereits to win her back. He triumphed in 1195, when he had defeated or gained the alliance of most of the wandering peoples of the High Altai:

Altan, Khuchar, Sacha-beki and all of them, after consulting together, said to Temujin, 'We appoint you as our khan. If you be our khan, we will go as vanguard against the multitude of your enemies. All the beautiful girls that we capture and all the fine horses, we will give to you. When

hunting is afoot we will give you the wild beasts that we catch.'
Such was the oath they made to serve him. They named him Genghis, or 'ocean'.

From Mongol legend in the *Secret History* we pass to Genghis Khan's later Persian biographer, Juvaini, whose *History of the World-Conqueror* is one of the great chronicles of the Middle Ages:

The home of the Mongols is an immense valley, whose area is a journey of seven or eight months both in length and breadth. Before the appearance of Genghis Khan they had no chief or ruler. Each tribe lived separately and there was constant fighting between them. Some of them regarded robbery and violence, immorality and debauchery as deeds of manliness and excellence. Their clothing was of the skins of dogs and mice and their food was the flesh of those animals. Their wine was mare's milk.

The sign of a great emir amongst them was that his stirrups were of iron; from which one can form a picture of their other luxuries. And they continued in this indigence, privation and misfortune until the banner of Genghis Khan's fortune was raised and they issued forth from the straits of hardship into the amplitude of well-being, from a prison into a garden, from the desert of poverty into a palace of delight.

Such was the view of the scholarly Juvaini, representative of a Persian civilization which the Mongols first conquered and then adapted when, in 1258, they sacked Baghdad. On this occasion they smothered the last Abbasid caliph for fear of shedding royal blood.

Genghis Khan's conquests were formidable. From the Year of the Cock (1201) to the Year of the Tiger (1206) he made himself master of Mongolia and set his nine-tailed white banner on the Onan river. Now he was great khan.

He then turned east and the struggle for China began. By 1213 the Mongols had stormed the Great Wall and were within the wide plain which stretches from Peking to the Yellow river. Two years later Peking fell.

Genghis Khan turned west. Bokhara, Samarkand, Nishapur and Herat were sacked and the Kwarazmian khanate extinguished. By 1222 Genghis' lieutenants had reached the shores of the Black Sea. Twenty years later the Golden Horde was to rule Russia and threaten Hungary.

Genghis Khan returned to Karakorum in 1224. He died on 18 August 1227, aged barely sixty. The funeral cortege visited the tents of each of his wives in turn. Mongol chieftains hastened from all corners of the new empire; some were three months on the way. Genghis Khan is buried in the Kentei mountains where he once hunted. The place became taboo and the forest was allowed to cover the spot, which is now completely forgotten.

The extent of Genghis Khan's conquests must be measured in degrees of latitude; about ninety-five percent of the earth's surface from the Black to the Yellow seas. How was it done? The Mongols were always a minority among their conquered peoples. The central army was led by ninety-five commanders of a thousand Mongols proper, but its masses were drawn from tributaries. The army was fast-moving with a high proportion of cavalry. The Mongols shot from the saddle.

The Horde became a byword for bloodthirstiness. This reputation is not altogether justified. In part it lies in the exuberant propaganda of the Mongol's own subject chroniclers. Their chief difficulty lay in taking walled towns, particularly on the silk road and in northern China, where they would advance behind ranks of hostages.

In sacking the desert oases the Mongols displayed all the nomad mistrust of merchant society, but also adopted the techniques of previous local wars between the trading stations themselves. In order to suppress the trade of a rival town, its inhabitants as well as its defences had to be extinguished. So towering mounds of the skulls of Mongol victims are still pointed out in Persia and Afghanistan, symbols of the Mongols' obsessive fear of the urban prosperity of the subjects who outnumbered them and mistrust of the decaying Abbasid and Chinese cultures which they overtook.

The Mongol Empire

The cohesion of the Mongol Empire lay in its long adherence to its early tribal structure. Genghis Khan codified Mongol clan law in the *yasa*, which remained the basis of the Mongol moral and civil code until the twentieth century. The early origins of the Mongols in the High Altai were never forgotten. Here at Karakorum the tribes would assemble in a *qiriltay* when a campaign was being prepared or a new great khan had to be elected and acclaimed.

The process of assembly was necessarily protracted, but communications within the empire were remarkably good. The Tartar relay post could take a message from Tabriz to Peking in two-and-a-half to three months, while merchant caravans took a year or so if all went well (which was rare).

When the Mongols captured Baghdad in 1258, they reopened the through trade route to the Far East. Caravans could make their way from Tana, Trebizond and Damascus to China. The heyday of the route ended in the fifteenth century when a number of factors put an end to the old overland route. These included the death of Timur in 1406, the fall of Constantinople and the Italian Crimean trading stations in 1453 and 1475, the Italian economic depression and the Portuguese penetration of the Indian Ocean from the Cape of Good Hope at the end of the century.

Italian merchants were not slow to follow up the opportunities offered by the Mongol Empire as a vast free-trade area (although local tolls could still be heavy) in the years after 1258. Pegolotti compiled a handbook for merchants trading with the east in the 1340s, which gives an indication of the nature of the goods which entered Europe from the Mongol Empire.

Luxury goods (always the last to stop coming from the east in any political and economic crisis) predominated. The medieval diet in Europe also required strong spices to disguise bad meat, and powerful purgatives.

The overland route began at Tana, on the Don, or at Trebizond, Smyrna and Damascus. From the Caucasus and southern Russia came amber, hides, honey and slaves (who were in increasing demand in Italian households after the Black Death precipitated a domestic servant crisis in the late fourteenth century). At Tabriz damask, brocades, quicksilver, mastic, spikenard, lign-aloes, camphor and ceremonial parasols could be obtained.

The Samarkand market offered rhubarb and silk, and the best silk and galangal came from Peking. The Tibetan rhubarb route was probably more important at this stage than the famous silk road. Very little Chinese silk was in fact imported to the West (where there had been excellent silk factories at Constantinople and in Sicily for centuries). Powdered rhubarb was the most drastic purgative known in late medieval Italy and figures among the most expensive items in household accounts.

The more important land route led down from Tabriz to the Persian Gulf and Ormuz. Here musk, borax, camel hair, galbanum, scammony, hyssop, and gum arabic could be obtained. Somalia was the source for

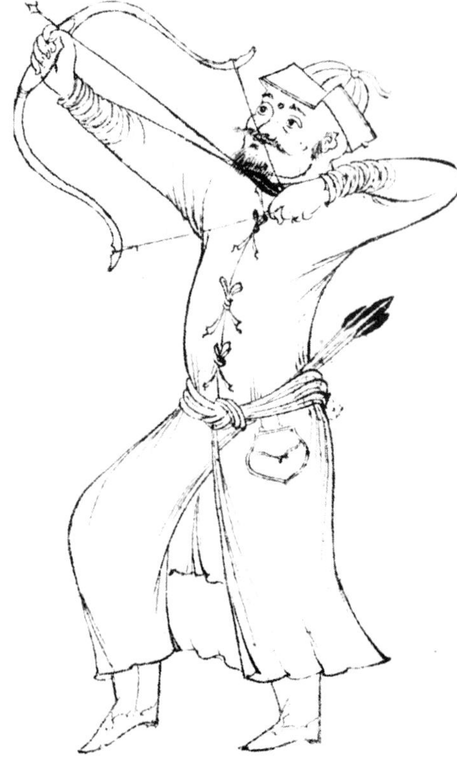

gold, frankincense and myrrh. Then dhows would bring goods on the monsoons from east Africa and India.

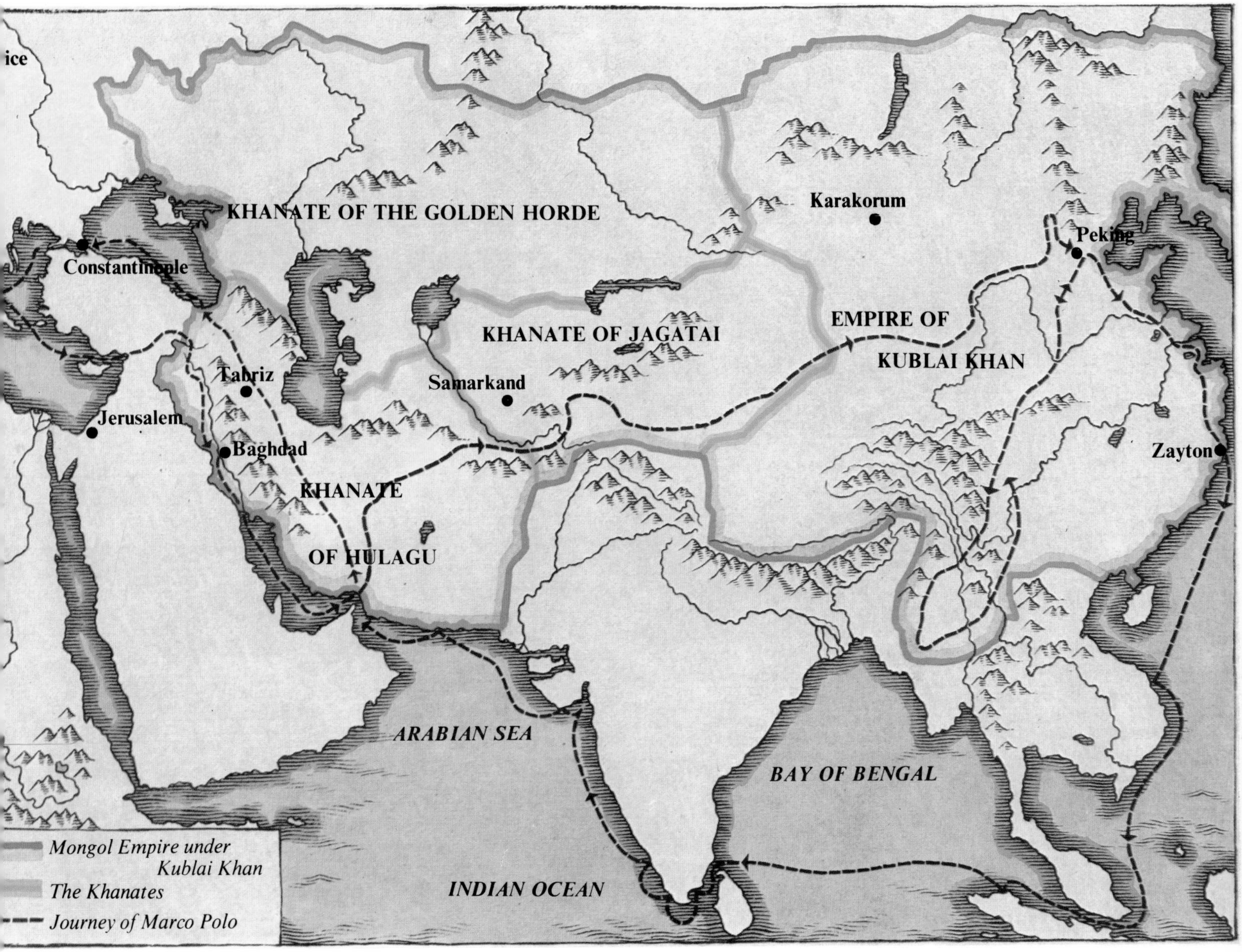

India produced indigo, wormwood, ginger, sugar, paper, cotton, carpets, amber and saffron. Sri Lanka sent zedoary, pearls and coral. Thence most ships sailed to the East Indies, source of the most important spice of all, pepper. From the East Indies came also brazilwood, cubebs, dragon's blood, cinnabar, cinnamon, mace, cardamon, nutmeg, asafoetida and cloves.

Visitors from the West

The Polo brothers were not the only westerners who reached the Mongol courts at Saray, Murghan, Karakorum and Peking. The West first became aware of the Mongols in 1238 when the Assassins of Syria implored Henry III of England to save Islam from the new enemies of civilization and when there was a glut of herrings at Yarmouth because their German buyers had stayed at home for fear of the Mongols.

In 1245 Pope Innocent IV decided to find out about the strange new Mongol power. Over the next century barefoot Franciscans regularly made their way to China. On 22 July 1246, John of Piano Carpini witnessed the enthronement of Guyuk as great khan, near Karakorum:

On a pleasant plain near a river among the mountains a tent had been set up. This tent was supported by columns covered with gold plates and fastened to other wooden beams with nails of gold, and the roof above and the sides on the interior were of brocade. A vast crowd assembled . . . and placed Guyuk on the imperial throne, and the chiefs knelt before him and after them all the people, with the exception of us who were not subject to them. Then they started drinking and, as is their custom, they drank without stopping till evening.

Guyuk was shocked by Pope Innocent's suggestion that he be baptized:

How do you know that the words which you speak are with God's sanction? From

Above, the camp of the Golden Horde; as nomads, the Mongols were used to a highly mobile existence and often feared urban life. Bibliothèque Nationale, Paris.

Top, the Mongol Empire at the time of Marco Polo; the unity brought to central Asia allowed renewed contact between east and west, and, after the initial wave of destruction, it brought prosperity as well.

Opposite, a Chinese illustration of a Mongol bowman. He is aiming the short bow normally carried in open warfare, but the bowmen also carried larger bows for use during sieges.

the rising of the sun to its setting, all lands have been made subject to me. Who can do this against the will of God?

He ordered the pope to submit to him also and concluded ominously:

If you do not observe God's command, and if you ignore my command, I shall know you as my enemy. Likewise I shall make you understand. If you do otherwise, God knows what I know.

It seemed impossible to communicate with such people. Perhaps they were not talking of the same god. Geographically the great khan was encamped two years' journey away; mentally he was even more distant. In the next half century the two sides edged towards each other like people in the dark.

There was so little information. Mandeville, the most popular late medieval arm chair traveller, peopled the improbable lands beyond Christendom with headless Singhalese giants and drunken Ethiopian monsters (who lay stupefied on their backs, each in the shade of his single huge foot).

After 1258 Italian merchants had more reliable information about the Mongols, but men like Polo were hardly believed unless they confirmed tales of pearls the size of ostrich eggs or of the Catholic piety of Prester John.

The papacy fancied that it could evangelize the Mongol Empire—and indeed in 1307 John of Monte Corvino became first Archbishop of Peking. Western kings such as Edward I of England and St Louis of France toyed with the idea of a Mongol alliance to save the crusader outposts in the Holy Land. The great khans thought the European emissaries were simply vassals bringing inadequate tribute, but forgave them their eccentricities. The ilkhans of Persia had a more realistic view of the situation, but firm proposals were rare. It is in one of these encounters between east and west that we have the account of the most remarkable ambassador-traveller of the time, a Nestorian monk called Rabban Sauma.

The travels of Rabban Sauma

Rabban Sauma was born near Peking in about 1225. He became a hermit in 1278 but was persuaded by a disciple to make the immense pilgrimage to Jerusalem. They set off with the approval of Kublai, the great khan. During their journey the pilgrims found that since the death of Genghis Khan, fifty years before, the Mongol Empire had become a loose confederation of principalities held by members of the imperial family, and sharing the same cultural and administrative traditions.

The khans of the Golden Horde ruled Russia from Saray, demanding tribute from the local princes (thereby strengthening the position of the Russian princes who were finally enabled to shake off the Mongol yoke in the fifteenth century). In Persia the Mongol ilkhans erected a semi-independent state. The centre of the empire had shifted from Karakorum to Kublai's stately pleasure domes in northern China.

The remoteness of the great khan clearly contributed to the remarkable lack of friction between the great and lesser khans, although every decade or so the clans continued to meet in *qiriltays* where the heroic past of Genghis Khan could be relived in splendid displays of horsemanship and massive drinking bouts. There were also a number of tributaries, native rulers who retained their thrones under Mongol protection on the fringes of the empire. They recognized Mongol suzerainty, supplied military contingents and paid annual tributes.

Local wars prevented Rabban Sauma from returning to Peking or visiting the Holy Land after he had reached Persia. Instead his disciple, Mar Yaballaha, was elected Nestorian patriarch and Rabban Sauma was sent by the Persian ilkhan, Arghun, as his ambassador to the west. To choose a Christian for this task was a shrewd move, but the Mongols were eclectic in religion, as in other things. Arghun's mother was a Christian, his own sympathies were for Buddhism (made fashionable at Kublai's court) and his vizier was a Jew.

Rabban Sauma's private interests were in seeing and securing as many Christian relics as possible. Constantinople showed him the most potent relics in Christendom. He observed Stromboli in eruption, met the infamous Charles of Anjou, and was delighted by the undergraduates at Paris University. In October 1287 Rabban Sauma met the only Christian king who had in fact fought briefly in alliance with the Mongols in the Holy Land—Edward I of England. Completely unaware who his guest was, Edward took communion from a heretic.

Edward sent English envoys in return to the ilkhan. Their daily accounts may still be consulted in the Public Record Office in London. They include shopping lists for items from butter to parasols, painstakingly noted in pence of England, bezants of Byzantium, aspers of Trebizond and dirhams of Persia.

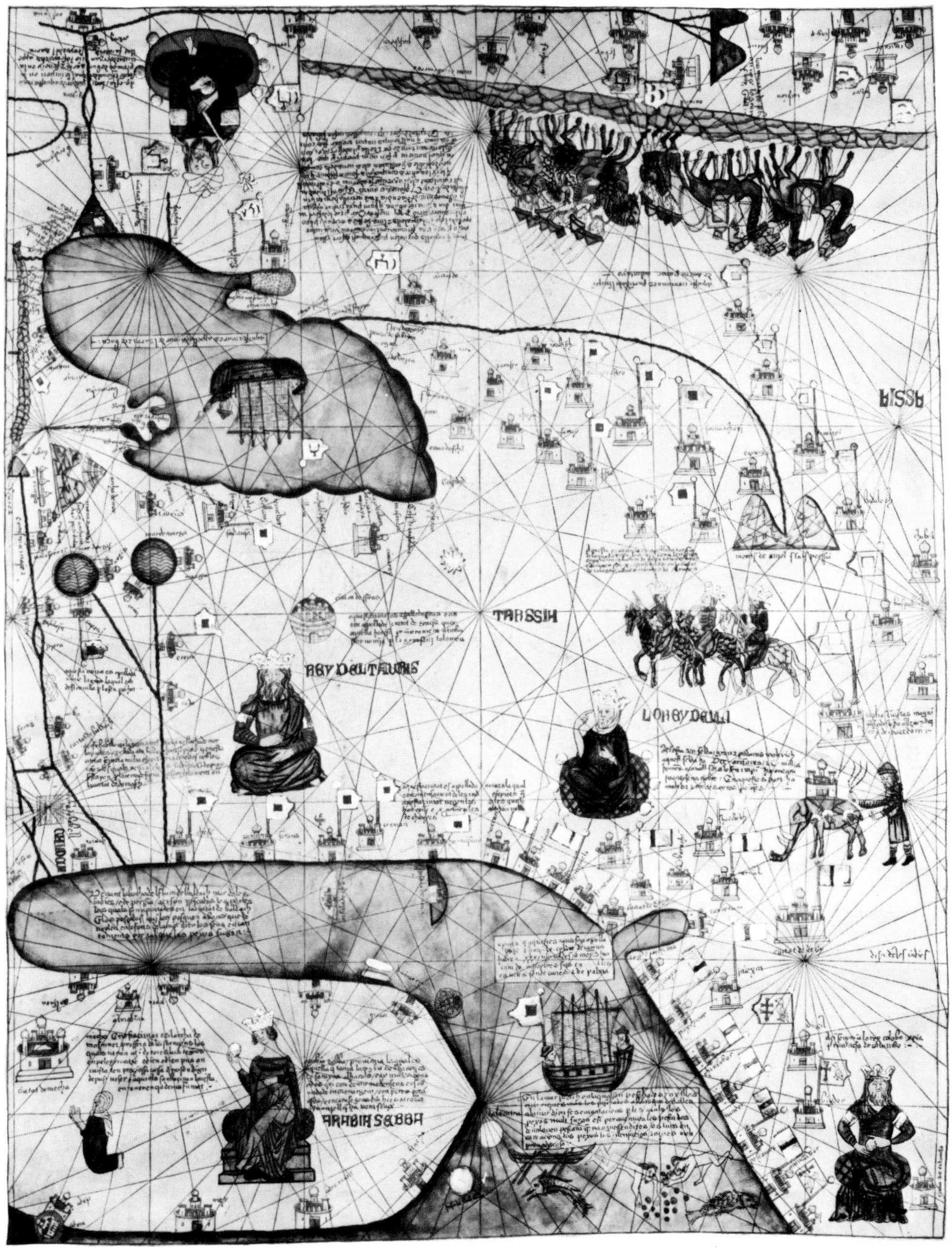

Above, a thirteenth-century Chinese painting of Mongol horsemen; the Mongols soon became integrated to the Chinese way of life, although they still appeared as barbarians to the Chinese themselves.

Left, a panel from the Catalan World Atlas *of 1375, showing the Asian trade routes of Mongol times and the route of Marco Polo to Cathay. One result of the Mongol empire was to make such long-distance trade relatively safe. Bibliothèque Nationale, Paris.*

Left, a Chinese painting of Mongol horsemen playing an early version of polo; they also played more brutal team games on horseback which are still known in Afghanistan today. Victoria and Albert Museum, London.

Opposite left, Genghis Khan telling the citizens of Bokhara, in central Asia, that he was the punishment of God. He took Bokhara in 1220. He was notorious for his cruelty to those who opposed him but rarely destroyed places that let him pass without difficulty. British Museum, London.

Opposite centre, a sixteenth-century Indian painting of Kublai Khan crossing the Yangtse-Kaiang river in China in the 1250s. The Mongols terrorized the Chinese population far less than others they conquered. Imperial Library, Teheran.

Opposite right, Genghis Khan besieging a Chinese fortress in the 1210s, according to a sixteenth-century Indian painting. The rifles and cannon are clearly anachronistic, but large siege engines were used.

Unfortunately, Acre, the last crusader foothold in the Holy Land, had fallen before the expedition reached Mongol territory in 1292 and the project was forgotten. All that remained were the diplomatic presents: English gyrfalcons flying high over Tabriz and a Persian leopard shivering in a cage in England.

In the fourteenth century European interests in the Mongol Empire diminished. Ghengis Khan's state disintegrated further and the Nestorians were now persecuted. Rabban Sauma's disciple and patriarch died a hunted man in 1317 and his church was finally wrecked, with the Mongol Empire itself, by Timur.

The Mongol Empire united once more before it destroyed itself. Timur (the name means 'iron') of Tamerlane, who was born in Transoxiana in 1336, was not a second Genghis. He was a Muslim and regarded his conquests as something of a holy war to remind other Muslims (such as the Ottomans) of their duties to Islam. Nonetheless, there are similarities in the careers of Genghis and Timur: the slow building up of the support of nomad peoples from small beginnings, the vast and speedy conquests and the same exalted concept of empire. Timur was a more reckless and ruthless destroyer than Genghis, but he was not an uncouth nomad. Under him was evolved the magnificent architecture and delicate decoration of the great mosques and mausoleums of Samarkand, which survive today.

Timur's earliest conquests, from his base beyond the Oxus river, were to the east in Kwarazmia and Moghulistan. He never reached China, but suspended tribute to the nominal khan and demanded his submission instead. In 1381–84 Timur campaigned in Khorosan, Sistan and Mazandaran. In 1386–88 he overran Azerbaijan, Georgia and Persia, and in 1391–92 he tested the strength of Tokhtamish, the last great Khan of the Golden Horde in Russia.

Between 1392 and 1396 he embarked on a campaign in the west and finally defeated Tokhtamish. Later, in 1398–99, he entered India, took Delhi and penetrated south. He launched in 1400 his final campaign in the west, starting from the Karabagh. The Anatolian emirates which Bayezid had been subduing were conquered in turn, and reinstated by Timur in the years 1400–01. In 1402 he seized Bayezid and wrecked his army (which included German gunners, one of whom survived to tell the tale). Then he retired east again.

Timur's restless conquests, from Smyrna to Karakorum, from the Volga to the Ganges, make Alexander the Great's expedition in the same area look small. However, in this final fling, the Mongol Empire burnt itself out. Timur first re-created and then destroyed it as thoroughly as he had razed the cities he captured. When he died in 1405 the huge state collapsed. In Persia the Timurids held out until 1502. In India his descendants ruled as great moguls from 1526 until 1857.

Ruy Gonzales Clavijo, a level-headed Spanish ambassador, reached Timur's court at Samarkand in September 1403. His description of the aged and lame (some say

Above, a Japanese drawing of the thirteenth century showing Mongol archers shooting on foot and not, as was more usual, from the saddle. The Mongols tried to invade Japan in 1274 and 1281. Imperial Household Collection, Tokyo.

Left, a fifteenth-century Persian painting of Timur besieging the town of Herat, now in western Afghanistan. Timur probably had little hope that his empire would hold together after his death. On loan to British Museum, London, from the Royal Asiatic Society.

Opposite top, the Mongol horsemen of Genghis Khan, dramatically illustrated by a Chinese painter. Their ferocity was held in equal awe and horror as far west as Hungary. Metropolitan Museum of Art, New York.

Opposite centre left, Timur building a tower with the heads of the defenders of Mikut. His cruelty was notorious; on one occasion he had the heads of the 70,000 defenders of Isfahan piled around the town's fortifications, while in 1381 he had 2,000 men buried alive in Herat.

Opposite centre right, a Persian miniature of Timur relaxing at his court. British Library, London.

Opposite bottom, Timur's armies attacking an Islamic fort. Few forts could withstand the Mongol method of siege warfare, which involved a continual all-out attack until sheer weight of numbers won the day. British Library, London.

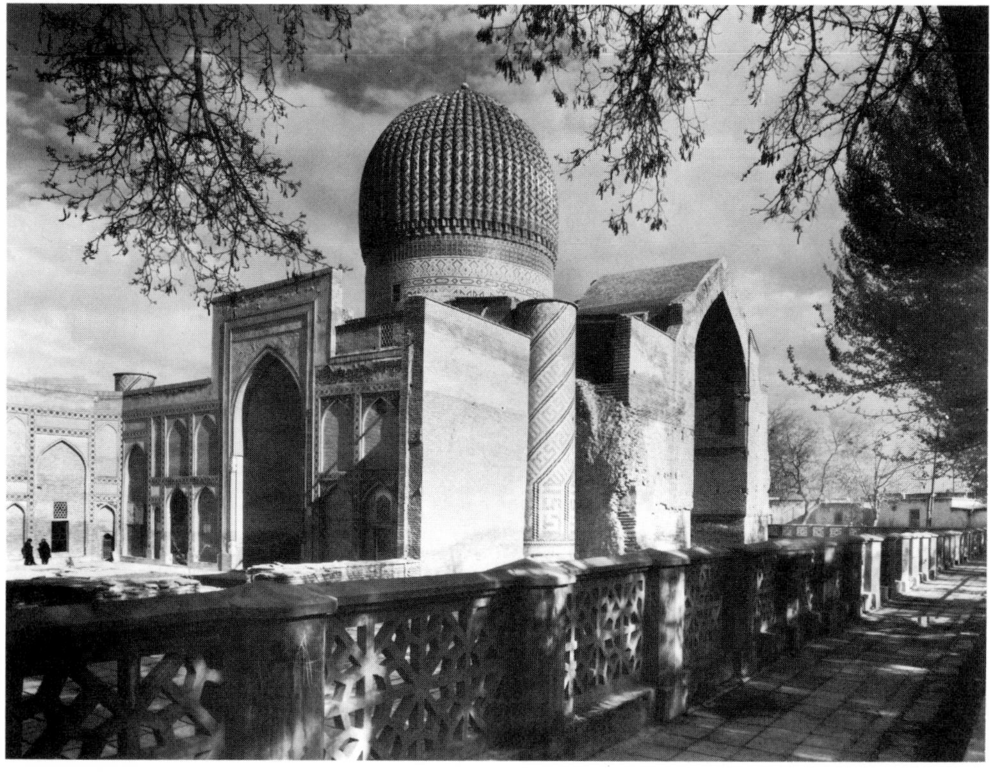

also albino) conqueror, and of the palaces and gardens of the capital, is one of the best. Clavijo was escorted to Timur who was

. . . seated under a portal which was before the entrance of the most beautiful palace. He was sitting on a raised dais before which there was a fountain that threw up a column of water in the air backwards, and in the basin of the fountain there were floating red apples. His Highness was dressed in a cloak of plain silk without any embroidery, and he wore on his head a tall white hat on the crown of which was displayed a balas ruby, the same being ornamented with pearls and precious stones.

Clavijo and his companions prostrated three times. Timur beckoned them to come closer, and the chamberlains who had been escorting them stood back,

for they dared not advance any nearer. His Highness commanded us to stand close to him so that he might the better see us, for his sight was no longer good. Indeed he was so infirm and old that his eyelids were falling over his eyes and he could barely raise them to see.

Such was the most powerful of all medieval emperors at the zenith of his rule.

Clavijo was feasted in many palaces. He noted all the old Mongol traits:

It is the custom of the Tartars to drink their wine before eating. No feast we were told is considered a real festival until the guests have drunk themselves sot. The attendants who serve them with drink kneel before the guests, and as soon as one cup of wine has been emptied another is presented.

Clavijo suffered diplomatic agonies for he did not like wine and always refused it.

The Spanish ambassador witnessed one of the last gatherings of the Mongol clans on the plain of Kanigil. The whole Horde gathered for a month's debate and festivities:

As soon as Timur's camp had been pitched all these folk of the Horde exactly knew where each clan had its place. From the greatest to the humblest each man knew his allotted position, and took it up. Thus in the course of the next three or four days we saw near 20,000 tents pitched in regular streets to encircle the royal camp, and daily more clans came in from outlying districts.

Mongol tribal cohesion had survived almost intact two centuries after Genghis Khan first led his Horde out of the High Altai. To the artisans and merchants of Samarkand the great tented encampment of the nomads who ruled them must have been as strange a sight as it was to the Spaniard Clavijo.

The days of the Horde were numbered. Soon they were to retreat back to the mountain pastures whence first they came. Timur's disapproving Arab chronicler saw the conqueror of the world throw himself wholeheartedly into the festivities for the last time at this particular gathering:

Everything succeeded according to desire and his wishes were satisfied until pleasure and bounding joy made him light and agile, and he linked his arm with another's and stretched out his hand to one who rose before him and they helped each other with arms joined. And when he was in the midst of dancing, he tottered amongst them because of his age and lameness.

Chapter 8

The Ottoman Turks

Byzantium's offspring and successor states rivalled those of the empire itself. The revived Bulgarian Empire of the Asen family (1187–1393), which nearly destroyed the Latin Empire of Constantinople (1204–61), was itself a confederation and culturally backward. Like Serbia, it shared with Constantinople the same Orthodox faith, most of the same legal and theological handbooks and some of the same classical textbooks.

Serbia was the most brilliant, faithful and dangerous of Byzantium's Balkan heirs. Milutin (Urosh II, 1282–1321) and Stephen Dushan (Urosh IV, 1331–55) tried to outdo the Byzantines in governmental forms and imperial splendour. The architecture of the great monasteries they founded (such as Grachanitsa and Studenitsa) may be described as Byzantine baroque. Yet their paintings have the same faithfulness to the Hellenistic forms which were being revived once more in Constantinople.

After its defeat at Kossovo in 1389, the Serbian Empire contracted to a minor despotate centred on the fortress of Smederevo (Semendria) on the Danube near Belgrade.

In the late fourteenth century, Russia, whose centres of power moved during the Mongol hegemony from Kiev to Novgorod and Moscow in the north, resumed its contacts with Constantinople. These were largely ecclesiastical and cultural. The names of Russian tourists of this period have been found scratched on the walls of the Hagia Sophia in Constantinople. Patriarchs looked to Moscow for alms.

Later some Russians claimed Moscow as the 'Third Rome', legitimate heir to the Empire of Constantinople, the Second Rome, and a defender of Orthodoxy unsullied by the betrayal of the Byzantine bishops who had signed the Act of Reunion with the Roman Church at Florence in 1439. It was, however, never more than a monkish idea and the importance of Byzantine features in the later Russian state have been much exaggerated.

Besides the tumbledown city of Constantinople, now just seven villages within the encircling walls, only the Morea remained to the Byzantine Empire. The Morea was a semi-independent despotate and inspired Greek hopes for the future. Even here, according to a contemporary inscription, the nobility 'breathed jealousy, deceit, strife and murder'. The despotate's little capital at Mistra, near Sparta, fell four years after Constantinople itself.

The Fourth Crusade of 1204 had brought Italian rulers to the Byzantine world. The Genoese ran the Black Sea trade from their outposts at Caffa, Trebizond, Moncastro (Akkerman) and Pera. They also controlled a few Aegean islands and the alum mines at Phocaea, near Smyrna. The Venetians ran the eastern Mediterranean trade with Beirut, Alexandria and the southern Aegean. Here they held Euboea (Negroponte), some other Aegean islands and the 'Great Island' of Crete. Candia (Heraklion), the Cretan capital, fell to the Ottomans only in 1669.

Before then numbers of Greek scholars, merchants and painters, including El Greco, had made their way to Venice and the University of Padua. Venice retained the Ionian islands, including Corfu, until Napoleon's day. Perhaps the most unexpected of western conquests in the Byzantine world was the Catalan occupation of Athens for most of the fourteenth century. The Catalan company, one of a number of European contingents in the Byzantine service, had, as was usual, run amok when they were not paid. These Spaniards simply took over the ruined city of Athens.

Mehmet II

The Ottoman Empire took two decades to recover from its defeat at Ankara. The civil war between Musa and Mehmet, the sons of Bayezid, resembled that between John V Palaeologos and John VI Cantacuzene in Byzantium half a century before. The lower classes, both Christian and Muslim supported Musa who was finally defeated by Mehmet I, the representative of the aristocratic party, in 1413.

Murad II (1421–51) resumed the work of conquest which Timur had interrupted. His son Mehmet II finally succeeded him in 1451, at the age of nineteen. Through his ancestry the new sultan was connected with the ruling families of Byzantium, Serbia, and Trebizond and also with the ruling dynasties of Mongol and Turkman Persia.

Anatolia had been settled by groups of Turkic peoples claiming common ancestors. The early histories of their clans are celebrated in heroic poetry and epic which has strong genealogical interest, such as the ballads of Dede Korkut or the deeds of Melik Danishmend. The most famous of these groups claimed descent from Othman.

The Greeks entered the new system of government even before they were conquered, from the day when Michael VIII Palaeologus married his illegitimate daughter to the ilkhan of Persia. The Greek Cantacuzene family was one of the groups which held together the Ottoman and Byzantine worlds, providing a coherence

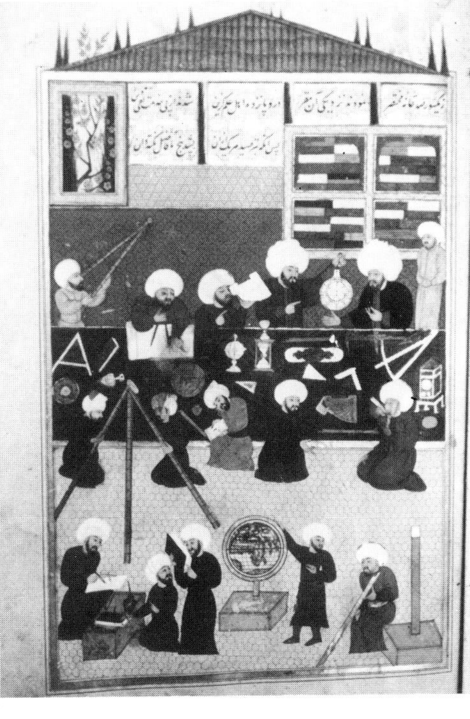

Above, sixteenth-century scholars following their ancient studies of geography and geometry; the Ottomans encouraged the traditional arts and skills of the cultures over which they ruled.

Opposite, the Gur Emir, or tomb of Timur at Samarkand. Despite his undoubted cruelty, Timur was a great patron of the arts and of science.

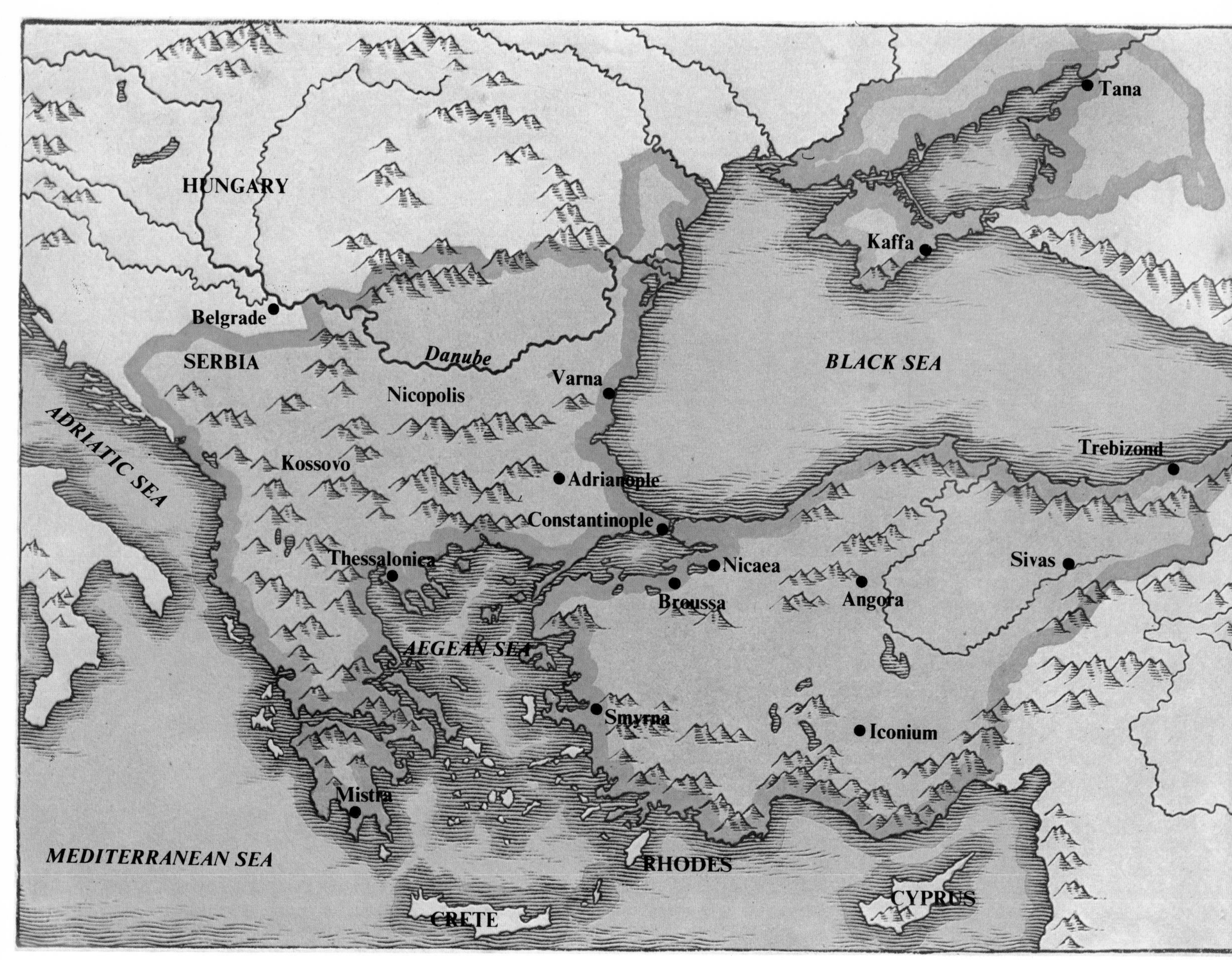

behind the political boundaries which were so complex at this time. George Amiroutzes, for example, Greek delegate at the Council of Florence, was related to the Trapezuntine and Serbian royal families as well as to Mehmet II's Begler Bey of the West, to whom he surrendered Trebizond in 1461. This sort of relationship was one of many which softened the blow of Ottoman conquest, for Amiroutzes' son went on to become Ottoman minister of finance.

Conquest often did not affect the position of the old ruling families. Where once they had held land in return for military obligations, now they became lords of hereditary military fiefs. For instance, Evrenos, last Byzantine governor of Broussa (Bursa) took office among his conquerors. His grandson conquered the Morea for the Ottomans and the family held the fief of Yenidje Vardar until the nineteenth century.

The Ottoman Empire

Constantinople finally fell to Mehmet II, henceforth called 'the Conqueror', on Tuesday, 29 May 1453, after a siege which, through the desperation of its inhabitants, had lasted several weeks. The event caused no great stir in the West and was in fact of importance only to the two peoples chiefly involved—the Greeks and the Turks.

For the Turks it was the final stage in the creation of a European empire out of an Anatolian border emirate. Mehmet II, with his largely Balkan armies, went on to conquer most of the Anatolian emirate and the Great Uzun Hasan of the White Sheep, as well as the Crimea, before he died in 1481. This was an essentially European conquest in Asia. The sultan with his wide-ranging intellectual interests was something of an Ottoman counterpart of the Renaissance princes of Italy.

The transference of the Ottoman capital to Constantinople, and the repopulation of the city (largely by Greeks) was, for the Ottomans, the symbolic claim to the old universal empire. Mehmet II became the padishah or emperor.

It is only partly true to say that the Ottoman Empire was heir to the Byzantine. Although in administrative and social detail there are no real parallels, the Ottoman and Byzantine Empires did rule the same peoples in the same areas from the same capital. From the subject peoples the Ottoman Empire largely drew its military and administrative institution, a non-hereditary ruling class, devoted to the sultan.

The Ottoman Empire was one of the most successful multi-national states which the world has ever seen. Its success was achieved only at the expense of the Turks, its dominant people. The Turks, and especially the Anatolian peasantry, became increasingly self-effacing and were the last of the component peoples of the empire to gain their own independence from it.

For the Greeks, the conquest was equally important, though only a fraction of them had lived in the Byzantine Empire for a century. When he appointed Gennadius II as patriarch, Mehmed gave his office greater spiritual powers than it had known for centuries, and more extensive political authority than it had ever enjoyed. Spiritually the ecumenical patriarch ruled

over almost all Greeks within the empire, and to these were even added the errant Serbs and Bulgars. The control of the Orthodox Church of Constantinople, hitherto largely confined to the shrinking boundaries of the Byzantine Empire, stretched once more from the Adriatic to the Caucasus. Greeks now looked to the patriarch, answerable only to the sublime porte, as their 'ethnarch' or national leader. The patriarchate assumed many of the functions and ceremony of the Byzantine emperors and its symbol was the double-headed eagle of the departed Palaeologus family.

The system which provided for semi-autonomous government within the empire, was shared by a number of other Christian peoples. However, the Greeks had peculiar advantages over their fellow subjects, since they were fitted to carry out tasks that the Turks themselves could not, or would not, perform. As Christians, as scholars, as official Ottoman diplomats, and as merchants they never lost touch with the western world, particularly Italy.

When Constantinople fell, Greeks began to think of 'The Great Idea', the dream of recapturing the City and restoring its Empire. A contemporary ballad describes how the news was received in Trebizond:

A bird, a beautiful bird, flew out from the City:
It shook one wing, and it was covered with blood:
It shook the other wing, and there was paper with writing beneath:
"Woe unto us, woe unto us: Byzantium is no more!
The ramparts are lost: the imperial Throne is destroyed!
The churches are devastated: the monasteries are wrecked!"

However, the refrain was: 'If Byzantium is lost now, she will flower once more and bear fruit.'

These words express 'The Great Idea', the dream of recapturing Constantinople and of restoring the old Empire which haunted the Greek mind until this century. What the Greeks did not realize until it was too late was that they had in fact achieved 'The Great Idea' under the Ottomans.

The Ottoman Empire was ruled not only through its provincial governors and native feudatories (*Dere beys*) but also vertically through the religious leaders, established in Constantinople, of the various peoples (*millets*) of which it was composed. Of these peoples only the hapless Turks did not enjoy the status and privileges of a *millet*. They bore the appalling human cost of military expansion in the fifteenth and sixteenth, and contraction in the nineteenth, centuries. The Ottomans themselves were not so much Turks as a great ruling extended family, wielders of the holy scimitar of Islam and as much the oppressors of the Muslim peasants of Anatolia as the Byzantine autocrats had been in their Christian ancestors.

The Turkish conquest had been made easier by the divisions of the enemies, both religious and political. During the fourteenth century the Byzantine emperors had been happy to recruit Turkish allies in civil wars against pretenders to the throne. Moreover, the Turks' reputation for victory attracted warriors of all persuasions to their ranks, including Christians. But perhaps the most important factor of all was that the Ottomans were prepared to allow their Orthodox Christian subjects, on payment of heavy tribute, to continue to practise their religion. This was a privilege which the Orthodox Christians knew from bitter experience would be denied them if their fellow Christians of the west should ever re-establish a Latin empire at Constantinople. In consequence the Christian allies and subjects of the Turkish armies fought loyally for their masters against the hated

Above, a miniature depicting life in sixteenth-century Istanbul; it was not until the next century that the Ottoman court began to decline in the face of corruption and favouritism. Fogg Art Museum, Cambridge, Mass.

Above left, contemporary miniature by Sinan Bey, a Turkish painter, of Mehmet II (1429–81), the conqueror of Constantinople. He was a fine administrator and patron of the arts as well as a commander and attracted several Italian artists to his court. Topkapi Palace Museum, Istanbul.

Above far left, a French painting of 1455, showing the siege of Constantinople two years previously. Despite the Ottomans' overwhelming superiority in numbers, they could only take the city by treachery and stealth. Bibliothèque Nationale, Paris.

Opposite, the Ottoman Empire in the late fifteenth century. At this point its extent was very similar to that of Byzantium in the eleventh century.

Catholic forces of the Holy Roman Empire or the kingdom of Hungary.

In addition to retaining certain of the administrative personnel of their predecessors, the Turkish rulers instituted a regular system of forcible annual recruitment of young Christian boys to be trained as soldiers and administrators of the empire. Brought from the provinces to the capital, they were put through a long and thorough course of indoctrination in the religion of Islam, were made proficient in the Turkish language and, on graduation from this cultural rehabilitation, were assigned either to the ranks of the famous Janissari corps of the army or posts in the administrative service.

The reign of Mehmet II was a time of vigorous consolidation. All that was left of an independent Serbia became Ottoman in 1459. Bosnia was subjugated in 1463–64. Along the lower Danube Ottoman influence was strengthened in the Christian principalities of Walachia (1462) and Moldavia (1476). A long war against Venice (1463–79) gave the sultan the island of Negroponte in Greece and also Scutari on the Adriatic.

The success of Mehmet was not confined to the territories in Europe. Sinope and Trebizond on the southern shore of the Black Sea came under Ottoman control in 1461. Moreover, in 1475 the sultan was able to seize Kaffa in the Crimea. Within Asia Minor the Turkish state of Karaman found itself incorporated into the Ottoman Empire during the years following 1464. Sultan Mehmet, near Terjan in 1473, was victorious, too, over the Aq Qoyunlu (White Sheep) Turcomans who then dominated much of Persia. Before the fall

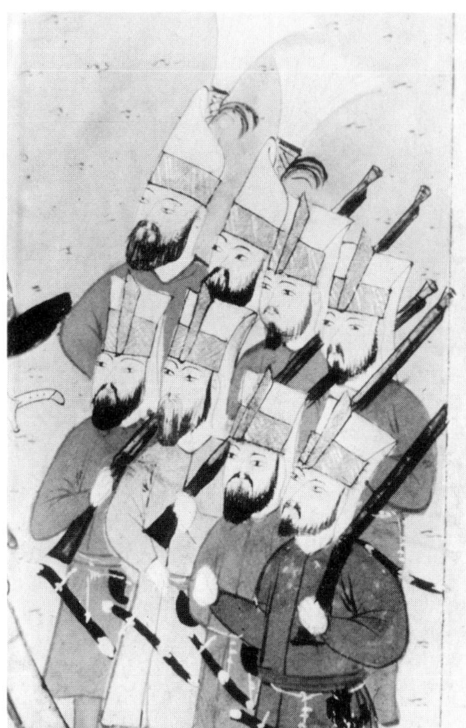

of Constantinople there had been a certain element of the provisional and even of the precarious about the greatness of the Ottomans. Now, as the Christian sources in particular make clear, the activities of Mehmet had established Ottoman greatness on a firm and enduring foundation.

The Mameluke Sultanate

The Ottomans had to face a grave crisis in the east—a crisis which involved two other Muslim regimes of the first importance, the Mameluke Sultanate of Syria and Egypt and the Safawid state in Persia. A military regime composed of slave soldiers (mamelukes) had ruled over Egypt and Syria since 1250. At first these soldiers were recruited mostly from the Kipchak Turks of the steppe lands north and east of the Caspian Sea. They were brought as slaves to Cairo, made Muslim, trained in the arts of war, then set free and advanced to the full status and privileges of a Mameluke. This meant that they became a member of a dominant warrior caste, non-Muslim in origin and ruling over the local populations of Egypt and Syria almost as a garrison in an alien land. After about 1400 recruitment shifted to a new geographical area, the Caucasus, most of the slave material being now of Circassian descent.

With the rise of the Ottomans in the fourteenth and fifteenth centuries political and military tension began to grow along the ill-defined borderlands separating northern Syria and Asia Minor. The Mamelukes and the Ottomans now strove, one against the other, to control the small Turcoman principalities located on the frontier. Two areas were of special significance—the region adjacent to Adana and Tarsus where the

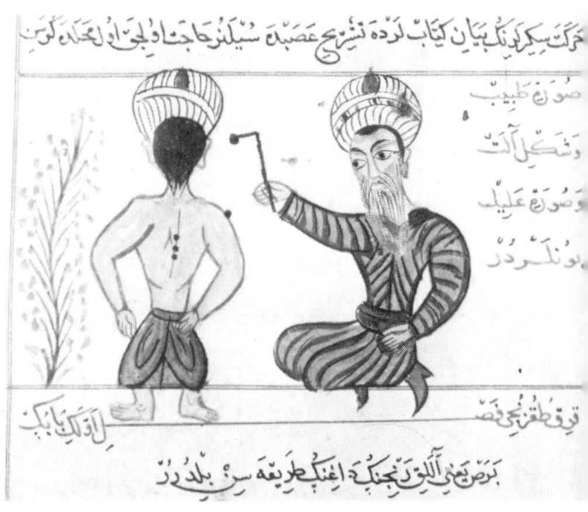

Cilician Gates offered one of the few practicable routes through the Taurus mountains, and the region of Albistan, where the river Euphrates cuts through the mountain ranges to flow southeast into Iraq.

The friction between the Mamelukes and the Ottomans broke out into open warfare for domination over Cilicia in the years 1485–91. At this time Jem, a brother of the Ottoman Sultan Bayezid II (1481–1512), was a captive in the hands of the Christians. As long as Jem remained alive (he died in 1495), the sultan was reluctant to commit himself to a major conflict in the east. He therefore undertook only a limited war in Cilicia.

The peace settlement of 1491 left the Mamelukes in control of that area—but it was no more than a negative success and one which, even so, had demanded maximum deployment of their military resources. A question had in fact been asked, though not yet answered: what would happen if the Ottomans ever felt themselves free to turn the entire weight of their army against the Mamelukes.

There was also tension between the Ottoman Empire and Persia. Much of Persia had been under the control of a Turcoman confederation known as the Aq Qoyunlu (White Sheep). After 1490 the power of the Aq Qoyunlu began to crumble as a result of dynastic feuds. A new regime emerged in Persia—a regime which was the creation of a formidable religious order bearing the name of Safawiyah. This order, which had its main centre at Ardabil near the Caspian Sea, had come to embrace, in the course of time, an extreme form of the Shii faith, the most important of the unorthodox versions of Islam.

To the religious aims of the order Shaykh Junayd (d. 1460) added objectives of a political and military nature. A series of campaigns, carried out between 1499 and 1503 against the Aq Qoyunlu led to the foundation of a strong Safawid state in Persia with Isma'il (d. 1524), as Shah.

These events constituted a grave danger for the Ottomans. The military strength of the Safiwiya had been drawn mainly from the Turcoman tribes located in Asia Minor. To control these tribes even under normal

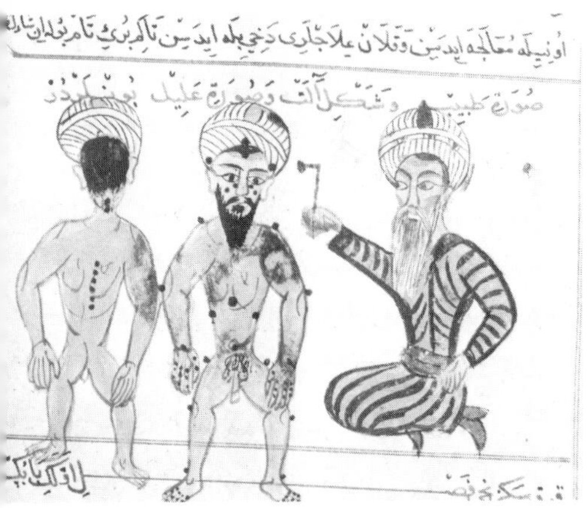

circumstances was a difficult task. Now, through the activities of the Safawiya, the Turcomans were being drawn into allegiance with a movement which was outside the control of the Ottomans. It also represented a form of the Islamic faith which was unwelcome to them as orthodox Muslims.

The situation was all the more perilous because the influence of the Safawiya was strong in the areas under dispute between the Mamelukes and the Ottomans, that is, the lands along and adjacent to the southern fringe of Asia Minor. Ottoman intervention in these lands to counteract the Safawid influence would disrupt the precarious balance of forces on the frontier and perhaps arouse the sultan at Cairo to a massive retaliation at a time when the Ottomans might be engaged in a major conflict with Persia.

A complicating factor was the bitter contention between the sons of Bayezid II for the succession to the Ottoman throne, notably between Ahmed, who was in charge of the province of Amasya in Asia Minor, and Selim, who was governor of the province of Trebizond. In 1511, Selim crossed the Black Sea to Kaffa in the Crimea. Aided by a force of horsemen from the khan of the Krim Tartars, Selim moved southward across the Danube, demanding of his father, Bayezid, a province in Europe from which he would be able to wage war on behalf of the Muslim faith against the Christians. Sultan Bayezid, worried over a great revolt of pro-Safawid elements then raging in Asia Minor and reluctant to take extreme measures against his own son, granted this request.

Meanwhile the grand vizier, Ali Pasha, with a strong contingent of Janissaries (the élite infantry of the Sultan) and the provincial levies of Asia Minor, among them the troops of Amasya under the command of Ahmed, had advanced against the rebels. Near Kaysari, in June 1511, the revolt was crushed, but in the course of the fighting Ali Pasha lost his life. Ahmed was therefore left in Asia Minor with a powerful force to his hand. This course of events so alarmed Selim that he marched against the sultan, hoping to strengthen his position by winning over to his side the Janissaries, among whom he was held in high esteem. Though well disposed towards Selim on account of his reputation as a soldier, the Janissaries remained faithful to their lord, Sultan Bayezid, and at Chorlu, between Adrianople and Istanbul, in August 1511 routed the troops of Selim.

With the battle lost, Selim fled for refuge to the Crimea, Ahmed, meanwhile, had resolved to make a bid for the throne, hoping to cross the water to Istanbul with aid of the forces at his command and also with the assistance of a strong faction among the great dignitaries at the court. It was now that the Janissaries, still inclined towards Selim, made a violent demonstration in Istanbul against the partisans of Ahmed, thus underlining their refusal to accept that prince as the future sultan in succession to the ageing Bayezid. Ahmed had no course left to him but open rebellion.

In order to strengthen his position he took over much of Asia Minor by force. The fear, at Istanbul, that Ahmed might turn for aid to the Safawid Shah Isma'il led to the abdication of Bayezid II in 1512 and to the accession of Selim I (1512–20). A rapid campaign fought in the spring of 1513 secured Selim in his possession of the throne, Ahmed being defeated in battle, captured and then put to death.

Selim I

After ordering a large-scale 'police operation' in Asia Minor against the Shii Muslims—an operation designed to safeguard his rear while he was engaged further to the east—Sultan Selim marched against Persia. At Chaldiran in August 1514 the Ottomans inflicted a severe defeat on the Persians. The battle did not lead to an Ottoman conquest of Persia; but it did set

Above, sixteenth-century painting of an astronomer in Istanbul following the course of a comet or meteor with a quadrant.

Above left, pages from a sixteenth-century Turkish treatise on medicine describing the point of nervous control on the surface of the body. Turkish medical knowledge was still far ahead of that of the rest of Europe. Bibliothèque Nationale, Paris.

Opposite left, Turkish miniature showing Mehmet II finally consolidating his power by killing King Uzun Hassan of Persia. Topkapi Palace Museum, Istanbul.

Opposite right, a corps of Jannissaries, Christian children raised as Muslim soldiers, at Van Castle. The Ottoman military power was based on the Jannissaries, who were also given great political power and were traditionally close to the sultan. Topkapi Palace Museum, Istanbul.

a limit to the expansion of Safawid influence in Asia Minor.

Selim was determined to subjugate those regions of Asia Minor where the Safawid influence was strong and he brought under his control Albistan in 1515 and Kurdistan in 1516. The state of balance which had existed along the frontier between the Mameluke Sultanate and the Ottoman empire was thus upset, and to the detriment of the Mamelukes. Qansuh al-Ghuri, the Mameluke sultan (1501–16), had taken no effective action in northern Syria at the time when the campaign of Chaldiran was in progress. He hoped no doubt that the Safawids would overcome the Ottomans. However, when this hope was unfulfilled and the Ottomans intervened in the borderlands between Syria and Asia Minor Qansuh al-Ghuri felt that a strong response was essential. In 1516 the Mamelukes mobilized their maximum strength and marched into northern Syria. They hoped that a demonstration in force would compel the Ottomans to restore the former situation on the frontier and make them renounce all further aggression in the east through fear of an effective Mameluke-Safawid entente.

A terrible disillusionment awaited the Mamelukes. Sultan Selim made it clear that war would ensure if the Mamelukes insisted on a return to the former position in the border territories. On 4 August 1516, in the plain of Malatya, Selim made one of the most dramatic decisions in the annals of the Ottoman Empire. He was presented with a choice—to advance once more against Persia or to penetrate into Syria and attempt to overwhelm the Mamelukes befor the Safawids could threaten him from the rear in Asia Minor. He resolved to move southward and give battle to Qansuh al-Ghuri.

On 24 August 1516 the Ottomans crushed the Mamelukes at Marj Dabiq, near Aleppo. The Mameluke sultan himself died in the rout. Most of the Mameluke equipment, funds and munitions of war was inside Aleppo. The indiscipline of the Mamelukes within the city had been unbridled, however, during the weeks preceding the battle. Now, as the defeated army streamed back from Marj Dabiq in disorder, the citizens closed their gates. This action meant that the Mamelukes could offer no further resistance in Syria. A withdrawal to Egypt, in order to equip a new army for a resumption of the conflict, was all that remained to them. The important towns of Syria, Aleppo, Damascus and Jerusalem, yielded to the Ottomans.

With Syria in his hands Sultan Selim had no reason to fear a Mameluke-Safawid entente, for such an alignment was now unrealizable. He therefore offered to leave the new Mameluke sultan, Tuman Bay (1516–17), in charge of Egypt, but as a vassal dependent on the Ottoman Empire. At Cairo the Mamelukes rejected this solution. A strong Mameluke force crossed the Sinai desert into Palestine, only to be driven back at the Battle of Gaza in December 1516. Selim, once his preparations for overcoming the arid wastes of Sinai were complete, moved against Egypt and at Raydaniyya in January 1517 inflicted another severe defeat on the Mamelukes. Tuman Bay and the remnants of his army fell back on Cairo, which the Ottomans occupied at the end of the

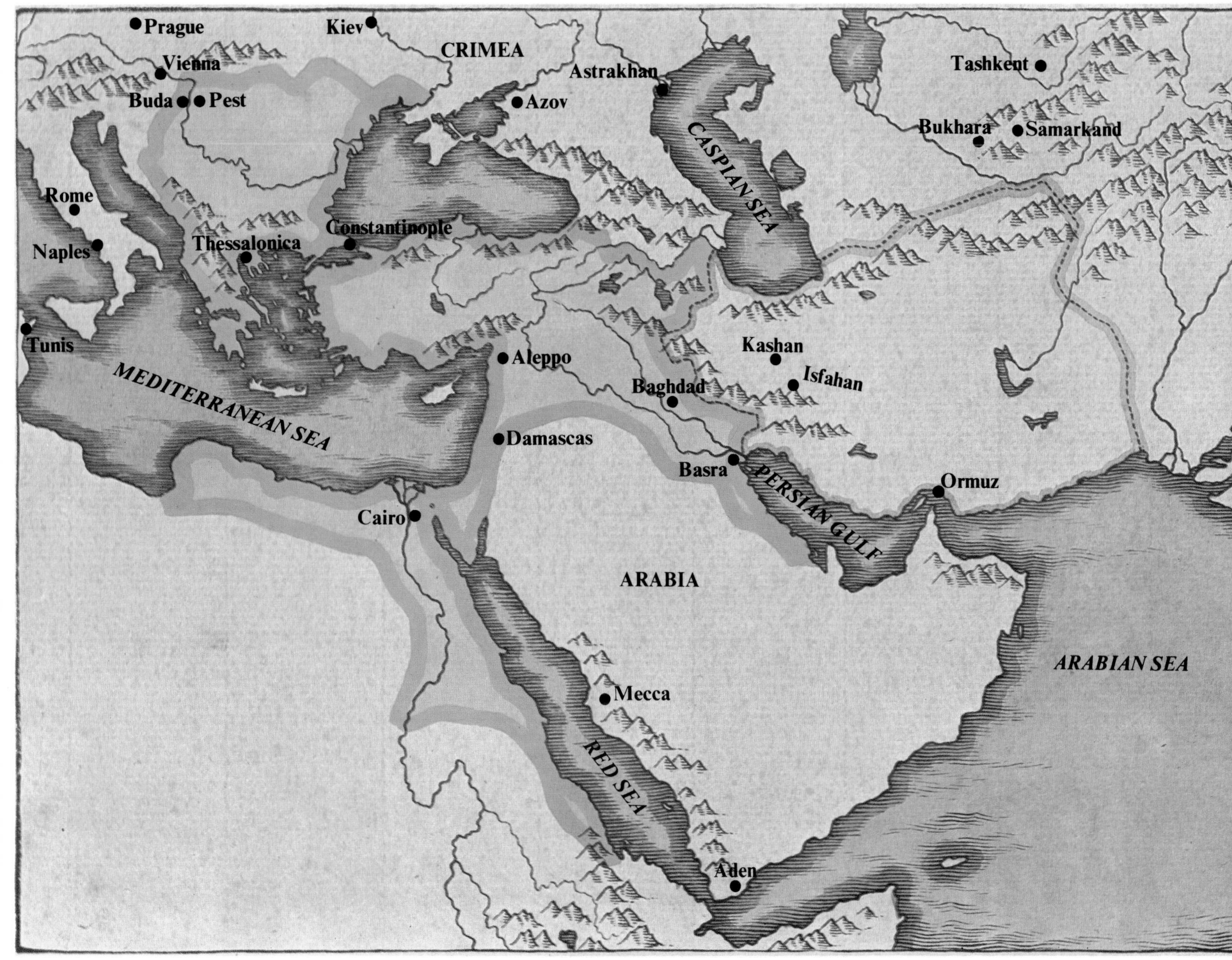

Above, the Ottoman Empire during the reign of Süleyman the Magnificent in the early sixteenth century.

Opposite, a fifteenth-century Persian miniature, depicting the Islamic interest in gardens, nature and hunting. Topkapi Palace Museum, Istanbul.

month, after several days of fierce street fighting. The Mameluke sultan, still offering what had now become a vain resistance, was at length captured in March and then executed at Cairo in April 1517.

Sultan Selim was now at the summit of his achievement. He was a prince who was renowned as a soldier and a statesman and esteemed as a poet, writing in the Persian tongue. He had a reputation for implacable ruthlessness. Among his own people, in order to wish ill of someone it sufficed to declare 'Sultan Selime vezir olsun'—'may you become a vizier of Sultan Selim'—so often did the men who served him meet their death at his imperious command.

After the death of Tuman Bay the Mameluke sultanate came to an end—but not the Mameluke regime, at least in Egypt. Ottoman 'colonization' on a large scale, of the large territories won in the campaigns of 1516–17 was out of the question. In Syria, it is true, the Ottoman system of provincial administration was introduced within certain limits. In Egypt, however, the old Mameluke regime continued largely in force, though not now in the form of an independent state. An Ottoman governor ruled at Cairo. A garrison of Ottoman soldiers (including a contingent of Janissaries) was stationed there.

The system of rule which Selim I 'improvised' in Egypt and Syria in 1517–18 did not settle down into a stable equilibrium. In Syria the 'diehard' Mameluke element attempted to throw off Ottoman control in 1520 on the death of Sultan Selim. This insurrection was suppressed, however, without great trouble. More serious was the revolt of the Mamelukes at Cairo in 1524—so serious in fact that the new Ottoman sultan. Süleyman (1520–66), sent no less a person than his grand vizier, Ibrahim, to Egypt in 1525. It was Ibrahim Pasha who now set the administration of the province on a durable foundation.

Campaigns against Hungary and Austria

On the death of Selim I the throne passed to his only son, Süleyman, whose reign was to see the Ottoman Empire at the height of its splendour. The princes of Christendom—so the Italian Paolo Giovio affirms—rejoiced at the death of Sultan Selim 'and certainly it seemed to all men that an enraged lion had left behind him as his successor a mild lamb, for Süleyman was young, inexperienced and of a quiet character'. Seldom can a first impression have been so wide of the mark. The new sultan was to be a most dangerous foe who would himself lead no fewer than nine campaigns against the Christians.

There had been a long and difficult conflict between the Ottomans and the Hungarians in the middle of the fifteenth-century—a conflict which ended in 1456 when Sultan Mehmed II tried unsuccessfully to capture the great fortress of Belgrade. Since that date no major confrontation had occurred between the two states. Now, in 1521, the young Süleyman marched against Belgrade and took it in a brilliantly organized campaign. Five years later the armed might of Hungary went down to ruin before the Ottomans at the Battle of Mohacs in 1526—the most famous of all Süleyman's victories and one which marked the end of the old medieval kingdom of Hungary. It was an event celebrated by the historian Kemalpasazade with all his command of the ornate artifice available in the rich Ottoman language:

One morning, when the furthest reaches of the plain of heaven were becoming tinted with the rose hue of the dawn, when the banner of the moon had been overthrown and the hosts of darkness were taking flight . . . then the Ottomans, seized with a sacred zeal, rose like waves in turmoil. . . .

Sword in hand (the Ottomans) rushed like searing flames against the infidels of stubborn heart. The glorious phalanxes, resembling mountains sown with tulip blooms, became stained at once, in the festival of combat, with blood vermilion-red like vials filled with wine. . . . The bright gleam of the scimitars, like narcissus wet with dew, became sullied.

The conflict was prolonged till the moment when the rim of the hippodrome of heaven grew tarnished with the blood-red hue of sunset . . . (the foe) saw the tree of his existence pitilessly despoiled of its leaves and fruits . . . the infidels having been defeated, the lance of their vigour was broken, the bow of their might was unstrung, the solid wall of their strength overthrown by the guns of war, the register of their greatness was torn. . . . Abandoning their baggage and tents, they scattered in all directions, the fumes of despair in their hearts, their face and eyes soiled with dust. . . .

The Hungarian throne fell now, by reason of a marriage alliance, to the Archduke Ferdinand of Austria, the brother of the Habsburg emperor Charles V. Among the Hungarians there were contending factions, one pro-Habsburg, the other a native party unwilling to see a foreign prince ruling at Buda. The Archduke Ferdinand in 1527 found himself confronted with a rival claimant, the *vaivoda*, or ruler, of Transylvania, John Zapolya. Zapolya, driven into the Carpathians by the troops and adherents of the Habsburg archduke, appealed to Süleyman for aid. The sultan, who considered that Hungary was his by right of conquest, agreed to establish Zapolya on the Hungarian throne as a vassal prince dependent on Istanbul. The scene was thus set for a prolonged conflict between the Habsburgs and the Ottomans for possession of the Hungarian realm.

Sultan Süleyman now sought to launch a lightning campaign against the Archduke Ferdinand—to deliver a blow so powerful that it would eliminate Austria as a factor of importance in Hungarian affairs. He therefore marched in 1529 against Vienna itself. Bad weather and also difficulties of terrain and logistics hindered the Ottoman advance. The arrival of the Ottomans before Vienna was so late in the campaign season and the resistance of the Christians so stubborn that the sultan had to raise the siege and make a laborious retreat to Belgrade.

A second attempt to strike a decisive blow was made in 1532 and again without success, the Ottoman forces being immobilized so long before the Hungarian fortress of Güns that the campaign ended as little more than a giant razzia through the borderlands of Austria. Although the resistance of the Habsburgs was not broken in these campaigns, Süleyman had nonetheless achieved much. Zapolya ruled now at Buda as his nominee. A series of subordinate principalities (the Khanate of the Crimea, Moldavia, Walachia and Hungary with the great Muslim lords of Bosnia as an additional defence in the extreme northwest) now covered the long northern frontier of the empire.

The death of Zapolya in 1540 left an infant son as heir and forced Süleyman to adopt a different attitude towards the Hungarian problem. With the disappearance of Zapolya from the scene. Ferdinand of Austria made a further attempt to take control of Hungary. To leave the affairs of that kingdom in the nominal charge of a young child and his mother was out of the question.

The sultan began therefore in 1541 a series of campaigns which led finally to the emergence of three distinct Hungaries—Habsburg, comprising the far northern and western fringes of the medieval realm; Ottoman, embracing the territories along the middle Danube from Esztergom to Belgrade; and Transylvania, a dependent state entrusted to the son of the dead Zapolya, John Sigismund, who ruled under the protection of the sultan.

The campaigns of Süleyman on the middle Danube revealed how difficult it was for the Ottomans to overcome the problems of time, distance, terrain and logistics inherent in military operations directed against territories far removed from the centre of the empire. A similar lesson was to be learned from the renewed hostilities with Persia. The campaigns of Süleyman in 1534–35, 1548–49 and 1553–54 brought to the Ottomans a notable measure of success—the extension of Ottoman control over large areas of eastern Asia Minor, for example, in the region of Erzurum and of Lake Van and also the capture of Iraq from the Safawids.

However, these campaigns did little to resolve the tensions existing between the two powers. Along the ill-defined borderlands in Armenia and Adharbayjan the border authorities, Ottoman and Safawid, and the restless Turcoman tribes, always hard to restrain, came repeatedly into conflict. Each time the Ottomans undertook a serious campaign, the Safawids resorted to tactics which the Ottomans found almost impossible to overcome. The Safawids retreated deep into their own territories, thus lengthening the enemy lines of communication. They engaged in a 'burnt-earth' withdrawal which swept the land bare of supplies; they harassed endlessly the advancing Ottoman columns; and they had an assured trust that the mountains and the harsh climate of the eastern lands would eventually compel the Ottomans to retire.

The acquisition of Iraq in 1534–35 was a logical complement to the conquest of Syria and Egypt in 1516–17. Ottoman control over the Fertile Crescent brought to the sultan at Istanbul advantages and also obligations of great importance. The territories newly incorporated into the Ottoman Empire made available to the sultan an abundance of rich resources not previously at his command. He was now, moreover, Khadim al-Haramayn, servitor of the two sacred cities of Mecca and Medina—a status which gave him a vast prestige in the Muslim world. On the other hand, as the master of Egypt he inherited from the Mamluk regime the task of resistance to the growing power of the Portuguese in the Indian Ocean.

It was not merely that the Portuguese advance might conceivably call into question the safety of the Hijaz. There were also mercantile interests at issue. The ancient transit trade in spices and other eastern products from India and beyond, through the lands of the Middle East, to the Christian states on the northern shores of the Mediterranean Sea had given considerable profit to the Muslim merchants and the Muslim governments who levied toll on this traffic. With the advent, in 1498, of the Portuguese in western India and the subsequent extension of their power in the lands around the Indian Ocean, the transit trade was for a while disrupted. As a result the flow of spices to Europe through the Red Sea and the Persian Gulf diminished greatly in quantity. However, the disruption did not last long. The traffic revived slowly until, in the second half of the sixteenth century, it attained once more its former importance. It was not until 1600 that the pre-eminence of the sea route via the Cape of Good Hope over the more ancient lines of commerce through the Arab lands would be established beyond all doubt.

The resistance of the Muslim states was one of the factors responsible for the incompleteness of the Portuguese achievement. In 1508–09 a Mamluk expedition—momentarily successful, but soon defeated—opposed the Portuguese in the waters off the coast of western India; a further Mamluk expedition was active in the Yemen at the time of the Ottoman campaigns against Syria and Egypt in 1516–17.

During the years following the visit of Ibrahim Pasha to Egypt in 1525 the problem of resistance to the Portuguese began to assume a more urgent importance in the eyes of Sultan Süleyman, not least because of requests for aid from the Muslim state of Gujarat in India. It was not, however, until 1537 that the Ottomans undertook the organization of a major campaign.

The construction of a fleet at Suez was an expensive and laborious affair—timber, naval stores, artillery and munitions had all to be brought to Egypt and then transported overland from the Nile to the harbour at Suez. In 1538 a strong force under the command of Süleyman Pasha, the governor of Egypt, set sail for India, where troops were landed to besiege Diu, which the Portuguese had taken in 1535. The Portuguese offered a fierce defence. Süleyman Pasha was so far from his home base that he was reluctant to become involved in a long and difficult conflict. He therefore raised the siege and withdrew to the Red Sea. It was now, in the course of the return voyage, that he achieved the most important result of the entire campaign—the establishment of Ottoman control over Aden as a means towards the more effective defence of the Red Sea area against the raids of the Portuguese.

Spasmodic warfare continued throughout the middle years of the sixteenth century around the shores of the Indian Ocean. The contact between Portugal and Christian Abyssinia at this time led the Ottomans to create a military administration at Massawa and Suakin in 1557. There was conflict, too, in the Persian Gulf. The Ottomans had taken over most of Iraq in 1534–35. It was not, however, until 1546 that Basra came under their immediate domination.

A conflict much more complex in character was fought out in the Mediterranean Sea. There had been war between the Ottoman Empire and Venice in 1463–79 and again in 1499–1503. To the Ottomans the main objective was the liquidation of the territories that the Signoria held along the shores of Greece and in the waters of the eastern Mediterranean.

There was tension too in the western half of the Mediterranean Sea. Here the Spaniards, having in 1492 defeated Granada, the last Muslim state in Spain, had extended their reconquest across the sea to North Africa, taking Oran in 1509.

The rise of the Muslim Corsair states

At almost the same time a sequence of events was set in motion which would lead, by 1529, to the emergence at Algiers of a new Muslim regime dependent on the Ottoman sultan to the emergence, in short, of the first of the Muslim corsair states in North Africa. A long battle was now to ensue between Spain and Algiers for effective control of the western Mediterranean.

The conflict of Christian against Muslim became more urgent in the years about 1530. Spain, under the Habsburg emperor Charles V, sought to achieve a firm hold over the central reaches of the Mediterranean Sea. The Spaniards enjoyed, in Naples and Sicily, a strong position on the northern flank of the narrow waters adjacent to Malta.

In 1528 Genoa, which possessed a powerful fleet, moved into the orbit of Spain. Also in 1528 the Knights of St John, whom the Ottomans had evicted from their island fortress of Rhodes in 1522, established a garrison at Tripoli in North Africa. More important still, the Emperor Charles V in 1530 made over to the Knights the island of Malta, henceforth to be their main base of operations. A little later, in 1535, the emperor carried out a successful campaign which left a Spanish garrison in command at La Goletta, close to Tunis. A direct

Above, Süleyman (ruled 1520–66), seen here on horseback, is best known in Christendom for his military successes, but within his kingdom he was known as Süleyman the Lawgiver in respect of his wide-ranging legal and administrative reforms. Bibliothèque Nationale, Paris.

Top, Murad III (ruled 1574–95), seen here supervising the building of a castle in Gurcistan, was for the most part indolent and subservient to his harem. This failing would be common in many later sultans. Topkapi Palace Museum, Istanbul.

assault that he undertook against Algiers itself in 1541 ended, however, in failure.

It was at this time—in 1529 and in 1532—that the Ottomans were making a determined effort to remove Austria as a factor in the Hungarian situation. The Habsburg emperor used the naval forces at his disposal to make a diversion at sea which might ease the pressure against Austria on the Danube. In 1532 a fleet under the Genoese admiral Andrea Doria took Coron in southern Greece, leaving there a garrison which held the fortress until the Ottomans recaptured it in 1533.

The increase of tension within the Mediterranean now induced the sultan to call from Algiers the famous corsair chieftain Khayr al-Din, known to the Christians as Barbarossa. The Ottomans had all the resources needed for the construction and maintenance of a large fleet—timber, naval supplies and also a sea-faring population located on the shores of the Aegean and able to provide crews for the ships. The only thing lacking was an efficient 'high command'. Khayr al-Din therefore brought with him to Istanbul the corsair captains who under his guidance had done so much to raise Algiers to eminence at sea. To Khayr al-Din himself the sultan now gave the office of *qapudan*, that is, high admiral of the Ottoman fleet.

A new war began between Venice and the Ottomans in 1537. There was endless friction along the borders of the territories that the Signoria still held on the coasts of Greece, Albania and Dalmatia. A further cause of tension was the fact that Christian corsairs often made use of Venetian harbours (for example in Cyprus and Crete) during the course of their raids against the Muslims.

Khayr al-Din, having reorganized and strengthened the naval forces at his command, led the Ottoman fleet with great success in the years 1537–40. Off Prevesa, in 1538, the Ottomans wrested from the combined armadas of Venice and Spain a marked initiative which was to remain in their hands until the Battle of Lepanto in 1571. During these years of conflict there was an entente between Venice and Spain, with the Knights of St John at Malta and the pope at Rome providing additional support. Nonetheless, effective cooperation between Venice, concerned with the defence of her territories in the Levant, and Spain, intent on the problem of the corsairs in North Africa and in the western Mediterranean, was difficult to achieve, Venice found the war unprofitable and expensive and therefore made peace with the Ottomans in 1540, surrendering to the sultan her last possessions on the mainland of southern Greece.

Khayr al-Din died in 1546, but he left behind him a number of able captains to continue the Ottoman offensive at sea. Of these none was more famous than Torghud 'Ali Re'is, the 'Dragut' of the Christians, who established at Tripoli in 1551 the second of the Muslim corsair states in North Africa. A Spanish attempt to undo this Ottoman success came to grief at Jerba in 1560. On the other hand the Ottomans failed to capture Malta in the great siege of 1565.

Soon there ensued yet another Ottoman-Venetian war in 1570–73 and a new alliance of Venice, Spain, the pope and the Knights of St John. The main objective for the Ottomans was the island of Cyprus, which fell to them in 1570–71. In this latter year, however, the Christians routed their foe at Lepanto. This celebrated victory, welcomed with great rejoicing throughout Europe, had little positive result. The divergence of interest between Spain and Venice made a fruitful prosecution of the war difficult to achieve on the Christian side. As for the Ottomans—an astonishing deployment of their rich resources, human and material, enabled them to build and equip an entire new fleet and to send it to sea for the campaign of 1572.

Venice, disappointed by the course of the war, negotiated a peace with the sultan in 1573, yielding Cyprus and obtaining in return a renewal of her trade privileges in the Ottoman Empire. Spain, however, continued the war a little while longer. Don John of Austria, the victor at Lepanto, led a successful expedition to Tunis in 1573, but his triumph was of short duration. The Ottomans seized Tunis in 1574—an event which marked the emergence of the third Muslim corsair state in North Africa.

The year 1574—of greater significance than the year of Lepanto, 1571—made it

clear that an answer had been given at last to the question posed after the fall of Granada in 1492: was north Africa to come under Christian or remain under Muslim rule? The verdict had been issued in favour of the Muslims.

During the later years of his reign, Sultan Süleyman had to face a bitter conflict between his sons over the succession to the Ottoman throne. Mustafa, the eldest son of Süleyman, who was born of Gülbahar, became a focus for the unrest, largely economic and agrarian in character, which was developing in Asia Minor. The danger from Mustafa seemed to be so great that Süleyman ordered his execution in 1553. Thereafter, Selim and Bayezid, the sons of Khurrem, most beloved of the consorts of the sultan, were rivals for the succession to their father. No decisive breach occurred, while Khurrem was alive. Her death, however, in 1558 led to civil war. Bayezid, defeated in battle near Konya in 1559, fled to Persia for refuge. In 1561 the Shah handed him over to the Ottomans in return for a large financial reward. Bayezid was at once executed and Selim, the last surviving son of Süleyman, remained as the undisputed heir to the throne.

The golden age of the Ottoman Empire

The reigns of Süleyman (1520–66) and of Selim II (1566–74) constituted a golden age for the Ottoman Empire. Now it was that the Ottoman system of government attained its 'classic' forms and dimensions. The household of the sultan included much more than the domestic and ceremonial apparatus of an imperial court. It embraced also the central regime of the Ottoman Empire, that is the great departments of state and also the numerous troops dependent directly on the sultan—the famous Corps of Janissaries (infantry equipped with fire-arms), the six regiments of household cavalry, and the various technical corps such as the bombardiers, the artillerists and the military engineers.

Most of the personnel belonging to the household had the status of slaves. These slaves recruited into the service of the sultan might be captives of war taken in hostilities, on land and on sea, against the

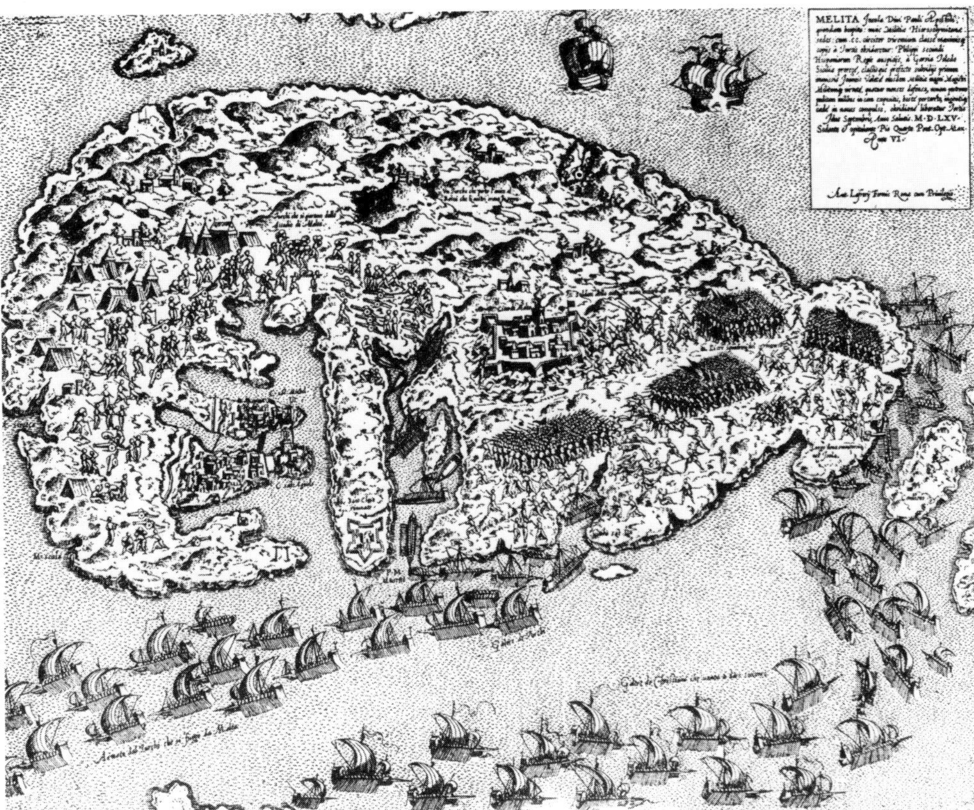

infidel Christians or youths obtained through the *devshirme*, that is the child tribute levied on the subject peoples of the empire and, above all, on the Slav races in the Balkan territories.

A large proportion of the young recruits spent some years in hard physical and manual labour on estates in the provinces. They then returned to Istanbul and were drafted into the armed forces of the central government (the Janissaries) where an expert training as soldiers awaited them. The smaller proportion, chosen because of their promise for the future, received in the schools of the imperial palace a long and elaborate education in language and literature, in physical development, in the routine of administration and in the practice of war. At length, having risen in the private and personal service of the sultan, the best among them were sent out to take charge of a province. A member of this élite, if he were fortunate, might even ascend to the highest appointment in the empire, the exalted office of grand vizier.

To the notable achievements of this age a large number of able men made their contrition: great officials like the grand viziers Ibrahim, Lufti and Mehemmed Soqollu; jurisconsults like Kemalpasazade or Abu Su'ud, learned in the Shari'a, the Sacred Law of Islam; sailors like Khayr al-Din and Torghud 'Ali; and figures of high renown like Baki, famed as a poet, or Sinan, the celebrated architect.

Amongst these men Sultan Süleyman must be given his due place. His fame is based on his military successes. Yet his reign is no less distinguished for the lavish expenditure that he devoted to the repair of

Above, the Marques de Santa Cruz (1526–88), a commander of the Spanish fleet at the Battle of Lepanto in 1571; the Christian fleet comprised an alliance of Spain, Venice and the Papacy. Museo Naval, Madrid.

Top, in 1565 the garrison of Malta faced this four-month siege by the Turks. The defenders were eventually relieved by the Spaniards, and the Turks were kept out of the western Mediterranean.

Above left, the galley, driven primarily by oars, was still the main method of transport and warfare in the Mediterranean in the sixteenth century, for both the Turks and the Venetians. National Maritime Museum, London.

Opposite, the Ottoman Turks, under Süleyman the Magnificent, besieging Vienna, the capital of the Holy Roman emperor, in 1529. This was the limit of their westward expansion, although they were to repeat the attempt in 1683. Topkapi Palace Museum, Istanbul.

the frontier fortresses (for example at Buda and Temesvar) and to the building of mosques, aqueducts, bridges and other public utilities (at Damascus and Kaffa, for example). He sought also to adorn the capital of his empire, Istanbul.

Of all the tributes made to the excellence of Ottoman rule in the golden age of the empire none is more remarkable than the account which Ogier Ghiselin de Busbecq, the ambassador of the Emperor Ferdinand I (1556–64), has given of his first audience with Sultan Süleyman. Busbecq underlines in a memorable passage the profound impression that the experience bestowed on him:

There was not in all that great assembly a single man who owed his position to aught save his valour and his merit. No distinction is attached to birth among the Turks: the deference to be paid to a man is measured by the position he holds in the public service. . . . It is by merit that men rise in the service, a system which ensures that posts should only be assigned to the competent. Each man in Turkey carries in his own hand his ancestry and his position in life, which he may make or mar as he will. Those who receive the highest offices from the Sultan are for the most part the sons of shepherds or herdsmen, and so far from being ashamed of their parentage, they actually glory in it, and consider it a matter of boasting that they owe nothing to the accident of birth; for they do not believe that high qualities are either natural or hereditary, nor do they think that they can be handed down from father to son, but that they are partly the gift of God, and partly the result of good training, great industry, and unwearied zeal. . . .

Süleyman was a monarch whom the Venetian, Andrea Dandolo, characterized as wise and just, but ruthless beyond measure to all who threatened or might endanger his empire or his own person.

A poet from Zara, Brne Krnarutic, who had fought against the Ottomans in the time of Süleyman, described in Croat the campaign of 1566, during the course of which the sultan died in his tent before the walls of Szigetvar, a fortress then in Christian hands. Of Süleyman he was to write that there was no evil in him and that never again would the Turks have such a great sultan.

Muslim and Christian alike declared their tributes to his greatness. His subjects knew him as Qanuni, the 'Giver of Laws'. To the Christians he was above all a great king—Il Magnifico, 'the Magnificent Sultan'.

Chapter 9

The Crusades and the Expansion of Western Christendom

Christendom was an ideological concept: it was the community that acknowledged as its head the pope, who was held to be the direct successor of St Peter. It had been in the making since the break-up of the Roman Empire in the fifth century. The pope thus also became the guardian of the Roman heritage. It was his mission to recover the provinces lost to the German tribes who had broken through the frontiers of the Roman Empire. His weapon was not to be the sword but the Bible.

The making of Christendom was essentially the extension of papal authority among these Germanic peoples, but its characteristic civilization and society was very much a fusion of its Germanic and its Roman inheritance. The German contribution was more obviously marked in northern Europe, where Roman civilization had been only a thin veneer. The Germans were able to impose their own language, customs and laws, while in Mediterranean Europe the Roman legacy remained all important. The contrast between northern and southern Europe is one of the most striking features of the medieval world.

The moulding of Christendom was interrupted by the Hungarian, Viking and Muslim invasions in the ninth and tenth centuries. These were beaten off, and the Vikings and Hungarians were converted to Christianity. The Muslims of Spain were driven back by the Christians from the mountains of Galicia and the foothills of the Pyrenees to beyond the rivers Tagus and Ebro. The islands of Corsica, Sardinia and Sicily were also recovered from the Muslims. It was a period of rapid development in almost every field, from agriculture to learning. The feudal system, which owed something to both Roman and German heritages, emerged. The papacy began to make its authority felt in all parts of Christendom; by the turn of the twelfth century it supervised almost every aspect of Christian life. Christendom had perhaps reached its greatest degree of unification.

The forces that determined the early expansion of Christendom were largely ideological. These forces weakened, however, in the last centuries of the Middle Ages and the new lands brought within the orbit of Christendom were retained within a European framework only where economic and political ties were sufficiently strong.

The expansion of Christendom took place along two main fronts: in the North into central and eastern Europe; and in the South into Spain and the eastern Mediterranean. It was directed very largely against the Muslims and the Byzantines. The Christian attitude towards the Muslims was fairly straightforward: they were enemies of Christendom and it was essential that the Holy Places should be rescued from them. This does not mean that in the lands conquered from Islam it was impossible for Christian and Muslim to live together in harmony. In Spain and Sicily tolerance prevailed and the more advanced Muslim civilization was absorbed by the Christians.

Much more complicated was the attitude of the West towards the Byzantine Empire, which was the direct descendant of the Roman Empire and formed part of the Christian world; its emperors claimed the right of representing the whole Christian world, which the popes asserted was their own. The struggle between Byzantium and the West was so bitter because it was a struggle for the leadership of Christendom.

In the eleventh century, the balance between western Europe and the Byzantine Empire changed radically. In 1071 the Byzantines lost Bari, their last stronghold in southern Italy, to the Normans. As a result the papacy recovered ecclesiastical jurisdiction over southern Italy, which had long been disputed with the Byzantine patriarch. So bitter was this quarrel that in 1054 the papal legate placed the Byzantine patriarch in schism.

In 1071 the Byzantines also lost virtually all Asia Minor after their defeat at Mantzikiert by the Seljuk Turks. The Byzantine Emperor Alexius I Comnenus (1081–1118) appealed for western aid. This was taken up by Pope Urban II, who in 1095 called for a crusade to rescue eastern Christendom from the menace of the Turks. His motives were many-sided; but, above all, he seized the

Above, the Council of Clermont, 1095, at which Pope Urban II called for a crusade for the first time and won a powerful response from all parts of western Christendom.

Opposite left, an example of seventeeth-century Turkish calligraphy, worked in metal. As the Ottomans lost ground to Persia in this period, many craftsmen left the Ottoman Empire and went to Isfahan. Topkapi Palace Museum, Istanbul.

Opposite top right, Selim II (ruled 1566–74), the successor of Süleyman and known as Selim the Drunkard. The succession to the sultanate was usually violent and was a permanent source of Ottoman weakness. Topkapi Palace Museum, Istanbul.

Opposite bottom, Selim II shown in a contemporary Turkish miniature. During his reign, the sultanate became subjected to the grand vizier for the first time. Topkapi Palace Museum, Istanbul.

opportunity to assert papal primacy by assuming the protectorship of the Holy Places, a role which the Byzantine emperor was no longer in a position to carry out.

The People's Crusade

A great Council met at Clermont in France in 1095 attended by over 200 bishops and many noblemen. Urban, who was French, made an eloquent speech to the assembly. 'Jerusalem', he said,

> is now held by the enemies of Christ. She longs to be liberated and ceases not to implore you to come to her aid. God has conferred on you Franks above all other nations great glory in arms. Accordingly, undertake this journey eagerly for the remission of your sins, with the assurance of the reward of imperishable glory in the kingdom of heaven.

So deeply moved were his hearers by these words that when he had finished they cried out, 'God wills it! God wills it!' Urban distributed to hundreds of knights the crosses of red cloth which they were to wear on their shoulders or their helmets and from which they acquired the name of crusaders. During the next few months Urban went about France, repeating his appeal and organizing the enterprise.

The pope's message was taken up by travelling preachers. One of the most passionate of these was a French monk, Peter the Hermit. He had himself seen the sufferings of the Christians in Jerusalem, and he rode on an ass through towns and villages, bearing a huge crucifix and sobbing and groaning as he urged the people with fiery phrases to deliver the city from the infidel. He was assisted by another Frenchman, Walter the Penniless, and there were other preachers of the same sort in Germany.

These preachers were responsible for what has been called the 'People's Crusade'. Their appeal was assisted by the continuing belief in the eleventh century that the Last Judgement was at hand.

Small enthusiastic groups of men and women, without arms or discipline, set out from France and Germany for the Holy Land. Some of the German groups massacred and plundered the Jews in the Rhineland towns. Many of them were later set upon and routed by Magyar soldiers as they passed through Hungary. Those French and German groups that reached Constantinople in 1096 were advised by the emperor to await the arrival of the crusading armies, but since they took to plundering the Greeks encouraged them to cross to the Asiatic side of the Bosporus where they proceeded to descend in great disorder to attack the city of Nicaea. There they were slaughtered by Turkish archers massed behind the defensive ramparts. Walter the Penniless was among those killed. Peter the Hermit, who was in Constantinople seeking help from the emperor, survived for twenty years the disastrous People's Crusade.

The First Crusade

Meanwhile, military precautions for the First Crusade were proceeding. Since none of the great sovereigns of Europe came forward to lead it, it was conducted by princes and noblemen. Some were inspired by religious devotion, others by a desire for travel and adventure and most probably by the hope of new lands and power.

The leaders and soldiers of the First Crusade were predominantly French. Each leader raised his own force. Godfrey of Bouillon, Duke of Lower Lorraine, gathered Germans, Flemings and Frenchmen from the region between the Meuse and the Rhine. Count Hugh of Vermandois, brother of the King of France, Count Stephen of Blois and Robert, Duke of Normandy, raised a force in northern France and attracted volunteers from England and even Scandinavia, while Count Raymond of Toulouse drew his contingent from southern France. Another group of Normans, from southern Italy, was led by Bohemund of Otranto, son of Robert Guiscard, and his nephew, Tancred.

It was agreed that the forces should meet in the neighbourhood of Constantinople in 1096 and from their begin their operations against the Turks. They proceeded to this destination by three routes. Godfrey de Bouillon's contingent went by the Danube through Hungary and Serbia, Count Raymond's and Count Hugh's contingents crossed the Alps and went through northern Italy and Dalmatia, and the Normans under Bohemund crossed the Adriatic from Apulia to Durazzo.

It was not until the late spring of 1097 that the scattered and poorly-organized forces drifted one after another into Constantinople. Their approach, preceded by stories from towns and villages of looting and destruction, alarmed the Emperor Alexius Comnenus. He had expected mercenary troops in response to his appeal for help and did not welcome the arrival of whole self-contained armies. He particularly feared the Normans from southern Italy. They were the best troops and, moreover, Bohemund and his father were old opponents of the Byzantine Empire, which they had already invaded several times.

In addition, while Alexius wanted to regain the provinces he had lost to the Normans, the leaders of the crusade planned

Above, the routes of the early crusades and the crusader kingdoms set up by the First Crusade.

Opposite, Peter the Hermit, one of the many wandering preachers who whipped up enthusiasm for the First Crusade throughout Europe in 1095. British Library, London.

to reconquer Syria and Palestine and share it among themselves. He therefore insisted that before he transported them across the Bosporus they should swear an oath of obedience to him. They agreed unwillingly to do this. It was also arranged that the emperor would furnish them with supplies and receive back his lost provinces.

After recapturing Nicaea, which was handed over to Alexius, the crusaders began to advance across Asia Minor. In front went the mail-clad horsemen, who wore over their chain armour white surcoats on which the red cross was sewn, behind them on foot came the archers, armed with crossbows or longbows. They were still a motley crowd and ill-prepared for the march. On their way across Europe, many knights had travelled as if they were going to a tournament, with falcons on their wrists, their hounds running before them and their chess-boards to relieve their tedious hours; now many of them did not think of carrying water-bottles. However, they defeated the Turks at Dorylaeum and eventually arrived at Antioch in October 1097.

The city was strongly walled, and the crusaders were not numerous enough to blockade it. They suffered severely from lack of supplies and the cold of the winter. Fortunately the local Turkish princes were on such bad terms with each other that they delayed the despatch of a relieving force. After eight months, the crusaders captured the city, only to be besieged in it themselves by a belatedly-assembled Turkish army. Dysentery now broke out among them, and their stores of food ran low.

In these desperate circumstances a Provençal monk, after having a vision, discovered beneath the pavement of an old church the 'Holy Lance of Antioch', the head of the spear with which the Saviour's side was pierced during the Passion.

The crusaders sallied out, led by Bohemund and won a decisive victory. Some crusaders said that they had been aided by St George and other saints fighting on white horses. Bohemund, however, felt that the tales of miracles were an aspersion on his generalship. He compelled the monk who had found the Holy Lance to undergo the ordeal of walking through a fire, which killed him. Bohemund also worsened relations with the Byzantine emperor by refusing to hand over Antioch to him.

The crusaders remained in Antioch for seven months. Not only were they exhausted by famine and sickness, they also quarrelled among themselves. Raymond of Toulouse resented Bohemund's claim to rule the city. It was not until 1099 that they resumed their progress southwards and advanced down the coast from Antioch.

In the end, however, their delay was fortunate for them. They began their journey again just as the two most important Muslim powers in the Near East were at enmity with each other. The Seljuk Turks were advancing westwards to fight the Fatimid caliphs of Egypt. Palestine lay between them and was the inevitable battleground. In 1099 the Fatimites had just succeeded in recovering Jerusalem from the Turks, but they could exert little control beyond the city. The petty Arab emirs who ruled in the country were unable to check the advancing crusaders. One by one the cities opened their gates to them—Tripoli, Beirut, Tyre and Acre. On 7 June the crusaders reached Jerusalem.

'When they heard the name of Jerusalem', a chronicler wrote,

> they could not keep back their tears. They gave thanks to God for having allowed them to achieve the aim of their pilgrimage, the Holy City where our Saviour had wished to save the world. . . . They advanced until the walls and towers of the city became clearly visible. They raised their hands in an act of supplication towards heaven, and humbly kissed the ground.

When the moment of devotion had passed, however, it was clear that the fortifications of the city would be hard to overcome. The siege lasted forty days. It was intensely hot and water was short, the crusaders lacked siege-engines until a Genoese fleet arrived at Jaffa with food and war *matériel*. Then they built two mobile wooden towers. From these they succeeded in setting a turret alight and overwhelming the defenders on that part of the wall.

The next day, Friday, at three in the afternoon, the day and hour of the Passion, Godfrey de Bouillon stood victorious on the walls of Jerusalem. 'The city presented a spectacle of such slaughter of enemies and shedding of blood that it struck the conquerors themselves with horror and disgust', declared the Archbishop of Tyre, unable to conceal his feelings. For three days the crusaders massacred the city's inhabitants and took immense booty. Muslim men, women and children were slain; Jews were burned in their synagogue; and seventy lamps and heavy vases of gold and silver were taken from the mosque.

The other side of the spirit of the crusade was seen that evening when the victors, barefoot and with fervent joy, visited the holy places. Everyone threw himself face down upon the ground, his arms crossed: 'Each believed that he still saw before him the crucified body of Jesus Christ. And it seemed also to them that they were at the gate of heaven.'

Eight days after taking the city (news which Pope Urban did not live to hear) the leaders of the crusade proceeded to elect a governor of Palestine. Bohemund wished to remain in Antioch, while the Count of Flanders and the Duke of Normandy planned to return to Europe. Raymond of Toulouse refused election, believing that a cleric would be the only suitable head.

The choice then fell on Godfrey de Bouillon, who refused to accept a royal title in the city where his Saviour had been crowned with thorns. He would only allow himself to be called the Defender of the Holy Sepulchre, but when he died the following year his brother, Baldwin I, was elected in his place, and he did not hesitate to term himself 'King of Jerusalem'.

The crusaders formed from their conquests, as well as the kingdom of Jerusalem, the principality of Antioch and the earldoms of Edessa and Tripoli, each under a Frankish lord. These states were organized on a feudal basis, and Palestine became almost like a European country with its churches, monasteries and castles. The states were divided into fiefs, the holders of which owed the customary homage and duties towards their rulers. The barons possessed their feudal courts, and the bishops were richly endowed and given powerful privileges.

Nevertheless, the position of the crusading states in Palestine were very weak. Most of the townspeople and peasants were Muslims, and hardly any attempt was made to convert them to Christianity. The crusaders themselves were disunited. Princes and barons, bishops and clergy, knights and merchants, all thought of their own interests. Only a few crusaders stayed in the Holy Land. Most went home after the fall of Jerusalem.

The crusading states never had sufficient knights to defend themselves properly or to fight in open warfare. Their most valuable soldiers were the members of the two military orders. These were men who took monastic vows but devoted themselves to a military life and made themselves responsible for the defence of a large part of the Christian territory.

The older of the two orders was that of the Hospital of St John of Jerusalem, which originated in a hospital founded in about 1070 to care for sick pilgrims in Jerusalem and became a military organization some fifty years later. Its members, called the Knights Hospitallers, wore a white cross on a black ground.

The order of the Temple of Solomon was founded in 1118 by Hugh de Payens, a knight of Champagne, to protect pilgrims on the road from the coast to Jerusalem. Its members, known as the Knights Templar, wore a red cross on a white ground and soon took to fighting the Muslims. Their houses had circular churches attached to them, as a reminder of the Church of the Holy Sepulchre in Jerusalem.

Shortage of numbers compelled the military orders to defend the Holy Land by erecting and garrisoning great stone castles in important places. These were highly developed types of castle construction and immensely strong. The most magnificent of them was Krak of the Knights built by the Knights Hospitallers in the twelfth century to guard the only pass from Christian territory to Tripoli and the coast. Its strategic position, massive walls and vast store-houses enabled it successfully to withstand at least twelve sieges. For a century and a half it remained, in the words of a Muslim chronicler, 'a bone stuck in the throat of the Saracens'.

The Second Crusade

In 1144, the Emir Zangi, a forceful Muslim chieftain from Mosul, who aimed to set himself at the head of the disunited Muslims of the coastal areas, captured the ill-guarded town of Edessa, the northern outpost of the Christian territory. Though this exposed the crusaders' northern flank in the Holy Land, they were not alarmed. They had become used to living side by side with the Muslims and had even made their own treaties with the local native rulers; they did not think it advisable to resume hostilities.

In Europe, however, the news of the fall of Edessa produced immediate alarm, particularly among the leaders of the Church. Islam seemed to be about to expel the Christians from the Holy Land. Pope Eugenius II entrusted the preaching of a new crusade to the most celebrated Churchman of the time, St Bernard of Clairvaux, in 1148. St Bernard had established a new Cistercian monastery at Clairvaux which had become famous for its austerity and piety. Although he had become the counsellor of popes and kings, he never accepted any post other than that of abbot of the house he had founded. He was convinced of the righteousness of the crusade he proclaimed. 'The earth trembles and is shaken he said, 'because the King of Heaven has lost his land, the land where once he walked.' A terrible Judgement Day awaited those who failed to take up the Cross, but to die in battle for the cause of Christ would be to gain the reward of eternal bliss.

When he delivered this awesome message, many devout men were inspired to join the ranks of the new crusading forces. Others who came forward, however, were of a different character. They were thieves, murderers, perjurers or adventurers in search of their own ends under the cloak of religious zeal. St Bernard acknowledged this but was not dismayed. Rather he hailed the departure of these men, saying, 'Europe rejoices to lose them and Palestine to gain them; they are useful in both ways, in their absence from here and in their presence there.'

St Bernard's eloquence also ensured that this time the crusade had royal leadership. His enthusiasm carried away the Emperor

Conrad III, and King Louis VII of France also joined. Nevertheless, the crusade was a complete failure. Many of the crusaders never reached the Holy Land at all. The two monarchs fell out with the Byzantines and laid fruitless siege to Damascus. Conrad returned to Germany in 1148 and Louis to France the next year. St Bernard called the failure 'an abyss so deep that I must called him blessed who is not scandalized thereby'.

The fall of Jerusalem

During the thirty years which followed the fiasco of the Second Crusade, the Holy Land underwent a complete and ominous transformation. For the first time the Muslims were united against the invaders and a formidable fighting force.

This was Saladin's achievement. He was a Kurdish officer who rose to be Sultan of Egypt and Syria and a remarkable man of great character and courage. Having reduced Mesopotamia and received the homage of the Seljuk princes of Asia Minor, he devoted the rest of his life untiringly to waging a *Jihad* or holy war against the Christians, whose territory was surrounded by his dominions. He was a brave fighter and a cunning statesman but also a chivalrous and generous warrior who gained the admiration even of his Christian opponents. He rejected the idea, generally accepted at the time, that massacres were an inevitable part of warfare. 'Abstain from the shedding of blood', he told his captains, 'for blood that is spilt never slumbers.'

The crusaders in Palestine were too disunited to put up effective resistance to Saladin. In 1187 he inflicted a disastrous defeat upon a force of knights, mostly Templars, in the region of Tiberias. This was the beginning of the end for the kingdom of Jerusalem, which was now practically denuded of its defenders. Saladin pursued his campaign unchecked. He was said to have intervened in the middle of battle on occasions to provide his opponents with ices and fresh horses so that they could continue to fight, but he still defeated them. One by one the crusaders' strongholds at Acre, Jaffa, Beirut and Ascalon fell to him.

In September Saladin's army appeared before the walls of Jerusalem. The city was full of Christian refugees, but few of them were soldiers. Within a fortnight the Muslims had undermined part of the walls, and the city had to surrender. Saladin allowed its defenders to ransom themselves and granted them a safe passage back to the nearest Christian territory. The great cross was taken down from the Church of the Holy Sepulchre and dragged for two days through the mire of the city's streets. The bells of the churches were melted down, and the floors and walls of the Mosque of Omar were purified with Damascene rosewater. Saladin continued his conquests until Tyre was the only town of consequence which remained in Christian hands.

The Third Crusade

The news of the fall of Jerusalem caused widespread consternation in Europe and a determination to retrieve the Holy Land. Pope Urban III died soon afterwards, and his death was attributed to grief at the Muslim victories. His successor, Gregory VIII, issued a Bull proclaiming a new crusade to the East.

The old emperor, Frederick Barbarossa, summoned a council at Mainz to discuss the crusade. His bishops and barons unanimously agreed to support it after they had been addressed by the Archbishop of Tyre. The archbishop also attended a meeting in Normandy with Philip Augustus, King of

Above, the castle of Krak des Chevaliers, the largest and best defended of the crusader castles in the Holy Land. It was eventually captured in 1271.

Above left, Christian pilgrims visiting the Church of the Holy Sepulchre at Jerusalem. The crusaders' main object was to free the important Christian shrines from Muslim control and to restore them as centres of pilgrimage.

Top, the conquest of Jerusalem by the First Crusade in 1099; the crusaders had to attend to their horses carefully, as they had no hope of finding new warhorses in the Holy Land. Bibliothèque Nationale, Paris.

France, and Henry II, King of England, and pleaded the cause of the crusade before them. Philip and Henry wept, embraced and vowed to go together to the Holy Land. Henry died in 1189 and was succeeded by his son, Richard, whose warlike spirit was keenly attracted by the idea of the campaign.

Frederick Barbarossa was the first to set out on the crusade. He left Germany with a vast army and took the overland route. His soldiers suffered greatly on the march from hunger and thirst as well as from the attacks of Turkish horsemen, and in 1190 he himself died of shock after bathing in a cold mountain stream. His much-depleted force reached Antioch, which it succeeded in capturing, since Saladin had withdrawn most of his troops from the area.

Meanwhile, the Christians in the Holy Land had at last taken the offensive and began to besiege the port of Acre, the best base from which to retake Jerusalem. They were then surrounded by Saladin, and for eighteen months besiegers, besieged and would-be-relievers fought fiercely and endured hunger and disease. By now Philip and Richard had set out separately by sea. Philip arrived first at Acre and became ill. Richard delayed to capture Cyprus from the Byzantine Empire, but on his arrival he took charge of operations and captured the town within a month in 1191.

The way to Jerusalem now lay open, but discord had already broken out among the crusaders. The Duke of Austria, angered by Richard's insistence that his own banner should be set above the duke's on the walls of Acre, had gone home. Above all, Philip and Richard quarrelled continuously before Acre. Since Richard, as Duke of Normandy and Aquitaine, was the French king's vassal, Philip considered that he should accept his leadership, but Richard continually criticized and ignored him. When Philip wanted to attack Acre, Richard went to dinner; when Richard wanted to attack, Philip had a headache. Finally, Philip abandoned the crusade and returned to France, where he proceeded to invade Richard's territory.

Philip's departure, however, did not weaken Richard's resolve to continue the crusade. He led his army southwards towards Jerusalem, advancing through the sun-scorched country. His skill in battle won him a victory over Saladin at Arnif which gained him the name of 'Lion-Heart'. He captured Jaffa, refortified Ascalon and before the end of the year was within a dozen miles of Jerusalem, only to withdraw to the coast because he had insufficient men to besiege the city.

He had established a remarkable understanding, even friendship, with Saladin. Each greatly admired the other, and a writer said at the time, 'Could each be endowed with the faculties of the other, the whole world could not furnish two such princes.' The two men exchanged presents and courtesies, and when Richard's charger fell in action Saladin sent him a new one. They also met and even discussed the possibility of dividing the Holy Land.

The negotiations, however, were fruitless. Richard again advanced on Jerusalem; this time he got with an advance party within sight of the walls but once more had to retreat. He won a brilliant victory at Jaffa but had to relinquish the crusade forever. News from Europe made him anxious to return home.

In 1192 Richard made a three-years' truce with Saladin by which the crusaders retained the coast from Ascalon to Acre with the right of access to Jerusalem. Small bodies of crusaders were permitted to visit the Holy Sepulchre on condition that they went unarmed.

Richard then set off on his journey back to England, though he was not to return home until he had suffered shipwreck and captivity at the hands of the Duke of Austria. That the Third Crusade should have failed while led by the three most powerful kings of the time brought severe disillusion.

The power of Islam under Saladin seemed formidable. When he died in 1193, the Muslims were downcast. 'Without Saladin', said his scribe, 'the great men perished, with him disappeared people of true worth; good deeds diminished, and bad ones increased; life became more difficult, and earth was covered with shadows; the century had its phoenix to deplore, and Islam lost its support.'

At the end of the twelfth century, the crusades seemed to be over. The great hope of delivering the Holy Sepulchre from the infidel had been eclipsed by the national struggles of the West and Latins and Byzantines were divided.

The Fourth Crusade

In 1198, when Innocent III became pope, the Church was in a difficult situation. The empire could still assert itself against the papacy, and secular rulers still managed to control the appointment of bishops. Jerusalem was still held by the Muslims. Most of the lower clergy were not celibate, and the monastic orders, including even the Cistercians, were losing their zeal and becoming wealthy. The beliefs of the Cathari were spreading, while criticism of the Church and anti-clericalism were common among lay people.

One traditional method of promoting the papacy was to preach a Crusade. Innocent did so himself in the belief that a renewed attempt to gain the Holy Land for Christendom would be bound to revive the old crusading spirit. Moreover, since no emperor or king was now likely to assume control of the expedition, he hoped that his success would be greater than that of his predecessors.

Events quickly proved that Innocent was entirely mistaken. The enterprise was begun in 1199 by a group of enthusiastic noblemen in northern France, led by Boniface, Marquess of Montferrat. Though they were zealously helped by papal preachers, they were motivated not by religious feeling but rather by personal ambition for wealth and power.

Ships had to be obtained from the Italian maritime cities—Venice, Pisa and Genoa. These cities had already gained enormous riches from constructing ships and transporting the crusaders and had also obtained commercial bases in the leading Syrian ports and built up a large carrying trade. Of these cities, Venice had prospered most and could best provide what the crusaders needed.

To Venice the crusaders therefore turned. By April 1201 their envoys had concluded their negotiations with the rulers of the city, who showed themselves to be hard businessmen. The sum of 85,000 silver marks, paid in advance, was required for the hire of ships and for provisions. The Venetians announced that they would also join the crusade, and the Doge himself, though old and quite blind, sewed the Cross on to his 'great cotton hat' as a sign of their earnestness and good faith. In return for its participation, Venice required an equal share in the direction of the crusade and half of any conquests.

When the crusading armies were assembled in Venice in August 1202, they could not raise funds to pay the agreed sum to the Venetian government, which interned them on a small island in the lagoon. There they were given the choice either of paying or of conquering for the Venetians the Christian town of Zara, on the Adriatic coast, from the King of Hungary. The crusaders discharged their debt by storming Zara, so completing Venetian domination over the Adriatic.

Pope Innocent III was indignant at this disgraceful diversion of the crusade. At first he excommunicated the whole army; later he forgave them, only to discover that the crusade had again been diverted. The young Byzantine prince, Alexius, offered them money, supplies and troops if they would re-establish on the throne his father, Isaac Angelus, who had been deposed by his brother, Alexius III. The crusaders accepted and sailed for Constantinople, reaching the Bosporus in July 1203. They captured the city without difficulty. Isaac and his son were made joint emperors but were unable to meet the terms they had promised to their benefactors.

In 1204 the crusaders and Venetians decided to sack Constantinople. Towers were erected on the decks of their ships and the attacking parties crossed on ladders, gained the walls and broke into the city. For three days it was sacked. Priceless treasures were lost, manuscripts burnt, paintings destroyed. Many metal statues, some of which dated from ancient times, were melted down for weapons and armour. Four famous bronze horses were taken to Venice, where they can still be seen above the portico of St Mark's Cathedral.

The aftermath of the Fourth Crusade

The conquest of Constantinople was the logical conclusion of the rivalry between Byzantium and the West. The closer contacts that developed in the twelfth century only intensified the already existing hostility. The Byzantines hated the westerners for their rough, barbaric and overbearing ways and also, not without reason, feared them as conquerors. The westerners despised the Byzantines, whom they thought effete and treacherous and considered them upstarts and usurpers of the Roman Empire; they were intensely suspicious of the overtly amicable relations that Byzantium

Above, a twelfth-century wall painting from Old Cairo, in Egypt, depicting a battle with the crusaders in chain-mail. British Library, London.

Top, the crusaders of the Fourth Crusade, in 1204, converging on the city of Constantinople; this episode represented the end of any real hopes in Christendom of recapturing the Holy Lands by a crusade. Bodleian Library, Oxford.

Opposite left, a typical Saracen warrior of the twelfth century, according to an Arabic illustration.

Opposite centre, the Battle of the Horns of Hattin, near Tiberias, in 1187, at which Saladin took a number of important prisoners. Here he is shown seizing the part of the True Cross carried by the crusaders as their battle standard. Corpus Christi College, Cambridge.

Opposite bottom centre, Richard I of England (ruled 1189–99), who was captured by his enemy Leopold of Austria on his way back from the Third Crusade, imprisoned, then handed over to the emperor. Burgerbibliothek, Bern.

Opposite top right, Richard I of England jousting with Saladin on the Third Crusade. British Library, London.

Opposite bottom right, Innocent III (ruled 1198–1215), the pope of high ideals who had the misfortune of calling the disastrous Fourth Crusade.

maintained with the Muslim countries of the Middle East. It was believed that the crusaders had been betrayed by the Byzantines. For the Venetians the conquest of Constantinople was the outcome of the dominant role they had won in the commerce of the Byzantine Empire. The Byzantine emperors of the twelfth century were only too well aware of the dangers that this held in store for their state. They tried to limit Venetians privileges, even in 1171 imprisoning all Venetians resident in the Empire and confiscating their goods. Compensation promised to the Venetians was never paid and the position of Venetian merchants at Constantinople remained extremely uncertain. In 1198, the Venetians were threatening to replace the Byzantine emperor Alexius III Angelos (1195–1203) with his nephew, who was also called Alexius—a threat realized in 1203 after the crusaders' first conquest of Constantinople. The Venetians did not necessarily want to destroy the Byzantine Empire; all they wanted was a pliable ruler who would uphold their commercial privileges.

Any hopes that had been pinned on the young Alexius were soon disappointed. Alexius was in no position to carry out the promises he had made to the crusaders and the Venetians: to recognize the primacy of the papacy, to aid the crusaders against Egypt, and to give compensation to the Venetians. Popular pressure was far too strong. He was overthrown in a palace revolution and in March 1204 the leaders of the crusade proceeded to draw up a treaty partitioning the Byzantine Empire. On the night of 12 April 1204 the crusaders stormed Constantinople; the Byzantine emperor and patriarch fled and in their place were set up a Latin emperor and a Latin patriarch.

It was the Venetians who profited most from the destruction of the Byzantine Empire; they took advantage of it to found a more durable empire than the Latin Empire of Constantinople.

The Venetians were mostly interested in obtaining possession of those regions and ports that had strategic and commercial value. They gave up many of the territories allotted to them by the partition treaty. while their title to their most valuable possession in the Levant, the island of Crete, was only secured in August 1204 by a separate treaty with Boniface of Montferrat, one of the leaders of the Fourth Crusade, Crete dominated the entrances to the Aegean; it was the vital link on the trade routes from western Europe both to Constantinople and to the ports of Syria.

There was less method behind the conquests of the crusaders, but the Greeks were in disarray and were at first inclined to accept the rule of the new lords of Constantinople. By early 1205 the Latin Empire had possibly reached its greatest extent. It dominated not only the coasts of the Sea of Marmora but also the European coasts of the Aegean from Thrace to the Peloponnese. It seemed that the Latin Empire might successfully replace the fallen Byzantine Empire.

In March 1205, however, the Latin emperor Baldwin I was ambushed near Hadrianople by the Bulgarians and was never heard of again. Shortly afterwards Boniface of Montferrat was also killed in battle against the Bulgarians. The frailty of the Latin Empire was only too apparent. Baldwin's brother, Henry of Hainault, had to abandon his conquests in Asia Minor and hurry to the rescue of Constantinople. He was elected emperor soon afterwards, and his firm rule did much to disguise the weakness of his empire. He was able to assert his authority over its more distant parts and he did his best to reconcile his Greek subjects to Latin rule.

The Fall of the Latin Empire

A serious weakness of the Latin Empire was that the conquest of western Asia Minor was never completed. There were as a result difficulties in provisioning Constantinople and these became more serious as the hold of the Latin over Thrace grew weaker. Furthermore, Constantinople could hardly act as the focal point of the Latin Empire; it was too distant from its main centres of power in Greece and the Peloponnese. It was also isolated by foreign enemies. In Europe it was threatened by the Bulgarians and in Asia Minor by the Greeks, who were reorganizing themselves. The Latin emperors were forced to fight on two fronts; this overtaxed their resources.

The dangers of Constantinople's position became more pronounced after Henry of Hainault's death in 1216. His successors as emperor were mostly worthless men, unable to give cohesion to the lands of the Latin Empire. The capture of Thessalonica in 1224 by the Greeks of Epirus isolated Constantinople still further. Yet the Latin Empire lingered on until 1261. That it lasted this long was for the most part because of quarrels among its opponents, the strength of the walls of Constantinople, and the protection afforded by the Venetian navy.

Even the Venetians, however, who had expected so much from Constantinople, seem to have been disappointed. By 1261 Venetian commercial interests were moving away to the crusader states. This was not only the result of chaotic conditions in Constantinople; it was also because the Black Sea trade, which had been falling off in the twelfth century, failed to revive after 1204. As a result the Latin emperors were always in financial difficulties. This was reflected in their growing military weakness. Western knights were reluctant to settle in the Latin Empire; many preferred to take service under the Greeks.

Any hopes that Innocent III might have entertained that the Schism between the eastern and western churches had been healed by the conquest of Constantinople were soon disappointed. The Greek people and priests were unwilling to yield to the Latin Church and ritual. Adherence to Greek Orthodoxy became the badge of resistance to the Latin conqueror. Byzantine civilization was deeply rooted and remarkably resilient. In the Peloponnese the Villehardouins were forced to introduce Greek landowners into the feudal system they established. The system itself, in which the registers of fiefs had to be kept in Greek, owed much to Byzantine institutions. The conquerors have left behind them practically no traces of Gothic architecture. One version of the *Chronicle of the Morea*, which celebrates the deeds of the Franks in the Peloponnese, was even written in Greek.

The Greek resurgence

The failure of the Latin Empire was a result of the lack of aid from the West and of its inability to adapt itself to the Levant; it was also a consequence of the resurgence of the Greeks. The main centres of the Greek revival were in Asia Minor around the city of Nicaea and in Epirus and arose immediately after the fall of Constantinople. The founder of the Nicaean Empire, Theodore Lascaris (1205–22), immediately set about recreating in exile the fallen Byzantine Empire. He took the most vital step in 1208, when he had a Byzantine patriarch elected at Nicaea, which thus became in a real sense the new centre of the Orthodox world. In 1219 the ruler of Serbia, who two years earlier had obtained a royal crown from the papacy, preferred to recognize the Nicaean patriarch. In return the Serbian archbishop was granted independent status. In 1235 the Bulgarians followed the Serbian example and the Bulgarian primate was raised to patriarchal rank. The Balkans were returning to the Byzantine orbit.

The Greeks of Epirus challenged the Nicaean claim to be the true heirs of Byzantium. In 1225, after destroying the Latin kingdom of Thessalonica, the Greek despot of Epirus was proclaimed emperor; but before his ambitions against Constantinople could be realized, he was captured by the Bulgarians. An alliance between the Bulgarians and the Nicaeans also failed to take the city, but it was the starting point for the Nicaean conquest of Thrace and Macedonia. The Nicaeans could not turn their energies against Constantinople until 1259, when these conquests were finally secured. It fell two years later to a small Nicaean force which penetrated the defences of the city while the Latin garrison was absent.

Although the old emperor had gone, the Patriarch, now called *Ethnarch* or 'national leader', stepped quite literally into his imperial buskins of purple and assumed his symbol of the double-headed eagle. Thus it was that a Sassanian silk design, adopted by the Seljuks in the twelfth century, became the imperial device of Russia and Germany and the symbol of the modern Greek Orthodox Church. The Patriarch's spiritual boundaries now extended from the Caucasus to the Adriatic—the Ottomans even restored the errant Churches of Bulgaria and Serbia to the Greeks—while his political powers in Constantinople were greater than they had ever been under the departed emperors. The history of the Great Church of Constantinople under the Ottomans is not particularly edifying (between 1453 and 1842 ninety-three Patriarchs enjoyed 140 reigns, usually buying their position from the Sultan at enormous cost to the faithful). But the Patriarchate at least preserved almost intact into the modern world the Byzantine political concept of a world order in which the Greeks had a special mission; and its servants used the Ottoman Empire as a practical vehicle for what amounted to a re-enactment of Byzantine methods of rule in many provinces. These prosperous Greeks, merchants, ecclesiastics and politicians whom even modern Greeks hesitate to call 'collaborators', lived in splendid wooden mansions in the Phanar quarter of Constantinople, where the Patriarchate itself was moved in 1601. The Phanariots, as they were called, some claiming descent from the great families of Byzantium, were vigorously anti-Western. Just before the fall of Constantinople the Grand Duke Luke Notaras had claimed that 'it is better to see in the City the power of the Turkish turban than that of the Latin tiara.' This view, and the appalling memories of the betrayal of Byzantium and of Orthodoxy to the West in 1204 and in 1439, held good until well into the nineteenth century. It made the Phanariots the most trustworthy diplomats the Ottomans could employ: when in 1793 the empire sent permanent chargés d' affaires to the European capitals, they were almost entirely Greek.

The Children's Crusade

Eight years after the sacking of Constantinople, there occurred the strange and tragic episode of the Children's Crusade of 1212. It is difficult to disentangle history and legend from the surviving records but it seems that bands of children, some thousands strong in all, gathered in France and western Germany and set out to march on a crusade with the intention of reaching the Holy Land and 'recapturing Jerusalem'.

It also seems clear that only a few of the children ever returned to their homes. Many perished from hunger and disease as they wandered across Europe. The few surviving parties of French children who got as far as Marseilles and other southern ports were lured by merchants aboard their ships and sold as slaves. Many of the German children died during their journey through the Alps, and none got any further than Italy. Those who reached Brindisi were persuaded by its bishop to go home. As they struggled back, however, some were taken as servants by peasants and townspeople, and some of the girls were seized for Roman brothels. The historical basis of the story of the 'Pied Piper of Hamelin' is apparently to be found in the Children's Crusade.

The Fifth Crusade

Though the crusades dragged on for another eighty years, the crusading spirit was now all but dead. Pope Innocent III is reputed to have said of the Children's Crusade, 'These children shame us. While we are asleep, they march forth joyously to conquer the Holy Land'; and at the great Lateran Council of 1215 he proclaimed a fresh crusade which was to start on 1 June 1217. The next year, however, he died, and few plans had been made.

Since the Christian states in western Europe were at hopeless variance, and a renewed and more serious struggle between the papacy and the empire was imminent, there was little hope that Christendom would take effective action against the reviving power of Islam. Innocent's successor, Pope Honorius III decided to make one more effort to liberate Jerusalem. In 1217 he persuaded the King of Hungary and the Duke of Austria to take an army to Egypt, which John of Brienne, titular king of Jerusalem and actual ruler of the little Christian state in the Holy Land, was proposing to invade.

Some 300 German ships took the crusaders to Acre in the autumn of 1217. After a lengthy siege, they took Damietta at one of the mouths of the Nile in November 1219. They now seemed to be in a strong position, and the Sultan of Egypt offered them all the Holy Places, the True Cross and the western half of the Kingdom of Jerusalem as far as the River Jordan if they would leave Egypt and make peace. The offer was rejected because the military orders considered that the territory assigned to them by the sultan was indefensible and also because the papal legate held that Christians might never make permanent peace with infidels.

The crusaders hoped to conquer the whole of Egypt, but they achieved no further successes. In the summer of 1221 the sultan threatened their position by flooding the low-lying lands of the Nile basin and they had to sue for peace. The sultan agreed to arrange for their evacuation and to give them the True Cross. So the Fifth Crusade ended, though not in tragedy, yet in complete failure. The crusaders did not even get the True Cross—the sultan could not find it. The Greek clergy of the Church of the Holy Sepulchre had presumably hidden it.

The Sixth Crusade

In many ways, the Sixth Crusade was the strangest of all. No pope gave it his blessing,

Above, Frederick II, the Holy Roman emperor (ruled 1220–50), shown as a baby in his mother's arms. Frederick's method of crusading without the Church's blessing was generally looked upon with horror, however successful its results. Burgerbibliothek, Bern.

Top, a mid-thirteenth-century Crusader, in the armour of the time. It comprised a coat of chain mail and similar leggings. The cloth surcoat was an innovation introduced in the Holy Land to try to protect the wearer from the heat. British Library, London.

nor was it undertaken from religious motives. Its leader was the Holy Roman emperor, Frederick II, the grandson of Barbarossa. He did indeed succeed in regaining Jerusalem, but by treaty with the Muslim rulers of Egypt rather than as a knight of the Cross.

Frederick had succeeded to the Sicilian kingdom at the age of four. During his minority, Pope Innocent III had acted as his guardian, obtaining from Frederick, when he came of age in 1216, acknowledgment of papal overlordship in Sicily. When, in his turn, Honorius III, crowned Frederick as emperor in St Peter's, Rome, in 1220, he exacted from him promises that he would uphold the rights of the Church and go on a crusade. Such heavy obligations to the papacy did not, however, prevent Frederick taking an independent attitude and being quite as determined as his predecessors to assert his independence.

Frederick was a very unusual monarch. He spoke fluent German, French, Italian and Arabic and read both Latin and Greek with perfect understanding. He had studied the ancient philosophers as well as contemporary writings on geography, medicine and the sciences. Such attainments had gained him the nickname of the 'wonder of the world'.

His activities increasingly alarmed the papacy. He seemed to be lukewarm and even sceptical in matters of religion. Having been brought up in Sicily, where Arabs were still numerous, he preferred to live as a Muslim ruler, with a troupe of Muslim dancing girls and a large harem guarded by eunuchs at Palermo. The main object of his policy was to conquer northern Italy, which the papacy saw as a threat to its independence. Finally, Gregory IX, who became pope in 1227, excommunicated him for his failure to keep his crusading vow.

Frederick, however, chose his own time for the crusade and his own way of undertaking it. Still under sentence of excommunication, he sailed with a small army for Acre in September 1228. He met with a very indifferent reception from the Christian barons in Palestine. The grand masters of the military orders forbade their members to obey him, and the friars openly preached against him. Frederick ignored them and entered into discussions with the Sultan of Egypt. He knew that the sultan was facing family dissensions and feared new Turkish invasions from the East.

After lengthy negotiations, emperor and sultan signed the Treaty of Jaffa in February 1229. This granted Frederick Jerusalem, Jaffa, Bethlehem and Nazareth. By right of marriage with the daughter and heiress of John of Brienne, he claimed to be king of Jerusalem but had to place the crown upon his own head in the Church of the Holy Sepulchre, since no priest had come to the shrine for the ceremony. When he embarked at Acre for Europe, his new subjects gathered in the streets to pelt him with filth.

The Seventh Crusade

Once again Jerusalem did not long remain in Christian hands. Frederick's attention was entirely given to the renewed struggle between the empire and the papacy. The older crusading barons ignored the representatives of the imperial government in Jerusalem. The Christian territory in the Holy Land became little more than a confederation of feudal domains and commercial cities in 1244 and the Sultan of

Egypt made an alliance with the Turks and recaptured Jerusalem.

The next year, Innocent IV, who had become pope in 1243, summoned the Council of Lyons to deal with what, in his opening sermon, he called the five wounds of the Church. These were the sinful lives of many of the clergy and people, the danger from the Saracens, the continuance of the Great Schism between eastern and western Christendom, the invasion of Hungary by the Tartars and the rupture between the papacy and Frederick II. The Council formally deposed Frederick. It also ordered the preaching of a crusade against the heathen in the Holy Land.

Little attention was given to the decisions of the Council. There would have been no Seventh Crusade had it not been for St Louis. He alone was able to rise above the factions which divided Christendom and threatened it with ruin. When the news of the fall of Jerusalem reached Europe, St Louis was desperately ill in Paris. He vowed that, if he recovered from his sickness, he would himself go on a crusade to retrieve this disaster. While the pope and emperor battled for political power, he gathered his forces for the enterprise. His preparations were so thorough, however, it was not until August 1248 that his expedition was ready to set out.

This crusade was remarkably similar to the Fifth; it was undertaken with the same aims, pursued with the same ignorance and came to the same disastrous conclusion. St Louis was persuaded to go to Egypt and fight its sultan, whose defeat would restore the Holy City to Christian possession. Once again Damietta was attacked and captured in 1249. St Louis took a prominent part in the assault on the town and inspired courage in others, but he was badly advised and led a force against Cairo. His men also were caught in the flooded streams of the Nile delta and in 1250 were surrounded and defeated at Mansurah and compelled to surrender.

St Louis and his followers were released after evacuating Damietta and paying a large ransom. Most of the noblemen, including the King's brothers, returned to France, but Louis stayed in the Holy Land for four years, trying to obtain favourable treatment for the Christian prisoners in Egypt and to gain support for yet another attempt on Jerusalem. The crusading barons, though of French descent, would not listen to him, nor would the leaders of the military orders. Attempts to gain fresh armies from Europe were equally unavailing. In 1254 the news of the death of his mother, Queen Blanche, compelled him to return to France. King Henry III of England was also menacing his realm. All he had been able to do was to secure some strengthening of the fortifications of the most important Syrian seaports. The Christian recapture of Jerusalem was as far off as ever.

Above, St Louis, wearing a golden helmet, leading the assault of the Seventh Crusade on the town of Damietta in Egypt in 1249. It was the only real success of the crusade. Bibliothèque Nationale, Paris.

Opposite, the dismemberment of the Byzantine Empire after the armies of the Fourth Crusade captured Constantinople in 1204.

The Eighth Crusade

The Christian cause was now far more at risk in Europe than in Egypt or Palestine. The popes were determined to destroy the power of the empire. After Frederick II died in 1250, they involved themselves in a policy which could eventually destroy their influence. They invited Prince Charles of Anjou, the ambitious brother of Louis, to conduct the campaign against the empire. He defeated the imperial army at Tagliacozzo in 1268, became King of Sicily and attempted to make himself powerful in Italy and the Mediterranean. Such a situation thwarted all hopes of uniting Europe in a crusade.

THE CRUSADES AND THE FRANKISH STATES

Date	Crusades	Frankish States	Islam
1050	Urban II preaches the First Crusade (1095) First Crusade (1095–9) Capture of Jerusalem (1099)	Latin Kingdom of Jerusalem established (1099)	Seljuk Turks in Asia Minor
1100	Crusaders capture Tyre (1124) Second Crusade (1147–9)	Godfrey of Bouillon 'defender of the Holy Sepulchre' Baldwin I (1100–18) Baldwin II (1118–31) Fulk I (1131–43) Baldwin III (1143–62)	Nureddin, atabeg of Mosul Muslims capture Edessa (1144)
1150	Third Crusade (1190–2)	Amalric I (1162–74) Baldwin IV (1174–83) Baldwin V (1183–6) Guy of Lusignan (1186–7) End of Latin kingdom of Jerusalem	Nureddin takes Damascus (1154) End of the Fatimids of Cairo Saladin captures Jerusalem (1187)
1200	Fourth Crusade (1202–4) Children's Crusade (1212) Fifth Crusade (1217–21) Sixth Crusade (1228–9) Frederick II recovers Jerusalem (1228) Treaty of Jaffa (1229) Seventh Crusade (1248–54)	Crusaders found Latin Empire of Constantinople (1204)	Mongols arrive in Mesopotamia Turks recapture Jerusalem (1248)
1250	Eighth Crusade (1270)	Loss of Tyre, Acre, Sidon and Beirut End of the Frankish States (1291)	Baibars, sultan of the Mamelukes (1260–77) Baibars defeats crusaders in Syria
1300			

Meanwhile, the military power of Egypt was steadily increasing. The Mamelukes, the Turkish soldiers who formed the bodyguard of the sultans, revolted, and in 1260 one of their number, Baibars, became sultan. First he attacked the Mongols, the fierce Asiatic race who had been advancing westwards, and drove them across the Euphrates. Then relentlessly he turned upon the Christians in Syria and Palestine. By 1268 he had captured many of their towns, including Jaffa and Antioch. Whenever he took a town, he either slaughtered the inhabitants or sold them as slaves. In the end he sent so many to the slave-markets that the price of a young Christian girl fell to one drachma.

When St Louis heard of these terrible events, he resolved to go on another crusade. He set sail with a force in 1270, but again he did not go to the Holy Land. This time he allowed the crusade to be diverted to Tunis, because he believed a fantastic report that its Muslim Bey would be baptized a Christian if the crusaders would protect him from the anger of his subjects. It is not certain whether this report was circulated by the Sultan Baibars or Charles of Anjou, who probably welcomed the chance of a campaign in North Africa.

No sooner had the crusaders landed in North Africa in July than they were blockaded inside Carthage by the Bey of Tunis. They were short of water, and soon plague began to spread. By the end of August, St Louis himself was dead. Charles, landing shortly afterwards, immediately made peace with the Bey and led the survivors of his brother's army back to France.

Prince Edward of England

In the summer of 1270 Prince Edward, the son and heir of King Henry III of England, had set out with a small force to join his uncle, St Louis, in Tunis. Since St Louis was dead by the time he reached North Africa, Edward wintered in Sicily and then sailed on to Acre in the spring of 1271, hoping to gather a crusading army around him. He received little support from the barons and hostility from the Venetians and Genoese, who wished to continue their lucrative exports of weapons, armour and galley-slaves to Egypt. A year later he had to make a truce with Baibars and prepare to go home, though he intended to return with a large army.

Before Edward's departure, Baibars hired an assassin to stab him with a poisoned dagger. The prince was seriously ill, though the story that the future Queen Eleanor sucked poison from his wound was only written down a century later. While he was still ill in Acre, he learnt that his father was gravely ill, and when he got back to England he found that the old king was dead.

For the rest of Edward's life the conquest of Wales and the attempted conquest of Scotland kept him occupied. He had no time for a crusade, and no one else organized another. Hugh III of Lusignan, King of Cyprus, assumed the crown of Jerusalem, but the lukewarmness of the barons and the avidity of the Italian merchants discouraged him as much as they had Prince Edward. The ever-ready Charles of Anjou, encouraged by the Knights Templar, replaced Hugh of Lusignan in 1277, but before he could do anything his power in his own kingdom was destroyed by the Sicilian Vespers of 1282, a massacre of the French in Sicily provoked by discontent with his rule.

The Knights Templar had been anxious for Charles of Anjou to intervene in the Holy Land because the sultan, Baibars, had turned against the strongholds of the military orders after the fiasco of the Eighth Crusade. In 1271 he besieged Krak of the Knights. Its garrison of Knights Hospitallers were experienced soldiers and fought with tenacity, but they were hopelessly outnumbered. The large perimeter of the outer ward was soon abandoned, but even so it was a month before one of the towers of the inner ward fell to the Muslims. The surviving knights then withdrew to the great redoubt. Baibars smuggled a forged letter into them, purporting to come from their commander at Tripoli and ordering them to surrender. They did so under promise of a safe-conduct to the coast. After that, many castles gave in to Baibars without a struggle.

Sultan Baibars died in the same year that Charles of Anjou briefly accepted the crown of Jerusalem. He drank by mistake from a cup of poisoned wine which he himself had prepared for someone else. However, his successors were as determined to destroy the last vestiges of the Christian states in Syria. In 1289 Tripoli was sacked, thus leaving Acre as the only notable Christian stronghold. It was stormed after a siege of six weeks and stubborn fighting in the spring of 1291 and all the inhabitants were massacred or enslaved. For half a century the city remained a desolate ruin of rubble, inhabited only by beggars and peasants.

Within two months of the fall of Acre, Tyre, Sidon, Beirut and a few minor places capitulated without fighting. Save as an empty title, the crusading kingdom was at an end. There remained only the island of Cyprus, sold by Richard Lion-Heart to the Lusignans, whose family held it as a feudal monarchy until 1489, when it became a Venetian colony, only to be conquered by the Turks in the next century. The same fate befell the island of Rhodes. After Palestine fell, the Knights Hospitallers went there and defended it against the Turks until 1523.

Islam continued to menace Europe. The Turks advanced steadily into the Balkans and in 1453 captured Constantinople. Pope Pius II subordinated all else to trying to arouse the European princes to the increasing danger but got no response from them. Eventually their selfishness and lack of solidarity led him to take the initiative and proclaim a crusade, and in 1464 he resolved to put himself at the head of it. He gathered together a fleet of ships at Ancona on the Adriatic. By now he was old and sick, and on the day set for the departure he was carried in a covered litter down to his vessels. He was not told that neither princes nor armies followed him. He did not even know that most of his sailors had deserted their ships. He died that night on board ship in the harbour.

The idea of crusades to expel the infidel from the Holy Land had finally died. The

Muslims now ruled over what had been for more than a thousand years eastern Christendom, the very cradle of the religion and the region of its earliest growth. Despite their high idealism and all the effort and courage they had inspired, these crusades had been thwarted by national rivalries and European disunity. 'The crusaders forsook God', a medieval chronicler said, 'before God forsook them.'

Yet the crusading ideal was not everywhere without results and the reconquest of Spain and Portugal was part of the same movement of Christian expansion.

The Reconquest

The ninth and tenth centuries were the golden age of Muslim Spain, as of the Islamic world generally. At the capital Cordoba, the Caliph built a magnificent mosque second only to the mosques of Mecca. Spanish Christendom then consisted of a few independent areas in the northern part of the peninsula where the people worshipped in low, cavernous churches barrel-vaulted like crypts.

In the next century, however, the Christian cause revived. The monks of Cluny organized pilgrimages to the great shrine of Santiago de Compostela in the remote northwest of Spain and made the road to it one of the great European pilgrim ways. With the monks and pilgrims came feudal knights, mostly Normans and Burgundians, to inspire the Reconquista, the war to reconquer the remainder of Spain from its Moorish rulers. Ten years before the First Crusade, the Spanish Christians, captured Toledo with the help of Burgundian soldiers.

This was the beginning of the Spain of the Cid. Rodrigo Diaz de Bivar (*c.* 1043–99), a nobleman of Castile, gained this name when the Moors called him *sidi* (lord). He was constantly at war from 1065; his greatest achievement was the capture of Valencia in 1094. Within a hundred years of his death, he had become the hero of countless legends and romances chanted by wandering minstrels. For Spaniards he was the ideal of knightly virtue, patriotic duty and Christian grace displayed in the struggle against the Muslims.

In the twelfth century, some English and Flemish crusaders, sailing towards the Mediterranean for the Second Crusade, anchored at the mouth of the River Douro. They were persuaded by the local people to stay to fight the infidels there. So, instead of Edessa they stormed Lisbon, slaughtered the Muslim inhabitants, took over their lands and founded the kingdom of Portugal.

The Reconquista was halted for a time in Spain during the twelfth century, partly because of rivalry between the Christians themselves. In the next century, however, the Christian advance was rapidly resumed, and by 1270, the year when St Louis died in Tunis, the Spanish crusaders had conquered the whole country except Granada, which remained under Muslim occupation until 1492.

The crusaders and a wider world

Though so futile in attaining their avowed aims, the crusades to the Holy Land, played a very important part in making possible European expansion into the New World and elsewhere. The Italian trading cities, particularly the republics of Venice and Genoa, were quick to appreciate the

Above, a banquet given by Charles V of France for Charles IV, the Holy Roman emperor, in 1378. At the banquet a drama was enacted showing the glory of crusading; but the crusading ideal was no more than a faded dream by this time. Bibliothèque Nationale, Paris.

commercial prospects opened up by the crusades. Their fleets brought the exports of the east to the countries of the west. They were not hampered by any religious considerations, being prepared to send their ships both to Alexandria and to the Christian ports of Acre and Tripoli and to exchange slaves for what they got from the Muslims.

In the thirteenth century the northerners of the European seaboard began to compete with the Italian merchants. The Baltic ports formed themselves into a Hanse or league, a virtual maritime republic with a grand master rather like that of the military orders. By the fifteenth century eighty-four cities had joined the Hanse, which had depots all over northern Europe, including several in England. It was now so powerful that it could defy kings and even popes.

Other seafaring nations also were stimulated into action by the crusades. Among them was Portugal. Prince Henry of Portugal, who died in 1460, was the first European ruler to follow a deliberate policy of extending sea-trade and inspiring the discovery of new routes and markets. He systematically constructed a large merchant-fleet and encouraged cartographers and mathematicians to draw up maps and charts which were fuller and more accurate than any previously produced. His ships sailed to Madeira, the Azores and the Canaries and then on down the west coast of Africa to bring back slaves and mixed cargoes. In 1486 a Portuguese mariner, Bartholomew Diaz, reached the Cape of Good Hope. Less than ten years later, influenced by his Portuguese predecessors, Columbus set out on his important voyage.

What did European traders bring from the East? Among them were new spices and foodstuffs which introduced greater variety into diet. Previously most households had eaten bread made of wheat, rye or barley and vegetables such as peas, beans, onions and leeks. Meat was salted and usually not very fresh. Only the nobility, who had the right to hunt, could get fresh meat. For inland regions, the only fish available was dried cod. The crusaders introduced spices such as ginger, pepper, cloves and nutmeg, fruits like figs, dates and raisins and also rice and almonds. Sugar was probably the most important innovation. Wealthy Europeans began to eat crystallized peaches, cakes covered with almond paste and fine sugar and cheese tarts flavoured with ginger and garnished with saffron.

Rugs and carpets came from the East, as did cushions and wall-hangings. The crusades also brought changes in costume and fashion. Ladies and gentlemen began to wear flowing robes made from imported materials such as silk, linen, velvet and brocade. Turbans were popular for a time, as were slippers. Knowledge of dyeing came almost entirely from Syria. Noble European ladies used rouge for their faces and henna for their hair. They also used glass mirrors, which had come to the West via Constantinople instead of polished metal discs. Aromatic scents for the dress and body also came from Syria. Finally regular baths, essential in the hot climate of the crusading lands, became popular in Europe for the first time since the days of the Romans.

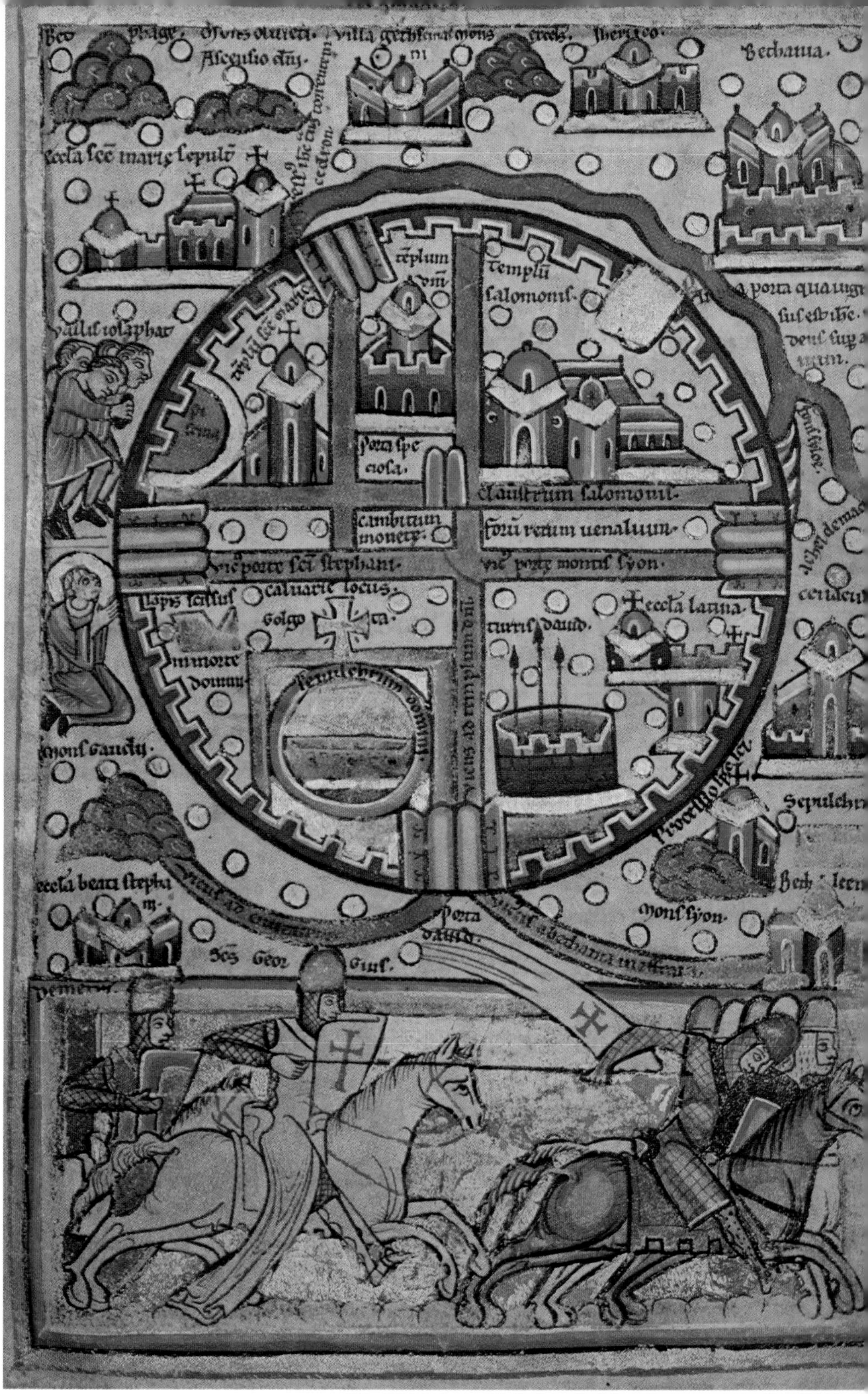

Castles and learning

Domestic and ecclesiastical architecture, except in the Moorish styles of Spain, were little changed by contact with the Muslims. The opposite was the case with military architecture. Before the crusades, European castles were usually little more than a single square stone tower, perhaps set on a mound, and encircled by a wall and moat. In Syria and Palestine the military orders learnt to build much stronger and more elaborate castles. In these the main fortifications were enclosed by a series of circular walls, all set with turrets, rounded to prevent mining at the angles and arranged with lines of fire that enabled each to protect others from assault. All the walls had projecting upper sections from which the defenders could counter-attack their opponents with molten pitch. In England, King Edward I, who had seen the castle at Acre, ordered the construction of such castles at Harlech, Conwy

Above, Alfonso X of Castile and Leon (ruled 1252–84), shown with his Moorish retainers. During his reign, there was a great mixing of Christian, Jewish and Islamic culture in Spain. Escorial Library, Madrid.

Top, an Arabic illustration of AD 1222 of a copy of the works of the Greek physician Dioscorides: Arabic scholarship was as important as Byzantine in preserving the learning of the ancient world.

Left, a fourteenth-century illustration of crusaders embarking for the Holy Land. The crusades represented western Europe's first attempt to come to terms with the civilizations beyond its boundaries.

Opposite, a schematic plan of Jerusalem from a thirteenth-century European manuscript. The Sixth Crusade won control of Jerusalem for a few years, but otherwise the city was under continual Turkish control from 1187. Royal Library, The Hague.

and Caernafon to subject the conquered Welsh.

Another military acquisition from the crusades was the complicated skill of blazonry and heraldic signs. The crusaders at first painted such signs on their shields but later embroidered them on their surcoats, linen garments which they wore over their armour to give protection from the hot eastern sun. These signs became known as 'coats of arms'. The Spanish knights of the Reconquista were especially quick to adopt these heraldic devices.

Muslim influence on the arts of peace was also considerable. The Arabs believed strongly in education. In 970, a century before the First Crusade, they had nearly thirty free schools in Cordova alone for poor Moorish and Spanish scholars. Their universities in Spain, Egypt, Mesopotamia and elsewhere were attended by Christian students who returned and in turn influenced the universities of Paris, Oxford and Italy. The Arabs studied ancient Greek philosophy and developed mathematics. They invented the decimal notation, created algebra and developed spherical geometry. In physics, they were the first to use the pendulum, and they set up observatories with telescopes. In medicine they pioneered the study of physiology and hygiene and used anaesthetics such as opium and myrrh in surgical operations. As chemists, they discovered fertilizers which made Syrian crops more fruitful than any grown on European farms.

The Arabs also made a very practical contribution towards the spread of learning the manufacture of paper from cotton, which they had learned from the Chinese and which the Europeans in turn acquired from them. Until then, all books had to be written on parchment or papyrus, and after the Arab conquest of Egypt Europe was deprived of its supplies of papyrus.

The crusades and feudalism

The crusades also had an important effect upon the feudal system in western Europe. Many of the smaller barons had to mortgage their estates in order to raise money for the crusades and lost them because they could not pay back the money-lenders. Others died in the Holy Land without male heirs so that their estates passed to daughters and then, by marriage, into other families. Between 1100 and 1300 many peasants were able to take advantage of baronial difficulties and increasing general prosperity to buy themselves out of their serfdom. Towns and cities also were able to buy privileges which freed them from the control of a feudal overlord. In England, Richard Lion-Heart sold many municipal charters which gave boroughs valuable rights of self-government in order to raise money for his crusading expeditions.

The crusades also emphasized to the rulers of Europe the value in any long campaign of a large army under a single command. National armies were now needed instead of small, territorial, feudal forces. Gradually feudalism was being replaced by nationalism.

The Mongols and the West

The failure of the crusades led some men to wonder whether missionary work among the Muslims might not meet with greater success. Even in the twelfth century there had been those who tried to take a more rational view of Islam. William of Malmesbury, the English historian, emphasized that the Muslims regarded Muhammed not as God but as his prophet. In 1143 another Englishman, Robert of Ketton, finished a translation of the Koran into Latin. In the thirteenth century members of the Franciscan and Dominican orders actually began the task of preaching to the Muslims. Ramon of Pennafort, a Spanish Dominican, worked during the period 1240–75 for the conversion of Muslims in Spain and North Africa. Another Dominican, William of Tripoli, emphasized to Pope Gregory X (1271–76) the connection between Christianity and Islam and advocated the peaceful conversion of the Muslims. By the middle of the thirteenth century, however, this new missionary enthusiasm had found a much more promising field than the stubborn Muslims.

The creation of the Mongol Empire by Genghis Khan in the early thirteenth century was to open up practically the whole of the Far East to western missionaries and traders. When he died in 1227 his dominions reached from the Pacific to the Caspian and the Indian Ocean. They were split up among his sons, but they continued as a loose confederation and further conquests were made. Persia, the Caucasus, and southern Russia were all incorporated in the Mongol Empire. The ferocity of the Mongols may not have seemed favourable for western missionary activity. Many of the tribes that formed the Mongol confederation were, however, Nestorian Christians—this was to give rise to the legend of Prester John—while the western Mongols were interested in the West because they saw there potential allies against their main enemies, the Mamelukes of Egypt.

In 1245 a Franciscan, John of Pian de Carpini, was sent by the papacy on a mission to the Mongols. This was the beginning of the exchange of numerous embassies and missions between the Mongols and the West. For almost a century western missionaries were able to work in the Far East. Latin missionaries established themselves in India on the Malabar coast, while others reached China, where in the early fourteenth century John of Monte Corvino became Bishop of Peking.

The work of these missionaries helped to prepare the way for western merchants. Between 1260 and 1269 Marco Polo's father and uncle reached the court of Peking. They returned to the West and in 1271 began the return journey to China, taking Marco Polo with them. He was to remain in the service of the Great Khan from 1275, when he arrived, until his departure in 1292. He recounts his life in fascinating detail in his book, *Il Milione*. Other western merchants have left much less trace of their activities in the Far East. In China the Franciscans established a factory for western merchants at Zaiton, opposite Formosa, which in the estimation of contemporary travellers was the greatest port in the world. By 1315 agents of the Genoese bank of Vivaldi had set up business in the ports of Gujerat and Malabar

Undoubtedly the most important market for westerners was Tabriz in northern Persia. It lay at the centre of caravan routes leading from China across Central Asia and from India by way of the Persian Gulf. It was in close contact both with the Black Sea through Trebizond (Trabzon) and with the Mediterranean through the ports of the Armenian kingdom of Cilicia. The Genoese established themselves at Tabriz soon after the middle of the thirteenth century and by 1304 had organized themselves into a colony. They entered the service of the Mongol rulers of Persia; they manned a fleet on the Euphrates, and they sailed the Caspian. The Venetians obtained the right to keep a consul at Tabriz only in 1324.

By that date the situation was becoming more unfavourable. The Mongols were being converted to Islam and were becoming more hostile to Christians. In 1339 Westerners were massacred at Almaligh, the chief city of Turkestan. In 1343 others were slaughtered by the Mongols at the port of Tana on the Sea of Azov. The route across the steppes which in the early fourteenth century had been described in the Florentine Pegolotti's handbook for merchants as 'quite safe' was now barred to western merchants. At the same time the collapse of the Mongol state in Persia virtually closed the market of Tabriz to westerners.

Mamelukes and Ottomans

The break-up of the Mongol Empire and the closing of Asia inaugurated a period of crisis for western Europe. The Mamelukes of Egypt had a stranglehold over the Red Sea trade route, which now became the main channel by which oriental spices, drugs and dyestuffs reached the West. They were able to demand excessive tariffs. In 1375 they finally destroyed the Christian kingdom of Cilicia. This deprived Cyprus of much of its commercial value, and in 1426 the island was terribly ravaged by the Mamelukes.

In the Aegean and the Balkans the West was faced with a new enemy, the Ottoman Turks. The Ottomans formed one of the many Turkish emirates that by the early fourteenth century had destroyed Byzantine rule in western Asia Minor.

The loss of its Asiatic provinces in the early fourteenth century sealed the fate of the Byzantine Empire. It no longer had the resources to resist its enemies, let alone continue the work of restoring its former greatness. The power vacuum created by the fall of Constantinople in 1204 still remained unfilled. Neither the Venetians nor the Genoese had the power or the inclination to dominate the Levant; they were only too content to exploit the commercial opportunities that the absence of any great power presented. At one stage in the mid-fourteenth century it looked as though the Serbian ruler Stefan Dushan might succeed to the Byzantine heritage. In 1345 he had himself proclaimed 'Emperor of the Serbs and Greeks'; but his death in 1355 showed how weak the foundations of his empire were, how impossible it was to bind together the many peoples of the Balkans into a single state. For one thing, the rivalries between the patriarch of Constantinople and the Serbian and Bulgarian Churches went far too deep. Such a situation helps to explain the rise of the Ottomans to power in the Balkans during the second half of the fourteenth century.

The Ottomans served as mercenaries in the civil wars that racked the Byzantine Empire in the mid-fourteenth century. In 1354 they were able to establish themselves

in the Gallipoli peninsula. The conquest of Thrace followed very rapidly. The Byzantines were forced to become vassals of the Ottoman ruler Murad I (1360–89). In 1387 Thessalonica fell to the Ottomans. Two years later they completely defeated the Serbs at Kossovo, and in 1393 Bulgaria was conquered. Ottoman authority extended in Europe from the Danube to the Aegean and the Gulf of Corinth. The areas of direct Ottoman rule were, however, rather more limited. In general they aimed to occupy strategic points; they were willing to allow local rulers a large measure of independence, as long as they remained loyal and provided troops and an annual tribute.

The dynamism of the Ottomans sprang from their *ghazi* mission to extend Islam at the expense of the infidel. The Tartar conqueror Timur claimed that they were neglecting this mission, and in 1402 he defeated the Ottoman ruler Bayezid at Ankara—though this setback was made good by Murad II (1421–51). The culmination of Murad's work, the conquest of Constantinople, was left to his son Mehmed the Conqueror (1451–81), who accomplished the task in 1453.

Western Europe and the papacy were well aware of the threat posed by the Ottomans, and the papacy took more drastic measures against them than it had against the Mamelukes. The aim had been to bring the Mamelukes to their knees by economic sanctions, but this policy was flouted by western merchants and even turned out to be a lucrative source of revenue for the papacy, which sold licences for trade with Egypt. In 1365, it is true, King Peter of Cyprus mounted a crusade against Alexandria. Apart from this, however, the crusade was employed in the fourteenth century for the defence of western interests against the Turks only.

In the early part of the century the main threat came from the Turkish emirates established on the west coast of Asia Minor, who had taken to piracy on the Aegean. In 1344 the chief of these pirate towns, Smyrna, was captured by a crusading expedition. This was perhaps the most successful of the later crusades; troops had been provided by the papacy, by the King of Cyprus, by the Venetians, and by the Knights Hospitallers. In 1350 the Knights Hospitallers were given the task of garrisoning the city. After the fall of the crusader states they had retreated to Cyprus and then in 1308 found a base on the island of Rhodes. The Hospitallers provided a small permanent force for the defence of Christendom in the Levant. From 1397 to 1404, for example, they occupied the citadel of Corinth and stood guard against Turkish invasions of the Peloponnese.

Meanwhile the Ottomans had come into conflict with the Hungarians along the lower Danube. The Hungarian King Sigismund (1387–1437) appealed to the West for a crusade against the Turks to rescue Constantinople, but this crusade was annihilated by the Ottomans in 1396 at the Battle of Nicopolis. It was the last genuinely western crusade. Others mounted against the Ottomans were mainly the concern of the Hungarians; such was the crusade of Varna in 1444, another disaster for Christian arms. The Ottoman hold on the Balkans was not to be shaken.

The emperors of Byzantium understood that the only hope of rescue from the

Above, the Mamelukes, or warrior caste of medieval Egypt, as seen by the German Ritter Conradgrunemberg in 1486. The Mamelukes were soon to be conquered by the Ottoman Turks. Forschungsbibliothek, Gotha.

Top, an English miniature of 1400 showing Marco Polo leaving Venice on his expedition to Cathay. Venice was the centre for Europe's trade with the East. Bodleian Library, Oxford.

Above left, a European view of the fall of Constantinople to the Ottoman Turks in 1453, an event of little practical importance to the west. Bibliothèque Nationale Paris.

Ottoman threat came from the West. Appeals were made to the papacy; the emperors John V (1341–91) and Manuel II Palaiologos (1491–1525) toured the capitals of Italy and western Europe in the search of aid. The papacy demanded in return the Union of Churches. In 1369 John V agreed to work for this and in 1439 at the Council of Florence the Union was formally proclaimed. Union with Rome had some backing in Byzantium among the intellectuals, but such was the popular antipathy that its implementation was almost impossible. Negotiations over the Union of Churches at least brought to Italy numbers of Byzantine scholars, who revealed to Italian humanists the treasures of classical learning preserved by Byzantium.

Venice and the Turks

The advance of the Ottomans into the Aegean and the Balkans touched the interests of Venice more sharply than those of almost any other western power. The Venetians pursued two main objectives: they wanted to bar the Aegean to Ottoman warships and to clear it of Turkish pirates; they also wanted to preserve Albania and the Dalmatian coasts from Ottoman conquest. If these fell to the Ottomans, Venice's control of the Adriatic might well be endangered. A policy of cooperation in the crusades and attempts to unite the Christian powers of the Levant against the Turks were not very successful. From the late fourteenth century Venice embarked on a deliberate policy of building up its territories both in Italy and in the Levant. Albania came under a Venetian protectorate and various ports in Greece and the Peloponnese were acquired. In 1423 Thessalonica passed under Venetian control, only to fall to the Turks seven years later. Thereafter, the Venetians were on the defensive and tried to follow a conciliatory policy towards the Ottomans. After the fall of Constantinople Turkish pressure on the Venetians grew stronger, until in 1463 war broke out; it was to last until 1479. The Venetians clung grimly to their Empire, but at the peace treaty they were compelled to cede the island of Euboea, and they had to give up their Albanian protectorate; they were being forced out of the Aegean and their hold on the Adriatic was threatened. The West was losing control of the Mediterranean, which had been one of the foundations of its commercial supremacy.

Competition between western merchants became fiercer. By the end of the thirteenth century Venetian merchants were being instructed by their government to form price rings to counter Genoese competition. There was a succession of bitter commercial wars between Venice and Genoa, lasting from the mid-thirteenth century until the close of the next century. The main prize was control of Constantinople and the Black Sea trade. The Byzantines were reluctantly drawn into these wars and were stripped of Lesbos, Khios and Phocaea by the Genoese.

The Venetians and the Genoese realized that their colonial possessions were not simply valuable as trading stations but that they also had natural riches to be exploited. In Crete and Cyprus, Venetian landowners began to plant sugar and cotton and the government encouraged the growing of dyestuffs. Wine was also exported. The Genoese worked the alum mines of Phocaea on the western coast of Asia Minor. At the same time there was a growing trade in raw materials. Corn was shipped from southern Russia and the Romanian principalities to Italy, as were the animal products of the Balkans and the Peloponnese. There was also a brisk trade in slaves from southern Russia. The great commercial centre of all this trade was the island of Khios. Thus just at the moment that western control over the Aegean was about to end, the Levant was more than ever before an economic colony of the West, providing it with raw materials and receiving in return finished goods.

More direct contacts were also made between the Mediterranean and northern Europe. At the turn of the thirteenth century the Venetians and Genoese began to pioneer the sea route to Flanders. There was even some direct trade between Flanders and Crete, which the Venetians did their best to prohibit. In the mid-fifteenth century the Italians were faced for a short while with the threat of English competition.

Italian trading interests had been moving westwards over a long period. Even in the thirteenth century Pisa found it more profitable to concentrate on trade with Tunis and Sicily, while the Genoese developed a well-balanced triangular trade between the Levant, Genoa and Morocco. It was only natural that once conditions became unfavourable in the Levant the Italians would tend to shift their interests more and more to the western Mediterranean and northern Europe. The rise of the Ottomans contributed to this, not because they were actively hostile to western commerce, but because they were in a position to demand customs duties; they also encouraged local industries and the development of a Greek merchant marine. Both helped to undermine the old bases of western commercial supremacy, though the Levant was never completely closed to the Italians in the Mediterranean.

Expansion in northern Europe

Western expansion in the Levant had been favoured by political conditions. There were no dominant powers; this allowed the westerners to control the seas and consequently the trade of the Levant. Their commercial supremacy was jeopardized and finally destroyed by the rise to power first of the Mamelukes and then of the Ottomans.

Western expansion in northern and central Europe also took place against a background of political disintegration. The thirteenth century saw the destruction of imperial power in the struggle between Frederick II and the papacy. The emperors no longer possessed a sufficiently strong basis of power in Germany itself, and with the removal of effective imperial authority Germany lost its cohesion, splitting up into numerous petty states. In the Slav states the power of the crown tended to be weakened by the claims of members of the ruling family and by those of the Church and nobility. The pagans of the Baltic coast possessed only the most rudimentary organization, while the Orthodox principalities of Russia had to bear the full brunt of the Mongol invasions. In 1240 they were brought under the authority of the Khanate of the Golden Horde and, with the exception of Novgorod, were virtually cut off from the West. In 1241 the Mongols invaded central Europe, but the threatened conquest never materialized.

The uncertainty of the situation in eastern Europe invited western expansion. The papacy hoped to convert the pagans and to bring the Orthodox of Russia under the authority of Rome. By the mid-thirteenth century it seemed on the point of achieving these aims. In 1251 the ruler of the pagan Lithuanians was baptized, and two years later the Orthodox ruler of the western Russians accepted a crown from Pope Innocent IV. But this chance of extending the frontiers of Christendom beyond the confines of Poland and Hungary came to nothing. Both rulers returned to their former persuasions; the latter because papal aid against the Mongols was not forthcoming, the former because conversion to Christianity did not save his people from their greatest enemies, the knights of the Teutonic Order.

The Teutonic knights

The Teutonic Order was founded at the end of the twelfth century for service in the Holy Land but later settled in Prussia at the invitation of Conrad of Mazovia. This Polish duke hoped that they would protect his territories from the pagan Prussians. It was his intention that the Order should remain under his control, but he was outwitted and the knights became an independent power. From their fortresses of Culm and Thorn, built by 1232, they quickly overran Prussia. They were soon faced with a violent Prussian uprising. It was put down with the utmost savagery, but resistance was not finally crushed until 1283.

In 1237 the Order took over another military order, the Knights of the Sword, founded in 1202 to convert the pagans of Livonia, after the latter's very existence had been imperilled by a defeat at the hands of a Lithuanian tribe. The Teutonic knights quickly restored the situation in Livonia and even initiated an aggressive policy against the Russians of Novgorod. This was brought to an end in 1242 when they were defeated by the Russian prince Alexander Nevsky. Thereafter their energies were mostly taken up in a vicious war against the Lithuanians, although in 1308 the Order was able to seize Pomerelia and the city of Danzig (Gdansk) from the clutches of the Poles. It was now approaching the height of its power, with territories that stretched along the Baltic coast from the Oder to the Narva.

The Teutonic knights succeeded in building up a German state along the Baltic coast. This was only part of a general spread eastwards of German political power. The imperial houses of Habsburg and Luxembourg hoped to find in the 'new lands' beyond the Elbe a basis of power which would give substance to the imperial office. The key to their plans was Bohemia. Under its native Slav Dynasty it was the most advanced and powerful state in central Europe during the thirteenth century. When this dynasty died out in the early fourteenth century, the Habsburg emperor Albert of Austria (1298–1308) obtained Bohemia for his family. After his death, however, it fell to the new imperial house of Luxembourg; the Habsburgs had to rest content with their Austrian lands.

Above, the Holy Roman emperor Sigismund I (1368–1437), who helped to heal the Great Schism by calling the Council of Constance and whose opposition to Huss caused him great unpopularity in Bohemia.

Opposite, Henry of Silesia leading the eastern European army at Leignitz in 1241, where they were wiped out by the Mongols. Although the way to Europe was open, the Mongols turned south and never threatened the west so dangerously again. Österreichische Nationalbibliothek, Vienna.

In the course of the fourteenth century the Luxembourg rulers of Bohemia succeeded in uniting under their rule virtually all the 'new lands' beyond the Elbe. This was mainly the work of the Emperor Charles IV (1347–1378). His ambitions then turned further east to Poland and Hungary, whose crowns were united in 1370 by King Louis of Hungary (1342–83). Louis left no male heirs, and both the Luxembourgs and the Habsburgs coveted his inheritance. Poland was to escape their clutches, but Hungary fell in 1386 to Charles's son Sigismund, who had married one of Louis's daughters, while the Habsburg plans came to nothing. The whole Luxembourg heritage was finally united under Sigismund when he became King of Bohemia in 1419. On his death in 1437 it passed to the Habsburg Albert of Austria; but when Albert died two years later, the entire Luxembourg edifice collapsed.

The conquests of the Teutonic knights and the development of the Luxembourg state were sustained by German migration into the lands beyond the Elbe. In the first half of the thirteenth century there was a general advance of German peasant settlement from the Elbe to the Oder, and from the close of the century a second wave of German colonization swept into Pomerania and Prussia. German settlement was on a massive scale. It has been reckoned that between 1200 and 1350 about 1,200 new villages were planted in Silesia. Rather more had been founded by the turn of the fourteenth century on the east Prussian lands of the Teutonic Order. Outside these main areas of colonization there were other regions of more scattered German settlement, in Bohemia, southern Poland, western Hungary and Transylvania.

Peasant migration was only one aspect of German expansion. Germans controlled the mining industry of central Europe; they opened up the gold and silver mines discovered in Bohemia and Moravia in the mid-thirteenth century and in Hungary during the next century. They also worked the saltmines around Cracow.

The Germans' success in colonizing the new lands owed a great deal to the towns they founded. Before the thirteenth century there were very few German towns beyond the Elbe, although German traders had established themselves in the most important Slav centres. Later it was not uncommon for an old Slav centre to be refounded as a German city. This is what happened at Cracow in 1257. At about the same date Brno comprised an old quarter inhabited by Czechs and a new town settled by Germans and a few Walloons engaged in weaving. German towns were most thickly scattered in the areas of heavy peasant settlement between the Elbe and Oder and on the lands of the Teutonic Order, where by 1410 ninety-three new towns had been founded. There were also large numbers of German towns in areas of less dense settlement, such as Bohemia and Poland. They were founded along trade routes and in the mining regions. They not only ensured German control of trade and mining in central Europe, but they might also open up new areas for peasant colonization. The towns provided the new German villages with protection and with markets. In the early thirteenth century it was already becoming the practice in Silesia to found new villages around an urban centre.

A practice which gave greater cohesion to German colonization was that of founding the new towns according to the laws of a particular German city. Although those of Magdeburg were perhaps the most popular, the German towns founded along the Baltic coast almost all took their laws from Lübeck; they came to be known as cities of the Hansa. Among the most important were Rostock, Danzig, Riga and Reval. Together with other cities of western Germany, they formed a loose confederation to ensure control of the trade route from Flanders to Novgorod; this was the basis of their prosperity. They brought to the West the raw materials of Russia and northern Europe—furs, timber and wax. They took back in return finished goods, especially Flemish cloth. They also helped to bring supplies to the German colonists and provided an outlet for their produce. By 1250 corn was being shipped from Brandenburg to England and Flanders.

Lübeck was the hub of the confederation of Hansa cities. Goods were trans-shipped there across a narrow neck of land to the Elbe, thus avoiding the long route round Denmark. Lübeck's prosperity was threatened by the Danes' ambitions in the Baltic and their control of Holstein. In 1227 it formed a coalition of Hansa cities which drove the Danes out of Holstein. This coalition was only temporary, and it was not until 1358 that the Hanseatic League was formally constituted. In 1370 the Danes were brought to their knees, but by then the high point of Hanseatic prosperity was already passed; the cities of the Hansa were going on the defensive against Dutch and English competition.

Slavs and Germans

Among the achievements of the Hanseatic towns was the integration of the Baltic lands in the economy of western Europe. The presence of German cities and merchants produced much the same result in central Europe, while the better agricultural techniques and implements brought by the German peasants improved the standard of agriculture. This may have helped to improve the lot of the Slav peasants, but they only accepted German laws and customs with great reluctance.

German colonization also brought central Europe more firmly into the framework of western culture. This was most marked among the upper classes. Many members of the thoroughly German nobility of Brandenburg had Slav ancestors, while the Czech and Polish nobility adopted the German practice of using family titles and crests as well as the building of castles.

The Church was a still more active agent of westernization. Two orders of monks, one founded at Prémontré in 1119, the other at Cîtreaux in 1098, were granted wide lands by the Slav princes. Gothic architecture was introduced and quickly assimilated by the Czechs; Bohemian Gothic was to be one of the glories of late medieval architecture. There also grew up in Bohemia a school of Latin religious poetry, and even the flowering of Czech literature from the mid-thirteenth century was inspired by the same currents as other western vernacular literatures. In the fourteenth century Bohemia was quickly caught up in the early Humanist movement.

Poland took longer to absorb western culture; ideas associated with the eleventh-century Gregorian reform movement were accepted only in the early thirteenth century. The spread of Gothic architecture and Latin religious poetry did not begin until the fourteenth century. The Poles were much influenced by the achievements of the Czechs. Polish students flocked to the University of Prague, founded in 1348 by the Emperor Charles IV. This influenced Casimir the Great of Poland, who in 1364 proceeded to establish a university at Cracow.

Slav reaction

The assimilation of western culture did not reconcile the Slavs to the Germans; if anything, it made them more conscious of their national heritage. The Slav reaction was fiercest in Bohemia, which was most open to German influences. The German domination of the economy was resented, and there were clashes between Czechs and Germans in the University of Prague, which was controlled by the German 'nation'. As a result the movement initiated by John Hus for the reform of the Bohemian Church, which was purely spiritual in origin, became tinged with the anti-German feeling that existed among Czechs of all classes. This flared up into a national rising in 1419 when Hus was condemned to death by the Council of Constance in 1415. Sigismund mounted expeditions called crusades against the Czechs, but they were all defeated. He was forced to negotiate and finally in 1434 was recognized as King of Bohemia. Bohemia returned only very briefly to German rule, however; after Albert of Austria's death in 1439 it was ruled by a Czech, George of Podebrady, first as regent for Albert's posthumous son Ladislas and then from 1458 to 1471 as king.

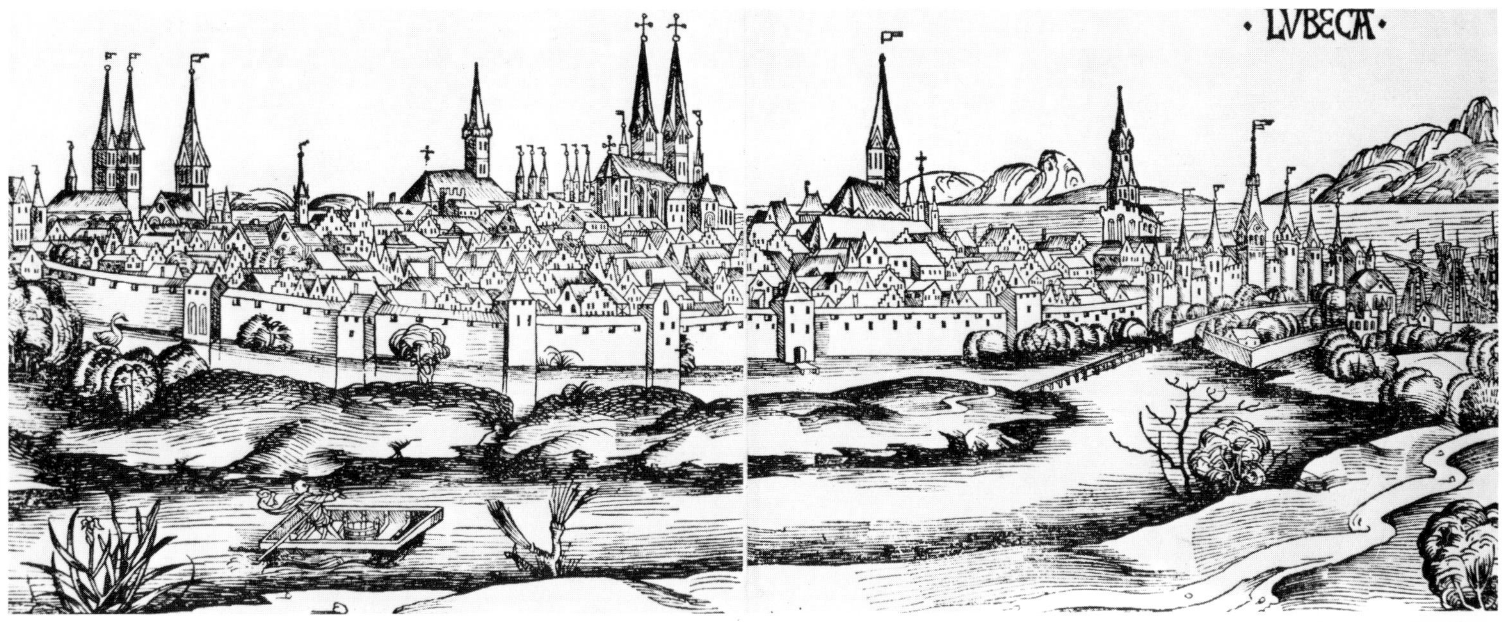

The Poles were never subjected in the same way as the Czechs to German domination, but they came under its shadow. In 1343 the founder of Polish unity, Casimir the Great (1333–70), had to renounce his claims to the Pomerelian lands seized by the Teutonic Order, and at about the same time Silesia was detached from Poland by the Luxembourgs. Casimir's ambitions turned eastwards to the lands of western Russia, which were then under the rule of the pagan Lithuanians. This prepared the way for the union of the Polish and Lithuanian crowns in 1386, as a result of which the Lithuanians adopted Christianity and were brought within the sphere of western civilization. The Lithuanian nobility proceeded to adopt the manners and traditions of the Polish aristocracy.

The Lithuanians and Poles united against their common enemy, the knights of the Teutonic Order, and at Grünwald in 1410 gained a crushing victory. Although the Order was forced on to the defensive, it took a succession of wars to bring the knights to their knees; only in 1466 were they at last obliged to give up western Prussia to the Poles.

The Polish and Czech reaction to the threat of German domination came at a time when German colonization was ending. By the mid-fourteenth century German migration into Prussia was slowing down. No more new lands were to be Germanized and the Germans were to lose those regions, such as Livonia, where conquest had not been followed by extensive German settlement. By the fifteenth century there were reports that villages were being deserted in areas of heavy German settlement, such as Brandenburg and Prussia. At the same time the prosperity of the Hansa was at an end. With a lack of surplus population, its cities ceased to grow, while restrictive policies aimed at foreign competition only led to stagnation.

At the same time as German expansion was coming to an end and the Italian supremacy in the Levant was being undermined, Portuguese and Catalan voyages were making known the Azores, the Canaries and Madeira. Under the inspiration of Prince Henry the 'Navigator', these islands were colonized by the Portuguese and voyages were undertaken down the African coast. By the time of Henry's death in 1460 Portuguese sailors had reached the Gulf of Guinea.

Europe stood on the threshold of the 'Great Discoveries'. In a sense these were part of the move westwards of the Italians. In 1291 the Vivaldi brothers of Genoa set off to discover the western route to the Indies. The Genoese were to play a large part in Portuguese and Spanish colonization. They introduced sugar and cotton, even the use of slaves, from the Italian colonies in the Levant. They dominated the market of Seville.

Though this all points to Europe's renewed expansion overseas, the legacy of the Middle Ages should not be forgotten. The lands of the Baltic and eastern Europe opened up by the Germans remained an essential part of the economic framework, and the Mediterranean continued to provide a market for the goods of western Europe. A European economy had been brought into existence. Its frontiers were not all that much different from those of Christendom in 1204, but spiritual bonds had been replaced by economic ones.

Above a Bohemian peasant, drawn in the early fifteenth century by Jacobus de Cesulis. Bohemian nationalism was to be an important stimulus to the Hussite movement throughout the fifteenth century.

Top, the north German city of Lübeck in 1497, the centre of the Hanseatic League of towns which controlled most of the carrying trade of the North Sea and Baltic Sea.

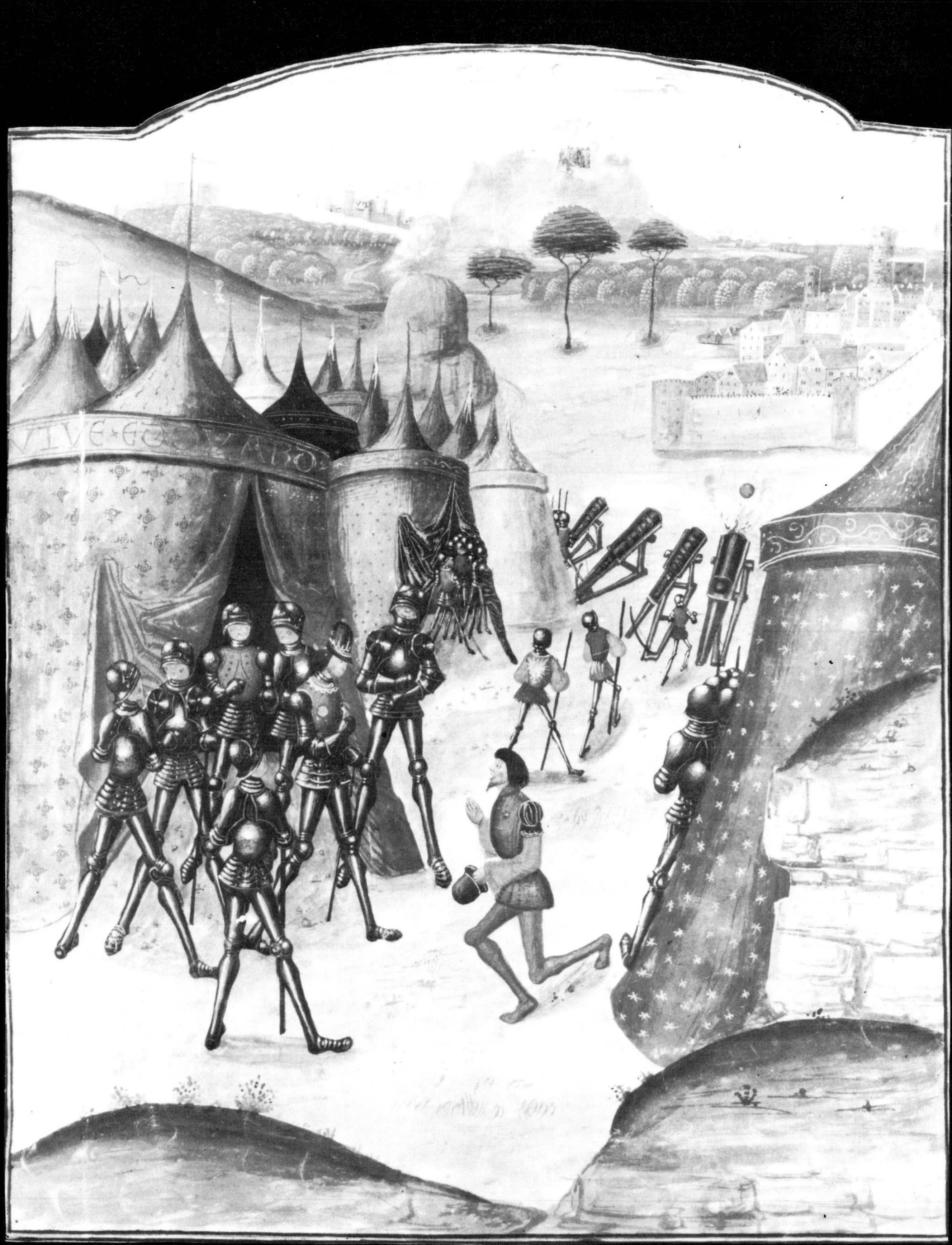

Part III

THE HIGH MIDDLE AGES

Introduction

The period between the eleventh and the fifteenth centuries—the central period of the Middle Ages—witnessed the full fusion of disparate historical and ideological strains The ancient Greco-Roman inheritance of Europe came to full fruition and eventually merged with the Germanic idea of society. Precisely by virtue of this, a number of features came about which not only coloured the complexion of the age itself, but also, and perhaps more important, laid the foundations of developments from sixteenth century onwards.

Though the character of the age was certainly more static than our own, there were nevertheless far more changes than is commonly assumed, both in the structure of society and above all in the ideas which sustained it.

What gave medieval society in these centuries its particular physiognomy was the virtually undisputed and uncontested sway of certain basic tenets of Christianity. The consequence of this was the great power which the papacy wielded from the time of Gregory VII in the late eleventh century and which reached its dizzy heights in the pontificate of Innocent III (1198–1216). From then on the papacy slowly but quite perceptibly declined in authority, standing and prestige: the conciliar movement which was a by-product of the Great Schism in the fourteenth century reversed the position and function of the pope by subjecting him to the power of a general council. The pope, hitherto an uncontrolled and uncontrollable monarch, was now subjected to the supervision of the council which acted as a representative organ of the whole of Christendom.

Similarly nurtured by an application of Christian principles was secular medieval rulership in the shape of 'the king by the grace of God'—the theocratic ruler—who derived his power from divinity through the administration of unction. This kind of rulership precluded the people from conferring any power on the king: thus what the people had not given, they could not modify, still less take away. The essential feature in both the institutions of the papacy and of kingship was the working of the monarchic principle: in each instance the individuals were subjects of the monarch. The great change which occurred in the thirteenth century and of which we are largely the beneficiaries was that the status of the individual as a subject was turned into that of a citizen fully partaking, through representative institutions, in the government of the State. This so-called ascending theme of government was instrumental in the diminution of the power of the popes as well as of that of the theocratic kings.

In the high Middle Ages Europe was no longer a mere geographical term but overwhelmingly an ideological notion: the unity of the Christian faith, underpinned as it was by the law of the Church, was largely responsible for bridging biological, linguistic and racial differences and for the emergence of a European commonwealth from the Orkney Islands to Sicily, from Sweden, the Prussian and Polish marshes to Castille and Aragon in the Iberian peninsula. This commonwealth was not conceived as an economic unit. Its sustaining factors were the fraternal as well as filial bonds forged by the ideological amalgamation of elements of originally Roman-Christian-Germanic paternity which produced common interests, aspirations and aims. The inner core of this European community in the high middle ages was religious and its structural organization overwhelmingly ecclesiastical. Hence this same period witnessed the split with Constantinople, because its religious and ecclesiastical principles did not accord with those of the West, with the consequence that the whole eastern empire ruled from Constantinople was no longer regarded as European. The contours of the East-West tension, of which we are the heirs, can clearly be discerned on the medieval horizon. Europe was what corresponded to the Roman-Christian-Germanic assumptions—Constantinople and its empire were Greek and therefore outside the European orbit.

The crusades assume their special significance within the precincts of this East-West tension. They began shortly after the formal breach with Constantinople (1054) and ceased to make much appeal by the late thirteenth century. They were the first large-scale mass movements which Europe witnessed. Military in conception, religious in aim, aggressive, adventurous and romantic in character and wasteful of man-power, they certainly were aimed at wresting from the Muslims the holy places in Palestine. They had also as a not unwelcome by-product the conquest of Constantinople, which symbolized the militarily achieved subjection of the eastern empire to Latin-western domination. That the direction and overall supervision was in the hands of the papacy is comprehensible, though the execution lay entirely in the hands of the western emperors and kings. Nevertheless, the crusades also had undoubtedly beneficial effects: they widened the intellectual horizon of their participants and helped to break down the self-imposed western isolation by familiarizing the crusaders with the riches of the East; they also put a new vigour into trade and commerce. Despite the wastage in blood, effort and good will, the crusades stimulated the crusading warrior and his leaders to look beyond their narrow parochial confines.

Within this central period there was progress in virtually all departments of public, social and economic life. New techniques were acquired both in agriculture and domestic industry and in the production of the necessary implements. Missionary activity was given a new impetus when the northeastern regions of Europe were converted and the missions penetrated as far as central Asia in the thirteenth century. New lands were opened up by novel methods of cultivation and thus made arable. The fairs and markets in western Europe became regular places for the exchange of goods. An orderly banking system emerged. The communal movement derived great profit from an elaborate system of taxes and tolls. New industries sprang up while old ones were developed.

In the course of the twelfth century intellectual advances made great strides forward. It was the time when some of the monastic and cathedral schools reached their peak and when the universities came into being. Initially specializing in either law or philosophy and theology, they soon had to widen their syllabuses. In course of time the demand arose for the extension of regular curricula, and by the fourteenth century Greek, Arabic and Hebrew were included in university studies as well as medicine and related subjects. The proliferation of universities in all countries, from eastern Poland to Portugal, from Scotland to Hungary, would sufficiently indicate that they were the response to educational and social needs. And the very institution of a university was a medieval invention: there was no such thing in antiquity and there was no model on which the medieval university could have drawn.

This was also the age in which a great many heretical sects—heretical by the standards of the time—flourished. Means were devised to combat them, partly by persuasion through the efforts of the newly founded itinerant mendicant orders (chiefly Dominicans and Franciscans) and partly by the repressive measures of inquisitorial proceedings and tribunals, the execution of their sentence having been imposed on the secular power. Throughout the thirteenth century there were incontrovertible symptoms that the traditional order of things no longer satisfied contemporaries. The Heretical movements were but one sign.

What the observer witnesses in the thirteenth century is a broadening of human perception, knowledge and fields of enquiry which resulted in a veritable intellectual revolution, notably through the absorption of the ideas of Aristotle. He opened up a new world, the physical world, in which hitherto little interest had been evinced. It was in the

thirteenth century that the very term of 'natural sciences' came to be coined, and well-conducted experiments as proper means of enquiry made their first appearance. Man himself and his nature became for the first time an object of investigation. Man was shown to be capable not only of conquering nature (a process that has not yet come to an end) but also of managing and manipulating his own affairs in public, that is, of governing himself and through appropriate representative organs his own community, the State. The thirteenth century might well be seen to mark the great divide between the medieval and modern world. It was the century which precisely by making man's humanity a central topic of study gave rise to naturalism and humanism in all their multifarious and fruitful manifestations, in scholarship, in the arts, in poetry, in vernacular products, and so on. Above all, the concept of the institution of the State was born. Observation, experimentation, critical approach and the individual's self-reliance began to replace the authoritative pronouncement by superior authority, with consequences which are still not fully appreciated. Man had been liberated from the tutelage in which he had been kept for so long: as a citizen he elected the government which remained responsible to him. Man and his State had become sovereign. This is one of the many bequests of the Middle Ages of which the decisive and formative influence on our own world has not yet found adequate recognition.

Above, Clement IV invests Charles of Anjou as King of Sicily in 1265; the conflict between political authority and spiritual power was one of the major themes of medieval history and was tied up with questions about the independence of rulers in their kingdoms and the unity of Christendom. Pernes les Fontaines, Tour Ferrande.

On page 110, Edward III laying siege to a French town in the Hundred Years War. A very early form of cannon are being used, their barrels held together by hoops of metal. Bibliothèque Nationale, Paris.

Chapter 10

The Papacy

The strength of the papacy lay in its continuously developed doctrine relating to the standing, function and authority of the Roman Church; it was a doctrine which had steadily evolved since the mid-fifth century. By the time of Innocent III it had reached the high-water mark of its logical consistency. From this zenith of evolution and actual power exercised there was, throughout the thirteenth century, a gradual decrease of papal authority, with consequential changes throughout Christendom.

The key to how these changes came about is perhaps to be found in the term papal monarchy. This can be defined as the exercise of supreme papal authority over all aspects of Christian life, both temporal and spiritual. Under Innocent III it was seen only as a means of fulfilling the papal mission to lead Christians to salvation by way of the Church; but under his successors it was increasingly obvious that preservation of authority was becoming an end in itself. The papacy found it more and more difficult to meet the spiritual needs of the time. This was perhaps at the basis of the changed position of the papacy.

Innocent III

The reign of Innocent III (1198–1216) was crucial to the development of papal monarchy. This does not, however, mean that his reign marked a break in papal history. He had the same concept of his office as his predecessors.

The papacy was held to be a divinely instituted office, set over the community of the faithful, the Church. Each pope was the direct successor of St Peter and, as such, possessed the fullness of power which the Apostle had received from Christ. This was pure doctrine. It only became enforceable in the fifth century AD when the power of law was harnessed to it.

This came about as the result of two developments. On the one hand, the pope was acknowledged as the sole interpreter of the Bible, and, on the other, the Bible was treated as a legal text. It meant that Christians were subordinated to the papacy not simply spiritually but also juridically. The pope became the supreme judge and legislator of Christian society.

The true importance of this development hardly becomes clear much before the middle of the eleventh century. The struggle between Rome and Constantinople for the primacy of Christendom led to a deeper elucidation of the nature of papal authority. It was found to be quite incompatible with any lay control over the Church. This was to become the basic issue in the Investiture Controversy.

The papacy's main opponent was the German emperor. Not only did he exercise a very tight control over the Church in his dominions, but his claims to be the head of Christian society cut right across papal ideology. The outcome of the investitute controversy was not a complete victory for the papacy. It had to compromise over the question of ecclesiastical appointments; and although the pope, and not the emperor, emerged as the universally recognized head of Christendom, the problem of the Empire was not solved.

During the second half of the twelfth century the papacy was faced with two outstanding German emperors, Frederick Barbarossa and his son Henry VI. They were determined to restore real authority to the imperial title. A very sharp distinction was drawn between spiritual and temporal power: the former belonged to the papacy, while the latter was to be exercised by the emperor. Additional support for imperial claims was found in Roman law. The emperor claimed to be heir to the supreme authority of the Roman emperor.

A deeper explanation of papal authority was needed in the face of such claims. It culminated in the concept that the pope was the Vicar of Christ. The pope was seen as the intersection between heaven and earth; he was, as Innocent III claimed, less than God but greater than man. He was set above the kingdoms of the world; it was his duty to see that no Christian was denied justice, and he was responsible for the welfare and good order of Christian society.

The relationship between the papacy and secular rulers had also to be put on a firmer footing. The view was gradually taking shape that the rulers were part of a hierarchy established by God for the fulfilment of his purpose and that there ought to be a division of labour between the secular rulers and the papacy; there must, of course, be cooperation, but the vital point was that sovereignty was to rest in the hands of the papacy.

Frederick Barbarossa had tried to dominate Italy. In the face of this threat, the papacy had been inclined to stress the division of labour between emperor and papacy and to mute its claims to sovereignty. The papacy was able to preserve its independence of action only because the cities of Lombardy refused to accept direct imperial control. They banded together, under the leadership of Milan and with the encouragement of the papacy, in an alliance known as the Lombard League. In 1176 they defeated

the imperial forces at the Battle of Legnano. It was clear the Barbarossa would not be able to dominate Italy and he reached some accommodation with the pope. Henry VI revived plans for controlling Rome. He had married the heiress of the Norman kingdom of Sicily; and because he possessed a firm base in Sicily he in some ways posed a far more serious threat to the papacy than his father had.

The immediate background to Innocent III's reign was not very promising. There was the threat from the emperors; Jerusalem had not been recovered by the Third Crusade; anti-clericalism and heresy were rife; papal control over the Church was not yet as tight as its ideology demanded; the Church was still in devious ways subjected to lay influence. On the other hand, Henry VI had died shortly before Innocent's election, and Innocent was able to impose his own solution on the disputed succession that followed.

During Innocent's reign the political background was favourable to the development of papal monarchy. The assertion of papal monarchy was not primarily the extension of papal authority in temporal affairs, nor was it the subjection of the territories of Christendom to the political control of the Holy See. It was simply a means of bringing right order to Christendom and of caring for its welfare. This could only be accomplished if the papacy had overall supervision of every aspect of Christian life. 'Nothing that happens in the world', wrote Innocent III, 'should escape the notice of the supreme pontiff.'

Innocent tried to make sure that suitable men were appointed to bishoprics because the bishops were the essential instruments for the proper functioning of the Church. He did not interfere in elections if they were

properly conducted, but he insisted that disputed elections should be referred to him for judgement and that in these cases the papal choice should be accepted. He was constantly urging the bishops not to neglect their pastoral work and to raise the standard of their lower clergy.

Innocent was naturally preoccupied with the behaviour of the clergy; they should do nothing to cause scandal in the Church, not even by the way they dressed. But he did not neglect the morals of the laity. The rite of marriage was not to be abused; and he delivered careful judgements, not just in the marital affairs of princes, but also in those of ordinary men and women. He patronized Fulk de Neuilly, whose work was devoted among many things to rescuing prostitutes.

These are relatively minor matters, but they show Innocent's determination to supervise all aspects of Christian society. His main task was perhaps to deal with the problem of heresy and to answer critics of the Church. He was faced with the dualist heresy of the Cathari of southern France and Italy. They believed in the world of the flesh created and dominated by the Devil and the world of the spirit created and dominated by God. This was particularly dangerous to the papacy, which was laying stress upon the unity of Christendom under a single ruler. Innocent believed that heretics were guilty of high treason, because they had rejected the faith which held society together, as well as of the theological deviations, for which they were excommunicated.

Above, the Holy Roman emperor Frederick I, also known as Frederick Barbarossa. For much of his reign (1220–50), he was occupied with Italian and papal politics, but his reign also saw increasing prosperity in Germany.

Above left, nuns in choir from a fifteenth-century psalter of Henry VI of England. Many nuns were from noble families, and an abbess could wield considerable political power.

Opposite, Henry VI (ruled 1191–97), the Holy Roman emperor. He failed in his attempt to make the Empire the hereditary kingdom of his family, the Hohenstaufens, and abolish the divisive procedure of electing each new emperor. Bibliothèque Nationale, Paris.

Though it was the duty of the secular ruler to aid in the extermination of the heretics found in his territories, Innocent received very little support from Philip Augustus of France against the Cathari of southern France, who were known as the Albigensians. The crusade against them was led by papal legates; it was enthusiastically received by the barons of northern France.

There were other ways of combating heresy. Innocent patronized the new preaching orders, the Dominican and Franciscan friars. They used the same methods as the heretics, going into their strongholds, preaching and holding public meetings. But it meant something more than this: Innocent was harnessing to the Church spiritual forces that until then had been outside and critical of the established Church.

The papacy not only had the task of confirming Christians in their faith; it also had to urge them to extend the faith among the heathen. Innocent encouraged the work of German missionaries in Livonia but characteristically insisted that conversion of the pagans should not be carried through with excessive rigour.

In addition the papacy held itself responsible for protecting the Holy Places; and Innocent III certainly felt that the recovery of Jerusalem was among his most urgent tasks. One of his first actions on becoming pope was to preach a crusade. The outcome of the Fouth Crusade, which set off from Venice in 1202, was not perhaps that envisaged by Innocent, but the conquest of Constantinople in 1204 was hailed by him because it seemed to be a solution to the age-old struggle between Rome and Constantinople for the primacy of the Church.

Innocent III's reforming activity culminated in the Fourth Lateran Council of 1215. A code of disciplinary decrees was enacted which was to serve as a legal basis for the exercise of papal government. It was the climax of a great burst of development in Church law which aimed at a better definition of papal authority. Uniformity was also encouraged by the spread of Roman liturgical practices, and centralization of the Church on Rome proceeded apace.

Papal administration at Rome was reformed; one of the first steps that Innocent III took as pontiff was to stamp out corruption among the hangers-on of the papal court. The chancery was reorganized and an attempt was made to deal with the mass of litigation that came flooding into Rome. Innocent also benefited from the effort made in 1192 to put papal revenues on a regular footing. Special officers were sent out in an attempt to obtain better payment of papal revenues; and in 1199 the first papal tax on clerical incomes was instituted to help to pay for the Fourth Crusade.

Papal government was further strengthened by the still greater use made of papal legates. They were sent out to all parts of Christendom and enabled the pope to exercise authority in areas that were not amenable to direct control from Rome. The legates held provincial councils, which provided an opportunity for putting papal legislation into practice. The legates were not simply agents in ecclesiastical affairs but often had an important part to play in purely political matters.

Innocent III's guiding aim was the reform and welfare of the Church, but it was quite impossible for him to carry out this task without at some point coming into conflict with secular rulers. His reign saw a more careful appreciation of the exact nature of the division of authority between the papacy and the secular rulers. It was part of a king's duty to help to lead his people to salvation, but the pope could intervene if he judged the king to be obviously failing in this duty, for otherwise the good order of Christendom would be endangered. Innocent III intervened in temporal affairs not so much because he was supreme sovereign of Christendom, but rather because the welfare of Christian society appeared to be threatened. This does not mean that he claimed to exercise only indirect power in temporal affairs; on the contrary, he could intervene directly, but only in exceptional circumstances which he was to define. Two hierarchies, a spiritual and a temporal one, were necessary for the administration of Christendom, but the pope claimed supreme and final authority over each.

If the papacy were to carry out its mission properly, it had to be free from external pressures. It must not again become the plaything of Roman politics, as it had so often been in the past. Innocent was determined to secure full control over the city of Rome; he succeeded, even though it meant temporary exile. A further step was to recover papal control over central Italy; this would not only protect the papacy from its enemies but would also give the papacy a temporal basis of power. Innocent obtained recognition of papal rights over a large part of central Italy from the rival candidates for the imperial title; and he tried, not with complete success, to organize it into a coherent state governed by rectors appointed from Rome.

Good order in Christendom demanded that the imperial office should go to a suitable candidate. By the end of the twelfth century the theory had been formulated that the Empire had been taken away from the Greeks and given by the papacy to the Germans. The papacy insisted that it had the right to examine the fitness of the man chosen by the German electors as so-called King of the Romans or, in the case of a disputed election, to make a choice between the rival candidates. The papacy refused to crown automatically as emperor the candidate presented by the German electors.

The disputed election after Henry VI's death (1197) meant that Innocent III was perhaps the first pope in a position to make good these papal claims. He chose Otto of Brunswick as the most suitable claimant. When Otto showed himself unworthy of his office by invading the kingdom of Sicily, which had passed to Henry VI's son Frederick, and by threatening the Papal States, Innocent excommunicated him and then supported Frederick's claim as King of Sicily. While in all this Innocent was motivated by a desire for the general welfare of Christendom, he was not indifferent to political considerations. He was determined to keep his freedom of action: central Italy must remain under papal control. This stand had far-reaching political implications.

Innocent III had fewer grounds for intervention in the affairs of the kingdoms of Christendom. He normally intervened for purely ecclesiastical reasons. His long-lasting quarrel with King John of England arose out of the disputed election of an archbishop of Canterbury; John refused to accept Innocent's nominee. England was placed under an interdict barring the country from ecclesiastical functions, as was Norway when its king, Sverre (1184–1204), refused to abide by an earlier Church settlement. Innocent III also quarrelled with Philip Augustus when he repudiated his wife without just cause.

Innocent considered it his duty to bring peace to Christendom. In 1199 peace was made between Philip Augustus and Richard I of England thanks to the good offices of the papal legate, Peter of Capua. In 1204, when Innocent tried to save John and forbade Philip to continue with the conquest of Normandy, Philip protested that the Pope was interfering in an essentially feudal dispute. Innocent justified his action on the grounds that the moral order was being threatened: Philip had broken a peace treaty concluded with the English king.

At the same time, it is true, the papacy did make use of its feudal connections. In 1207 Poland again placed itself under papal protection. The papacy's feudal control over England was tightened as a result of John's submission to Innocent; this also happened in Sicily, where under the terms of Constanza's will Innocent had become regent for the young Frederick. Innocent III exploited his feudal overlordship, which also extended to Portugal, Aragon and Hungary, not in order to introduce direct papal control but to secure favourable conditions for papal legates and the local hierarchy.

Innocent III handed on to his successors not only the lines of policy that they would have to follow but also the main problems with which they would have to deal; for despite his great achievements his work was hardly finished at the time of his death. Heresy had not been destroyed; there remained the problem of the crusade and the Greek Church; control over the Papal States was very precarious, threatened by internal unrest and Frederick II's lieutenants. In 1220 Frederick added the imperial title to his Sicilian crown; and the spectre of imperial domination of the papacy was to lead to a bitter struggle between the papacy and Frederick II; the disposal of the Empire and the kingdom of Sicily was to be of major concern to the papacy.

The thirteenth-century papacy: theory and practice

The thirteenth century did not really see more extreme claims advanced for papal sovereignty but rather a greater insistence upon the papacy's role as the head of Christendom.

The nature of papal authority did not alter: the pope was still seen as a divinely appointed vicar of Christ, fully empowered to look after the needs of Christian society. Regard for the welfare of Christendom was still the foremost duty of the papacy. The fight against heresy was continued: the Albigensian crusade was brought to a successful conclusion; the Franciscans did much to clear Italy of heresy. The culmination of Innocent III's work against heresy came with the adoption of the inquisitorial machinery for judicial purposes under Gregory IX (1227–41) and Innocent IV (1243–54).

The possibilities of missionary work among the Mongols were explored. Innocent IV despatched emissaries to the Mongol ruler from the first Council of Lyons (1245). At about the same time efforts were made to bring the pagan Lithuanians and the Orthodox Christians of Russia within the papal fold, while a little earlier the Order of Teutonic Knights was established in Prussia under papal patronage.

Serious efforts were made to implement papal primacy over the Greek Church; negotiations begun under Innocent III between papal legates and representatives of the Greek Church continued intermittently throughout the period leading up to the Greek recovery of Constantinople in 1261. They came to a head in 1274 at the second Council of Lyons, when a Union of Greek and Latin Churches was formally proclaimed. The primacy of the pope was recognized by the council, and Latin practices were to be introduced into the Greek Church.

Gregory X (1271–76) had called the Council of Lyons with the express purpose of uniting Christendom in preparation for a crusade. The crusade was still central to papal policy; and there was an effort to obtain closer control over the actual expeditions. Like Innocent III, the thirteenth-century popes had one fundamental answer to the multitude of problems that confronted them. Papal control must be made ever tighter over all aspects of Christian life.

Bottom left, the Norman king of Sicily Tancred (ruled 1189–94) hearing the appeal of a bigamist. Sicily was one of the main routes for the introduction of Arabic culture to Europe; the kingdom was taken over by the Holy Roman Emperor Henry VI shortly after Tancred's death. Burgerbibliothek, Bern.

Left and bottom right, the Holy Roman Emperor Frederick II (ruled 1220–50) fought a lifelong battle with the papacy, primarily because of his overwhelming power in Italy, as he was King of Sicily as well as Emperor. He was also a highly cultured man, and wrote a book on falconry from which this illustration is taken. Vatican Library.

Below, a mid-thirteenth-century English illustration of the papal court, where deputations from all over Christendom were continually being heard.

The power of papal legates in all parts of Christendom was one of the characteristics of the thirteenth-century papacy and helps to explain its great authority. The importance and the very great work of some of the papal legates is perhaps best seen in England. After John's death in 1216 the government of the country was entrusted to a regency council in which the papal legate was one of the leading figures. Throughout the troubled reign of Henry III (1216–72) papal legates were at hand to help the king to patch up his quarrels with the barons. The high standard of the English Church during the thirteenth century is another tribute to the legates' abilities.

Closer papal supervision also meant increasing centralization. Administration began to be departmentalized. By the end of the thirteenth century separate judicial, financial and administrative sections had emerged.

The growth of administration and the scope of papal government demanded increased revenues. The incomes derived from papal estates and from various tributes did not suffice. Income taxes on clerical revenues were turned towards the costs of administration; dues paid by prelates on the occasion of receiving their office from the pope ceased to be customary gratuities and became a fixed tax and the papacy's most lucrative source of revenue. A scale of fees was fixed for hearing a suit before the papal courts and for papal letters and bulls obtained from the chancery. But the systematization of revenues was not sufficient to pay for the upkeep of the rapidly expanding civil service. To meet this difficulty, by the reign of Innocent IV it was becoming necessary to reserve more and more benefices for papal nominees. These two developments, increased papal taxation and increased control over ecclesiastical patronage, perhaps more than anything else brought home the power of the papacy.

The struggle with Emperor Frederick II

The increased centralization of the Church and the greater range of papal authority were in part the logical conclusion of Innocent III's work; they were also a reaction to the threat posed by the Emperor Frederick II.

He wanted to restore dignity and authority to the imperial office, but this could only be achieved if the pope's power was strictly limited to the spiritual sphere. He laid emphasis on the supreme authority accorded to the emperor by Roman law; subsequently, perhaps influenced by the ideas of the Greek philosopher Aristotle he did advance beyond old positions when he claimed that a human form of organization, the state, and not the divine institution of the Church was the natural object of the human community. He also demanded that the pope should stand trial before a general council, because in his view it represented the whole Church, from which papal power was derived. But such claims should not be allowed to obscure the fact that the imperial case rested on the old concept of the world order, in which all power ultimately went back to Christ. This played right into the hands of the papacy; for the pope was still universally regarded as the Vicar of Christ.

The struggle with Frederick was so bitter because Innocent III's legacy was placed in jeopardy not only by imperial demands that papal power should be limited to spiritual matters but also by the attempt to restore imperial control over Italy.

Frederick had promised Innocent III that he would give up the kingdom of Sicily as soon as he became emperor. He failed to keep this promise. Sicily was too valuable; also he was attached to it by the ties of a childhood passed for the most part in Palermo. The early part of his reign as emperor was spent reorganizing his Sicilian kingdom and bringing it thoroughly under his control. It was to be the base from which he would subordinate northern Italy and then set about restoring imperial authority in Germany.

Frederick's ambitions aroused the suspicions of the papacy. A state of undeclared war had existed for many years before 1239, when the struggle began in earnest. In 1229 a papal army invaded Naples while Frederick was away on a crusade. The papacy also encouraged the resistance of the Lombard cities to imperial control. The Lombard League was revived under the leadership of Milan.

Not all cities joined. Pavia and Cremona, traditional enemies of Milan, preferred to enter the imperial camp. Italy was split into two opposing groups: the one supported the papacy and was known as the Guelf party; the other, which was called the Ghibelline party, supported the imperial cause. Their rivalry divided Italy for nearly 200 years; it led to faction within cities and to feuds within families. The main alignments were decided not so much by loyalty to pope or emperor as by purely local considerations. In Tuscany Florence supported the Guelf cause; its main commercial rival Lucca entered the Ghibelline camp. Pisa, with a large stake in the trade of Sicily and Naples, supported the emperor; its great trading rival, Genoa, was usually true to the papacy.

The Papal States were a constant source of friction. Frederick needed some control over them to keep open his lines of communication from Sicily to Lombardy and Germany. After the outbreak of war he had comparatively little difficulty in reducing them to obedience. Pope Innocent IV, realizing that at Rome his freedom of action was severely circumscribed by imperial power, fled to seek safety outside Italy. In 1245 he called a general council which met at Lyons—a stone's throw from French territory—and deposed Frederick.

The papal legate was sent to Germany to exploit local differences and to ensure that Frederick obtained no support from that quarter. Frederick was in fact rather weak militarily; it was all he could do to hold down Lombardy. In 1248 his small army was destroyed at Parma by a papal force.

Frederick died two years later. Innocent IV might exult, but the threat to the papacy was not yet over: neither Germany nor Sicily immediately passed to rulers amenable to papal control. Frederick's son Conrad kept his inheritance together; and after the latter's death in 1254 Sicily and Naples fell to Frederick's bastard son Manfred. By 1261 Manfred was in a position to dominate Italy. To avert this threat the papacy gave the kingdom of Sicily to Charles of Anjou, brother of the French king Louis IX. In 1266 Charles invaded Naples, defeating and killing Manfred. The kingdom thus passed to the Angevins.

It took the papacy a little longer to find a satisfactory solution to the German problem. There was a period until 1272 when there was no ruler because the papacy was unwilling to crown as emperor either of the two foreign princes chosen by the German electors. But with the accession of Rudolf of Habsburg the dangers which had threatened the papacy for so long seemed to be over: Rudolf was ready to abandon imperial pretensions and build up a German monarchy with papal backing.

Criticism of the papacy

The struggle with Frederick II amply demonstrated the power of the papacy, but other dangers were in store. There was perhaps too great a reliance on the support of the kings of France; and there was also the possibility that the Angevins would come to dominate Italy, thus placing in jeopardy once more the papacy's freedom of action.

The threat to the papacy went deeper than this. It received mounting criticism. It was argued that it was becoming too much of this world and increasingly neglecting its spiritual work; it seemed to have too little regard for the ideals of Apostolic Poverty. These were points of view well exploited by Frederick II's propagandists, but even so faithful a son of the Church as St Louis could complain to Innocent IV about his fiscal exactions and his reservations of benefices. This sort of criticism is also to be seen in England in the work of Matthew Paris. Satire against papal venality grew more virulent. Men objected to the dues paid by prelates consecrated by the pope and to fees involved in carrying through a law-suit at Rome: it was nothing other than the sin of selling justice and ecclesiastical offices. The growth of papal taxation was extremely unpopular and resulted in tax riots. The practice of presenting aliens with Church property on English soil was also strongly resented, and in 1231 a small Yorkshire landowner called Robert Tweng led an armed protest against it.

Criticism of the papacy was uncoordinated; it was often no more than personal pique. Usually it expressed only a vague disquiet with the state of the Church and was mainly directed against what were considered to be the excesses of papal power. There was no attack on papal authority as such.

Dissatisfaction of this sort became much more dangerous when allied to other forces taking shape during the thirteenth century. Together they were to do much to undermine the very basis of papal monarchy.

The growth of royal government was perhaps the most important of these new forces. At first this development was welcomed by the papacy, which did not appreciate the dangers it held in store. It was seen as a means of bringing good order more easily to Christian society. There were certainly clashes between the growing papal and royal administrations, but they could be settled without any violent struggle because both king and pope had roughly the same concept of sovereignty.

On the other hand, the growth of royal government during the thirteenth century produced a state of affairs at variance with the ideology to which both sides subscribed. The increasing range of royal administration gave greater definition and unity to the territories belonging to the king. Contemporaries became increasingly aware that the primary allegiance of a subject was owed to the king rather than to the pope. Within his lands the king must not have any superior, and his kingdom was not to come under any superior authority.

These political developments were given the necessary ideological backing by the spread of Aristotelian ideas, which cut right to the heart of papal authority. Political power did not come from God; the state was not a divine creation. Instead, Aristotle emphasized the natural origins of the state; while power within the state, far from being derived from above, sprang from below. Sovereignty rested with the whole community, though it could in practice be exercised by a ruler as the representative of the community.

With this went an even more fundamental change: all members of the community had a natural right to participate in the government of the state.

Above, the Hohenstaufen Empire in 1250; Frederick II's control of the kingdom of Sicily was implacably opposed by the papacy, which felt encircled by a hostile power.

Opposite, an early medieval miniature of Lawrence of Durham, a monk and scholar. After the rise of the universities in the thirteenth century, monasteries soon lost their importance as centres of learning.

These new ideas held danger for royal authority as well as for papal monarchy. Kings were, however, able to come to terms with them more easily, for the ground had already been prepared by feudalism; the king's power was in varying degrees limited by the feudal contract with his vassals. No such adjustment was possible for the papacy. Popes saw the ills of the Church but could only supply old-fashioned remedies—the crusade and the policy of centralization. The papacy was failing to meet the true needs of the time. Alienation from the established Church was increasing; and it is not surprising that during the later Middle Ages the papacy was faced with a series of crises both in and outside the Church.

Boniface VIII and Philip the Fair

Serious tensions within the Church had already begun to show themselves by the time of Boniface's accession in 1294. His predecessor Celestine V had been forced to abdicate because of his alleged incompetence. This gave rise to claims that Boniface's election had been irregular. There seems to have been a split in the college of cardinals; and Boniface was to be hounded by the Spiritual Franciscans, who had been patronized by Celestine. The circumstances surrounding his election were to be a constant source of weakness to Boniface.

They were exploited by his main opponent, Philip IV of France (1285–1314). A first clash over clerical taxation in 1296 was patched up very quickly. It had no direct connection with the real struggle, which began in 1301. The actual pretext seems trivial enough. A French bishop was arrested and tried before the royal court for slandering the king. Boniface insisted that the case should come before him for trial, because bishops came under direct papal jurisdiction. The actual cause of the quarrel was not so important as the principles at stake. It turned into a conflict of opposing concepts of sovereignty. Boniface re-stated the now traditional papal case: the papacy possessed supreme authority in both temporal and spiritual affairs. Philip was willing to recognize that the papacy had supreme spiritual power, but claimed that in temporal matters no outside power could claim suzerainty over his kingdom.

The clash gave rise to a spate of propaganda defending the position taken up by Philip the Fair. Some of it was official; some of it was composed by masters of the University of Paris. Of the two main themes in the royal defence, the first was that the king was simply protecting his kingdom against the claims of the papacy. The other theme hinged on defining the respective spheres of ecclesiastical and secular authority. One of the royal propagandists, obviously much influenced by Aristotelian ideas, saw the state as the only source and sole foundation of real power; and this was to be exercised by the king. Consequently, the Church in its temporal existence ought to be subordinated to the king. These claims were not so very different from the position taken up by Frederick II's defenders, who provided the French propagandists with many of their arguments. Even Philip IV's strategy of bringing Boniface for judgement before a general council went back to the men around Frederick II. What was new was that French propaganda had a firm footing in the Aristotelian view of the state.

This had practical implications. The victor would be the one who had the support of the French people united as a nation and of the Church universal. Boniface, claiming that he was protecting the Church in France from royal oppression, called a council of French bishops to meet in Rome to consider reform of the Church in France. Only half the French bishops came, and nothing was accomplished. Philip, on the other hand, was able to demonstrate the support he had from the people of France: representative assemblies of both clergy and laity were called together, and the royal case was explained to them. The king appeared to be acting in his quarrel with the papacy not as a ruler whose power was divine in origin but as the representative of his people, making them believe that he spoke as the agent of the nation.

While the French people stood solidly behind their king, the situation in Italy exposed the weakness of the papacy. Boniface relied on French and Angevin aid in the struggle between the Guelfs and the Ghibellines; he was also faced with the hostility of the powerful Colonna family. In 1303 Philip's minister William Nogaret, with the support of the Colonnas, took Boniface prisoner at Anagni; he was to be brought for trial before a general council. Boniface was rescued by the local inhabitants, only to die a few weeks later.

Philip continued his struggle against Boniface beyond the grave. He demanded that the measures taken against him should be disavowed. The problem confronting Boniface's successors, Benedict XI (1303–05) and Clement V (1305–14), was how to come to an agreement with Philip and yet preserve papal authority intact. They were willing to absolve Philip from his excommunication by Boniface and to declare that Boniface had not intended to assert any new claim by the papacy to lordship over France. This did not go far enough. Philip brought pressure to bear on the papacy, on the one hand by suppressing the Order of Templars, on the other by threatening a posthumous trial of Boniface. Clement V agreed to open such a trial. He prevaricated and it was allowed to drop, but only after he had ordered the deletion from the registers of the papal chancery of all matter that might be injurious to the King of France.

The popes at Avignon

The need to come to a compromise with the King of France was one of the reasons which led Pope Clement V to fix his residence at Avignon. It also lay close to Vienne, where a general council assembled in 1311; Clement had to be sure that this council would be controlled by the papacy and not dominated by the French king. A return to Italy was then out of the question because of the turmoil there; the struggle between the Guelfs and the Ghibellines was resumed with new fervour after the Emperor Henry VII's Italian expedition in 1312. Another consideration may have been that Avignon was much better situated for administrative purposes than Rome.

The encounter with Philip the Fair and the exile of the papacy at Avignon has usually been taken to mark one of the great turning points in papal history; but this is true only in a rather limited sense. The

Avignonese popes continued to assert the claims of papal monarchy and followed the politics of their predecessors.

The administrative machinery developed during the thirteenth century was brought to a peak of efficiency. The great organizer was John XXII (1316–34). The papal fiscal system was regularized, and new sources of revenue were found. Papal tax-collectors were given permanent commissions and had powers of excommunication to enforce payment of papal taxes. Italian bankers were employed on an increasingly large scale to transmit revenues from all corners of Christendom. At the same time the judicial system was perfected to deal with the growing volume of appeals; these came before the tribunal called the *Rota Romana*. Increased centralization was also to be seen in the policy of reserving more and more benefices for papal nominees. This was the cause of bitter criticism, but it should be stressed that the candidates were examined scrupulously.

The Avignonese papacy was only too conscious of its duty to bring peace to Christendom. This was seen as essential to a successful crusade. John XXII intervened in Edward II's difficulties in Scotland and Ireland and helped to negotiate a peace with the Scots. Later, a more urgent task was to restore peace between England and France. From 1337 to 1341 Benedict XII forbade Philip VI of France to take the offensive against Edward III. One can hardly doubt the papacy's sincerity, but the result of papal intervention, far from bringing about peace, was to ensure that neither side would gain outright victory, in other words to prolong the war. The French were helped by papal loans and the papacy did everything in its power to prevent Flanders coming under English control.

In this the papacy was motivated by a desire to preserve the status quo, defence of the established order was essential if papal authority were to be upheld. Kings were to be protected from their barons and their subjects. Edward II was forced to rely on papal support when faced with baronial opposition. John XXII dissolved a feudal league which threatened Philip V of France. He also waged a long and unsuccessful campaign on behalf of the Brienne family, which had been driven out of their duchy of Thebes by Catalan mercenaries.

The way was being prepared for a compromise between the papacy and the princes of Christendom. This first became clear over papal taxation and appointments. Popular pressure sometimes forced the king into legislation designed to limit the effects of papal patronage and jurisdiction, but this did not reflect the essence of royal policy. The papacy might present candidates to the great ecclesiastical offices, but a man acceptable to the ruler was almost always chosen. In England the provision of aliens to bishoprics was virtually unknown during the fourteenth century. Patronage was an

Sexta etas mūdi

Anno mundi. 6504. Anno xpi. 1305

Linea summoꝝ pontificū
Clemens quintus

Clemens quintus papa. natione vascon⁹. burdegalēsis eps bernardus got tho antea vocatus. pře bertrādo milite nat⁹. post longā ꝯtentionē pontifex creat. Cardinales eni coartati a perusinis in coclaui tandē in hūc bernardū burdegalensem epm tūc agentē i gallijs cōuenerūt. Is decreto electionis de se facto apud burdegallā accepto. lugdunū se ꝯtulit. Et clemētis quinti noie assum pto. cardinales illuc ad se litteris accersiuit. q oia facta parandi mora mēse Augusto anni salutis quinti terdecies q centeni accesserūt. Fuitq ea curie translatio annis septuagintaquoꝝ. Que multas dei ecclie preuaricatōnes. multa incuerit xpiano pplo detrimēta. Interfuerūt lugduni pōtificis coronationi philippus rex francie. carolusq frater suus. in frācia ex ytalia reuersus. Joannes dux britannie ⁊ quequid nobilitatis omīs gallia tūc habebat. Dumq pompa eius celebritatis ex more ⁊ p vrbē duceret. muri pina gētiū pressura incubantiū impulsa corruit. Cui⁹ casu dux britānie ⁊ multi ignotiores oppressi interiere. carol⁹ regis frater debilitatus. ⁊ pōtifex ipe adeo in turbā pceps deturbatus ē. vt mitra ex capite excussa iaspidē pciosissimū amiserit. Creauit vo clemens cardinales ex gallijs tam multos vt facile tūc cōiectura omēs assequi potuerit. pontificē romanū deinceps nō nisi ex gallicis creari posse. ytalie aūt ⁊ vrbi rome visus ē satisfecisse in duobus iacobo ⁊ ioanne colūnēsibus. quos ad capellum ⁊ integrā dignitatē restituit. Ne aūt romani curie absentiā diuturniore sicut sibi cōscius erat. futurā egreferētes animo rebellarent. tres cardinales attributa senatorij muneris potestate romā accedere curauit. Quorum auspicijs ipa roma ⁊ ytalia omīs gubernabat postmodū eius iussu dulcini heresis oppressa ē. ac templarioꝝ religio penitus extincta. venetos ꝑterea ꝑter ferrariā occupatā anathemate notauit. ac sacramenta interdixit. Idem in florentinos ⁊ lucenses egit. ideo florentini grauissimis exactionib⁹ clerum grauare cepe rūt. Cū ad cōponendū ecclesie statum animū adiecisset ꝯcilia habuit. vbi clemētinaꝝ liber postea confectus est. Ubi etiā celestinū papā sub nomine petri sanctis confessoribus aggregauit. Deinceps vo varijs egritudinibus afflictatus. nūc eni dissinteria. nūc stomachi ⁊ lateꝝ dolore cruciabat. Octauo pontificat⁹ sui anno. mense decimo. die quintodecimo moritur. Uacat tum sedes annis duobus. mēsibus tribus. diebus. xvij. dum non satis inter cardinales constat quem potissimū deligant. Nec minoꝝ quidē discordia inter electores imperij tum fuit. mortuo heinrico. Eius autem corpus in vasconiā patriā suam defertur. vbi in beate marie de vzesta templo diocesis vasatensis sepelitur.

Dulcinus ⁊ margarita vxor sua heresiarche. apud vrbē lōgobardie nouariā. cū anno salutis septimo terdecies centeno in rebus xpianis varij motus agitationesq inciderūt. sectatores vtriusq sexus ad mille nacti virus diffundere ceperant. Eo perniciosius quo sacerdotes ⁊ religiosos in populoꝝ inuidiam adductos. spernentes simulatā puritatē quādam ⁊ innocentiā vite ꝑponebant secūdū quā immixti femellis mares. lasciuia ad libitū debaccari. Que pestis duobus annis perdurans. Eos itaq a clemēte romāo pontifice nūcij in montem coactos excelsum alpibus cōtinentem. fame ⁊ frigore confectos ad vnū sustulerunt. Captis deniq dulcino ⁊ margarita vercellas perduci iubentur. ⁊ primo lacerari inde eorum offa cōcremari ⁊ in ventum dispergi precepit. Nec hec pestis omnino deleri potuit. quin adhuc in mōtibus tridentinis alique eius reliquie remanserunt.

Concilium Uienense

Anno domini millesimo. cccxi. kal. Nouēbris concilium generale in vrbe narbonēsis gallie viēna celebrari cepit. vt ante fuerat publicatum. in quo aderāt plusq. ccc. epi vltra alios plātos de varijs regionib⁹ orbis. Et cum clemens vt satisfaceret ꝑmissioni facte regi francie de delēda memoria bonifacij cū rex illum hereticū fuisse ꝑbare intēdebat. conciliū assentire noluit. ꝑcessum tū in regem francie iniustū declarauit. Statutū fuit q omīa bona ⁊ possessiōes q fuerāt templarioꝝ mansioni hospitalis hierosolimitani assignerētur. Facte fuerūt in eo cōcilio ꝯstitutōes generales ꝯcernētes statū religiosoꝝ. Et librū clemētinaꝝ a se cōpositū i eodē viēnē si ꝯcilio clemēs edidit. Petrū qz morroneū q celestinus fuerat in numeꝝ retulit beatoꝝ. In eo ꝯcilio ad alterius anni medietatē ꝑtrahens. de subueniē do hierosolime multa vba fecit. Que i irritū cecidere. Et decreta ꝑmulgauit extantia quibus de suo nomine clementinā appellatio perseuerat.

Above, Pope Clement V (ruled 1305–14) convening the Council of Vienne in 1311, at which the decision was taken to suppress the Knights Templar. Victoria and Albert Museum, London.

Left, the papal palace at Avignon, where the popes lived between 1309 and 1378. One reason for the move was that Avignon was more convenient as a centre for Christendom.

Opposite, the Pope Boniface VIII (ruled 1294–1303) in council; the papal court included a civil service that ran the affairs of the church all over Christendom and also heard cases brought before the ecclesiastical courts. British Library, London.

essential part of both royal and papal government. It was tacitly agreed that it should be shared to their mutual advantage. In the same way, it was usual for the king to take a large share of papal taxation.

This type of compromise certainly had its roots back in the thirteenth century, if not before, but now it was on the point of becoming the foundation on which the exercise of papal monarchy depended. It was now virtually impossible to find new means of assuaging religious discontent. The Franciscans revived the question of apostolic poverty. John XXII's only answer was to persecute them and in 1323 to condemn the doctrine of poverty. New constitutions were provided for the religious orders. The solutions of the Avignonese papacy were essentially administrative; and its false position became clear when its administration grew more oppressive as a result of papal involvement in Italy.

The return to Italy

It was always the intention of the popes to return to Rome. Plans were made under John XXII and Benedict XII to move to Bologna in preparation for an eventual return. Urban V set out for Rome but was driven back to Avignon. It was clear that the papacy had to have control of the situation, but this was not conceived just in terms of restoration of papal authority in Rome and the surrounding region. It was hoped that the turmoil of Guelfs and Ghibellines would provide an opportunity to assert papal authority over the whole of northern and central Italy. Temporal power was needed to back up the spiritual and administrative strength of the papacy.

There were two major obstacles to papal ambitions. The cities of Lombardy and Tuscany, even those sympathetic to the papal cause, would tolerate only a very limited degree of papal control. Florence, which prided itself on being a most faithful daughter of the Church, preferred to go to war with the papacy rather than let the papal legate obtain any real measure of control of Tuscany.

Secondly, the designs of the papacy conflicted with the ambitions of the German King Louis of Bavaria (1314–47). He too sought to take advantage of the struggles within Italy to revive imperial claims.

It was a strange encounter. On the ideological level it was fought with the full panoply of arguments and counter-claims developed since the investiture controversy; these were reinforced on the imperial side by the work of Marsiglio of Padua and William of Ockham. It underlined the bankruptcy of both sides: it confirmed that as an international institution the Empire was a thing of the past, but this in turn meant that papal intervention in the affairs of Germany was unlikely to have much meaning. Papal appointees to German benefices were often rejected. John XXII could claim that the administration of the Empire lay with the pope until he had crowned the electors' choice as emperor; but this mattered little when real power in Germany was coming to rest with the territorial princes.

After Louis' death in 1347 his rival Charles of Luxemburg was universally recognized as King of Germany; he was crowned emperor in 1355 and agreed that he would never interfere in Italian affairs. This gave him freedom to settle the situation inside Germany. The next year he laid down procedure for the election of the German king so as to exclude papal interference.

The Great Schism

By 1376 the situation in Rome and the surrounding district was sufficiently peaceful for Gregory XI to return. On his death two years later, however, the papacy, which had survived two external crises, was faced with an internal one. The Archbishop of Bari was elected pope amid the demonstrations of the people of Rome and took the name Urban VI (1378–89). His career had until then been undistinguished. It was assumed that he would allow the cardinals a large part of the framing of papal policy, as had been usual under the Avignonese papacy. In 1353 the cardinals had made an electoral pact which bound the next pope to associate the cardinals in the major decisions of government; similar pacts were made during subsequent vacancies. The cardinals were claiming a share in the fullness of power enjoyed by the papacy.

Urban VI, however, refused to have papal authority diminished by the claims of the cardinals. The cardinals therefore decided, that he was not fitted for the papal office; in the summer of 1378, using the excuse that they had chosen him under duress, they proceeded to elect one of their number, Pope Clement VII (1378–94).

In its origins the schism was a purely internal affair connected with the problem of how an unworthy pope was to be removed. But it was complicated and made much more difficult to resolve by the political situation: the Hundred Years' War had divided Europe into two power blocks. Even though France and the Iberian kingdoms made a show of examining the credentials of the rival popes, there can be no doubt that allegiances were determined by predominantly political motives. England and its allies supported Urban VI, while France and its allies recognized Clement VII, who took up residence at Avignon.

The conciliar movement

The schism may have had its political advantages, but these were outweighed by a consciousness that a terrible scandal had been perpetrated which threatened the whole fabric of the Church.

But how could it be solved? Neither pope would willingly renounce his claims, and they became still more firmly entrenched once they had set up their rival administrative machines. Nor was there any body that clearly had the right to sit in judgement over the two popes. Furthermore it was not just a matter of settling the schism: it became increasingly clear that any solution involved the whole question of authority within the Church.

The 'conciliar movement' was essentially an attempt to meet this difficult problem. It did not provide a coherent system of Church government, but within it one can detect two distinct strands which corresponded to different concepts of the Church. On the one hand, there were the cardinals who claimed that resolving the schism was properly their duty; for they argued that power within the Church resided in a corporation consisting of the college of cardinals with the pope as its head and that as a result the pope was responsible to the college. On the other hand, there was a wider body of conciliarist or church council opinion. While admitting that the pope was head of the whole Christian community, it held that sovereignty lay not with the pope alone but with the whole Christian people; the latter was represented by the general council to which the pope was subordinate. This body was to be responsible for reforming the Church and ending the schism. The one represented an oligarchic view of the Church, the other a democratic one.

The Avignonese cardinals were determined to impose their own solution. They had the backing of the French government, which canvassed the possibility of simultaneous withdrawal of obedience by supporters of both popes. In 1398 the French implemented their part of the scheme, but this method of forcing both popes to resign—thus allowing the cardinals to end the schism by electing a new pope—failed because supporters of the Roman pope refused to follow the French lead. The cardinals next tried to arrange a meeting between the rival popes to secure their abdication. This plan was sabotaged by the natural reluctance of the Roman pope.

Dissident cardinals of both obediences then called a general council to meet at Pisa in 1409. Both popes were deposed and a new one elected. This attempt by the cardinals to put themselves at the head of the growing support for a general council was doomed to failure. They were unable to implement their sentences of deposition, and there were now three popes instead of two.

The Council of Constance

A general council meeting to reform the Church now seemed the only hope. The cry for reform grew louder. On the one hand, there were those like Hus in Bohemia who were disillusioned with the established Church; on the other, there was a more orthodox body of opinion that called for reform because they saw in the work of Hus and Wycliffe a threat to established order.

Reform of the Church was to be the theme of the council that assembled at Constance in 1414, but the actual outcome turned very much on the political interests of the rulers of Christendom. The council was called by the Pisan pope John XXII, but under pressure from the German king Sigismund, who was to be its moving force. Sigismund was not inspired by conciliarist ideals, though his desire for reform was genuine enough, if a little vague. His main interest in the council was political. He calculated that if he could help to bring the schism to an end he would become the leading prince in Christendom and in a position to overawe the papacy. This new-found power would then enable him to reassert imperial authority in Germany. He was to be disappointed.

Nevertheless, much that the council achieved was due to him. Thanks to his energy and presence of mind, John XXII was deposed, the Roman pontiff was forced to abdicate and the Avignonese pope deprived of any secular backing. The question now before the council was whether to proceed to a general reform of the Church or to elect a new pope first.

After the pattern of the universities, voting at the council was by nations. The English and German nations were for reform. The French, Italian and Spanish nations, supported by the majority of cardinals, determined on election first. The deadlock was broken when, for purely political reasons, the English delegation gave up its insistence on reform. A compromise was reached. A decree *Frequens* was issued laying down regular meetings of the general council, to which, it was asserted, everyone, including the pope, was subjected and from which there was no appeal. These enactments were thought to be a guarantee that the work of reform would go on. The council then elected Pope Martin V.

Victory for papal monarchy

The council of Constance that had promised so much achieved precious little save the ending of the schism. No new structure of Church government came into being. On the contrary, it soon became clear that the papacy would re-emerge with its old authority virtually intact. Even before the council broke up, Martin V had prohibited appeals from the pope to a general council in matters of faith. Doubt arose on the validity of the decree which claimed that the pope was responsible to the council, because Martin V did not specifically confirm it. After his return to Rome he turned his energies to restoring control over the Papal States.

Martin V and his successor Eugenius IV were not opposed to the councils in themselves and faithfully carried out the provisions laid down in the decree *Frequens*, but they were determined that the councils should remain under papal control.

The internal contradictions of the conciliar movement soon became apparent. The council of Basle that met in 1431 could do little more than defy Eugenius IV's attempts to dissolve it; there were quarrels about which was the right approach to the reform of the Church. Should it concentrate on the papal administration or should it begin from below? Most of the higher clergy gradually deserted the council to join Eugenius IV. Although in 1439 the council proclaimed its superiority over the papacy, it was clear that it offered no real alternative to papal monarchy for the representatives at Basle were frightened of the democratic principles on which conciliar theory was based. The laity were not allowed any real part in their deliberations and decisions. The council acted less as the representative of the Church than as a body standing above society by virtue of divine authority.

There is another side to the restoration of papal monarchy. The alliance with the princes of Christendom was resumed. The papacy needed their support in the struggle with the conciliarists. But the compromise with secular power now went further than it had under the Avignonese papacy. The popes were forced to accede to the increasing royal control over the Church which had been won during the schism.

The policy of compromise with established order initiated under the Avignonese papacy at least preserved the outward forms of papal monarchy, but it was now deprived of much of its spiritual content. Disillusion with the papacy continued to grow; it seemed to be an obstacle to any reform of the Church.

Above, Urban VI (ruled 1378–89), elected pope partly because the Roman people demanded an Italian pope. He was almost immediately deposed and an antipope elected, thus creating the Great Schism that lasted until 1417.

Above left, the order of the Knights Templar was founded in about 1118 to fight in the Holy Land; but the order eventually became so rich and powerful that the church and kings of Europe attacked it. Its last leader, Jacques de Molay, is shown here burned at the stake for heresy in 1314. British Library.

Chapter 11

Clerks, Scholars and Heretics

'Doubtless good works are better than great knowledge, but without knowledge it is impossible to do good.' The famous words with which Charlemagne (in a capitulary written shortly before 800) announced his own educational policy still provide the fundamental guide to the patterns of thought in western Europe between the twelfth and fifteenth centuries. The central assumption that all branches of intellectual activity should be centred on God and subserve Christ's purposes is difficult if not impossible to recapture in a more modern and less religious age. But the world of medieval learning is unintelligible except in terms of a concerted attempt to 'justify the ways of God to man'. Indeed the history of thought between 1000 and 1500 is best interpreted as the most ambitious, sophisticated and sustained effort ever made by human reason to comprehend a divinity which was by definition never capable of comprehension.

This paradox was one of which medieval thinkers were themselves only too frequently and painfully aware. St Bernard, St Francis and many others expressed grave doubts as to the validity of conclusions based on rational enquiry; and even Abelard, arguably the most significant figure in the movement towards uninhibited speculative thought, faced the same dilemma. In the celebrated words of his letter to Héloise after his condemnation in 1141, 'I will never be a philosopher, if that is to speak against St Paul: I would not be an Aristotle, if that were to separate me from Christ.' It was probably inevitable that this basic conflict between faith and reason should lead not to a long history of intellectual heresy but to the late medieval disintegration of the previous attempt to synthesize human knowledge under the aegis of the divine.

New learning and the new law

The decades immediately before and after 1100 have long been recognized as a period which marks a genuine revolution in the history of western Europe. As in the case of its fifteenth-century Italian counterpart, the true nature of the so-called 'twelfth-century renaissance' has been obscured rather than clarified by its now conventional title. This was fundamentally a new age, characterized by its willingness to adapt the teachings of the early Christian Fathers and eventually of Aristotle to its own purposes.

The genuinely characteristic feature of twelfth-century intellectual activity, as perhaps of medieval society as a whole, was an attempt by the clerical estate, widely regarded as God's representatives upon earth, to maintain and define their special position in society. Members of the priesthood, under the leadership of bishops, metropolitans and the pope, formed a clerical élite but not an absolute theocracy. And it was the need to resolve the ambiguities of their role—in this world but not entirely of it—which provided both the social and intellectual mainspring of the new order.

The eleventh century saw the first massive and sustained attempt by the clergy, under the undisputed direction of the papacy after the reign of Gregory VII (1073–85), to claim an absolutely distinctive place against that of the laity. The ambitious and ultimately remarkably successful reform programme of the Church, its attack on clerical marriage, its denunciation of simony and insistence on clerical celibacy was specifically aimed at differentiating the clerk from the layman.

Inevitably this movement led to a new and more violent phase in the already vexed and complex history of the relationship between spiritual and secular authority. The investiture controversy began a conflict which was certainly not ended by the Concordat of Worms in 1122. On the assumption, made by St Augustine and commonly accepted throughout the Middle Ages, that both pope and emperor—and, by implication, all kings and all priests—were agents of divine authority, the precise limits of their rival claims to obedience was always a matter of practical concern and often of spiritual urgency.

The fundamental issues thus raised by the investitute controversy compelled its protagonists to become articulate. Resistance to the pope or emperor, opposition to a Henry II or a Becket, had to be justified and rationalized. Theologians, philosophers and political theorists have rarely been offered so exciting an opportunity to contribute towards a public debate. The collision between the spiritual and temporal powers at the end of the eleventh century led to an almost instantaneous outburst of controversial literature. For the first time for centuries there was a concerted attempt to analyse and re-define the theoretical concepts which underlay the ordering of society: the nature of law and of right, the source and limitations of authority.

In the first place, however, the investiture controversy provoked an intensive interest in the study of the law. From the beginning the papacy's assertion of supremacy over its lay rivals had been founded within a framework of jurisprudence. The appeal to legal precedents or Church authorities was the Church's most familiar method of argument and exhortation: it can be seen at a relatively crude and embryonic stage in Gregory VII's famous *Dictatus Papae* of 1075, which included the explicit claim that a pope could depose an emperor. Such extremism rapidly provoked a reaction from the lay party. As early as the 1080s Peter Crassus of Ravenna, himself a layman, was invoking Roman civil law and assisting in the contemporary rediscovery of Justinian's great legal codes. In the first years of the twelfth century the University of Bologna not only replaced Pavia and Ravenna as the main centre of legal studies in Italy but was itself centred upon the lay schools of Roman law.

Lay participation in legal and medical studies within the Italian universities remained one of their important characteristics—largely because Italian towns, unlike most of those north of the Alps, possessed a semi-professional class of literate lawyers and notaries with a practical interest in technical training. But even in Italy it was the clergy who reaped the most startling fruits from the resurgence of learning and controversy. Throughout the Middle Ages the spokesmen for the lay or, more accurately, imperialist cause tended to be clerks rather than laymen—as did those, like the Englishman John of Salisbury (*c.* 1115–80), who attempted to produce a sophisticated reconciliation between the claims of the rival authorities.

At Bologna itself legal studies were rapidly dominated by the work of the ecclesiastical canonists. Master Gratian of Bologna regarded Roman law with suspicion and his *Concordia Discordantium Canonum*, compiled by about 1140, provided both the essential legal sources and the textbook for the universalist Church. Gratian's work was almost immediately adopted in the schools as the basis for the study of all canon law. In 1159 one of Gratian's most ardent disciples and pupils, Master Roland Bandinelli, became Pope Alexander III: the era of the great lawyer-popes had dawned and with it the firm establishment of a Church that was legally corporate and catholic as well as holy and apostolic.

Faith and reason

The intellectual activity within the new universities was, like the institutional form those universities took, latent in the developments of the previous century. The trend towards a greater sense of cohesion and common purpose was as evident in the one sphere as the other. Before 1200, the most ingenious and daring speculative thinkers wrote, like St Anselm of Canterbury (*c.* 1033–1109), St Bernard (1090–1153) and Peter Abelard (1079–1142), with a markedly individual tone and spirit. Unlike each other in almost every respect, these three famous figures were all typical of the pre-university age. They were still the masters and not the servants of the very logical skills and academic techniques they helped to promote. By the end of the century individual philosophers and theologians as well as lawyers were beginning to seem less important than the movement within which they took their place. Scholasticism was in process of becoming, for good or ill, more important than the scholar.

To a very large extent the process by which intellectual enquiry (and eventually university syllabuses) came to centre on a relatively small body of universally accepted subject matter was dictated by the very nature of the source material available. The texts available to twelfth-century scholars, the Bible, the Early Fathers and St Augustine, were theoretically guides to the whole range of human thought—especially when supplemented by the contemporary influx of Islamic ideas and interpretations of classical works via Spain and Sicily. But the transmission and copying of books was a slow and expensive business. Few scholars, even in a big cathedral school or university, had a large library at their personal disposal. More often than is easy to imagine in the modern world such practical limitations controlled the development of a scholar's thought.

The most obvious solution to these problems was the provision of large quantities of one common textbook, which accordingly then became extremely influential—often beyond its merits. Gratian's *Concordia* is an example of a supremely successful as well as popular manual. Its theological counterpart is the *Four Books of the Sentences*, written in the early eleven-fifties by Peter the Lombard, educated at Bologna and Reims and a teacher in the cathedral school of Paris from 1140 until his death twenty years later. Peter's systematic compilation of questions from the Bible and patristic authorities (especially St Augustine) did more than any other single work to determine the aims and principles of scholastic thought for the next two centuries.

The emergence in the last half of the twelfth century of the mature critic was the result of a long and arduous process of technical enquiry. Ivo of Chartres (1040–1117) had directed attention to the need to group texts intelligibly; it was probably under the influence of the canonists that in his *Sic et Non* of about 1122 Abelard took the essential step of providing a carefully planned proof that 'careful and frequent questioning is the basic key to wisdom' and that 'by doubting we come to questioning, and by questioning we perceive the truth'.

Never a rationalist but always a logician, Abelard's immense influence on philosophical and theological study was not seriously undermined by the personal tragedy and ecclesiastical censure of his last years. With his attack on the Platonic concepts of Forms or Ideas ('the universal is a mere vocal sound' or at most a 'mental image'), Abelard liberated philosophy from the very real danger of a descent into a wilderness of confused metaphysics.

So was inaugurated one of the world's greatest debates. Twelfth-century learning left no greater legacy to the future than the belief that it was the Church's duty to reconcile, or at least to try to do so, the miraculous workings of God's grace with the rational speculation of the human mind. This fundamental issue was not of course an entirely new one; but it was during the age of Abelard and his successors that it came to dominate the intellectual scene. The developing skills and sophistication of the scholar, together with an increasing view of the divinity in human forms, gave the issue an urgency it had previously lacked. Before the twelfth century theology as a discipline can hardly be said to have existed, except in the limited sense that it justified the obvious —man's enslavement to the Devil and need for redemption by an all powerful and inscrutable divinity. But the new emphasis on Christ himself, on God made Man (more fundamental to the 'humanism' of the twelfth century than its interest in classical authors), gave grounds for a more optimistic enquiry into the nature of the Godhead.

Such optimism is already apparent in the writings of St Anselm of Canterbury. Anselm's famous assertions that 'he believed in order that he might understand' ('*Credo ut intelligam*') and that faith sought understanding ('*fides quarens intellectum*') had been shared by St Augustine. But in his famous study of the Atonement, the *Cur Deus Homo?* of about 1097, Anselm laid a novel emphasis upon the humanity of God as Man. During the next 200 years this new doctrine had exhilarating effects. If God was man he would accept and approve all men's attempts to understand him.

This belief seems central to Abelard's life as well as his writings: it accounts for his readiness to embark upon the dangerous passages of intellectual adventure. Several of Abelard's opinions were condemned at the Council of Sens in 1141 through the influence of St Bernard, who wrongly believed that 'this most excellent doctor prefers free will at the expense of grace'. But the spirit in which Abelard conducted his logical investigations long survived his personal downfall. The view that Christ could be directly comprehended through the scope of human intellect or emotion is

Above, the famous twelfth-century lovers Peter Abelard and Heloise, his pupil who bore him a son. Abelard thereafter became a monk and Heloise went to a monastery, but their correspondence continued for many years. Musée Condé, Chantilly.

Below, a twelfth-century miniature of scholars in a ring around their teachers at Canterbury Cathedral. Before the foundation of the universities in the early thirteenth century, the cathedrals were the centres of scholarship. Trinity College, Cambridge.

the common denominator among such various movements of the late twelfth century as the extension of heresy, the emergence of the friars and the passion for academic and eventually university learning.

The problem of heresy

The social and intellectual ferment of the twelfth century consolidated the theoretical supremacy of the Church at the cost of presenting it with its most explicit challenge. In the year 1000, organized heresy, as opposed to pagan survivals and individual eccentricity, seems to have been virtually non-existent in Latin Europe. By 1200 heresy was not only relatively common but potentially dangerous. It is now difficult and perhaps impossible to make an exact assessment of the severity of this threat to the existence and cohesion of the Church. What is clear is that successive popes and members of the ecclesiastical hierarchy considered the danger to be very great indeed. The need to combat and suppress heresy added a note of urgency to the work of scholars and theologians.

The central paradox of twelfth-century heretical movements was that they shared many of the assumptions and ideals of the Church reformers themselves. Heresy rarely took the form of a frontal attack on the institutions of the Church as such and was generally impelled by an intense devotion rather than hostility to the moral tenets of Christian belief. Like the founders of the new monastic orders, the early heretics were almost all inspired by a desire to return to the primitive purity of the communal life led by Christ and his apostles.

The chronological development of medieval heresy was, accordingly, closely related to the extension of ecclesiastical power and influence throughout western Europe. Only after the middle of the twelfth century did a hitherto diverse series of unorthodox doctrines crystallize into organized sects and communities—at exactly the time that orthodox schools of thought were solidifying into coherent academic and university disciplines. Before that date, the history of heresy, like that of all abstract learning, tended to consist of a series of isolated individuals, sometimes able to attract a group of disciples but rarely able to promote a general movement.

Nevertheless, even in this early period heretical opinions had to be condemned, however academic and esoteric they might appear. St Bernard took considerable pains to combat the ingenious if perverse distinction drawn by Gilbert de la Porrée (1076–1154) between the 'essence' and 'substance' of the divine. But neither Gilbert de la Porrée, nor his contemporary Abelard, nor Berengar of Tours, excommunicated in 1050 for his unorthodox conception of the Eucharist, held opinions likely to provide the mainspring of popular heresy. Arnold of Brescia (died 1155) owed his mob support in Rome and other Italian towns not to his doctrinal heresies (according to tradition he was a pupil of Abelard at Paris) but to a violent attack on clerical property.

Much more menacing was the rapid growth, in the years that followed Arnold of Brescia's execution, of the sect whose members called themselves the Cathari, the 'Pure'. Known in southern France as the Albigensians because of their centre at the city of Albi in the department of Tarn, the Cathari owed much of their evangelical success to the practical argument that they attained a higher standard of morality than the established priesthood. What made this heresy particularly dangerous and indeed unique was its combination of well-defined and revolutionary doctrine with a sophisticated organization.

Although twelfth-century Catharism remains a mysterious movement because the surviving evidence usually compels us to see it through the eyes of its Christian persecutors, certain themes emerge quite clearly. Catharist teaching was based on a form of Manichaean dualism apparently synthesized in the Byzantine Empire and especially by the Bogomil sect in Bulgaria: its stark antithesis between the eternal principles of good and evil appealed on intellectual grounds to the learned as well as emotionally to the ill-educated or illiterate lesser clergy and urban poor of northern Italy and southern France. Above all, members of the Cathari derived cohesion and strength from their belief that they were members of an exclusive sect: both its leaders, the *perfecti*, and the much larger group of ordinary believers, the *credentes*, could hope to die in purity and be assured of an everlasting life in paradise.

So attractive a creed won the sympathetic interest and eventually the support of many nobles in southern France, an area which had not previously experienced the full weight of orthodox Christian reform movements. By the close of the twelfth century the Albigensian heresy in the Midi could no longer be contained by the local agencies of the Church. Fortunately for the papacy, when in 1208 Innocent III preached a crusade against the heretics after the murder of his legate at the court of Raymond VI, Count of Toulouse, he unleashed the territorial appetites of the northern French nobility.

But the experience of the Albigensian heresy left a permanent adverse legacy to the organized Church. The papacy allowed itself to be forced, initially against its will, into the belief that all proposals for radical reform of the clergy were dangerous. The popes' fears that they might lose their spiritual leadership led them to proclaim as heretical movements which, at the beginning of the eleventh century, would have been legitimized and incorporated within the Church. The career of Peter Valdès or Waldo (died 1217) provides the classic example of this process.

Waldo, a rich merchant of Lyons, was, according to a familiar medieval tradition, so moved by the words of *Matthew* xix 21 that he distributed his money to the poor and adopted the life of a mission-preacher and mendicant. His followers, the Waldenses or *Vaudois*, initially settled in communities on the French side of the Alps and appealed in vain for ecclesiastical recognition at the third Lateran Council in 1179. Five years later Pope Lucius III placed the Waldenses under the ban, and they were compelled to elaborate their own primitive ministry and moral code. Only after Innocent III instituted a crusade against them in 1209 did they come to attack the papacy as anti-Christ and condemn themselves to a centuries-long endurance of sustained but never completely successful persecution.

Against the background of the Albigensian heresy it is understandable that the Fourth Lateran Council of 1215 should have required bishops to hunt out and bring to justice all persons suspected of heresy. More questionable was Pope Gregory IX's decision in 1233 to entrust the friars with independent authority to try and sentence proved heretics in southern France. The delegation of the work of combating heresy to local agencies and secular governments was administratively convenient but deprived the papacy of effective control over inquistorial methods and procedures.

The coming of the friars

And as ye go, preach, saying, The Kingdom of heaven is at hand. Heal the sick, cleanse the lepers, raise the dead, cast out devils: freely ye have received, freely give. Provide neither gold, nor silver, nor brass in your purses, not script for your journey, neither two coats, neither shoes, nor yet staves: for the workman is worthy of his meat. (*Matthew*, x 7–10).

These words, interpreted by St Francis (1182–1226) as a personal call when he heard them read in the church of the Portiuncula two miles below Assisi one morning in or about 1208, lie at the heart of the extraordinary success of the new mendicant orders in thirteenth-century Europe. There is no doubt that St Francis and his Order were the single biggest factor in reawakening primitive Christian faith during the years after the 1215 Lateran Council. By forging a link between clergy and laity, the Franciscan and to a lesser extent the Dominican, Carmelite and Augustinian friars helped to save the organized Church from indifference and contempt. They postponed, and this is their most significant historical achievement, the slow disintegration of the universalist Church for at least one and possibly several generations.

The mendicant orders (living entirely on alms) of the early thirteenth century were a genuinely revolutionary force eventually compelled to subserve conservative ends. St Francis himself stands quite apart from all the other founders of religious orders within the Catholic Church. Unlike Saints Benedict and Bernard before him or Teresa and Ignatius Loyola at a later period, he was both unable and deliberately unwilling to provide a code of moral and public conduct by which his followers should live. At a period when the development of the Church was characterized by the extensions of legal and administrative procedures, St Francis's refusal to codify his principles or organize his disciples stands out in stark contrast.

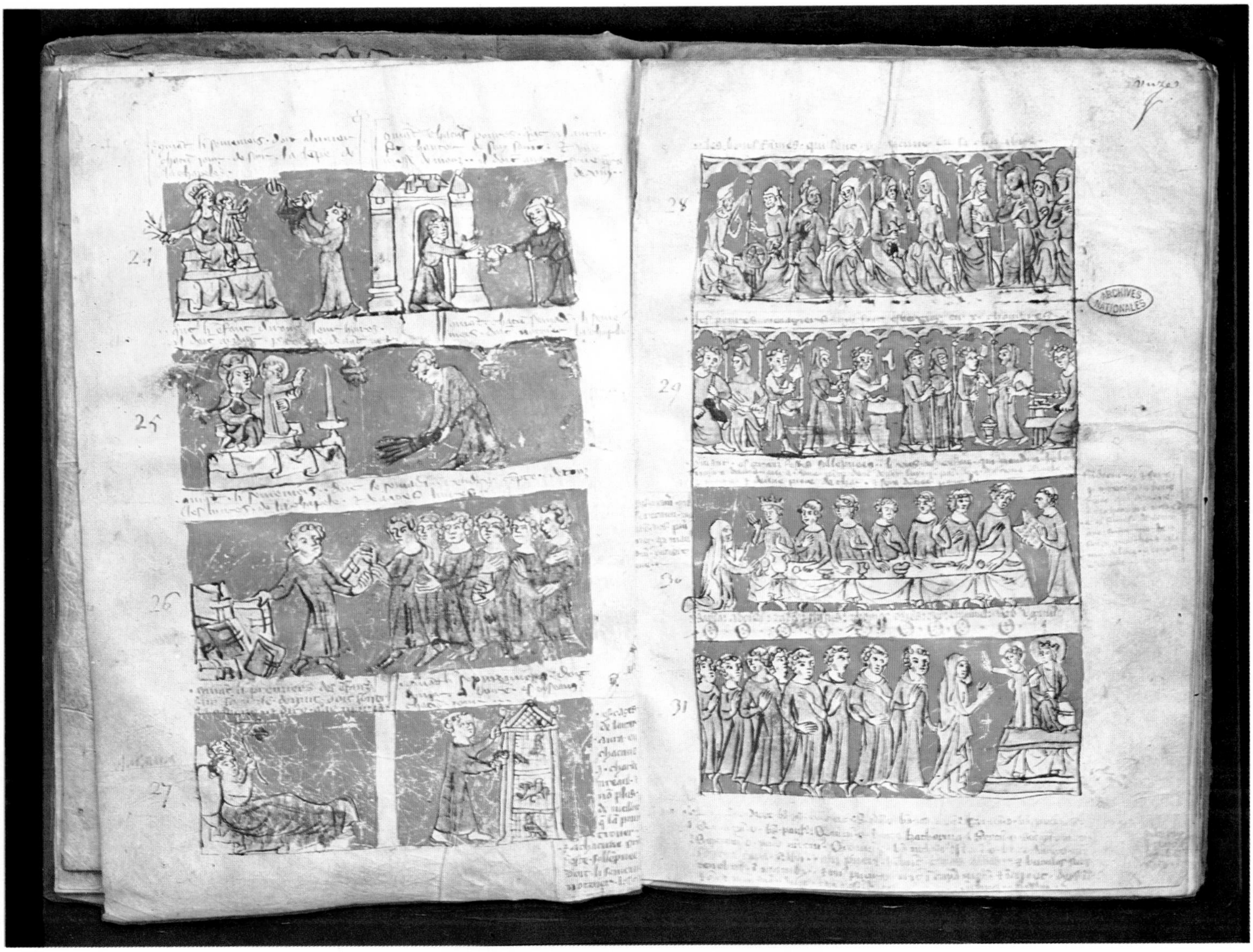

This refusal owed its roots to two deeply felt conclusions. The only necessary guide to a perfect human existence was Christ's own life; for that reason obedience might be withheld from any command which ran contrary to each individual's personal conception of spiritual perfection. In the words of the first Franciscan rule, later modified, the *Regula Prima* of 1221, 'If any official orders a brother to do something against our life and his own soul, the latter shall not be obliged to obey.' Secondly, it was a fundamental feature of St Francis's message that he addressed—on Christ's behalf—all inhabitants of Christendom and indeed the

Above, in the thirteenth century schools and universities were founded in many cities of western Europe. This painting shows the intellectual, social and religious training given at the school of Ave Maria in Paris. Archives Nationale, Paris.

Left, St Bernard preaching in the main square of Siena in the early twelfth century; medieval Christianity was continually revitalized by reformers winning popularity amongst the laity rather than by initiatives from the papacy. Siena Cathedral.

earth. In his own words, 'I tell you truly that the Lord has chosen and sent out friars for the profit and salvation of all men in this world.' No religious reformer or leader has ever preached a less exclusive creed.

The early mendicants were therefore sharply divided from previous reforming movements within the Church, all of which had been intent upon the creation of a saintly and usually contemplative élite. If the first Franciscans and Dominicans have any ancestors, they must be sought within the ranks of twelfth-century heretics rather than among the monastic orders. The intriguing analogies between the careers of Peter Waldo of Lyons and his contemporary Francis of Assisi have often been noticed. Like Waldo, St Francis came from a wealthy urban background and renounced the secular life in order to become a hermit. His personal experience of penury not only taught him the religious rewards of poverty but enabled him to appeal to the poor in northern Italian towns. Very little can be known for certain about the social origins of the first generation of Franciscan friars; but it seems very likely that they drew their recruits from a much lower level of society than the contemporary monastery or nunnery.

More important still, the mendicants deliberately addressed and cultivated a religious audience among the urban middle-class and working-class groups whose spiritual needs had never been fully met by the monastic orders nor even—as far as we can tell—by their parish clergy. Many of the latter were widely criticized, probably with justice, for their neglect of preaching duties. Accordingly, the friars' success in establishing themselves within the town environment was immediate and remarkable. In Venice the two enormous brick churches of the Franciscans and Dominicans, the Frari and SS. Giovanni e Paulo, still tower above the numerous other Gothic, Renaissance and Baroque churches within the city.

Apostolic poverty, with its implied rebuke for the life being currently led by the higher clergy, had consequently a practical as well as doctrinal significance for the history of the mendicants. From the very early days of the movement it was predictable that this issue would raise great controversy within as well as without the Order. When in 1322 Pope John XXII finally condemned the traditional Franciscan thesis that the poverty of Christ and the apostles was absolute, he did so only at the cost of antagonizing many of the more ascetic 'spirituals', who established small communities of *fraticelli*, especially in the hills of southern Italy. A century earlier apostolic poverty had in fact been crucial to the Franciscans' evangelical success, for it made movement from town to town economically essential as well as spiritually desirable.

The mobility of the first members of the mendicant orders is startling even by modern standards. Within six weeks of their landing at Dover on 10 September 1224 (four days before St Francis himself received the stigmata on Monte Alverna), the first small group of Franciscans to reach England had established three important settlements at Canterbury, London and Oxford. St Francis' own two most ambitious preaching tours—to southern France and Spain in 1214–15 and to eastern Europe and Egypt in 1219—seem to have been conducted at breakneck speed. The friars' ability to carry both the faith and diplomatic messages over vast distances remained one of their most spectacular characteristics; Carpini, the Franciscan head of a mission sent by Innocent IV to the Mongols between 1245 and 1247, is said to have travelled 3,000 miles in 106 days—a feat which is both physically more impressive and historically more significant than Marco Polo's more famous journey a generation later.

It was within rather than outside Christendom that the itinerant preaching of the early friars had its most profound effect. As early as 1256 there were 1,242 Franciscan friars in the English provinces dispersed among forty-nine houses sited in the largest cathedral and county towns. By this date, however, general mobility on the part of the rank and file of the mendicant orders was already on the wane. Though the itinerant ideal survived and the friars were never restricted like the monks by an oath of *stabilitas loci* (literally 'stay in one locality') it was a feature of their extraordinary expansion that they should become increasingly preoccupied with financial and administrative concerns. Similar pressures were forced upon the friars by the papacy itself. Although Innocent III tentatively supported the principles advocated by the early friars, and later popes gave them formal approval and took them under their personal protection and authority, they insisted in return that the new orders should have a series of official rules and some form of internal disciplinary organization.

The gradual transition from radical idealism to institutional conservatism was as familiar and disillusioning a process in the Middle Ages as it is today: but by their very nature the friars were exposed to particularly scathing criticism on these grounds. Before the end of the thirteenth century the mendicants were already beginning to assume their conventional role in the popular and literary imagination: they were the predestined scapegoats for the sins of all the clergy as well as their own.

Equally remarkable although more understandable was the rapid evolution of a mass evangelical movement into an élite of literate intelligent people. Among the renunciations which St Francis had required from his disciples was that of all human learning. A strong and often explicit anti-intellectual tendency is as evident in the early Franciscans of North Italy as in contemporary heretical sects. But even before Francis's death in 1226, his own Order was gravitating towards the universities. All successful evangelism requires a modicum of intellectual argument: evangelism against a background of organized heresy demands mental subtlety and learning as well. This was a lesson learnt by the Spaniard St Dominic (1170–1222) during his ten years' mission among the Albigensian of Languedoc. His Order of Friars Preachers, which held its first general chapter at Bologna in the year before Dominic's death, was specifically directed at combating heresy by means of the spoken word and eloquent sermon. Both the need for technical training and the fear, probably misplaced, of a revival of influential academic heresy drove the Dominicans and Franciscans towards the universities—above all to the universities of Paris and Oxford.

The universities

The Dominican friars arrived at Paris in 1217 and the Franciscans two years later. Both orders were intent on founding schools for their own members, the most talented of whom were soon to be enrolled for degrees in the theological faculty of the university. They could hardly have chosen a more auspicious moment. In 1215 a papal legate had at last recognized the right of the *studium generale* of Paris to make statutes of its own: the tortuous process by which the cathedral school of Notre Dame evolved into a self-governing university corporation was almost complete. For the next two centuries this greatest of the 'masters' universities' was to be the dominant centre of logical, metaphysical and theological studies within western Europe.

Not, of course, that Paris, at which surprisingly few of the outstanding teachers were ever Frenchmen, enjoyed a complete monopoly of higher learning. The origins of the university of Oxford, where Robert Pullen had been lecturing in theology as early as 1133, are even more mysterious than those of Paris; but in 1214 the schools there acquired not only corporate recognition by the papacy but a chancellor, deriving his authority from the Bishop of Lincoln although soon to become the elected master of the schools.

Throughout the early thirteenth century the University of Cambridge, which seems to have owed its establishment to a migration of dispersed Oxford students in 1209, tended to exist in the shadow of England's first university. But by the lifetime of Robert Holcot (*c*. 1300–49), a Dominican teacher deeply influenced by William of Ockham, Cambridge had developed a genuinely distinctive approach to theological and philosophical problems and its reputation already rivalled that of Oxford.

In southern Europe the early thirteenth century was a period of more dramatic expansion in the number of universities. Within Italy, Bologna continued to tower above its rivals, and its three most characteristic features—lay participation, the primacy of legal studies and the constitutional subordination of the teaching masters to the student 'nations' and their rectors—proved the dominating influences. The Universities of Vicenza (1204) and Padua (1222) were in fact the products of student migrations from Bologna. Naples, founded by Frederick II in 1224, as well as the early Spanish Universities of Palencia (*c*. 1208), Salamanca (*c*. 1220) and Valladolid (*c*. 1250), were more artificial creations, promoted and sponsored for political and bureaucratic purposes by a secular prince. All were modelled on the Bolognese rather than the Parisian pattern and all concentrated upon the study of law.

The new French universities of this period, Angers (1229), Toulouse (founded by papal bull in 1229) and Orléans (1235), were also most famous for their provision of a technical training in canon and civil law. At Montpellier a celebrated medical school in existence by 1137, rapidly eclipsed its Italian counterpart at Salerno, arguably the oldest of all European universities although not recognized as such by any public authority until 1234. All these southern European and French universities were of great social and cultural significance in spreading the ideal of the cosmopolitan and professional scholar: Thomas Aquinas himself studied at Naples University for a period before his move to Paris in 1245. But their preoccupation with legal and practical studies and the influence exerted upon them by lay sovereigns, municipal authorities and the students themselves tended to inhibit them from the free pursuit of speculative and theological enquiry. Bologna itself had no regular theological faculty until 1353.

It was therefore at Paris and Oxford that the thirteenth century saw the most determined and comprehensive attempt ever made to apply the disciplines of an academic university training to the abstract issues of philosophy and theology. In these two centres the complete ascendancy of theology, now best defined as the philosophical interpretation of theological texts, would have been inconceivable in the pre-university age. As several contemporaries noted and lamented, the traditional seven liberal arts were seriously neglected and the university arts course was directed towards an intensive study of logic and the dialectic, *grammatica speculativa*, at the expense of grammar and science.

Despite the obvious disadvantages of increasing inflexibility and the use of a highly technical jargon, the assets of the new professionalism and restriction to sharply defined theological and philosophical problems rapidly made themselves apparent. Perhaps most students suffered rather than profited from a sophisticated university syllabus by which a master's degree in theology depended upon fourteen years of severely technical training in the intricacies of the theological argument. But a handful of extremely talented thinkers, among whom Alexander of Hales (died 1245), Bonaventure (1221–74), Albert the Great (*c*. 1200–80) and Thomas Aquinas (1226–74) are the most famous, were able to exploit their extraordinary academic expertise for the widest possible purpose—the production of the *summa*, a comprehensive and systematic treatment of the full range of human knowledge and experience.

The age of synthesis

Like most universities at most times, those of thirteenth-century Europe owed their greatest achievements to the tension set up between the self-enclosed corporate community and the more radical influences of contemporary society and culture. The

Above, all education in the thirteenth century was in the hands of the monks and the friars, and now many highly educated men, including university graduates, sought careers in the Church and the civil service. British Library, London.

Top, a thirteenth-century painting of St Francis of Assisi, from the church in Subiaco. Francis had been rich and pleasure-loving before he became a mendicant preacher sworn to absolute poverty. Chiesa Inferiore, Subiaco.

Opposite, a friar preaching outside a church; in the thirteenth century the friars won considerable authority by their preaching, in which they were prepared to attack social and political injustice and to defend the weak. Fitzwilliam Museum, Cambridge.

great scholastics of Paris and Oxford depended for lasting influence on factors quite other than their connection with the university world, its agreed syllabuses and conventional teaching methods.

In the first place, the great majority of the productive thinkers of the thirteenth century were friars: Hales and his pupil Bonaventure belonged to the Franciscan Order, while Albert and Aquinas were Dominicans. Membership of a mendicant order provided such men with a sense of purpose and cohesion which the confused tangle of university affairs alone would have made impossible. Dominican and Franciscan scholars, previously educated within their Orders' own schools and hence permitted to proceed directly to the study of theology on arrival at a university, possessed an organization and *esprit de corps* which made them the acknowledged leaders of speculative thought in both Paris and Oxford.

At the same time, the rivalry between the two orders and, more significantly still, the jealousy displayed towards them by the secular masters tended to polarize intellectual activity within fairly well-defined and self-generating schools.

More direct influential was the intoxicating effect on Paris and Oxford scholars of the works of Aristotle, by any standards the greatest single determinant on the patterns of their thought. Many translations from Aristotle had reached the West, usually from Arabic sources, as early as the middle of the twelfth century. But it was only after the formal establishment of the new universities that revised Latin translations directly from the Greek fully revealed the implications and basic premises of Aristotle's own thought. For the first time medieval philosophers were presented with a detailed, comprehensive and apparently self-sufficient analysis of a universe in which the Christian God played no part. The dangers of indiscriminate Aristotelianism were rapidly appreciated: as early as the 1220s Pope Gregory IX warned the University of Paris against the use of Aristotle's texts until they had been 'examined and purified'. In one sense perhaps the greatest achievement of the thirteenth-century scholastics was their limitation and restriction of the potentially explosive effects of Aristotle's pagan philosophy.

To the great Aristotelian challenge of the age (all the greater because by contrast so little of Plato was either read or understood) three responses were possible. The first was that of the so-called 'Latin Averroists', whose acceptance of Aristotle's philosophical tenets wherever they might lead broke the link between reason and faith and led directly towards heresy and their outright condemnation and suppression in the last quarter of the century. The second and, generally speaking, most speedy response was essentially conservative: it might prove possible to counter Aristotle's influence in the interests of traditional 'Augustinianism' by denying the validity of his metaphysical assumptions and emphasizing the supremacy of providential revelation over the human 'active intellect'.

The most famous and eventually most influential of all attempts to grapple with the Aristotelian legacy, however, was that of Aquinas and his associates. The latter decided not only, like Bonaventure, to annex but positively to incorporate Aristotle's teachings (including his metaphysics) within the Christian world-view. No one before or since has ever mastered Aristotle's thought more thoroughly than Aquinas; by common assent the latter's 'Great Synthesis', originally planned by his master, Albert the Great, is the most elaborate and ambitious intellectual structure of the Middle Ages and perhaps of all time. Before his death at the age of forty-eight in 1274, Aquinas had written an extraordinary number of separate but interlocking works, whose implications, sometimes conservative and sometimes very much the reverse, are impossible to summarize in brief. Even the author's own synthesis and introduction to his entire corpus, the *Summa Theologiae*, was started in 1266 but never completed.

For modern philosophers Aristotle's astonishing readiness to take sensible reality as the starting point of all philosophical enquiry ('Nothing exists in the intellect unless first in the senses') has led to his enduring relevance. But for medieval thinkers, despite grave doubts both before and after his death, Aquinas immediately became the central and inescapable figure simply because his speculations marked the climax of the continuous desire to press reason into the service of faith. Opinion is still inevitably divided as to how far Aquinas achieved a successful reconciliation of such contrasting views as those between the divine and natural law, the Christian God and the 'prime mover', faith and reason themselves. It seems indisputable that Aquinas's own intentions were conservative in every sphere: like his predecessors, he was very conscious of his membership of Christendom's clerical élite and never faltered in his exaltation of the Eucharist and the status of the priesthood. Equally clearly, and by a strange paradox, the conception of Aquinas was never in its own period given the benefit of a genuinely fair trial and investigation. Aquinas's contemporaries lacked Aquinas's own intellectual nerve: within three years of his death, many of the more Aristotelian elements in his thought were officially condemned by the Bishop of Paris.

Rationalism and the natural sciences

It has been said that fourteenth-century thinkers were obsessed with the limits rather than the scope of reason. Certainly they had few other characteristics in common. It is accordingly not surprising that the work of men like Duns Scotus, William of Ockham, Thomas Bradwardine, Marsiglio of Padua and Bartolus of Sassoferrato was based on different premises and came to even more different conclusions. What is startling by comparison with the thirteenth century is the failure of the universities to attempt a serious reconciliation of the many discordant voices.

The history of thought, like that of art, is prone to move in cycles; and it was probably inevitable that a long period of uncoordinated criticism should follow the coherent theories on philosophy. In particular, the most powerful techniques of the twelfth and thirteenth centuries became the most serious liabilities of the later Middle Ages. The systematization of logic and dialectic as the fundamental weapon of intellectual enquiry finally led to a serious chasm between life and thought. The ascendancy of theology, which had once liberated, now inhibited detached philosophical enquiry. Fourteenth-century intellectuals speak to the modern world more forcefully and cogently than those of any other medieval period; but they were the last representatives of a gradually dying common purpose.

By common agreement the three greatest figures in the history of the critical reaction against Thomist (Thomas Aquinas) philosophy and the authoritarian claims of the Church were Duns Scotus, William of Ockham and Marsiglio of Padua. Of these Duns Scotus was certainly the most complex and probably the most profound thinker. Before his death at the age of forty in Cologne (1308) the 'subtle doctor' had prepared the way for a widespread retreat from the intellectual positions of the thirteenth century. Indeed his works, and particularly the two *Commentaries on the Sentences,* take the form of an attempt to grapple with the conclusions of Aquinas in the light of their partial condemnation by the Bishop of Paris, Etienne Templier, in 1277.

Like Aquinas, Duns Scotus drew heavily

on Aristotle, but in his case for the paradoxical purpose of liberating Christian theology from the stranglehold of pagan philosophy. Duns replaced the Thomist emphasis on knowledge and reason by stressing the primacy of God's love and will. If God only does as he wills it follows that no human attempt to explain divine action can ever be successful; for by its very nature God's Will is beyond the grasp of a purely rational enquiry. On the other hand, Duns believed that human reason and divine revelation still complemented each other and that there was no contradiction between the two.

It was William of Ockham (*c.* 1300–49) who took the vital step of denying that there was any inherent connection between faith and reason at all, thus dealing the deathblow to the central assumption upon which the great intellectual structures of the twelfth and thirteenth centuries has been built. Ockham's basic premise was the sovereignty of the individual thing or being; this alone was real, this alone could be known. It therefore followed—by the principles of Ockham's razor—that the introduction of abstract terms or concepts would destroy clarity of perception and comprehension. 'Beings shall not be multiplied without necessity (*entia non sunt multiplicanda praeter necessitatem*).' If intuition rather than abstraction was the means of acquiring knowledge, the road to complete intellectual agnosticism was open. As God himself can never be known intuitively, his existence can presumably never be proved. Such a belief even had destructive effects on the political theory of the age. The papacy's claim to a distinctive knowledge of God's purposes could not be defended in a world where there could never be any certainty as to His actions.

Ockham's hostile and personally stormy relationship with the fourteenth-century papacy was shared by his contemporary, Marsiglio of Padua (*c.* 1275–1342). Accepting the basic premise that the nature of God's intervention on earth had to be taken on faith and could never be explained by reason, Marsiglio went on to consider how 'peace and tranquillity' could best be attained in this world. In his *Defensor Pacis*, completed in 1324, Marsiglio subordinated the Church to a state whose authority was derived from the sovereign people. The papacy enjoyed no inherent jurisdiction either in the temporal or, the spiritual fields, for in the latter too the principal authority should be a general council representing the views of all members of the Church, laymen as well as priests. Such views, associated with Ockham's philosophical scepticism, achieved a short-term theoretical success during the conciliar movement. Their long-term effect was even more revolutionary for they attacked the central medieval thesis of an authoritarian clerical order with an undisputed right to guide the fortunes of the laity.

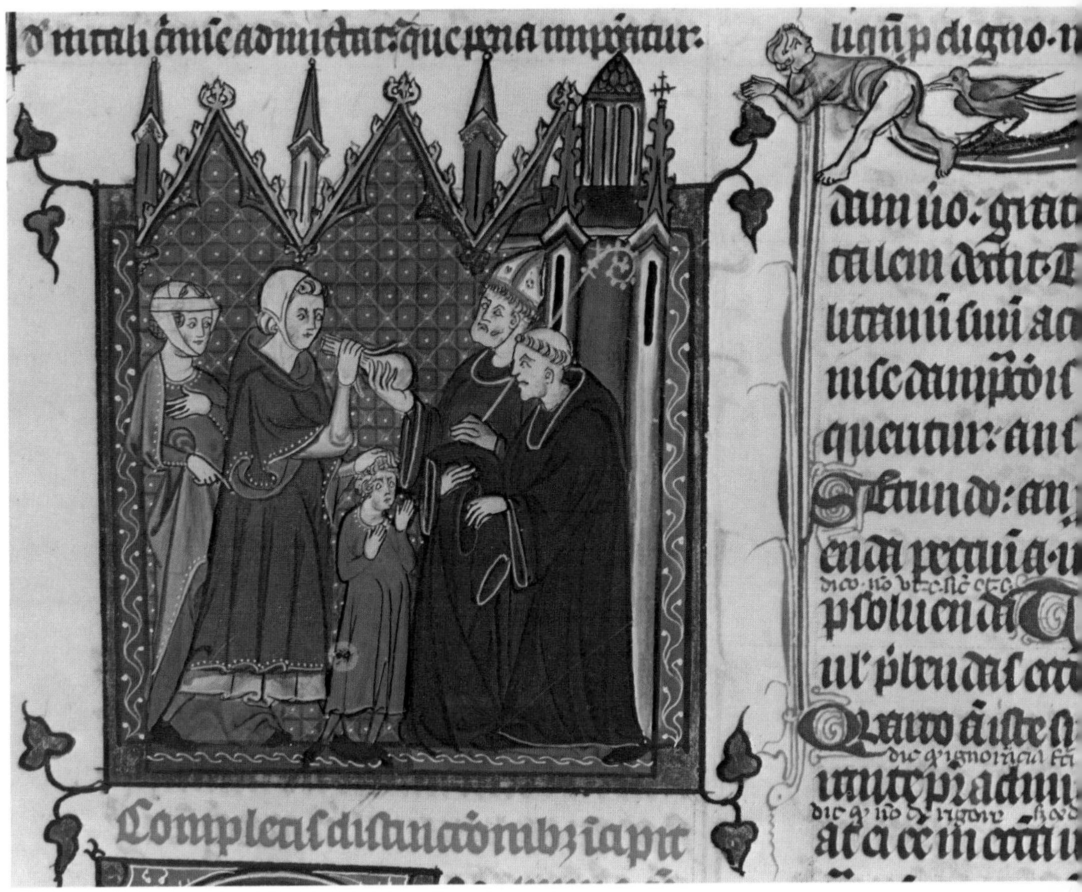

Ockham's theory of knowledge had equally revolutionary effects in the field of scientific enquiry. The thirteenth century had seen important developments, especially at Oxford, within the study of mathematics, optics and astronomy; but poor communications restricted knowledge of the new discoveries to a small circle of university scholars, often uninterested in the practical application of their theories.

The work of Roger Bacon (*c.* 1214–92) at Paris and Oxford is the most famous example; it was characteristic that he should advocate experiment as a method of rational investigation without—as fas as is known—engaging in much experimental work on his own account.

The dawning realization—at first very tentative—that a gulf had opened between the principles behind natural and supernatural knowledge lies at the basis of the scientific renaissance at the University of Paris in the late fourteenth century. Jean Buridan (*c.* 1300–58) and Nicholas Oresme (*c.* 1320–82) shared Ockham's own preoccupation with dynamics—a topic which raised in a practical form the problems of physical reality and causation.

But despite recent claims to the contrary, the academic study of science in the medieval university was trapped within an intellectual blind alley. The ability of the French scholars in question is undoubted; but it could hardly prevail against the technological limitations of their period and the disruption of the University of Paris which accompanied the renewed outbreak of the Hundred Years' War in the decades after 1400.

Above, a twelfth-century drawing of the mandrake, a plant believed to have the body of a human and used as a painkiller. Medieval scientists had little interest in experiment or controlled observation, and most medical and botanical knowledge came from the herbalists. Walters Art Gallery, Baltimore.

Top, parents offer an abbot a bag of money to accept their son as a novice. As centres of learning, rich landowners and the main source of the civil service in most kingdoms, the monasteries could provide talented people with a successful career.

Opposite, a fresco in S. Maria Novella church in Florence depicting St Dominic, St Peter and St Thomas Aquinas refuting heretics. Aquinas achieved the union of Greek and Christian philosophy by explaining the separate roles of reason and faith. Santa Maria Novella, Florence.

The collapse of universalism

Although the intellectual synthesis of the age of Aquinas was destroyed by self-inflicted wounds, it could in any case never have survived the political, social and economic changes of the fourteenth century. The decline of the papacy's ecumenical authority, the failure of the international crusading ideal, the outbreak of sustained and disruptive warfare in northern Europe, and the economic crisis which preceded and followed the incidence of widespread bubonic plague were symptoms of the general disintegration of a previous world order. Throughout western Europe this disintegration can be observed in a concrete geographical form: provincial tendencies triumphed at the expense of central authority and claims to universal dominion. The political history of Germany after the period of 1257–75, when the country had no effective ruler, is the classic example of the success of these separatist forces at the expense of imperial power; but developments there can be paralleled in Italy, France and Scotland.

It must be emphasized that the characteristic political unit in the age of Petrarch and Chaucer was usually the dynastic, sometimes the city, but never the 'nation' state. Nevertheless the new or newly articulate political localism of the period helped to promote the rapid acceleration of cultural and intellectual differentiation within Europe. In this sphere, a decisive role was often played by the prince's 'court', a social milieu which acted as a magnetic force on artists and writers to an extent that would have been unthinkable in the period of Abelard or even Aquinas.

It would be misleading to draw too sharp a line between the world of court and university. One of the major social functions of the latter was to prepare intelligent clerks and sometimes laymen for the service of their prince. The talented group of writers who clustered around the entourage of Charles V of France and his sons at the end of the century, men like Nicholas Oresme and Pierre D'Ailly (1350–1420), always preserved close links with the University of Paris from which they had received their training. On the other hand, and by its very nature, the prince's court encouraged both its clerical and lay members to adopt a more secular approach to life and learning than was possible or desirable in a medieval university. It is a suitable and symbolic commentary on the new situation that Boccaccio (1313–75) attempted but quickly abandoned the study of canon law, while Geoffrey Chaucer (1345–1400) probably never experienced the dubious benefits of a university education at all.

Boccaccio and Chaucer are of course most renowned for their central role in the literary development of their respective languages. Without question the fourteenth was the decisive century for the emergence or revival of the spoken literatures of western Europe. Here too was another threat, at first indirect, to the primacy of the medieval university. The persistence of the belief that the universal language of Latin was the most suitable vehicle for the communication of serious intellectual enquiry must not be underestimated: it was to encourage fifteenth-century Italian humanists in their ambitious but fundamentally misguided attempt to revive Ciceronian Latin as an all-sufficient language. But by 1400 many writers were already and often painfully aware of the challenge to medieval Latin. Of the three major works of the English poet John Gower (*c.* 1330–1408), the *Miroir de l'omme* was written in French, the *Vox Clamantis* in Latin and the *Confessio Amantis* in English.

More significantly still, the fourteenth century revealed the advantages of the spoken word as a medium of instruction and edification within the Church itself. A large proportion of European parish priests at all times in the Middle Ages would have been unable to read the Latin Vulgate, let alone the writings of Aquinas or Ockham. But the effect of such developments as the inflammatory vernacular sermons of John Milic in Prague during the 1360s or the early English versions of the Bible which appeared a few years later was to make clear as never before the divorce between the language of the university lecture-room and the world of practical Christianity.

However, the rapid expansion in the number of European universities during the later Middle Ages reminds us that these institutions continued to fulfil an important social function, as well as testifying to the strength of national differences. In 1300 Christendom possessed twenty-three universities, all situated in Italy or the Spanish peninsula except for five in France (of which Paris alone was in the first rank) and Oxford and Cambridge in England. Two centuries later there were seventy-five universities, including three in Scotland as well as sixteen in areas east of the Rhine.

It is clear that the foundation of universities like Prague (1348), Vienna (1365) and St Andrews (1411) represented a reaction against the previous ascendancy of Paris, Oxford and Bologna, in the interests of Bohemian, Austrian and Scottish regional needs. Similarly these and other universities attracted local aristocratic interest, patronage and even participation to an extent unparalleled before 1300. The rapid growth of colleges within the *studium generale*, most dramatically seen at Oxford and Cambridge, can readily be interpreted as part of the general trend towards a view of the university as a centre of local privilege rather than international learning. On the other hand it might be argued that the multiplication of European universities, nearly all deriving both their institutional and educational patterns from the Parisian and Bolognese archetypes, delayed for a while the complete collapse of an international intelligentsia.

The career of Nicolas Copernicus (1473–1543), who studied at the Universities of Cracow, Bologna, Padua, and Ferrara, and who lectured in mathematics at Rome itself (before settling at Frauenburg on the Baltic), illustrates the survival of the ideal of the cosmopolitan scholar. Copernicus was reading a text of Thomas Aquinas in the week before he died.

Late medieval heresy

The heresies associated with the English John Wycliffe (*c.* 1329–84) and the Czech John Hus (*c.* 1369–1415) brought the disruptive forces within fourteenth-century thought and society to an extreme but not illogical conclusion. Both movements eventually took the form of a localized protest against the powerful position of the papacy as the spiritual and doctrinal ruler of Christendom. Lollards and Hussites exploited not only the prevailing anticlericalism of their age but also the spoken or written word as an essential instrument of propaganda. Wycliffe and Hus represented the more detached critical spirit of fourteenth-century thought; at the same time they revealed both the strengths and weaknesses of its universities. Academic unorthodox opinion might develop, given the appropriate social conditions, into popular heresy; but academic influence on the world outside the university walls was too insecure and slight to control or guide that heresy's future.

John Wycliffe, more or less permanently resident at Oxford as a university teacher, administrator and writer during the 1360s and 1370s, was, is and will always remain a controversial figure. He can only be understood, if at all, within the context of the Oxford schools. Attempts to explain his career in terms of a series of personal outbursts of moral indignation at the corruption of the Church, or alternatively as the

result of bitterness at his lack of ecclestical promotion, make him a less rather than a more intelligible figure. Wycliffe's intellectual force had intellectual roots. His audacious attacks on traditional doctrines of the Church were grounded in his detailed knowledge of the works of his immediate predecessors.

Wycliffe first acquired a reputation through his vigorous attack on the conclusions of Duns Scotus and William of Ockham. At the same time the nominalists' denial of the value of human reason for the interpretation of divine truth and their consequent emphasis upon God's *potentia absoluta* opened the way to Wycliffe's own eventual belief that revealed doctrine could be derived from the Bible alone. More precisely still, it was Wycliffe's own participation in one of the continuing debating issues of the fourteenth-century university that led to his central conclusion that lordship depended on God's grace alone—with its result that everyone in a state of grace has true lordship. More influential and corrosive because more intelligible was Wycliffe's attack on the doctrine of transubstantiation; but here too the heretical leader's attitude to the Eucharist betrays the ambiguous and academic approach of an ingenious and logic-chopping schoolman.

Perhaps the greatest paradox of Wycliffe's career is that this notorious university scholar founded a popular heresy but not an intellectual school. Sympathy for Wycliffe's ideas in Oxford itself was never very enthusiastic and crumbled away away completely under relatively slight pressure from the English ecclesiastical hierarchy. The complete collapse of university support condemned Lollardry to a sterile future.

Below left, John Wycliffe (c. 1329–84), the English heretical theologian, at first had considerable support at court, which he lost by his refusal to compromise. In the end his greatest achievement was his translation of the Bible into English, completed, after his death, in 1388.

Bottom left, New College, Oxford, founded in 1379 and shown here in a drawing of 1463.

Below, an illustrated edition of Aristotle, produced in Naples in the 1480s. His work was still held in great respect but would shortly be challenged by the revival of Platonism. Vienna State Library.

Opposite, a fifteenth-century woodcut of scholars and their teachers; by this time, many secular schools for the children of the nobility had been founded. Staatsbibliothek, Munich.

Significantly, it was the critical rather than the positive elements within Wycliffe's teachings which gave his 'poor priests' a transitory period of missionary success. The disendowment of the English Church was a programme attractive to many who had little sympathy with Wycliffe's doctrinal heresies. But with one or two exceptions, notably the Herefordshire knight Sir John Oldcastle, who led an ill-organized and abortive rising in early 1414, Lollardry failed to win gentry support. The history of fifteenth-century Lollard survival makes pathetic reading, and the view that it had little direct influence on the English Reformation is undoubtedly correct.

The history of the Hussite movement in Bohemia was very different and much more complex. Like Wycliffe, Hus was a university-trained theologian who eventually came to deny papal supremacy. But his general attitude towards the Church and the priesthood was essentially orthodox: in particular he was intent on exalting rather than disparaging the sacrament of the Eucharist. The most radical feature of English heresy had been Wycliffe's own ideas: there was no parallel for the dramatic political, social and religious consequences which followed the burning of Hus at Constance on 6 July 1415. The religious programme of the Utraquists, who adhered to the principle of communion in both kinds by the laity, appealed to the provincial sentiments and economic self-interest of the Bohemian and Moravian nobility.

In the confusion that followed the collapse of central government in Bohemia, the social extremism of the lower orders in Prague and various Czech villages exploded into a form of wild religious radicalism. The long series of military invasions by imperial expeditions intent on crushing Bohemian resistance positively postponed the restoration of social and religious order. The talented leadership of the Czech knight John Zizka and (after his death in 1424) his successor, the priest Prokop the Shaven, held the anti-Hussite crusades at bay. Only in the 1430s was a compromise settlement arranged. By the 'Compacts' of Prague in 1433 the laity of Bohemia were conceded the right to communion in both kinds; but the papacy recovered its formal control over organized religion in central Europe.

It is dangerously easy to overestimate the significance of the Wycliffe and Hussite movements. Although neither heresy was absolutely annihilated, both were ultimately absorbed within the framework of the medieval Church. Despite the attempt of Prokop's 'warriors of God' to carry their radical creed to Silesia, Saxony, Bavaria and even (in 1433) to Poland, these principalities remained orthodox. Heresy at the subterranean level was regularly found in later medieval Europe, but there is little evidence that it spread significantly in the years immediately after 1400. Events in both England and Bohemia proved that the Church could still contain a direct heterodox attack on its doctrines and authority—not least because such an attack aroused the conservative instincts of the socially dominant nobility and urban patriciates.

The withdrawal from authority

The cultural and intellectual life of fifteenth-century Europe has recently been described as one of 'a strange standstill between seed-time and harvest'. Such a standstill is of course largely illusory; but the remark makes a valid comment upon an age whose religious currents and mental tensions are difficult to define and grasp. A central characteristic of the period was the cultivation of a deliberately individual, informal and unorganized attitude to the problems posed by the existence of this world and the next. It is no coincidence that the most influential book of the period was *The Imitation of Christ*, a manual of personal and austere devotion traditionally assigned to Thomas à Kempis (*c.* 1380–1471), one of the most self-effacing of all Christian teachers.

The greatest failure was without doubt that of the Church itself. There is much truth in the view that the conciliar movement was one of the greatest lost opportunities in the history of the Christian Church. The prelates, theologians and canon lawyers assembled at the councils of Constance and Basle between 1414 and 1442 lacked neither ability nor intellectual courage: they provide an indirect tribute to the continuing strengths of a medieval university education. But like academics at most times, they were unable to convert their proposals into concrete reforms.

The conciliarists suffered from the fact that national and local divergencies had already so divided Christendom that it was even more difficult to establish a unanimous council than an acceptable Pope. Accordingly their movement was less a genuine party than a collection of talented individuals like the French Jean Gerson (1363–1429) and the German Dietrich of Niem (*c.* 1340–1418). By 1450 few conciliarists remained: they had always comprised a small minority within the Church itself and gradually drifted back—through inertia rather than conviction—to the traditional view of papal monarchy.

The conciliar movement also exemplifies the second of the great weaknesses of the organized Church in the fifteenth century: the failure to take the laity into real and meaningful partnership. The exclusion of representatives of secular interests from full

participation in the work of the councils contradicted not only the logic of conciliarist theory but the political realities of a situation in which the will of the lay prince was always the decisive factor.

More serious still was the Church's failure at the local level to provide satisfactory outlets for the religious aspirations of the increasingly literate and self-confident gentlemen and urban parishioner. Neither the religious orthodoxy nor the pious generosity of the great mass of fifteenth-century laymen is seriously in doubt. Their patronage of such institutions as the academic college and, above all, the chantry within an existing parish church showed few signs of slackening during the course of the fifteenth century. The chantry indeed might be interpreted as the late medieval Church's grudging and inadequate concession to the religious enthusiasms and needs of its secular flock. For the layman the chantry priest, rather than the monk, friar or dignitary of a large collegiate church, was the most significant figure in organized religion; for the ecclesiastical hierarchy he was a poor and insignificant member of the clergy, never fully integrated into the life of the Church.

But the popularity of the chantry foundation was only one of the many symptoms of the growth of a more popular and devotional religion in the later Middle Ages. Mysticism, the quest for direct personal experience of God, was of course a traditional medieval and indeed Christian ideal; but in the fifteenth century it became increasingly the concern of the laity and poor priests rather than the clerical élite.

Margery Kemp, an illiterate and truculent Norfolk woman who died in about 1440, had more confidence in the validity of her own visions of the divine than in the words of the Church's own preselected contemplatives, the English monks and friars. The corporate mysticism of the Rhineland and Low Countries owed its success to the pious aspirations of the urban laity rather than to the direction of the official Church. Under the initial inspiration

of Ruysbroeck (1293–1381) and his disciple Gerard Groote (1340–84), the Brethren of the Common Life continued to embody the *nova devotio*, the ideal of a devout lay community, until the Reformation.

Such developments represented not only a withdrawal from the traditional institutions of the Church but an indirect reaction against the role of reason in the religious life. This is not to deny that the religious movements of the period often owed their origins to the works of scholars and universities; orthodox mysticism owed much to Dominican theologians of the thirteenth century, while the survival of Averroism perpetuated an academic heresy in popular form. But it is hard to resist the conclusion that the most vigorous forms of religious life and worship in the fifteenth century were explicitly or implicitly anti-intellectual. Perhaps it was possible after all, to 'do good without knowledge'. Or perhaps what was needed, as both Erasmus and the Quattrocento Italian humanists believed, was a new definition of learning to replace an outworn ideal.

Above, the friar, from the earliest edition of the Canterbury Tales, *composed by Geoffrey Chaucer (c. 1340–1400) after 1387. The tales, which represent some of the earliest court poetry written in English, demonstrate the wide interest in humanity felt by the court and the London merchants, Chaucer's patrons and audience. Henry Huntingdon Library, California.*

Above left, Thomas à Kempis (c. 1380–1471), a German Augustinian monk usually said to have written the Imitation of Christ, *a work of mystical devotion dealing with prayer, recollection and the freedom from worldly desires.*

Above far left, a German woodcut of the 1490s showing a school teacher and his pupils. The rapid spread of printing since the 1450s brought knowledge within the reach of all and helped to encourage the spread of schools. British Library, London.

Opposite left, John Huss burned at the stake in 1415; his fellowers, who believed in the supremacy of the Scriptures over the immoral pope and who also saw in this movement a chance to express their Bohemian nationalism, continued to trouble the church for twenty years. National Museum, Prague.

Opposite centre, monks of the fifteenth century depicted in a prayer book of Henry VI of England; by this date the monastic ideal was spent, and with the foundation of lay schools and almshouses the usefulness of monasteries would soon be questioned.

Opposite right, a woodcut taken from a mid-fifteenth-century book produced by the Brethren of the Common Life. This community, centred in the Low Countries, believed in lay devotion, and this illustration suggests that they were prepared to consider violence against the monarch to promote virtue.

Chapter 12

England and France at Peace and War

On 6 March 1204 the troops of King Philip Augustus of France (1180–1223) captured the formidable fortress of Château-Gaillard, recently built by Richard I of England to defend his duchy of Normandy against Capetian attack. There are few more significant dates in the history of either France or England. Within a few months Richard's younger brother, King John (1199–1216), had lost Normandy for ever; for the first time since a duke of Normandy had seized King Harold's crown in 1066, the rulers of England were effectively debarred from playing a decisive military role in northern France.

Throughout the rest of the thirteenth century the two kingdoms experienced very different types of political evolution; but their divorce was never final. Similarities between the French and English political, social and cultural traditions remained more striking than their divergencies from a common pattern. By a strange irony it was these similarities, and more precisely the persistence of the belief that both kingdoms formed one coherent and viable political unity, which led—four generations after John's loss of Normandy—to the longest Anglo-French war in the history of western Europe.

The ascendancy of France

Throughout the Middle Ages the fortunes of England and France were inextricably intertwined within a network of close and binding influences. It was an alliance within which France, during the thirteenth century above all, was usually the dominant partner. In the age of St Louis and Philip the Fair, northern France rather than Rome or Germany was the heartland of the characteristic values of medieval Christendom. Nowhere was French influence more pervasive than across the English Channel.

The ruling English dynasty of the Plantagenets was itself French in origin and continued to be French in outlook and attitude. Every king of England between 1199 and 1461 married a French princess or heiress. The English aristocracy, like the English court, not only spoke French but its ranks were continually filled by recruits from the French mainland. Simon de Montfort, now remembered as the leader of a native English opposition to the crown, was himself a first-generation immigrant from the kingdom of France. Edward I, conventionally known as 'the founder of the English nation', chose as his personal friends favourites who—like his military captain, Otto de Grandison—were French by birth.

In the artistic and intellectual fields, French primacy and influence were equally obvious. Although several areas gradually evolved their own distinctive styles of Gothic architecture, thirteenth - century English masons all worked within the general framework of the technical discoveries and aesthetic assumptions pioneered in the north of France during the late twelfth century. The rebuilding of Westminster Abbey in the years after 1245 marked a deliberate and successful attempt by an English king, Henry III, to build a great church in the contemporary French style. Similarly the reconstruction of St Stephen's Chapel in Westminster Palace after 1292 was the result of Edward I's desire to emulate its earlier and more famous counterpart—St Louis' *Sainte Chapelle* on the Ile de la Cité in Paris. In a very different sphere, the intellectual life of the new English universities at Oxford and Cambridge tended to revolve around the great debating issues already raised at Paris.

The Plantagenet monarchs, could never afford to be indifferent to the extraordinary success with which the thirteenth-century Capetians extended their authority over a kingdom three times as large as that of England. Successive English kings, notably John in 1214, Henry III in 1230 and 1242–43 and Edward I in 1294–97, unsuccessfully attempted to reverse the humiliation of the loss of Normandy by means of armed attacks on the French kingdom. Admittedly these three kings did preserve their control over a much reduced duchy of Gascony, but this area of southwestern France was rarely of urgent concern to the Capetian dynasty.

English kingship under attack

Nothing is more remarkable in the whole of English history than the early date—unparalled in Europe north of the Alps—at which a relatively remote kingdom had been subjected to the will of a central lord. Thanks to the precocious achievements of William the Conqueror, his successors, Henry I (1100–35) and Henry II (1154–89), stand out as the most forceful—as opposed to the most pretentious—rulers of their age. King John's inability to prevent Normandy from falling into the hands of Philip Augustus in 1204 was both a symptom and a cause of the decline of royal authority within England. Already by the end of the twelfth century there were signs that the exceptional power of the Anglo-Norman and Angevin monarchy was beginning to provoke its own counterpoise and antithesis: a series of opposition movements to the crown.

It was of course inevitable that this opposition should be conducted by members of the English baronage, sometimes in association with groups of knights as well as reforming churchmen like Archbishop Stephen Langton of Canterbury (1207–28) and Bishop Robert Grosseteste of Lincoln (1235–53). Although the twelfth- and thirteenth-century ruler owed much of his strength to his position as feudal king, he was inevitably vulnerable to attack by lords who renounced their fealty to him on the grounds that he had broken the principles of the feudal 'contract'. In themselves, isolated aristocratic protests against the misrule of an oppressive or negligent king were the most characteristic form of political struggle in medieval Europe. But baronial opposition in thirteenth-century England presented its kings with a more permanent challenge: it was often sustained over periods of many years, it was sometimes successful and, above all, it found expression in written programmes and legal enactments. Resistance to the king had in fact become articulate.

The events of the last two years of John's reign (1214–16) provided a detailed demonstration of the vulnerability of the English crown to baronial attack. John died in the middle of a savage civil war which it is unlikely he could ever have won. Even more significant than his military failure was his enforced consent to Magna Carta at Runnymede in June 1215.

The Great Charter deserves its fame. By the end of the year it had already become what it has ever since remained—a document less important for its contents than as an abstract and ill-defined expression of the monarch's obligation to respect the traditional rights of his more substantial subjects. Most of the Charter's detailed provisions, especially those relating to the complexities of feudal land tenure, were rapidly outdated by developments within the English social order. But for the rest of the Middle Ages Magna Carta was frequently reissued as a reminder that the authority of a monarch over his subjects could and might be limited.

In a more subtle way the kingship of John's long-lived son, Henry III (1216–72), was also controlled and conditioned by the attitudes of a restless and potentially hostile baronage. The contemporary ideal of a harmonious relationship with the king cannot conceal the grave weaknesses of Henry III's position. He deservedly lost the confidence of most of the English nobles at an early stage of his reign and thenceforward his room for manoeuvre was extremely limited. In particular the resistance to taxation displayed by his baronage consistently prevented him from tapping the considerable wealth of his kingdom.

Financial insolvency compelled Henry to

submit to the radical reform plan forced upon him by the majority of his barons in 1258. The Provisions of Oxford of that year contained detailed proposals for the replacement of traditional royal supremacy by a series of consultative, legislative and executive committees, all strongly representative of baronial interests. Not surprisingly, Henry III soon attempted to extricate himself from his oath to observe the Provisions. In the armed struggle which followed, the weaknesses within the baronial movement, never an organized party, were inevitably exposed and the *status quo* restored. But in the year before his death at the Battle of Evesham, Simon de Montfort had proved not only that an English king might be defeated and captured in battle (Lewes in May 1264) but that England might be governed without a king.

English monarch vindicated

'By God's blood I will not be silent but will defend my rights with all my strength!' Edward I's angry outburst against Archbishop Winchelsea of Canterbury in 1300 reflects the characteristic theme and tone of his attitude to kingship. According to his most sympathetic historian, Edward I was 'a conventional man in a changing age'. A conservative by temperament and inclination, he nevertheless presided over a revolution in the principles and practice of government. No ruler between William the Conqueror and Henry VIII made a more lasting contribution to the cause of English monarchy.

The essential condition for Edward's success was his ability as a war-leader. His personal participation in a crusade to the Holy Land (1270–74), the well-planned campaigns of 1277–94 which deprived Wales of its political independence and his prominent role as a European statesman all established Edward's prestige within his own country. As a result a remarkably able group of royal servants, most notably Robert Burnell, Chancellor of England from 1274 to 1292, were able to carry through a vast programme of complicated reforms in the spheres of governmental administration and the land law.

Of all the achievements of the reign, however, none was more valuable than Edward's success in solving the financial problems which had consistently defeated the efforts of his father and grandfather. In 1275, the year after his return from Syria and Italy, Edward persuaded his first parliament to accept the tax of a national duty of half a mark on a sack of wool or 300 wool fells and a mark on a last of hides. This 'Great and Ancient Custom', to use its later title, paved the way for a massive exploitation of taxes on and in wool by later medieval English governments.

Of greater constitutional significance was Edward's success in imposing regular direct

Below, Henry III, according to a contemporary sculpture. As well as opposition from the barons, Henry faced the aggressive expansion of papal authority. National Portrait Gallery, London.

Left, the seal of Simon de Montfort (c. 1208–65), who believed that the government should represent the full community of the realm and who summoned a prototype parliament, including knights and burgesses, to further his campaign against Henry III in 1265. British Museum, London.

Centre left, 'tally sticks' of the thirteenth century, with details of payments to the Royal Exchequer recorded in notches. Raising adequate taxes was a perennial medieval problem, and summoning a broad-based parliament was the chief expedient tried by Edward I to win acceptance of his new taxes. Public Record Office, London.

Below left, Henry III (ruled 1216–72) had Westminster Abbey rebuilt, as shown in this thirteenth-century drawing. But his reliance on French favourites brought opposition from his barons, culminating in the rebellion of Simon de Montfort in the 1260s.

taxation in the form of subsidies on movable property upon both laity and clergy. Against bitter opposition from the reluctant taxpayer and the ecclesiastical hierarchy, Edward was the first English monarch to familiarize his subjects with the doctrine that the king could not 'live of his own' but had a right, however ill-defined, to frequent levies of extraordinary taxation.

The need to secure respresentative assent to royal taxation lies at the very heart of the early history of the English parliament. Much ink has been expended, often fruitlessly, on the quest for the origins of this famous institution. At once a supreme lawcourt, an enlarged royal council and a general deliberative assembly, the early English parliament was first and foremost and instrument of royal power and not of opposition to the crown. It owed its most distinctive feature, the regular attendance of burgesses and knights of the shire as representatives of the English commons, to the king's desire to extract taxation from his subjects as frequently and as painlessly as possible. Within a generation of Edward I's death the commons were to become an indispensable component of every English parliament. The county gentleman and burgess were accorded an important role in a frequently summoned if short-lived assembly; an arena within which, very hesitantly and many years later, they learnt to express their own political grievances and aspirations.

But to the many valuable legacies of his reign Edward I added a conflict which for the next generation threatened to prejudice the rest of his achievements. Tempted by the accidental death in 1286 of the Scottish king, Alexander III, and the resulting

succession dispute, Edward attempted to force the northern kingdom into political subjection to himself. The outbreak of Anglo-Scottish hostilities in 1296–97 marked a genuine watershed in the history of the two kingdoms. An able and ruthless monarch had overreached himself by overestimating his own resources and underestimating the Scot's capacity for resistance.

Edward I died at Burgh-on-Sands in July 1307 during a last great campaign designed to achieve total victory over Robert Bruce, by then the recently crowned King of Scotland. The new English king, Edward II (1307–27), lacked the personal force to prove a successful ruler; but it was his complete inability to withstand the aggressive activity of Robert Bruce, particularly during the disastrous years which followed the Battle of Bannockburn in 1314, that led to the complete collapse of his authority and his eventual deposition and murder. Only when the English kings learnt to appreciate that the Scottish problem could never be solved, but might be contained or ignored, were they able to resume their traditional preoccupation with their role in France.

Capetian kingship

By comparison with the vicissitudes of royal authority in thirteenth-century England, the fortunes of the late Capetian kings presented to contemporary observers a spectacular example of growing power and prestige. In the age of Henry III and St Louis the historical tables seemed to have been neatly turned: the traditional supremacy of English kingship had proved illusory, while in France strength had grown out of weakness. After 1204 the Capetian dynasty, finally liberated from what Marc Bloch called its long period of 'vegetation', was at last able to build its own success story upon the strong foundations of the kingdom's prosperity.

The career of King Louis IX (1226–70) and even more his posthumous reputation as St Louis is central to the French political tradition in the Middle Ages. The assiduously calculated cultivation of St Louis's personality after his death was not only successful in securing his canonization in 1297 but makes it difficult to set his achievements within the context of his own lifetime. Thus what seem to be his greatest failures, the abortive Egyptian crusade of 1248–51 and the expedition to Tunis on which he met his death in 1270, did more than anything to establish his contemporary reputation.

The transmutation of a French king into a European saint was the ultimate proof of the theory that the Capetian monarch was not as other rulers. This view had its roots in earlier Capetian history and gradually developed into the famous claim that the King of France was 'emperor in his own kingdom'.

Upon this assertion of absolute feudal overlordship were grafted the more extreme principles of Christian kingship and possibly even the influences of Roman imperialism. Although he was not a priest himself, the king's office was sacramental in quality and carried in its train a complex variety of supernatural attributes and legends, ranging from the ability to cure scrofulous diseases by touch through such mysteries as the 'secret du roi' to the doctrine of the blood royal.

The success with which the Capetian monarchs persuaded their own subjects of their semi-divine status has never been satisfactorily explained. Even Matthew Paris, a thirteenth-century St Albans chronicler with no reason to admire the kings of France, quoted with approval the reply of St Louis' brother, Robert of Artois, when he was offered the imperial crown. He refused 'because we believe that the noble kingship of France with its line of royal blood going back to the sceptre of the Franks is much more excellent than any imperial throne, which can only be awarded by election.

These were sentiments common to all the late Capetians, above all to Philip IV (1285–1314), who brought respect for the dignity of the royal office to a great and formal if sometimes artificial climacteric. Philip the Fair's utter ruthlessness towards any challenge to his authority, whether from pope, the Templars or adulterous members of his own family, was that of a king who acted, as he is said to have looked, 'not like a man, not like a beast, but like a graven image'. After Philip's death, the kings of France were to suffer every conceivable political and personal humiliation, from capture in battle to complete inbecility. But respect for the divine institution of monarchy was never lost and proved continually capable, as Joan of Arc quite correctly believed, of wresting recovery from disaster.

Capetian government

The crowing achievement of the Capetian dynasty shortly before its extinction in 1328 was the establishment of a sophisticated system of central administration, the creation of a governmental machine and a state apparatus. The kingdom of France had proved relatively slow, by the standards of the papacy or England, to evolve a fully professionalized central bureaucracy. All the more impressive is Philip the Fair's success in presiding over the rapid development of new administrative agencies during the critical years immediately before and after 1300.

At this period the French kingdom acquired what it had previously lacked except in a very slight form, a fixed geographical centre, a political pivot around which the heterogeneous confederation of semi-autonomous French principalities could begin to revolve. For at least a century before Philip the Fair's accession in 1285 Paris had been the major European city

Above, the French Cour des Comptes, or Exchequer, in the fourteenth century. Philip IV's taxes were so unpopular that after his death there was the general uprising known as the Jacquerie. *Archives Nationales, Paris.*

Left, Philip IV (ruled 1285–1314) of France, known as Philip the Fair. He asserted the power of France over the papacy and successfully expanded his influence over Lyons, although he was less successful in Flanders. Bibliothèque Nationale, Paris.

Opposite left, Robert Bruce (ruled 1306–29), King of Scotland, in battle with the English. He was defeated by the English king Edward II early in his reign but himself defeated Edward II at Bannockburn in 1314 and was recognized as rightful King of Scotland in 1328. Bibliothèque d'Arsenal, Paris.

Opposite right, Edward I of England (ruled 1272–1307) attending a session of parliament: he was the first to give real standing to this institution and to expand it from the old King's Council to include representatives of the shires and boroughs. Royal Library, Windsor Castle.

north of the Alps, but it was the new king who made it the incontrovertible political capital of France. In conjunction with an ambitious building programme in the city and the development of a more glamorous and static court life than France had yet experienced, a complex linkup of new or newly adapted government departments was established upon the Ile de la Cité.

The real dynamic behind the governmental reforms of the late thirteenth century was less the idea of a new and more 'absolutist' ideology of kingship than Philip's fanatical quest for a larger revenue. The rapid evolution of novel administrative techniques in the financial field was accompanied by a series of ingenious experiments designed to find new forms of taxation. At the calculated risk of provoking outbursts of political resistance, particularly from the papacy, Philip's government imposed a long series of general tenths on the clergy as well as a variety of quota and assessment taxes on the laity. But in the last resort the late Capetians failed to bridge the gap between their massive expenditure and their income. Philip the Fair was condemned to purgatory by his even more famous contemporary, the Italian poet Dante, because of his deliberate devaluation of the French coinage and because of the reputation he enjoyed as a 'false coiner'.

The failure of Philip the Fair and his three sons to find a satisfactory solution to the monarchy's financial problems was to prove its crucial defect during the first phase of the Hundred Years' War. It is symptomatic of its weakness during this critical period that the French kingdom never evolved a regular tradition of national representative assemblies of a type similar to the English parliaments. The occasional experiments in that direction, like the embryonic Estates General of 1302, never took firm root.

The wave of spontaneous protest and rioting by the French provincial nobility which followed Philip the Fair's death in 1314 pointed an obvious moral. There had been a genuine 'revolution in government' during the preceding decades, but this new administrative centre had been imposed somewhat arbitrarily and artificially over the realities of the French political scene. Edward III was soon to show how much more readily he could mobilize the wealth and manpower of his three or four million subjects than could his French rivals tap the resources of a larger, richer and more populous kingdom of perhaps twenty million inhabitants.

The accession of the Valois

When Philip the Fair died in 1314 the continuity of the Capetian dynasty as the leaders of the most powerful political unit in western Europe seemed well assured. Philip was the father of three healthy and vigorous sons, each of whom in turn succeeded to the crown of France: Louis X 'the Quarrelsome' reigned from 1314 to 1316, Philip V 'the Tall' from 1316 to 1322 and Charles IV 'the Fair' from 1322 to 1328. All failed in the primary duty of a hereditary monarch: not one proved himself able to produce a male heir.

So, by a curious irony, the genealogical good fortune of the Capetian dynasty, their greatest single advantage over other west European rulers since 987, now deserted them not once but three times. It was indeed the absence of any previous succession disputes in the history of the French monarchy that made the crises of 1316, 1322 and 1328 so controversial and potentially explosive. In these three years the French prelates, magnates and university scholars who debated—at great length and in reasonably good faith—the question of the succession to the crown had neither precedent nor law to guide them. The principles of the so-called 'Salic Law', by which it was held that a woman could neither inherit the French crown in her own right nor transmit a claim to the throne to her children, were evolved in the later fourteenth century to justify the coups d'état which replaced the Capetian with Valois kings.

On Charles IV's death the only alternative to a Capetian queen or her descendants was a non-Capetian king. In April an assembly of French barons cut the Gordian knot with commendable speed and decisiveness. They chose as their monarch Philip Count of Anjou and Valois, first cousin of the late Capetian kings. This first Valois king, Philip VI (1328–50), was, by all the pragmatic tests of the year, much the most realistic choice. He was thirty-four years old, a great-grandson of St Louis, experienced in both French and European politics, and had already begun to exercise effective royal power as Regent of France.

The unanimity with which the French nobility accepted their first Valois king in 1328 nevertheless proved deceptive. Philip VI was always to remain a victim of circumstances of his own accession. Although it would be unjust to describe him as a usurper, he undoubtedly suffered from the weaknesses of a usurping king. For at least a generation after 1328 the Valois monarchy forfeited part of the unquestioning loyalty enjoyed by the Capetians. In 1328 Philip VI had been compelled to make concessions to several members of the aristocracy, particularly the dukes of Burgundy, in return for their support.

Moreover, the accession of the Valois inevitably antagonized the other contenders for the throne in 1328. Of these Philip, Count of Evreux initially seemed the most formidable, for he was not only the senior surviving nephew of Philip the Fair but had married Joan of Navarre, Louis X's eldest daughter and arguably the rightful Queen of France since 1316. Philip's claim to the French throne was never entirely forgotten, and after his death in 1343 it was inherited by his eldest son Charles, King of Navarre, whose ambitious conspiracies continued to undermine Valois power for at least the next twenty years. Much more dangerous, however, was the challenge presented by Edward III of England (1327–77), whose claim to the crown rested on the fact that his mother, Isabella, was the daughter of Philip the Fair.

The origin of the war

At the time of Philip of Valois's accession in 1328 Edward III was only sixteen years old, a new king under the tutelage of his mother, Isabella. After an initial protest Edward showed himself ready to recognize the fait accompli. In the summer of 1329 he travelled to Amiens cathedral in order to render his personal act of homage to Philip VI. For several years thereafter Edward allowed his claim to the French throne to remain dormant. For obvious reasons it was never completely forgotten. Opinion is still divided as to whether Edward III ever seriously expected to become King of France; but his title to the crown could always be relied upon to embarrass the Valois diplomatically and to exploit any tension within the French kingdom.

Throughout its course the Hundred Years' War showed many of the characteristics of a series of civil wars within the kingdom of France. Edward III's great advantage in the late 1330s, like that of Henry V eighty years later, was that he could present himself as an alternative king to dissident sections of the French aristocracy and bourgeoisie. His claim to the throne offered the discontented nobleman legal justification for acts of rebellion against the Valois monarchs. In the years immediately preceding the outbreak of hostilities Edward's court became a centre of refuge for men like Robert, Count of Artois, who fled to England in 1334 after a violent quarrel with Philip VI and his ally, the Duke of Burgundy.

There were, however, many other reasons why war between England and France always seemed likely. As we have seen, official relations between the two kingdoms had long been strained. The traditional sources of conflict—the role of the English king as Duke of Gascony, overlapping spheres of influence in the county of Flanders, rivalry between English and Norman merchants and sea-captains in the Channel—remained unresolved. But these were familiar problems, apparently no more acute in the first ten years of Edward III's reign than they had been in any previous decade: they should not have too high a place in any list of the 'causes' of the war.

In the last resort the outbreak of war was due to a personal act of will on the part of Edward III. Ever since his marriage to Philippa of Hainault at York Minster in 1328, the young king had been surrounded by a group of highly bellicose courtiers and nobles, strongly influenced by contemporary chivalric ideals. During the first years of the reign it seemed possible that their military ambitions might find a suitable outlet through Edward III's determination to undo the work of Robert Bruce and reduce Scotland to a position of legal subjection to the English king. But a series of strenuous Scottish campaigns ended by bringing him no nearer his objective. In 1336 Edward began to entertain thoughts of armed intervention in France—on the explicit grounds that Valois assistance to the Scots had deprived him of his rightful victory there. But it is hard to resist the conclusion that Edward had now realized the futility of fighting a war of diminishing returns against Scotland: the excitement and profits of successful war might be gained, and much more gloriously, in northern France.

The openings of the war

Anglo-French war began—as it was to continue intermittently for the next 106 years—against a confused background of feverish diplomatic activity and complicated military preparations. As befitted a conflict which had little unity and owes even its name to the superficial hindsight of later generations of Englishmen and Frenchmen the Hundred Years' War cannot be said to have begun with a formal 'declaration of war'. Neither Philip VI's confiscation of Edward's Gascon fief in May 1337 nor Edward's own feudal defiance of 'Philip of Valois, who calls himself King of France' a few months later, were necessarily decisive. The drift to war was unchecked by adversaries who could not possibly foresee the length, vicissitudes and complexities of the forthcoming struggle.

In 1337, as ever afterwards, the major military problem confronting the two opponents was the need to mobilize a sufficiently large force of troops to take advantage of a relatively short summer campaigning season. As both kings, and not just Edward III, were required to reward their armies by means of regular and substantial wages, military success depended on effective war finance as well as commissariat arrangements. In most years during the early phase of the Hundred Years' War the Valois kings were able to raise an army of up to 10,000 men. But so large a force lacked cohesion and definition. It was liable to mass desertion and could, in any case, never be sustained in the field for more than a few weeks without a ruinous strain on the monarch's finances.

At first sight Edward III's financial problems in launching English military expeditions across the Channel seemed even more serious. In time the English king proved himself remarkably adept at exploiting parliamentary tenths and fifteenths, as well as wool customs duties, in the interests of his war expenditure. During the first few years of the war, however, Edward was consistently unsuccessful in obtaining the revenues necessary to sustain his ambitious military designs. His first campaign on the Franco-Flemish border could not be mounted until 1339 and then proved an expensive and abortive failure. At the end of the following year Edward returned from Flanders to England in a state of near-bankruptcy. His reckless borrowing ruined both Italian and subsequently English consortia of money-lenders to the crown and also provoked a constitutional crisis of confidence (1340–41) in his own kingship. But Edward weathered the storm; there is no greater tribute to his qualities and charm as war-leader than his ability to persuade both his nobility and parliamentary commons to continue to support a war which brought them few material rewards until 1346.

During these first years Edward III was also unable to solve his greatest strategical problem—the most effective point at which to exert pressure on the Valois monarchy. A complicated and costly series of alliances with a varied collection of dukes and counts in the Rhineland and the Low Countries never had much practical effect and collapsed completely in 1341. The promising opportunity offered by the rise to power in Ghent and Flanders of an Anglophil popular leader, Jacques van Artevelde (1338–45), eventually proved equally illusory. The English naval victory over a combined French and Catilian fleet at Sluys (June 1340) had little permanent significance in an age when sea-power was a meaningless phrase. Only the outbreak of a particularly complex and vicious succession dispute within the duchy of Brittany, precipitated by the death of Duke John III in 1341, enabled English troops to sustain a limited series of military operations within the confines of the French kingdom.

Crécy and Calais

On 11 July 1346 Edward III, guided by the advice of Geoffrey de Harcourt, a prominent nobleman of the Cotentin recently exiled by Philip VI, landed in Normandy with 15,000 men. At long last French territory had been invaded by a major English force—numerically the strongest expedition ever dispatched by the English government during the whole course of the Hundred Years' War.

Despite the size of his army, Edward's war aims in 1346 seem to have been very limited: he probably planned no more than a slow march across northern France in order to demonstrate his power and prestige. The news of a large French army advancing towards him under the leadership of Philip VI was sufficiently alarming to induce Edward to move rapidly northeast in an attempt to reach the coastal ports near Boulogne. But at Crécy, on the plain at

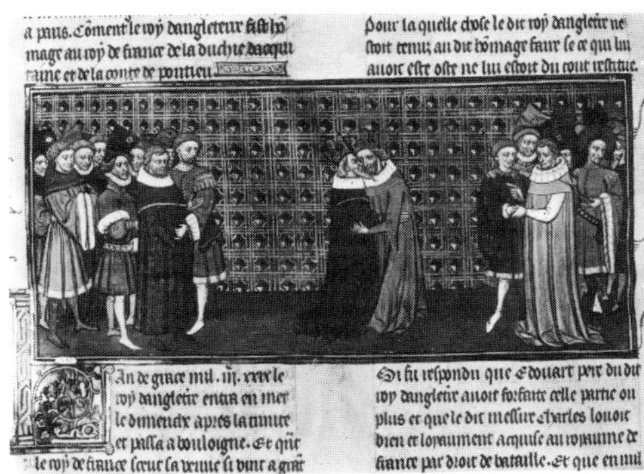

Above, Edward III of England sailing to Calais to conduct a campaign in France. The war proved an important stimulus to English shipping and many other industries associated with supplying the armies. Musée Dobrée, Nantes.

Centre, Philip VI of France (ruled 1328–50), the first king of the Valois dynasty. His accession was challenged by Edward III of England and precipitated the outbreak of the Hundred Years War. Bibliothèque Nationale, Paris.

Top, Edward III paying homage to Philip VI of France in 1329, in respect of his fiefs in France. Edward only asserted his claim to the French throne when he had the support of the Flemish and other French nobles. British Library, London.

Ponthieu, the English army was compelled to take up a defensive position and to prepare to fight. By the evening of 26 August the improbable had happened: Philip VI was in full flight and the French nobility decimated as a result of their own impetuosity.

The Battle of Crécy marked a genuine turning point in the history of the Hundred Years' War. In military terms it solved nothing, and Edward found himself incapable of bringing the war to a rapid and triumphant conclusion. But he had proved —and that dramatically—that it was possible for an English army to win a crushing victory over its French opponents.

In 1346 Edward III had established a glorious precedent. In the following year he provided his successors with an equally important but more concrete legacy: a gateway into the kingdom of France. The conquest of Calais, which surrendered on 4 August 1347 after a long and arduous siege, was Edward's most lasting military achievement. Henceforward a concrete garrison could be maintained, admittedly at extravagant cost, on French soil. Until its surrender by Queen Mary as late as 1558, Calais provided successive English governments with the opportunity of putting aggressive intention into offensive action.

The collapse of France

The Battle of Crécy and the successful siege of Calais ensured that Edward III would continue to fight the war, not that he would win it. For six years after the king's triumphant return to London in October 1347, English military efforts languished. Most of the limited resources available were squandered in Brittany at a period when the English economy was temporarily dislocated by the initial ravages of the Black Death. France suffered even more seriously from the first onslaught of bubonic plague in 1348, a catastrophe which confirmed the provincial and national Estates in their unwillingness to grant war taxation to the Valois king. The death of Philip VI in August 1350 and the accession of his son, John II (1350–64), replaced a quietly competent if much maligned monarch with one whose suspicious temperament and outbursts of vindictive rage further exacerbated the serious tensions within the French aristocracy.

The fragility of Valois control over the French kingdom was brutally exposed in 1355 and 1356 when John II proved himself unable to resist a series of simultaneous marauding raids launched at various parts of his domain. Edward's own sortie from Calais in the autumn of 1355 was succeeded in the following spring by an attack on Normandy. Meanwhile, Edward's eldest son and heir, the Black Prince, established himself in Bordeaux with the object of leading large plundering expeditions into southern and central France. On his return south from the second of these raids, the Black Prince was overtaken by the French army and compelled—like his father ten years earlier—to stand and fight. The Battle of Poitiers (19 September 1356), where a force of 6,000 English troops sustained the attack of a larger French army, was an even more resounding success than Crécy. Among the many French lords in English hands at the end of the day was the French king himself, soon conveyed to London as the most remarkable trophy of the war.

The loss of the Valois king and the need to find large sums of money with which to pay his ransom brought royal authority within France to the point of complete collapse. The Estates of Languedoil, summoned to Paris in order to vote subsidies, seized the opportunity to make a violent attack on the maladministration of the French government. More sinister was the uneasy alliance between Charles of Navarre, Robert le Coq, Bishop of Laon and Etienne Marcel, provost of the merchants of Paris, a popular leader prepared to use riot and terror in order to gain his ends. In May 1358 moreover the area southeast of Paris experienced the full horrors of a peasant revolt, the *Jacquerie*.

Gradually the forces of conservatism rallied around John II's heir, the young Dauphin Charles. The *Jacquerie* was brutally suppressed. Marcel assassinated

Above, a French version of their disastrous defeat at Crécy in 1346; in the main, though, the war consisted of raiding parties rather than set battles. Bibliothèque Nationale, Paris.

Top, the Battle of Poitiers (1356), an important victory for the English in the Hundred Years War; the French king, John II, was captured and later ransomed. In the middle of the picture can be seen a herald; his duty was to observe that the conventions of war were properly followed. Bodleian Library, Oxford.

Opposite, Philip V of France disinheriting Robert d'Artois in 1322. Robert went to England where he encouraged Edward III to undertake a war against Philip.

(July 1358), and a modicum of law and order restored.

The failure of Edward III to exploit the abasement of the French monarchy in the crisis year of 1356 to 1358 provides eloquent testimony to his inability to fight the war to a finish. In an attempt to achieve a total victory he led his own last great raid into northern France in October 1359. Although a magnificent display of English power, this expedition too failed to produce a decisive result. It finally came to an end in May 1360 at the little village of Brétigny near Beauce, where the Dauphin and the Black Prince agreed on provisional peace terms.

The resulting Treaty of Brétigny-Calais (1360) concluded the first major phase of the Hundred Years' War. Although Edward III temporarily renounced his claims to full sovereignty over the kingdom of France, he was acknowledged as supreme lord of a vastly enlarged duchy of Aquitaine in the southwest, as well as of Ponthieu, Calais and the county of Guines in the north. In addition, the French committed themselves to paying no less than three million gold *écus* as ransom for their king, John II.

The art of war

'When the noble Edward first gained England in his youth, 'wrote Jean le Bel, the most famous chronicler of the first phase of the Hundred Years' War, 'nobody thought much of the English, nobody spoke of their prowess and courage . . . Now, in the time of the noble Edward, who has often put them to the test, they are the finest and most daring warriors known to man.'

More than 600 years later, the sustained military superiority of the English over their French adversaries remains astonishing. The greatest, if most obvious, advantage of the English troops was that the war took place almost exclusively on French soil. From this fact alone it followed that the prizes and profits of war normally fell to Edward III whereas the kingdom of France bore its devastation and suffering. Once an English force had crossed the Channel its solidarity and cohesion were well assured.

The difficulties involved in transporting companies of men and horses across the Channel were very considerable. Despite several blunders, some maladministration and much corruption, Edward III's government was generally remarkably successful in solving problems of recruitment, supply and transport. The king himself was ideally suited to the role of a great fourteenth-century war-leader. Despite recent attempts to prove the contrary, he was no great strategist and usually had no precisely defined military or indeed political objectives. However, he enjoyed fighting, he could win the confidence and loyalty of his nobles and knights and he was willing to delegate authority in the field.

Edward therefore fostered a deliberately informal and decentralized attitude to war. The typical military operation of the fourteenth century was the *chevauchée* or armed raid, conducted by a few hundred and occasionally by a few thousand men under the leadership of a skilled commander. Sometimes the *chevauchée* might lead, nearly always by accident, to a major pitched battle; but its primary objectives were plunder, devastation and a display of military strength. Until 1416–17, when Henvy V decided upon a series of slow sieges of Norman towns, the Hundred Years' War was characterized by a series of extremely mobile expeditions in which a small *cadre* of fighting men inflicted considerable damage while proving almost impossible to intercept or capture. These companies, or *routes*, often irresponsive to superior authority, were both the scourge of France and the effective military units of the war.

War and chivalry

The length and vicissitudes of the Hundred Years' War are incomprehensible unless it is understood that the leading combatants on both sides positively desired to fight—within the context of a complicated series of military assumptions, conventions and ideals. As Froissart, the most famous spokesman for such ideals, wrote:

Mankind is divided into three classes: the valiant who face the perils of war to advance their persons and increase their honour; the people who talk of their successes and fortunes; and the clerks who write down and record their great deeds.

For contemporaries the best, and perhaps the only, justification for the war was that by providing a long and splendid series of opportunities for individual 'feats of arms', it put the all-important chivalric qualities to the test. These qualities themselves were in essence those common to all military élites during periods of continued war. Like the Homeric hero or Japanese samurai, the fourteenth-century knight placed a high premium on personal bravery or *prouesse*, a type of courage which included the willingness to carry out audacious, dangerous and, if necessary, foolhardy exploits. Intense loyalty towards the fellow-members of one's exclusive company or caste was also essential and can be seen at a developed stage within the Black Prince's entourage in Gascony during the 1250s and 1260s.

To these familiar ideals, fourteenth-century chivalry added its own characteristic appurtenances and trappings. The great war-horse or *dextrarius*, in increasingly short supply as the war progressed, was even more valuable as a status symbol than an instrument of war. A rapid expansion in the science of heraldry and a remarkable increase in the number of heralds reflected an increasing obsession with the nuances of the social order. During the early years of Edward III, the English court was opened, as never before, to the influence of the originally southern French ideal of courtly love: both the king's wife, Queen Philippa of Hainault, and his daughter-in-law, Joan of Kent, brought great talent to their roles as conventional *grandes dames*, presiding benignly over the fortunes of their knights. Both the English and the French kings cleverly exploited the popularity of the highly formal and extravagant vow to perform an honourable deed of arms by founding the exclusive military orders of the Garter and the *Chevaliers de l'Etoile*.

It need hardly be said that chivalric ideals, like religious ideals at all periods, were never completely achieved in practice. As most contemporaries were well aware, many chivalric practices—like the numerous challenges to personal combat interchanged between the Plantagenet and Valois kings—were merely formal and stereotyped gestures. But it would be a mistake to regard chivalry as nothing more than a veneer which overlaid an unscrupulous and brutal war. Chivalric theory and military practice often complemented each other extremely well. It was not only honourable, according to the international 'Law of Arms', to spare the life of a defeated knightly adversary: because of the prevalence of a systematically organized traffic in ransoms, it was profitable too.

The *chevauchée* itself had a chivalric as well as a military rationale. A small and highly mobile mounted raid provided the optimum conditions for the performance of deeds of valour. In this way military operations themselves might be converted into a series of hand-to-hand jousts and skirmishes. French and English knights learnt the art of war in the highly artificial context of the tournament: as a consequence official periods of warfare are often impossible to distinguish from the innumerable tournaments which preceded and accompanied them. Whenever possible war itself was transformed into a perpetual tournament.

The effects of the war

Considerable controversy continues to surround the effects of the war on the economy and society of France and England. Even more than in the case of the German Thirty Years' War, it seems impossible to isolate the results of military operations from those of more profound economic forces like population decline, falling production and rising wages. By its very nature the Hundred Years' War—a long, rambling but spasmodic war conducted over a very large area—is difficult to assess in terms of human suffering. It is impossible to know how many people died as a result of the war or even the number of those engaged in the war effort on each side.

Some sections of English society clearly did make material gains during the first phases of the war. Military preparations were inevitably concentrated in the south-east of the country and accordingly set the seal on London's slow evolution 'from commune to capital'. Edward III's urgent need for war finance led to a great expansion in the number of parliamentary subsidies and hence ensured that the English parliamentary commons would play a more rather than less integral role in national politics. The English government's massive exploitation of the country's most important export trade by means of a variety of heavy wool-taxes (over which the commons had secured the right to consultation by 1362) had even more significant results. The differential between heavy customs duties of over forty percent on raw wool and less than five percent on finished cloth encouraged the trend towards a thriving domestic cloth industry. By the end of the century, England had already become—what it has ever since remained—primarily an exporter of manufactured commodities rather than raw materials.

This transformation of the English economy was not accompanied by any profound social revolution. In the first instance the profits of successful war tended to fall into the hands of the established aristocracy and, above all, of the king's own relatives. As a career open to talent, war did of course raise the fortunes of several obscurely born military captains. But remarkably few of these military adventurers or their counterparts, the bourgeois entrepreneurs, forced their way into the higher reaches of the English nobility. Those who did so had already invested their newly acquired capital in landed estates and adopted the traditional behaviour pattern of the existing aristocracy. Sir Walter de Manny (died 1372), a Hainaulter who was probably the most competent of all Edward III's war captains, used his wealth to promote the foundation of the London Charterhouse in 1367–68.

In France too the disasters of the period between Crécy and Poitiers dislocated the economic order without inaugurating a major social transformation. Though certain areas—Artois, Picardy, parts of Brittany and Normandy and, above all, the Bordelais—suffered severely at the hands of English troops and companies of marauding *routiers*, a relatively primitive system of arable farming showed itself remarkably resilient: rapid recovery from the immediate effects of military devastation was apparent throughout most of France during the 1360s. Ultimately more serious and pervasive were the long-term ills caused by governmental debasement of the coinage. In 1345–47, and more severely still in 1356–58, the Valois kings precipitated a major monetary crisis as well as general inflation by their devaluation of the French currency in an attempt to raise the revenues with which to meet the English challenge.

Charles V and the recovery of France

For de Tocqueville the reign of the third Valois king, Charles V (1364–80), was decisive for the history of France: it marked the period when the *ancien régime*, which survived until 1789, was born. Despite the political disasters of the fifty years after his death, Charles's achievements were never completely sacrificed. Often seriously ill, emaciated, unable to ride a horse into battle, no French king could have been less prepossessing: none was more influential.

In the first place Charles V showed himself able to call upon the latent reserves of loyalty towards the French crown. Like St Louis, he laid great stress on the duties and sacramental nature of his kingly office; like Philip the Fair, he deliberately encouraged the elaboration of a sophisticated and centralized government machine based on Paris. But Charles's own greatest contribution to the cause of French monarchy was his success in solving the financial problems which had crippled his two predecessors. He forced his subjects to accept, in fact if not always in theory, the principle that the king had a right to demand extraordinary taxation from them. A complex series of administrative expedients and financial levies, of which the hearth-tax and the *gabelle* or salt-tax were the most lucrative, made the king of France the richest sovereign in western Europe.

By contrast Charles V's achievements in the military sphere were singularly unimpressive. The memory of his father's humiliation at Poitiers seems to have had a permanently inhibiting effect on a king

Above, English soldiers looting a French town in the Hundred Years War. Most bands of soldiers expected to make their profits from sharing out such plunder in proportions agreed before the expedition began; for many loot and ransoms made the war a highly profitable enterprise. British Library, London.

Top, English soldiers besieging a French town in the early fifteenth century. Appointments such as head of the garrison in a captured French town, or the grant of estates in captured French territory, were the rewards sought by successful English soldiers. British Library, London.

Opposite, English soldiers scaling the walls of a fortress in Gascony; this region was important to England, both because it was an ancient fief of the English crown and because of its close trading links with England. British Library, London.

FRANCE IN THE THIRTEENTH AND FOURTEENTH CENTURIES

Date	France	The war	England	Date	France	The war	England
1200		Philip Augustus completes the conquest of Normandy	Magna Carta (1215)	**1320**	Charles IV 'the Fair' (1322–8) Last Capetians of the direct line Philip VI of Valois (1328–50) The Black Death John II 'the Good' (1350–64)	Edward III claims the French crown (1328) Opening of the Hundred Years' War French naval defeat at Sluys Crécy (1346)	Organization of parliament
	Louis VIII (1223–6) St Louis (1226–70) Death of St Louis at Tunis (1270)	Henry III defeated at Taillebourg	Henry III (1216–72) Henry III captured by the barons (1264)				
1270	Philip III 'the Rash' (1270–85)	Treaty of Paris (1286)	Simon de Montfort master of England	**1350**	Etienne Marcel The *Jacquerie* Charles V (1364–80)	Poitiers: capture of the French king (1356) Treaty of Brétigny (1360) Treaty of Avignon (1365) Du Guesclin frees France	Revolt of John of Ghent The Good Parliament (1376) Richard II (1377–99)
1300	Philip IV 'the Fair' (1285–1314) Persecution of the Templars	French defeat at Courtrai (1303)	Edward I (1272–1307) Edward II (1307–27) Edward III (1327–77)	**1400**	Charles VI (1380–1422)	Death of Du Guesclin (1380)	Wat Tyler

who took no personal pleasure in the conduct of war. The weakness of English control in southwestern France had long been evident before Charles allowed himself, under pressure from Gascon noblemen at odds with the Black Prince, Prince of Acquitaine from 1362 to 1372, to provoke a renewal of Anglo-French war in 1369. During the succeeding eleven years all the major military initiatives were taken by the English rather than the French.

In the last resort, therefore, Charles V failed to make quite the most of his great opportunities. Although at the time of his death in 1380 English domains in France had been reduced to a few Channel ports and a coastal strip near Bordeaux, the war still continued. On the other hand, it seemed to all intelligent contemporaries that France had now resumed her traditional supremacy among the powers of western Europe. Not only was southeastern England experiencing the horrors of war at first-hand through the agency of naval raids by joint Franco-Castilian fleets; in 1377 the death of the long-senile Edward III and the succession of his ten-year-old grandson, Richard II (1377–99), added the problems of a minority to those of baronial faction and war-weariness. By contrast, the kingdom of France was enjoying a cultural as well as economic revival.

Chapter 13

Town and Countryside

One of the most striking features of medieval Europe is the contrast between its outward unity and its inner division. This appears very clearly in its economy. On the one hand, there was a flourishing international commerce, following well-worn routes and linking the great cities of medieval Europe; and, on the other, there was the half-closed economy of much of the countryside, where communications were poor and money was scarce.

Town and countryside correspond very roughly to those two aspects of the medieval economy. This does not mean, however, that a rigid division should be drawn between town and countryside: even the largest towns had orchards and gardens, and many even had their own fields. Towns were of all shapes and sizes; they varied from the great cities of Flanders and Italy to market towns that were scarcely distinguishable from villages, and they were at widely differing stages of economic development. This makes it difficult to trace the economic history of medieval Europe, for one is always in danger of forgetting that the pace of economic change varied from place to place. The causes of economic change in the Middle Ages are rarely clear; but the relations of town and countryside do seem to offer a key, because the development of the medieval economy depended to a very large extent on bringing together the wealth of the countryside and the trade of the towns.

The twelfth and thirteenth centuries have left an impression of prosperity: they were a time of economic expansion. The merchants of the Hansa acquired a virtual monopoly of the Baltic trade, while the Italians dominated the Mediterranean. Safe markets were won in Russia and the Levant and were to be one of the foundations of industrial growth in Flanders and Italy. The increasing importance of the Italians in international trade was underlined in 1252, when first Genoa and then Florence issued a gold coinage. That of Florence was the more successful and was soon to supplant the failing Byzantine coinage as the basis of international credit and exchange.

Europe's thriving commerce was reflected in the growth of towns. Not only were new towns founded in almost all parts of Europe, but many towns, both great and small, were bursting out of their walls. New lines of fortifications had to be constructed to shelter their expanding suburbs. The countryside too was apparently prosperous, for the growing urban market ensured rising prices for agriculture produce.

The foundations of prosperity

The wealth of medieval Europe was founded on its agriculture, which was very largely geared to arable farming. Since about 1100 great progress had been made in clearing land. This reached its height in western Europe during the twelfth century: on both sides of the North Sea coastal marshes were drained and brought under cultivation; in Lombardy the marshlands of the Po Valley were being reclaimed; everywhere the remaining forests and wastes were under attack, and the most inhospitable regions began to be settled. At the same time, as we have seen, colonization was begun in the Slav lands beyond the Elbe, and it gathered force during the thirteenth century.

The initial cause of this great movement is not at all clear; it was probably compounded of a variety of factors. Among the most important were overpopulation in certain areas and the ending of the period of invasions. Once begun, however, it gathered speed under the impetus of the growing population that pioneer conditions demanded. It is not possible to say exactly how great or how rapid this growth of population was. Obviously it varied from place to place, but all the signs are that it was of considerable proportions. New parishes had to be carved out of old ones, and chapels had to be provided for new settlements. The numbers of tenants on some estates increased enormously. On the estates of the Bishop of Worcester, for example, they went up by sixty-five percent between 1182 and 1299.

The economic growth of Europe in the Middle Ages was above all a question of increased land under cultivation and of growing population, but it was also helped by some improvements in agricultural techniques. By the end of the thirteenth century, and in some places possibly long before, the open-field system with its three course rotation of crops had been perfected in those regions of northern Europe best suited to arable farming. During the twelfth century there seems to have been a general increase in the number of plough teams, while a more advanced plough with coulter and mouldboard came into wider use. Tools were increasingly made of iron. Where these improvements were adopted, the soil could be prepared much more thoroughly; and this presumably produced more corn.

Land was the most valuable of Europe's natural resources, but among others there were, of course, supplies of timber, and water in abundance. With the construction

Above, a fourteenth-century Genoese Treatise on the Vices, *depicting drunkenness. Wine was one of the most important luxury goods, the subject of long-distance trade. British Library, London.*

Opposite top, burial of victims of the Black Death at Tournai in Flanders in 1349. The plague swept over Europe in ten years and in some towns may have killed up to half the population. Royal Library, Brussels.

Opposite bottom, Charles V and his leading general, Bertrand du Guesclin (1320–80). Du Guesclin took Castile for France in 1369 and recaptured Poitou from the English in the 1370s, but he was unwilling to help Charles to take Brittany, his home country. Bibliothèque Saint-Genevieve, Paris.

Opposite right, Charles V of France (ruled 1364–80), known as Charles the Wise. He re-established royal authority over his kingdom and was an important patron of the arts but had little military success against the English. Cathedral of Saint-Denis, Paris.

of water-mills a valuable source of power could at last be properly exploited. The water-mill seems to have been invented at about the beginning of the Christian era. probably in Syria. It spread only slowly to western Europe, but by the end of the eleventh century very great numbers of water-mills had been built, as the Domesday Book shows in the case of England. The windmill harnessed another source of power. This too seems to have come from Syria; the first European examples date from the end of the twelfth century.

Medieval Europe was comparatively well supplied with minerals. In about 1170 rich silver deposits were discovered in Saxony; these supplemented the mines of the Harz mountains, which had been worked since the tenth century. The Alps were also a region of great mining activity; gold and silver were extracted, and base metals too were mined. From Germany miners fanned out into central Europe to work the mines of Bohemia and Hungary. England was well endowed with mineral resources: the southwest provided silver, tin and lead; and elsewhere there were deposits of iron, coal and lead. Most parts of Europe possessed local iron-workings; the richest were in northern Spain, the eastern Alps and Sweden.

Another aspect of Europe's economic expansion during the twelfth and thirteenth centuries was the growth of towns. This was closely bound up with developments in the countryside, for towns relied on the surrounding district for their supplies of foodstuffs and other raw materials. They also drew a very large proportion of their inhabitants from neighbouring villages. It was, however, a two-way process; the growing towns gave added stimulus to agricultural expansion, and the prosperity of the countryside soon came to depend more and more on the presence of urban markets.

In northern Italy this was transformed during the eleventh and twelfth centuries into direct control of the countryside by the towns. The institution responsible for this was the urban commune, a body of private citizens sworn to uphold common interests. With a greater or lesser degree of violence, it was grafted on to existing municipal institutions, and it became the holder of real political power within the city. Its chief aim was to further the city's commercial prosperity, for which domination of the countryside was considered essential.

The communal movement was much less successful in northern Europe. In England and France it was carefully controlled by the royal government. The situation was confused in Germany, but the cities of the Hansa and the Rhineland were able to obtain a considerable degree of independence. In Flanders it was in the count's best interests to allow the towns a large share in

their internal government. Political domination of the countryside by the towns was quite another matter. Even so the towns of northern Europe exercised indirect control through their markets.

Towns were the centres of local trade. It was through their markets that the natural wealth of the countryside was turned into something negotiable. Their growing demands meant that local trade, mostly in raw materials, would increase. This brought new wealth to the merchants and the landlords and allowed the rapid growth of long-distance trade.

International trade never completely came to a standstill, not even in the darkest days of the invasions of the ninth and tenth centuries. There was always some demand among the nobility and the Church for the precious cloths, spices and drugs imported from the Levant and for wax and furs of eastern Europe. Until the twelfth century the West had little to offer in return except raw materials, and large amounts of gold and silver had to be found to pay for the

Opposite above left, English officials weighing and receiving coins as tax payments in the late twelfth century. The expansion of trade made coins of all denominations far more common than earlier.

Opposite below left, a mason and a carpenter undergoing an examination before being allowed entry into their guild. The guilds aimed to protect the standard of workmanship and in times of depression only accepted the children of existing members as apprentices.

Opposite right, the weavers' guild at Bologna; within the towns both the industries and the trades were controlled by guilds. Museo Civico, Bologna.

Above left, harvesting, in the month of June, according to the Très Riches Heures du Duc de Berri, *in the early fifteenth century. Despite this romantic picture most of Europe had not recovered from the ravages of the Black Death by this date. Musée Condé, Chantilly.*

Below left, a thirteenth-century treatise on surgery, showing methods of curing a head-wound. Methods of surgery remained primitive, if not brutal, until the sixteenth century. British Library, London.

Bottom, bricklayers at work in the thirteenth century; the great castles and cathedrals of this time were built by these methods, with only wooden scaffolding and hand-driven cranes. Trinity College, Dublin.

Below, an illustration from Liège, dated about 1150, showing an operation for cataracts and the removal of adenoids. British Library, London.

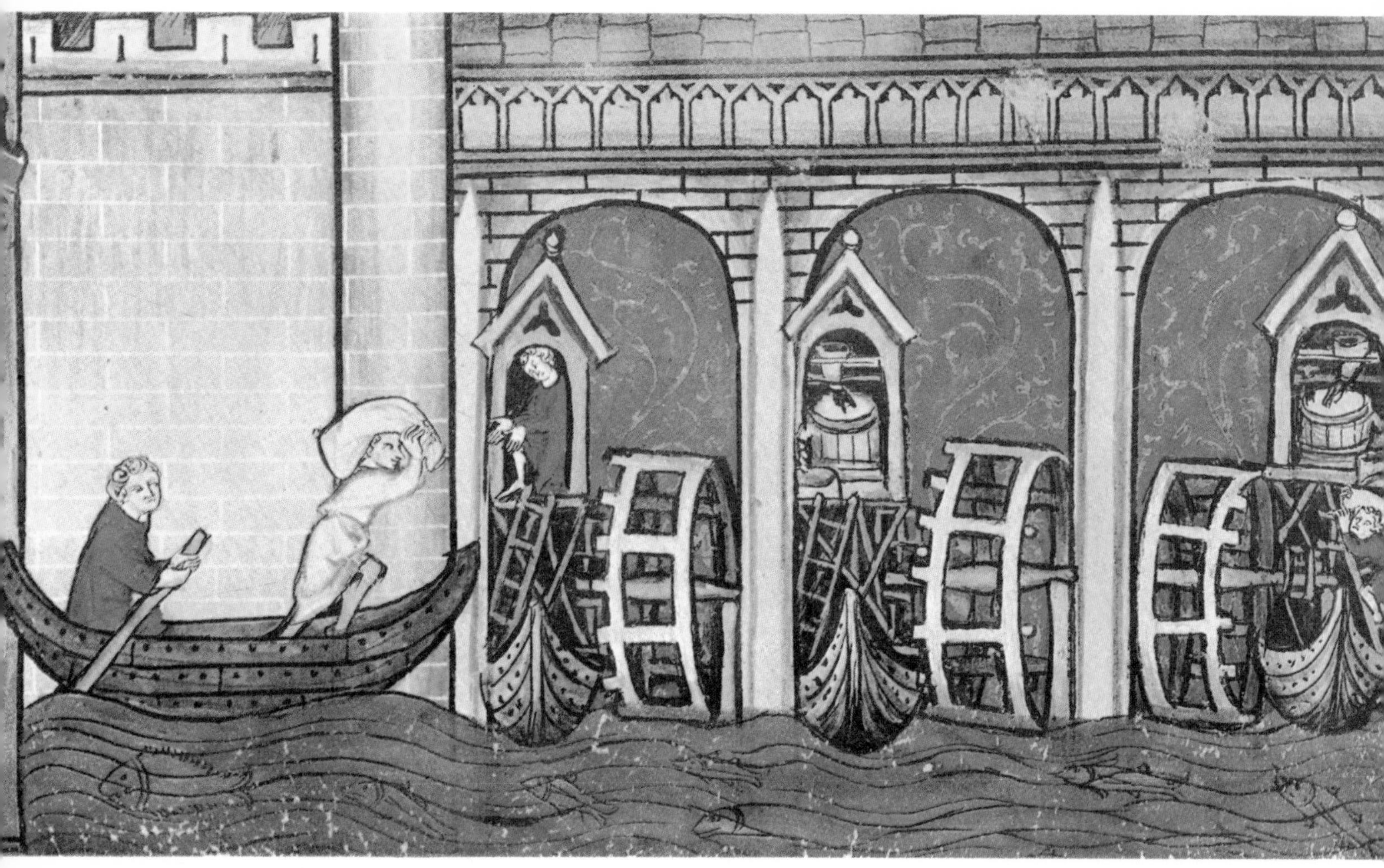

imports. This in itself limited the volume of long-distance trade, which was also restricted by the lack of integration between the various parts of Europe. The result was that the wealth of northern Europe filtered only very slowly into international trade.

These obstacles were beginning to be overcome in the twelfth century. Much closer contacts were forged between Italy and Flanders with the rise of the fairs of Champagne; these fairs provided a permanent place of exchange between Italy and northern Europe. The growing wealth of northern Europe could now be employed more directly in trade with the Levant. Western merchants also began to dominate the markets of the Levant and eastern Europe. These provided an outlet for Flemish cloth, and a rapid growth of the Flemish cloth industry followed. Long-distance trade was no longer so dependent on the amount of bullion that western Europe could supply.

The success of the Flemish cloth industry was outstanding, but other trades were also coming to be concentrated in the towns. This development was most marked in Flanders and northern Italy, where the metal, leather and fur trades were becoming urbanized. The growing importance of industry in the towns is underlined by the appearance of craft guilds alongside the provisioning trades established earlier.

The organization of industry in the towns remained rudimentary. It was still for the most part a household activity. But once confined in a small area, the different stages of production could be supervised by a single man, usually a merchant. He bought the raw materials, put them out to the artisans, and marketed the finished product. The artisans often worked in shops rented from the merchant and were paid miserable wages. The system was brutal, but production was swift and cheap.

The direct contribution of industry to urban wealth was comparatively small, for very little value was added to the raw materials in the course of production. Indirectly, however, the presence of industry stimulated the growth of the urban market: there was a greater demand for raw materials to be made up and for foodstuffs to feed the workers. More products were put on the market, and this favoured the expansion of trade, both local and long-distance.

The greater volume of trade demanded changes in the organization of commerce. The comparative lack of money and its slow circulation were among the main obstacles to the swift growth of commerce. These began to be overcome from the turn of the twelfth century by the development of better credit facilities. There were advances in banking methods, and rudimentary bill of exchange was devised. There was also a tendency to keep clearer accounts.

Progress in business methods stemmed in part from the greater literacy of the merchant class. It was no longer necessary for a merchant to accompany his goods; he could now conduct his affairs from a central office with the aid of correspondents in the cities where he had business. The 'sedentary merchant' could deal with a much greater range and volume of trade than his 'travelling' predecessor. This stage had been reached in Hanseatic trade by the turn of the thirteenth century, but the Italian merchants, above all those of the inland towns of Lombardy and Tuscany, were rather more advanced. The business houses of Siena and Piacenza had already begun to establish permanent branches in some of the main towns of northwestern Europe.

Economic decline

The prosperity of Europe was founded on an expanding agriculture and a fast developing commerce. The towns in a sense played the key role, for they channelled off the surplus wealth of the countryside into trade and industry. Already in the thirteenth century, however, at the height of medieval prosperity, there were signs that conditions favourable to continued economic expansion were coming to an end.

In western Europe the clearing of new lands was being brought to a halt. In the Lincolnshire fens no more land was reclaimed after about the middle of the thirteenth century, when the last great sea

dyke was built. There was little good land still available; furthermore, it was more expensive to clear because scarcity had put up the value of forest and waste.

The demand for foodstuffs did not slacken, and the land had in some places to be farmed more intensively. This could lead to impoverishment of the soil. By the late thirteenth century there was less manure available, for the extension of arable at the expense of the waste and grazing lands meant that proportionately fewer beasts could be kept. The numbers of livestock that a peasant could turn out on the village waste had to be strictly limited; the price of meadowland rose rapidly, and elaborate arrangements had to be made for pasturing livestock on the stubble after harvest. Surveys from some English counties show that at the end of the thirteenth century the peasantry were very badly off for livestock. As a result of the rapid expansion of arable farming the essential balance between arable and livestock may well have been lost.

In these conditions there was a serious danger that, if population continued to grow at its old rate, it would begin to press very hard on available resources. But there are signs that the rate of increase was falling. Indeed, from about the middle of the thirteenth century the rural population in some parts of Tuscany began to decline slowly but steadily. A similar trend may possibly have existed from the turn of the century in some East Anglian villages.

On the other hand, there were economic and social pressures that aggravated the growing shortage of land and made it difficult for the peasants to adapt themselves to the new conditions. An active land market allowed some peasants to build up holdings that were much larger than the standard ones. These were often subdivided to meet the growing pressure on land. There was greater stability where the standard holdings were maintained, but they tended to stay in the hands of the same family, and this, too, aggravated the problem of overpopulation. In most villages, there were fewer peasants with adequate holdings; the majority had to try to make a living off their smallholdings and wage labour.

Far more serious was the growing pressure exerted in many places by the landlords. This might take many different forms, for the relations between landlord and peasant varied from region to region, from village to village, and even within each village. Above all there was a distinct contrast between conditions in England and those existing in many parts of Europe.

In England many landowners tended to farm their estates directly in order to take advantage of the high prices being paid for agricultural products. They could either cultivate their estates by exacting labour services from their peasants or, what was more usual, they could employ cheap wage labour and keep such services owed by their peasants as they still found useful; the other services could then be commuted for a money payment which helped to meet the cost of wages. The peasant owed a great variety of dues to his lord. Perhaps the most burdensome of these were the entry fines that he had to pay when he took up his holding.

On the Continent direct farming by the landlords was not so marked. It was more usual to rent or lease estates out. This had its disadvantages, for while the value of land was rising the real value of money was falling. On the other hand, rent may only have been a small consideration beside the profits obtained from justice and entry fines. The lords were also able to impose direct taxes on their peasantry. To escape these burdens, many French peasants were willing to purchase charters of liberty from their lords; but these often left them even more heavily in debt. The peasantry were also weighed down by tithes.

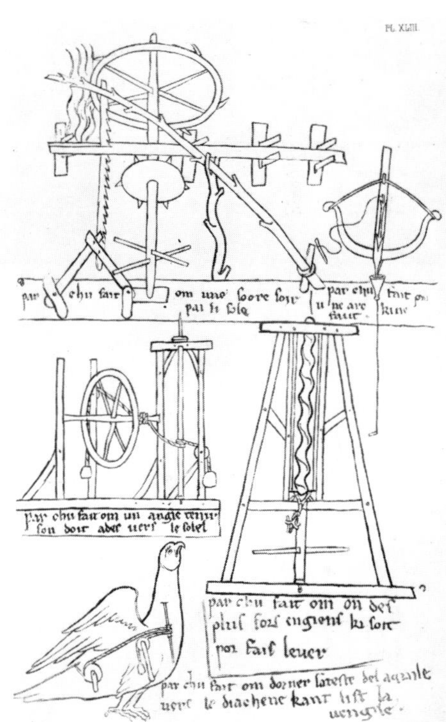

Above, sketches of various mechanical contrivances, including a hydraulic saw, from the work of Villard de Honnecourt of about 1130. Medieval mechanics never got far beyond crude gears, used as often in toys as in machines.

Top, a medieval banquet as depicted in an . illustration to an Old Testament story. Except in periods of great prosperity, the nobility preferred to consume their wealth rather than reinvest it in agricultural improvements or industry. University Cathedral, Basel.

Above left, a French thirteenth-century feast. As many as twelve meat courses might be served, and often, when whole animals were cooked, all the left-overs were given to the poor. Bibliothèque Nationale, Paris.

Opposite, a complex watermill on the River Seine. The largest cities, such as Paris, Naples and Rome, had more than 100,000 inhabitants and a large-scale industry was required to feed them.

Very little of a landlord's revenue was put back into his estates; the vast proportion went into conspicuous consumption. This became all the more marked from about the middle of the twelfth century, when the nobility began to form a closed military caste. Its characteristic way of life demanded heavy expenditure on fine apparel and rare foods and wines. Even the equipment of a knight became more elaborate and expensive. The peasants might benefit from building operations carried on by a lord at his country residence, but the greatest part of his revenue would be spent on luxuries obtainable only in towns. Many nobles found it very difficult to keep up their aristocratic way of life and fell increasingly into debt either to the Jews or to merchants.

The roots of a crisis

Although agriculture was ceasing to expand in western Europe during the thirteenth century, there was no need for trade and industry to stop growing, since an increased proportion of agricultural wealth was finding its way either directly or indirectly to the towns. It was a vicious circle. To pay for their luxuries the landlords had to extract more money or services from their estates and more corn had to be put on the urban market. This led to overfarming and in some places to deteriorating soil. By 1300 English corn yields were showing a tendency to fall.

Some of the new urban wealth returned to the countryside. Merchants increased their investment in land; it was the only secure investment, and it gave status. Yet in the conditions of the thirteenth century such investments may well have led to a further draining off of the wealth of the countryside into the towns. In northern Italy, and perhaps in Flanders, the cities helped to ease the problem of rural overpopulation. The rapid development of the cloth industry in Florence and Pisa during the second half of the thirteenth century demanded large-scale immigration from the countryside. In this way the city was still very closely attached to the countryside.

Nevertheless, it was becoming possible for expansion in Flanders and northern Italy to go ahead with less and less reference to conditions in the countryside. The growth of royal and especially of papal taxation during the thirteenth century not only added another burden to the others that weighed upon the rural economy; by creating a pool of urban wealth it also gave the Tuscan bankers the necessary security for the rapid development of credit which, as we have seen, was one of the bases of continuing commercial expansion. The presence of overseas markets for cloth allowed the industries of Flanders and northern Italy to develop to a degree out of all proportion to the needs of western Europe.

The Flemish and Italian towns also became less dependent on the surrounding countryside for supplies of food: the strongest tie uniting town and countryside was in danger of being severed. By the middle of the thirteenth century Flanders was importing corn from the Baltic coasts, while the Italian cities were able to obtain cereals not only from southern Italy but also from the Black Sea region. In Tuscany the city authorities embarked on a deliberate policy of providing cheap corn; this would keep down wages and thus the costs of cloth making. By the early fourteenth century the price of corn was beginning to fall. This cut right at the heart of the rural economy of western Europe.

The balance between town and countryside was beginning to be upset. A relatively advanced commercial and industrial structure had been imposed on top of a fairly primitive agriculture. From about the middle of the thirteenth century the advances made in commerce and industry had been increasingly detrimental to the well-being of the countryside. It was increasingly becoming clear that policies suitable to an expanding urban economy were harmful to a declining agriculture. This was of course most noticeable in northern Italy, but the increasing control exercised by the Italians over European commerce and credit brought similar problems to northwestern Europe.

The agricultural base of the economy was becoming impoverished; the peasantry were increasingly in debt and badly fed. The crisis of the later Middle Ages was essentially agricultural, but it was to have its repercussions on the urban economy once the towns of Italy and Flanders had lost the protection of safe overseas markets.

The seriousness of the situation did not become clear until perhaps the 1340s, but there were earlier signs of impending crisis. Between 1309 and 1317 much of western Europe was in the grip of a terrible famine, during which there was considerable loss of life. Corn prices were beginning to fall, though this was disguised by violent fluctuations that confused the situation still further. Real wages do not seem to have started rising. France and Flanders were faced with severe monetary troubles.

Yet this crisis did not affect all parts of Europe either to the same degree or at the same time. The areas that suffered most were those, such as large parts of France and southern Italy, given over almost exclusively to corn production. Though the lands east of the Elbe were another great corn-producing region, they came through the early stages of the crisis almost unscathed, for the land was not overworked and the peasants were not yet oppressed by their landlords. From about the turn of the fourteenth century, however, these new lands felt the full weight of the crisis. The losses of the Black Death were not made good; the demand for corn slackened, and clearing was brought to a halt. England and Holland, with more varied agricultures, suffered far less.

The more urbanized parts of Europe did not escape the crisis. The fourteenth century was a period of internal struggles in the Flemish cities, and soon after the middle of the century their industries began to decline. About the same time Hanseatic commerce was contracting. In Tuscany agriculture was disrupted for more than half a century following the disastrous famine and plague of 1339–40. The great Tuscan cities were faced with industrial, financial, and social difficulties. Some—Lucca, Siena and Pisa for example—never recovered and went into permanent decline; but Florence profited from their misfortunes and was able to maintain a high degree of prosperity. Northern Italy remained far in advance of the rest of Europe; while a general recovery seems to have begun there from the early fifteenth century, in most other parts of Europe this was delayed until towards the end of the century.

The Black Death

The shape and timing of the crisis depended on local conditions, but in many regions its onset seems to have coincided with the outbreak of the Black Death, a combination of bubonic and pneumonic plague which ravaged Europe from 1347 to 1349. The effects of the plague varied from place to place. Some areas—Holland is perhaps the best example—seem almost completely to have escaped its toll, while elsewhere as much as half the population died.

These losses, however appalling, seem to have been made good very quickly, for the majority of plague victims were apparently drawn from either the aged or the very young. This single visitation of plague was not in itself disastrous; but it was followed over the next fifty years or so by repeated outbreaks which made rapid recovery almost impossible and further exhausted a population already on the verge of starvation.

The losses sustained during the second half of the fourteenth century were obviously very serious to an economy that depended so much on manpower. In many areas they produced temporary chaos—though this must not be confused with crisis. It is a little too easy to attribute the economic difficulties of the later Middle Ages simply to the drastic reduction in population. Its effects were far from uniform. The countryside was no longer overpopulated, and in England and perhaps in France this undermined the landlord's domination over the peasantry. In the lands east of the Elbe, on the contrary, the landlords were able to take advantage of the peasants' difficulties to increase their control over the countryside and gradually to reduce the peasantry to serfdom. In northern Italy the fall of population allowed landowners and entrepreneurs from the towns to build up estates and to dominate the rural economy. The

Left, a procession in Chantilly praying for the end of the Black Death; the plague was felt most strongly in the towns and the monasteries, and it has been argued that its effects were greatly exaggerated. Musée Condé, Chantilly.

Below left, Florentines giving help to the poor of Siena during the famine of the early fourteenth century; after this famine European agriculture never recovered its former efficiency, and it is possible that Europe had become overpopulated by 1300. Biblioteca Laurentiana, Florence.

Bottom, the Black Death, which seemed to progress inexorably and strike without warning, was seen as a punishment from God; in many regions flagellants such as these in Bruges in 1349 wandered the countryside whipping themselves as atonement for their sins. Royal Library, Brussels.

Opposite left, a thirteenth-century English caricature of the Jews, who were important money-lenders. Aaron of Lincoln (fl. 1170–80) lent money to the English king and even to the Archbishop of Canterbury to help finance the cathedral. Edward I expelled the Jews from England in 1290. Public Record Office, London.

Opposite right, a fourteenth-century German miniature of a Jewish teacher and his pupil; throughout the Middle Ages the Jews played an important role in financing business on both a large and a small scale. British Library, London.

Black Death had the effect of speeding up processes already begun. Thus, while in some places it may even have contributed to economic growth, elsewhere its effect was to intensify the crisis and delay recovery further.

The repercussions of war

War was as terrible a scourge as the plague. Its effects were much the same; it increased misery and chaos and favoured trends in the economy and society that were already under way. The Hundred Years' War certainly contributed to the agricultural depression in France, but it helped the development of the English cloth industry, which grew rapidly under the protection afforded by Edward III's war finance. Northern Italy was ravaged by repeated wars in the course of the fourteenth and fifteenth centuries; city and countryside alike were terrorized by companies of mercenaries. The outcome of these wars, however, was to affirm the dominance of Florence over Tuscany and of Milan over Lombardy.

Rural depression

The effects of war and plague must not be minimized because they appear to be only secondary. They deepened and gave substance to a crisis that might otherwise have followed a rather milder course.

The immediate reaction of landlord and peasant alike to the slump in corn prices was to put more corn on the market; this made a bad situation worse. In England the landlords, especially the great ecclesiastical corporations, tried to cut their losses by reintroducing labour services on a wide scale; this aroused deep resentment among their peasantry.

The difficulties of the landlords increased after the Black Death; the losses of population led to a rapid rise in wages. In all parts of Europe there were attempts to peg wages at pre-plague rates. This intensified the militancy of the peasantry and produced a situation in which peasant uprisings were easily sparked off. They were practically always of local character. Even the greatest of them—the Peasants' Revolt of 1381 in England—was limited for the most part to the southeast and East Anglia.

In the face of peasant non-cooperation and sometimes violence, the landlords' policy of repression was bound to fail. Wage legislation was rarely strictly enforced. However it was managed, the large estate geared to corn production became increasingly unprofitable. Even the most conservative of landowners were forced to rent or lease out their estates, so as at least to do away with the mounting costs of administration.

The attachment that existed between a lord and his estates now became weaker. It is exactly at this period that many English estates passed out of the hands of the old families into the possession of new owners; these rarely kept them for more than a generation. The same tendency is also to be seen in some parts of France. The new families were often drawn from the ranks of the prosperous peasantry. Such frequent changes of ownership, especially marked among the smaller landowners, must have contributed to the instability of the countryside.

Where estates were divided up and passed into the hands of the peasantry, the old system of corn production geared to the market was normally doomed; for the peasantry must have been forced to fall back on subsistence farming to escape the worst effects of the agricultural depression. In some regions it was even becoming more usual to pay rent owed to a landlord in kind. In this way he protected himself against the constant fluctuations in the value of money.

The less direct control exercised by the landlord and the changes in agriculture shook village life. In many places communal life in the village was threatened. The tendency for some peasants to build up large holdings was now intensified; in England many villagers came to be dominated by a few prosperous peasants, who tended to take over the estates when they came to be rented out. This upset the stability of the village community, which had depended on a rough equality among the various classes of peasant holdings; such equality was now fast disappearing.

The Black Death itself does not seem to have brought much disruption to the organization of village life: the vacant holdings were soon taken up by the survivors. After the Black Death, however, it became far less usual for a particular holding to stay in the possession of a single family; this undermined another of the mainstays of village solidarity. It made for greater mobility among the rural population, which the landlords vainly tried to curb. Holdings were now abandoned more easily, and court rolls are full of cases of dilapidation of property.

The weakening of the village community and of the attachment of a particular family to a holding, as well as intensified rural migration, are developments common to both England and the continent. Nevertheless one must not exaggerate the effects: most villages recovered their stability. The absence of a lord often compelled the peasants to take greater initiative in the regulation of their affairs. In England it became more usual for village bye-laws to be enacted. In Germany there was a further growth of 'mark' communities, associations of peasants bound together to regulate the use of wastes.

The end of the urban boom

The depression of the later Middle Ages did not pass the towns by. The urban boom continued well into the fourteenth century, but it was increasingly apparent how unstable its foundations were. Western domination of markets in the Levant and Russia was coming to an end. From about the middle of the century western Asia was virtually closed to Italian merchants. Western exports still found their way to these markets, but in smaller quantities; profits fell heavily because the Italians were now forced to work through middlemen. The declining market for cloth and other industrial products both at home and abroad brought bitter competition. During the fourteenth century Florence was continually at war with its industrial rivals in Tuscany, while Bruges, Ghent and Ypres stamped out competition from smaller Flemish towns and from the rural cloth industry.

War was one answer to the economic crisis, but it was more usual for towns to

adopt a policy of protectionism in an effort to preserve their share of the dwindling market. The guilds increased restrictive practices in the hope of protecting the interests of their members. These policies were, however, the opposite of those that had favoured commercial and industrial expansion; they only led to further decline. In the Flemish cities this change of policy was associated with a change of government. There was a bitter conflict between the merchant-class that had grown rich on long-distance trade and the weavers, who favoured a protectionist policy and tried to guard against the decline of the long-distance trade by ensuring absolute domination over the local market. The surrounding countryside was brought under direct political control. The dangers are clear. The urban boom had been largely possible because commerce and industry had not been closely tied to the local market. Now the situation was reversed.

The expansion of commerce had been founded to a very large extent on the extension of the credit system. Its frailty was exposed in 1343 by the bankruptcy of the two greatest Florentine business houses, those of the Bardi and the Peruzzi; the kings of Naples and England had found themselves unable to honour their debts. The confidence on which trade depended was shattered; and credit was thereafter controlled more tightly.

Towns were forced back more and more on their local markets; but with agriculture impoverished and dislocated, these usually had little to offer. Many towns tried to guard against the chaos in the countryside by restricting immigration. This was to have disastrous consequences, especially after the Black Death had decimated the urban population, for the towns depended on immigration from the countryside to keep up their numbers.

Change in the later middle ages

The later Middle Ages were a period of depression; they were also a period of change which paved the way for economic recovery. The extent of recovery must not, however, be overemphasized: it seems unlikely that the heights attained in the thirteenth century were reached again before the end of the Middle Ages, and population was only just beginning to approach its former levels. It has been argued that there was a general rise in the standard of living; certainly the impressive farm houses and town houses that survive from the fifteenth century in many parts of Europe bear witness to the wealth of certain sections of society.

Certainly there are signs that by the end of the Middle Ages a more efficient economic structure had been forged during the period of depression. Economic activity seems to have been better spread over Europe. Southern Germany became one of the major industrial regions of Europe, while England and Holland appeared as mercantile powers, eager to seek out new markets. The English efforts in the Baltic and the Mediterranean proved largely abortive, but merchants from Bristol broke into the Iceland trade, while the Dutch nearly wrested control of the Baltic trade from the Hanseatic cities.

The Italians still dominated European trade. Their business houses had branches in most of the important European centres. Italian ties with northern Europe had been tightened by the opening up of the sea route through the Strait of Gibraltar. Merchants

Above, hunting was the main obsession of most medieval monarchs and noblemen; these illustrations are taken from a fifteenth-century edition of a French manual on hunting, written in 1382. British Library, London.

Opposite left, a group of flagellants during the Black Death. Such groups were most common in eastern Europe and north Italy; a few visited England, but the movement never caught on there. Staatsbibliothek, Munich.

Opposite right, as the three-field system of crop rotation spread throughout Europe in the Middle Ages, sowing winter wheat became a regular part of the agricultural year. Here the job is illustrated in an early sixteenth-century missal, depicting the month of October. Bibliothèque Nationale, Paris.

and bankers from the northern Italian cities performed the essential task of keeping trade moving and did much to preserve the economic unity of Europe at a time when there was a danger that it might completely disintegrate.

Within northern Italy international banking and commerce were becoming concentrated in four metropolitan centres: Venice, Genoa, Florence and Milan. Previously a large number of Tuscan and Lombard cities had had European interests. Thus, while the small Tuscan town of Pistoia had in the thirteenth century boasted business houses with international interests, by the fifteenth century it had become little more than a market town with some light industry geared to the Florentine market. Francesco Datini, one of the most successful fourteenth-century business men, came from another small Tuscan town, Prato. He built up his business at Avignon, but when he returned to Tuscany he made Florence, not Prato, the centre of his affairs.

The rise of metropolitan centres was not just limited to Italy; it was during the later Middle Ages that London came to dominate the English economy so completely. The

Left, a fifteenth-century painting of shops in Paris. The spread of lock-up shops rather than stalls in the market square is evidence for the growing importance of consumer goods in the late medieval period. Bibliothèque Nationale, Paris.

Opposite top, an English painting of castle-building in the fifteenth century – perhaps an indication that the economy was on the decline, as wealth was once more spent on vast building projects rather than on trade. British Library, London.

Opposite bottom left, a scribe recording the transactions of a late fourteenth-century Genoese banker; double-entry book-keeping was introduced in the 1340s to facilitate this work. British Library, London.

Opposite bottom right, a Sienese painting of about 1310 showing a treasury official counting money. Royal or civic finances, like those of private individuals, needed hordes of cash, which might be supplemented by occasional loans from the bankers. Victoria and Albert Museum, London.

result was better defined economic regions and a clearer division of labour between different towns; but it relegated many towns that had formerly enjoyed an international standing to a position of local importance only.

Economic recovery demanded a return of prosperity to the countryside. It is no coincidence that during the fifteenth century northern Italian agriculture was flourishing. It was now much better balanced, less dominated by arable farming. The decline of the urban corn market allowed more diversification of agriculture and this made for greater flexibility. In England there were the beginnings of an enclosure movement. More enterprising farmers escaped the restraints of communal farming, which was still largely given over to corn production. In many areas open-field farming was also becoming more flexible. The lands of the village were not divided up into any set

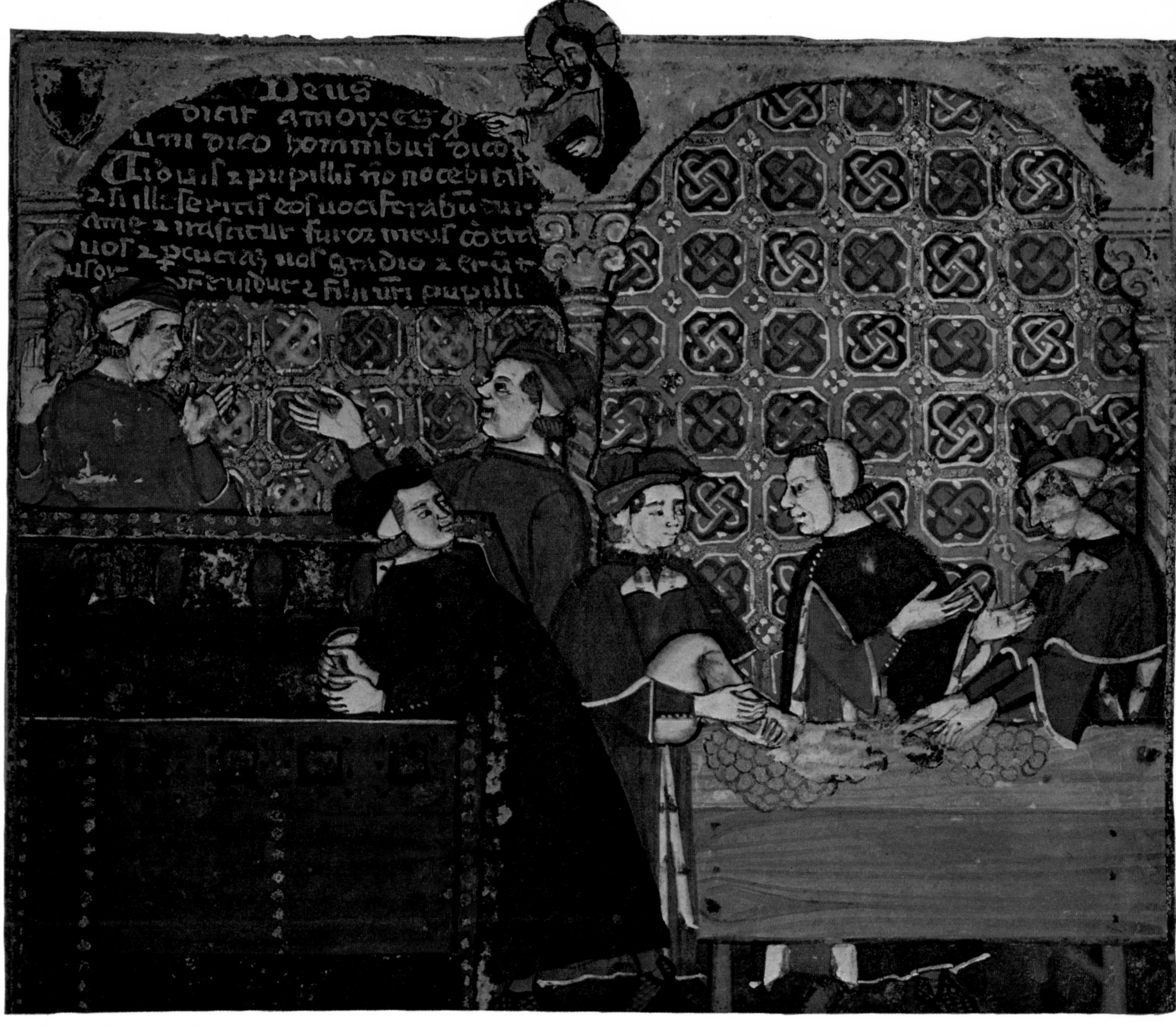

number of fields but into as many as were suited to the lie of the land and the type of crops sown.

New crops were introduced. In England beans were being grown on a much larger scale from the early fourteenth century; they not only gave the peasantry a better diet but could also be used as a winter feed for sheep and cattle. In Lombardy beans were deliberately planted to improve the quality of the soil. More land was given over to industrial crops. Woad, cultivated on an increasingly large scale in Lombardy, was not only employed as a dye-stuff but also provided valuable fodder for livestock. Mulberry trees were planted in the hilly regions of Lombardy to supply the growing silk industry of Milan.

Perhaps the most important change was the greater emphasis on pastoral farming; this can be considered one of the early pointers to economic recovery. Much of Holland's prosperity seems even then to have stemmed from dairy farming. Lombardy became a great cattle raising region, while in England more land was used for sheep farming. From about 1450 villages were being depopulated and their lands enclosed for sheep farming.

In many parts of Europe the prosperity of the countryside increased with the growth of rural industries. The rural cloth industry produced cheap fabrics as an alternative to the expensive materials of the town-based industry which the peasantry could not afford. While its early growth was part of the agricultural depression, in England its rapid development was favoured by the abundance of wool and by the difficulties of the Flemish industry, so that by the end of the fourteenth century England was one of the largest exporters of cloth in Europe. The rural industry had decided advantages over that carried on in the towns. It did not have to face the same guild restrictions and was able to profit from the increased mobility of labour in the countryside. The rural industry may also possibly have derived some slight advantage from the increased use of fulling mills.

The success of other rural industries was not as spectacular as that of the English cloth industry. Nevertheless a flourishing linen industry grew up in the Flemish countryside; and in Italy the metal trades were increasingly carried on in the mountains, where there was water and timber in abundance.

The towns played an essential part in the reconstruction of the countryside. Stock raising requires more capital than arable farming, and the towns supplied much of the capital needed, as they did for the industrial crops, which were mostly cultivated within easy reach of a town. It was partly because of shortage of capital that agriculture in France took so long to recover. Increased investment by the towns in land may well have been just a natural reaction to economic depression, but it was to form one of the foundations of the recovery of agriculture.

With the decline of the urban corn market the towns were no longer in a position to overexploit the countryside. Investment was

UNIVERSITIES AND CULTURAL LIFE

Date	France	Italy	Europe
1100	*Chanson de Roland*		St Anselm
	St Bernard founds Clairvaux Abelard Suger's *Life of Louis VI* Chrétien de Troyes *Roman de Renart* Notre Dame cathedral in Paris	Saracen style in Sicily Palatine Chapel at Palermo St Francis of Assisi	Tristram and Isolde Averroës John of Salisbury Walther von der Vogelweide
1200	University of Paris Villehardouin's *Chronicles* Chartres cathedral William of Lorris *Roman de la Rose* Aquinas' *Summa Theologiae* Jean de Meung Rutebeuf	University of Padua St Bonaventure St Thomas Aquinas Siena cathedral Nicola Pisano Marco Polo Dante	Roger Bacon Toledo cathedral Westminster Abbey Duns Scotus Meister Eckhart
1300	Joinville's *Memoirs* Jean Buridan Papal palace at Avignon Nicholas Oresme William of Machaut	Giotto Petrarch Boccaccio Brunelleschi	William of Ockham John Ruysbroeck Geoffrey Chaucer
1400	Froissart's *Chronicles*	Leonardo Bruni	

now likely to be more beneficial to agriculture. This was certainly the case in Tuscany: perpetual rents in wheat had been a heavy burden on the peasantry, but in the fifteenth century they brought in only a very moderate return on capital. People from the towns began to take a more direct part in Italian agriculture. When the great ecclesiastical estates in Lombardy broke up under the pressure of heavy taxation, much of the land was taken over by speculators from the towns; and they had the necessary capital to effect improvements. At the same time there was a spread of commercial leases of land, under which the owner was commonly expected to provide the lessee with some capital or stock. The increased interest shown by the Italian cities in agriculture is perhaps reflected in the more equitable division of taxation between town and countryside. In Lombardy rural taxation was deliberately reduced in the early fifteenth century.

In the English Midlands cattle rearing was carried on less by farmers than by graziers from the towns. It is noticeable that their standing was rising within the towns. But throughout northern Europe relations between landlord and peasant were perhaps more decisive for the recovery of agriculture than they were in Italy. They were no longer dictated so much by claims of lordship as by supply and demand for land. This shift was very much in the peasantry's favour. Labour services virtually disappeared. Landlords were often forced to provide stock or other capital equipment, while the rents paid by the peasantry were falling sometimes to purely nominal sums. In England these changes are reflected in the rise of a class of prosperous yeoman farmers; this gave a solid base to English agriculture.

A much better balance was being established between town and countryside, which helped the recovery of both. The rural industries are a case in point. The towns provided markets for their products, but did not dominate them. The merchants from the towns were mainly responsible for marketing the products but they did not control the raw materials, and capital was now dispersed along the various stages of production. Profits seem to have been shared out fairly evenly between town and countryside.

The dawn of modern economy

The later Middle Ages were a time of preparation, not a time of fruition; they hold the key to later developments, but it is easy to forget how very backward Europe's economy still was. Agriculture remained its essential base, while the towns derived most of their prosperity from trade. The great companies had not yet begun to specialize in any particular branch of business but would take on almost anything from international banking to purely local affairs. A capital market hardly existed beyond shares in shipping and mining, for industry had not yet passed beyond the craft stage and its equipment required little capital. Land remained the only real long-term investment.

At the same time the foundations were being laid for renewed commercial expansion. The money market became more flexible with the perfection of the bill of exchange, while the development of double-entry book keeping made for more efficient business organization. The profit motive was certainly present earlier in the Middle Ages, but now it was better directed.

The increasingly large role that the state was to have in shaping the economy is also prefigured in the later Middle Ages. The city was now brought more firmly within the framework of the state. The great Flemish cities lost their independence and passed under the direct control of the dukes of Burgundy. Governments were also forced to borrow more and more heavily, to devise more efficient methods of taxation, and even to devalue the coinage, in order to meet their rising expenditure. The economic foundations of the state were being laid.

The growth of the state in the later Middle Ages went hand in hand with the emergence of better defined regional economies. London and Paris came to dominate the economies of their respective countries partly because of the role of each as administrative capital. The state was in future to play a large part in re-establishing the much-needed balance between town and countryside.

Opposite, the Italian bankers were, with the Jews, the main source of finance in the later Middle Ages. At first they dealt only in money-lending, but in the fourteenth century transactions involving bills of exchange, and even deposit banking, became more common. British Library, London.

ud it phelippe descendy tresex
cellent et tres redoubte price
Charle par la grace de dieu

Part IV

THE SHAPING OF EUROPE

Introduction

The late fourteenth and fifteenth centuries in western Europe were marked by uncertainty and confusion. The solid faith of the age of St Thomas Aquinas, St Louis and Dante gave way to anxious questionings in many spheres of human activity. The Holy Roman emperor was no longer a serious power in Europe. The papacy was rent by schism. The universities were full of ferment and disagreement, which were reflected at all levels of society.

Italy, deserted by the popes, led the way towards a new era. Venice, triumphing over its rivals, gained in wealth, stability and reputation. In Rome there was a new interest in ancient Roman history, which showed itself in the writing of men like Rienzi, with his wild dreams of a revival of the republic, and Petrarch, whose interest in Greek and Latin studies was soon to spread. Before the fourteenth century was out, Greek was being taught in Florence and whatever else the Italian Renaissance brought, the study of Greek letters was certainly not the least of its contributions.

Elsewhere the common people, if not yet coming into their own, were at least demonstrating (sometimes noisily) their discontent. The times were hard and the population had decreased, never having fully recovered from the ravages of the Black Death and later epidemics. Thus, a smaller labour force brought demands for increased wages and then revolts or risings which were the equivalent of twentieth-century strikes. The worker wanted more. In the words of the poet, William Langland:

Penny ale will not do, nor a piece of bacon,
But if it be fresh flesh or fish fried or baked.

In Switzerland a peasant democracy made its first appearance. Eminently practical, it proved singularly successful, secure amid the mountains and with a larger defence in proportion to its numbers than any of the other emerging states. Elsewhere in western Europe it was the monarchical ideal that triumphed. It was a king's duty to govern, to administer justice and to lead his warriors to successful and profitable combat.

It was in France, England and, to a lesser degree, in Scotland and the Iberian peninsula that kingship became identified with government. But the process still depended on individual personalities: Charles V and Louis XI of France, Henry V and Edward IV of England and Ferdinand of Aragon showed how determination and character could shape the destinies of countries.

For they were communities rather than nations: the concept of nationhood was not yet born. Besides allegiance to Church and king there was everywhere a strong sense of local grouping. Despite the growth of trade and the movements of armed men, most people saw little beyond their own country or city. This was particularly true of the Holy Roman Empire where the pull towards Rome as the centre was irresistible, partly because tradition, geography and religion favoured it.

It is easy to read history backwards, to see signs of the Renaissance, the Reformation or absolute monarchy long before these really appear. Contemporaries were not gifted with such hindsight and accepted the world as they found it. Nonetheless, as the fourteenth century came to a close, even simple people began to realize that theory and practice differed and that changes must come about. The existence of two serious claimants to the papacy, each supported by powerful governments, could not continue indefinitely. It could not fail to modify men's views about the institutions of the Church, although not about its divine mission. And so, whether it was English Lollardy, Czech Hussitism or the criticism of Italian humanists like Poggio or Valla, the new movements towards religious reform added up to a critical approach which was bound to lead to a re-examination of the teaching of the Bible.

This was made easier because the Bible was now more accessible. The first printed translation, the Gutenberg Bible, had appeared. If it dates, as is likely, from 1453, when Constantinople fell to the Turkish sultan, the coincidence is striking. Important as the printing press was to be, it was so only because literacy was no longer confined to the clergy and increasing numbers were able to read. The German-speaking peoples in particular, who had previously sent their ablest young men to study at Paris, Oxford or in Italy, were now provided with greatly increased numbers of local universities. The foundation and endowment of universities like Prague, Vienna, Heidelberg, Cologne, Mainz and Tubingen, all within a century or so, demonstrated that learning and scholarship did not depend upon imperial and papal initiative. The new universities recruited their students from the many song-schools and grammar schools. For these pedagogues could now be found in sufficient strength to whip the elements of Latin into ever-increasing numbers of boys.

Some of these would turn to the law for a livelihood. Violent as the times often were, force was not the only way of settling disputes. There was a great deal of litigation in the England of the Wars of the Roses and in war-torn France. The study of law flourished

at the Inns of Court in London, at Bourges and Orleans, and at the Italian universities. Notaries public, chartered by emperor or pope, were familiar figures in every walled city. As much subtlety was spent in comment on the civil law as on canon law, its ecclesiastical counterpart, and earlier training of the commentators in the arts faculties of the universities had helped to bring this about. The young men had learnt there how to argue logically according to fixed rules, and how to dispute publicly and draw out nice distinctions of meaning.

At the same time there was apparent a new passion for antiquity, together with a growing demand for the Latin of Cicero and Pliny and a new-found interest in the life of the ancient world. Men began to cultivate elegance of style, so that an Eneas Sylvius could make his way to the papal throne by his achievements as a writer rather than by piety, patronage or wealth.

The restoration of the authority of the popes was accompanied by the increasing activity of the papal court, itself the training ground of humanists as well as theologians. The Italian Renaissance, of which Florence was the first focus, was made possible largely because rulers were also patrons and the profits of successful enterprise were turned into objects of beauty.

While the Italians were seeking for and transcribing neglected manuscripts, or translating the rediscovered Greek poets and philosophers, their northern neighbours were making their own special contributions to the rising nation states of the future. The English parliament not only survived the dynastic struggles but even benefited from them. Again and again the government appealed for its authority to statutes enacted in parliament. Thus, although very little public participation in affairs was implied, government was far from being a personal autocracy. Significantly, the reign of Richard II saw both the crushing of the Peasants' Revolt and the removal of a monarch who spoke of the laws as emanating from his own breast.

To be influential in northern Europe it was necessary to own or control land, which was almost the sole source of wealth and power. From it came the produce on which the people lived and the fighting men who followed their leaders to battle. War was, or could be, a profitable trade and it was governed by its own laws and conventions as clearly defined as those relating to matrimony or the transmission of property by inheritance.

It was in the later Middle Ages that chivalry became a code of conduct. The French chronicler Froissart gives more space to the exploits and the inter-relationship of French and English knights than to any other aspect of the years whose events he related in such detail. The Knights of the Garter were chosen personally by the monarch for their bravery in combats which were regulated struggles of expensively armoured men and horses. As the vassal of his overlord, as the champion of his lady and as the upholder of the Church, the knight went in search of trouble. As the upholder of the Church he was happiest in fighting infidels, and now that the Muslims were too powerful to be attacked in the Holy Land he could crusade in Lithuania or Prussia. In this way he also pushed the basically French civilization of western Europe ever further eastwards against the Slavs.

Writing a century ago, Bishop Stubbs characterized these years as futile, bloody and immoral. The epithet 'futile' can certainly not be applied to the age of Henry V, Joan of Arc, Louis XI and Prince Henry the Navigator, of Botticelli, Lippo Lippi and Leonardo da Vinci, or of Gutenberg and Caxton. Immoral and bloody, certainly, but not exceptionally so, judged either by the ethical standards or by the war record of the twentieth century.

The Spanish and Scandinavian kingdoms emerged full of hope for the future. Poland, Bohemia and Hungary were mighty states not yet crushed by the Turk, and the Old World stood poised ready to usher in the New. It was an age full of vitality and hope. Something new was being born. The labour was long and hard. The offspring was modern man.

Above, Joan of Arc besieging Paris in September 1429; she was unsuccessful in this venture and was captured by the Burgundians six months later. Bibliothèque Nationale, Paris.

Opposite, a meeting of the Order of the Golden Fleece, founded by Philip the Good of Burgundy in 1429. The Order was the most idealistic of the late medieval chivalric organizations. Fitzwilliam Museum, Cambridge.

On page 160, Charles the Bold of Burgundy and his advisers; his lands included Flanders, Artois, Luxembourg, Holland and Zeeland as well as Burgundy; and he aimed to add Alsace and Lorraine to them.

Chapter 14
The Triumph of the Monarchy in Europe and France

There are remarkable superficial resemblances between the histories of France and England during the late fourteenth century. Charles VI of France and Richard II of England were both under age when they came to the throne and, within a few years of their accession, both faced popular uprisings against social injustice. In both countries the government of the realm was disturbed by the ambitions of the uncles of the king—in England the Duke of Gloucester and in France primarily the dukes of Burgundy and Anjou. Finally, both the young kings endeavoured to assert their own government and appoint their own ministers, with varying degrees of success.

It is, however, the differences which are interesting and significant. First the kings themselves. Whatever his failings, it certainly cannot be said of Richard II that he was feeble minded, whereas from 1392 until his death thirty years later, the French king was subject to periodic attacks of madness.

France was a deeply divided nation. There were vast tracts of the kingdom where the king's writ did not run. With varying success the English kings, lords of Gascony since the twelfth century, ruled as the sovereign power in Normandy, Champagne, Maine, Aquitaine and Toulouse. Throughout this period the counties of Flanders, Artois and Nevers and the great duchy of Burgundy were part of the territory of the dukes of Burgundy, which was in all but name an independent country. In Périgord, Angoulême and Blois the Duke of Orléans wielded an almost equal power, and in Berry and Poitou the Duke of Berry was supreme. The allegiance of the dukes of Brittany to the French crown was still more tenuous.

Despite the restriction of the French king's authority, the monarchy still enjoyed the right to certain feudal levies, and the royal treasury could still be a very profitable object of plunder. Moreover, with all their pretensions and the splendour of their courts, the two most powerful men in France, Duke Philip the Bold of Burgundy and Duke Louis of Orléans, proved themselves little better than bandits in their administration of the royal finances to the benefit of their own estates. In England the objective of aristocratic ambition was the crown itself, that is to say, the power of directing the government of the country rather than the ability to exploit it in order to build up a private state within the state.

Charles the Mad

When Charles V died in 1380 at the age of forty-three, the tide seemed to be on the point of turning for France in its long struggle with England. It had succeeded in its fight to nullify the terms of the Treaty of Brétigny. The English had been driven out of all the territories previously ceded to them and were left with only their age-old province of Gascony. With the help of competent, if low-born, ministers, Charles had restored royal authority, laid the foundations of an effective standing army and initiated other important reforms.

From 1382 to 1388 Philip the Bold of Burgundy was chief counsellor to the King of France. Through his wife he succeeded to the countship of Flanders in 1384. The royal exchequer paid him 100,000 francs towards the cost of entering upon his new county and two years later a further 120,000 francs to defray his expenses in enforcing its allegiance to the French crown.

Although, by the terms of his father's will, Charles VI had come of age in 1381, it was not until a full seven years later that the regency was declared at an end. France seemed to be on the point of disintegration during this period. Quite apart from the depredations of Philip the Bold, his brother, John of Berry, was in receipt of an annual pension of some 20,000 francs and their nephew, Louis of Orléans, was awarded in his turn a duchy at the expense of the royal domain. He, too, was to plunder the French treasury and powers of royal patronage to his own advantage, and the four years of Charles's personal rule were too brief a period for radical changes to be affected. It is probable that the plot which led to the overthrow of the government of the dukes in 1388 was organized by the constable of France, Olivier de Clisson, and he it was who headed the new administration.

Nevertheless, in the new administration of 1388 Charles VI had at least provided his country with a somewhat less rapacious regime than the one which had gone before. Men like Bureau de la Rivière introduced a measure of order into the business of the French state. Some attempt was made to conciliate the bourgeoisie of Paris, whose bitter discontent with the level of taxation and corrupt administration had broken into violence with the rising of the *Maillotins* at the begining of the new reign. The government, both local and national, was purged of Burgundian officials.

The new government of professionals, many of whom had served under Charles V, was despised by the court because of the low births of its members, who were dubbed the *Marmousets* (the best English translation for this is perhaps 'funny little men'). A state of affairs in which such men could win and hold control of France cannot have struck Philip of Burgundy as particularly amusing, and it must have been with considerable relief that he heard the news of the king's madness in 1392.

Although Philip of Burgundy had recovered his influence at court, he was to experience strong opposition in the years that followed. Louis, the king's brother, had secured his duchy of Orléans in the year before the king's final relapse. Then, showing an ambition equal to that of his uncle, he added to this substantial holdings in France, among them Blois, Angoulême and Périgord and also territories outside the kingdom including Luxembourg. As the fifteenth century began, the dismemberment of France must have seemed imminent to many contemporary observers.

Left, Edward III of England with the founder members of the Order of the Garter, the Order that he founded to honour his greatest soldiers in the Hundred Years War, whether members of the nobility or professional soldiers. Library of the Victoria and Albert Museum, London.

Opposite top, Philip the Bold, Duke of Burgundy (ruled 1363–1404), the son of John II of France and regent during Charles VI's minority and insanity. He was the chief architect of the Duchy of Burgundy of the fifteenth century. Musée de Dijon.

Opposite bottom, in 1393 Charles V of France attended a court ball dressed as a savage, with several attendants. Their costumes caught fire, and four of Charles' companions were killed. The incident intensified the king's madness. Bibliothèque Nationale, Paris.

The rising power of Louis of Orléans threatened not only Philip the Bold's ascendancy at the French court but also the future of the new state which he was slowly, skilfully and unscrupulously building up on the eastern borders of France. Furthermore, during his occasional moments of lucidity Charles VI tended to turn to his brother, Louis, for help.

In 1407, a fateful year for France, the Duke of Burgundy's son, John the Fearless, had Louis of Orléans assassinated. This act let loose the long and bitter strife between the Burgundians and Armagnacs, which was to cost John his life and was to be ended only thirty years later at the Congress of Arras.

Richard II

In 1399 Richard II formally abdicated in favour of his cousin, Henry of Bolingbroke, asking only that the new king be a good lord to him. Months later Richard was dead and his body was exhibited in Westminster Hall. Then the way was clear for Henry IV to consolidate the position which he had won by a display of force and confirmed by the approval of parliament.

The reign of the boy-king Richard had begun in 1377 in troubled circumstances. His father, the Black Prince, darling and hero of England's triumphant wars against France, had died the year before, worn out by a fever contracted fighting in Spain on behalf of Peter IV of Castile. Richard's grandfather, Edward III, the architect of the English success against its two traditional enemies, Scotland and France, had ended what had been the most glorious reign in English history in the dotage of old age.

In the country at large, the mood was one of disillusionment. The French king, Charles V, and his general, Bertrand du Guesclin, were successfully assailing the English position established by the Treaty of Brétigny. French, and later Castilian, privateers pillaged the south coast of England and even the Thames estuary, and the government was powerless to prevent them. The peasantry was increasingly dissatisfied with its lot and more self-assured in the aftermath of the Black Death which, owing to the sharp decline in population, had effectively made labour a seller's market. However, despite these inauspicious beginnings, Richard's first move in the role of king was an unqualified success.

The discontent of the ordinary people had finally come to a head in the rising known as the Peasants' Revolt in 1381. The affair had all the makings of a major rebellion. The rebels gained the sympathy of the citizens of London. The great Savoy palace of the Duke of Lancaster was burnt to the ground, two bishops were murdered and the insurgents forced the king to meet them to hear their demands. In this dangerous and dramatic encounter his boyish courage and good looks endeared Richard to the populace, and his advisers were soon able to execute the ringleaders and disperse the mobs. But during the next ten years Richard showed that it was his aim to clip the wings of the nobility as well as to discipline the peasants, and his bid for personal autocracy nearly succeeded. The aims and ambitions which inspired him were the same as those which a century later were to inspire the Tudor monarchy.

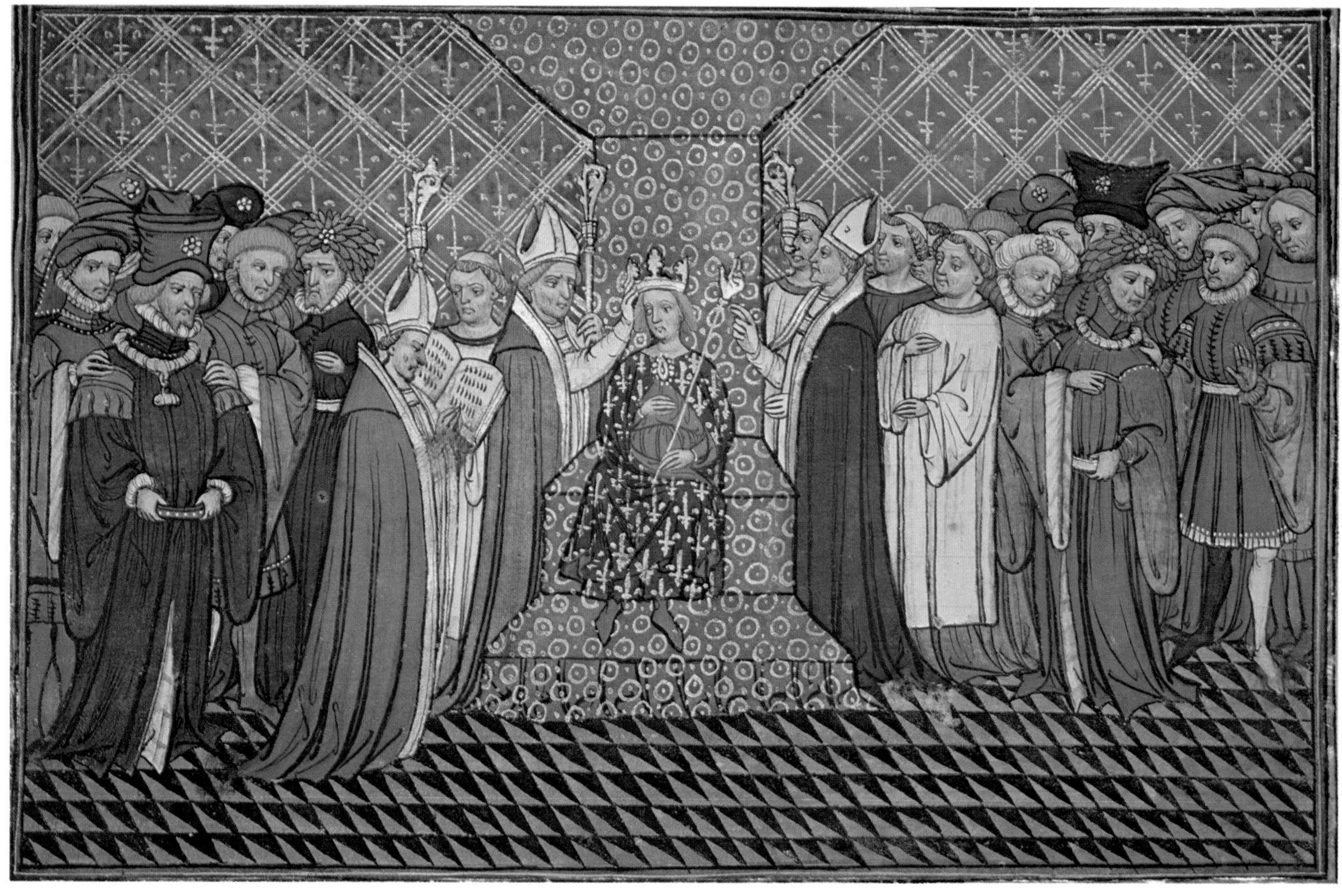

The Peasants' Revolt

On Saturday 15 June 1381, the youthful Richard rode down to Smithfield, outside London, with his counsellors for a further meeting with the rebellious peasants under their leader Wat Tyler. We are told that despite Richard's willingness to grant almost all the terms demanded of him, Wat Tyler remained unconvinced and indeed launched a hot-tempered tirade against the king and his counsellors. Weapons were drawn and Tyler was struck down and murdered on the spot. After this breathtaking piece of provocation the royal party seemed paralysed by fear. Only Richard kept his head and rode straight at the hostile ranks, calling out, 'Good people, will you kill your king? I am your leader now.' Taking advantage of the respite, some members of the royal party made for safety, while the Lord Mayor rode off to call out the garrison of the Tower of London. By the time they arrived, however, the temper of the crowds had changed and they were already dispersing.

There is no need to search for the general causes of peasant risings during the Middle Ages. Life was hard, the winter months regularly brought conditions of near-starvation and the extremes of luxury and poverty were both widespread and conspicuous. Often the rural labourers were subject to the manor court which was presided over by the very lord whose own high standard of life rested on their oppression.

Yet in the later fourteenth century there were additional burdens. In an attempt to combat the effects of the general European economic depression which followed the boom conditions of the previous century, many great landholders, hoping for financial security, leased out their lands to the peasants, commuting labour services for a fixed money rent. In this way the mark of servitude—the obligation to work on the lord's land to the neglect of one's own—became less obvious, and with the scarcity of labour following the depopulation caused by the Black Death the peasant labourer held a commanding position. The consequent high rise in the costs of labour produced a further reaction from the landowners who, in many cases, tried to reimpose labour services.

The general market conditions and the increasing mobility of the labourer himself in search of better terms further dislocated the social order, already undermined by the Black Death. For Englishmen the outlook seemed still bleaker. A war with France which had formerly paid for itself and brought rich profits to the country was by the 1380s, beginning to be an expensive burden. Moreover, the Scots were raiding across the border more frequently.

The government of the regency needed money desperately, but the influential and rich men who controlled parliament were reluctant to carry the brunt of a failing war with France. Consequently, instead of approving a levy of a fifteenth on the total value of the movables of the taxpayer (a customary tax which of course took more from the wealthy) parliament agreed in 1380 to a poll tax of three groats to be levied on all irrespective of means. The system of collection was so slow and inefficient that in the spring of 1381 the government established commissions for fifteen counties; these were to gather the whole levy at all costs and to imprison defaulters. This provided the spark which set alight the fires of rebellions.

Discontent first boiled over in the south-east. In Kent the leadership of Wat Tyler was reinforced by the fiery sermons of the vagrant priest, John Ball, freed from the archbishop of Canterbury's prison. His theme was summed up in the popular couplet:

> When Adam delved and Eve span
> Who was then the gentleman?

On Tuesday 11 June the Kentish rebels marched on London. There they were met by Richard on the Friday at Mile End. They demanded the trial of all those ministers of the king whom they saw as responsible for the country's parlous state and the abolition of servile status. The young king agreed to these terms, promised that charters should be delivered in confirmation and, according to the French chronicler Froissart, gave the rebels standards bearing his insignia as an earnest of good intentions.

It is a remarkable fact that the promised charters were in fact drawn up and in many cases handed over to local representatives, large numbers of whom began to return to their villages. However, once the danger had passed and the mobs had been dispersed after the Smithfield encounter, the government called in the charters and executed more than 100 of the ringleaders of the revolt. By the end of the year the *status quo* had been restored and the only lasting effect of the Peasants' Revolt was that no further poll tax was ever levied by an English parliament.

It is surprising, in view of the inflamed passions of the insurgents, how little violence was practised. It is true that the Duke of Lancaster's palace, the Savoy, was razed to the ground, but this seems to have been an act of vengeance by the Londoners in pursuance of their own private feud. Four of the king's counsellors, including the Archbishop of Canterbury, were beheaded, but these as members of the government fell into the class of traitors whose heads the rebels had demanded. By and large there was no indiscriminate killing or wanton destruction, the target in almost all cases being the manorial records of the hated servile conditions, which were systematically sought out and destroyed.

The revolt affected many counties. It was a spontaneous and partly co-ordinated rising of the lowest orders of society and, in some cases, even found allies among disaffected local gentry. It constituted a real threat to an unprepared government, but its aim was to gain a recognition of rights, not to bring about wholesale destruction.

The king asserts himself

Richard's route from his minority led inevitably through the hazards of baronial opposition. Lords of the council had exercised effective power throughout the 1370s and when early in the next decade Richard began to build up an administration of his own choosing it was to be expected that the great lords would move against him. He was growing up in a world where the old ties of feudal allegiance based on land tenure were gradually giving way to a new and less stable order of 'affinities'. These were groupings of men round the great, determined not so much by land tenure but rather by indentures or contracts of fees to be paid and protection given in exchange for specific services, whether military or administrative. The system had been consolidated by the practice of indentures developed in the formation of the new army and extensively used in raising the forces for the French campaigns.

As a result of his father's senility and his own youth, the king found himself without any such strong and loyal band of retainers, and one of the main endeavours of his reign was to build one up. The first tentative attempt was thwarted when, in 1386, he was forced to dismiss his counsellors and to suffer the impeachment of his competent chancellor, Michael de la Pole, who was a merchant by origin.

It seemed as though Richard's tutelage might be indefinitely extended after he was defeated by an army under the leadership of his uncle, the Duke of Gloucester. Moreover, when, in the parliament of 1388 (the 'Merciless Parliament'), his supporters were exiled and executed by the orders of the Lords Appellant, as the opposition now called itself, his position seemed even more precarious. Yet, within a year Richard was back in control, the appellants having alienated support, partly because of their avarice and incompetence and also because they had been obliged to continue the policy of peace with France which they had condemned as cowardly when it had been pursued by the king.

Richard had the good sense to seek the support and advice of his uncle, John of Gaunt, and must at this time have met on friendly terms Gaunt's son, his cousin, Henry of Bolingbroke, who was later to overthrow him.

The years of peace

For the next ten years the court and realm of England enjoyed comparative peace. It was the first great age of English courtly culture. The native talents of men such as Geoffrey Chaucer and the painters of the new school of manuscript illumination were combined with the cosmopolitan influences of the international courtly culture of Europe (fostered by Richard's two queens, Anne of Bohemia and Isabella of France) to produce a brilliant period in the history of the arts in England. It was the age which saw the creation of the first great masterpieces of the English language—Chaucer's *Troilus and Criseyde* and *Canterbury Tales*—which were without parallel in contemporary Europe. In architecture, too, there were striking achievements, most notably the Great Hall at Westminster.

During this period, in which the king's government remained pretty much the king's affair, Richard and his ministers pursued policies intended to establish the position of the monarchy beyond doubt. They continued to recruit reliable members to the king's 'affinity' with gifts of land and offices and built up a large body of retainers. Men-at-arms bearing the device of the White Hart became a numerous and formidable body. Complementary to this was the stocking of the royal arsenal with modern artillery. so that on his second expedition to Ireland Richard was able to leave more than thirty cannon in the Tower of London.

Richard's policy in Ireland may be seen as part of a general policy aimed at building up the authority of the king. While retrenching on the expenses of the fruitless campaigns

Opposite, the coronation of Charles VI of France, whose reign (1380–1422) saw the continual decline of French fortunes, both in the Hundred Years War and in royal authority in his own kingdoms. Charles himself suffered from insanity after 1392. British Library, London.

in France, he initiated a policy in Ireland which if continued might well have effectively established the claims of the English crown there.

By 1397, Richard felt strong enough to move against his former enemies. His marriage with Isabella of France in 1396 had gained him an extension of the truce with France for a further thirty years and had brought with it a dowry of £50,000 to the royal coffers. His estimate of his power seemed triumphantly vindicated by the ease with which he was able to arrest Gloucester and the Earl of Arundel, who was active in Gloucester's factions, and have them killed. However, within two years Richard himself was deposed and murdered. The way in which his support melted away can be partly explained by the arbitrary nature of his acts, particularly the confiscation of the Lancastrian inheritance of Henry of Bolingbroke. Equally important, however, was the steady erosion of confidence in the king's word and the increasing fear of his growing power.

Richard also alienated the powerful by gradually placing his own servants in positions of authority in local government; by 1399 eleven of the counties were governed by sheriffs who were members of the king's household. But his desperate need for money led him to ever more objectionable infringements of the traditional liberties of his lesser subjects, such as forced loans and the notorious 'Plesaunce'. This was a fine levied on individuals and districts who had supported the king's enemies in the early years of the reign and whom the parliament of 1397 branded as traitors.

The king overthrown

In 1399 Thomas Mowbray, Earl of Norfolk, accused Henry Bolingbroke, Earl of Derby and heir to the great Lancastrian estates, of high treason. The charge was denied and Richard ordained that the affair should be settled by trial by combat. It was arranged that the contest should take place at Northampton and the two rivals arrived with their followers for the joust. At this point Richard intervened and exiled both contestants, Henry for ten years and Thomas for 'a hundred winters'.

Although Richard's position was undoubtedly strong he was surrounded by a powerful baronage jealous of its rights and needing skilful handling—something beyond Richard's capabilities. Therefore, when two years later John of Gaunt, Duke of Lancaster, died Richard looked for a quick and simple solution to the problem presented by the wealth and power of the house of Lancaster by extending Henry's exile to a life term and forbidding him to take up his inheritance. Thus he not only alienated Henry of Lancaster but all the magnates. If the huge duchy of Lancaster could be confiscated, who was safe?

Richard now embarked a second time for Ireland with a sizeable army, which could be turned back to counter any move by Henry. But he had miscalculated in leaving the realm under the regency of his weak and politically untried uncle Edward, Duke of York.

Henry returned from exile in 1399, landing at Ravenspur in Yorkshire with only fifteen men-at-arms. He could however rely not only on his own Yorkshire retainers to join him but could also count on the sympathy of many great lords and the active help of the powerful Henry Percy, Earl of Northumberland.

Henry's publicly proclaimed intention was merely to recover his inheritance, but more was obviously in the wind. The exiled Archbishop of Canterbury returned with him and Henry's adroit moves ensured that the members of the king's council were outmanoeuvred and that only a handful of supporters were at Conwy to greet Richard on his return from Ireland. At their meeting in Flint castle Henry swore that he would respect Richard's kingship if only his lands were returned to him.

Again Richard failed to judge the situation and the man. By returning to England, Henry had committed an act of rebellion and sooner or later the final test must come. If Richard hoped that he would be able to outmanoeuvre Henry he was day-dreaming. The duke escorted his sovereign back to London and the Tower. Richard summoned a parliament, but its first business was to hear the news of his abdication. Henry assumed the throne by the 'right of inheritance and conquest, confirmed by the community of the realm' and was crowned with full solemnity. An attempt to reinstate Richard was followed by his murder in 1399.

This attempted counter-stroke was by no means the last threat which Henry IV had to face. Two years later the Scots invaded England claiming that Richard was still alive. Their total defeat by Henry Percy of Northumberland was a mixed blessing for the new king, contrasting as it did with his own unsuccessful expedition against the Scots. In 1402 the Percies themselves formed a grand rebellious coalition with the Welsh under Owen Glendower and the Scots. It is a mark of Henry's insecurity that the great family most responsible for his gaining the kingship and most lavishly rewarded for its efforts should have joined forces with the Scots, England's chief enemy.

Left, Henry of Lancaster escorting Richard II of England back to London in 1399, to imprison him in the Tower of London and force him to abdicate soon afterwards. Richard had lost the sympathy of the nobility by his tendencies to autocracy. British Library, London.

Opposite left, the crucial meeting between Henry of Lancaster and Richard II at Flint Castle in 1399. Henry's rebellion was virtually declared, and Richard found himself almost friendless. British Library, London.

Opposite right, Henry IV of England (ruled 1399–1413). He brought the great wealth of the Duchy of Lancaster to solve some of the monarchy's financial problems but was never confident of his hold over his kingdom. National Portrait Gallery, London.

Henry's speed and adroitness enabled him to intercept the Percies and the Earl of Douglas on their way to join with their ally in Wales. At the Battle of Shrewsbury in 1403 Northumberland's son, Sir Henry Percy, called Hotspur, was killed and the Earl of Douglas taken prisoner.

The victory established the Lancastrian dynasty, but Glendower remained a serious menace for many years and was for some time supported by the French. In 1405 the old Earl of Northumberland rose again and was not finally defeated until three years later. Moreover, the new dynasty remained vulnerable to rebellion even after Henry's death. On the eve of the departure of his son, Henry, for France in 1415 the plot by the Earl of Cambridge to assassinate him was unmasked and Cambridge and his associates executed.

It is not suprising that there should have been such persistent unrest. The magnates who supported Henry Bolingbroke's claim to his inheritance did not necessarily want him as king. His usurpation was an example to other powerful lords and had cost him dear in buying support. His resultant weakness made Henry dependent on the good will of the House of Lords and the generosity of the House of Commons for the finances necessary for running the country. The Lords gained increasing power in the King's Council and the Commons asserted their control over money grants.

While explicitly disclaiming any role in government, the Commons had by the middle of the reign made their grants of taxes dependent on the remedy of abuses by the government. Apart from this increase in power the Commons also gained in corporate sense and procedural expertise as a result of the greater frequency of parliaments. Finally, it was becoming more common for royal statutes to be passed only after parliamentary consent.

The Lollards

Besides political unrest and financial stringency, the reign of Henry IV also saw the consolidation of the Lollards, a heretical sect which continued to flourish among the lower orders of society up to the time of the Reformation. The beliefs of the Lollards reflected a disillusionment with the clergy and the established church which was general throughout Europe. They denied the doctrine of transubstantiation and thereby the unique function of the priest in the sacrament of the eucharist. They attacked the confessional and the practice of clerical celibacy and claimed for laymen the right to use a vernacular Bible and to interpret it for themselves. In essence, all these beliefs can be seen to be an attack on the special status of the priestly office and an assertion that the virtuous layman needed no mediator between himself and God.

In the later years of the fourteenth century the Lollards represented a sizeable section of the population, finding support in all classes of society. They derived their inspiration and teachings from the Oxford scholar, John Wycliffe, whose anti-clericalism had won him influential support and whose increasingly heretical views exerted a considerable influence at Oxford University.

Wycliffe was officially condemned as a heretic in 1380 but died unmolested in his Lutterworth rectory four years later.

Henry IV, however, tightened up the laws against heretics. The penalty of death by burning was confirmed by statute and the bones of Wycliffe disinterred. The quickening pace of religious persecution largely affected the lower classes at first, but Lollardy retained its strength amongst the increasingly literate merchant and artisan classes in the towns. Even so there were a number of Lollard gentry in parliament who petitioned the crown for the disestablishment of the Church. Moreover, in Sir John Oldcastle, a friend of Henry, Prince of Wales, the movement seemed to have one powerful ally.

The measure of this English protest movement against the Church is given not only by the standing of Oldcastle, a wealthy landowner and a valuable military leader in the Welsh campaigns, but by the fact that after his imprisonment in the Tower he was able to escape and organize a rising. Henry V promptly suppressed the rebellion and, with the capture and burning of Oldcastle in 1417, Lollardy ceased to be a threat.

An English hero

Henry V was twenty-six when he succeeded his father in 1413. To his contemporaries he was a pious and noble warrior king, to later ages the symbol of triumphant England. To many modern scholars, however, he has appeared as a cold, brilliant, somewhat hypocritical diplomat and military leader. In fact, Henry so completely epitomized the virtues and weaknesses of his time and of aristocratic and feudal Europe that it is very hard for an age so remote in ideals and sympathies as our own to see the diverse elements in Henry's character as parts of an integrated whole.

When Henry announced his intention to retrieve his inheritance in France, he believed that his rights to it were ordained by God and that He would help him vindicate his claim. Such principles of action were understood and respected by contemporaries. Nor need we question Henry's honesty in his desire to bring peace to the kingdom of France and justice to its people.

Another aim which Henry would have admitted was the union of the two crowns so that their resources could be combined in a joint crusade against the Turks. With his dying words he spoke of the crusade and many other princes of western Europe were to pay lip service to this great ideal before the century was over. These kinds of beliefs were those of a Christian monarch. Henry's piety also showed itself in his appointment as bishops of men with qualifications in the Church rather than in administration. his keen interest in the liturgical conduct of his own private chapel and in his strict persecution of heretics.

These were some of the attributes of the medieval Christian king. There were, however, others just as important—the willingness to defend one's rights with arms if necessary, generosity and bravery in battle, merciless reprisals against enemies who refused to acknowledge the justice of the king's cause, and mercy to the innocent. Unlike Edward III, Henry forbade his army to molest non-combatants but like Edward's son, the Black Prince, he showed no quarter in punishing stubborn opposition.

War with France

Whatever the genuinely held beliefs of the king, it is obvious that foreign distractions were an excellent cure for the discontent which had been growing during the last years of Henry IV and was threatening to get out of hand. The strain on the resources of the central exchequer had brought bitter complaints from the country's representatives and increasingly rigorous parliamentary control. War with France would, in the long run, inevitably add to the country's financial burdens. But, in the short term, a couple of resounding victories would make the new dynasty immensely popular after forty years of French successes and English policies of peace.

In view of the unrest he left behind him, Henry's departure for France was something of a gamble. It was successful, thanks to a reasonable share of luck and Henry's own genious for war. His experience in Wales had taught him a lot and shown his qualities. These were demonstrated even before the expedition to France sailed. To mobilize and supply a medieval army of any size was in itself a major undertaking. The army comprised not only the men-at-arms, recruited by indentures or contracts between the king's agents and the captains, but also the numerous service corps, such as the armourers, miners and sappers, probably recruited from the mines of the Weald of Kent.

As always in an English army of the period, the archers formed a major contingent, drawn from the yeomen peasantry of the villages whose skill in archery was encouraged by government decrees. It is interesting to learn that each of the great

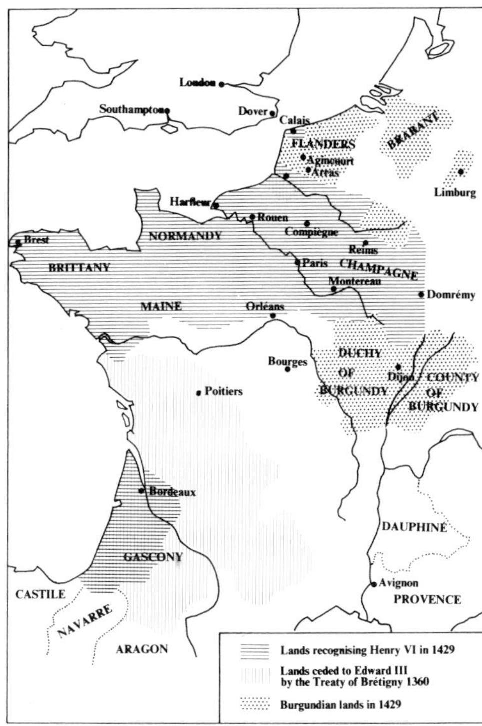

Above, France during the Hundred Years War; although the English won control of substantial areas by the Treaty of Bretigny in 1360, they were never able to assert their authority over the whole country.

Above left, an English view of the Battle of Agincourt (1415), one of the great English victories of the Hundred Years War. The longbowmen on the left have been described as the main reason for the overwhelming victory.

Opposite left, the funeral of Richard II of England (ruled 1377–99) a year after he was driven from the throne by Henry IV. Richard had been responsible for introducing the style of French courtly art to England during his reign. British Library, London.

Opposite right, Henry V of England (ruled 1413–22), though considered a hero by Shakespeare and his contemporaries, left the monarchy in debt and committed to an expensive war in France. National Portrait Gallery, London.

household officers of the king, among them the king's smith and the king's master of music, brought his own bowmen to the army.

Henry made a show of being willing to conciliate, and negotiations were continued with French representatives until the month of his departure for France. It is difficult to tell how sincere these English manoeuvres were. The French offered marriage with the king's daughter and a dowry of 850,000 gold crowns, but Henry demanded in addition the restitution of Aquitaine and Normandy, declaring that if this were not granted he as the rightful king of France would come and claim them. When, in reply, the French emissaries told him that he was not rightful king of England, let alone of France, matters had gone too far for peace and Henry completed his preparations. On 11 August 1415, Henry set sail with about 9,000 men, landing three days later near Harfleur.

Agincourt

After a siege of a month, during which time no French commander had made any attempt at relief, the town was forced to capitulate and Henry entered in triumph having sent news of his victory posthaste to London. The aim was now to build up Harfleur as an English enclave—a second Calais—at the mouth of the Seine. But before returning to England the king was determined on a demonstration of force in Normandy, although the army was much depleted by dysentery.

The gamble was being played out to the last throw. To have returned to a sceptical London, whose merchants had so generously financed the campaign, with only the capture of Harfleur to show for his efforts (a victory which could have been easily reversed by determined French effort) would not have been very impressive. Henry had to risk flaunting English power in France and pit his weakened force in battle for the sake of a great victory. The French armies obligingly made a battle possible, when after shadowing his march for several days in an attempt to drive him into a trap, they finally forced the English to stand and fight near the little village of Agincourt (now known as Azincourt).

The fame of this victory resounded throughout England and earned Henry a hero's welcome home and an immortal reputation. Repeating their old errors of ill-discipline and refusal to make proper use of the terrain, the French knights allowed themselves to be mown down by the English archers and butchered.

A mistaken report that the French were attacking the baggage train and the camp followers in the rear of the English army led to the fateful and expensive order to kill all prisoners. That day the French lost more than 1,500 knights, among them three dukes and the English the opportunity of collecting many thousands of pounds of ransom money.

But Henry's campaigns had so far produced few tangible gains. It was essential to follow up the victory at Agincourt as soon as possible, and thus Henry set about the conquest of Normandy from 1417 onwards.

After his triumphant return from France he could be certain of the support of the House of Commons and in fact they granted him the customs receipts on wool and leather for life. The next two years were occupied in negotiations for a peace settlement, but it is most unlikely that Henry for one moment abandoned his intention of a new campaign. Indeed, his demands on the French based on the Treaty of Brétigny, were so extreme that war was bound to be the only way to settle them.

Nevertheless, many approaches were made in an attempt to gain these demands by peaceful negotiations with both the Armagnac and the Burgundian parties in France. The most fascinating series of exchanges, however, was that initiated by the Holy Roman emperor, Sigismund. These illustrate well the characteristic assumptions of the fifteenth century and the practice of medieval diplomacy.

As in all diplomatic encounters the aims of the parties were divergent. For his part the emperor wished to secure the success of the Church Council at Constance which had been convened under his auspices to end the long protracted schism of the Papacy. His first objective was to persuade the French to abandon their support of the pope of Avignon, Benedict XIII. This achieved, he began to seek a reconciliation between France and England as a preliminary to gaining their united backing for German policy at Constance. Secondly, Sigismund was worried by the increasing power of the dukes of Burgundy on the western frontier of the Empire and hoped to win over the English to a grand alliance with him and the Armagnacs against John the Fearless.

The Armagnacs also had an interest in the emperor's activity. Quite apart from the unreal scheme of a joint Armagnac–English venture against Burgundy, they hoped that the emperor would be able to act as an effective mediator between them and the rapacious English. Finally, the English hoped that Sigismund would ally himself with them against their opponents in France.

Having detached the French from their allegiance to Pope Benedict XIII, the emperor decided on a state visit to England to continue his diplomatic campaign in London. He was received with great ceremony. Parliament was kept in session so that the illustrious foreign visitor could see the workings of the English king's great council of Lords and Commons, and the emperor himself was made a member of the Order of the Garter.

It seems that Sigismund did make some progress and persuaded Henry to consider new French peace offers. But the French were probably playing for time. Their aim was to drive the English from the dangerous and vulnerable bridgehead of Harfleur, and their blockade of the port was gradually having its effect. The emperor himself finally became convinced of French duplicity and in August 1416 signed the Alliance of Canterbury with Henry. Of all the conflicting aims which had underlain the emperor's negotiations, only the King of England's had been successfully accomplished. However, Sigismund had at least the assurance of English support for his policy at Constance and emphasized the fact in his letter to the council fathers to justify his long absence.

The expedition to Normandy

In July 1417 Henry set sail for Normandy. The blockade of Harfleur had been raised the previous year as a result of a naval victory on the Seine by John, Duke of Bedford. The king was determined not on mere demonstrations of force but on the effective reconquest of the duchy. But his plans were increasingly in jeopardy as the old enemies, Burgundy and Armagnac, whose civil war had been such an important factor in the English successes, moved towards an alliance against the foreign invader.

Both parties had been in negotation with the English, hoping to win their support in the bitter conflict between them, but neither had gained the terms it sought. Finally, in desperation it would seem, they agreed to settle their differences. A meeting was arranged to take place on the bridge of Montereau and the utmost precautions were taken to guard against treachery, since memories of the murder by the Burgundians of the Duke of Orléans were still vivid. They were too vivid for the Armagnacs. On a fateful day for France in August 1419 Duke John the Fearless of Burgundy was done to death with an axe in the presence of the Dauphin, within the very enclosure which had been erected to protect the two parties. Orléans was avenged: England was jubilant.

Immediately Henry pressed his advantage. He gave the new Duke of Burgundy, Philip the Good, two weeks to declare his interest. The duke's decision was a foregone conclusion. With Burgundy's support guaranteed, Henry was bound to succeed. This success was sealed by the Treaty of Troyes between Henry and King Charles VI. By its terms Charles was to remain King of France for his lifetime, but Henry, who was to marry Catherine, the French king's daughter, was declared his heir. Henry was also committed to conquering the territories still held by the Armagnac supporters of the Dauphin.

There could be no pretence that the settlement was popular with, or even to be tolerated by, the people of France. Even in the duchy of Normandy, where the English regime was most fully established and most efficient, only a fraction of the taxes were collected and that with great difficulty.

After the signature of the Treaty of Troyes and his marriage to Catherine, Henry settled his affairs in France. He returned to England in February 1421 for the coronation of Catherine in Canterbury cathedral and for the parliament, which was convened in May. Between these two events Henry is recorded as having toured the country, presumably to re-establish himself in the affections of his subjects after an absence of three and a half years and also, it may be assumed, to win support and funds.

Henry's successes in France had cost his exchequer heavily and he was unwilling to approach parliament yet again. Instead, he instructed his chancellor to raise loans privately from over 500 lenders, who included not only the wealthy and powerful Bishop Beaufort of Winchester but hundreds of small towns and village communities as well as merchants and members of the gentry. Henry's death from dysentery at the siege of Meaux in the following year made such generous investment in the French venture even more unsafe and called into question the position of his dynasty even in England.

Murder and faction

Although some contemporaries explained the murder of Louis of Orléans as a *crime passionel,* claiming that he had seduced the Duchess of Burgundy, and other may have accepted John the Fearless' outrageous justification of his crime, the assassination of 1407 was a political act. The rise of Louis was a threat to Burgundy even before the death of Philip the Bold, and not only in France. By his marriage to Valentine Visconti of Milan, Louis had established claims in Italy, and it was only the consistent opposition of Philip which prevented these from yielding any concrete results.

Rivalry was fierce and continuous. At one point the armies of the two dukes were mustered about Paris and only the intervention of the dukes of Berry and Bourbon averted civil war. The prestige and statecraft of Philip the Bold had been able to restrain the ambition of Orléans, but within months of his death Louis had won a commanding position. He was able to arrange his son's marriage to the king's daughter, Isabella, the widow of Richard II of England, who received from her royal father the immense dowry of 300,000 francs.

The regime of Orléans was not only corrupt but also oppressive and quickly became very unpopular. With some skill in timing, John the Fearless exploited this growing discontent and put himself at the head of it by raising a strong protest in the royal council and at a meeting of officials against the taxes imposed by Orléans. His stock rose considerably and, with the good will of the capital assured, he intercepted the Duke of Orléans' attempt to abduct the Dauphin and rode back into the city with the young prince to a tumultuous welcome from the populace.

Once again the private armies mustered and once again peace was secured by the dukes of Bourbon and Berry. But the outcome was John's virtual exclusion from the government. Moreover, his enemy continued to have control of the purse strings. Despite his manoeuvres, his popular following and his power John saw the position of Burgundy increasingly jeopardized both at the French court and in Flanders.

Armagnacs and Burgundians

On the night of 23 November 1407, returning from a visit to the queen, Louis, Duke of Orléans, was struck down in an attack by nine armed men and his brains spilled in the gutters of a Paris street. John the Fearless' guilt soon became public knowledge and he took flight.

Although he had fled the capital John was careful to maintain contact with his agents there and in the following year felt sufficiently confident to return, being greeted by enthusiastic crowds. From the first he had made no attempt to conceal his responsibility for the crime and now he was prepared to justify it as an act of patriotic statecraft.

Neither the court nor the family or party of the dead man was satisfied by this justification. However, John's popularity with the Parisians was undiminished and at one point the court withdrew from the capital for fear of a popular rising. In a suitably elaborate ceremony at Chartres in the following year the Duke of Burgundy was reconciled with the son of his victim. Before the end of the year the victory was made complete when the Dauphin of France was put in the keeping of Duke John.

John's position continued under constant attack from the partisans of Orléans, who were revitalized by Bernard d'Armagnac, the brother-in-law of the new duke, Charles. The party gained the support of several great noblemen, among them the dukes of Bourbon and Berry. In 1411 the banishment of the Armagnac princes and their excommunication was formally proclaimed. When the news broke in the following year that they had allied with Henry IV of England this simply enhanced John's already strong position.

An Armagnac attack on Paris was driven off and a new reconciliation took place at Auxerre in August 1412. This time the two dukes rode on the same horse to demonstrate their friendship—John of Burgundy convinced of his mastery of the situation, Charles of Orléans no doubt toying with the secret treaty which he had recently negotiated with the English.

The Cabochiens

The struggle with the Armagnacs continued but John the Fearless may reasonably have felt that his position was secure for some time to come. Nevertheless, in the following year he had to flee Paris once again and spent the next two years trying to fight and negotiate his way back to power.

A contributory factor in his fall was the revolt of the Cabochiens, so-called after one of its leaders, a butcher named Caboche, which broke out in Paris in the spring of 1413.

There was a serious move for reform behind all this, as well as perhaps a certain amount of Burgundian scheming, and the sponsors included some senior members of the Duke of Burgundy's household. The numerous intelligent proposals in the ordinance—for more efficient, less expensive and more equitable management of the king's affairs—are witness to their influence. However, in August the Cabochien leaders lost the support of Paris and fled the capital. John the Fearless made good his escape to Flanders, his reputation considerably tarnished by his dubious involvement with the Cabochiens.

During the next two years John was fighting for his political life. His exclusion from any part in the government of France was complete, and his territories were invaded by Armagnac armies. But, thanks both to his diplomatic skill, which culminated in the ambiguous Treaty of Arras, and his military expertise he weathered the storm with comparative ease.

Despite his skill, however, John was not able to prevent the increasing influence of the Armagnacs over the king or dislodge them from the capital. The two factions were still squabbling over the terms of the settlement when news came of Henry V's preparations for invasion. Throughout the previous year John had been conducting protracted negotiations with the English and one of the terms of the Treaty of Arras was that he should not conclude an alliance with them. He respected this clause and letters from the ducal archives suggest that he intended to join the French royal army in the Agincourt campaign.

However, like a number of other French princes the Duke of Burgundy was not on the field of battle on that fateful October day and the French defeat could more accurately be described as the defeat of the Armagnac party, most of whose leaders were eliminated from French politics either by death or capture. The Duke of Orléans himself was taken back to captivity in England where he was held in the Tower of London until he was ransomed by the son of his enemy, Philip the Good of Burgundy, in 1440.

Nevertheless, despite the apparent destruction of his enemies by the English, John the Fearless found the position at Paris little changed. When the Dauphin Louis died in December 1415, and the moderate body of councillors which had grown up around him was disbanded, John's last hope of influence at court faded. Bernard of Armagnac became constable of France and John remained excluded from government.

Above, the murder of Louis, Duke of Orleans, the virtual ruler of France, in 1407 at the hands of John the Fearless, Duke of Burgundy. The King of France very soon pardoned the murderer. Bibliothèque Nationale, Paris.

England, Burgundy and Orleans

The weakened Armagnac regime, faced with the imminent threat of an English return, played for time. The negotiations merely delayed the inevitable. In 1417 Henry V invaded in force and set about the systematic conquest of Normandy.

As Henry V set about the methodical reduction of the towns of the north of the duchy, John of Burgundy proclaimed his case against the Armagnacs in a document which, in the fashion of the age, accused them of a whole catalogue of crimes, including the murder of the Dauphin and his successor. He then systematically forced the towns in the south to accept his rule and threw a ring round Paris, virtually reducing it to a state of siege. Much more important than this, however, was the fact that he was able to win back the queen mother to the Burgundian cause and with her the king. A Burgundian administration was now set up at Troyes in opposition to the regime in Paris, of which the new dauphin, Charles, was nominally head of state.

In 1418, under the cover of peace negotiations, John finally recaptured Paris and imposed his rule on the capital after a reign of terror in which the Count of Armagnac and all the members of his party who could be found were viciously murdered. The Duke of Burgundy and the queen mother now controlled the capital and its environs, but the rest of France eluded them. The young Dauphin, displaying remarkable vigour and determination for a fifteen-year-old boy, refused to follow the example of the senior members of his family in accepting the rule of the Burgundian. After a bold and almost successful attempt at a counter-coup, he retired to set up a provincial government at Bourges.

The Burgundian and Dauphinist parties now at last began to seek a new agreement. Exploratory meetings ended in the disastrous encounter on the bridge of Montereau on 10 September 1419. Most contemporaries and many later commentators have accepted the Dauphinist version of events—that John the Fearless, Duke of Burgundy, was struck down, in a sudden fracas, begun, it was suggested, by his own attempt on the life of the Dauphin.

The King of Bourges

Burgundy was the decisive factor in French politics and in December 1419 John's son, Philip the Good, entered into an alliance with the invaders. In May of the following year the matter was sealed at the Treaty of Troyes, which set out terms of the change of

Below, the murder of John of Burgundy in 1419. The Dauphin is shown here as an innocent bystander, but it is likely that he was well aware of the assassination plot.

Opposite, the Tower of London, an important centre of English royal power throughout the Middle Ages, but as London itself became wealthier, its merchants won a high degree of autonomy for the city. British Library, London.

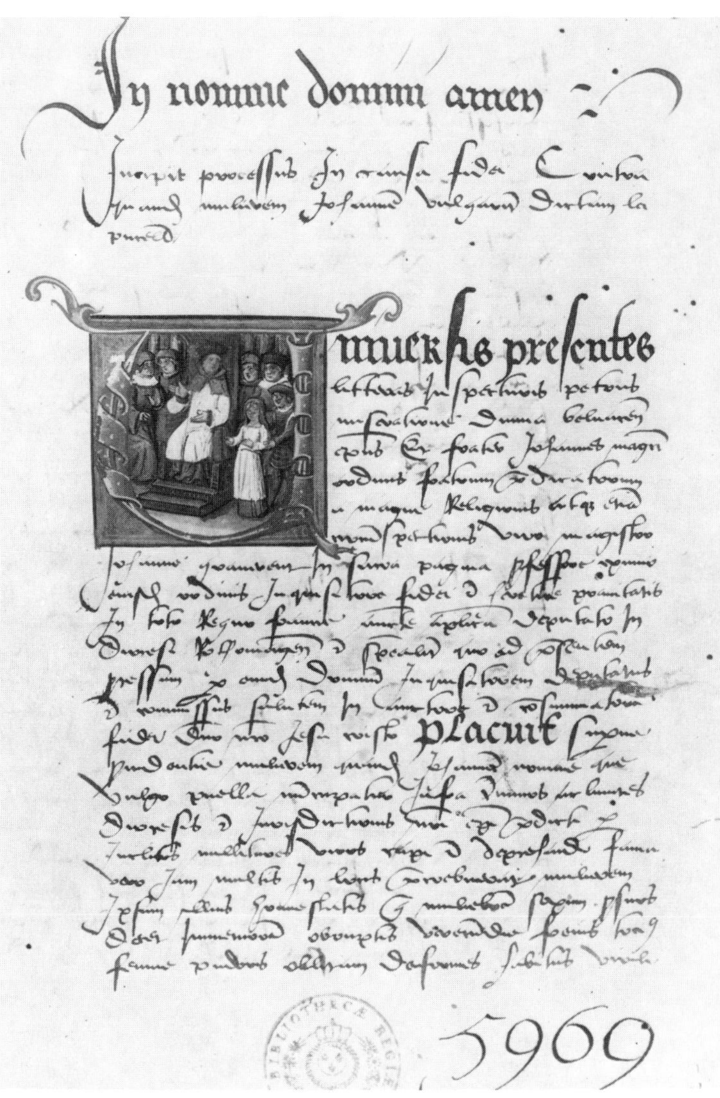

dynasty when the ailing Charles VI died. Henry V of England, who had married Catherine, the mad king's daughter, was declared heir to the throne and the king's 'true son'.

The phase has special significance as the disinheritance of the Dauphin was validated on the grounds that he was in fact the queen's illegitimate son. Remarkably, the queen herself explicitly confirmed this and Charles's supine inactivity in the following years has often been put down to his tormented doubts as to his legitimacy.

For whatever reason, Charles certainly did not display much energy in advancing his cause. His rule was restricted to the lands south of the Loire, including the Dauphiné itself, but they formed a sizeable area and, properly exploited, could have been used as the base for a counter-attack against the invaders. Despite the problem of his legitimacy, most Frenchmen, whether ruled from Bourges or from Paris, were prepared to accept Charles' claim and, after his coronation at Reims, his right to the throne would not be questioned by any true Frenchman.

Up to the mid-1420s the English had not only held their own but were slowly and surely beginning to push back the frontiers of their newly won French territories. Indeed, with John of Bedford's resounding victory over a Franco-Scottish army at Verneuil in 1424, it seemed as though the great days of Agincourt had returned. The English won no kind of popular support in the occupied duchy of Normandy.

There was a considerable resistance movement against the English in occupied France and if Charles VII had been more confident of his cause and more aggresive in his policies the English would have been pushed back sooner than they were.

Despite differences with their Burgundian allies the English proceeded with their remorseless advance, recapturing Maine and Anjou and numerous towns. By 1428 the whole of France north of the Loire and a vast area from Poitou to Gascony and the Pyrenees recognized Henry VI of England.

Joan of Arc

Joan was born of yeoman stock in the village of Domrémy on the eastern frontier of France about the year 1412. Theories have been advanced that she was the bastard child of an aristocrat, even of Charles VI, and her parents in fact foster parents, but this has not been proved and seems an unnecessary hypothesis. She was an intelligent and straightforward young woman, who, despite her claim to be inspired by the voices of the saints, had none of the characteristics of a religious hysteric. Her basic shrewdness and common sense emerge from the records of her interrogation.

In 1428 the little community of Domrémy was driven to take refuge at Vaucouleurs. Then, possibly because her voices instructed her or because she had simply decided that this had to stop, Joan demanded letters of introduction from Robert de Baudricourt, a French royal commander, for a visit to the king at Chinon on the Loire. Eventually the commander agreed and the maid set out for her famous interview with Charles.

A test was arranged to see what these claims amounted to. A courtier was instructed to sit on the royal throne and Joan was left to identify the real king—which she did without hesitation. She was then permitted a private interview with Charles and seems to have persuaded him almost at once that he was indeed the legitimate heir to the crown of France and that with her help he could do something about it.

With the authority of a revitalized king behind her, Joan was now free to move to the next stage in her mission—the relief of Orléans. Fighting alongside soldiers, she wore the armour of soldiers and fought like a soldier, but hers was a mission of faith and

Above, Henry VI of England being crowned King of France at Paris in 1431, when he was ten. The ceremony only served to emphasize the hollowness of his claim to rule France by comparison with Charles VII, who had been crowned at Reims two years earlier. Bibliothèque Nationale, Paris.

Left, the people of the town of Troyes give up their keys to Charles VII and Joan of Arc; Troyes was the first town taken by Joan on the way to Reims. Bibliothèque Nationale, Paris.

Opposite left, a scene from the life of Richard Beauchamp, Earl of Warwick, showing his successful siege of Rouen in 1418. The town became a centre of English control in Normandy until the French recaptured it in 1449.

Opposite right, the trial of Joan of Arc in 1431, as recorded in a manuscript of the end of the fifteenth century. It was said that, despite the efforts of the officers of the Inquisition to give her a fair hearing, the trial was a mockery. Bibliothèque Nationale, Paris.

for the time she was probably content to leave the military arrangements to the professionals. However, after the victory at Patay, which seemed to have opened Normandy to the French, it was she who insisted on the coronation of the king. On 17 July 1429, Charles was crowned 'King of France by the grace of God' in Reims Cathedral, with Joan standing at his side. Her mission was over, but her career as a soldier was not. Although Charles subsequently failed to follow up the French military advantage, Joan continued her career with the bands of French troops operating independently against the English. It was as a member of one of these that she was captured at the seige of Compiègne by a Burgundian captain.

The English attempt to minimize the impact of the Reims ceremony by having the boy-king Henry VI crowned at Paris as King of England and France was unsuccessful. It succeeded in revealing English pretensions which could be advertised only by the coronation of a weak-minded boy in the wrong church and by the wrong prelate.

The main reason for the English collapse was not financial problems or war weariness at home but the sudden revival of the morale and determination of the French people, and at the heart of this revival stood the figure of the maid. Like all occupying powers, the English were from now on to suffer the persistent and increasingly effective resistance of the local population within their own borders as well as the growing strength of the legitimate regime beyond those borders. To have any hope of stemming the tide, the English had to discredit the French symbol of national revival. Consequently, when at the siege of Compiègne the maid fell into Burgundian hands the English authorities paid the huge ransom of some 10,000 golden crowns.

From that point there could of course be no doubt as to Joan's fate, unless her king should take up her cause. This Charles failed to do. He was no doubt influenced by counsellors like La Trémouille, jealous of her success, but he too may have shrunk from the thought of a future overshadowed by such a woman.

Joan had claimed that she acted under the instructions of the saints and that, through them, she was the chosen instrument of God for the restoration of France and of its rightful king, Charles VII. The English aim was to discredit these claims as the ravings of an unbalanced heresiarch. To this end they endeavoured to convict Joan of heresy and to get her to confess that her voices came from the devil. Pretended sympathizers were introduced into her cell in order to trick her into a confession. Besides the officer of the inquisition who questioned her, there were two concealed observers, whose notes, so the inquisitor reported, bore no relation either to what Joan said in her defence or to his own notes. But, of course, this state trial like most state trials, was brought to a successful conclusion and the young girl of Domrémy was burnt to save her from her sins and the English from the consequences of her actions.

The Congress of Arras

Before Joan the cause of the 'king of Bourges' had seemed on the point of collapse. After her it was only a matter of time before the English were driven out of the realm of Charles VII of France.

The real turning point in France's military fortunes came four years after her death, when the Duke of Burgundy was reconciled with the king at the Congress of Arras. It had been difficult previously to dispute the legalistic claims of the English. On grounds of legitimacy alone the right of Henry VI of England stood up well against the claim of the supposedly illegitimate king of Bourges. Joan had established once and for all the legitimacy of Charles VII and at the same time had introduced a sense of national identity and purpose to France which found ever-increasing expression in the years which followed.

Despite their treaty obligations and their common interests in many matters, England and Burgundy had proved uneasy partners. The breach caused by Duke Humphrey of Gloucester's invasion of Hainault on behalf of his wife, Jacqueline of Hainault, had been healed only with difficulty. The danger of a Burgundian desertion was hinted at when the duke failed to attend the coronation of Henry VI in Paris. When, in the following year, Philip's sister Anne, wife of John, Duke of Bedford, died, one more tie between the allies was broken.

Further evidence of the gradual shift in the international situation against Burgundy was the success of Charles's diplomatic activity on her eastern borders. The possibility of a strong France in alliance with the Holy Roman Empire and the German princes was a disturbing one for Burgundy. The situation demanded that Philip switch alliances, and negotiations began with the French court.

The great Congress of Arras of 1435 was a suitable setting for the Burgundian volte-face. Delegations were sent not only by the English, Burgundians and French but also by the pope and the Council of Basel. From Armagnac there came, in addition to the royal embassy, numerous embassies from aristocratic and civic authorities in the provinces.

Despite the banquets and the jousting the reconciliation of the English and French positions proved impossible, as everyone must have known it would. The English would not relinquish Henry VI's claims to France and the French could not entertain such claims. The English delegation left the conference early in September, leaving Burgundy and the French to work out their differences.

Philip had chosen his own time and he in a position to dictate his terms. The change in his alliance was worth almost any price to Charles, and the price was heavy. Charles publicly declared his own innocence of any part in the murder of John the Fearless. Philip was exempted from the duty of paying homage for his French fiefs during the lifetime of Charles VII. He was allowed to keep the territories granted him by the English and, above all, to hold the important line of towns on the Somme, although Charles reserved for France the right to redeem them at some future date for the sum of 400,000 crowns.

In the short term, the Treaty of Arras was a triumph for Burgundy. For France, no

matter what concessions had had to be made, the return of Burgundy was decisive. For England the agreement was an unqualified disaster and, within a year, the English had been forced to relinquish Paris. But they were tenacious and Normandy was not finally cleared of the invaders until 1450. Three years later, however, they were expelled even from their centuries-old province of Gascony.

Charles VII

In 1440, the year after the great ordinance designed to repress military excesses and give the monarchy the sole right to recruitment, a number of princes, the dukes of Brittany and Bourbon, the Dunois, the hero of Orléans, under the leadership of the Dauphin (later Louis XI), rebelled against Charles VII. The rising was known as the Praguerie, so-called apparently in association with the Hussite risings in Bohemia. Sparked off perhaps by the evidence of growing royal power, exemplified in the ordinance of 1439, it was further proof of the determination of the French magnates to maintain their position of privilege, which had flourished so splendidly during the turbulence of the preceding eighty years. Supported by the country at large and by much of the nobility, Charles assembled an army from the ranks of the free companies which still plagued his kingdom and rapidly dealt with the rebels.

Perhaps Charles VII's most important achievement was to establish the basis of an effective professional army. This consisted of a regular cavalry force of fifteen *compagnies d'ordonnance,* each consisting of some 600 men, who were billeted throughout the regions of France. To maintain such a force demanded healthy finances and here, too, the king began to set his house in order, He regularized the system of taxation and appointed four royal receiver-generals to administer the finances of the realm. To round off his military arrangements he provided his army with a modern artillery train and with the *francs archers* ('free archers') tried to set up an infantry equivalent to the regular cavalry force.

The reign of Charles VII was an eventful one for France. After decades of humiliation and ineffectiveness the monarchy was once again a viable institution. The English presence had been reduced to the town and district of Calais, a move had been made towards curbing the disruptive power of the great feudatories, and the kingdom's commerce was in full revival, as the sensational career of the merchant and financier Jacques Coeur showed.

The ideal of chivalry

The fourteenth and fifteenth centuries witnessed a recession in European economic life, a considerable depopulation of the continent, and wars of a magnitude and a destructiveness hardly seen since the barbarian invasions in which the states of Europe had been born. Concurrent with, and partly as a result of, these upheavals was an increased mobility, both geographical and social, in the lower ranks of society. As a consequence of this there was an upsurge from below of an oppressed majority demanding its fair share in property rights, in city government and in general well being. This seething multitude was ruled by a class blatantly devoted to the full exploitation of its immense privileges and delighting in the gross extension of those privileges wherever possible. The result was a profusion of splendour and extravagance which was in sharp contrast to the misery and poverty of the masses.

The nostalgic revival of a legendary age of chivalry, lost in the mists of antiquity, dominated courtly life in the later Middle Ages. The new humanism in Italy regarded

Above, the German poet Wilfram von Eschenbach on his way to the Holy Land in the early thirteenth century; as the author of Parzifal, *and a renowned soldier, he was an ideal knight of his age.*

Left, Charles VII of France (ruled 1422–61), painted by Jean Fouquet; after an inauspicious start to his reign he proved a successful king, finally driving the English from France and reorganizing the royal administration. Musée du Louvre.

Opposite left, the two great dukes of Burgundy, Philip the Good (ruled 1416–67) and his son Charles the Bold (ruled 1467–77). They both outshone their feudal overlords, the kings of France, in the splendour of their courts and the extent of their ambitions. Bibliothèque Municipale, Arras.

Opposite right, Charles VI of France (ruled 1380–1422), painted in about 1411. His reign saw a divisive conflict between the French nobility which almost caused the destruction of his kingdom. Bibliothèque Publique et Universitaire, Geneva.

antiquity as a past completely separated from the present and a fit object for study. for the medieval mind, however, the great ages of antiquity formed a continuing link with the present and were a legitimate source of inspiration, romance and learning.

The Goths had been awed by the marvels of Rome and their descendants at the court of Burgundy retained something of the same spirit. The past was thought to be governed by the same laws of knightly chivalry which contemporaries wished to believe governed the present. It was believed that, if only the true spirit of chivalry could be revived, so would the virtue of the ancients.

South of the Alps the virtues of the ancients were being recovered by a new spirit of practical research. This was essentially different from the mentality which could lead men to say of Henry V that 'he maintained the discipline of chivalry as well as did the Roman before him'. But throughout Europe men of civilization honoured the memory of antiquity in their own fashion. During this period the Italians themselves could not shake off old habits of thought all at once. A particularly bizarre example of the 'new learning' occurred during the siege of Constantinople by the Turks in 1453. Most men in the west were horrified at the fall of the great city. There was, however, a body of thinkers who, thanks to a mistranslation in which the Turks were described as *Teucri* ('Trojans' in Latin), declared that the Greeks were at last getting their deserts for the atrocities they had committed at the sack of Troy.

The cult of chivalry at that time affected the whole of western Europe. The archangel Michael's overthrow of Lucifer was 'the first deed of knighthood and chivalric prowess' according to the French writer, Jean Molinet, and the all-pervading legend of King Arthur was cultivated at the court of John I of Portugal as well as in the elaborate rituals of Burgundian *courtoisie*. It even had its adherents at the court of Lorenzo the Magnificent at Florence.

The code of chivalry was not reserved merely for courtly pageantry. It determined the behaviour of even so calculating a

monarch as Henry V of England. It is recorded that during the Agincourt campaign he had to spend the night in the open because, marching with the vanguard and having gone beyond the scheduled stopping place for the night, he would not 'retreat' while accoutred for battle. It was only after receiving the fullest advice that the Duke of Burgundy, 'who loved honour more than his life and a good name more than a crown', decided that he could break his agreements with the English without loss of reputation and make his peace with the Dauphin.

With high-flown ideas of reputation went the trappings of outward display and munificence and the most carefully prescribed rules of polite behaviour. The Burgundian chronicler, Olivier de la Marche, recorded that 'when Frederick III, the King of the Romans, was pleased to dance, two knights carrying torches always danced before him'. When a member of the ducal house of Brittany visited the wife of Charles the Bold of Burgundy, while he was still count of Charolais, it required a council of state to prepare the meeting and to ordain that the visitor should first make two obeisances and that the Countess of Charolais might then advance three paces.

More astonishing to a later age than even these matters of ritual is perhaps the vast meals which a nobleman seems to have been obliged to consume. Yet, while it is true that when the Earl of Warwick sat down to breakfast at his London house as many as six oxen might be roasted for the meal, it should be remembered that anyone who knew a member of his household was free to take as much food as he could carry on a long knife. Status symbols of this kind always appear absurd to another age, but a modern writer is perhaps nearer the mark when he said: 'The feudal sense that the enjoyment of wealth is inseparable from public responsibility chiefly distinguishes medieval ideas of ownership from classical and modern.' Societies may fail to achieve their ideals but it is significant that they have them.

In the matter of artistic patronage self-interest and public good fortunately coincided. Both the Duke of Burgundy and the Duke of Berry plundered the treasury of France without stint and without shame, but posterity is greatly indebted to them for the purpose to which they chose to put some of their stolen wealth. The famous and exquisite book of hours, the *Très Riches Heures* of the Duke of Berry, is only the best known in the duke's vast treasury of art. In Portugal the House of Avis proudly stands before us in the immortal work of the great artist Nunez Gonzalvez, and at the court of Richard II there flowered some of the richest blooms of late medieval European culture.

Bouciquaut, a French contemporary, believed that 'two things sustain the order of divine and human laws, chivalry and learning', and in England again the high

Above, Guillaume Dufay and Gilles Binchois, the leading composers of the Burgundian school. They worked together at Cambrai from about 1445 until 1460. Bibliothèque Nationale, Paris.

Left, Johannes Ockeghem, surrounded by his students of music at the Burgundian court. Ockeghem himself was the student of Dufay and Binchois. Bibliothèque Nationale, Paris.

Opposite top, Sir Geoffrey Luttrell, an archetypal English knight of the 1340s, with his wife and daughter-in-law; in the chivalric tradition the woman was the idealized epitome of virtue, for whom the knight had to prove his worthiness. British Library, London.

Opposite bottom, a fifteenth-century manuscript of the French thirteenth-century love poem Le Roman de la rose, *showing the current ideal of courtly love, in which the men are very much the submissive servants of the ladies. Bibliothèque Nationale, Paris.*

traditions of medieval culture were carried by the saintly if woefully inadequate king, Henry VI, founder of Eton and of King's College, Cambridge. But patronage was by no means the preserve of the monarch and the king's uncle, John, Duke of Bedford, employed the greatest musician of the age.

Whatever political disasters the Agincourt campaign and its aftermath inflicted upon a war-torn continent, the composers of the court of Burgundy, such as Dufay and Binchois, must have blessed the chance of war and politics which brought the great John Dunstable and his colleagues into their orbit. It was the only time in history that an English composer was to divert the course of European music, but for the Netherlanders and later the Italians it was a 'new art' and launched them into discoveries from which were to emerge the glories of sixteenth-century polyphonic music. Throughout Europe the privileged courts of the nobility were a focal point for high ideals, high culture and, of course, high living. None of them, however, could vie with the magificent and grandiose pretensions of the House of Burgundy.

The expansion of Burgundy

At his death in 1477 Charles the Bold of Burgundy possessed territories comprising the modern countries of Belgium, the Netherlands and Luxembourg, the great duchy of Burgundy in France, the county of Burgundy adjoining it across the border in the Holy Roman Empire, and numerous counties and principalities between these two major areas of territory. He met his death while trying to consolidate his authority in a vast new region in Alsace.

There were European kings who controlled less land, but few European rulers controlled more wealth. It was, moreover, an open secret, that Charles himself was aiming at a crown. He was the last of a line of four dukes who for a century had dominated the politics of northern Europe and whose lands contained the biggest industrial and commercial complexes north of the Alps. Their subjects numbered among them the greatest musicians and painters anywhere in Europe.

It was all part of a unified whole. The driving force behind the dukes of Burgundy was political and something more than the natural ambition of any noble house to increase its possessions. Commercial wealth and artistic talent were harnessed to it for explicitly political ends and no means were ignored which could increase the standing and reputation of the house of Burgundy.

The impetus behind the development of Burgundy derived from the reign of the first duke, Philip the Bold, who received the duchy from his father King John II of France. According to the legend, the massive fief was handed over as a reward for the bravery which the young knight had shown in defending his father on the fatal field of Poitiers. However, modern research presents a rather different picture. King John had hoped to incorporate the duchy into the royal domain on the death of the last of its Capetian dukes. But his manoeuvres lacked subtlety and he was obliged to compromise. The Assembly of the Estates demanded that the land of Burgundy should retain the virtual independence of the French crown which it had traditionally enjoyed, and John was forced to give them a new duke of their own.

The history of Burgundy is rich in splendid occasions and grandiose gestures which reveal the very essence of the new state. Typical of these was the crusade which ended in disaster in the Battle of Nicopolis in 1396. It has a special significance for Burgundy in that it was the country's debut as a European power.

Although the crusade as an effective military operation was defunct by the end of the thirteenth century, the ideal continued to inspire individuals who could find ample scope for their ambition in service with the Teutonic knights against the heathen Lithuanians. At least one campaign on a crusade was essential for any knight aiming at the highest reputation for chivalry. Chaucer's paragon of the knight in the *Canterbury Tales* had fought in eastern Europe, and the annual season's campaigning there was so popular that Charles V of France forbade knights and squires to leave France to join it without an authorized royal permit.

It was therefore only natural that the great paladin of Christian chivalry, Philip of Burgundy, should wish to join battle with the infidel. The original plan was for a joint enterprise managed by him, John of Gaunt and the Duke of Orléans. However, in the event, none of these was to go and the army which set out for Hungary was led by Philip's son, the young Count of Nevers, and was an entirely Burgundian enterprise.

Where others were content to discharge their obligations to knighthood in the routine campaigns of the Teutonic knights it was only fitting that the heir to Burgundy should seek out the traditional enemy of Christendom, the champion of Islam. It was, moreover, sound strategy which dictated the frontier between Hungary and the advancing Ottoman Empire rather than a more idealistic target.

Arriving in the territories of Hungary, the Burgundian leaders ignored the advice of King Sigismund of Hungary, the man on the spot, both on strategy and tactics. He advised a concentrated defensive action on the Danube, but the crusaders crossed the frontier and penetrated deep into Turkish-controlled territory and laid siege, without siege artillery, to the town of Nicopolis.

When the Turkish army of Sultan Bayezid came up to relieve the town, Sigismund's advice was again ignored, and the Franco-Burgundian forces launched themselves on a magnificent and completely successful charge in which much glory must have been won. The Christians did great slaughter and drove back the Turks, but when the impetus of their attack had spent itself the sultan threw his reserves into the battle and won a complete and crushing victory.

The pride of Burgundy was destroyed or captured and the scale of the ransoms can be judged by the fact that nearly 500,000 francs was paid for the return of the duke's heir, John. Yet despite this, when John and his companions returned to Flanders, they were welcomed as conquering heroes in town after town and the prestige of the House of Burgundy had never stood higher. It is impossible now to understand how a major military reversal could receive such acclaim. It may be that the mere fact of having fought the infidel with honour was considered a noteworthy deed. Certainly Olivier de la Marche states quite flatly that John received his nickname of 'the Fearless' because, while many others boasted of their intentions to go against the infidel, he had had the courage actually to do so.

The Burgundian Court employed the painters Jan van Eyck and Rogier van der Weyden, the sculptor Claus Sluter and the musicians Dufay, Binchois and Ockeghem. It had moreover, within its boundaries the great tapestry factories of Arras and could draw on the riches of the Flemish towns. For all these reasons it could regard itself as the most splendid and one of the most powerful courts in Europe.

Its power was buttressed by an impressive central administration, with regional capitals at Dijon and Lille (and later Brussels), but directed in many matters from the Duke of Burgundy's residence in Paris.

Louis XI

The new king of France was in his thirty-ninth year when he came to the throne in 1461 and had waited for supreme power with an impatience which three times burst out into revolt. He took his place at the head of the Praguerie revolt when he was only eighteen. Six years later he again rose against his father in protest at the influence wielded at court by the king's mistress, the beautiful and witty Agnès Sorel. He spent the last years of his father's reign in virtual exile at the court of Philip the Good of Burgundy.

Immediately on his accession, Louis determined to demonstrate forcibly that a new regime had arrived. He dismissed the ministers who had served his father so well and replaced them with his own nominees. He even repudiated the Pragmatic Sanction of Bourges, the important act by which Charles VII had guaranteed the crown's freedom of action in Church affairs.

It was indeed a new regime. In France as elsewhere it owed much to the personality of the monarch. In France Louis XI, in England Edward IV and Henry VII, and in Castile-Aragon Ferdinand II brought a new professionalism to kingship, which renovated it so completely as to make it appear a new institution. Thus it was that the French chronicler, Comines, could say of Louis, 'He did not appear or dress or speak like a king, yet he was the most terrible king there ever was.'

His chief enemy was Burgundy. Early in the reign the young count of Charolais mobilized the rebellious elements who opposed Louis' developing mastery into the League of the Common Weal. The League nominally under the leadership of the king's brother Charles, comprised the dukes of Brittany and Bourbon, the Count of Armagnac, and John of Anjou. It was an episode in the continuing protest of the great magnates against the revival of royal power begun by Charles and continued by Louis.

Yet, although their aims were selfish, the aristocratic rebels represented a profound tendency in French life. The forces of regionalism, although not so strong as in the Spanish kingdoms, were nevertheless very real in France. The spirit of independence in Brittany, reflected in the ducal pretensions

Above, Edward IV of England on an expedition against Louis XI of France in 1475 and to assist Charles the Bold of Burgundy. Louis paid Edward to withdraw. Until the wars of religion of the next century, many wars were undertaken purely as diplomatic manoeuvres, with more hope of profit than glory or bloodshed. British Library, London.

Opposite, a nobleman encouraging an itinerant musician, from a collection of lute songs of about 1500. Interest in learning and the arts among the nobility greatly increased during the fifteenth century.

to an independent foreign policy, was not by any means an artificial creation of the dukes. However, Louis was able to recruit support from the other regions and in the years following the indecisive Battle of Montlhéry and the damaging Treaty of Conflans he managed by degrees to recover his position.

In 1468 Louis attempted to carry the war into the enemy's camp and stirred up a rebellion against Burgundy in the town of Liège. But for once he had badly overreached himself and 'the universal spider', as a contemporary called him, was caught in the meshes of his own web. At the very moment when the people of Liège were on the point of rebellion Louis, with a rashness equal to that of Charles the Bold himself, visited the new Duke of Burgundy in his town of Peronne for negotiations to avert the threat of a renewed Anglo-Burgundian alliance.

Even as the two princes were opening their discussion news reached the conference chamber of the revolt at Liège. The king was held under house arrest throughout the night. Charles himself is reported to have passed the night with his advisers, pacing up and down his room, threatening revenge and, at times, almost incoherent in his rage. The following day he compelled the king to go with him to witness the suppression of the rising and the execution of the royalist ringleaders. When Louis was finally allowed to return to his realm he had been forced to agree that Flanders should be independent of the parliament of Paris.

For ten brief months during 1470–71 it looked as if Burgundy's English ally, Edward IV, had finally lost his kingdom and France could breathe more easily. However, not only did Louis fail to rob Charles of his powerful ally but he had to stand by while Burgundy consolidated its power on the eastern frontiers of France.

New vistas for France

The death of Charles of Burgundy opened up great possibilities for the expansion of French power, but Louis seems to have been surprised by the unexpected news of the death of his arch-enemy. Louis sent troops into Artois and the duchy of Burgundy, who had no wish to see the rich self protector of Charles's nineteen-year-old heiress, Mary of Burgundy and proposed the marriage between her and his seven-year-old son and heir.

The brutality of Louis' troops in the occupied territories did not fit in with their master's protestations. Moreover, Mary looked about for a more likely protector than the seven-year-old Dauphin and accepted the advances of Maximilian of Austria, son of the Emperor Frederick III of Habsburg.

A confused war with France followed, and, by the Treaty of Arras in 1482, Louis was confirmed in possession of Artois and the duchy of Burgundy but had to surrender his claims to the Flemish counties. The consequences of this marriage were to become still more far-reaching when the Burgundian inheritance eventually passed to Charles V, Holy Roman emperor and King of Spain.

Nevertheless, Louis had recovered an important part of the Burgundian lands. Moreover, with the death of René of Anjou, and his heir during the two years prior to Arras, extensive possessions in Anjou, Maine and Bar reverted to the French crown, which also acquired the Angevin claims to the throne of Naples.

Louis went a long way in consolidating the territorial position of the French crown and the process was hastened when in 1491, a few years after his death, the duchy of Brittany was at last reunited with France by the marriage of King Charles VIII to Anne of Brittany, despite the fierce opposition of the Bretons.

Louis had also made considerable achievements in administrative and financial reform. During his reign the revenue from taxation trebled and the royal grip on the administration became absolute. Louis convened his council to save appearance but, as far as was possible in a still restless and potentially unruly France, his will alone governed the kingdom.

Louis did not neglect the rising commerce of France, which he viewed as essential to the wealth and power of the kingdom. He not only flattered the merchant classes with honours and offices but also actively promoted the great international fair at Lyons and founded and encouraged new fairs at Caen and Rouen. He set up the French silk industry which was to become a strong competitor to the Italians and, most important of all, established a strong currency.

Louis was an extraordinarily superstitious man, with one of the largest collections of holy relics in Europe. He passed his final years in seclusion at Tours, fearful of death and paying his doctors ever more extravagant fees to prolong his life. When he died in 1483 he was succeeded by his thirteen-year-old son Charles.

The regency crisis in England

It was England's tragedy that, of the descendants of John of Gaunt who survived the death of his grandson Henry V in 1422, it should have been a babe-in-arms who became the titular head of state. England was faced with a regency crisis at the very moment when its economic position at home and its vast commitments abroad demanded an imperious will and iron statecraft. And it was a double tragedy since the three men who now found themselves at the head of affairs were talented and strong-willed princes, whose qualities were never to be deployed to the full in their country's interest.

John, Duke of Bedford, the dead king's eldest surviving brother, was best fitted beyond doubt for the office of regent, but he was to exhaust his great abilities in the thankless task of governing and defending the English position in Normandy. His younger brother, Humphrey, Duke of Gloucester, was an intelligent and high-spirited prince who in happier times would have been gratefully remembered for his generous and enlightened patronage of learning and the arts. As it was, the University of Oxford was indebted to him for the finest library in the kingdom, and the first tentative steps of English humanism were taken with his encouragement.

The third of this talented triumvirate was the duke's uncle, Henry Beaufort, Cardinal Bishop of Winchester. His family was descended from John of Gaunt's misalliance with Catherine of Swynford. The legitimacy of the line had been confirmed by Richard II. By his expert deployment of the revenues of the rich diocese of Winchester, Henry made the name of Beaufort one of the most powerful in the land.

Despite the fact that the will of Henry V had certainly made Gloucester guardian of the young king and, according to the duke's reading of it, had also created him regent of England in the absence of his elder brother, a council of regency was set up at the request of parliament. The council had a large membership and was determined to see that no single one of its members should achieve a position of supreme control—not even the late king's brothers and certainly not Gloucester.

Statesmanship and tact were not among Gloucester's obvious qualities and he unwisely accepted the council's summons to attend parliament which was addressed to him as Duke of Gloucester. The council, which had determined to set aside even the will of Henry V if it attempted to 'change and abroge the governaunce' of the realm without the assent of parliament, began to work with great vigour. From the outset it established that all its acts should be attested and signed by at least four of its members.

As a compromise gesture Gloucester was granted the title of protector of the realm and chief councillor of the king, but the titles had little real weight. When in 1428 he tried to force the recognition of his claims to the full regency he was told that the council had no knowledge of any special authority which he enjoyed. He was reminded that he had accepted the council's summons at the very beginning of the reign, in common with other lords of the kingdom. Moreover, in the previous year members of the council, as tactfully as possible but quite firmly, had interviewed both Gloucester and Bedford to learn their views as to where the ultimate authority lay during the minority.

From the very first years the House of Lancaster was desperately short of ready cash. The old theory that the king should live off his own resources still had force enough to make parliament reluctant to vote supplies. Nevertheless, it is a remarkable fact that, without the expense of the war in France, the king's own income, together with such parliamentary grants as came his way, would have brought solvency within sight. As it was, the Lancastrians were forced to borrow, and to borrow without even the luxury enjoyed by Edward III of renouncing his debts and bankrupting his Italian bankers.

The rising power of the Medici in Florence was not to rest on the unsure foundations of royal favour, and the advisers of Henry VI had to be content with creditors uncomfortably near home, who, becuase they were wealthy enough to maintain the government, were too strong to be trifled with. Such men were the merchants of the burgeoning city of London and Henry Beaufort, Bishop of Winchester. It had been calculated that he lent a total of £35,000 to Henry V and more than £45,000 to the regime in the first ten years of Henry VI. Moreover, it must be remembered that in a society which did not yet have an efficient and reliable money market, the bishop could charge interest rates (suitably disguised to circumvent the Church's ruling against usury) of up to thirty per cent. There may well have been more profitable and surer investments, but the bishop was paying for power and won an increasingly firm grip on the finances of the kingdom. At one point the royal jewels were consigned to him as security.

It is understandable that Gloucester should have viewed such a powerful magnate as a threat to the kingdom, but Beaufort's manoeuvres in the council also threatened him personally. The conflict between the two men came to head in the autumn of 1425. Duke Humphrey accused Beaufort of treason against both Henry IV and Henry V and forced him to refute these damaging charges both publicly and in full parliament. Moreover, Beaufort's power was not limited to financial affairs; early in the reign he became a cardinal and papal legate.

At the Council of Constance (1414–18), which had met to put an end to the schism in the Church, the German delegates had demanded the reform of the Church before the election of a new pope. However, largely becuase the English changed sides and deserted the Holy Roman emperor's representatives, the council elected a pope before any serious reforms had been effectively implemented. The impetus of the conciliar movement was spent and the pope, Martin V, set out upon the recovery of the full powers of his predecessors.

Above, John, Duke of Bedford (1389–1435), the brother of Henry V, shown here with St George in the frontispiece of the Bedford Hours. *He was nominally protector of England during Henry VI's minority but was in France for most of the time. British Library, London.*

Below, Richard Beauchamp, Earl of Warwick, shown here as one of the protectors of the infant Henry VI. British Library, London.

Opposite left, Louis XI of France (ruled 1461–83) in council, declaring war on Charles the Bold of Burgundy, his continual enemy.

Opposite right, Charles the Bold of Burgundy besieging Liège in 1468 to put down the revolt of that town against Burgundian rule.

After years of fruitless work, however, he was obliged to confess that 'in England it is the king rather than the pope who rules the church'. Among the most important buttresses of royal power in the Church were the status of Provisors and Praemunire which forbade English churchmen the right to appeal to Rome or to receive from Rome any appointment to a benefice without the approval of the king. In his long struggle to get these statutes repealed, Martin had the active support of Beaufort, who under Henry V had actively sought and accepted a cardinalate without the king's knowledge and had thus himself infringed these statutes. Henry had forced him to choose between voluntary exile and refusal of the cardinal's hat, and Beaufort decided on the latter.

The struggle for power

The basic weakness of the Lancastrian claim to the throne meant that the Lancastrian kings had to be powerful and effective rulers and it is therefore surprising that the insecure throne of Henry VI lasted as long as it did. Under Henry the crown was falling into contempt, but in the early years the Council of Regency on the whole showed itself equal to the demands of the situation. However, with the ascendancy of the Earl of Suffolk, who unashamedly used his position as leading councillor of the king for factional advantage, the Council, too, became discredited.

Suffolk's ascendancy rested on the king's marriage to his candidate, Margaret of Anjou. The dowerless queen, whose main advantage seems to have been her close dependence on Suffolk, was the last in a succession of French princesses proposed as wives for Henry VI to symbolize the truce between the two kingdoms. Various factors disqualified the others. In one instance the painter sent over to take the lady's picture for the king to make his choice fell ill and thus delayed matters. With his protégé safely installed and the king's infatuation for her growing daily, Suffolk's position was strong, but he still had to face the continuing opposition of the Duke of Gloucester.

Gloucester's position was first eroded in 1441 by the trial and conviction of his wife, Eleanor Cobham, on charges of attempting to cause the king's death by magic and witchcraft. The duke himself was not held responsible in any way but inevitably became implicated in his wife's guilt. Continuing in his advocacy of the war in France against the policy of the king's senior advisors, Gloucester, who was largely without support in the council, showed his characteristic lack of political realism. By degrees he forced himself into isolation and thus made his own position increasingly vulnerable. Suffolk was probably implicated in Gloucester's arrest on charges of treason in February 1447 and the duke's death in the same month proved to be of considerable advantage to him.

In the following year Suffolk was created duke and his position seemed assured. However, by mismanagement of affairs he provoked discontent on all sides and at this point the Duke of York had his first brush with the government. The issue was a straightforward matter of arrears in payment to York for his services as commander in Normandy. The duke made accusations of sharp practice. Following the classic pattern of English governments in trouble with overmighty subjects, the council appointed York as king's lieutenant in Ireland. But this was not enough to save Suffolk. The growing discontent in the country at large led to his indictment in parliament for mismanagement. Attempting to flee the country, he was captured and lynched by pirates in the English Channel in 1450.

The parliamentary opposition to the regime was an accurate reflection of the state of feeling in the country, as was shown by the rising of the men of Kent under Jack Cade. Cade's rebellion of 1450 was in no way as serious a threat as the rising of the peasantry seventy years earlier, although like their predecessors, Jack Cade and his followers occupied London for three days in their attempt to force reforms on the government. Far more than the Peasants' Revolt, the Cade Rebellion was a rising of the middle orders of society against an inefficient and oppressive officialdom.

The fall of Suffolk made little difference to the inadequate and partial way in which affairs were run. He was succeeded as the most powerful man in the king's council by Edward Beaufort, Earl of Somerset, who, it was rumoured, had designs on the crown. Affairs were going badly abroad as well as at home. The collapse of English hopes in France which began with the resurgence of French morale after Joan of Arc was complete with the loss of Gascony in 1453.

York and Lancaster

The flagging energies of the administration were indeed becoming apparent in many fields. York's demand to occupy his rightful place in the king's council and his call for reform became increasingly difficult to resist. The weakening of the central authority in Lancastrian England had left the magnates free to pursue their local rivalries unmolested as well as to contend for the control of the central government. As a consequence, the strong challenge made by York in the interests of his own house against the administration of the Beaufort party had the effect of polarizing the numerous conflicting interests throughout the country behind the two court parties. The opposing factions of York and Lancaster now came into being. The struggle known to later generations as the Wars of the Roses really began in 1452 when Richard, Duke of York, marched on the capital in an attempt to bring his grievances to the attention of the king against the opposition of his chief minister and to persuade the monarch to dispense with that adviser.

As so often in his subsequent career, York miscalculated and was forced to withdraw. However, within two years the first of Henry VI's attacks of madness opened the way for him and he was declared protector of the realm by an enthusiastic House of Commons, for the Yorkist cause, although opposed by the court party and disliked by

the king, was enthusiastically supported by the merchants and the citizens of London, who wanted an end of the misgovernment of the Lancastrians and a more positive mercantile policy.

When the king recovered his wits in 1455 the ten-months' rule of the Yorkists came to an abrupt end. Always willing to march against his king, York took to arms again but this time with more success. At the First Battle of St Albans he took custody of the king, escorting him back to London and there appointing a second Yorkist administration. The most important of the new appointments was that of the brilliant and dynamic young Earl of Warwick as the Captain of Calais, who commanded for the Yorkists the 'largest single force in the king's pay'.

The earl certainly deserved this prize command. He had led a bold flank attack at St Albans which had virtually decided the issue of the day and continued to serve the Yorkist cause to great effect in the outpost across the Channel. But, despite a period of brief reform under York's second protectorship, the cause lost ground in England and within a year the Beauforts were back and York himself retired to Ireland.

From 1456 onwards the Lancastrian government more or less abandoned even the pretence of a national administration, devoting its energies exclusively to the maintenance of the dynasty. Commissions were sent out into the country to investigate charges of treason and their ruthless conduct provided fresh grievances against the ailing administration.

The Yorkists also accused the government of preparing for the introduction of native Irish forces into England and in 1460, judging the time ripe for a comeback, they made a combined attack on the central government from Calais and Ireland. This time despite initial reverses York made good his march on the capital and forced the government's hand. Even now, however, true to form, he miscalculated the temper of the magnates who, although ready to support a move for reform, were not yet prepared for a change of dynasty and the accession of the duke as king.

The situation was crystallized in the famous scene at the Palace of Westminster in October. Following the victory of his supporters at Northampton, York had returned from Ireland not only to secure the reversal of the attainders passed on him and his party but also to make an open claim to the throne.

On 10 October, backed by a force of some 300 armed men, he went to Westminster Hall. A naked sword was carried before him as he entered the Hall before the assembled lords and, marching the length of the floor, he went to the empty throne and laid a hand on it. Instead of the shouts of acclamation which the duke had hoped would grace his attempted act of usurpation there was a sullen silence. The awkward pause was broken by the Archbishop of Canterbury, who asked whether the duke wished to see the king. The angry reply has become notorious: 'I know of no one in the realm who would not more fitly come to me than I to him.'

The scene had lacked all preparation and had, in any case, been badly stage-managed. York followed up this reverse with a written statement, setting out his claim to the throne on hereditary grounds alone, but still the prize eluded him. The claim was good and indeed virtually unanswerable. It rested on the fact that the House of York was descended from Edward III's third son Lionel Duke of Clarence, whereas John of Gaunt, the founder of the House of Lancaster, was the fourth son. Against this it was argued that Henry IV had rested his claim not only on his descent from Henry III but also on the acclamation of parliament. Furthermore, it was pointed out that the succession had been confirmed on Henry IV and his heirs by parliamentary statute. Richard declared that his hereditary claim, confirmed by divine law, took precedence over any parliamentary statute.

Above, Edward IV of England (ruled 1461–83). His reign saw the start of far-reaching changes in the powers and administration of the monarchy and of an alliance between the Crown and the merchant classes. National Portrait Gallery, London.

Above left, Henry VI and his wife Margaret of Anjou being presented with a book by Talbot, the Earl of Shrewsbury. Margaret was the most energetic proponent of the Lancastrian cause until her defeat at the Battle of Tewkesbury at the hands of Edward IV in 1471. British Library, London.

Left, Henry VI of England (ruled 1422–61; 1470–71). He came to the throne at the age of one and never had the character to overcome the nobles who controlled the kingdom during his minority. National Portrait Gallery, London.

Opposite, a genealogical table drawn up in England in the 1440s, showing Henry VI as the direct descendant of St Louis, by both the French and the English lines. Despite this reassertion of the English claim to rule in France, the final English withdrawal from France took place in 1450, bringing the Hundred Years War to an end. British Library, London.

The points discussed were not merely academic nor were they merely the attempts to reconcile the fact of a mighty subject's ambition and power with the theory of constitutionalism to government. The debate about York's claims was a debate on the very nature of that constitutionalism itself. Could parliamentary statute override the prime feudal law of hereditary succession? Was the realm in fact to be governed by the same laws as landed property? Could it be regarded as the personal domain of the monarch and as such subject to the same laws of devolution as the great estates of his magnates? The questions were real and pressing. They were also difficult and dangerous.

The king's judges and the sergeants-at-law refused to advise on the matter, claiming that it was too high for the law and above their learning and should be decided in the House of Lords. The outcome was compromise. The claims of York were recognized as just and he was proclaimed heir apparent. Henry was to remain king for life only, to be succeeded by York or his heirs.

The settlement was similar to that reached in the case of Henry V's claim to the throne of France, and for the same reasons. The claimant was too strong for his wishes to be ignored but not strong enough to be able to push his claim to its logical conclusion.

After being proclaimed heir-apparent and protector in November, York left London for the north to subdue the Lancastrian lords who were refusing to accept the settlement. It is perhaps characteristic of the man that immediately after he had achieved everything he had been struggling for he should die as the result of underestimating the opposition. He was killed in December at the Battle of Wakefield. Thus, within a month of its triumph, the Yorkist cause was thrown into confusion once more. It was to be saved partly by the strength of the Earl of Warwick but far more by the skill and political sense of Richard's eighteen-year-old son, formerly Earl of March and now Duke of York and heir apparent to the throne of England. Despite his father's reverse, Edward defeated a large Lancastrian force coming to Queen Margaret's aid and then made across country to London, providing the rallying point for the scattered forces of the Earl of Warwick. In an inexplicable fit of lethargy the latter had allowed himself to be defeated by the army of the queen and had even lost the king to her.

This was the turning point in the war. Up to this stage whoever had held the king could more or less dictate terms. The opposing party had for the time being to accept what came and watch for an opening. But now the swords were out and the Yorkists could look forward only to large-scale confiscations, exile and proscriptions. The alternative was to cut the Gordian knot and to proclaim a new king. Thanks both to Edward's rapid marches and to the outrage caused by the excesses of the queen's troops in the territory they passed through, London opened its gates to the Yorkist leaders. In March, Edward was formerly acclaimed as king by the soldiers and citizens of the capital. His title was confirmed in a specially designed religious service which was intended to serve until his coronation.

Edward marched north before the end of March to seek out and destroy the forces of his opponents, joining up on the way with the Earl of Warwick. At the Battle of Towton near York, in the same month, he routed the army of Margaret of Anjou, who was forced to flee to Scotland. Because of the support of the Scots for the former queen she was able to make good her escape to France. But in the ensuing months Edward and Warwick mopped up the remaining pockets of Lancastrian resistance, executing many of their leading opponents.

Edward IV

It was above all strong and effective rule which England needed. The long minority of the saintly Henry VI had been a period of financial insolvency, military humiliation in France and corrupt and incompetent administration at home. Moreover, this dark period ended with the discovery that the child-king had developed into a weak, mentally unbalanced man, undoubtedly of virtuous life and a great benefactor to education but a failure as a ruler.

The House of Lancaster had owed its elevation to the ranks of European monarchy to the ability and ruthlessness of its founder Henry Bolingbroke. Its fortunes prospered under the brilliant and distracting foreign successes of his son, but the memory of the usurpation was still strong in men's minds. The increasing need for a sound and undemanding foreign policy and for security and stable conditions at home meant that the dynasty could feel secure only under the rule of a strong and efficient king.

Richard's son, Edward IV, was one of the most engaging and stimulating men ever to have occupied the throne of England. Barely twenty at the time of his accession, he was handsome, physically strong, notoriously successful as a womanizer and very calm and effective in his manipulation of the political world.

Behind his rise to power lay a long history of dynastic conflict and political manoeuvre. This road ended in his coronation under the aegis of the powerful and brilliant Earl of Warwick. The problem of Warwick's ambition was not to be finally resolved until ten years later and only after Edward had again lost his throne. However, the brief 'readoption' of Henry VI in 1470–71 marks a break in the reign not only in time but also to a large extent in character. During the first ten years Edward made good his claim to absolute authority. Thereafter the successful deployment of that authority can be seen in the rehabilitation of life and government within the realm.

It is worth examining the roots of the conflict between Edward and Warwick and seeing why, indeed, there should have been any conflict. Edward was a lusty young man with a strong taste for the good life, and at his right hand was a man whose abilities and loyalty were proven. Admittedly Edward never very strongly resisted the temptation to sensual indulgence, but he was, from the first, determined to be master in his own house. And there were good precedents in the career of Gloucester and the reign of his unhappy predecessor. The medieval king was expected to be the source of power. If he relinquished his grasp of this, he could expect disaster.

At first there was no dispute between the two victors. Warwick was confirmed as captain of Calais, and created great chamberlain and constable of Dover Castle and the Cinque ports. For the moment it seemed that Edward was prepared to submit to all his mentor's demands. For the moment the centre of attention was not in England but at the French court. There Margaret of Anjou was wooing the support of the new French king, Louis XI, who was fascinated by the opportunity which now presented itself of keeping the arch-enemy of France in a permanent state of turmoil. A representative of his had been with Edward on his march to Towton but now that the Yorkists looked like becoming securely established it was natural for Louis to support their rival. And there were inducements. Margaret, who had already traded the border town of Berwick for the Scottish king's assistance, was now prepared to offer Calais to France in exchange for a loan.

There were two courses of action open to England: to counter the Franco-Lancastrian alliance by an agreement with Louis' other great enemy, the Duke of Burgundy, or to seek to undermine the Lancastrian understanding with France. Warwick favoured the latter alternative. The alliance between England and France, which was his grand objective, was to be secured by the marriage of the young English king to Bona of Savoy, Louis' sister-in-law.

In the summer of 1463 a truce was signed between England and France, with Philip the Good of Burgundy concurring, and all seemed set fair for the triumph of Warwick's policy. But there were serious weaknesses. Burgundian compliance could not be relied on indefinitely and English commercial interests were far more heavily engaged with Burgundy than with France. The average Englishman may have hated all foreigners, but he hated the French most of all. The prospect of an alliance with France was violently resented and the attempt to foist another French queen on the country after the troublesome Margaret of Anjou was to invite opposition. Nor was Edward at all satisfied at the prospect, having already set his eye on an altogether more experienced bedfellow. Finally, quite apart from his sexual proclivities, the king had determined to break the plan which clearly set the seal on Warwick's pretensions to determine all important matters of policy.

The conflict with Warwick

The sensation which rocked English society in September 1464 was a nice compound of romance, high state policy and the humiliation of the senior minister. What Edward had to announce offended many others besides the Earl of Warwick. It was nothing less than his secret marriage, six months previously, to the beautiful but penniless Elizabeth Woodville, the widow of a Lancastrian lord. At one stroke Edward had wrecked the plans for a French alliance, thus opening the way to a more solid agreement with Burgundy. He had won still greater popularity with his subjects both by backing their commercial interests and by appealing to their hearts with his romantic alliance. Finally, he had served notice on Warwick of his intention to be master and had won his lady, not to mention a whole new clan of relations, who would make a satisfying counterbalance to the crowds of Nevilles in high places.

Warwick accepted the situation with the best grace he could, but he continued in his plans to resurrect the French alliance and drew closer to Louis. For his part Louis was delighted that earl and king were at odds with each other. He was eager to encourage Warwick's advances, hoping that by supporting the powerful magnate he could break England's alliances with Burgundy and also with Francis of Brittany, both of whom were involved in the League of the Common Weal against the French crown.

Edward's understandings with Burgundy and Brittany were formalized as alliances with important commercial clauses in 1468, and the marriage of the king's sister, Margaret, to the Count of Charolais was officially agreed. Although Warwick still had sufficient influence to persuade the king into an unwise policy of hostility towards the great German trading league of Hansa, the breach between the two was virtually complete. Warwick received the offer of a principality in the Burgundian Low countries from Louis as the price of overthowing Edward. In 1469, collecting reinforcements from Calais, he headed an open rebellion in favour of the king's brother George, Duke of Clarence.

Uncharacteristically, Edward, caught wrong-footed, was captured and forced to sign a series of documents granting the rebels' demands. But Warwick discovered that Edward was apparently indispensable. The mounting unrest in the country at the news of the coup made it impossible to convene the parliament at which the earl had planned to make his arrangements and he had to grant Edward more freedom than he had intended. Displaying his usual resilience, Edward secretly summoned his supporters to his side and by May 1470 Warwick had to flee to France, having been proclaimed traitor throughout England.

The struggle was, however, by no means ended. Louis, who not only wished to see the overthrow of the powerful Yorkist regime in England but also desperately needed the English alliance against Burgundy, achieved the almost impossible task of reconciling the two arch-enemies, Warwick and ex-queen Margaret, in a common cause to restore the pitiful Henry VI to his English kingdom. For ten brief months the 'readeption', as Warwick termed it, seemed to have succeeded. Edward, again caught off his guard and again betrayed by his brother Clarence, had to flee his kingdom to the court of his brother-in-law, Charles the Bold. But, although her husband was reestablished, Margaret delayed her own return with the young prince of Wales and the Lancastrian magnates, doubtful of the outcome and opposed to the French alliance against Burgundy, withheld their full support from the restored regime.

Displaying characteristic adroitness and determination, Edward returned to England in May 1471, landing at Ravenspur as Henry Bolingbroke had done and claiming like him to have come only to claim his inheritance. His small force met no opposition and many lords including his brother Clarence flocked to his banner. Three weeks after landing he was in London, having outmarched Warwick to the capital.

With the crushing victories of Barnet and Tewkesbury, which took place within days of each other, Edward ended all opposition. Warwick was slain at Barnet, and at Tewkesbury the young prince of Wales was killed and Margaret herself captured. Meanwhile, Edward's loyal brother, Richard of Gloucester, had defeated a last attempt by Margaret's allies to seize the capital. On his return there Edward, after the death of Henry VI, which he ordered, was beyond all question the supreme power in the land.

The achievements of Edward IV

Edward displayed considerable tenacity in pursuing his policy of alliance with Burgundy—more so indeed than Charles the Bold himself, who was becoming increasingly concerned with his plans to gain the title of kingdom for his extensive but vulnerable ducal territories. Nevertheless, Edward continued with his plans for an invasion of France in association with Burgundy and, in addition, extracted several sizeable loans from parliament in order to have the means to fit out an expedition.

Finally, Charles came to the conference table. The two rulers agreed on the division of the spoils after their defeat of France

Above, Bodiam Castle, in Sussex, was built in the fifteenth century; such massive building projects reflected both the economic stagnation and the political instability of the age.

was assured and also that Edward should be free to hold his coronation at Reims. They further agreed that if Edward or his heirs wished to be crowned elsewhere they should be entitled to take the sacred ampula for the coronation on condition it was returned.

Despite Duke Charles's continuing delay before the seige of Neuss Edward finally crossed to Calais in July 1475. There he was met by the duke who calmly advised him to press his attack into French territory while he, Charles, completed his commitments at Neuss and then came to join him.

Edward was confronted by a large and powerful French army and, without the certainty of Burgundy supporting him on the flank, his position in France could not be firmly established. Edward had himself brought over a large and well-equipped army and Louis was eager to detach him from his Burgundian alliance. The ease with which the French king was able to buy Edward off has given rise to the suspicion ever since that the French expedition had been from the start largely intended as a bargaining counter to win French financial support.

English claims to the crown of France were referred to a future committee of arbitration and Louis agreed to pay over 75,000 crowns there and then so that the English would withdraw their forces. He agreed further to the astonishing annual pension of 50,000 golden crowns, to be paid to Edward in the city of London. It says much for the success with which he had established Yorkist rule in England that Edward evidently presented a sufficient threat to Louis for this pension to be paid with fair regularity.

Three years later Edward received additional funds from the confiscated estates of his brother Clarence, who was killed by drowning in the Tower in February 1478, though probably not in a butt of Malmsey wine as tradition has it. In the previous year, the duke's name had been connected with rumours of plotting, and one of his servants had been found guilty of trying to bring about the king's death by means of magic. Clarence had committed sufficient treason against his brother to merit his punishment, but, even after having himself brought the bill of attainder before parliament, Edward could not give the word for the execution. Sentence was, however, finally carried out on the authority of the House of Lords.

The extent to which Edward had restored the crown's finances after the period of the impecunious Lancastrian kings may be measured by the fact that the treasury was able to consider the repayment of outstanding debts. Edward's credit had always been sounder than his predecessors' and, from the first years of his reign, he had been able to borrow from Italian bankers—the first English king to do so for sixty years. His financial success was based on both the wealth of his family and the sound commercial policies he pursued. He fostered relations between England and its market in Burgundy and worked to re-establish a good understanding with the Hanseatic League, whose ships carried him and his forces across the North Sea on his return to England in 1471.

Modern scholarship is increasingly coming to regard the reign of Edward IV as one of the decisive periods of English history. First, he achieved something remarkable in English late medieval history—a solvent monarchy. In the second place, by his own genuine interest in justice and his ability to enforce it, he gradually restored the essentials of constitutionalism and right procedure to English life. Third, his reign saw the establishment of administrative practices whose worth was proved by the succeeding dynasty of the Tudors.

Richard III

On the death of the king his brother, Richard, Duke of Gloucester, found himself and his dynasty in a dangerous situation. The young Prince Edward was proclaimed king as Edward V and his mother, Queen Elizabeth, and her family, the Woodvilles, seemed firmly entrenched. The country was faced with a minority dominated by an ambitious and avaricious clan. Richard, on the other hand, could expect political extinction. He had been a loyal servant to his brother, had proved his abilities both as an administrator and a soldier while lieutenant in the north, and undoubtedly had more than his fair share of ambition. But Richard was not unpopular and when, with the aid of Henry Stafford, Duke of Buckingham, he succeeded in taking custody of the young king and had himself proclaimed protector of the realm there was no opposition in the country at large.

Richard's next move, however, was not so popular, for he now declared Edward and his young brother, Richard, to be bastards, claiming that their father had in fact contracted a secret marriage prior to that with Elizabeth Woodville. Again, with the support of Buckingham, Richard had himself proclaimed king. Discontent in the country mounted when he confined the young princes in the Tower of London and rumour began to report that the new king had murdered his nephews. Later in the year Buckingham turned against the king and although his rebellion was put down it served as a warning that Richard could expect continuing opposition to his claims.

The most serious threat was posed by the Earl of Richmond, Henry Tudor, in exile at the court of Brittany, and despite strenuous efforts Richard was unable to gain his extradition to England or arrange his assassination. When Richmond landed at Milford Haven in 1485, the Yorkist king was able to go to meet him in overwhelming force. The Battle of Bosworth, at which Richard was killed and with him the hopes of his dynasty, was decided, after a long-fought contest, by the desertion to the enemy of a body of Richard's troops.

Richard's short reign revealed his talents for kingship and his love of justice. His acts included the banning of the forced loans or 'benevolences' extorted in the reign of his brother and measures to defeat the corruption of justice. His courage was demonstrated by his refusal to flee from the defeat of Bosworth. Moreover, all the evidence available suggests that the Richard III of Tudor propaganda (a misshapen monster from birth, murderer of Henry VI, Edward the Lancastrian prince of Wales and his own brother Clarence) can be totally discounted. It is even possible to have reasonable doubts about the most notorious of his alleged crimes—the killing of the princes in the Tower. However, such judicial murders were commonplace in the fifteenth century and Richard may well have been guilty. Henry Tudor and his son were obliged to kill many more to secure their own position.

The Burgundian chronicler, Comines, said of the civil wars in England:

> England enjoyed this peculiar mercy above all other kingdoms, that neither the country nor the people nor the houses were wasted, destroyed or demolished; but the calamities and misfortunes of the war fell only upon the soldiers and the nobility.

It was true. The Wars of the Roses had involved small forces and had been settled in pitched battles, from which the country at large had been more or less spared. France, on the other hand, had suffered the depredations of the English invaders and of the bands of mercenaries employed by the warring factions. England, except for the atrocities committed by the Lancastrian armies at the beginning of the wars, had avoided this.

Yet the state of the country was inevitably unsettled by the periodic armed conflicts over the succession to the throne. The constant change of parties had produced a welter of lawsuits to decide the tangled claims to property and these in turn had brought the whole process of law into decay. The profession of lawyers flourished as never before, but litigants often as not decided their own cases by strong-arm methods. The jury, the coping-stone of the judicial system, was discredited by intimidation and corruption.

In all walks of life violence had become, even more than usual, the natural method of settling disputes. However justified the Yorkists claims to legitimacy (and they had been weakened by the accession of Richard III), the decision had nevertheless been made by force. To the country as a whole the claims and counter-claims of the noble factions can have held little interest.. What was needed was a strong king, whatever his colour.

Henry Tudor

Victory in battle as the only legitimizer was never more convincingly demonstrated than in the succession of Henry VII. His claim by heredity could hardly have been weaker, deriving as it did through the bastard line of Beaufort from John of Gaunt (legitimized but debarred from the succession) and the misalliance between Henry V's queen, Catherine, and her Welsh chamberlain, Owen Tudor. Yet, after the death of Henry VI and his son Edward, Prince of Wales, Henry Tudor had been adopted as the official Lancastrian candidate. As a consequence, he had spent much of his life a fugitive on the continent from the agents of the Yorkist kings.

His claims were contemptible, yet at the magic word of victory, spoken on Bosworth Field, this wily and persistent adventurer was transformed into the king of England and, following its custom in such cases, the country and its capital gave him a hero's welcome, until the next time. But, as things turned out, there was to be no next time and gradually, thanks to the pertinacity and skill of this latest winner in the monarchy game, the English came to the conclusion that the Battle of Bosworth had been the last major engagement in the century of civil war.

His reign was certainly not to be uneventful, for Henry had to face his fair share of pretenders. One of his first acts was to imprison the young Earl of Warwick, who, as the son of Richard III's elder brother Clarence, was the senior claimant to the throne. This, however, did not prevent an imaginative priest from having his young pupil, Lambert Simnel, declared the true Earl of Warwick, escape from confinement

Above, Richard III of England (ruled 1483–85), regarded as a monster in Elizabethan times but today seen to have been intelligent, peaceful and a supporter of advanced political ideas. National Portrait Gallery, London.

Top, a stained-glass window at Canterbury Cathedral showing, on the left, Edward V and his brother Richard, Duke of York, the 'princes in the tower'.

Opposite, the English Court of the Exchequer; litigation about financial affairs was a major occupation of fifteenth-century landowners in England. Many cases were heard at the Court of the Exchequer. Lambeth Palace Library, London.

and proclaimed as King Edward VI in Ireland. After his capture Simnel was lucky to suffer only from Henry's sense of humour, being employed as a scullion in the royal kitchens. The next pretender, the Earl of Lincoln, Richard III's designated heir, was defeated at the Battle of Stoke.

Perhaps the most dangerous imposture of all was that of the draper's assistant, Perkin Warbeck. The Yorkist cause was by no means dead, its fiercest advocate being the dowager Duchess of Burgundy, Margaret of York. She it was who launched the regal-looking Warbeck on his career, recognizing his claim to be Richard of York, one of the 'princes in the tower', and assisting him in eight years of troublemaking to win the impressive, if worthless, recognition of the Emperor Maximilian II. In the last year of the century Henry ended the most serious threats to his dynastic position with the execution of Warbeck and Warwick. But there were to be other scares and in 1502, when his heir, Prince Arthur, died (named after the semi-legendary King Arthur for fairly obvious propaganda reasons), the succession was again in doubt for a while.

Although he found his position contested by the old-style court faction, Henry was increasingly able to rely on the support of the country as a whole, which was wearied by the unsettling events of the previous century. Even the city of York, which after Bosworth had formally recorded its sorrow at the death of the last Yorkist king, welcomed the usurper with all pomp on his visit in the following year. Moreover, Henry's marriage to Elizabeth of York, Edward IV's daughter, went far to reconciling discontents in the party itself.

Henry, however, had no intention of letting his title rest on this dynastic alliance and had proclaimed his right to the crown as a hereditary one, vindicated by the judgement of God revealed in his victory. Whereas the parliament which had confirmed the claims of Henry IV a century before had been convened by his predecessor to ensure its legitimacy as a parliament, the body which in November 1485 ordained that the crown 'abide with our now sovereign lord king Henry' was convened by Henry himself.

At home Henry was accepted as long as he showed himself to be king. The recognition of foreign princes, equally vital, was another matter and led him into continental diplomacy. Henry was able to exploit the conflicting interests of Spain and France in the jungle of Italian politics to win the important recognition of both the great powers. In this context, even the hoary claim to the throne of France, which no English king, least of all one so insecurely placed as Henry, could afford to renounce, was brought into play.

An alliance with Ferdinand of Aragon was cemented by the betrothal of Henry's baby heir to Catherine of Aragon. In return, Henry was to make war on France and this he duly did with a token expedition against Boulogne. Henry paid for the war (always a cruely expensive business) with a parliamentary grant and the raising of forced loans. Then, by the Treaty of Etaples in 1492, he earned a handsome pension from the French king in exchange for abandoning the war and allowing his claims on the French throne to fall into abeyance. Like his predecessor Edward IV, Henry had converted an unenforcible gain into ready cash and had also gained the recognition of the two major European powers.

However, Ferdinand for one was not convinced of the English king's staying power. The dowry was to be paid in instalments (never in fact completed) and the Spanish princess was permitted to sail for her wedding only in the year 1501 when her father was satisfied that Henry was securely established. Henry's first international exercise had yielded positive results, but his later continental manoeuvres were to reveal England's essentially peripheral position in a Europe still orientated towards the Mediterranean.

The renovation of the monarchy

The English monarchy, which had once wielded more complete sway within its dominions than any other in medieval Europe, had suffered a steady erosion of authority up to the middle of the fifteenth century. The reign of Edward IV had done much to restore the situation and that of Henry VII confirmed this increase in royal power.

From the first Henry set out to establish the pre-eminence of the crown. His ministers were drawn from all ranks of society, from the emerging middle class to the great aristocracy, but they all had in common their dependence for position on the will of the king. Nor did Henry neglect the immense value of splendour and display for impressing on men's minds the greatness of the king. Careful of his resources, he nevertheless did not regard the lavish ten-day festivities which celebrated the brilliant marriage of his son and heir to the king of Aragon's daughter as waste, and he maintained a court whose brilliance impressed such a hardened observer as the Venetian ambassador. Silks and ceremony were a part of statecraft. Henry used every means available to heighten the awe in which the monarch was held but also exercised in a very practical manner the vague but powerful prerogative which pertained to the king.

The reign of Edward IV had demonstrated the obvious truth that financial independence was the only firm basis of power, but to achieve this even he had to resort to the highly unpopular or forced loan. Henry, after the one instance already mentioned, never again raised revenue in this way. By the most rigorous interpretation of his rights, by careful economic management, and by the studious avoidance of war, Henry VII, who started his reign in debt, left a full treasury to his heir. Yet it has been pointed out that the balance of royal finances was still precarious when even the limited wars of the next reign could reduce the surplus to a debt. But Henry himself. managed to achieve and maintain solvency.

The most important source of income was land and Henry dramatically increased the crown's lead over its rivals as the greatest landowner in the kingdom. The possessions of Lancaster and York naturally fell to him and, by the simple expedient of dating the beginning of his reign on the day before Bosworth, he was able to confiscate the lands of the loyal supporters of his predecessor with a show of legality. In addition, he declared null and void all grants of land made since the death of Henry VI and in the first six years carried out a thorough survey of all the lapsed feudal rights pertaining to the crown.

Henry's other main sources of income were the proceeds of the customs duties on wine and other produce (tunnage and poundage), granted to him for life by his first parliament, and the profits from the administration of justice derived from the fees payable to obtain royal writs and the fines imposed as penalties. Ultimately, of course, the prosperity of the king was a direct reflection of the prosperity of his kingdom. Under Henry the statute book shows numerous measures designed to protect and encourage English trade, and the treaties with Spain and Flanders contained important commerical clauses.

However, the crown had reservations in the matter of one of the most profitable of English industries, the production of wool. The landlords had begun to abolish the patchwork of small peasant holdings and substituted in its place wide open fields on which to graze their sheep. The monarchy objected to the social effects. The dispossessed peasantry were ruined and joined the swelling ranks of vagabonds, able-bodied but unemployed men who travelled the English countryside in their thousands and presented a potential source of discontent and rebellion. In an attempt to stem the tide, Henry passed two acts against enclosure in the early years of his reign.

In his search for funds Henry ignored almost entirely the parliamentary grant, which had been for earlier kings a standard source of extraordinary revenue. But such income was bought at the price of parliamentary scrutiny of expenditure and demands for reforms. Authorizing taxation was, in the late fifteenth century, the major function of parliament, and a king who could live of his own could dispense with this troublesome body. Increasing the royal revenue, at which Henry was so adept (though his revival of customary obligations and feudal dues often proved very unpopular), would be of no use unless the administration of royal finance were also improved.

Henry, as always following the precedents of his medieval predecessors, bypassed the cumbrous and semi-independent institution of the exchequer, substituting for it a household office, namely the chamber. As the reign progressed this department took over more and more of the operations of receipt and audit, and the final scrutiny was made by the king himself, whose autograph monogram appears on page after page of the chamber accounts. Never before, and not for a long time afterwards, was there an English or for that matter a European king whose financial position was so secure and so carefully controlled.

However, the strength of the monarchy which Henry bequeathed to his son lay not only in financial solvency and an exalted monarchic idea but also in the restoration of the processes of royal justice. The king's chief executive instrument was the royal council. This had always had judicial functions and, by extending these, Henry made available a new standard of judicial efficiency and rectitude which bypassed the discredited jury service and administered justice which, if sometimes partial in the king's interest, was energetic and incorruptible in its dispensations between subjects. Henry, like all medieval kings, was constantly travelling about his kingdom. Consequently, the membership of the council was divided between those attending on the king and those operating from Westminster, where they had met in the traditional hall of the king's council since the days of Edward III, the Star Chamber.

Henry's success was the result of single-minded concentration on the affairs of his own country. European ambitions were not extravagantly pushed; Ireland was soon abandoned to its own devices and the problem of Scotland was temporarily shelved by the marriage of Margaret Tudor to James IV. The medieval English monarchy had been restored to a new potency and, to later generations, the spectacle provided such a radical contrast to the state of affairs before Henry's accession that it seemed as if he had established a 'new' monarchy. But, in the words of one modern historian, 'The centre of Henry's government, as of all medieval government, was the king himself.' At his death he left a system that once again functioned smoothly but that bore few signs of innovation and required, as it always had done, the strong and effective supervision of a hard-working king.

Above, Henry VII of England (ruled 1485–1509). He consolidated the power of the Crown and gradually improved the country's prosperity but introduced few innovations in government or political institutions. National Portrait Gallery, London.

ENGLAND AND FRANCE FROM 1380 TO 1500

Date	France	England	Europe
1380	Charles VI (1380–1422) Rising of the *Maillotins* Charles marries Isabeau of Bavaria The *Marmousets* Philip the Bold, Duke of Burgundy, inherits Flanders (1384) War with England resumed (1385)	Richard II (1377–99) Peasants' Revolt (1381) Richard marries Anne of Bohemia Richard marries Isabella of France Chaucer's *Canterbury Tales* Henry IV (Lancaster) deposes Richard II	Turks capture Byzantine Asia Minor and Bulgaria Swiss League Tower of Strasbourg Cathedral begun
1400	John the Fearless, Duke of Burgundy (1404) Duke of Orleans murdered by Burgundians; start of civil war (1407) Duke of Burgundy defeats French at Liège	Marriage of Henry IV to Joan of Navarre Rebellion of the Percys; Henry Percy (Hotspur) killed (1403)	Florence overthrows Pisa Ghiberti begins work on Florence Baptistery Donatello's *David* Council of Pisa
1410	John the Fearless murdered (1419) Philip the Good, Duke of Burgundy Treaty of Troyes	Henry IV joins Orleanists Henry V (1413–22) Henry V invades France; defeats French at Agincourt (1415) Henry V—Alliance with Sigismund of Germany and Duke of Burgundy Henry V marries Catherine of Valois	Peace between Portugal and Castile Council of Constance
1420	Death of Charles VI Charles VIII (1422–61) Joan of Arc relieves Orleans (1429) Coronation at Reims (1429)	Death of Henry V Henry VI (1422–61) proclaimed king of England and France	Constantinople besieged by Turks
1430	Congress of Arras: Duke of Burgundy abandons English alliance and unites with Charles VII		Cosimo de' Medici Henry the Navigator
1440	Renewal of war with England (1448)	Marriage of Henry VI and Margaret of Anjou Rival political groups in England: Lancaster and York English cede Rouen to French	War between towns and princes in Germany
1450	French regain Cherbourg End of Hundred Years' War (1453)	Jack Cade's rebellion England surrenders French claims except for Calais Richard, Duke of York, named protector of England during Henry's insanity Edward (son of Henry VI) made prince of Wales	Mehmet II becomes sultan of Turkey Constantinople captured by Turks (1453)
1460	Death of Charles VII Louis XI (1461–83) Charles the Bold becomes Duke of Burgundy Liège (1468)	Henry VI captured at Northampton Edward of York becomes king as Edward IV Edward marries Elizabeth Woodville Edward IV defeated by Warwick 'the Kingmaker' (1469) Edward IV flees to France	Marriage of Ferdinand and Isabella (1469) Lorenzo de'Medici becomes leader of Florentine Republic (1469)
1470	Charles the Bold defeated and killed by French at Nancy	Henry VI restored to the throne by Warwick (1470) Edward IV defeats Warwick at Barnet (1471) Henry VI murdered Alliance between Edward IV and Charles the Bold	
1480	Death of Louis XI Charles VIII (1483–98)	Edward IV succeeded by Edward V Richard Duke of Gloucester proclaimed Richard III Richard killed at Bosworth Henry Tudor becomes Henry VII (1485) Marriage of Henry VII to Elizabeth of York (1486)	Spanish Inquisition Leonardo da Vinci Vienna captured by Matthias Corvinus of Hungary (1485) Ivan III subdues Khanate of Kazan
1490	Brittany united to France by marriage of Charles VIII to Anne of Brittany (1491) Louis XII succeeds Charles VIII and marries Anne of Brittany		Ferdinand of Aragon ends Muslim rule in Spain (1492) Ludovico Sforza of Milan invites Charles VIII to invade Naples Savonarola burnt at Florence Switzerland becomes independent republic (1499)
1500			

Chapter 15

The Rise of Spain and Portugal

By the end of the reign of Alfonso X the Wise of Castile, the political boundaries of the Iberian peninsula had settled along lines which were to remain by and large fixed for the next 200 years. From the end of the thirteenth to the end of the fifteenth century, the major powers were the three Christian kingdoms of Portugal, Castile and Aragon. The tiny Basque kingdom of Navarre in the north played only a small part in events and the once great power of Islam was reduced to the restricted territories of the Emirate of Granada in the south.

By the early years of the sixteenth century, the Moors had been eliminated as an independent political entity and, of the Christian kingdoms, only Portugal and the united crowns of Aragon and Castile remained. Yet the veneer over the cracks was thin and the divisions of the new Spain were too deep ever to be lost sight of. Thus, even today the Catalan and Castilian languages are quite distinct and the hostility between Barcelona and Madrid still lingers.

The kingdom of Aragon was made up of Aragon proper, land-locked, rural and aristocratic in its constitution, the southern seaboard territory of Valencia (reconquered from the Moors during the thirteenth century), and the dynamic, commercially orientated county of Barcelona, whose great capital city was one of the dominant forces in Mediterranean trade. In many ways fourteenth-century Aragon is the most interesting of all European states, since here two of the most powerful forces of late medieval Europe were finely balanced: the drive to increasing centralization by the developing monarchies and the fiercely independent and centrifugal force of the towns. During the days of Aragon's power these two forces complemented each other to produce a commercial empire with territories throughout the Mediterranean and a constitution in mainland Aragon which afforded to merchants and nobles alike a degree of status in their relationship with the monarchy which was enjoyed in no other state.

The House of Aragon, like that of Castile, was descended from a son of the eleventh-century King of Navarre, Sancho III, the Great. Under him the Navarre had for a brief time been the greatest power in Christian Spain, but in his will he divided his empire between his sons and the two young kingdoms of Castile and Aragon soon came to dominate the peninsula through their reconquest from the Moors.

The first important accession to the crown of Aragon took place in the mid-twelfth century, when the premier count of Catalonia, Count Berengar of Barcelona, married into the royal house to become King of Aragon. Catalonia joined the kingdom as a senior partner, jealously preserving its own laws and customs, and for the next two and a half centuries the House of Aragon was descended in the male line from the counts of Barcelona.

In the thirteenth century, James I, the Conqueror (died 1276), drove the Moors out of Valencia and the Balearic Islands. He was also able to bring under control a nobility which had taken advantage of his minority and to reach an understanding with the French king by which each monarch surrendered the longstanding claims to each other's territories.

New grounds for conflict with the French royal house were soon discovered in the reign of James's successor. James I had divided his kingdom between his sons, leaving the little kingdom of Majorca to a junior line which maintained its independence up to 1344. Aragon went to his eldest son, Peter III, who happily seized the opportunity offered by the revolt of the Sicilian subjects of Charles of Anjou, uncle of the French king, of extending Aragonese rule still further into the Mediterranean. Charles's harsh rule provoked his Sicilian subjects to rebellion, and his overweaning ambition united many powerful enemies against him, chief among them the Byzantine emperor and the King of Aragon. The revolt of the Sicilian Vespers in 1282 drove Charles from the island and put Peter of Aragon on the Sicilian throne.

Three aspects of Peter's conquest should be noted. First, the success of the king's imperialism chimed well with the commercial aims of Barcelona in the Mediterranean. Second, diplomatic activity on the international scale was to become a distinguishing feature of Aragonese affairs and was to yield some of the richest archives of medieval Europe. Third, the naval victories of Admiral Roger of Loria presaged the future power of the Catalan navy.

As a direct consequence of the Sicilian adventure, the House of Aragon extended its claims even to Greece. One of the most famous bands of mercenaries was the Catalan Gran Company, which, after service in the Sicilian wars, was called in against the Turks by the emperor at Constantinople. The company conquered the duchy of Athens (1312) and held it in the name of Aragon for the next seventy years. The loss of the tenuous association with Athens was compensated for by the establishment of Aragonese claims in Sardinia during the reign of Alfonso IV (1327–36).

The far-flung territories of fourteenth-century Aragon are correctly called an empire, but the origins of this empire lay rather in the commercial drive of the cities, chief among them Barcelona, than in a planned policy of conquest by the kings. The organization of the empire reflected the separatist elements in the mainland kingdom and rested on the simple but apt and original concept of the viceroy, who exercised the full powers of the king in his absence. Originally held by close members of the royal family, the position later came to be held by officers of the crown, and was to be adapted by the great Spanish empire of the sixteenth century.

The constitutional arrangements of mainland Aragon, like those of most medieval states, were the subject of many bitter conflicts between the kings and their subjects, both noble and middle class. But the famous Aragonese oath of allegiance provides the setting of constitutional theory for these struggles:

> We who are as good as you, swear to you who are no better than we, to accept you as our sovereign king and lord, provided you observe all our liberties and laws, but if not, not.

The idea of contract between ruler and ruled was central in aristocratic Aragon as well as in urban-dominated Barcelona, and in the late thirteenth century the principle was established that the laws of the state were only valid with the consent of both king and *cortes*.

The *cortes* of medieval Aragon was one of the most important constitutional bodies of the Middle Ages and, from the first, enjoyed an independence of the monarch far greater than anything known elsewhere. Each of the three constituent lands of the kingdom had its own *cortes*, an assembly which represented the estates of the clergy, the nobility and the towns, each jealously defending their liberties. It was convened every three years, irrespective of the monarch. From the middle of the fourteenth century the *cortes* of Catalonia achieved a still more important place in the affairs of the kingdom when it established a standing committee, the *generalitat*, designed at first to ensure that the money grants made by the assembly were properly spent but soon accumulating judicial and military functions.

Aragon and Valencia developed similar institutions and in Aragon there was yet another check on the monarchic principle in the office of the *justicia*, elected by the lesser nobility (caballeros) to protect their interests against the encroachments of royal officials and answerable to the *cortes*. The last great element in the Aragonese constitution was the city of Barcelona, as powerful a commercial force as its Italian rivals but, unlike them, not a republic but a 'royal town'. However, through its *Consolat de Mar*, a corporation recognized by the monarchy, it exercised an independent authority

Left, the Alcàzar castle in central Spain, built by the Moors in the Middle Ages and later taken over by the Knights of St Johns.

over matters of commerce and administration.

This array of powerful and determined constitutional bodies among his subjects was the King of Aragon's main problem, but he was also faced with the usual tribulations of the medieval monarch in the form of aristocratic factions. The most serious of these in the fourteenth century was the opposition to Peter IV (1336–87). At the opening of his reign he had to contend with the hostility of a party grouped round his father's second wife, Eleanor of Castile, and then was involved in a struggle to get his chosen heir accepted. He was eventually successful, but not before both sides had called in Castilian help and thus involved Aragon to some extent in the great Castilian civil wars of the period.

Castile

Castile was neither so commercially nor so constitutionally advanced as Aragon. Its society was essentially pastoral and aristocratic and its direction not outwards towards the possibilities of trade but inwards towards the continuing struggle of the reconquest against the Moors. Major advances were made in the reign of Ferdinand III (1217–52). He formally united the ancient kingdoms of Castile and Leon, led them to the capture of Cordoba and Seville and exacted homage from the remaining Muslim kingdom of Granada. However, whereas the King of Aragon was able to exercise comparatively effective royal control in the newly conquered territories of Valencia, Ferdinand was obliged to yield immense privileges and lands to Castilian nobles in Andalusia.

Ferdinand's son, Alfonso X, the Wise, continued his father's campaigns against Islam though at a slacker pace. His reign was marked chiefly by his enlightened patronage of Jewish and Arabic scholarship. It was also interesting in a quite different respect because of his candidature for the office of Holy Roman emperor during the great interregnum. Two and a half centuries later a Spanish king was to win this somewhat tarnished and by that time anachronistic honour when Charles V of Habsburg became Holy Roman emperor. Alfonso's reign ended with his deposition in 1282 and his succession by his son Sancho IV.

The years of anarchy which followed provided ample opportunity for foreign intervention, and the pattern was repeated on a large scale seventy years later during the fateful reign of Peter I, the Cruel. The civil wars between Peter and his half brother, Henry of Trastámara, the illegitimate son of their father Alfonso XI (1312–50), have been described as an overspill of the central conflict in fourteenth-century Europe, the Hundred Years War between France and England.

Peter's troubles began when he repudiated his French wife, Blanche, and thereby provoked the enmity of the French king, Charles V, who sent a force to Castile, in the cause of Trastámara, under the great commander Bertrand du Guesclin. Not unnaturally, Peter found support from England in the shape of an army commanded by Edward, the Black Prince, which won for him the great but unproductive victory of Najera in 1367. The Castilian cause continued to enjoy English support from Peter's brother-in-law, John of Gaunt. But whereas his chivalrous brother Edward lacked the diplomatic finesse to exploit his victory, John, however, lacked the necessary military qualities to establish for himself a position strong enough for effective diplomatic manoeuvre.

With Peter's final overthrow in 1369 the dynasty of Trastámara was firmly established on the throne of Castile. But for the two non-Spanish powers there was more at stake than a game of dynastic politics in a foreign land. There was also the important factor of the Castilian fleet of galleys. This impressive fighting force, which derived much of its navigational skill from the Arabs and its essential justification from the growing Castilian wool trade with the ports of northern Europe, was turned against England after the defeat of Peter I, the Cruel, their candidate in the civil wars. The results were important, affecting English communications with its possessions in the south of France and laying the south coast of England open to the depredations of Castilian raiders.

If fourteenth-century Castile lacked the commercial power and international reach of Aragon, it was nevertheless laying the foundations of an economy which was to outstrip by far that of its eastern neighbour. Its prosperity was based on the wool trade. The high plateau lands of Castile offered poor agricultural soil, but from the thirteenth century their potentialities as pasturage were increasingly exploited. The movement of the flocks from winter pasture in the south to summer pasture in the north established a pattern of drover's routes and guilds, which introduced the *Mesta,* a new and increasingly powerful organ, into the social and economic life of the country. The vitality of the medieval Spanish wool industry was assured by the introduction of the hardy and heavy-fleeced Merino strain from north Africa, with the result that, as the fourteenth century progressed, Spanish wool was able to compete in the markets of Italy and Flanders even with the celebrated English product.

As in England, wool provided a new dynamic in social, economic and political development. The growing contacts provided by trade widened the horizons of Castile. Similarly, as in England the new source of revenue was quickly tapped by the monarchy. In this respect the already existing organization of the *Mesta* was ideally suited to the role of monopolistic agent to the monarch in his dealings with the industry. Dominated by a handful of noble producers owning enormous flocks of as many as 40,000 head, it regulated the movements of the shepherds, defended and extended their privileges and was in addition closely involved in the international and highly profitable fair at Medina del Campo.

The great aristocratic families made this new source of wealth their sphere of influence, and this pattern of aristocratic domination was characteristic of Castile. We have already seen how aristocratic factions threw the country into turmoil in the reign of Peter the Cruel. In the long reign of John II (1406–54), distinguished by the king's patronage of the arts and a court whose brilliance and pageantry emulated the splendour of the court of the dukes of Burgundy, the government was in the hands of the king's favourite, the constable Alvaro de Luna. He in his turn provoked the anger of the nobility by a tough policy intended to strengthen the power of the crown but was finally overthrown the year before the king's death by a faction centred on Queen Isabella, King John's second wife. The situation in Castile during the reign (1454–74) of Henry IV, the Impotent, was similar to that experienced in Portugal during the long reign of Alfonso V: the power of the nobility was temporarily out of control and the condition looked likely to become permanent.

Compromise and conflict

In Aragon the century had opened with a potentially disastrous situation, when the death of the last of the house of Barcelona in 1410 had left six contenders disputing the succession. The civil war which ensued was, however, quickly brought to an end. The issue was settled in a remarkable manner when, in June 1412, delegates from Aragon, Valencia and Barcelona agreed upon the so-called Compromise of Caspe. This settled the kingdom on Ferdinand I, a Castilian who was also a nephew of the late Martin of Aragon. The decision was not questioned, even by Barcelona which would have much preferred a Catalan claimant.

In the reign of Ferdinand's son, Alfonso V, Aragon's Mediterranean empire gained a new territory when, in 1443 he successfully made good his claim to the throne of Naples. From that time onwards Alfonso stayed in his Italian kingdom, where his court became one of the most brilliant in Renaissance Italy and a natural channel for conveying the cultural and social ideas of the Renaissance into Spain. Alfonso died in 1458 without legitimate issue, leaving Naples to his bastard son Ferrante and Aragon to his brother John.

John II of Aragon began his reign auspiciously, bringing the little kingdom of Navarre to the crown as a result of his marriage to its heiress Blanche. On her death in 1442 he had remarried and, possibly under the influence of his second wife, became convinced of the treasonable intentions of his son, Charles of Viana, the acting ruler of Navarre. As the eldest son of the king of Aragon, Charles held the traditional office of lieutenant-general of Barcelona. When, therefore, acting on his suspicions, John had his son arrested, the Catalans, never fully reconciled to the Castilian dynasty, rose in revolt and there followed ten years of civil strife confused by the rivalries of the city factions of Barcelona. For a time John gained French support by the cession of Roussillon and Cerdagne to Louis XI but, even when in 1472 the Catalans finally submitted, John had to agree to respect the *fueros* or traditional privileges of the county.

In 1469, Ferdinand, John of Aragon's heir by his second wife, had been married to Isabella, sister of Henry IV of Castile. Ferdinand's father was fighting to retain his crown and Isabella's claims on Castile were soon in jeopardy. A year after her marriage, her brother reinstated his daughter, Joanna, nicknamed *La Beltraneja* by a rival faction, who claimed that she was in fact the daughter of the court favourite, Beltran de la Cueva.

After the death of Henry IV in 1474, Isabella and her husband successfully defeated the Portuguese army of Alfonso V who had come to claim the hand of Joanna and with it the Castilian crown. In 1479 Ferdinand succeeded to the throne of his father and, from the welter of Iberian dynastic politics, the laws of chance had extracted a winning combination, which, by uniting the crowns of Castile and Aragon, paved the way for the formation over the centuries to come of the modern state of Spain.

The Catholic Kings

There was indeed nothing inevitable about the succession of either Ferdinand or Isabella. He was, after all, the second son of the king's brother, while she was sister of a king with a recognized heir, whom only his own weakness prevented from succeeding to the throne. Nor was there anything inevitable about the union of the two crowns of Aragon and Castile. Relations had been equally close between Castile and Portugal and Alfonso V's invasion of Castile was in the tradition of Iberian politics. Without the help of Ferdinand of Aragon and his military advisers, Isabella might well have been defeated.

Isabella I of Castile (1474–1504) and Ferdinand II of Aragon (1479–1516) joined their countries in what was in effect a federation—sovereign in their own states, they were merely consort in that of their partner. But from the beginning Castile was the dominant partner. Ferdinand was to live in his wife's country and was not to leave without her permission. Moreover, only Castilians were to be appointed to the council of Castile and Ferdinand was not to levy war without the consent and advice of Isabella.

Clearly Isabella's aristocratic supporters were determined to prevent the subjection of their country to the will of a foreigner and, if Ferdinand had been of different temperament, these provisions would not have been worth the paper they were written on. However, in the event, the almost intuitive human and political relationship which husband and wife developed ensured the harmonious and astonishingly effective working of the delicate and somewhat idealistic arrangements.

After the heroic conquests of the thirteenth century, the much reduced kingdom of Granada in the south was the only remaining Muslim state in Spain. Spurred perhaps by the papal call to the crusade following the fall of Constantinople in 1453,

but more probably anxious to exploit the revenues raised on that pretext, Henry IV had led token expeditions against the Moors and had even succeeded in recovering Gibraltar.

Ferdinand and Isabella took the war more seriously. The campaign, which opened in 1482, lasted ten years, during which time the Castilian army took the first steps towards its sixteenth-century greatness and Ferdinand exercised his talents as a diplomat to exploit the conflict between the rival rulers of Granada, El Zaque and his nephew Boabdil. Resistance came to an end with the fall of Granada in January 1492. The terms of the surrender were generous. The Moors retained the right to bear arms, their property, their laws and even their religion. A year later Boabdil and 6,000 of his followers were persuaded to emigrate to North Africa.

The kingdom of Castile had won a new province and the powers of Islam had at last been driven out of Spain. Yet the crown had gained little real advantage. The conquest had still further enriched the already powerful nobility, and during the tolerant reign of Hernando de Talavera, the first Archbishop of Granada, few Muslims were converted to the Christian faith.

A more repressive policy was introduced by the new Archbishop of Toledo, Francisco Jimenez de Cisneros. In 1502 the liberty of religion allowed by the capitulation ten years previously was withdrawn and all adult Moors who refused baptism were expelled. A large number nominally surrendered their religion for their motherland and a new class was added to the diverse population of Spain, the *Moriscos*. Yet, despite statutes passed by both Ferdinand and his successor, Charles, prohibiting Moorish dress and customs, the *Morisco* community of Granada proved too valuable to the trade and commerce of Spain and was able to buy exemption from religious legislation until the reign of Philip II.

Compared with the Jews in the rest of Europe, those in Spain had enjoyed both toleration and respect. The example of the treatment accorded to Jews in the neighbouring Islamic states may have shown the Christian rulers the way to moderation. But, as the tide of Muslim power receded, so the Jewish community suffered increasing restrictions, until, in the last decade of the fourteenth century and the first years of the fifteenth, a wave of pogroms swept Aragon and Castile. The mass baptisms of these years swelled the class of *conversos* (converted Jews), although, in many cases, the new Christians remained secretly loyal to their true faith.

In 1480 Ferdinand won permission from Rome to set up the Castilian Inquisition, under royal control, to investigate the crypto-Jewish *conversos*. Seven years later he imposed this institution on Aragon and it became increasingly identified as an agency of the centralizing royal power, although its importance in establishing a common faith throughout the peninsula continued. The temptations for a *converso* to relapse must have been very strong in the presence of the Jewish community.

Within months of the victory over Granada, the Catholic Kings (the title was conferred by the pope in 1494) outlawed Judaism. Many Jews left rather than accept baptism, and although the authorities made strenuous efforts to prevent Jewish doctors from taking their talents elsewhere they could not stop a flood of skilled artisans and experienced businessmen from emigrating. These valuable citizens were in due course replaced, but largely by Flemish, German and Italian immigrants who had to be heavily bribed with remitted taxation and then, as like as not, left the country.

The Inquisition was not only a powerful organ of state, it was also a symbol of the control which Ferdinand and his successors came to wield over the Church in Spain. Its wealth and privileges were immense and, like those of the nobility, had to be limited. Even before the final conquest of Granada Ferdinand, in return for help against the pope's enemies in Italy, had gained the right to make appointments to all the major benefices in the new province. His successor extended this to all the bishoprics in Spain. Even more remarkable was a series of three papal bulls which made the Spanish crown absolute master of the Church in its American territories. In addition, Ferdinand also won considerable control over Church revenues.

Besides these benefits to the crown the reign of the Catholic Kings also witnessed a marked reform in the body of the Church itself. Under the auspices of Cardinal Cisneros discipline in the monasteries was drastically tightened up—400 Andalusian friars were so shocked at the thought of losing their concubines that they deserted to Islam. Moreover, by his foundation of the University of Alcalà and patronage of the

Above, a Jewish family in fourteenth-century Spain at their Passover Feast. The Jews made a greater contribution to the culture of medieval Spain than anywhere else in western Europe. British Library, London.

Opposite, Ferdinand and Isabella, the architects of sixteenth-century Spain, expelled the Jews, encouraged exploration of the New World and established the Spanish Inquisition. The Convent, Madrigal de las Altas Torres, Avila.

Below, a coin of Ferdinand and Isabella, whose marriage in 1469 united the kingdoms of Castile and Aragon and whose policies ensured that this union became permanent. British Museum, London.

Complutensian Polyglot bible, the cardinal made notable contributions to the advance of scholarship.

By the end of the century Ferdinand and Isabella had also done much to curb the anarchy which had distracted the previous reigns. But although the final result of increased royal control was something new, the means employed were traditional. In Castile the town guilds of peace-keeping vigilantes, the *Santa Hermandad,* were revived to counteract the excesses of an irresponsible aristocracy and the *consejo real* was established as the central governing body in which the nobles could now participate only in the capacity of observers.

In Aragon Ferdinand aimed to pacify the continuing unrest in Catalonia by restoring the medieval constitution of the country, and he himself scrupulously observed the contractual relations it embodied. In both kingdoms the crown began to assume more direct control in local affairs, when the old office of *corregidor,* a municipal official formerly appointed by the commune to represent it in dealings with the kings or its local lord, was reinvigorated and appointed by the crown. As might be expected, no attempt was made to abolish the military orders, bastions of privilege and anti-monarchical by nature. Instead, the Catholic Kings won from the pope the right to be appointed to the grand masterships of the orders of Santiago, Calatrava and Alcantara. In 1523 Charles V secured a papal bull confirming the integration of all three under the crown.

By such means Ferdinand and Isabella were able to restore their troubled kingdoms to peace and order and exact grudging recognition of the crown's position. But nothing could undo the squandering of resources by previous kings. In an act of resumption in 1480 the great lords were required to return crown lands acquired since 1464, but nothing was done to check the growth of dynastic alliances.

It has been calculated that some twenty-six families owned more than half the land of Spain, and it was not only these great families which enjoyed the privileges of nobility. The hereditary status of *hidalguía,* which gave exemption from royal taxation, from imprisonment for debt and many other privileges, was enjoyed by thousands of men, both rich and poor. From the third decade of the sixteenth century the situation worsened, as the crown sought to raise short-term funds by the sale of patents of nobility. As elsewhere in Europe the lot of the peasant was hard, but his troubles were compounded as the limited supply of agricultural land was reduced still further by the encroachments of the ubiquitous shepherds of the *Mesta.* By a law of 1501 any tract of land which had once been used as pasturage was to be retained for that use in perpetuity. Thus the crown, in return for immediate financial support, undermined still further an already decaying agriculture.

'The greatest monarch in Christendom'

At the end of his reign Ferdinand was king in his own right of Aragon, Naples and Sicily and Navarre. He was regent of Castile for his grandson, Charles V of Habsburg, and was thereby lord of the Castilian territories in North Africa and the ever-growing empire in the New World of America, which had been discovered by the Genoese, Christopher Columbus, in 1492 under the aegis of Isabella and was rapidly being explored.

Through the intervention of Charles VIII and Louis XII of France, Naples had been lost to Aragon; and Ferdinand had set about the isolation of France, although he first recovered the lost Catalan territories of Rouisslon and Cerdagne by seeming to countenance Charles's Italian ambitions. His first great triumph was the formation of the Holy League of 1495, by which England, the Emperor Maximilian and the pope allied with Spain to counter French designs in Italy. From this period Ferdinand maintained representatives in Rome, Venice, Brussels and London and at the Austrian court. He thus became one of the first rulers outside Italy to employ a permanent ambassadorial service, which, however rudimentary, was one of the forerunners of modern diplomatic practice. When France nevertheless made war on Naples, Ferdinand took up the challenge and, thanks to the brilliance of his general, Gonzolo de Cordoba, and the seasoned Spanish infantry, veterans of the campaigns in Granada, Aragon emerged victorious. The Italian wars proved another important milestone in the development of the Spanish army, which was to dominate the battlefields of the world in the sixteenth century. Cordoba, defeated at first by the cumbersome but murderous Swiss infantry, evolved a phalanx formation, which combined fire-power and cut-and-thrust-weapons in a single fighting unit. With only slight modifications this formation proved itself both more deadly and much more manoeuvrable than anything before it.

By strength and cunning Ferdinand had restored his house to the throne of Naples. However, his position in Castile, where for thirty years he had held the title of king and had sat at the centre of power, was brusquely terminated by his wife's will. She left her kingdom not to her husband and co-ruler but to their weak-witted daughter, Joanna, wife of Philip the Fair of Habsburg.

The separateness of the kingdoms could hardly be more graphically stated. Not only did the various territories retain their quite mutually-conflicting constitutions but they lacked even a common currency. Isabella had jealously excluded Catalan merchants from the riches of the New World on the grounds that it had been discovered at the cost of Castile. In the same vein, although rather less effectively, Ferdinand had annexed Navarre not to the joint kingdom but to Aragon alone.

In 1504, therefore, when Isabella died, Ferdinand found his position as regent for his daughter challenged by her husband Philip, who enjoyed the almost unanimous support of the Castilian nobility, determined to save themselves from Aragonese domination. In June 1506 Philip landed in Castile and was acclaimed king in his wife's right. Ferdinand was obliged to retire to Aragon. But Philip died the following September and eventually, in answer to the appeals of the ageing Cardinal Cisneros, acting as regent, Ferdinand returned to take up the regency, appointing an administration of Aragonese officials.

The mounting discontent in Castile was ended only on Ferdinand's own death in 1516. When the young Charles arrived in Spain the following year his demand to be crowned king and his refusal to act as regent for his mother were both accepted.

The emergence of Portugal

The history of medieval Portugal begins under the walls of Toledo. When in 1085 Alfonso VI of Leon and Castile captured this great centre of Muslim power and civilizations, he regarded his leading captains generously. Among them was the French count, Henry of Burgundy, his king's son-in-law, who received a fief to the south of the river Minho in the district of Oporto. By the middle of the next century, Henry's son and successor, Afonso Henriques, had gained effective independence for his country, which now extended from the Minho to the Tagus in the south. To strengthen his position with respect to strife-ridden Leon and Castile, Afonso, who had proclaimed himself king in 1139, put himself under papal protection in return for an annual tribute. Nevertheless, the pope did not acknowledge his claim to kingship until some forty years later.

In 1147 Afonso had pressed into his service a body of English crusaders destined for the Holy Land to help him to take the great town of Lisbon from the Moors. Afonso's status was further confirmed by the marriage of one of his daughters to Ferdinand II of Leon and when his son Sancho succeeded him the kingdom of Portugal was established. To assist him in the task of reconquest to the south, King Sancho I (1185–1211) called in the military orders of the Templars, Santiago and Calátrava whose power was later to be a considerable embarrassment to the Portugese crown.

Sancho himself led a successful expedition against the Sultan of Morocco's lands in the Algarve. This was the first naval expedition in Portuguese history, but its success was short-lived. Sancho devoted himself to the administration of the reconquered territories and to combating the threatening power of the Church. His son, Afonso II (1211–23), continued the policy, instituting searching enquiries into ecclesiastical privilege. This provoked such determined opposition that his successor, Sancho II (1223–46), was overthrown by a faction of nobles encouraged by the Church in Portugal and the pope and headed by Sancho's brother, Afonso, who became king as Afonso III in 1248.

It was not long before he, too, was conducting investigations into the tangle of property rights which had resulted from the steady process of reconquest and which favoured the power of the Church and nobles at the expense of the crown. Inevitably he, too, came into conflict with the Church.

The Portuguese reconquest was completed in the first years of his reign with the final conquest of Algarve. This brought troubles in its wake from his Christian neighbour Afonso X, the Wise, of Castile, who had been receiving tribute from the Moorish population. The conflict was resolved at the Treaty of Badajoz in 1267, which fixed the boundary between the two countries on the line which it has held ever since.

Afonso married the illegitimate daughter of Afonso of Castile and his reign, like that of his neighbour, was a period of cultural advance, during which the elements of Provençal civilization were introduced into the country. Equally important were measures taken towards the emancipation of the serfs, the encouragement of trade and the introduction of representation of the towns in the *cortes*.

The progress begun by his father was maintained by Dinis (1279–1325), called 'the Farmer'. Some of his most important work was the encouragement he gave to agriculture, including special inducements to nobles who wished to develop their lands.

He continued to promote the industry and trade of the country, signing a commercial treaty with Edward I of England in 1294. In politics his major effort was directed against the military orders. He brought the Spanish order of Santiago within his territories under Portuguese control and, like many other European sovereigns, took

Above, Ferdinand and Isabella riding into Granada in triumph. The city, in the extreme south of Spain, was the last outpost of Moorish control in that country and was not taken by the Christians until 1492. The Royal Chapel, Granada.

Opposite, John of Gaunt at a banquet given by the King of Portugal. John, son of Edward III of England, travelled to Portugal in 1386 to conclude a treaty with that country which has lasted until the present day. He also helped King John I on his campaigns in Castile. British Library, London.

advantage of the French king's unprincipled destruction of the Order of the Temple by incorporating its lands in the new Portuguese Order of Jesus.

These solid achievements in government were paralleled by a brilliant advance in literature and learning. The king was himself a poet, writing a number of magnificent love lyrics which, however real their debt to Provençal culture, mark the arrival of a new national idiom in the literature of Europe. He made an equally great contribution to the growth of scholarship in his country by the foundation of the university of Lisbon (later moved to Coimbra).

The glorious reign of Dinis, like that of his grandfather, ended in civil war, and he was succeeded by his rebellious son Afonso IV (1325–57). Afonso in his turn was faced with the insurrection of his heir, Peter, and the episode became one of the most famous in Portuguese history and literature. Peter had married Constanza of Castile but fell desperately in love with one of her ladies in waiting, the beautiful Ines de Castro. After the death of his wife in 1345, Peter and Ines retired to a palace at Coimbra where she bore the young prince four children. Their idyll lasted for ten years, but finally the king was persuaded to agree to the death of Ines by courtiers who feared the growing power of her relations.

It is told how the ageing Afonso himself went up to Coimbra but was won over by the pitiful pleas of his grandchildren. His courtiers nevertheless carried out the assassination and Peter, distraught with grief and fury, rose in rebellion. The rising was quelled and the prince was made to reconcile himself with the murderers. Immediately after his accession, however, he succeeded in tracking down two of his enemies and had them killed by having their hearts drawn out of their bodies.

Such brutality was exceptional even in the fourteenth century. During his ten years' reign (1357–67) Peter's addiction to the dispensation of justice and his frequent practice of administrating the penalties himself struck his contemporaries as something more than a laudable concern for the just processes of law. They dubbed him variously: Peter the Justicer, Peter the Severe, and Peter the Cruel.

It is not suprising that the history of Portugal was often bound up with that of its powerful neighbour Castile. However, with the marriage in the next reign of Peter's grand-daughter Beatrice to the Castilian heir this involvement threatened to decline into subservience. Consequently, when Ferdinand I of Portugal died in 1383 and John I of Castile had himself proclaimed King of Portugal, there was a popular revolt in favour of John, grand master of the Knights of Avis (formerly the order of Calátrava) and bastard son of Peter I and Ines. The Castilian enjoyed the support of numerous Portuguese nobles and confidently advanced to claim his new kingdom.

However, in addition to the support which he had from the people at large and the commercial interests of the cities, John had a powerful ally in the English duke, John of Gaunt, still pursuing his claims to Castile. When the armies met at the field of Aljubarrota, the company of English archers in the small Portuguese army made a major contribution to the crushing victory won by John of Avis and his able counsellor, Nun' Alvares Pereira. John's election by the *cortes* was confirmed and his friendship with John of Gaunt was cemented by his marriage to Gaunt's daughter, Philipa of Lancaster. A treaty was signed with England which established the longest-lived alliance in history, and a new, heroic age of Portuguese history, presided over by the House of Avis, began.

Industry, notably textiles trade, particularly with England, and the standing of Lisbon as an international entrepot of commerce, all of which had been given a strong impetus by the enlightened policies of Dinis, now enjoyed again the full benefits of royal encouragement. But the immense dynamic potential of the proudly independent Atlantic state was now directed by the House of Avis to an outward-looking policy of exploration which made the fifteenth century the golden age of Portugal.

The capture of Ceuta on the north African coast from the Moors in 1415 was the symbol of what was to come, and the school of navigation established by John's famous son, Prince Henry the Navigator, at Sagres in southern Portugal, was the operations room from which the great enterprise was directed.

John was succeeded by his son Edward (1433–38) who codified the laws and was an enthusiastic patron of the work of his brother, Henry the Navigator. During the minority of his son, Afonso V (1438–81), the country was again torn by civil war, which lasted intermittently until the decisive Battle of Alfarrobeira in 1499, when the king's uncle, the competent second son of John I, was defeated and killed by the forces of Afonso, Duke of Braganza, the illegitimate son of John of Avis before his marriage to Philippa of Lancaster.

Unlike his half-brother, Afonso could claim to be of pure Portuguese descent, but his power derived from his influence with the king, whose reign was distracted by attempts on the throne of Castile and by the dramatic, although not very productive, capture of Tangier in 1471. After the death of Afonso, called 'the African', his son, John II, inherited a kingdom humiliated by its defeat at the hands of Ferdinand of Aragon and Castile two years before and dominated by the arrogant and powerful aristocratic houses. His first act was to administer a new and more stringent form of the oath of homage, and he followed up this initial attack on the nobility with an investigation into the titles by which they held their vast estates. In the searches which followed treasonable correspondence between Braganza and the King of Aragon-Castile came to light and the king seized this opportunity for the execution of the turbulent aristocrat.

John combined the talents of a statesman with the inclinations of a patron. Under his auspices Portugal was open to the inspiration of the new forces in art generated by the Italian Renaissance. Like his predecessors he actively encouraged the endeavours of the Portuguese explorers. Although he refused to help Columbus, whose plan to reach India by a western sea route to India he thought would prove far longer than the

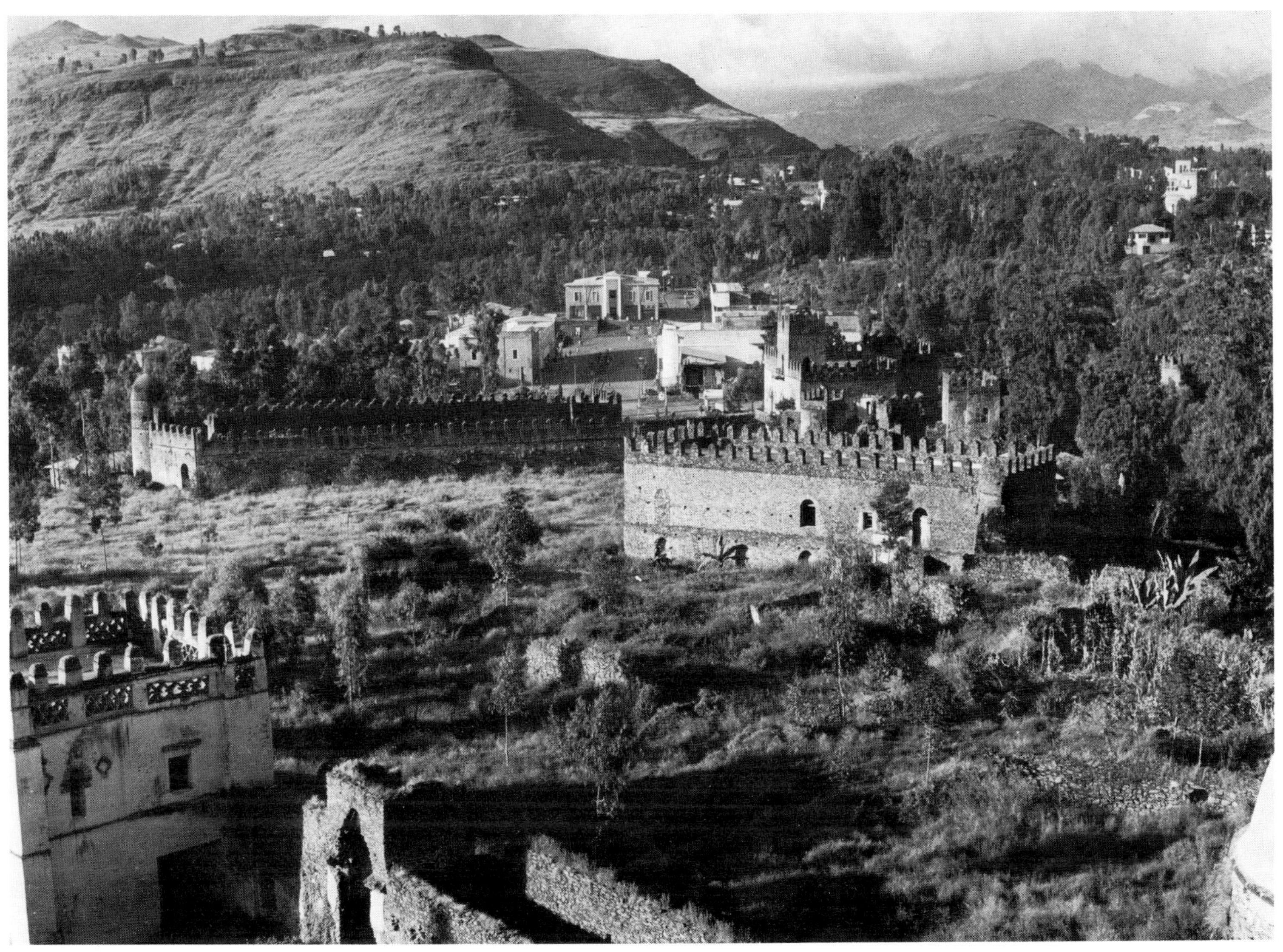

eastern routes being opened up by his own countrymen, he nevertheless negotiated a sizeable stake for Portugal in the New World at the Treaty of Tordesillas in 1494. Under his rule the impetus of Portuguese expansion was fully maintained, while at home the House of Avis, secured for the time against the ambitions of a powerful nobility, was the undisputed ruler of a country seemingly on the threshold of a new golden age.

Above, the ruins of Gondar in Ethiopia, which the Portuguese visited in the fifteenth century in search of Prester John.

Opposite top left, the victory of John I of Portugal over the Castilian rebels led by John of Aviz at Aljubarrota in 1385. This victory ensured that Portugal retained its independence from Castile.

Opposite top right, English painting of the late fifteenth century depicting the marriage of King John I of Portugal with Philippa of Lancaster, the daughter of John of Gaunt, in 1386. British Library, London.

Opposite bottom, Henry the Navigator (1394–1460), Duke of Viseu, who founded a centre for exploration in 1416 and promoted voyages that reached as far as Sierra Leone. Lisbon Art Gallery.

SPAIN, PORTUGAL AND ITALY IN THE FOURTEENTH AND FIFTEENTH CENTURIES

Date	Spain and Portugal	Venice and Florence	Other Italian cities
	Alfonso X, king of Castile (died 1284)	Conflict between Genoa and Venice	
1300	Ferdinand IV, king of Castile and Leon (1295–1312) Alfonso XI, king of Castile and Leon (1312–50) Peter IV, king of Aragon (1336–87)	The Guelfs crush the Ghibellines—exile of Dante (1307) Florence at war with Pisa and Lucca War between Venice and Bologna	The Visconti in Milan The Black Death ravages Italy The Scaligeri in Verona
1350	Peter I, 'the Cruel', king of Portugal (1357–67) Battle of Najera (1367) Henry II, king of Castile and Leon (1369–79) Battle of Aliubarrota (1385) Martin I, king of Aragon (1395–1410)	Plot led by Marino Faliero in Venice (1355) Florence forms a league against the pope Revolt of the Ciompi	The Este family in Ferrara Verona Padua, Siena and Perugia under the control of Milan
1400	Compromise of Caspe John II, king of Castile and Leon (1406–54) Alvaro de Luna	Verona annexed by Venice Conflict between Venice and Milan (1426–54) Cosimo de'Medici	Genoa in rebellion: restoration of the republic Filippo Maria Visconti seizes Bologna
1450	John II, king of Aragon and Sicily (1458–79) *La Beltraneia* (1468) Marriage of Isabella of Castile and Ferdinand of Aragon (1469) The Inquisition—Torquemada Capture of Granada (1492) Discovery of America (1492)	Peace of Lodi between Venice and Milan (1454) Lorenzo the Magnificent Pazzi conspiracy Death of Lorenzo (1492)	Giovanni Bentivoglio in Bologna The Sforzas assume power in Milan Francesco Sforza Ludovico the Moor
1500			

Chapter 16

Northern and Eastern Europe

For a thousand years before the emergence of the recognizable features of unitary states in the tenth century, the Scandinavian peoples had been spreading out across Europe and fertilizing it with new blood. The last great wave of emigrants, the Vikings, made a lasting mark on the kingdoms which had arisen from the impact of their ancestors, the Goths, on the Roman world.

The Norsemen from Denmark and Norway settled in great numbers in the east of England and set up kingdoms in Ireland and the Isle of Man. They established the duchy of Normandy in northern France, which the French king was obliged to recognize, and from here within a century was launched the most sensational and enduring achievement of the Norsemen, the conquest of the kingdom of England. In the south of Europe the Norman kingdoms of Sicily and southern Italy established themselves at the expense of the Byzantine and Islamic empires. In the north Varangian adventurers from Sweden founded the states of the Russian empire, which was to claim the inheritance of Byzantium itself some six centuries later.

About the tenth century the homeland kingdoms began to achieve some stability. The problems facing any central government trying to establish itself in a region after such a history are obvious, but, by the eleventh century, the kingdom of Denmark at least could claim parity with any of the states of western Europe. For a brief period under King Canute it subjugated the lands of Norway and the kingdom of England. After Canute the Danish empire broke up and for the remainder of the eleventh century the rulers of Denmark were fighting off the attacks of the pagan Wends, a Slav people settled between the Oder and Elbe rivers, and attempting to consolidate their power with help from the recently established Christian Church.

Anarchy prevailed with little interruption until the reign of Waldemar I (1157–82). The kingdom of Waldemar was considerably bigger than modern continental Denmark, comprising the southern provinces of modern Sweden—Skane and Blecking—and important possessions on the Baltic coast of Germany. At first Waldemar did homage to the German emperor Frederick I but, by the end of his reign, he was strong enough to conquer the Island of Rügen, to assert Denmark's dominion in its Baltic possessions and to renounce the act of vassalage. Waldemar also did much to formalize and strengthen the position of the monarchy in Denmark itself, relying heavily on the assistance and advice of Denmark's first great churchman, Bishop Absalon.

By this time the country had been Christian for about 150 years and the Danish Church, having been first under the sway of English ecclesiastics and then those of Hamburg, won its independence in the twelfth century with the foundation of the archbishopric of Lund in 1104. Absalon was a political cleric like the great chancellors of the Holy Roman Empire and the kind of right-hand man whom Henry II of England thought he had gained by the appointment of Thomas Becket. In 1170, the very year of Becket's martyrdom, Absalon greatly enhanced the prestige of the Danish monarchy by canonizing Waldemar's father and solemnly crowning his son as heir. Absalon proved himself as a military leader in the war against the Wends and by his fortification of Copenhagen, but he also furthered the cause of learning by his patronage of the chronicler Saxo Grammaticus and the introduction of canon law.

Danish expansion continued in the first years of the reign of Waldemar II, second son of Waldemar I. He won new territories, received the homage of the Norwegian king and in 1214, largely as a result of the troubled state of affairs in the Holy Roman Empire, won recognition of Danish suzerainty in its north German territories from Frederick II. For a short period Waldemar extended Danish rule over Estonia but an aristocratic rebellion forced him to surrender many of his gains and to make dangerous concessions to the nobles. Waldemar's codification of Danish laws was a valuable achievement, but the decline of royal authority increased so much that in 1282 King Eric V was forced to agree to a charter which entrenched the aristocracy firmly in the councils of the realm.

Internal weakness was compounded by the encroachments of foreign powers. Skane and Blecking were lost to Sweden for a period and, at the accession of its next great king, Waldemar IV, Denmark's fortunes were at a low ebb. Waldemar restored the internal authority of the monarchy, recovered the Swedish provinces and even enjoyed a brief triumph over the mighty Hanseatic League. He had allied with the other kingdoms and had cemented Dano-Norwegian relations by the very important marriage of his daughter, Margaret, to Haakon VI of Norway. But in 1370, opposed by the Hansa allied with Sweden, Denmark was forced to the humiliating settlement of Stralsund, which gave the league a virtual monopoly of Scandinavian trade.

On the death of Waldemar in 1375 and the accession of his daughter Margaret, a new period opened in the affairs of the Scandinavian kingdoms, which was confirmed by the Union of Kalmar in 1397. The importance of this great act of state is frequently minimized, but it determined the history of Norway as a vassal kingdom for the next 500 years. The whole of fifteenth-century Scandinavian history is dominated by the unrelenting struggle of the Swedes to throw off Danish supremacy.

Sweden

In the earliest times Sweden was inhabited in the north by Finno-Ugrian peoples, from whom the Lapplanders are descended, in the central lands by the Svear and in the south by the Gotar, the putative ancestors of the Goths. By the sixth century AD, the Svear were dominant and by the eighth century their descendants, the Rhos or Rus, known as the Varangians to Byzantine historians, had begun to penetrate the great plains of European Russia. They followed the river systems, above all the Dnieper, and by the mid-ninth century had established themselves in the districts of Novgorod and Kiev. Their advance brought them into contact with Orthodox Christianity from Constaninople, while the Frankish missionary St Ansgar brought Catholicism to the Swedish homeland at about the same time.

However, it was not for another three centuries that Christianity was fully established. The Swedish Church was first organized along conventional European lines in the reign of Eric IX (died 1160), who soon after his death was revered as a saint. Whatever his qualifications for the honour, he certainly capitalized on his religion and led a crusade to conquer the pagan Finns.

After his reign the authority of the monarchy declined again and the land was ruled in effect by the powerful nobles. The great thirteenth-century regent, Birger Jarl, attempted to extend Swedish power over Novgorod but suffered a decisive defeat in 1241 at the hands of Alexander Nevsky. During this period, too, Finnish pirates were a continuing menace and Stockholm first emerges into history as the main fortress in the coastal defence system.

The fourteenth century opened with a familiar picture of royal impotence. The king was exiled and his three-year-old nephew, Magnus VII of Norway, was chosen by the nobles as his successor. A long minority was ideal for their purposes and Magnus was not declared of age for another thirteen years, that is, in 1319. He had been brought up and educated in Sweden and his consequent unpopularity in Norway forced him to recognise his son Haakon VI as king there. Despite this and the continuing baronial turbulence, Magnus enjoyed a brief success when he took the southern provinces from Denmark and even felt strong enough to ally with Waldemar of Denmark against the Hansa.

However, the growth in royal power which would have followed a successful overthrow of the German merchants could not be contemplated by the nobles who deposed Magnus and Haakon of Norway and elected Albert of Mecklenburg as king. But the humiliation of Waldemar of Denmark was avenged on the Swedes at the Battle of Falköping in 1389 when his daughter Margaret, who had never relinquished her husband's claims on the crown, defeated and captured Albert. In 1397 at Kalmar she conducted the coronation of her heir, Eric of Pomerania, as king of the united kingdoms, having succeeded in forcing acceptance from the three diets.

Norway

As we have seen Margaret's position in Norway derived from her marriage to Haakon VI. The kings of Norway, like their Danish and Swedish cousins, were troubled with powerful nobility, but during the thirteenth century the monarchy had enjoyed a period of glory in the reign of Haakon IV (1204–63). He had come to power as the candidate of the so-called *Birkebeiner* party. Composed of members of the gentry and lesser nobility, the party had grown up in the civil turmoil of the previous century and had been welded into an effective military and political force by King Sverre in his successful bid for power. It would be misleading to describe the *Birkebeiner* as the party of the common people, but it was certainly opposed to the great magnates, both lay and ecclesiastical, and generally supported the monarch.

Haakon IV, elected king in 1217, had his position further strengthened by the imposing and novel ceremony of coronation in 1247. His prestige was again enhanced when he added Greenland and Iceland to Norway's overseas colonies, which, since the ninth century, had consisted of the Orkneys, Hebrides and Man. His reign was also distinguished by the brilliant achievements of Norse literature and its greatest figure, Snorri Sturlusson, the Icelander.

Haakon's successor, Magnus VI, brought to an end the wars with Scotland over Man and the Hebrides by ceding them to Alexander III of Scotland. He continued the cultural advance of his kingdom by codifying the laws. After him Norway lapsed into a century of royal ineffectiveness, which was followed by the long Danish hegemony, confirmed by the Union of Kalmar and did not end until the post-Napoleonic settlement in 1814.

The union had sought to allow each of the kingdoms to keep its old constitutions, proclaiming only the unitary kingship. But in fact such an arrangement was bound to profit the most powerful and populous country, Denmark. The Danes were able to maintain their position with respect to Norway and for a time it seemed as though their growing might would even be sufficient to subdue the Hansa. Margaret and, after her death, Eric sought to extend Danish rule over the neighbouring province of Schleswig and for a brief time even exercised supremacy over Lübeck. But the Hansa after a period of disunity once again regrouped and in 1435 compelled Eric to sue for peace and cede Schleswig.

Four years later Eric was deposed by his own nobles, who elected Christopher of Bavaria in his place. The new king was unable to restore his authority either within Denmark or over the increasingly independent Swedes and was in his turn deposed in 1448 in favour of yet another German prince, Christian of Oldenburg. The dynasty he founded was to rule Denmark for the next four hundred years, and, through his accession to the duchies of Schleswig and

Above, the death of Olaf II (ruled 1015–28), who introduced Christianity to Norway and unified the country. National Library, Iceland.

Top, a sixteenth-century map of Scandinavia by Klaus Magnus, expressing the ambitions of Sweden over her immediate neighbours.

Holstein, he brought Denmark important new territories. However, he was no more able than his predecessors to activate the feeble hold of Denmark over Sweden and in 1471 was crushingly defeated at the Battle of Brunkeberg by the Swedish noble leader, Sten Sture.

The struggle for Sweden continued into the reign of Christian's grandson, King Christian II. This talented ruler did much to reform Danish society but earned the bitter opposition of the still powerful aristocracy by his legislation in favour of the gentry and merchant classes and by his furtherance of the reformed religion of Luther. Despite his gifts, Christian was brutal and despotic and his reign ended in disaster. His attempt to assert Denmark's dominion in Sweden by force and the massacre of all the great leaders of Sweden at the notorious 'Stockholm bloodbath' of 1520 precipitated the final Swedish rebellion and the accession of Gustavus Vasa as king in 1523—in the same year that Christian was deposed in Denmark itself.

The rising of 1523 was the last in a series of Swedish rebellions which had begun with that of Engelbrecht Engelbrechtson in 1431. Engelbrecht was a member of the lesser nobility and his rising had a strongly social as well as nationalist flavour. He succeeded in throwing off Danish rule and, for a brief period, controlled Sweden. But the success of this movement, which was composed essentially of the peasants and gentry, was too dangerous for the great magnates to let go unchecked, and in 1436 Engelbrecht was assassinated by the orders of a noble, Karl Knutsson. The latter established himself as the ruler of the country and forced considerable concessions from the Danes including control of Finland.After Knutsson's death in 1470 his power was inherited by the great family of Sture. Sten Sture also played an active part in the cultural life of the country, being closely involved in the founding of the University of Uppsala. Between 1497 and 1501 Sture was forced by Danish pressure to relinquish his position as regent but after his return to power his family continued to rule the country until shortly before the accession of Gustavus Vasa.

The growth of Switzerland

Even before the death of the last Hohenstaufen emperor, Frederick II, in 1250, conditions in the Holy Roman Empire were unsettled. The collapse of the central authority had led to the founding of local *Landfrieden,* associations of towns formed for mutual protection against the depredations of brigands, or the petty nobility, or even the greater magnates struggling to increase their states. For twenty years after Frederick's death all semblance of imperial authority was lost as various rivals tried to make good their claims to be emperor. During this period (known as the Interregnum) any community enjoying the legal status of an imperial fief was in an enviable position at law. Since the only authority to which it was legally subject was quite powerless, it was in effect an independent state—if it could defend itself.

Liberty defended by legalism and strength is the heart of the Swiss ideal and that ideal can be said to have been born in the year 1231 when the community of free peasantry of Uri was formally incorporated as a fief of the empire. Nine years later the neighbouring valley of Schwyz, until that time belonging to the Habsburg family, won a similar status, although with a less clear title. Moreover, by a course of events still somewhat obscure, a third community at Unterwalden came to lay claim to the same privileges. In 1291 these three 'cantons', as they later called themselves, signed an alliance for mutual security and independence.

The signatories to what was for the time a fairly commonplace form of association had a number of very important advantages over many others like it. All the cantons had rural mountain populations, all were free (serfdom being unknown), all had territories adjacent to one another, and all lay on the shores of Lake Lucerne. Thus they were strategically placed on the international route which ran between Germany and Italy through the town of Lucerne, across the lake and thence to the St Gotthard pass. Finally all had come to see the House of Habsburg as their common enemy.

The family of Habsburg had been a dominant political factor in the area since the eleventh century. When in 1273 the great Count Rudolf was elected Holy Roman emperor, the three valley communities found that their much vaunted imperial allegiance put them completely in the hands of the most powerful of their neighbours. It seems that Rudolf was prepared to respect their liberties, but during his reign the three cantons were gradually being welded into a territorial lordship stretching from the St Gotthard to the Rhine. Rudolf died in July 1291 and the alliance already mentioned was signed the following month.

During the years which followed the valley communities were free of imperial interference, even during the ten-year reign of Albert of Habsburg. When he died the Luxembourger Henry VII succeeded him as emperor. Henry and his successor, Louis IV, gave tacit confirmation to the new grouping, appointing a single administrative officer or *Vogt* to the three cantons. But the house of Habsburg, after years of involvement with the problems of its Austrian territories, began to show fresh interest in its lapsed rights in southern Germany. Consequently, when in 1314 the election to the imperial throne produced two claimants, Louis of Bavaria and Frederick of Habsburg, the forest cantons sided with Louis.

In November 1315 Frederick's brother Leopold led an army against the Swiss, but the campaign ended in disaster when, at the Battle of Morgarten, the flower of the Austrian army was slaughtered. It seems from a contemporary account that the duke nearly led his army into a prepared ambush, but this could not lessen the shock of such a massacre of trained knights at the hands of peasants. It was an ominous echo of the Battle of Courtrai, twelve years earlier, in which Flemish commoners had scored a short-lived victory over the chivalry of France, and the Swiss infantryman was soon to become the most dreaded of continental fighting men.

A month after the battle the victorious Swiss signed the union which was to be the legal basis of their association for the next five centuries. Its most important new clause was the one which forbade any member to make alliances without prior consultation with the others, and the cantons pledged themselves to defend their independence.

William Tell

William Tell, like Robin Hood, is a legendary national hero, and yet there is nothing particularly unlikely about his story. After the death of Count Rudolf, it is said, his successors no longer respected the freedoms of the Swiss and the cantons were soon subjected to the extortions of Austrian officials. Still worse was to come after the Habsburg line died out (possibly the chronicler means 'after the Habsburg imperial line died out', i.e., on the death of Albert in 1308). Local petty nobles were installed as administrative officials and of these the worst was Gessler, the *Vogt* of Uri, who compelled the people to do homage to the symbol of his authority, a cap on a pole. Tell refused and saved his life by his skill as a marksman in shooting an apple from his son's head. While being taken by ship to prison, Tell won his freedom with a mighty leap to the shore and subsequently ambushed and killed Gessler. This was the signal to the Swiss to rise up and expel their oppressors.

However great their valour as soldiers, the independence of the Swiss was all too vulnerable. Nevertheless, after 1332, Lucerne, recognizing its common interest with the powerful guardians of the St Gotthard pass, joined the confederacy and made it seem really viable.

Lucerne's loose association with the three founders was typical of many of the subsequent compacts. It retained its own municipal law and even remained a Habsburg town, but it subscribed to the essential provisions of mutual defence and consultation before making alliances or war.

Some twenty years later the confederates were joined by the great cities of Zurich (1351) and Berne (1353), in both cases for reasons connected with their own internal power politics or foreign policies rather than with any intention of contributing to the common good. About the same time the forest communities of Glarus and Zug also attached themselves to the union. Together the eight *Alten Orten* ('old places') formed a potentially powerful confederation of urban and rural communities.

Although both Zurich and Berne reserved the right to opt out of the traditional Swiss feud with the Habsburgs, the family could not afford to ignore the growing and aggressive power of the confederation. When, in 1385, Lucerne encroached on Habsburg territory, taking among other places the town of Sempach, Leopold III, Count of Tyrol, led another Habsburg army against the Swiss. He ordered his troops to dismount and use their long lances as pikes, and the Battle of Sempach in 1386 was a hard fought one. But the outcome was nevertheless a decisive Swiss victory. Two years later, with the defeat of Leopold's brother at Näfels by the people of the valley of Glarus, Habsburg pretensions to authority in the area came to an end.

In 1415, taking advantage of Frederick of Habsburg's disfavour with the Holy Roman emperor, Sigismund, the Swiss went over to the attack and conquered the province of Aargau. This acquisition was valuable from a strategic point of view but was to gain still greater significance in the constitutional history of the confederation, which still had no council, no treasury, no seal and no executive. Since Aargau was a joint conquest it became a jointly administered territory. Indeed, a growing sense of corporate identity began to make itself felt at the end of the fourteenth century. With the signing of the Priest's Charter of 1370 the members agreed to disallow privilege of clergy throughout their territories. By the important Compact of Sempach of 1393 the members agreed to declare war only after consultation with their partners and also agreed on the rules of war and plunder which their troops should observe in the field.

It is clear, indeed, that the cantons must have had strong bonds of interest to keep them together through the intercantonal wars which took place between 1436 and 1446. In the course of these wars Zurich, bitterly jealous of the growing might of Berne in the west, was nevertheless forced to surrender its territorial ambitions in the east and to abandon its alliance with Frederick of Habsburg. It was during this dispute that the band of troops which Charles VII of France lent to Frederick took part. But, after a brush with the Swiss, their commander withdrew them from the fight and the Dauphin Louis signed a truce with the Swiss Confederation on France's behalf.

Some years later the Dauphin, now Louis XI of France, was able to use the terrible might of a Swiss army to destroy Charles the Bold, Duke of Burgundy. The speed of Charles's advance from 1469 onwards in the territories of Alsace, adjacent to the confederation, worried the Swiss, but after two centuries of fending off the power of dangerous aristocrats they took the matter in their stride. In due course they eliminated the Burgundian army which Charles brought against them at Morat in 1476. They finally destroyed Burgundian power at the Battle of Nancy in 1477, at which Charles met his death.

No sooner had they settled this external enemy than the confederates were involved in serious internal conflict over the admission of Fribourg and Solothurn, allies of Berne. However, a compromise was reached and in 1481, at the Compact of Stans, the confederates made further agreements on the restraint of rebellion and the raising of armed forces.

In the last years of the century the Swiss fought off an attack by the Holy Roman emperor, Maximilian I. In the first years of the sixteenth century, with the admission of Basle, Schaffhausen and Appzell, the number of cantons was complete until the changes following the Napoleonic settlement 300 years later.

The Slav world

To describe Europe as a continent is strictly speaking incorrect, since it is in effect a peninsula of the Asian land mass. This fact had a continuing although frequently unrecognized influence on the medieval history of western Europe. For the frontier zones it was of decisive importance.

From the beginning of the Christian era these frontier zones had been inhabited by a group of tribes known collectively as Slavs whose area of occupation stretched from the Baltic coast east to the Ural mountains and southwest to the Balkans. To their west lay the Germanic kingdoms of western Europe and to the north the Scandinavian peoples. To the east were the nomadic tribes of Asia, which periodically coalesced into massive empires and lordships, extending over the central Asian steppes and bringing into their orbits the more settled cultures of the great Chinese Empire on their eastern border and the backward, petty tribal units of the Slavs on the west.

The Hunnic Empire of the fifth century AD, stretching from the Caspian Sea to the Baltic and embracing the Slav heartlands, was followed in the second half of the sixth century by the sixty-year dominion of the Avars. By the ninth century Avar power had dwindled away, to be succeeded by that of the Bulgars in the south, who shared a common boundary with the Frankish empire and thus cut off the southern Slavs on the Adriatic coast from the main body of their brothers in the north.

To the east a group of Finnish tribes, the Magyars, had established themselves in an area stretching southwards to the coast of the Black Sea. To the northwest the virile power of the Vikings was beginning to balance its seaborne migrations round the coast of western Europe by equally daring explorations of the landmass of western Eurasia.

Above, Santa Sophia Cathedral in Kiev, built in the eleventh century and modelled on the church of the same name in Constantinople. Kiev was the earliest centre of Christianity in Russia.

Top, a sixteenth-century version of the legend of William Tell, the Swiss hero of the late thirteenth and early fourteenth centuries.

For many centuries this region had been the home of the Slavs, ruled by successive conquerors, but it was the Varangian (Dano-Swedish) principalities of Kiev and Novgorod which planted the seeds of a new permanent force. This gradually welded the Slavs themselves into an imperial power.

The State of Kiev

The two Varangian principalities set up under the semi-legendary princes, Rurig at Novgorod and Igor at Kiev, were on the axis of one of the great trade routes of medieval Europe. This went from the Baltic by river and overland portage to the Dnieper and thence to the Black Sea where it linked up with the Byzantine routes to Constantinople. The wealth and power of these new states were built on the trade in furs, slaves and timber going south and Byzantine luxury goods coming north. Novgorod was at the junction of this route with the east-west route from the Baltic to central Asia, while Kiev controlled the great trunk route to the south.

By the last quarter of the ninth century these two states had been united under Oleg of Kiev and it is in this period that the first great Russian state under the princes of Kiev came into being. With the defeat of the Magyars by the Patzinak Turks the new Russian state was able to extend its boundaries to the Black Sea coast. For the next century the Varangian-Slav principality of Russia held undisputed sway over a vast tract of land between the Baltic and the Black Sea.

Within a comparatively short period the Varangian ruling class lost its separate identity by intermarriage and assimilation. By the latter half of the tenth century a new and decisive element was added when, during the reign of Grand Prince Vladimir (980–1015), the nascent state abandoned its heathen past and formally adopted Christianity. Despite the attempts of his western Catholic neighbour, Boleslav the Mighty of Poland, or perhaps because of them, Vladimir accepted baptism from the representatives of the Greek Orthodox Church of Constantinople and married the sister of the Byzantine emperor. A metropolitan see was established at Kiev, subordinate to the metropolitan of Constantinople—a fact of tremendous importance in Russian history.

After the death of Vladimir in 1015 the Russian state fell apart in a period of civil war involving his descendants, which was temporarily resolved by the division of the state between the princes of Kiev and Chernigov in the east. After the death of the prince of Chernigov in 1035 there began the golden age of Byzantine Kiev under Yaroslav, the greatest ruler of Russia in the Kievan period. The churches of the capital bore witness to the civilizing influence of Byzantium in their architecture and their frescoes. Under Yaroslav, too, the principality enjoyed its last close diplomatic contact with western Europe for several centuries, a contact epitomized by the marriage alliances he contracted. His son married the daughter of Harold of England and, of his daughters, one married Harald Haardraade of Norway and the other Henry I of France. The brilliance of the court of Kiev at this period may be judged by the fact that the new queen of France was more than a little disappointed by the conditions of life which she found at her husband's court. However, Kiev's period of brilliance was soon to be undermined.

In 1061 the important outlet to the Black Sea was lost when the combined armies of the sons of Yaroslav were defeated by the Rurkic tribes of the Cumans, who thereby extended their frontiers to the kingdom of Hungary. A still more severe blow was struck at the trading position of Kiev some twenty years later when the Byzantine Empire concluded a commercial treaty with the rapidly growing power of Venice.

Although geographically severed from Byzantium by the Cuman conquests of the tenth century, Russia retained its strong dependence on the metropolitan of Constantinople and was thus isolated culturally from the west.

The formation of the principalities

After the death of Yaroslav the Wise in 1054 the divisive forces within the state reasserted themselves. His sons and grandsons founded a number of dynasties whose rivalries form the framework of Russian political history for the next 400 years. But, throughout this period, the successive grand princes of Kiev and then of Vladimir kept alive as a vital part of the Russian political ethos the principle of a single grand prince, to whom all ultimately owed obedience. It is worth considering the significance of this. Medieval Russia was a vast territory and there was no reason why it should have developed into a unitary state. After the great days of Kiev, it might have been expected that the process of fragmentation would have led to the evolution of a group of independent nation states, as happened in Europe on the breakup of Charlemagne's empire.

There were numerous reasons why this did not happen. Obviously, geography is very significant. In the whole vast region from the Carpathians to the Urals there is no natural frontier to compare with the Alps, the Pyrenees or the English Channel. The populations of this region, although they were to develop distinctive national characteristics, were never as divided by languages, traditions and identity as the peoples of western Europe. Another important factor to be taken into account was the period of Mongol rule.

The dynastic system of the ruling houses was also of great significance. Each of the many princes enjoyed sole authority within his domain, limited only by the obligation to send troops to the aid of the grand prince of Kiev, and later of Vladimir, if they should need them. The office of grand prince descended through all the branches of the family from brother to brother down through the generations. Thus, until the mid-fourteenth century, when Moscow secured the title to itself in perpetuity, all the princely lines had a vested interest in retaining the office of grand prince in no matter how attenuated a form. In this way the theory of a central authority survived with sufficient vigour for it to be taken up by the house of Moscow in the fifteenth century as the tool with which to shape the autocracy of all the Russias.

Medieval Russian society

Chief among the states was the great principality of Kiev itself. To the north of it was the principality of Novgorod and to the northeast the principality of Suzdal (later called Vladimir, then Moscow). To the east of Kiev and south of Suzdal lay the principality of Chernigov. The rivalries between these states and their neighbours were set in the pattern of princely ambition but were not determined by this alone. By the eleventh century a clearly articulated society was beginning to emerge, comprising various groups whose interests might have to be taken into account in the shaping of princely policy. Thus, while the princes were sometimes blamed by the chroniclers for allowing their pride to prevent them uniting against the heathen Cumans or the Bulgars on the Volga, their actions often met the approval of their powerful subjects.

In its early years Russian society consisted basically of a warrior aristocracy, the merchant class of the cities on which trade, the main source of wealth, depended and the peasantry, ruthlessly exploited to provide food, cannon fodder and slaves. However, as conditions became more settled within each state, the aristocracy, now recruiting to its ranks successful merchants who had invested their profits in land, came to take a more solicitous interest in the peasantry as a source of income. The aristocracy of the *boyars* was divided into two groups: the *druzhina* or courtiers who followed the travelling court of the prince, and the provincial magnates who stayed on their large estates.

In addition to the *druzhina* the prince had to reckon with the growing power of the towns represented by the militia or *veche,* which was largely controlled by the merchant oligarchies. To these classic divisions of secular society must be added the whole hierarchy of the clerical estate which rapidly came to play a decisive part. Indeed, one of the chief marks of political ascendancy was to be the establishment of a metropolitan or ecclesiastical hierarchy independent of Kiev.

With the opening up of new trade routes, such as the northern one from the Baltic through the principality of Suzdal to central Asia, the trading interests of the states inevitably came into conflict from time to time. Another important factor was the gradual emergence of separate national identities represented by the three main racial groups: the great Russians to the north, the White Russians or Byelorussians to the west, and the Ukrainians, whose territory included Kiev, to the southwest.

Kiev and Novgorod

In the 1130s the last grand prince of Kiev to exercise in any effective way the theoretical supremacy of his house died. Within thirty years the great principality had been overrun and its capital, the glory of old Russia, sacked by the prince of Suzdal, Andrei Bogolyubsky. Kiev's position had already been in decline both politically and commercially, but its fate was sealed when Andrei, incread of moving his capital to the ancient centre of the Russian state, installed a regent in Kiev and continued to rule from his own capital of Vladimir, which now gave its name to his principality.

Following his triumph at Kiev, Andrei attempted to subjugate its client state to the north, but his armies were routed before the walls of Novgorod in 1170. Although the great republic eventually acknowledged the suzerainty of the princes of Vladimir, it remained effectively independent.

The title, 'Republic of Novgorod' is, strictly speaking, inaccurate, since the city continued with a prince as the official head of state throughout its independent history. Yet as early as 1126 the city oligarchs had elected his chief official or *posadnik*. The explanation of this state of affairs is to be found in part in the peculiar geographical advantages of the city. Benefiting to the full from its position as a junction of trade routes, Novgorod had the further advantage over the other Russian states of being effectively shielded by them from the depredations of the Asian Nomads. Thus at first it found it had less need than its neighbours of the services of a military aristocracy. In consequence, this class was less able to assert itself.

Furthermore, the very barrenness of the huge wastes which formed the city's hinterland (stretching to the coasts of the White Sea and the Arctic Ocean) was a positive advantage. These wild tracts of country supported a sparse population of hunters, with whom the Novgorod merchants were able to conduct a very favourable trade in walrus ivory, falcons for the hunt and, above all, the valuable furs that formed so essential a part of the wardrobe of the wealthy classes throughout Europe. Throughout this territory the commercial oligarchs held large and profitable estates, but neither the manpower nor the economics of the region provided the temptation to found rival political units.

Above, a battle between Novgorod and Suzdal in the late fifteenth century; at this time Moscow was extending its influence over the whole of Russia, and both these cities were forced to recognize Moscow's sovereignty by 1478. State Tretyakov Gallery, Moscow.

Left, a fourteenth-century painting of St George and the Dragon, from Novgorod. At this date the city's population may have been as high as 400,000 – far larger than any in western Europe. Russian State Museum.

The oligarchic republicanism of Novgorod increased still further in the middle of the twelfth century when the bishop as well as the prince's chief officer became elective. It must, moreover, have been reinforced and encouraged by the close ties which the city had with the powerful and increasingly independent merchant oligarchies of the north German towns. These were coming to dominate Baltic trade, in which their factory at Novgorod played a vital part. Their combined strength, increasingly effective through the agency of the Hanseatic League, enabled them to exercise decisive political as well as commercial initiatives—a lesson which cannot have been lost on their Russian colleagues.

The rulers of Novgorod continued to accept the provision of princes and *posadniks* by the rising state of Vladimar, as they had from the old principality of Kiev. To some extent this represented a more real dependence, since the city depended for its corn supplies on the region of Niz in the territories of Vladimir. The princes of Vladimir were well placed to cut Novgorod's trade to the east.

The unwilling partnership was valuable to the princes of Vladimir both because of the annual tribute but more particularly because of the opportunity it gave them of playing a major part in the direction of policies of the greatest commercial power in Russia. In the constant struggle for ascendancy between the prince and the oligarchy, the latter managed quite effectively to restrict the princely power. The vital matter of commercial law, for example, was entirely outside the prince's jurisdiction and much power lay with the popular assembly of the town's *veche*. This in turn was controlled by the boyar aristocracy of landowners, bankers and capitalists, who held all the magistracies and through these controlled the true merchant classes and their guilds.

This rigid oligarchical system in which the vast majority of the citizens was allowed no part was to prove the essential weakness of the state of Novgorod when eventually Moscow was able to devote its energies to its conquest. The appeal to the unrepresented citizenry proved irresistible. But in the early years of the thirteenth century this threat lay in the distant future. The more immediate danger was building up to the west from the two aggresive powers in the Baltic region: the kingdom of Sweden and the Teutonic knights of Livonia.

Once again, however, Novgorod was blessed with good fortune. Her enemies did not combine their forces and Prince Alexander Nevsky proved a heroic war leader. One of the great soldiers of medieval Russia, he was the son of Yaroslav, great prince of Vladimir. He gained his title of honour, Nevsky, from his resounding defeat of the forces of Earl Birger of Sweden on the banks of the river Neva in the year 1240. Two years later he won a still greater triumph over the army of the Teutonic Knights in his sensational and dramatic victory on the frozen surface of Lake Peipus. Their prince having so effectively discharged his essential function, the citizens of Novgorod were free to conduct their ever more profitable affairs for the next 150 years. During this time they were at liberty to enjoy the undisputed position of Russia's leading city, both economically and culturally, for the rest of the nation had entered the long night of the Tartar supremacy.

Mongol power in Asia

To appreciate as fully as possible the position of Russia during the thirteenth and fourteenth centuries it is necessary to realize that during this period Russia was merely the westernmost client of an empire bounded in the west by the kingdoms of Sweden and Hungary and in the east by the Pacific. The Mongol Empire ruled for two centuries not only the area covered by the bulk of the modern Soviet Union but also the Chinese Empire and the states of Persia and Afghanistan.

From 1240 until the collapse of Mongol power two centuries later the Russian states were part of the western Khanate of the Mongol Empire—the khanate of the Golden Horde (from the Mongol word *ordu* meaning camp). This great empire did not survive for more than two centuries by the use of terror alone. The central administration, set up by the khanate and based on the capital Saray on the Volga, provided a lesson in central government which was not lost on the Russian princes, who eventually inherited the power of their conquerors.

This administration was divided broadly into two areas. The former territories of the Cumans and the Volga Bulgars, parts of the western Russian principalities of Galicia, Volniya and the whole of the principalities of Kiev and Chernigov were directly under Mongol control. The remaining Russian principalities, chief among them was the principality of Tver and the great principality of Vladimir with its dependant, the republic of Novgorod, continued under the rule of their princes. They reigned, however, by permission of the khan, carrying out his policies and collecting taxes on his behalf. Under the Mongols trade remained an essential activity of the region and the most important agents of this trade were the Muslim merchants who for a short time were given the task of farming the taxes and exercised their authority very oppressively.

To ensure the most thorough exploitation of the population both for purposes of taxation and recruitment into the army, the Mongol administration carried out the first census of Russian history and, indeed, the first census of any medieval European state. They possibly derived the principles involved in conducting a census from their great client state to the east, the Chinese Empire. Further examples of their centralizing drive were the development of overland communications and the institution of a regular post system considered so important that a special tax was levied to maintain it.

Russia under the Tartar yoke

From the moment of the Tartar conquest the history of the Russian principalities was like a kaleidoscope, colourful, changeable and dramatic, but always contained within the framework of Tartar policy. The khans allowed the Russian states to run their internal affairs more or less as they wished, as long as the annual tribute was regularly paid. But for close on a century they exploited the rivalries between the states in their own interests.

Overshadowing everything else was the great rivalry between Moscow and Tver which came into prominence when the office of the grand prince of Vladimir became vacant on the death of Andrei, the son of Alexander Nevsky, in 1304. Andrei's younger brother, Daniil of Moscow, had also died. The laws of succession traditionally accepted over the previous century excluded from the succession the descendants of Daniil and gave the throne to the late grand prince's oldest surviving cousin, Mikhail of Tver, Moreover, Andrei's own boyars seem to have anticipated the natural course of events by moving to Tver. But, despite his apparent right to the office by Russian custom and his consistent success on the battlefield, Mikhail was assassinated in 1318 with the connivance of the Mongol khan at the Horde. Ivan I of Moscow finally succeeded as grand prince in 1331.

The exact history of the conflict between Tver and Moscow during these years is obscure, but it seems clear that Mikhail and

Above, fragment from a sixteenth-century illustration of 'The Church Militant', showing Alexander Nevsky, who submitted to Mongol rule to save Novgorod from being destroyed. State Tretyakov Gallery, Moscow.

Left, Tartar soldiers in a battle with less disciplined oriental nomads. The Tartar domination over such tribes gave a new unity to central Asia. Österreichische Nationalbibliothek Vienna.

Above left, Ivan I Kalita of Moscow with the Metropolitan Pyotr; by uniting his interests with those of the Church, Ivan helped to make Moscow the religious centre of Russia.

Opposite, the Korsun Doors of Santa Sophia Cathedral in Novgorod, made in the 1150s by German craftsmen and so symbolizing the close contact between Novgorod and the civilization of western Europe. Cathedral of Santa Sophia, Novgorod.

his son Dmitri were able to prove their ascendancy among the Russian princes both on the field of battle and in the struggle for the control of the vital city of Novgorod. It is equally clear that the khans consistently supported the weaker power of Moscow against the princes of Tver.

With the accession of Ivan I Kalita (as he was called) of Moscow to the title of Grand Prince of Vladimir, the house of Tver was finally eliminated from the running. By this time also the Tartars were faced with a new problem: the very real threat of the princes of Lithuania, Gedimin and Olgerd, who by an effective policy of peaceful infiltration had established their authority throughout the territories of the historic principality of Kiev. They were, moreover, beginning to make inroads in the more northerly territories of Rus in Novgorod and Pskov. To meet this new menace the khan proclaimed the succession of Ivan of Moscow's son, Semen, to the grand principality of Vladimir.

Thereafter the khan appears to have pursued a shrewd policy of supporting the rivals of Moscow to the south and east, while ensuring that the Muscovite state was strong on its western frontiers, where the power of Lithuania was an everpresent threat to the Mongol hegemony. It is in this context that the Mongol policy of encouraging divisions in the declining state of Tver should be seen.

An essential element in the rise of Moscow was the goodwill and support of the khans, which the princes of Moscow generally sought. But, of almost equal importance, was the support which they received from the Church. The value of this was demonstrated on many occasions, notably in the latter part of the thirteenth century when Yaroslav of Vladimir, expelled from Novgorod by its citizens, was reinstated on the orders of the metropolitan Kirill, and again forty years later, when the metropolitan brought to an end a campaign conducted by the young crown prince Dmitri of Tver, by simply ordering the army to return home.

The authority of the Russian metropolitans would have been the envy of their Catholic counterparts, the popes of Rome, whose great days were by this time more than a century past. But this authority was not merely spiritual. To a large extent it rested on the remarkable sponsorship which they enjoyed from the khans. The Orthodox branch of Christendom was protected by its infidel masters not only from the excessive enthusiasm of their own agents but also from the encroachments of the Christian princes. Indeed, the Mongol *yarliki* ('patents') were so highly valued by the Church that as late as the sixteenth century it went to the extent of forging them.

The decline of the Tartars

In the second half of the fourteenth century the power of the Mongol khans in Russia began its long decline. After the death of Khan Janibeg in 1357 the Horde was divided within itself by the wars of his sons. In earlier years such dangerous civil wars in one of the provinces of the empire would have been subject to disciplinary action from the capital, but the empire itself was in dire trouble, since the Yuan dynasty had been expelled from China in 1368.

In addition to these internal troubles the khanate of the Horde was faced by the powerful and successful armies of Olgerd of Lithuania who, after a major victory over the Mongols, had made himself master of large parts of the Ukraine. During this period of unrest even the long docile principality of Moscow rebelled, and at Kulikova Pole on the Don in 1380 Grand Prince Dmitri Donskoi gained the first victory of Russian troops over a Tartar force. The victory was not long-lived and two years later Moscow was sacked by Tokhtamysh, the victor in the Tartar civil wars.

However, the triumph of Tokhtamysh was brief. In the late 1380s he was faced with the new terror of central Asia, the armies of Timur (Tamerlane) the Great. By 1395 all the great cities of the Golden Horde had been sacked and its armies subdued. With their masters thus beaten to their knees, the Muscovites were doubly lucky that Timur turned back from his march on Moscow and left Russia. He had achieved a radical reversal in the balance of power but had not made any permanent conquests or established a new imperial power in the place of the broken Tartars. From that time onwards the struggle was very much a war between equals.

The reign of Vasilii II (1425–62) set the seal on the Russian liberation from the Tartar yoke. He himself had been defeated and captured by the Tartars. He had been restored by Tartar arms and many of the towns of Vladimir had been overrun, but, by the end of his reign, these losses had been recovered. A number of Tartar nobles had entered his service and in the mid-fifteenth century a Tartar khanate was established by patent from Moscow.

The reversal of roles could hardly go further and yet, through force of custom and constitutional conservatism, the grand princes of Moscow, as the territories of Vladimir could now be called, continued to pay tribute to, and accept their patent from, one rival khan after another. However, finally in 1479, Vasilii's successor, Ivan III (1462–1505), refused the patent of the khan and declared the total independence of his state after an enemy 'occupation' of more than two hundred years.

The supremacy of Moscow

More important than this dramatic, but somewhat belated, gesture was Ivan's final subordination of Novgorod to Moscow. His predecessor had already defeated the city, but it was only in 1487 that the great port was forced into permanent submission. After years of punitive expeditions followed by truces by which the Novgorodians retained most of their rights, Ivan dealt with the city very harshly and resettled thousands of its leading families in other parts of Russia.

In the next reign, the last of the independent Russian states, Pskov, was absorbed into the new grand duchy of Muscovy. Besides the obvious political and military advantages enjoyed by a unitary Russia in confrontation with the power of Poland Lithuania to the west, the unification of all Russias had also brought with it the problem of the boyars of the respective courts. To prevent conflict over privilege, which could so easily grow into civil war, an elaborate hierarchy was established, which determined to a large extent the appointments by the grand duke, later the tsar, to the high offices of state. The first grand duke actually to be crowned tsar was Ivan IV, 'the Terrible', but the title had been borne from time to time since the death of the last Eastern Roman emperor at the capture of Constantinople in 1453.

The fall of the Byzantine Empire had a considerable impact on Russian thought. For Orthodox Christians it was the home of the true faith and for all Orthodox states the Byzantine emperor was the premier ruler of the Christian world. In the same century in which they had thrown off the last vestiges of their old servitude to the infidel Tartars, the grand dukes of Moscow found themselves the heirs to the Christian emperor himself. Ivan III married Sophie, the daughter of the last emperor, and their son, who succeeded Ivan as Vasilii III, was hailed by the abbot of Pskov as the sole protector of the Greek Church. Ivan IV's coronation as tsar in 1547 can therefore be seen as a natural progression, although the metropolitan of Constantinople withheld his recognition for fourteen years.

Ivan the Terrible

Ivan the Terrible is one of the most notorious rulers in European history and his unstable personality led him into acts of brutal violence which fully justify his traditional title in English. Yet the main target of his often oppressive rule was the unruly and potentially dominant aristocracy, and the examples of Lithuania and later Poland show how easily the powerful eastern European nobility could entrench themselves in the seats of power.

Ivan was only three years old when his father died and, for the first thirteen years of his reign, Russia was ruled by his mother (who died, probably poisoned, when he was eight) and then by a regency council. Of this council, the only man whom he could trust was the metropolitan, Makari. It was probably on his advice that in 1546 Ivan declared the end of boyar rule and in the following year had himself crowned tsar. When he was only twenty years old, Ivan established the *zemsky sobor*, a two-chamber body which contained representatives of the gentry and the merchants as well as the nobles and thus to some extent acted as a check on the power of the boyar class.

Ivan IV was the first of the grand princes of Moscow who, in theory at least, enjoyed undisputed sway over all the territories which called themselves Russia. He was the first tsar to inherit all the Russias and in this

sense his reign was crucial to the development of a centralized Russian state. The boyars who plundered and insulted the young Ivan were, in fact, in many cases either themselves the senior councillors of recently absorbed independent states or the sons of such men. The dangers of a renewed separatism were very real and, without the harsh rule of Ivan IV, might well have been realised.

Besides changes in the system of taxation Ivan also reformed the army and achieved his first great success with the conquest of the Tartar Khanate of Kazan. This was followed by the annexation of the Khanate of Astrakhan. By now the tsar was in his late twenties and was determined to rule independently. Accepting the rumour that the death of his wife, like that of his mother, was caused by poison, he broke with his advisers, who included notably Prince Kurbsky.

A symbol of his new independence was the well grounded but, as it turned out, not well conducted policy of establishing a Baltic seaboard for Russia. This involved him in war with the powerful state of Poland-Lithuania and lost him once and for all the services of his adviser and gifted general, Kurbsky, who after a defeat by Lithuanian forces deserted to Poland-Lithuania.

Kurbsky's desertion brought a neurotic response in Ivan who saw in it a confirmation of all his worst suspicions of the boyar class. He secretly left Moscow and sent notice of his intention to abdicate unless he be given absolute authority to deal with the 'traitors' as he saw fit. The result was the full powers which he had demanded and there followed the establishment of the *oprichnina*. This was the first of the notorious secret police forces which have plagued Russia from the time of Ivan to the twentieth century. The *oprichnina* (meaning 'a separate household') was staffed mainly by members of the gentry and lower aristocracy and was organized as a semi-monastic body. But the monastic avocation of the *oprichniki* ended with their organizational structure. They were the scourge of the boyars. many of whom were executed as traitors and whose estates were confiscated to finance the new body. Their depredations of the *oprichniki* extended beyond the aristocratic class and reached even the great towns such as

Novgorod and Pskov. Eventually they were disbanded by Ivan himself and in the early 1570s the administration of the state was put on a more normal basis.

The eventful reign of Ivan the Terrible ended in characteristic fashion when the tsar, in one of his unpredictable rages, killed his eldest son, Ivan. Thus at his death, Ivan left the virtuous, if slow-witted, Theodore as his successor.

The Time of Troubles

The young tsar Theodore reigned until his death in 1598, but the real power in the state was exercised by his uncle, Boris Godunov, who was elected tsar by the *zemskl sobor* on Theodore's death. The other son of Ivan IV, Dmitri, was an epileptic and died in 1591, probably by his own hand. Boris, who had Tartar blood in his veins and was not a member of the old dynasty of Danilovichi, followed Ivan IV's repressive policies and became increasingly unpopular with boyars and peasants alike. He acquired a monstrous reputation as the murderer of Ivan the Terrible, Theodore and even Dmitri.

Despite numerous important measures such as the promotion of Russian industry and commerce by calling in western experts, and the creation of the Russian Church as an autonomous body no longer subordinate to the metropolitan of Constantinople, Boris was dogged by ill fortune. His boyars became increasingly powerful and when a pretender claiming to be the dead Dmitri advanced into Russia with the backing of the king of Poland he found ready support. He entered Moscow in May 1606, but his triumph lasted only a few weeks, when it was apparent that he was not willing to accept the tutelage of the boyars. He was replaced for a few years by the Boyar leader, Basil Shuisky.

Russia now experienced a period of reaction after the strong rule of Ivan the Terrible, and the Times of Troubles, as it is known, ended only in 1613, after a second false Dmitri had attempted to make good good his claim and the king of Poland had intervened and been defeated. With the election as tsar of Michael Romanov, son of the powerful Bishop Philaret, the dynasty was founded which was to rule the empire of all the Russias for the next 300 years.

Bulgaria

While the princes of the state of Moscow were throwing off the long and oppressive rule of the pagan Tartars, their distant Slav cousins in the Balkans and their old enemies the Bulgars at the mouth of the Danube were struggling for their very existence against the new infidel power of the Ottoman Turks. This part of the world had long been the scene of conflict between the Byzantine

Above, Ivan the Terrible (ruled 1533–84), the first man to take the title of Tsar of Russia. His name derived from his determination to break the power of the boyars and establish an autocracy. National Museum, Copenhagen.

Above left, Boris Godunov, Tsar of Russia (ruled 1598–1605). He tried to pursue similar policies to those of Ivan the Terrible, supporting the administration and the towns against the boyars. Museum of the History of Moscow.

Opposite, a scene from the life of Ivan the Terrible, showing him fighting outside Moscow.

Empire, the encroaching waves of nomadic invaders from the steppes of Asia, and the Slav tribes on the Adriatic coast.

The Danube Bulgars, who with the Volga Bulgars had constituted the khanate of Great Bulgaria round the Sea of Azov, were the distant descendents of the great empire of Attila the Hun. In the mid-seventh century the khanate had been dispersed. One group of tribes migrated to the upper reaches of the Volga, where they emerged as an independent power some ninety years later to be the uneasy neighbours of the young Russian principalities. A second group settled on the delta of the Danube on the northwestern frontier of the Byzantine Empire. From here they not only found rich plunder in frequent raids into Byzantine territory but also, in the last years of the eighth century, were able to extend their power north and west into the territories of the formerly powerful Avars.

This expansion was, however, comparatively short-lived and, within a century, a large part of their gains north of the Danube were lost to the invading Magyars. The Magyars in their turn had been driven from their lands on the north coast of the Black Sea by a new wave of invaders from central Asia. The defeat of the Magyars at the Battle of the Lech in 955 by the German emperor Otto I halted their advance into Europe and they settled on the Hungarian steppe lands.

A few years before the incursion of the Magyars, the Bulgars and their Slav neighbours had undergone a far more momentous change in the epic campaign of conversion to Christianity conducted by Saint Cyril and Saint Methodius. This important accession to the Orthodox Church did not have any very notable impact on the secular policies of the newly Christian state. Deprived of its lands north of the Danube by the Magyars, it extended its conquests to the south, so that, up to the latter part of the tenth century, the empire of the Bulgars comprised more than half the former Balkan provinces of the Byzantines.

However, as a result, first of the victories of the Russian Prince Sviatoslav of Kiev and then of the campaigns of their own emperor, Basil II the 'Bulgar Slayer', the Byzantines recovered their lost provinces and the Bulgars became subjects of the emperor at Constantinople. Their Slav neighbour, the principality of Serbia, became a client state of Byzantium.

Some two centuries later the Bulgars were able to reassert their independence. A paralysing defeat inflicted on them by the Seljuk Turks towards the end of the twelfth century left the Byzantines virtually defenceless and awaiting the next blow on their southern frontier. Throughout the thirteenth century the revived Bulgarian empire maintained itself, although within much reduced borders.

To the north the Cuman Turks had thoroughly established themselves on the banks of the Danube, and this situation was not dramatically altered when, in the second decade of the fourteenth century the Cuman prince Basaraba founded the principality of Walachia with a largely Vlach (Romanian), Romance-speaking population. He and his successors, while acknowledging the suzerainity of the Hungarian king, successfully kept themselves free of his authority. To the south the Bulgarians were able to maintain their position against the rival Latin and Greek states which emerged in the aftermath of the eclipse of Byzantium by the Fourth Crusade. Indeed, it was the expansionist ambitions of the neighbouring Slav state of Serbia in the fourteenth century which most seriously reduced independent Bulgaria before it was overrun by the Turks.

Serbia

Together with their northern neighbours the Croats, the Serbs represented the southern members of that great mass of Slav tribes which had once dominated the central European landmass. The establishment of the Magyar state in the Hungarian plains confirmed the separate destinies of Poland to the north and Croatia and Serbia to the south. Their conversion to two different creeds of Christianity, the Croats to Roman Catholicism and the Serbs to Orthodoxy, confirmed the growing divergencies within the South Slavs themselves.

For a hundred years the two states maintained their independence against their powerful neighbours, but in the last decade of the eleventh century Vladislav of Hungary conquered Croatia. However, despite periods of vassaldom and subjection to the Byzantine Empire during the twelfth century, the Serbs survived until, like the Bulgarians, they regained their independence in the latter part of the century and emerged with the pretensions of a kingdom. The little mountain state survived for another two centuries and, during the brief but dazzling reign of Stevan Dusan, took on the dimensions as well as the ambitions of a major power.

In 1331 Stevan became king of Serbia and, through his marriage to the sister of the former lord of Bulgaria, the ruler of that country also. Exploiting the exhausted prostration of the Byzantine Empire, he extended Serb sway as far south as the Gulf of Corinth and as far east as the frontiers of Macedonia, proclaiming himself emperor of the Serbs and the Greeks. But he failed to capture the vital prize which might have given substance to his claims, the great city of Constantinople itself.

After his death in 1355 at the age of forty-six his empire fell apart into a congeries of petty principalities. Louis of Hungary took advantage of the collapse to seize Bosnia and the northern part of Serbia itself. The defeat of a combined Bulgar-Serbian force in 1371 by the Turks was followed by sixty years of alternate clienthood and vassaldom under the Ottoman Empire before complete conquest and subjection in 1439.

The Christian kingdom of Hungary

The defeat of the Magyars at the Battle of the Lech in 955 by the Emperor Otto I had put an end to any further hopes they may have had of conquest in Europe. They settled in their new home on the Hungarian plains and by the early years of the eleventh century during the reign of their first great king, St Stephen (977–1038), adopted the Roman Catholic faith, becoming the latest addition to the growing family of Christendom.

During the next two centuries Hungary was able to maintain its northern frontier more or less intact against the incursions of its northern neighbour Poland but lost a considerable tract of land to the southeast. Moreover, in the latter half of the eleventh century, the Patzinaks, fleeing from the invading Cumans (the latest arrival from the steppes), carved out a new home for themselves in the area later to become the autonomous principality of Walachia. But this loss to the southeast was balanced by the incorporation of the neighbouring Slav state of Croatia which, besides a considerable increase in territory, also brought Hungary a valuable coastal frontier on the Adriatic. Until the beginning of the sixteenth century Croatia was to remain a part of the Hungarian state, except for a brief period of Byzantine dominion.

The divisions in Hungarian society between the warrior Magyars, from whom the great noble houses were descended, and the conquered Slavs and Croatians who by and large supplied the lower orders of society and the peasantry was never wholly eliminated. Moreover, because on every frontier there was a usually aggressive neighbour, a powerful provincial military aristocracy was a valuable shield. But this could all too easily become a danger to the state if the provincial lord felt his rights infringed. The power of the nobility in Hungary remained a constant threat to the monarchy.

In 1241 Hungary was overrun by the marauding Mongols. When, thirty years later. King Bela IV, the last of the Arpad dynasty to exercise effective control over the powerful landed aristocracy, died, the country entered a period of aristocratic anarchy. On the death of the last of the Arpads in 1301, the leading nobles supported the claims of Wenceslaus I of Bohemia.

However, the triumph of the Bohemian house was short-lived and, after some years of dynastic warfare, another claimant (through the female line), Charles Robert, of the Angevin house of Naples, was crowned in 1310 as Charles I of Hungary. His reign ushered in the period of Hungary's greatness. He was a strong and able prince, well assisted by his French and papal advisers. When, after years of campaigning, he

Left, the Battle of Nicopolis (1396), when the Turks, led by Bayazid, defeated Sigismund of Hungary and an army which included crusaders from all over Europe. Only Timur's attack on the Turks prevented their overwhelming central Europe. Bibliothèque Municipale, Valenciennes.

finally brought the dismayed nobility to heel in 1327, he exploited the new power of the central authority to provide his adopted kingdom with one of the most effective economic and administrative machines of medieval Europe. He also sought to protect his frontiers from the growing power of the Habsburgs by a solemn alliance with the kingdoms of Poland and Bohemia. His son inherited a Hungary more secure and better governed than at any other time in its history.

After the consolidating reign of Charles I, his son, known as Louis the Great, who was crowned in 1342, initiated a period of imperial expansion. Despite his failure to make good his claims to the Angevin kingdom of Naples, he succeeded in re-establishing Hungary's position on the Dalmatian coast, which had been lost for a time to the Venetians. His other triumphs included the acquisition of Bosnia and parts of Serbia, the acknowledgment of Hungarian suzerainty by the principalities of Walachia and Moldavia and even his own coronation as King of Poland after the death of his uncle, Casimir III.

His father had shown the Hungarian aristocracy who was master of the house, Louis, with an administration now able to fund his ambitious policies, kept their cooperation by confirming their liberties and allowing them a considerable degree of autonomy within their estates, in return for their military support in his campaigns. The nobles thus strengthened their position at the expense of the liberties of their subjects, above all of the peasants.

RUSSIA, EASTERN EUROPE AND SCANDINAVIA: 950–1600

Date	Russia	Eastern Europe	Scandinavia
950	Vladimir the Great (980–1015) Adoption of Christianity (989)	Bulgaria reconquered by Eastern Empire Stephen king of Hungary (997–1038)	King of Denmark baptized (965) Christianity in Norway
1000	Yaroslav the Wise, Grand Prince of Kiev (1015–54) Sons of Yaroslav defeated by Cumans (1061)		Canute II king of England (1016–35) and of Denmark (1018–35)
1100	Vladimir II, Grand Prince of Kiev (1113–25) Novgorod independent of Kiev (1136) Sack of Kiev by Andrey Bogolyubsky	Kingdom of Bohemia founded Second Bulgarian Empire Bulgaria throws off Byzantine yoke	Waldemar I king of Denmark (1157–82) Christianity fully established in Sweden
1200	Genghis Khan defeats the Russians on the Kalka (1224) Tartars capture Kiev (1240) Alexander Nevsky: victories over Swedes (1240) and Teutonic Knights (1242)	Tartars invade Poland and Hungary Defeat of Hungarians by Ottakar II of Bohemia	Waldemar II king of Denmark (1202–41) Danish conquests in northern Germany Haakon IV, king of Norway (1217–63)
1300	Ivan I Kalita, Grand Prince of Moscow (1328–41) Moscow the dominant state in Russia Dimitri Donskoi, Grand Duke of Moscow (1362–89) Tartars defeated at Kulikovo	Wencelas II of Bohemia king of Poland Charles Robert of Naples becomes Charles I of Hungary Casimir III, the Great, king of Poland (1333–70) Stephen Dusan, king of Serbia (1335–46) Jagellon dynasty in Poland	Sweden and Norway united under Magnus V Union of Kalmar: Eric of Pomerania king of Norway, Sweden and Denmark
1400	Vasili I (1389–1425) Vasili II (1425–62) Ivan III (1462–1505)	Union of Poland and Lithuania Matthias Corvinus, king of Hungary (1458–90) Serbia and Bulgaria absorbed into Ottoman Empire	Eric of Pomerania deposed (1439) Revolt in Sweden led by Engelbrecht Engelbrechtson Christian I, king of Denmark (1448–81) and of Norway (1450–81) Swedish victory over Denmark at Battle of Brunkeberg (1471)
1500	End of the Golden Horde (1502) Vasili III (1503–33) Ivan IV, the Terrible (1533–84) Boris Godunov The Time of Troubles	War between Poland and Russia (1512–22) Hungary conquered by Turks Sigismund Vasa, king of Poland (1587–1632)	Stockholm 'bloodbath' Gustavus Vasa, king of Sweden (1523–60)
1600			

The sixty years which followed the death of Louis the Great and ended with the humiliating defeat of Varna were a period of decline for Hungary both at home and abroad. After five years of bloody civil war Louis' son-in-law, Sigismund of Bohemia, finally won the crown against the opposition of the late king's Neapolitan relations. But from the first Sigismund was beset with troubles. His own interests and ambitions were far-reaching. In 1411 he won the election as Holy Roman emperor and, after the death of his brother, Wenceslaus of Bohemia, in 1419, he spent twenty years trying to make good his claim to that kingdom against the ardent opposition of the Hussites.

In the early fifteenth century Ladislas of Naples had revived his house's claim to Hungary, and a more determined attack from Venice in the second decade of the century resulted in the loss of the Dalmatian coast. The crown of Poland had been lost with the death of Louis and the Turks had annexed Bosnia and Walachia. Moreover, Hungary's resources were not now sufficiently well administered to support the extravagance and imperial ambitions of the king. At his death he left a once prosperous and powerful state poor and distracted by internal division.

It was only the nobles who profited from the reign of Sigismund. Each new demand was granted only in exchange for a large grant of new rights and liberties. As the nobles prospered and increasingly avoided the burdens of supporting the state and their expensive monarch, so the peasants were more harshly oppressed to provide the necessary revenue. By the end of Sigismund's reign the peasant serf was paying something like a quarter of his income in dues to the Church, his lord and the king. In addition he had to perform forced labour on his lord's land and to contribute to the maintenance of the huge standing army required to fight the king's wars abroad.

The Hungarian aristocracy had so successfully recovered its commanding position in the country that, after the death of Sigismund, it was able to select from the available contenders to the throne his impecunious successor as emperor, Albert II of Habsburg. After Albert's death from the plague in 1439, his posthumous son, Ladislas, was crowned king by one group of nobles. Some months later a second group summoned the young Polish king, Wladyslaw, to be crowned King of Hungary. He was killed at the Battle of Varna and a regency council was set up, headed by John Hunyadi.

John Hunyadi died in 1456, the very year of his victory at Belgrade. When the young Habsburg puppet king, Ladislas V, died in the following year, Hungary was again without a ruler, although there were various legitimist claimants from a series of related royal houses. However, the Turkish threat from the south demanded a popular king behind whom the country could unite. Mathias Corvinus Hunyadi, son of John Hunyadi, was elected king, with his uncle as regent, a tutelage with which the strong-willed young monarch soon dispensed.

Matthias Corvinus combined wide-ranging territorial ambitions in Europe with the clear aim of keeping the Turks at bay to the south, and on the whole he was successful. After a long struggle as the champion of the faith in Bohemia against the Hussites he acquired large tracts of the Bohemian state for Hungary.

Turning his attention to the Habsburg zone of influence in Austria he conquered much of the province of Styria, the province of Salzburg and finally the city of Vienna itself. His successes had depended in part on military and financial reforms and at the end of his reign Hungary seemed to have recovered the brilliant position which it had enjoyed under Louis the Great.

On the death of Matthias Corvinus in 1490 the nobles again chose their king from the distant and weak dynasty of Poland. For the next forty years this monarch and his successor ruled by courtesy of the magnates and great clerics who were able to bolster still further their positions of privilege at the expense of the towns and the peasantry. The once powerful kingdom of Hungary again assumed the character of a loose federation of virtually autonomous despots, and its divisions made it an easy prey to the Turkish invasions of the sixteenth century.

Chapter 17

Italy: the Achievement of the City-States

During the fifteenth century Italian history is best seen in terms of the relationships of five major powers. These were the papal states, the republic of Florence, the republic of Venice, the duchy of Milan and the kingdom of Naples. Each of these powers exhibited distinctive modes of government; each was in a continuing state of tension, not only with its great neighbours but also with many lesser states both on and within its borders.

The Italian peninsula was essentially a collection of numerous small city-states. Although a number had been forced to submit to their powerful neighbours, many even of these managed to keep alive the fire of their independence. Some never succumbed to domination by others. In the papal states, in particular, theoretical dependence was belied by powerful *signorie* who conducted their own affairs without regard to the Holy See: the Montefeltre at Urbino (a lordship founded on professional soldiering and responsible for some of the most enlightened patronage of the Italian Renaissance), the Malatesta at Rimini, the Bentivoglio at Bologna.

Even the smallest of these Italian states showed a tenacious grip on that much-prized commodity, liberty. Two of them have survived even to our own day: the little mountain republic of San Marino, an impregnable rocky fortress in the one-time states of the Church; and the principality of Monaco, an enclave surrounded by the lands of Savoy.

It was a remarkable paradox that in the Italian peninsula, populated by some of the richest and most politically advanced communities in Europe, the claims of the two universal authorities of the medieval world (the Church and the Holy Roman Empire) continued as a part of political theory longer than anywhere else in western Europe. The kingdom of Naples was, in theory, a papal fief and this had positive results when the popes exercised their legal rights to nominate candidates for the throne. The dukes of Milan held their title from an imperial grant, purchased easily enough but still a significant indication of their desire to lend an aura of legitimacy to their seizure of power.

In an attempt to square the facts of the autonomy of the city-state, observable throughout north Italy, and the theory of imperial suzerainty, Italian political theorists, notably Marsiglio of Padua and Bartolus of Sasoferrato, evolved the doctrine that a free people could be its own sovereign. The theory that the people were the source of all public power had venerable antecedents, even going back to the days of imperial Rome, but Bartolus introduced the concept of law into the argument. If one aspect of law, the common law, were already determined by the people, even if only

Above, the Italian city states in the fifteenth century; the strongest were Florence, Venice, Milan, the kingdom of Naples and the Papal States.

tacitly, it followed, so Bartolus agreed, that the people could equally well make statutory or written law. It was their consent which gave validity to laws, whether that consent were tacit or explicit. Just as the kings of France and England were arguing that a king is emperor in his own kingdom, so the various kinds of republican or aristocratic constitution in Italy had acquired a theory which legitimized their rejection, in practice, of the age-old doctrine of imperial suzerainty.

The papal states

Even though Italian rulers did covet the lofty titles which the Holy Roman emperor could bestow, his power in Italy was long dead largely as a result of the consistent opposition of his great rival for universal allegiance, the papacy. Yet the popes had bought their victory dearly. The champion of the Church had been gravely weakened and his spiritual standing impaired by long and increasingly obvious involvement in political affairs. The slow but steady decline of the papacy in European affairs was confirmed by the period of the Avignon papacy (1309–78) and was completed by the Great Schism.

The schism was mended only by the agency of the Council of Constance, convened by the emperor and dominated by the clamours of the party of conciliar reform. Elected pope in 1417 by a conclave of the council and owing allegiance to the acts which it had passed, Martin V, however reluctantly, was obliged to agree to its wishes and to convene a further council, which met at Pavia. But, setting a precedent for dealing with unwanted councils whose purpose was to perpetuate the original council's rule over the Church, he had his legates transfer the council to a new meeting place at Siena. There it was soon dissolved, but not before it had fixed Basle as the meeting place for its successor. Martin died before this council met and it was his successor Eugenius IV, who had to deal with the assembled fathers of the Church.

Martin V's pontificate set the pattern for much that followed. His policy was anticonciliar and his delaying tactics weakened the impetus of the council. He began the gradual restoration of the city of Rome, patronizing among other artists the great Masaccio. He also set about recovering for the Church its rights in the papal states, although again he set a precedent for the future by the extensive favours which he bestowed on his own family, the Colonna.

The failure of a papal crusade against the Hussite religious reformers had obliged Martin V finally to yield to the pressures of the Emperor Sigismund to convene the council at Basle. Its willingness to negotiate with the heretics so angered and disturbed the new pope, Eugenius IV, that he soon ordered its dissolution. Pope and council struggled for the next fifteen years and in 1433 the pope revoked his anti-conciliar bulls, including one which had declared the doctrine of conciliar supremacy to be heretical.

The council pressed its advantage and voted numerous important reforms in Church administration and finance. These had a direct, practical result when, by the Pragmatic Sanction of Bourges in 1438, the French king adopted many of the reforms for the French Church. But, by its abolition of many papal revenues, the council was in fact attacking the papacy's very means of support. In 1437, Eugenius again condemned the council and, following the strategy of Martin, transferred it to Ferrara and then to Florence. The papacy's ultimate triumph over the council was helped by the immense boost to its prestige when it successfully concluded the union of the Catholic and Orthodox Churches in 1439.

The revival of Rome continued with a quickened pace under Pope Nicholas V. The celebrations of the mid-century jubilee marking the end of the schism, followed two years later by the imperial coronation of the Emperor Frederick III, with all the splendour that surrounded these events, brought prosperity to the city. The reign of Nicholas V was important in other respects for, following his natural bent as a scholar, he founded the Vatican library and commissioned artists and scholars. Among these was the famous humanist Lorenzo Valla who, in one of the first works of textual criticism, exposed as a forgery the long-suspect Donation of Constantine. This was the document of the eighth century which purported to contain the transference of imperial privileges to the Church by the Emperor Constantine (fourth century).

The last years of Nicholas were darkened by the fall of Constantinople, which despite its ecclesiastical surrender to Rome at the Council of Ferrara-Florence had received no help from the west. The power of the popes to rally Europe in the cause of the true crusade was dead, despite all the eloquence and efforts of Pope Pius II (1458–64). Under the name of Aeneas Sylvius Piccolomini, Pius had begun his career as an ardent supporter of the council and had even supported the anti-pope Felix V. Pius had a reputation as a humanist and was appointed as court poet and secretary to the chancery of the Emperor Frederick III. His conversion to the strictest theories of papalist supremacy was confirmed during his reign and his Bull, *Execrabilis,* forbade appeals from the pope to any future council.

It came to be seen that the papacy's authority in all matters derived in practical terms from the allegiance of the princes of Christendom. The Great Schism showed to these same princes that they were in a way arbiters of the Church. It is interesting to note also that the last great military expedition against the Turks, the Nicopolis crusade, took place independently of the

papacy. Indeed, originally it was to have been a joint enterprise between John of Gaunt who supported the pope at Rome and Burgundy which favoured the Avignon pope, an expedition to which neither pope could have given his blessing. The sovereigns of Europe, who had long since denied even the theory of imperial overlordship, now hastened to force the clergy within their borders to abandon more and more of their traditional ties with Rome.

Everywhere the power of the popes was in retreat and, by the middle of the fifteenth century papal income from Italian revenues exceeded that from all the rest of the Christian world combined. Inevitably the popes acted more and more as Italian princes.

The century closed with the reign of the most remarkable and unregenerate of all the occupants of the papal throne. Although belonging to the Spanish house of Borja (Italian, Borgia), Pope Alexander VI confirmed all the tendencies of his predecessors. Under him Rome became one of the greatest centres of patronage in the arts. In addition, the papal states were brought more completely under control than ever before through the military activities of his son, Cesare Borgia.

With the active encouragement of his father, Cesare Borgia, the last of the great *condottieri* and a cardinal at the age of seventeen, conquered the cities of the Romagna and was made Duke of Romagna by his father. Cesare, often considered the perfect model of the Renaissance prince, because of his reckless yet intelligent use of treachery and brutality to further his own ends, showed his utter ruthlessness by the murder of his chief opponents, who, he convened for this purpose at the castle of Sinigaglia.

His territorial acquisitions were crowned by the conquest of the duchy of Urbino and other small states, but his attempt to win complete independence of the papacy was defeated by the implacable opposition of

Pope Julius II. Julius, came to the papal throne soon after the death of Cesare's father, drove Cesare from Italy and incorporated his extensive possessions into the papal states. Thus, by the end of the fifteenth century the once great universal power of Rome was becoming increasingly identified with the ambitions and policies of an Italian territorial state.

Florence

Florence, aggressively proud of its republican institutions, entered the fifteenth century as an independent state, after having beaten off an attack from the powerful and ambitious Duke of Milan, Giangaleazzo Visconti. In its life-and-death struggle, Florence needed all the friends it could get and attempted to woo the smaller towns by posing as their defender against the machinations of the Milanese. Owing to a number of circumstances, not least among them the expertise of their English *condottieri,* Giovanni Acuto (Sir John Hawkwood), the Florentines fought off their enemy and saved their republic, although they had to face a renewed Milanese threat in the first decades of the fifteenth century.

Within a generation they had revealed their quality as the defenders of liberty by their subjugation, after a bloody and ruthless war (1496–09), of the important coastal state of Pisa. Within another generation they were to find even their own liberties circumscribed by the family of the Medici and its first great representative, Cosimo I. Honoured with the title of 'Father of his Country' throughout his long period of power Cosimo never held any official post of real authority in Florence but used the wealth and power of his family to win an unshakeable grip on the republican institutions of which his fellow citizens were so proud.

The rise of the Medici was the final episode in the struggle of the powerful families of semi-aristocratic oligarchs whose strength rested on their commercial enterprises. In 1434 Cosimo dei Medici returned to Florence with popular support from a twelve-month exile and expelled the rival family of the Albizzi. The success of Cosimo rested partly on the skill with which he manipulated the organs of government in his own interest and partly on the way in which he exploited his control of affairs to weaken the positions of his rivals. A typical means was the graduated income tax (the *castato*), which not only eased the burden of the poorest sections of the community but also seemed to rest most heavily on the wealthy family opposed to the Medici. But perhaps the most important ingredient in Cosimo's success, and the basis of his family's future greatness, was the assiduity with which he furthered the advance of the family bank. It has in fact been suggested that one of the elements in the decline of the bank towards the end of the century was the inadequate control exercised over it by his grandson Lorenzo the Magnificent.

The Medici banking system

During this period Florence was the centre of the Europen banking system and the Medici branches at Milan, Naples, Pisa and Venice in Italy, at Geneva, Lyons and Avignon in central Europe, and at Bruges and London in the north played an essential role in the system of European trade. Legally each of the branches was a separate entity and the man in charge of each branch could not necessarily expect any debts he might incur to be borne by the parent company. After the death of his friend and debtor, Charles the Bold of Burgundy, in 1478 Tommaso Portinari, the flamboyant and unsound controller of the Bruges company found himself abandoned to his creditors by Lorenzo, whom he had already involved in considerable loss.

This episode reveals one of the chief weaknesses of the Medici structure. At the top was the head of the family assisted by his general manager as chief adviser and director, next came the heads of the branches who were, in effect, junior partners with the family and operated as autonomous entities. The whole operation depended on their integrity and competence. Consequently, in the absence of auditors, everything rested on the skill of the head of the firm in selecting his branch managers and also in detecting discrepancies in the often falsified books sent each year to the head office.

Like any banking system the Medici organization played a vital part in European trade by arranging transfers of credit over long distances without the need actually to shift bullion from one place to another. The aspect of the Medici operations was of particular value to the papacy. During most of the fifteenth century the Medici acted as bankers to the popes and so important was this business to them that they even opened temporary branches at Constance and Basle for the duration of the councils there.

The pope might sometimes discharge debts he had incurred with the Medici by granting them the annates paid by a bishop

Above, Sir John Hawkwood, an English mercenary who served as a notable condottiere *in Italy between 1362 and 1394. He was known as Giovanni Acuto and was most often employed by Florence. This portrait was painted by Uccello.*

Above left, fourteenth-century panorama of the city of Florence, dominated by the octagonal Baptistery. As the main centre for cloth trading in southern Europe, as well as a banking centre, Florence was both large and powerful. Loggia del Bigallo, Florence.

Opposite, Cesare Borgia (1476–1507), the son of Pope Alexander VI. An illness in 1503, possibly caused by poison, destroyed his hopes for an independent duchy in north Italy, and his lands became incorporated into the Papal States. Accademai de Belle Arti, Bergamo.

on the first year's income of his see. In 1448 the Cardinal Archbishop of York received a remarkable letter from the pope's bankers in which they informed him that they held the bull appointing his nephew to the see of London but would regretfully have to return it to Rome if the annates were not paid within the month.

On his succession to his father in 1464, Cosimo's son, Piero di Cosimo, ordered a general review of the bank's position and this led to a policy of retrenchment and the calling in of debts. Tightening of credit by the Medici restricted funds in all Florentine business associations, and in fact a number of companies with interests in the Levant failed at this time. This was probably because of increasing Turkish hostility, but Florence blamed Piero and the Medici bank. When the London branch decided to call in its debts and to withhold credit facilities from Edward IV, the king prohibited the export of English wool to Florence. Starved of its raw material, the woollen industry had to dismiss workers and the resulting unemployment caused increased popular discontent with the Medici.

Lorenzo the Magnificent

In the future men were to look back on the time of Cosimo as a golden age. The nobles grumbled at the domination of the powerful family, the populace sometimes attributed their financial troubles to the Medici bank's conduct of its affairs, and the businessmen complained against the level of taxation (one half percent of taxable income) as a gross imposition and a disincentive to initiative. Nevertheless, the state had enjoyed a long period of external and internal peace. Cosimo's realistic alliance with the Sforza of Milan contributed to international stability and was an important check to the ambitions of Venice. By his determination to defend the interests of the bank, his son Piero had made the family highly unpopular, and there had been two conspiracies against him. Nevertheless, Piero had fully maintained the family's position and, on his death, he was able to leave it intact to his two young sons Lorenzo and Giuliano. Later Lorenzo was to record (somewhat ingenuously it may be thought) the events leading to his 'accession'.

The second day after my father's death, although I, Lorenzo, was very young, being about twenty years of age, the principal men of the city came to us in our house . . . to encourage me to the charge of the state. This I did, though on account of my youth and the great responsibility and perils arising therefrom, with great reluctance, solely for the safety of our friends and our possessions. *For it is ill living in Florence for the rich unless they rule the state.*

Lorenzo was well aware of the need to keep his popularity with the citizens as a body and also to maintain close connections with the other powerful families of Florence. In this he followed the precedent by arranging dynastic marriages which linked the Medici with their old enemies the Rucellai and even with their great rivals, the Pazzi.

In his handling of the revolt of the subject town of Volterra, however, Lorenzo stirred up hostility. The trouble grew out of a dispute over the ownership of the alum mine which had been controlled by a Florentine company but in 1471 had been taken over by the Volterrans. Lorenzo's decision to settle the matter by force, taken just as negotiations seemed likely to succeed, was a mistake and was opposed by some city councillors. The sack of Volterra which followed when his troops got out of hand ensured that the town became a natural refuge for all future malcontents.

If opposition could be overcome, it could not be eliminated and in 1478 it almost gained its objective. Lorenzo had come into conflict with the pope, Sixtus IV, and, pursuing his feud against the family, the latter gave his support to the attempted *coup d'état* organized by the Pazzi family who aimed to expel the Medici and take over their banking interests. The move was to be initiated by the murder of the Medici brothers in the cathedral at Florence during the Easter service of April 1478. Giuliano was in fact killed and, although Lorenzo escaped and rallied the citizens of Florence against his enemies, his position was critical. Matters were coming to a head at the Bruges banking company and Sixtus appropriated the property of the Rome branch, expelled its agent and repudiated his debts. Even so, after three years of conflict, the pope was obliged to come to terms with his enemy and reinstate him as papal banker.

Lorenzo's victory seemed to be complete and in 1484 death relieved him of his arch-enemy, the pope. But the affairs of the bank continued to deteriorate and in his later years Lorenzo saw his family threatened with bankruptcy. To avert the danger he even diverted money from the public funds of the city. The worst was staved off but in 1492, two years after his death, the democratic party in Florence, taking advantage of the disruption of Italian affairs caused by the French invasion, were able to expel the government of his son.

The Medici as patrons

Throughout later medieval European history the courts of princes and kings were, with the Church, the richest and most important centres of patronage for the high arts.

Fifteenth-century Italy witnessed the establishment of numerous aristocratic courts. The court of Naples had, from the previous century, been one of Europe's greatest centres of cultural activity. During the fifteenth century the papal court began to play an increasingly important role as patron, and outside the centres of the other greater states (Florence, Milan and Naples) there were numerous important centres of patronage such as Urbino, Mantua and Ferrara.

The most famous of Renaissance courts was nevertheless that of Lorenzo de' Medici, called the Magnificent. The reputation of the Medici family as patrons had been founded by Lorenzo's grandfather Cosimo. Under his aegis the great names of the early Florentine renaissance had flourished (men such as Donatello, Ghiberti and Brunelleschi) and he had commissioned a translation of recently discovered Platonic texts by the humanist Marsilio Ficino.

The other great names who enjoyed the patronage of Lorenzo were Botticelli, Michelangelo, Verrochio and Ghirlandaio, and in literature Poliziano, one of the prince's closest friends. Lorenzo himself was a considerable poet, delighting above all in the beauties of nature and the Tuscan countryside. He always wrote in the vernacular Tuscan and even composed songs in the metres of popular verse and on popular themes.

At the court of Lorenzo, the mysticism of Egypt, the wisdom of Greece, the common people of Florence and to devotional literature of popular religion were all fit sources of inspiration. The romances of chivalry which were the theme of *Morgante Orlando* by one of the court poets, Luigi Pulci, were particularly favoured. The story of Roland provided the inspiration of the great contemporary poet at the court of Ferrara, Matteo Boiardo, and the Arthurian legends were to find a sympathetic echo at Lorenzo's court. The cult of chivalry, revived with such splendour and with such hopes north of the Alps, formed yet another strand in the varied texture of Italian court life. If other aspects now seem more important in

the fabric of European civilization, to contemporaries these knightly observances were evidence of a common heritage in the noble traditions of Christendom.

Industry and commerce

Commerce was the mainstay of Italian prosperity as a whole, but industry was also immensely important. As early as the thirteenth century the silks of Lucca had gained a European reputation, at the same time as Venice and Florence were establishing factories. In many towns the art of the armourer was a vital and profitable business, but nowhere so much as in Milan, famed in Italy and far beyond for the quality of its work. The size of the Milanese industry may be gauged from the fact that in the early fifteenth century two of the city's master armourers were able to equip a force of 4,000 cavalry and 200 infantry at a few days' notice.

Perhaps the largest single industrial enterprise in fifteenth-century Italy was the arsenal at Venice. By the end of the century this state-run shipyard covered an area of some sixty acres and produced the war galleys of the republic's navy as well as building commercial vessels which were leased to private merchants. The activity at the arsenal represented only a part of the total output of Venetian shipyards, but it is particularly interesting because it was a true state enterprise, being financed out of public funds and employing full-time officials and technical advisers. The labour force was, of course, recruited as required but, although the wages might often be lower than work in private shipbuilding, the output of the arsenal was about six to eight galleys a year, making employment more secure.

Italy was not entirely without raw materials of its own. From the second part of the fifteenth century alum was the most important of these. This was an essential chemical agent in the manufacture of glass, the preparation and tanning of leather and, above all, as a mordant in the dyeing of cloth. Until 1460 the highest-quality alum was imported by Genoa from Turkish Anatolia, subject to the payment of a toll. When, however, large deposits were found at Tolfa near Civitavecchia in the papal states and, a decade later, still larger deposits at Volterra, the situation changed.

The popes immediately set about exploiting this new source of wealth, farming out the mining operation itself to the Medici. Then, by setting aside the proceeds of this toil for the purposes of a crusade, they claimed the right to a monopoly, despite the prohibitions of canon law.

The Medici's mining interests also extended to the iron-ore mines on Elba. Not only did they provide a banking service but could also procure virtually anything which

Above, the Battle of San Romano, painted by Uccello in about 1451, demonstrates the warfare of late fifteenth-century Italy. War was dominated by mercenary bands of condottieri *who could be hired by the highest bidder and did their utmost to ensure that battles were won and lost with as little bloodshed as possible. Musée du Louvre, Paris.*

Opposite, a mural of Siena's finances in times of war and peace. Siena was one of the richest Italian cities in the fifteenth century and managed to stay independent of its powerful neighbour Florence. Palazzo Publicco, Siena.

a customer might demand. Their services included boy singers for the papal choir from the renowned choir school at Cambrai, Flemish tapestries for Italian clients (either ready made or tailor-made to designs drawn up by Italian artists) and panel paintings by Flemish artists for the Italian markets. Moreover, all over Europe the agents of Italian merchant houses were on the look out for ancient manuscripts of the classics—we hear of one buying a manuscript of the Roman writer Pliny from the Dominican monks of Lübeck.

The variety of Italian commercial and industrial activity was immense and it was dominated by the large textile industry of Florence. Florence and Flanders virtually divided the market for fine cloths between them, although the growing cloth industry of England was providing serious competition and compelling a search for new sources of wool.

Despite its sizeable output the industry was mainly a cottage one. Many of the operations in the processing of wool, and in silk also, such as spinning, weaving and fulling, were put out to families working in their own homes, the women doing the spinning, the men the weaving. The intermediaries between the managers and the workmen were the foremen called *capo dieci*. They toured the cottages and outlying villages in the region, distributing the raw material and collecting the finished work and ensuring that the workmen did not substitute poor-quality materials for those originally provided. The looms were often bought from the manufacturer on what would now be called hire-purchase terms, and payment in kind rather than money was often the rule. The city was governed by the merchant guilds. Working men's associations of all kinds were banned.

The social order

The artisans who provided the labour force of industry and the small traders together made up the so-called *popolo minuto*. Despite their rebellions in the fourteenth century, they were never able effectively to throw off the government of the powerful merchants and entrepreneurs (the *popolo grasso*).

In Italy as a whole there was no clear distinction between aristocratic families and the greater merchants. From an early period nobles had entered commerce and merchants had invested their surplus profits in land. Most merchants spent a period of their youth abroad, but the aim was to return to the city as soon as possible. Moralists inveighed against the dangers of the merchant's spending his time away from home, but in fact the Italian merchant almost always married a girl from his own town.

For the upper classes marriage was an important event and brought heavy commitments. The beautiful *cassone* or marriage chests of the period were often decorated by the greatest artists of the day. The all-important matter of the dowry gave rise to a unique form of insurance, the so-called *monte del dote*. The father would begin paying premiums at the birth of a girl and the policy matured when she had reached the age of fifteen. If however she should die, the policy lapsed and the sum paid in premiums remained with the state. In Italy, as elsewhere in Europe, the rich lived in great state and the demand for domestic servants could probably not have been met had it not been for the large slave population.

Slavery

A slave was a natural member of any moderately well-off household in southern Europe and would frequently be found in clerical as well as lay establishments. In 1488 Pope Innocent VIII received a gift of 100 slaves, which he distributed among his cardinals. The Church tolerated slavery as a necessary evil, reasoning that the body might be in chains but the soul, the immortal part of man, nevertheless remained free. Between 1414 and 1423, 10,000 slaves passed through the market on the Venetian Rialto alone. Most of them came from territories under Infidel control which had been conquered from the Byzantine Empire.

In theory the Church forbade the selling of Christian slaves to the Infidel and endowed the children of Christian freemen with the right to buy back their liberty after a fixed term. In practice both these rulings were ignored and the Genoese in particular did a flourishing trade with the Tartar khans. On the market these unfortunate captives were true slaves in every sense of the word. Their faces were cut with identifying marks, they were, like any other object of commerce, insured against damage, although insurance policies specifically excluded damage by suicide. A female slave lost value if she were pregnant and a Florentine statute of 1452 ordained a fine or death by hanging for the seduction of another man's slave. Of course slaves could expect harsh punishments for any misdemeanours but, on the whole, their treatment must have been fairly lenient, since the housholders often found their slaves as much a threat as a convenience. Petrarch called them 'the domestic enemy'.

Warfare

Inter-city warfare was an endemic condition in medieval Italy. Rival commercial interest and aristocratic factions were the main causes.

Two special features shaped the evolution of political theory and practice of Italy. First was the absence of any feudal aristocracy governed by a recognized code of hierarchical subordination and headed by a supreme overlord, whether a king or prince. Second, there was the absence of any form of higher sanction, represented in other parts of Europe by the consecration ceremony of the coronation. Nothing could conceal the fact that in the north Italian plain the sole arbitrator of legitimacy was force.

However, the busy populations of the thriving cities could not spare essential, productive manpower for the conduct of these wars, and to meet the demand there grew up in the fourteenth century a class of professional commanders, the *condottieri.* They were, in effect, military contractors recruiting their men from the poorer part of Italy itself or from the floating population of soldiers of fortune who made up the ranks of the 'free companies' enlisted for the perennial struggles of the Hundred Years War in France. The profession of commander could earn a man not only considerable wealth but also respect, occasionally a principality and even (in the case of Baldassare Cossa) the papacy itself. The most famous of these mercenaries turned princes was Francesco Sforza who, as the result of his marriage to the illegitimate daughter of Filippo Maria, the last of the Visconti dukes, finally succeeded in winning control of Milan and assumed the much coveted title of duke in 1450.

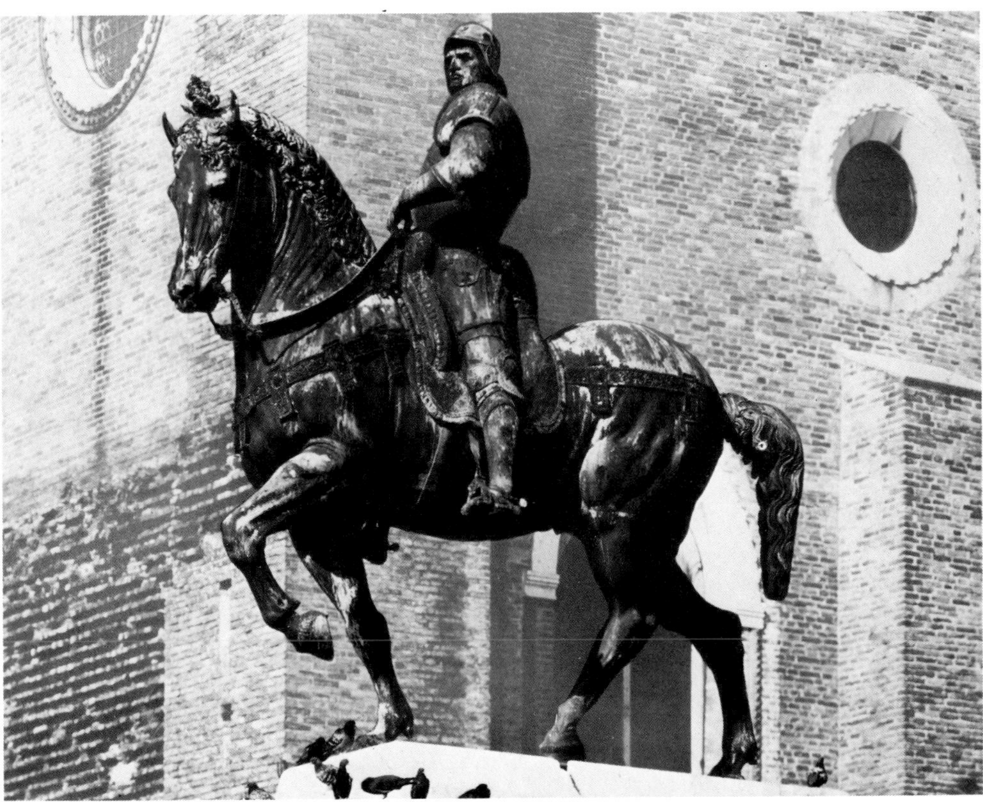

Milan

The vast extent and considerable power of the state which Sforza inherited were largely a result of the ambitions of the first great ruler of the Visconti family, Giangaleazzo, who died in 1402. His family had emerged in the late thirteenth century as the successful contenders in a typical conflict of aristocratic and merchant factions. The founder of the family's fortunes, Archbishop Ottone Visconti, had secured the election of his nephew Matteo as 'captain of the people'.

After a ten-year period of exile, Matteo was able to re-establish himself and have the term of his elective office gradually extended and its powers increased, with the result that the hereditary governorship of Milan remained with the Visconti for the next 130 years. Matteo had tried to bestow an aura of legitimacy on his position by buying the title of 'imperial vicar' from the emperor. Almost exactly a hundred years later, in 1395, his great descendant Giangaleazzo, purchased the still more exalted title of duke.

During the fourteenth century the Visconti lords of Milan had extended their territories through the 'voluntary' submission of their weaker neighbours, through intrigue, marriage and occasionally conquest. Thus when Giangaleazzo became sole ruler in 1385, after the murder of his uncle Bernabo, he exercised, through a variety of titles, direct authority over a united territory stretching from the Alps in the north down to the frontiers of the republic of Genoa, and from the frontier with Savoy in the west to the territory of Verona in the east.

It was a considerable area but it was only during the reign of Giangaleazzo that Milan seriously threatened the patchwork pattern of Italian politics. He extended his sway over Bologna, theoretically in the papal states, and for twenty years even established the Visconti supremacy over the lordship of Verona, where he overthrew the Della Scala family. His campaign against Florence has already been mentioned and, with his conquest of Verona, he aroused a still more powerful enemy in Venice, its eastern neighbour.

From the first, the Visconti had discounted the feeble opposition of republican Milan, which became more of a dictatorship than any of the other Italian states. The Visconti dukes had pursued a consistent and persistent policy of foreign aggrandisement and, perhaps most important of all, they enjoyed a far more complete control of the revenues of the state than their republican opponents, for whom any sizeable expenditure was only possible with the authorization of various municipal bodies. To these practical advantages may be added the memories of the Lombard kingdom of the eighth century to lend shape to Milan's ambition and the absence of any natural frontiers south of the Alps to impose bounds upon it. But after the death of Giangaleazzo the city was forced on the defensive by the Venetian conquest of Verona, the resistance of the Florentines and the overthrow of Visconti power in Bologna.

Like the dukes of Burgundy, those of Milan held power through a variety of titles and, like them, they evolved a remarkably efficient system of central administration, with a salaried bureaucracy to control matters of finance and jurisdiction and a body of lieutenants in the provincial centres. Sforza tightened the central hold on local matters still further and also strengthened the military organization of his newly won state. There was, however, one other important weapon in the armoury of the Milanese dukes one on which they spent heavily: diplomacy. The techniques and

Above, the coronation of Giangaleazzo Visconti as the first Duke of Milan in 1395. The cathedral of Milan was begun during his reign. Biblioteca de la Basilica de St Ambroise, Milan.

Top, the Colleoni Monument in Venice, made in the 1480s by Andrea del Verrocchio, commemorating one of the most notable condottieri *of the age.*

Opposite, a fresco from the Palazzo Communale at Siena painted in the late 1330s by Ambrogio Lorenzetti, depicting the allegory of good government. Palazzo Communale, Siena.

organization of modern diplomacy were, to all intents and purposes, worked out and developed in later medieval Italy.

The birth of diplomacy

For the reasons outlined above it may be said that the first true secular states of modern Europe developed in Italy. Because of their comparatively small size and considerable wealth they evolved as fully centralised and articulate units earlier than the large but incohesive kingdoms in the rest of continental Europe. Nor were the Italian rulers troubled with the revered and divisive traditions of feudal legalism. What they could hold was theirs. The situation in fifteenth-century France, where there could be genuine doubt as to the relative merits of the rival claims of the kings of England and France, would have been unthinkable in contemporary Italy.

In the patchwork of European sovereignties communications between rulers had developed considerably during the Middle Ages, and the leisurely and splendid progress of a special embassy was a common enough sight on the roads of Europe. Conventions about the conduct of such embassies were gradually being established. The formal entry into the presence of the monarch was one of the most important parts of the ambassador's proof of his credentials. Behind the ceremony lay the influence of Byzantine diplomatic practice, but fourteenth-century Europe, particularly Italy, was evolving its own procedures.

In these procedures the formal address or oration by the ambassador was very important. The men of the period had strong convictions about the power of words and an elegant, powerful and convincing opening address by the ambassador or orator could have a great impact on the host state. Consequently, the position of orator gained considerable prestige and the art of oratory was intensively cultivated. For a state in the predicament of late-fourteenth-century Florence the eloquence of its representatives was of special significance, and from that time the post of public orator was held by a succession of scholars expert in the increasingly popular study of the Latin of Cicero.

These humanists, as they came to be known, continued to enjoy official encouragement both for their services to the state and also for their studies. A direct connection can thus be seen between the birth of a new movement in European thought and scholarship and the political exigencies of determined statesmen. It is, however, more significant for the study of the history of European diplomacy to notice another development of the late fourteenth century in Italy. This was the establishment by some towns of permanent embassies for a period of years, a practice which increased during the fifteenth century and was given a special impetus by the events of the Milanese wars.

Fighting to establish himself in the duchy of his father-in-law, Francesco Sforza dispatched his agents throughout the length and breadth of Italy. The other states followed suit and all soon established permanent representation at Rome, a court which endeavoured to remain neutral in the Sforza dispute and consequently became the natural listening post for the combatants. The states of Italy were compact, powerful, aggressive and unavoidably close to one another. The distances between capitals were small and well within the scope of contemporary methods of transport. It was possible to be in almost daily touch with events at the capitals of one's neighbours and, since they might well become enemies at a moment's notice, it was important to keep in contact. Forerunners for resident ambassadors were no doubt to be found in the consuls who had for a long time protected the interests of Italian merchants abroad and, of course, in the agents of the banking houses. By the year 1500 every Italian state of any size had its permanent agents at the capitals of its main rivals and at least one non-Italian ruler, Ferdinand of Aragon, had begun to adopt this new weapon for international affairs.

The rise of Venice

Called the 'city of the lagoons' and the 'queen of the seas', Venice reached the apogee of its power in the first half of the fifteenth century. Its problems, like those of its great rival, Genoa, were not the same as those which faced the other towns of Italy. Until the fifteenth century Venice had not seriously concerned itself with the intercity rivalries which set its neighbours at one another's throats in the struggle for the control of land and the extension of their power over one another. Growing out of settlements on the cluster of islands at the head of the Adriatic, Venice had in the tenth century provided asylum for refugees fleeing from the invasions of the Magyars. The isolation from the mainland which had been its salvation then was to mark its history for the next 500 years.

The wealth of Venice rested on the trade which flowed through the city on its way from the east and Constantinople to the markets of northern Italy and Europe. As early as the tenth century the desire to protect these routes from piracy had led the Venetians to extend their sway over the communities of the Dalmatian coast. This essentially commercial impetus pushed Venetian power further south and east during the following centuries, until the city-controlled islands of the Aegean had established garrisons on the island of Crete and had even attempted to break into the Black Sea. In all these enterprises the cooperation of the Byzantine emperors could be of decisive importance and the embattled opposition of the republic of Genoa could be guaranteed.

During the twelfth century the Genoese, through the favour which they enjoyed at the court of Constantinople, seemed to threaten the existence of Venetian trade in the Levant. The decision to divert the armies of the Fourth Crusade to the sack of Constantinople in 1204 was the result of the self-interest of the Venetians, who provided the Crusaders with their transport. Not unnaturally, the Latin emperors established by the overthrow of Byzantium revoked the privileges of Genoa and fostered Venetian interests.

Even the cynical connivance at the destruction of the frontier post of Christendom was not enough, however, to guarantee Venice's position in the Levant. When, in 1261, the Byzantine Empire was re-established with Genoese help, the war between the Italian republics was renewed with all its former vigour, the advantage lying once again with Genoa. In addition, the new power of the Ottoman Turks provided a growing threat to all the Christian interests in the area. Although Venice had not previously hesitated to trade with the Arabs, this new champion of Islam was less amenable to the arguments of mutual self-interest.

The Genoese threat increased until in the 1370s a Genoese fleet under the great admiral Doria attacked Venice itself and came within an ace of victory. Only a supreme effort inspired by patriotic fervour enabled the 'queen of the seas' to retain even its independence. The War of Chioggia of 1379, so called after the Venetian port which the Genoese occupied for a time, was seen by later generations as the turning point in the struggle between Venice and Genoa.

However, the Venetians now found themselves threatened from another quarter by the massive expansion of the duchy of Milan under Giangaleazzo Visconti. The war between the two states, which went on for some seventy years, was the dominating feature of northern Italian politics until it was resolved at the general peace of Lodi in 1454. This left Venice deeply entrenched in former Visconti territories, ruling the towns of Bergamo and Brescia, and with its western frontier reaching even to Lake Como. Venice was now fully committed to involvement with the politics of Italy proper.

In 1425 Venice had allied with Florence against the threat from Filippo Maria Visconti, and the alliance lasted until in 1451, when Cosimo de' Medici, fearing the increasing power of Venice, switched Florentine support to the new ruler of Milan, Francesco Sforza. The death of Filippo Maria Visconti without legitimate issue in 1447 had sparked off a number of tentative rebellions throughout the Milanese state and there seemed nothing to halt Venetian advance through the lands of its old rival. Venice was brought to accept Sforza as Duke of Milan only after seven more years and then only in the context of a general Italian peace.

It was not merely by chance that the main Italian states joined in a common pact to preserve the internal peace of the country and defend it from all corners in the year after the fall of Constantinople. The capture of the Christian capital on the Bosporus is regarded by some historians as the turning point in the creation of the Ottoman Empire out of an army of conquest. It is therefore not fanciful to say that in 1453 the folly of the sack of Constantinople in 1204 was finally brought home to the Venetians. From then on Venice, together with other Mediterranean powers, found itself engaged in an even more fierce struggle with the new Turkish power.

Alone among the states of Italy, Venice had a regime whose legitimacy in the strictest legal terms was not open to serious question. The office of doge (derived from the Latin *dux*—'leader' or 'general') had a history stretching back to the earliest days of the republic in the tenth century. Until the twelfth century the doges (elected for life) had exerted an almost royal power, but subsequently their real authority was circumscribed just as their ceremonial splendour increased. Some doges, notably Marino Falieri and Francesco Foscari, made isolated attempts to reverse this tendency but without permanent success. There grew up an oligarchic constitution, dominated by the great aristocratic merchant families whose strength and stability were the envy of many an Italian ruler.

The main legislative body was the Great Council, constituted exclusively of aristocrats and with a membership of close to 1,000. Nevertheless, true executive power rested with much smaller specialist bodies grouped together in a Lesser Council of the Senate. Supreme power in the state was held by the Committee of Ten, which was first set up in 1310 with the functions of a 'committee of public safety' and from 1335 was established as a permanent organ of state. The committee controlled an extensive system of secret police which operated at all levels of the life of the republic and from whose attentions not even the aristocracy or the doge himself could feel free.

To a modern observer it may seem that when the sixteenth century opened Venice was already set on the path to decline. But to contemporaries the republic appeared unshakeably established. The longevity and apparent strength of its political institution were unequalled in Italy. The dignity and splendour of the ceremonial which surrounded its head of state, and which were displayed in all their glory at the annual marriage of the city to the sea, echoed the splendours of Byzantium where they had found their source. The brilliance and magnificence of the city, crowned by the great church of St Mark, were persuasive testimonies to its wealth.

The enemies of Italy

Although there were many independent political units in the Italian peninsula the Italians themselves had a strong sense of communal 'nationhood' (using the medieval sense of nation) against the foreign powers. This sense was fostered by the movement of scholars and artists among the towns, by the political attempts to establish general peace throughout Italy during the years following the Peace of Lodi and, not least, by the threat of foreign intervention. The

Above, the port of Genoa as it appeared in 1493. Despite having a flourishing trade, and providing some of Italy's most successful condottieri, *Genoa was subservient to France or Milan until the 1530s.*

Opposite left, Venice in the mid-fifteenth century according to the painter Carpaccio, still a great port, and a major political power in the north of Italy. Accademia, Venice.

Opposite right, Venice in 1480, with shipyards in the foreground; Venice's shipbuilding industry was remarkable and contributed significantly to the city's trading wealth.

King of France, the King of Aragon and the Holy Roman Emperor all held claims in Italy of varying weight. The claims of the medieval Holy Roman Empire had received a renewed stimulus from the Visconti purchase of the ducal title of Milan from the Holy Roman emperor Wenceslas. His Habsburg successor, Frederick III, whose long reign was among the least glorious in the annals of the empire, nevertheless performed a valuable service for his successors by refusing to relinquish the theory of imperial suzerainty. Without any power to enforce his will, Frederick consistently refused to recognize the Sforza usurpation of the title of Duke of Milan. When his son, Maximilian, married a daughter of one of the Sforza dukes, imperial interest in Milan became more active.

The Spanish interest in Italy was even greater. Alfonso V, the Magnanimous, of Aragon had ruled over the kingdoms of Aragon, Sicily and Naples, but on his death in 1458 these dominions were divided at his wish between his illegitimate son, Ferrante, to whom he left Naples, and his brother, John II, who became King of Sicily and Aragon. John and to an even greater degree his son, Ferdinand, regarded their claims as the legitimate line to be just as valid as those of Ferrante and were determined, whatever else might happen, to oppose French ambitions in Naples.

French ambitions in Italy, in fact, presented the greatest dangers. Through the marriage of Louis of Orléans to Valentina Visconti in the late fourteenth century his descendants laid claim to the duchy of Milan. On the other hand, the House of Anjou had venerable claims to the kingdom of Naples and Sicily. For the first fifty years of the fifteenth century there was no question of serious French attempts to push these claims, although René of Anjou had devoted much of his life to asserting his rights in Naples. But, with the ending of the English menace and the accession of Louis XI French interests in Italy once again became active and they were increasingly accepted by the Italian rulers themselves as part of the Italian situation. Indeed, they came to play on the possibility of French intervention with astonishing unconcern and used the threat of an alliance with France against one another.

There were three major French interventions in Italy. The first occasion was during the war of Ferrara in which Venice, fighting to establish itself in the territories of that city, found itself opposed both by Milan and Naples. In their search for allies the Venetians unhesitatingly offered their assistance both to the Duke of Lorraine, the Angevin claimant to Naples, and to the Duke of Orléans if they would come to Italy to vindicate their families' rights there. The second of these diplomatic forays quickly induced Sforza to drop his opposition to Venice and in the peace settlement which decided the matter of Ferrara the Venetians made substantial gains.

The second invitation to France came from Pope Innocent VIII. In 1485, the year after Venice's triumph, he decided to assert his rights as suzerain over the kingdom of Naples by forcing King Ferrante to resume the payment of tribute and to meet the demands of his barons whose cause the pope had espoused. In this conflict, as in many others, Lorenzo de' Medici exerted all his powers and considerable influence to bring about a reconciliation between pope and king. His efforts were successful, but not before the pope had invited the Angevin Duke of Lorraine to march on Naples and claim his kingdom.

Within ten years the French invasion, used so freely as a diplomatic counter by the Italians, became a reality. The issue again involved Naples, but this time in its dealings with Milan. Lorenzo had been dead two years and the states of Italy were powerless to avert the invasion. This was no doubt partly because no Italian statesman had the stature or influence of the dead Lorenzo but chiefly because the French armies were now led by the king in person. The weak but young Charles VIII, eager for glory, had inherited the claims of Anjou.

Milan and France

On his death in 1446 Francesco Sforza was succeeded by his eldest son, the cruel but highly intelligent and cultured Galeazzo Maria. Under him the court of Milan took on a new brilliance, epitomized on his visit to Florence in 1471. His patronage of such men as the architect Bramante set a pattern which was to be followed by his brother, the great Lodovico. Although a capable ruler and the firm ally of Florence in defence of the peace of Italy, Galeazzo provoked violent hostility among the younger members of the aristocracy nostalgic for the long-lost days of the republic. During the Christmas festivities of 1476 he was assassinated. Although the citizenry as a whole united in proclaiming his young son Gian Galeazzo the new duke, Milan was to be torn by civil conflict during the following years.

The conflict was resolved only in 1480, when the dead duke's brother, Lodovico il Moro (so-called because of his dark complexion), succeeded in wresting the regency from the duchess. From that time onwards he was ruler of the city, holding his young nephew in close confinement. When Gian Galeazzo died in 1494 his uncle officially succeeded to the duchy and, indeed, was the first Sforza to enjoy the official recognition by the Holy Roman emperor of his title. Under him and his wife, Beatrice d'Este, Milan attained a new stature among the centres of Italian patronage. From 1482 it was the home of the great Leonardo da Vinci, enticed from his native Florence by an invitation to build a statue to the new duke's father, the great Francesco Sforza.

Lodovico sought to establish his position by the marriage of his daughter to Emperor Maximilian I, but he was under continual threat from the ambitions of the young duke's wife, Isabella of Aragon, and her Neapolitan relations. The danger from Naples led Lodovico into the classic strategy of Italian diplomacy—alliance with France—and it was with his support that Charles VIII of France marched into Italy in 1494 to claim the kingdom of Naples. The barbarian was finally within the gates.

Milan's immediate danger was averted, but Lodovico, now fully aware of the drawbacks of a permanent French presence in Italy, joined forces with the enemies of France, so that only a year later Charles was obliged to withdraw. The respite was, however, only temporary. The dam had been breached and the long history of European intervention in Italy had begun.

Charles died soon after his return to France, but the Italian enterprises remained the centre of his successors' ambitions. In 1499, taking up the other option available to French ambitions (the claim to the kingdom of Naples), the new King of France, Louis XII, attacked Milan and drove out Lodovico himself. France, the Holy Roman Empire and the Spanish kings now made Italy their battleground; and the popes, taking advantage of the turmoil, through their agent Cesare Borgia were able, as has been seen, to recover much of their former territories. Lodovico, whose attempt to return was foiled at the Battle of Novara, was not the only ruler to lose his throne.

Savonarola

The French invasion of 1494 had had repercussions throughout Italy, above all in Florence. After the death of the great Lorenzo, the traditional powers and privileges of the 'chief citizen' fell to his twenty-year-old son. In common with his ancestors, Lorenzo, however great his power, had been careful to maintain at least the forms of republicanism, giving due respect to the elected officers of the state and exercising his considerable wealth in ways which by and large benfited the city as a whole. His son, Piero, flaunted his position too much like an absolute ruler and quickly became unpopular.

The news of the impending French invasion obliged Florence to declare its interest. Largely for economic reasons, the city as a whole favoured the French. The senior advisers seem to have counselled supporting Naples against the invader in accordance with the spirit of Lodi. Piero followed this advice but his popular reputation sank still further when the consequent loss of the essential French trade brought large-scale unemployment. His attempt to put matters right by a hasty change of front in favour of France and the imprudent surrender of four Florentine fortresses to

Charles lost him all support among the city fathers and, on his return from the French court, he was obliged to flee.

The Medici power was at last broken and the Florentines, disillusioned by the last representative of aristocratic rule, set up a new republican constitution, with a grand council modelled on the Venetian institution and the most rigorous safeguards against the rise of another family of potential despots. With freedom, however, there returned the evils of delay and conflict which had marked the old republic, and the Medici were able to re-establish themselves in Florence within a generation.

During the first four years of its existence, the new republic was dominated by the figure of Savonarola, a Dominican friar. Born at Ferrara, he had first come to Florence at the age of thirty in 1481, as a member of the community of San Marco. At first his sermons were poorly attended and he visited other Italian cities, between periods at Florence, until he was finally recalled by Lorenzo, acting, it is thought, at the request of Pico della Mirandola.

From 1491 Savonarola was Prior of St Marks and from its pulpit enveighed against the corruptness of the Church and of Italian society. The most fiery and apocalyptic representative in a tradition of popular preaching, which included such names as San Bernadino of Siena at the beginning of the century, Savonarola now began to draw huge crowds. This was not only because of his traditional, if vehement, denunciations of the great in Church and state but also because of his prophesies of doom, which gained authority from the accuracy of his prediction of the death of Innocent VIII.

After the expulsion of Piero, Savonarola's influence, which was growing even in the Florence of Lorenzo himself, became immense. A great wave of religious fervour swept the city and the ceremonial 'burning of the vanities', which had precedents in the career of Bernadino, took place. Men and women threw treasured possessions and fashionable fripperies into the flames. Many works of art almost certainly perished too. Attempting to silence the friar's continuing attacks on him, Alexander VI forbade Savonarola to preach and then excommunicated him when he ignored the ban. Savonarola now declared the pope no true pope and when Rome threatened the city with interdict he was implored to stop preaching.

From the first there had been a considerable body of opposition to his influence and the riots which followed a public ceremony at which one of his followers was to prove the friar's holiness by ordeal provided a pretext for his arrest. Savonarola was tried by a papal commission which found him guilty of schism and heresy and he and two of his disciples were hanged and burned in the public square of Florence in 1498.

By declaring the pope an imposter, he may have been guilty of the charge of schism, but there is no hint of heresy in Savonarola's pronouncements. His attacks on the morals of Alexander VI were fully justified. He nowhere denied the office of pope, nor were his demands for church reform doctrinally suspect. But, in the violent world of Renaissance Italy, the penalty of failure was very often death.

Above, Ludovico il Moro, Duke of Milan (ruled 1494–99), with his family, praying to Mary and Jesus. Ludovico was a typical Italian Renaissance prince, intriguing for his political advancement and patronizing the arts lavishly. Pinaceoteca, Milan.

Part V

RENAISSANCE AND REFORMATION

Introduction

The late fifteenth and sixteenth centuries form a fascinating period. This is not only because of the great intellectual, artistic, religious and economic forces that arose within it and that have influenced our lives ever since but also because it is the first period of history we can visualize with any clarity.

It was a time when many people voiced feelings recognizably akin to our own. The mastery of realistic techniques in painting and sculpture enable us to see their faces, houses, towns and even, to some extent, the countryside of Renaissance Europe. Moreover, the survival of personal correspondence, the growing habit of writing self-revealing autobiographies and the preserving effect of printing further enrich our knowledge of the way in which people lived during this time.

Scholars, many artists even, were increasingly conscious that their achievements had to be measured against those of the ancient Greek and Roman civilizations. At the same time Europeans, who suffered invasion from the east and were threatened from North Africa by the Turks, extended their knowledge and control of the world through the great voyages of discovery. The traders and colonists were soon to follow and before long had reached southern Africa, the Americas, India, the East Indies and Japan. The unparalleled extension of knowledge and opportunity brought by these discoveries was as much a tribute to the imagination as it was to the courage and avarice of the men and the governments and merchant syndicates who backed them. Even the successes of space travel today are less inspiring, since the astronauts have more information before they set out and their discoveries can have less immediate effect on men's lives.

The people of that time also lived in a period of religious turmoil. Not since the adoption of Christianity in Europe had men engaged in such a profound rethinking of the nature of worship and the significance of religion in everyday life. We have to wait until modern times and the widespread acceptance of Marxism before we can find issues which caused as much dissension as those between Catholic and Protestant.

It was not, however, an age in which we should find ourselves readily at home. Scepticism was unusual, atheism, to the overwhelming majority, literally unthinkable. Yet we would recognize the cruelty and immoderation, the persecution of Jews, and the frightened intolerance of any minority view that threatened the political or economic *status quo*. Indeed, in some respects we are better able to understand the sadder aspects of the period because of the tensions of our own time. However, it must be realized that there had been no Industrial Revolution on a scale which as to alter the whole way of life of large numbers of men and women. Europe was still overwhelmingly an agrarian society and in this respect, as in religion, the nature of Renaissance life was radically different from our own, even though its most important cultural achievements were centred on the towns.

It was a period of flamboyant individuals (like those rivals Henry VIII and Francis I of France), of artists like Leonardo and Michelangelo, of writers whose names, like Machiavelli, have become slogans.

Treated briefly, the age must appear as one of constant, and frequently violent change. In politics we watch the changing fortunes of dynastic wars. Europe is transformed into an immense battleground, as Habsburg and Valois enlist the other western nations in their struggles. Italy, whose culture made it the most splendid and tempting prey found itself a victim of these campaigns, which were waged on a vaster scale than any conflict in previous times.

Italy was not, of course, a unified country. The peninsula contained a number of mutually jealous states which lived restlessly together and were incapable of forming lasting unions which could keep out the armies of France, Germany and Spain. However, this lack of unity between the states brought about an extraordinary diversity which greatly enriched Italian Renaissance culture. Within Italy were to be found states not only with different governments and social structures but also with varying intellectual attitudes. By the middle of the sixteenth century, though, only Venice and the Papal States had managed to retain their freedom. Milan and Naples were Spanish dependencies and Florence had been forced to change from a republic into a duchy ruled by the Medici family which was dependent, if not formally, on Spain.

Fifty years ago this was looked on as a disaster. The republican freedom of Florence was contrasted with its enslavement, and Italy was seen as a nation left faint and bleeding from the guns and lances of its cut-throat neighbours. Coupled with this view was the theory that the Italian Wars of 1494 had been responsible for spreading Italian civilization from the early sixteenth century. Thus the legend grew up that Italy had to die in order that the rest of Europe might live.

New evidence has disproved this legend as well as many others. 'Liberty' under the Florentine republic had scarcely a flavour of democracy, and the rule of Cosimo, the first duke of Tuscany, was on balance beneficial to his subjects. Moreover, Venice, though checked as an expansionist power, was neither grieviously maimed by war nor destroyed commercially by the Portuguese spice trade round the Cape of Good Hope to India.

Equally, the Alps had never proved a barrier to the transmission of Italian humanism and artistic ideas to the rest of Europe. Indeed, Italian culture itself owed much to the importation of new ideas from the north. Finally, in the sixteenth century Italy, far from dying, was the most potent cultural influence in Europe. The poets Ariosto and Tasso were more influential than Petrarch and Boccaccio, as were the painters Andrea del Sarto, Primaticcio and Titian in comparison with Masaccio and Botticelli. Likewise, the architect Palladio had more influence than Brunelleschi.

Chapter 18

The Renaissance

The word Renaissance can be interpreted in different ways. It is often used to describe a period of time, broadly the fifteenth and sixteenth centuries, in the history of Europe. Alternatively, it is applied more narrowly to a movement in literature, learning and the arts. This double usage has often led to confusion, for it has been wrongly assumed that everything that happened in the Renaissance as a period bore the imprint of the Renaissance as a cultural movement. In fact, the cultural Renaissance was not universal: it began in Florence in the fourteenth century and spread only gradually.

The word 'Renaissance', meaning rebirth, was first used by the great French historian, Jules Michelet, in 1855. In its Italian form, *rinascità,* it can be traced back to a work of 1550 by the Italian artist and art historian, Giorgio Vasari. But the idea of a cultural rebirth was expressed by a number of Italian authors in the fourteenth and fifteenth centuries. On the assumption that the fall of the Roman Empire had been followed by centuries of barbarism, they believed that they were witnessing a great revival of literature and the arts.

Boccaccio, writing in about 1350, claimed that the painter Giotto (*c.* 1266–1337) had 'restored to light this art which for many centuries had been buried under the errors of some who painted in order to please the eyes of the ignorant rather than to satisfy the intelligence of the experts'.

He praised Dante (1265–1321) for having restored dead poetry to life. The idea of rebirth was soon extended to sculpture, architecture and learning. Lorenzo Valla wrote.

I do not know why those arts which most closely approach the liberal ones—painting, sculpture, modelling, architecture—had been so long and so greatly in decline, and had almost (together with literature) died out altogether; nor why they have revived in this age, and so many good artists and writers appeared and flourished.

Below, The Holy Family *(1507) by Raphael; for a long time the purity of his drawing and the nobility of his figures led Raphael to be considered the greatest artist of the Renaissance. Staatsgemäldesammlungen, Munich.*

Bottom, Giuliano de Medici (1479–1516), painted by Botticelli; he was restored to Florence in 1512 and was a major patron of Michelangelo. Staatliche Museen zu Berlin.

Below left, The Wedding Feast of Nastagio degli Onesti and the daughter of Paulo Traversaro, *painted by Botticelli; its classical architecture reflects the preoccupations of the Renaissance designers.*

On page 226, The Adoration of the Kings, *a work of 1445 by Fra Angelico and Filippo Lippi.*

During the nineteenth century the Renaissance was given a much wider interpretation. Michelet described it as nothing less than 'the discovery of the world, the discovery of man', and in 1860 Jacob Burckhardt, the Swiss art historian, set out to capture the whole spirit of the Renaissance. In his classic work, *The Civilization of the Renaissance in Italy,* he argued that it was in Italy that man first became aware of himself as an individual and that this was because of the place occupied by despotism in the Italian political system. When this individualism was combined with a powerful and varied nature it produced the universal man of the Italian Renaissance and provided the driving force behind the discovery of the world and of the full nature of man. But exceptional individualism predisposed the Italian to wickedness and scepticism.

Burckhardt belonged to a school of historians who liked to regard every event or movement as possessing a well-defined character of its own. For him the Renaissance was an isolated phenomenon. Other nineteenth-century historians preferred to trace the links between events and movements. As medieval scholarship got under way it became clear that the concept of a cultural rebirth in the fourteenth century rested on a false assumption. Culture had not died with the fall of the Roman Empire. It was found that medieval civilization owed much to antiquity (e.g., Roman law and Christianity itself) and that medieval art was not as absurd as Vasari had imagined. The Middle Ages were not blanketed by religious uniformity and there had even been earlier Renaissances under Charlemagne and in the twelfth century.

Scholars are now agreed that the Renaissance was basically a revolution in thought which began in Italy during the fourteenth century. It was characterized by the formulation of a new educational programme—the humanities—intended to prepare young men for an active life of service to the community. The medium of instruction was a Latin purified of medieval barbarism by the study of classical writers. The study of ancient writings became regarded as essential to a full life. The humanities comprised grammar, rhetoric and style, literature, moral philosophy and history. But those who taught these subjects—the humanists—were not simply educators: they wrote for each other and their concern for moral problems led them into the public domain. Some assumed a neo-Platonic philosophy which placed man at the very centre of the universe. The visual arts inevitably reflected this philosophical movement.

The Renaissance began in Italy probably because of the unique conditions that existed there in the Middle Ages. These included the absence of any strong feudal monarchy, the importance of town life, the preponderance of Roman law, the wide use of Latin by the laity and the survival of many ancient buildings.

The Florentine Renaissance

The Renaissance can be said to have started in Florence in the fourteenth century. For centuries people had been taught to believe that the good life could be attained only by withdrawing from the world and its material wealth. The Florentines, however, put forward a different philosophy of life. They showed that an active life in the world and possession of wealth were not incompatible with virtue. At the same time they advocated a new programme of lay education centred upon the study of classical Latin literature. Whereas in the past this had been frowned upon as pagan, it was now avidly studied for its own sake, not simply as a means to an end.

All this happened in Florence probably for political reasons. From about 1385 until 1440 it was almost a beleaguered city. For twenty years its chief enemy was the Duke of Milan, Giangaleazzo Visconti, who died in 1402. The threat from Milan was followed by another from Ladislas, King of Naples. After his death in 1412 Florence had to face another Duke of Milan, Filippo Maria Visconti. These enemies were dukes and kings, whereas Florence was a republic. Though its constitution was basically democratic, it was ruled in practice by an oligarchy of important merchants belonging to its seven major guilds. Yet civic responsibilities occupied an important place in the lives of many Florentine citizens. The enemies of Florence looked back to the Roman Empire as the golden age. Giangaleazzo Visconti believed that peace depended upon the rule of a strong man.

It was in the course of its struggle against Milan and Naples that Florence became the centre of Renaissance humanism. Though essentially a literary and scholarly movement, it could be used for political ends. As students and teachers of rhetoric the humanists were admirably equipped to produce effective propaganda. Coluccio Salutati, who became chancellor of Florence in 1375, wrote innumerable letters and manifestoes in praise of the city as a bulwark of freedom against despotic oppression. His work was so effective that Giangaleazzo Visconti was said to have considered his pen more dangerous than a detachment of Florentine cavalry.

Salutati's example was followed by his pupil, Leonardo Bruni, who was appointed chancellor in 1427. In one of his works he traced the Florentine love of liberty to the Roman republic, for he believed (contrary to medieval tradition) that the city had been founded by the republican Sulla, not by the imperial Caesar. Bruni applied to history the methods of textual criticism evolved by the humanists. He imitated Livy in his vast *History of the Florentine People* but also made use of archives.

The important role played by public office in the lives of the Florentine patricians obliged them to consider the problem of the relative value of the active and contemplative life. While Petrarch had shared the preference for the latter, Bruni asserted that man 'achieves his perfection only in political society'. This new fusion of the active and contemplative was exemplified by varied groups of citizens who gathered round the learned Ambrogio Traversari in the 1420s. Not all the early humanists were creative scholars or professional writers. Some were

book-collectors, notably Niccolo Niccoli, whose library contained more than 800 volumes. He received help for his book buying from the Medici bank and at his death he asked that his collection should be made accessible to the public.

Humanism was necessarily confined to a relatively small section of the Florentine population, but art and architecture had a wide appeal. The patronage of architecture which the commune shared with the greater guilds was often competitive. The bronze statues by Ghiberti and Donatello which adorn the facades of Orsanmichele, Ghiberti's bronze doors for the baptistery and Brunelleschi's cupola for the cathedral—all resulted from competitions. The great families of Florence commissioned artists to decorate their private chapels. The frescoes commissioned from Masolino and Masaccio by Felice Brancacci for his family chapel in Santa Maria del Carmine marked a turning point in Renaissance painting.

It was in Florence in the 1420s that a specifically Renaissance style in painting, sculpture and architecture was developed. Instead of adhering to the non-naturalistic style of an artist like Gentile da Fabriano, Masaccio set out to create the illusion of a three-dimensional world by means of perspective, controlled lighting and firmly modelled forms. Donatello was responsible for a parallel change in sculpture, while Brunelleschi discovered by studying Roman architecture that proportion is the essence of architectural design. The heroic style practised by these three men soon underwent changes, however.

Above, The Annunciation, *painted by Sandro Botticelli in the late fifteenth century, demonstrates the emphasis on the artist's individual vision and style that was becoming required in the competitive artistic world of fifteenth-century Florence. Uffizi Gallery, Florence.*

Opposite top, the library of Lorenzo de' Medici at Florence, housed in a building by Michelangelo. Lorenzo collected and copied many classical texts, as well as supporting contemporary Italian writers.

Opposite bottom, The Annunciation, *one of the panels of the Doors of Paradise by Lorenzo Ghiberti, on the Baptistery at Florence. In 1401 Ghiberti won a competition against Brunelleschi for the design of these doors.*

After Masaccio's death (*c.* 1427) Donatello's style moved in the direction of dramatic expressiveness, conveyed by the use of sharply delineated forms, dramatic gestures and distorted facial expressions. In architecture Brunelleschi developed a heavier classical style than he had used for his Foundling Hospital (1419. In the second half of the fifteenth century Florentine painting became characterized by a use of contour rather than modelling. While some artists like Pollaiuolo continued to seek naturalism, Botticelli was prepared to abandon it in his own search for perfection of linear harmony. Yet if perspective did not interest him, the draughtsmanship of his figures was more naturalistic than that of any artist of the fourteenth century.

The greatest Florentine patron of his day was Cosimo de' Medici, who dominated the political life of the city after 1434. He took an active personal interest in the New Learning and in art. He rebuilt the convent of San Marco and gave it a great library, erected the noviciate of Santa Croce and continued the rebuilding of San Lorenzo. Yet Cosimo was restrained in his private building. His palace, designed by Michelozzo, served as the model for the houses erected by the Florentine patricians later in the century. Though strong enough to resist attack, they looked outward into the streets and formed an integral part of civic life.

The Renaissance is often associated with Lorenzo de' Medici, called the Magnificent. He was a man of letters and a collector of antique works of art and of manuscripts, but his architectural projects lagged behind those of other Florentine patricians like Filippo Strozzi. Lorenzo became virtually the ruler of Florence after the failure of the Pazzi conspiracy in 1478. This change in the political climate had philosophical consequences: the decline in republican institutions and civic values caused scholars to adopt a less active and more contemplative way of life.

Marsilio Ficino (1433–99), the leading spirit in the Platonic revival, believed that philosophical knowledge and moral perfection could be reached through contemplation. His villa, which he called Academy, was not an educational institution but a sort of club dedicated to the memory of Plato. Its membership was made up of professional scholars and leading citizens. As Ficino's reputation grew, scholars from outside Florence came to join his circle of friends, the most important being Pico della Mirandola (1463–94), who derived his philosophical views from a wide variety of sources, including the Kabbalah, the Jewish mystical philosophy.

Alongside the complex and esoteric discussions of the Florentine Academy, humanism of a more traditional kind continued to flourish. Its chief exponent was Politian (1454–94), who combined admiration of classical literature with an appreciation of the Tuscan language as a literary medium. The influence of humanism on Florentine civilization was all pervasive, so that both Politian and the Platonic school left their mark on the art of Botticelli. Narrow specialization was absent from the civilization of the age of Lorenzo.

The Renaissance in Florence was an indigenous movement which grew out of her society and political institutions. In other parts of Italy, where social and political conditions were different, it was often imported and superimposed by a ruler for the sake of his own pleasure and glorification.

The papacy and the Renaissance

In Rome the movement was bound up with the cultural interests and patronage of the popes. By his employment of the Tuscan humanists, Poggio Bracciolini and Leonardo Bruni, Pope Innocent VII (1404–06) established an important tradition of learned Latinists in the service of the papal court. Poggio, who visited England in the course of his travels on ecclesiastical business, made a number of important discoveries among classical manuscripts in the great monastic libraries of Europe. He was also interested in the antiquities of Rome and built up a collection of ancient inscriptions and works of sculpture.

Rome in the early fifteenth century was a neglected and decayed city, but Pope Martin V (1417–31) undertook a rebuilding programme which was continued by his successors more or less consistently.

An important event under Pope Eugenius IV (1431–47) was the summoning of a council with a view to reuniting the Greek and Roman Churches. It met first at Ferrara, then at Florence, and attracted to Italy a number of Greek scholars, notably Cardinal Bessarion (1403–72) who decided to spend the rest of his life in Rome. He was a great book-collector and presented his volumes to Venice, where many are still preserved in the Marciana Library. Greek, however, was never considered as important in the Renaissance as Latin, which Lorenzo Valla (1407–57) acclaimed as the universal language in his *Elegantiae*. Among his other achievements as a humanist Valla produced evidence to show that the *Donation of Constantine,* a document on which the papacy based its temporal power, was fraudulent.

Apart from promoting peace, Pope Nicholas V (1447–55) was chiefly concerned with 'books and buildings'. He was the founder of the Vatican Library and enlarged its collection of manuscripts by employing many copyists and illuminators and by commissioning original works and translations from the Greek. Pius II (1458–64), who was himself a humanist, was also favourable to the arts and letters in Rome, but his successor, Paul II (1464–71), was intensely suspicious of classical studies. Members of the Roman Academy, a group of scholars who met at the house of the rhetorician, Pomponio Leto, were accused of heretical and pagan beliefs and practices.

Yet Pope Paul was not hostile to all aspects of the Renaissance. He collected antiques, medals and coins, built the Palazzo Venezia, the loggia of St Peter's and a new bridge over the Tiber and supported the Vatican Library and University. The introduction of printing into Italy by Sweynheim and Pannartz during his pontificate facilitated the production of new editions and commentaries on the classics.

Though marred by nepotism, the pontificate of Sixtus IV (1471–84) was culturally one of the most brilliant. The Sistine Chapel was started and Rome was given new bridges, roads and squares. Among the artists and craftsmen who flocked there from Florence and from other parts of Italy were Signorelli, Botticelli, Perugino and Mantegna.

All this activity was sustained under the Borgia pope, Alexander VI (1492–1503), despite the unworthiness of his pontificate. The bellicose Julius II (1503–13) founded the new basilica of St Peter's to Bramante's design and assembled at the Belvedere statues and antiquities unearthed in excavations. Raphael was commissioned to decorate the Stanze della Segnatura and Michelangelo to execute the pope's tomb and to decorate the ceiling of the Sistine Chapel.

The Roman Renaissance reached its peak under the Medici pope, Leo X (1513–21). Building, both papal and private, continued on an unprecedented scale. Painting and architecture were represented by outstanding artists; Bembo and Sadoleto issued elegant Latin epistles from the papal chancery; the Vatican Library continued to

grow under a succession of famous prefects. But all this was achieved without regard for the papacy's religious function. The reform of the Church was neglected and no effective response given to Luther's challenge. Nemesis came under Clement VII (1523–34) in the form of the sack of Rome (1527). Yet the Roman Renaissance did not really come to an end until the pontificate of Paul III (1534–50), when there was a reaction against the cultural values of the preceding epoch.

Naples and Milan

The Renaissance in Naples, though comparatively short-lived, was significant. It owed its existence largely to Alfonso V, under whose enlightened rule the traditionally quarrelsome Neapolitan baronage gave little trouble and the economy improved. Among the humanists who enjoyed his patronage was Lorenzo Valla (1407–57), and the tradition of scholarship was kept up by Alfonso's son, Ferrante, whose library became one of the most remarkable in Italy.

The chief figure of the Neapolitan Renaissance at its height was the humanist, Giovanni Pontano (1426–1503), who was also an able civil servant and diplomat. As a Latin poet he was surpassed only by Sannazaro (1456–1530). The only major painter who worked in southern Italy during the fifteenth century was Antonello da Messina (*c.* 1430–79). He was entirely cut off from the stream of experiment which started in Florence and spread to the rest of central and northern Italy. In fact he was closer to French or Flemish painters of the period, though there is no evidence that he ever went to Flanders.

It is often argued that the liberal arts can flourish only in an environment of political freedom, and the Florentines themselves

made much of this argument. Nevertheless, it was under the despotic Giangaleazzo Visconti (1347–1402) that the Milanese first felt the impact of the Renaissance. A spectacular building programme was launched and official encouragement was given to the University of Pavia, which became an important centre for the study of law. The Milanese Renaissance is associated particularly with Lodovico Sforza, *il Moro*, who became duke in 1494. He was encouraged in his patronage by his wife, Beatrice d'Este. Leonardo da Vinci and Bramante were among the distinguished artists who joined his court and a contemporary wrote,

> The court was full of men of every skill and talent, especially musicians and poets and no month passed but they were to present, besides other things, some eclogue or comedy or tragedy or other new production or play.

This brilliant period was cut short by the death of the Duchess Beatrice in 1497 and by the French occupation of the duchy in 1500.

Above, a bas relief by Donatello (c. 1386–1466) showing an incident in the life of St Anthony. Donatello was a pioneer of the use of perspective in such works.

Left, Marsilio Ficino (1433–99), a philosopher who, under the auspices of Cosimo de' Medici, founded an academy at Florence devoted to the rediscovery of the work of Plato. His work heralded an important strand in Renaissance humanism.

Below, a bust of Lorenzo de' Medici made by Verrocchio in the 1470s; Lorenzo participated actively in the group of artists that he patronized, writing poetry and introducing new ideas as well as sitting for his portrait. National Gallery of Art, Washington.

Opposite, Cosimo de' Medici, painted by Bronzino (1503–72), who specialized in portraiture. The desire to capture a personality in a portrait was a new interest of the Renaissance.

Ferrara, Mantua and Urbino

Before the ideas of the Renaissance could take root they needed to be embodied in educational theory and practice. The key figures in this work were two great schoolmasters, Guarino da Verona and Vittorino da Feltre. Both studied Latin in and around Padua in the late fourteenth century. Guarino also studied Greek and visited Constantinople. Eventually both men established schools which were associated with princely courts.

Vittorino taught at the Gonzaga court in Mantua from 1373 to 1446 and Guarino at the Este court in Ferrara from 1429 to 1460. Their pupils included middle-aged men as well as teenagers, poor children as well as sons of the nobility. The aim of their teaching was to encourage the full development of the individual through the study of the classics and a combination of moral and physical instruction. It was on this ideal that European education was to be based for centuries.

Among the pupils of Guarino and Vittorino were three important patrons of the Renaissance: Leonello d'Este Duke of Ferrara (1441–50), Lodovico Gonzaga Duke of Mantua (1444–78) and, most famous of all, Federigo da Montefeltro Duke of Urbino (1444–82).

It was under Leonello d'Este that Ferrara became a great centre of Italian poetry. Ariosto (1474–1533), the author of *Orlando Furioso,* which has been called 'the most perfect poem of the Italian Renaissance', spent most of his life there. In the late sixteenth century this literary tradition, which also extended to drama, was upheld by Tasso (1544–95).

Lodovico Gonzaga imported the artistic ideals of the Renaissance into Mantua. The Florentine architect Leon Battista Alberti (1404–72), designed the churches of Sant' Andrea and San Sebastiano. Among his many accomplishments (it is recorded that he could jump over a man's head with his feet close together!) he wrote a treatise on painting and another on architecture modelled on Vitruvius, the newly rediscovered Roman writer on architecture. Alberti was not just a dry theorist; he had an imaginative and creative mind. His design for San Sebastiano prompted a cardinal to remark 'I can't see if this is going to turn out to be a church, or a mosque or a synagogue.' Lodovico was also the patron of the painter, Andrea Mantegna (1430–1506), whose austere classicism provides a link between the work of Donatello in Florence and that of Giovanni Bellini in Venice.

The Renaissance in Mantua continued under Duke Francesco II (1484–1519) whose wife, Isabella d'Este, received praise from the most famous writers of the day for her enlightened support of poetry and drama. In 1524 Duke Federigo invited Raphael's pupil, Giulio Romano, to undertake work at Mantua. He drained the marshes, restored many buildings and built the Palazzo del Tè in the style called Mannerism, a self-conscious flouting of the classical principles followed by earlier architects of the Renaissance.

Federigo da Montefeltro is well known because of his unforgettable broken-nosed profile painted by Piero della Francesca. In the course of his reign (1444–82) he consolidated and trebled the size of his duchy of Urbino, which remained nevertheless one of the smaller Italian principalities. As a *condottiere,* or soldier of fortune, he could command a high price for his services for he was trustworthy, prudent and kept good discipline among his troops. He is remembered not for his battles, however, but for his transformation of Urbino into one of the chief cultural centres of Europe. The library which he collected was unrivalled.

The duke was a competent Latinist and an enthusiastic supporter of Greek studies. His cultivated tastes were embodied in his famous palace at Urbino, designed by Luciano di Laurana. According to Castiglione, who chose Urbino as the setting for his delightful *Book of the Courtier* (1528), the palace was so well furnished by the duke that 'it seemed not a palace but a city in the form of a palace'.

Venice

Renaissance ideas reached Venice later than elsewhere. By the end of the fifteenth century, however, it had become an important centre of the book trade. Aldus Manutius (1450–1515), who specialized in Greek texts, was one of the outstanding scholar-printers of the age. In the arts the golden age of Venice was the sixteenth century, when painting was represented by the Bellinis, Giorgione, Titian, Tintoretto and Veronese and architecture by Sansovino and Palladio.

The city was also important for its music. The Venetian calendar was punctuated by great religious and secular festivals, during which the doge and Senate would go in procession to the basilica of San Marco, where music was provided by two organs and two choirs. The greatest musician associated with Venice was Claudio Monteverdi, who came there from Mantua in 1611, probably to supervise the performance of his *Vespers*.

Leonardo da Vinci

The two outstanding artistic geniuses of the Renaissance are undoubtedly Leonardo da Vinci (1452–1519) and Michelangelo (1475–1564).

Leonardo showed unusual gifts from his earliest years and was placed by his father, a Florentine lawyer, in Verrocchio's studio. In his early works, more particularly his drawings, Leonardo tried to adapt his fleeting visions to the severe standards of academic Florentine art with its overlapping traditions of linear grace and fancy (e.g. Botticelli) and of scientific naturalism (e.g. Verrocchio).

In 1482 he went to Milan after recommending himself to the duke almost exclusively as a military engineer. His earliest notebooks contain drawings of engines of war. Architecture also interested him but his plans and elevations of domed churches were probably not intended to be built. He compiled notes on the art of painting and made numerous studies of the human body.

In addition to painting portraits and supervising small engineering projects, Leonardo undertook two important works for the Duke of Milan: an equestrian statue of Francesco Sforza and the mural of *The Last Supper* in the refectory of Santa Maria delle Grazie. He made a full-scale model of the statue in clay in 1493, but the monument was never completed. *The Last Supper*, despite its appalling condition, bears witness to Leonardo's inventive genius. Whereas earlier painters had chosen the moment of communion, Leonardo's treatment would seem to depict the terrible moment when Christ says 'one of you will betray me'.

In 1500 Leonardo returned to Florence and it was during the next five years that he painted 'Mona Lisa', the wife of an obscure

Above, the interior of S. Andrea Basilica, at Mantua, designed by Alberti in about 1470 in the classical style of Renaissance architecture.

Top, this painting by Benozzo Gozzolli, nominally of the journey of the Magi, in fact shows the magnificence of the Florentine Renaissance court, with Lorenzo de' Medici on a hunting expedition in the foreground. Medici Riccardi Palace, Florence.

Opposite, the Pietà, *sculpted by Michelangelo in 1498 in Rome.*

Florentine citizen. In her famous smile Leonardo achieved his aim of capturing and fixing the complex inner life in durable material. When he returned to Milan in 1508 he was employed in various capacities by the French governor, Charles d'Amboise. His frequent travels during these years enabled him to observe nature closely. After the expulsion of the French in 1512 Leonardo went to Rome. Finding the atmosphere distasteful, however, he retired into melancholy solitude until 1516 when he accepted Francis I's invitation to settle in France where he died three years later.

Michelangelo

Michelangelo was the son of an impoverished Florentine gentleman. After serving as an apprentice in the studio of the painter, Ghirlandaio, he joined Lorenzo de' Medici's school of sculpture under Bertoldo and produced works which tried to rival those of antiquity. In 1496 he went to Rome and produced his first major work, the 'Pietà', which broke new ground by combining two life-size marble statues in one group. After returning to Florence in 1501 he carved his famous *David,* the final expression of fifteenth-century Florentine naturalism. Michelangelo also painted his *Holy Family* at this time.

In 1504 he was commissioned by the Florentine republic to paint a large fresco in the Palazzo Vecchio. By showing an incident from the Pisan War in which soldiers were surprised while bathing he was able to introduce a wide variety of movement into his treatment of the human body. Michelangelo was the first artist to reveal the body in its entire range of action.

Julius II then commissioned him to work on his tomb, a project which was to occupy him on and off for forty years. He was soon diverted, however, to decorate the vault of the Sistine Chapel. Despite extremely difficult conditions he finished this 'tremendous biblical symphony' in a remarkably short space of time. The original design for Julius II's tomb was never completed, and Michelangelo was responsible only for the awesome statue of Moses in the present monument.

Michelangelo's career as an architect began in 1520 with the Medici chapel at San Lorenzo in Florence, in which architecture and sculpture were intended to complement each other. By his unorthodox treatment of classical themes he prepared the way for the Baroque style. The dome of St Peter's was among his subsequent architectural works. His last major painting, *The Last Judgement,* on the altar wall of the Sistine Chapel showed by its command of movement in space the course Italian art was to follow in the next century.

The Renaissance outside Italy

Renaissance Italy was not cut off from the rest of Europe. Rome was the centre of the international Church and the universities of Padua, Bologna and Salerno (to mention only a few) were famous for the study of law or medicine. There was a continuous traffic of churchmen and students between Italy and other countries, so that the Renaissance was almost bound to be exported sooner or later. But it was never copied exactly. In every country it was blended with native elements. In architecture, for example, classical themes like columns, pilasters and pediments were at first added to the façades of buildings which remained structurally Gothic. Only gradually did classicism become integrated into the architecture of northern Europe. And the same kind of compromise occurred in scholarship where humanism had to establish itself alongside the medieval scholastic tradition.

Signs of an interest in the New Learning appeared in France in the 1450s when two Italians, Tifernate and Beroaldo, lectured in Paris. A printing press in the cellars of the university of the Sorbonne began to produce editions of classical and humanistic texts. The most important of the early French humanists was Robert Gaguin, who wanted knowledge and eloquence to serve theology. This alliance of humanism and theology was one of the characteristic features of the northern Renaissance. Later in the century Greek studies were introduced into France by George Hermonymos and John Lascaris. In the work of Jacques Lefèvre d'Étaples (*c.* 1450–1536) classical learning became combined with mysticism. His scholarship was surpassed by that Guillaume Budé (1468–1540), whose works on the Roman coinage and the *Pandects* (the fifty books of Roman civil law which Justinian ordered to be drawn up in the sixth century AD) were remarkable even by Italian standards.

The cradle of English humanism was the household of Humphrey, Duke of Gloucester, who employed Italian secretaries. He was an enthusiastic bibliophile and gave many books to Oxford University. Partly because of his encouragement, a number of young Englishmen went to study in Italy. By the end of the fifteenth century the principal exponents of humanism in England were William Grocin, John Colet, Thomas Linacre and Sir Thomas More, whose *Utopia* showed that it was no longer essential for an Englishman to study in Italy to become an accomplished humanist.

Antiquarianism was one of the keynotes

Left, Desiderius Erasmus (1466–1536), painted by Hans Holbein. Erasmus brought the ideals and the learning of the Renaissance to northern Europe and linked them to the religious traditions of his home country.

Far left, the Galérie François Ier *at the Château de Fountainebleau, built and decorated by Italian artists in the 1530s. This was the first Renaissance building in France and displays the stylized forms of the Italian Mannerists.*

Opposite top left, a self-portrait by Leonardo da Vinci (1452–1519), whose universal genius and attention to the workings of nature embody the finest achievements of the Italian Renaissance.

Opposite top right, Bacchus, *sculpted by Michelangelo in about 1447, typical of that artist's use of the human body to express all kinds of feelings, including inebriation.*

Opposite bottom right, a sketch for the fresco The Battle of Cascina, *by Michelangelo (1505); Michelangelo was a student of anatomy and made careful studies of all his figures, to a far greater extent than earlier artists had done. British Museum, London.*

of German humanism. Scholars sighed after a German past which in their view was as great if not greater than that of Rome. While Conrad Celtis rescued texts proving that his countrymen had not been illiterate in the Middle Ages, Peutinger collected ancient German inscriptions. With the appearance of Luther, humanism was able to supply his movement with a strongly nationalistic propaganda against Rome.

Spain too felt the influence of the Italian Renaissance. Antonio de Nebrija (1444–1522) applied its lessons to fields of scholarship ranging from historiography to biblical studies. His patron, Cardinal Jiménez de Cisneros, was responsible not only for the foundation of the university of Alcalá de Henares (1508) but also for the publication of the *Complutensian Polyglot Bible*, in which the text was printed in Hebrew, Aramaic, Greek and Latin.

Erasmus of Rotterdam

The greatest representative of the Renaissance outside Italy was Desiderius Erasmus. The illegitimate son of a priest, he was born at Rotterdam in about 1469. Though he was not much affected by the artistic achievement of the Renaissance, he was in several respects the key figure of his age. He formed a link between the mystical movement known as the *Devotio moderna*; which flourished in the Low countries during his childhood, and the classical revival in Italy.

Erasmus began his career as a monk but, finding the life distasteful, he escaped to Paris under the pretext of improving his theology. In fact, he was keen to study the classics but only as a means to an end. In his *Enchiridion Militis Christiani* (1501) he showed that the classics, poetry and philosophy were only the prelude to the highest study of all, Scripture. The aim of Erasmus was to fuse the two worlds of antiquity and Christianity and his career illustrates the fact that, in northern Europe, the Renaissance was largely dedicated to a Christian purpose.

By his very active correspondence Erasmus established close ties with many of his fellow humanists in other countries. He also travelled a great deal, visiting England, France and Italy before eventually settling down in the printing centre of Basle, where his great edition of the New Testament appeared in 1516. Its preface is full of the spirit of the New Learning: while accepting the doctrine of the Fall, it expresses unbounded confidence in the goodness of man and in his ability to better himself.

Though Erasmus' health was poor and he was deeply disturbed by the troubles of the Reformation, his literary output was maintained until his death in 1536. His fame rested as much on his humorous writings, the *Praise of Folly* (1508) and the *Colloquies* (1526), as on his more serious works. He mercilessly lampooned worthless monks, vain schoolmen and warring popes, yet his approach to contemporary problems was also constructive. In the *Education of a Christian Prince* (1516) he laid down the principles upon which the ideal state might be built. In his advocacy of international peace and mutual toleration Erasmus embodied ideals which are often wrongly ascribed to a more modern age than his.

Chapter 19

The Italian Wars

The achievements of the Italian Renaissance did not take place in a vacuum. They need to be set against their political background. For forty years after the Peace of Lodi (1454) Italy was relatively peaceful. A finely balanced equilibrium was established between the five principal states, Naples, the Papacy, Venice, Florence and Rome. In 1494, however, this was upset by the intervention of France in the affairs of the peninsula. The invasion of Naples by the young French king, Charles VIII, marked the beginning of the Italian Wars which lasted on and off for more than half a century, involving more or less directly all the major powers of western Europe.

The wars inevitably affected the lives of the great men of the Renaissance. When Leonardo da Vinci offered his services to the Duke of Milan he stressed the qualities which he felt would be most readily appreciated:

I have kinds of mortars most convenient and easy to carry, and with these I can fling small stones resembling a great storm; and with the smoke of these cause great terror to the enemy, to his great detriment and confusion. . . . I will make covered chariots safe and unassailable, which, entering among the enemy with their artillery, there is no body of men so great but they would break them.

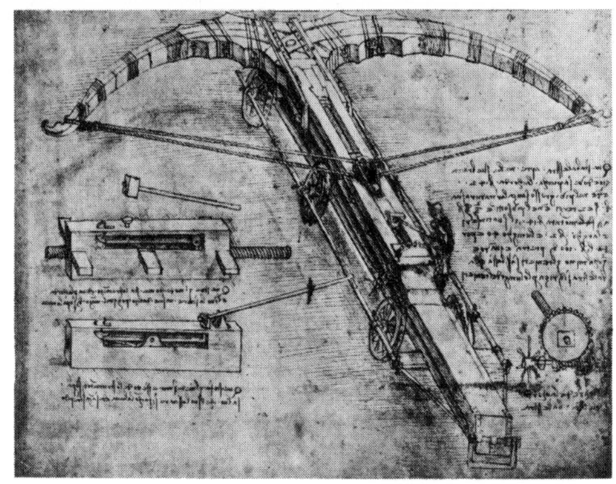

The Italian Wars were once regarded as the first manifestation of the aggressiveness inherent in the modern nation-state, but all the evidence points to a traditional motivation. War was the chief business of the medieval aristocracy, while a just war was condoned by the Church. The King of France was not seeking to round off his kingdom with natural frontiers, nor was he looking for economic advantages. His policy was dynastic rather than nationalistic and designed to satisfy the thirst for war of his aristocratic entourage.

The revival of the French monarchy

The end of the fifteenth century was marked by a revival of monarchy in certain countries of western Europe. These have been called 'new monarchies' but the term is misleading as the kings used traditional methods to consolidate and extend their power.

France was not a unified kingdom in 1450. The royal domain covered only about half of it, the rest being controlled by powerful princes and magnates. The crown nevertheless was able to exploit certain advantages, for example the Salic Law debarring females from the royal succession and the right of arbitrary taxation. Nothing comparable with the English Parliament existed in France. The nearest equivalent, the Estates-General, which seldom met, lacked legislative authority.

One of the main architects of royal centralization was Louis XI (1461–83), though his successes were often a result of good fortune rather than a policy. On the death of the Duke of Anjou in 1480 and of the Count of Maine, the French crown acquired Maine, Anjou and Provence by reversion. Marseilles became a French port and the inheritance also comprised the Angevin claim to the kingdom of Naples. In addition to these territories Louis XI acquired Roussillon from the King of Aragon. Thus, by 1483 the territorial power of the French monarchy had been doubled.

Louis XI was not a reforming monarch. His government differed from its predecessors simply by reason of its tyrannical character. No one was spared, no privilege respected. Two great nobles, the Constable of Saint-Pol and the Duke of Nemours, were beheaded. The king's old minister, Cardinal Balue, was imprisoned for eleven years.

When Louis XI died in 1483, leaving a thirteen-year-old son, Charles, as his heir, it seemed as though France would again lapse into civil turmoil. However, the early collapse of an aristocratic rising known as the *Guerre Folle* (1485) served to underline the effectiveness of the king's achievements.

The conquest of Naples

The year 1494 is often taken as the dividing line between medieval and modern history, but it is merely a date of convenience. The chief event of that year, Charles VIII's invasion of Italy, was not a startling innovation. Italy had been invaded by northern armies for centuries. In fact, Charles founded his ambitions on earlier successes of the French royal house in the peninsula. The House of Anjou had reigned in Naples for a time and the House of Orléans had intermarried with the Visconti of Milan. But the claims advanced by Charles and his successors were pretexts rather than causes of war. France was now a strong and reasonably unified nation; so was Spain. Italy, on the other hand, was a tempting prey by reason of its disunity. Thus, it became the duelling ground of the two rising nation-states.

Italy was not prepared to defend herself. Piero de' Medici, who had recently replaced Lorenzo the Magnificent as ruler of Florence, and Pope Alexander VI tended to side with Naples but were not willing to exert themselves in its defence. Lodovico Sforza, who had recently quarrelled with the King of Naples, encouraged Charles to invade. Naples itself was torn by faction and its king lacked ability.

None of the European powers was anxious to intervene at this stage, but Charles had to sacrifice some of his father's territorial gains to ensure that his neighbours would stay neutral. Thus Ferdinand of Aragon was given Roussillon while the Emperor Maximilian got back Artois and Franche-Comté. As for Henry VII of England, he was content to accept a large annuity under the Treaty of Étaples (1492).

The army which Charles VIII led across the Alps during the summer of 1494 was about thirty thousand strong. His artillery was more efficient than anything the Italians possessed, but as yet it was not the decisive weapon. The French king still relied mainly on his *gendarmerie*, that is, men-at-arms heavily clad in armour and armed with lances.

The invasion was more like a triumphal progress than a military campaign. The Neapolitan fleet, which should have blockaded Genoa, failed to arrive in time so that the Duke of Orléans was able to occupy the port. As Charles VIII, after passing through the Milanese, penetrated Tuscany, Piero de' Medici threw himself on his protection and a number of fortresses including Pisa were handed over to him. In November Charles was honourably received by the Florentines as the God-sent regenerator of their country, whose coming had been foretold by the Dominican preacher, Savonarola. The city formally acknowledged the king as the protector of its liberties and promised him financial aid.

Meanwhile the Neapolitan army under Alfonso's heir, Ferrantino, which should have prevented the French from crossing the Apennines, retreated southward. Charles reached Rome without encountering resistance and obtained from Alexander VI right of passage through the Papal States. Finding himself deserted by his allies, Alfonso abdicated in favour of his son, Ferrantino, but the French advance continued and on 22 February 1495 Charles entered Naples. As Ferrantino fled to Ischia, almost the whole of his kingdom passed to France.

However, French victories in Italy were never secure. Ariosto wrote,

All who hold the sceptre of France shall see their armies destroyed either by the sword or by famine or by pestilence. They will

Above, Louis XII of France (ruled 1498–1515) on his triumphal entry into Genoa in 1507 after the city had rebelled against his rule the previous year. Bibliothèque Nationale, Paris.

Top, fifteenth-century Naples, the capital of Italy south of the Papal States, one of the main prizes disputed in the Italian Wars between France and Spain.

Opposite, a design for a giant catapult by Leonardo. British Museum, London.

bring back from Italy short-lived rejoicing and enduring grief, small profit and infinite loss, for the lilies may not strike root in that soil.

While the French in Naples made themselves thoroughly unpopular by their greed, licentiousness, corruption and brutality, a league of mutual defence was formed by Venice, Milan, the pope, the emperor and Spain.

Fearing that he might be cut off from his base, Charles VIII left a garrison in Naples and marched north. The league's army under Francesco Gonzaga waited for him near Fornovo on the northern side of the Apennines. The king's position was so precarious that he tried to negotiate a passage, but battle was engaged while the talks were still on.

Although it lasted only a quarter of an hour the fighting was fierce. Both sides claimed a victory, but the advantage lay with Charles, who was able to reach Lombardy, albeit without his baggage. While the king returned home, the garrison in Naples surrendered to the Spaniards.

The French invasion precipitated a revolution in Florence where the popular desire for more political freedom had been fanned by the preaching of Savonarola. The government of Piero de' Medici was overthrown and a Grand Council of three thousand members on the Venetian model was set up in its place. Savonarola's preaching was also directed against the moral laxity of the age. In this he typified the strongly Puritan streak in fifteenth-century piety. Everywhere in Europe people were expressing disgust for the extravagances of the secular life and for

the corporeal existence. Savonarola could move an audience to a near-frenzy of self-denial. As a result of his preaching many so-called 'vanities' were thrown into bonfires.

The friar's hold on Florence, however, depended on the fulfilment of his prophecies. As the city became involved in a long and costly war against Pisa and isolated from the rest of Italy, disillusion set in among its people. Savonarola's influence was further weakened when he was forbidden to preach and excommunicated by the pope. In 1498 he was arrested and tried for his claim to prophecy and his political action. After torture had been used to extract a confession he was burnt at the stake on 23 May. His death did not produce any change of constitution or policy. Florence continued to be virtually a vassal of France till 1512 when the Medici were restored to power.

Louis XII and the conquest of Milan

Charles VIII was succeeded by his cousin, Louis XII, who also had a dynastic interest in Italy. As the grandson of Valentina Visconti he had a claim to the duchy of Milan and was encouraged to make it good by his chief minister, Georges d'Amboise, Archbishop of Rouen, who had papal ambitions. The king could count on the support of Pope Alexander VI, who was mainly concerned to establish his family as the supreme power in central Italy. A series of mutually satisfactory transactions ensued.

In exchange for an annulment of his marriage Louis bestowed the duchy of Valentinois on the pope's son, Cesare Borgia, and gave him the hand of the heiress of Navarre. When Cesare came to France to fetch his bride he brought with him a cardinal's hat for Georges d'Amboise. The

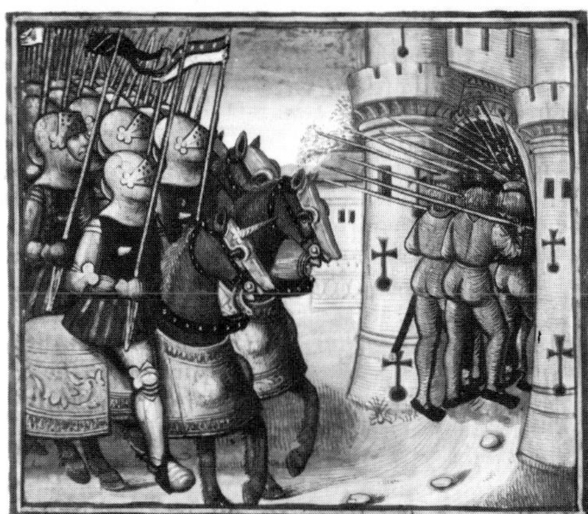

Above, soldiers leaving Milan castle; the wars had little effect on the ordinary people of Italy, although trade was often disrupted.

Top centre, Louis XII's conquest of Milan in 1500, which secured control of northern Italy, although he was unable to defeat Venice until 1509. Bibliothèque Nationale, Paris.

Left centre, the entry of Ludovico Sforza into Como; his support for Charles' original invasion of Italy in 1494 was a principal cause of the outbreak of the Italian Wars. Bibliothèque Nationale, Paris.

Far left, the citizens of Genoa acknowledging the authority of the French king in 1507 after the failure of their rebellion the year before. Bibliothèque Nationale, Paris.

Opposite left, the fleet of Naples was unable to arrive in Genoa in 1494 in time to prevent the French armies from occupying the town without serious opposition. This illustration is taken from a French chronicle of the campaign. Bibliothèque Nationale, Paris.

Opposite right, Girolamo Savonarola (1452–98), the Dominican friar who won power in Florence in 1494 with his programme of extreme asceticism.

King of France won Venice over by promising to give it Cremona. He signed agreements with England, Spain and the emperor and obtained permission to levy troops in the Swiss cantons at the price of an annual subsidy to each of them.

In Septemebr 1499 a French army under Gian Giacomo Trivulzio, a Milanese exile, captured Milan effortlessly, while Lodovico Sforza fled to the imperial court in Austria where he was hospitably received. The tide of events soon turned in his favour. The Swiss, being dissatisfied with their treatment by the French, offered him ten thousand men. This enabled him to return to Milan in the spring. As he approached, the citizens, who had soon grown tired of the French occupation, rose and opened their gates to him. On 8 April 1500, however, Sforza was betrayed by his Swiss troops at Novara and fell into the hands of the French as he tried to escape. He was taken to France where he remained a prisoner till the end of his life.

Instead of resting content with this success Louis directed his attention to Naples. In the Treaty of Granada (November 1500) he and Ferdinand of Aragon agreed to conquer and partition the kingdom. Finding himself under fire from two directions, Federigo of Naples threw himself upon Louis' mercy. He was sent to France and given the duchy of Anjou in compensation.

Louis now controlled the northern half of Naples while Ferdinand held Apulia and Calabria. But trouble very soon arose over territories not specified in the partition treaty, especially Capitanata, where profits were made from the tolls levied on livestock going to and from their winter and summer pastures. Gonsalo da Córdoba won a decisive victory at Cerignola in April 1503 and the French retired to Gaeta. Their capitulation early in the following year placed Naples under Aragon.

The French invasion enabled Alexander VI to assert his authority in the states of the Church, which had become a conglomeration of virtually independent lordships. His efforts were directed not only to strengthening the temporal power of the papacy but still more at founding a permanent state for his family. Between 1499 and 1501 his son, Cesare Borgia, conquered most of Romagna and was created its duke. Machiavelli wrote,

This lord is very proud and fine, and as a soldier is so enterprising that nothing is so great that it does not seem small to him, and for the sake of glory and of acquiring lands he does not rest, and acknowledges no fatigue or danger. He arrives at one place before he is known to have left the other; he endears himself to his soldiers; he has got hold of the best men in Italy, and these factors, together with continual good fortune, make him victorious and dangerous.

But Cesare's good fortune ran out just as he was thinking of deserting the French alliance, which was an obstacle to an extension of his power in Tuscany. In August 1503 Alexander VI died and without his support Cesare's states began to fall apart.

The League of Cambrai

The benefits of Borgia policy in central Italy were reaped by Giuliano della Rovere who became Pope Julius II in November 1503. Julius was a man of vast ambitions and boundless energy. His initial aim was to recover all the territories of the Church. After two years of preparation he set out

from Rome on a campaign of conquest accompanied by all but the most infirm cardinals. In 1506 he made a triumphal entry into Bologna. Standing among the crowd that watched him go by was Erasmus, to whom the satire, *Julius Exclusus,* has been attributed. This set out to show the incompatibility between the aims and achievements of the greatest Renaissance pope and the Christian ideal. St Peter refuses to recognize in the warlike figure with his magnificent tiara and pallium the representative of the apostolic succession.

Julius II's next move was directed against Venice, which had occupied Rimini and Faenza after the fall of the Borgias. At his instigation France, England, Spain and the empire formed the League of Cambrai in 1508 and in the following year a French army invaded Venetian territory, winning a decisive victory at Agnadello. Once Julius had recovered the cities of Romagna, however, he devoted all his energies to expelling the French from Italy. He tried to foment a rebellion in Genoa, attacked the Duke of Ferrara who was France's ally and secured the military assistance of the Swiss cantons.

By the end of the fifteenth century the Swiss had become the leading military power in Europe. Their confederation consisted of thirteen rural and urban cantons without any central executive authority. Common policy was determined by a diet of cantonal representatives which met at regular intervals. The Swiss were largely dependent on pay and loot acquired as mercenary troops in the service of foreign powers. 'This fierce and primitive people', wrote Guicciardini, 'have won great renown by their union and feat of arms, for by their natural ferocity and military descipline they have always defended their won country and won great fame fighting in foreign service.'

Because of their geographical situation the Swiss were able to play a decisive role in the Italian Wars. Until 1510 they served France more or less consistently. In March of that year, though, they were persuaded by Matthias Schinner, Archbishop of Sion, to place six thousand men at the pope's disposal for five years in return for an annual subsidy to each canton.

Louis XII retaliated by calling a general council to reform the Church. This move was welcomed by his Gallican subjects and was even supported by the Emperor Maximilian. But the council which opened at Pisa in November 1510 soon ran into trouble and was moved to Milan to be under the protection of the French army. In 1511 Julius took

Above, the capture of Pisa by the troops of Charles VIII of France in 1494; this became inevitable after Piero de' Medici had gone over to the French. Bibliothèque Nationale, Paris.

Left, Cesare Borgia (1476–1507), the younger son of Pope Alexander VI, who sought to create an empire for himself by exploiting his father's position. He has been thought to be the model for Machiavelli's Prince.

Below, the siege of Siena in 1554–55 by the Emperor Charles V; by this time, companies of musketeers were the most effective soldiers, and the heavy armour of fifty years before had been abandoned.

Opposite, Savonarola's burning for heresy in the main square in Florence in 1498; he had been spiritual leader to the city for the previous six years but aroused opposition for his moral severity.

the wind out of its sails by summoning the Fifth Lateran Council, which was enthusiastically acclaimed by most of Christendom. The Council of Pisa-Milan retired to Lyons and dissolved itself.

The conflict between the French king and the pope came to a head in 1512, when a French army under the command of the brilliant young general, Gaston de Foix, swept across the Po valley and defeated a combined Spanish and papal army at Ravenna (11 April). This victory was not followed up, however, for Gaston was killed and no one of comparable ability could be found to replace him. As a powerful Swiss army descended into Lombardy the French hastily retreated.

Henry VIII of England and his father-in-law, Ferdinand of Aragon, chose this moment to plan a joint conquest of Gascony,

but the wily Spanish monarch merely used an English expeditionary force as a cover to annex part of the small kingdom of Navarre. Even so, Henry did not give up the idea of armed intervention across the Channel.

Louis XII would have been well advised to seek a respite from war, but the death of Julius II and a change in the attitude of Ferdinand of Aragon encouraged him to try his luck again in Italy. Yet another French army overran Lombardy, only to be decisively routed by the Swiss at Novara. This was followed by another humiliation for French arms in northern France when a cavalry force was intercepted by the English as it was on its way to relieve the beleagured garrison of Thérouanne. The French fled from the field so fast that the engagement became known as 'the Battle of the Spurs'. On the Anglo-Scottish border, Louis XII's ally, James IV, was defeated and killed at Flodden.

Changes in warfare

The Battle of Ravenna was one of the earliest in which artillery played a decisive role, but this was not the only change in the art of war during this period.

The victories won by the Swiss infantry against the Burgundians in the 1470s had proved that wars could no longer be won by cavalry alone. The use of infantry, however, presented serious disciplinary problems. Most countries could not afford to keep up permanent armies on a large scale. They were therefore obliged to hire mercenaries who fought only for money; if this ran short they became insubordinate or disbanded. Native troops raised in an emergency were easier to manage but they were not as well trained as professionals. Only the Swiss cantons and Spain possessed an infantry which was at once native and professional.

The best mercenaries were undoubtedly the Swiss pikemen who fought in compact squares of about six thousand men, eighty-five shoulder to shoulder on a hundred-yard-long front and about seventy ranks deep. If possible they used three squares in echelon. The success of the Swiss formation depended on a strict discipline: cowards were executed and no prisoners taken. The Swiss wore little armour and were therefore able to attack fast. Their method of fighting proved so effective in the early stages of the Italian wars that it was copied by the *Landsknechte* (German infantry armed mainly with pike and often employed as mercenaries). It had certain disadvantages, however; the squares were easy targets for missiles and were not suited to rough terrain or well adapted to siege work.

Despite the growing prestige of infantry, heavy cavalry continued to be the aristocracy of war. The men-at-arms mounted on strongly armoured horses were equipped with the lance, axe or mace and their tactic was always to charge furiously in bodies of four to five hundred men. In the course of the wars there was a growing tendency to emphasize the distinction between heavy and light cavalry. The latter was, of course, especially useful in foraging and raiding.

Artillery changed considerably during the Italian Wars. Mere size was abondoned in favour of mobility and accuracy. The French continued the Burgundian tradition of light artillery capable of keeping up with an army on the march. The use of iron instead of stone balls also spread. But the wide variety of calibres complicated the task of supplying and carrying ammunition. Portable firearms gradually emerged as the dominant missile weapon during the Italian Wars. Although the range of the arquebus was barely four hundred yards, its heavy bullet caused the crossbow to be relegated to sea warfare and siege work in the 1520s. At first arquebuses were mainly used to defend fortified positions, but by 1512 they came into the open. They were fired over the heads of pikemen who protected them.

The development of artillery inevitably led to changes in the art of fortification. The success of the French guns in 1494 had shown that tall, thin walls were no longer adequate as a protection. The main innovation was the bastion—a solid construction projecting from the curtain with supporting guns—but for a long time old fortifications were modified rather than new ones built. The first large-scale works were undertaken at Verona in 1520.

Machiavelli

The standard of political morality in the sixteenth century was probably no worse than in any other age, but standing diplomacy, perhaps because it was not yet firmly established, often appeared cunning, furtive and treacherous. No one was better acquainted with this political atmosphere than Niccolò Machiavelli (1469–1527), whose name has been turned into an adjective to describe it. From 1498 until 1512 Machiavelli served the Florentine republic as chancellor and secretary and as ambassador to Louis XII, Cesare Borgia, Julius II and others. Being an exceptionally acute observer of the political scene, he soon became aware of the low esteem in which Florence was held abroad.

After the expulsion of the French from Italy in 1512, the Florentine government was overthrown and the Medici restored to power. Machiavelli was dismissed and in February 1513 he retired to his country house ten miles from the city. His letters to Vettori and Soderini reveal his boredom, frustration, bitterness, anxiety and nostalgia for politics. 'Fortune', he wrote, 'has so devised that since I cannot talk of the silk trade or the wool trade or of profit and loss, I have to talk of politics.' His mind ran on recent events and why they had happened. He came to the conclusion that policies should be judged solely by their results, not by the means used to attain them.

The lessons drawn by Machiavelli from his bitter experience of politics are embodied in *The Prince* (1513) and the *Discourses on Livy* (1515–17). Though he regarded man as basically anti-social and anarchical, he thought he could be educated to desire strong government. Strength alone mattered since 'fortune will not help those who will not help themselves'. To avoid mistakes in the present it was necessary to study the past and imitate its successful men. For examples of political wisdom Machiavelli turned to the Roman republic with its well-balanced society, efficient consulate and citizen militia and socially binding religion. At heart he was a republican, but he was ready to admit that despotism might be the answer to the needs of sixteenth-century Italy.

Machiavelli has been frequently misrepresented and misjudged. Cardinal Pole was convinced that Satan had held his pen; Frederick the Great called him 'the doctor of villainy'. In fact, Machiavelli was not a bad man but a realist passionately searching for the truth. Whereas writers in the past had mixed up politics with ethics and religion, he had the courage to affirm that politics are politics.

Chapter 20

Economic and Social Change

Europeans had travelled beyond the limits of their continent before the Renaissance, but in the fifteenth century a number of countries which had so far played no part in exploration began to send expeditions into uncharted seas. As a result of their efforts new lands were discovered, old superstitions shattered, hitherto respectable theories disproved and new sources of wealth tapped. The great overseas discoveries of the fifteenth and sixteenth centuries, in addition to being remarkable achievements in themselves, had far-reaching effects on the economic and social life of Europe. The opening up of the Cape route to the Spice Islands by the Portuguese threatened the monopoly hitherto enjoyed by Italian, particularly Venetian, merchants, while the discovery by the Spaniards of gold and silver Central and South America led to an increase of the amount of money circulating in Europe.

Among the goods which reached Europe from the Far East in the Middle Ages spices were particularly important. By the fifteenth century most of this trade came to Europe by sea. The goods were carried by Arab merchants from places like Malacca or Calicut across the Indian Ocean to ports along the Persian Gulf or Red Sea, whence they were carried by boat or overland to markets in Egypt or the Levant. Here they were bought by Venetian merchants who carried them the rest of the way to Europe. In short, the goods were bought and sold several times over, each time becoming more expensive. Moreover, the various governments straddling the route imposed heavy tolls and duties, so that the ultimate cost of the goods far exceeded their original price.

The Portuguese doubtless hoped that by discovering an alternative route to the Far East they would be able to obtain cheaper spices at least for themselves, but they were less successful than was once assumed. Although the Cape route to the East was free from tolls and duties and could be controlled from one extremity to the other by a single trading interest, it was almost twice as long as the old route. The risk of shipwreck and of cargoes deteriorating was consequently greater. The Portuguese were also less experienced than their rivals in handling and shipping goods, while Lisbon was less conveniently situated than Venice for the distribution of spices to the rest of Europe. Furthermore, the Portuguese were obliged to take military action in the Indian Ocean to protect their trade and, in an attempt to destroy that of their competitors, they had to spend a large amount of money on forts, ships, armaments and men. Thus it appears unlikely that they made large profits out of the spice business.

Had the Portuguese succeeded in destroying the trade of the Venetians and Arabs they would have been completely successful, but this did not happen. After a temporary setback early in the sixteenth century the old trade through the Levant revived. By 1560 it was so brisk that a Portuguese diplomat in Rome even suggested that his master should seriously think of importing spices that way himself if only he could come to terms with the Turks!

The recovery of the old trade was largely a result of the corruption and inefficiency of Portuguese officials in the East, who were ready to ignore it in return for a share of the profits. Thus the Portuguese spice trade was only a qualified success. The once popular notion that it caused the decline of Venice is no longer tenable. Piracy in the Mediterranean undermined the Venetian commercial structure to a much greater extent.

While the Portuguese were founding an empire in the Far East, the Spaniards created an empire of their own in Central and South America. Though the settlers were interested mainly in cattle, horses and sheep, they established sugar and tobacco plantations on coastal areas and discovered gold and silver.

During the first forty years of the sixteenth century the chief metal export from America was gold, either taken from the natives as barter or booty or mined in a primitive way by the conquistadores. However, in the 1540s, large deposits of silver were found at Potosi and Guanajuato. Mining was left to private enterprise but the Spanish government reserved to itself a proportion of the metal, known as the *quint*, approximately a fifth. Government agents were posted in America to prevent concealment and smuggling. All the bullion had to pass through the House of Trade in Seville, which was under the jurisdiction of the Council of the Indies. The government also controlled the supply of mercury which was used for extracting the silver from the ore.

Originally the bullion was carried to Spain by individual merchant ships which were armed and expected to defend themselves if attacked. Piracy, though, developed to such an extent that, in 1564, the Spanish government set up a system of convoys which sailed twice a year, in April and August. This proved quite efficient. The convoys reached their destination safely, except in 1628 when one was captured by the Dutch and in 1656 when another was intercepted by the English. On arrival the ships were carefully inspected by representatives of the

Above, merchants of the city of Hamburg in the 1480s. Ports throughout the northern and western coasts of Europe flourished at this time, as trade shifted from the Mediterranean to the Atlantic.

Below, a fifteenth-century Venetian galley, armed with both cannon and infantry; its power at sea formed the basis of Venice's expansion during the Italian Wars of the early sixteenth century. National Maritime Museum, London.

House of Trade before anyone was allowed ashore. The treasure was then transported to Seville where it was weighed and stored pending its disposal. Officially some eighteen thousand tons of silver and two hundred tons of gold reached Spain between 1521 and 1660.

The price revolution

A most important phenomenon of the sixteenth century was a rise in prices which affected the whole of Europe. This had serious social repercussions: people who depended on fixed incomes suffered, while others who lived by trade or speculation could grow rich quickly. Political life reflected these social changes.

The extent of the so-called price revolution is not easily assessed, for the documentary evidence available to the historian is difficult to interpret and often incomplete. Evidence exists only for certain areas and particular commodities. Little is known about the price of ordinary commodities like butter or cheese in England, but a fair amount about that of woollen cloth and other textiles. Variations in the size and quality of cloth, however, are not always indicated, so that it is often impossible to compare the prices of goods. The evidence for cereals is good but the price varied from year to year according to the harvests and even from district to district. Thus, it is impossible to compile a really accurate price index for the sixteenth century.

Despite these technical difficulties it would appear that the prices of basic consumable goods in England tripled by 1580 and quadrupled by 1600, a process which was reflected in other countries as well. In Flanders the price of wheat was 93 percent higher in 1521–22 than in the previous year, and in Hainaut 115 percent. In Antwerp there was a sharp rise in the price of fuel and the value of rents. In Spain there was a 2·8 percent average annual increase in prices from 1501 to 1562 and a 1·3 percent increase from 1562 to 1600. By comparison with more modern times the inflation of the sixteenth century was not particularly severe. It has been calculated that prices went up 400 percent in ninety years, whereas in the twentieth century they may have risen by as much in only forty years. But the price revolution came at the end of a long period of stable prices and sixteenth century society was less able to adapt itself to changing conditions than its modern counterpart.

Inflation occurs when 'too much money chases too few goods'. In the sixteenth century the scarcity of food and other commodities was blamed on such human weaknesses as idleness or greed. Sir Thomas More in *Utopia* blamed 'the unreasonable covetousness of a fewe' for 'the great dearth of victualles'. He believed that food was running short because greedy landlords were turning their land over to sheep on account of the profits to be made out of the sale of

wool. In 1533 Thomas Starkey asserted that 'a great part of these people which we have here in our country is either idle or ill-occupied.

In 1556, however, another explanation of the price revolution was advanced by Martín de Azpilcueta of the University of Salamanca. He showed that 'money is worth more when and where it is scarce than where it is abundant. We see by experience', he wrote,

> that in France, where money is scarcer than in Spain, bread, cloth and labour are worth much less. And even in Spain, in times when money was scarcer, saleable goods and labour were given for very much less than after the discovery of the Indies, which flooded the country with gold and silver.

This theory was further expounded in 1568 by the French lawyer, Jean Bodin, in a published reply to M. de Malestroit, who had blamed successive debasements of the coinage for the inflation.

Recently, however, the theory that the importation of precious metals from America was the principal cause of the price revolution has been largely discredited. American treasures did not begin to reach Europe in sizeable quantities until the middle of the sixteenth century, yet prices had begun to rise in the preceding fifty years. Moreover, much of the silver that reached Spain was immediately re-exported to pay for its imports, to maintain its armies abroad and to repay loans made by foreign bankers. As a result Spain suffered from a dearth rather than a surplus of gold and silver. This meant that in the seventeenth century it was obliged to adopt a billon currency, that is, base metal mixed with gold and silver. It would seem, therefore, that the price rise in Spain was a credit, not a monetary, inflation.

Population growth

In recent years the view has been adopted that a major cause of the price revolution was a rise in the population of Europe. This created a growing demand for food, fuel and clothing. As productivity failed to keep pace with this demand, goods became scarce and prices rose.

Again the sources available to the historian are unsatisfactory: no censuses or reliable estimates exist for any whole country in the sixteenth century. Information has to be pieced together from materials like parish registers, tax returns or muster rolls, which are frequently inaccurate or misleading. All the available evidence, however, points to a general rise in the population of Europe during the century. Some towns even doubled in size. In 1500 there were only five European cities with 100,000 inhabitants or more; by 1600 the number had grown to twelve or thirteen. The population of London may have gone up from fifty thousand to two hundred thousand. Certainly the city was making very heavy demands on the hinterland for food supplies, as were other towns like Bristol and Norwich.

In 1500 Seville had about sixty thousand

inhabitants. During the next two or three decades the number dropped as a result of epidemics and emigration, but it had risen to one hundred and fifty thousand by 1588. Smaller towns expanded to such an extent that they often had to build outside their walls and in the large cities there was much overcrowding. The growth in population was also felt in the countryside where there was fierce competition for limited amounts of farm land. Yet by modern standards sixteenth century Europe was thinly populated: the population of England rose from three and a half million in 1500 to five million in 1600 and that of the Holy Roman Empire from twelve to twenty million.

It is not difficult to see how the rise in population of the sixteenth century would affect prices. Wherever peasants farmed their land on temporary leases landlords could, and often did, raise their rents. Those tenants who could not afford the new rents left the land and either joined the armies of vagabonds who roamed about the countryside or flocked to the towns.

The rise in population meant an increased demand for food. To some extent this was met by improved methods of agriculture and the introduction of new crops such as rice in the Po valley. But most European farmers were illiterate and unable to read the new manuals of husbandry or, if they could, they lacked the capital necessary to carry out the improvements recommended. Consequently demand outstripped supply.

The price of other agricultural products was also affected by the rise in population. Until about 1550 wool prices in England and Spain (the only two countries which produced wool for an international market) rose even more rapidly than grain prices. This encouraged landlords to turn arable land into pasture. They enclosed common land and depopulated villages to make room for their flocks. This inevitably aggravated the problem of food supplies.

In Spain sheep-farming was practised on a huge scale in Castile where the soil and the climate were not favourable to other forms of cultivation. Each year enormous flocks of sheep were moved from the mountains of Old Castile to winter in the south. They were supposed to follow certain predetermined tracks but would often damage crops and cause soil erosion. Continual disputes arose between ordinary farmers and the guild of sheep farmers, called the Mesta, which enjoyed the full backing of the crown.

Above, sixteenth-century illustration from an edition of Marco Polo's voyages; Europeans were beginning to discover other races and societies and consequently found a new interest in earlier travellers.

Top, Harvesting, *by Pieter Brueghel; the paintings of peasant life of the mid-sixteenth century by Brueghel, despite their emphasis on hard work, show the relative prosperity and stability of the Low Countries. Metropolitan Museum, New York.*

Opposite top, Portuguese carracks of the mid-sixteenth century; at this date the Portuguese controlled much of the carrying trade of the Far East.

Opposite bottom, a sixteenth-century French port with ocean-going trading ships.

In 1501 the Mesta was given the right to use for ever and at fixed rents any land it had once used as pasture. The Spanish monarchy supported the Mesta in this way because it received a quick and sure revenue from taxes on sheep and the sale of wool. Arable farming was discouraged by this policy and Spain accordingly suffered from a serious shortage of grain. After 1506 it become more independent on foreign imports.

Spain was not the only country which failed to produce enough food for its growing population. After a severe famine in 1590–91 all the countries bordering on the western Mediterranean had to import grain from the Baltic. More Dutch and Hanseatic ships than ever before passed through the Sound between Denmark and Sweden laden with rye from Poland, Prussia and Pomerania. The newly constructed port of Leghorn (Livorno) became the main distributing centre in Italy for northern grain. The number of ships entering the port shot up from about 200 in 1592–93 to nearly 2,500 in 1609–10. The northerners had better crews and cheaper ships than the Italians, who began to lose the commercial dominance in this and in other aspects of the carrying trade which they had hitherto enjoyed.

If European agriculture failed to cope with the rising demand for food, the manufacturing industries proved more adaptable. Most of them did not require much fixed capital and they could use the increased labour force available. Only the guilds with their regulations limiting the number of apprentices and journeymen a master might employ stood in the way of greater productivity. But capitalist entrepreneurs could always go into the countryside or small country towns, where the people were only too glad to earn a little extra money by spinning and weaving at home. Alternatively the capitalists could take over the guilds and employ the master craftsmen on piece rates. Because the manufacturing industries were better able to keep abreast of the rising demand the price of their products did not go up as much as that of grain.

Although wages tended to go up in the sixteenth century they were seldom able to catch up with prices. In England and other countries, for example, the wages of building workers doubled during the century but food prices rose four or five times above their original level. It cannot be doubted, then, that wage earners were worse off in terms of real wages at the end of the century than at the beginning even allowing for the fact that retail prices did not go up as much as wholesale ones and that manufactured goods cost relatively less than food.

When the disparity between wages and prices became apparent in about 1530 a serious undercurrent of discontent developed among the labouring poor, occasionally flaring up into open revolt. If unemployment and low wages became combined with revolutionary religious propaganda the result could be devastating, as was shown by the Anabaptist take-over of Münster in 1534. Only those wage-earners who held land fixed at the old rate actually benefited from the price revolution, since, as their rent declined in value, they were able to get more for their produce on the local market.

Much has been written about the so-called 'rise of the gentry' in sixteenth-century England, but the picture is still far from clear. Some country gentlemen who held moderately large estates certainly did very well at this time, but it is difficult to say whether their success was a result of favourable market conditions or to royal favour. Other members of the gentry declined but no one has yet been able to work out exactly the ratio of 'declining' to 'rising' gentry. Nor was there anything new about merchants putting their capital in land with a view to becoming gentlemen or even members of the aristocracy. English society had always been fluid and the expanding economy of the sixteenth century simply offered wider opportunities for the movement of persons and capital.

A similar dearth of statistical evidence precludes a clear assessment of the effects of the price revolution on rural society in other parts of Europe. In Hainaut, and perhaps in the other Walloon provinces of the Netherlands, owners of reasonably large estates did better out of rising prices than smaller landowners. In France, on the other hand, it would seem that the lesser nobility were less successful in adjusting their rents to the economic situation. This would explain why so many were ready to join the armies engaged in the Wars of Religion. It is possible, however, that most of these were younger sons who had suffered as a result of the legal devices employed by their seniors to prevent the fragmentation of their estates.

On the whole the nobility in France, Spain and Italy managed to weather the storm of the price revolution quite well by raising rents or entry fines (premiums on transferring tenancies) at least as fast as prices and by exacting feudal dues and seigneurial monopolies. The upper nobility received gifts of pensions, lands and offices from the crown in return for their military and administrative services.

In Germany the social effects of the price revolution varied from one locality to another. In the west the nobility found it difficult to raise rents except in Bavaria and

Left, Jakob Fugger (1459–1525), the German banker whose control of the central European silver mines and position as financial backer of the Holy Roman Emperor made him one of the most powerful men of his day. Kupferstichkabinett, Berlin-Dahlem.

Far left, a sixteenth-century woodcut of a potter; most industry was still carried out in small workshops with few employees, and only capital-intensive industries such as mining, iron-founding and printing were worked on a larger scale.

Below, a fifteenth-century stained glass window from York, showing a nobleman visiting a prison as an act of charity. Many almshouses were endowed at this time as poverty became a chronic social problem.

Opposite top, The Poor Kitchen *and* The Rich Kitchen, *caricatures by Pieter Brueghel (1525–69) emphasizing the great differences in living standards even within the ranks of the peasantry. Inflation condemned some to poverty while others managed to consolidate their estates and attain the status of the gentry.*

Opposite bottom, a ship of the Hanseatic League, drawn by Pieter Brueghel in about 1500. By this date the League was facing serious opposition from the indigenous merchants of England and the Netherlands.

Austria where the ruling princes supported their claims to raise entry fines. In southwest Germany the princes provoked a considerable amount of peasant unrest by substituting autocratic Roman law for local custom, by taking over village and seigneurial jurisdiction and by imposing new taxes.

In Holstein and Denmark the nobles profited from high prices by acting as middlemen between the peasants and foreign merchants seeking grain and dairy produce. In northeast Germany and Poland they made the most of the growing market for rye, timber and furs in western and southern Europe. They raised a cheap labour force to farm their huge demesnes by tying the peasants to their holdings and exacting heavy labour services from them. The local princes did nothing to protect the peasants from this 'new serfdom' as they depended on the landowners or *Junkers* for money grants.

The golden age of Antwerp

European expansion overseas widened the scope of international trade and stimulated far-reaching changes in its organization and methods.

In the course of the sixteenth century the main focus of international trade shifted from the Mediterranean to the North Sea and the Atlantic, and Antwerp rose to a preeminent position. Within fifty years this city attracted to itself a high proportion of Europe's trade, becoming at the same time one of the largest money markets and an industrial centre. Its population rose from about fifty thousand in 1500 to around one hundred thousand in 1550, and these figures do not include a large floating population of foreign merchants.

Experience had shown that Lisbon was not a convenient centre for the distribution of spices to the rest of Europe. The Portuguese needed to exchange them for grain, metals and cloth. For centuries the Netherlands had been an important trading centre accessible to traders from many countries. In 1499, therefore, the Portuguese decided to establish their spice staple at Antwerp. Important as this event was, it was not the only reason for the city's golden age. The deepening of the river Scheldt linking Antwerp to the North Sea enabled ships which had been obliged previously to anchor in the estuary to go up river and unload directly at the port instead of having to trans-ship their cargoes. As a result the number of ships paying anchorage dues rose steeply during the century.

Antwerp was situated close to a network of rivers leading to the south. It was the terminus of a comparatively toll-free land route from Germany, so that even before the coming of the Portuguese it was thronged with German merchants who traded mainly in metals and fustians. Many English cloth merchants were there too. All these traders were attracted not only by the city's geographical situation but also by the favourable conditions attached to its two annual fairs. By the 1540s it was handling eighty percent of the Netherlands trade and exporting about three times as much as London.

In addition to being a clearing-house for goods, Antwerp imported a considerable quantity of food for its fast-growing population and this in turn gave rise to local industries like fish-curing and sugar-refining. Its main industry, however, was the finishing of English cloth, which necessitated the importation of dyes from southern Europe and America and of alum (used to fix the colours) from the papal states. Antwerp manufactured armaments and church bells and exported a wide range of goods such as furniture, tapestries, paintings, jewellery, glassware, books, paper, maps and musical instruments.

The growth of capitalism

Antwerp was also one of the foremost money markets in Europe. Originally merchants would transact business with each other directly but by the sixteenth century they had begun to work through bankers. These had often started their careers as merchants in various commodities and had then switched to trading in money, which

offered larger and quicker returns.

This was true of the great family business of Fugger, based at Augsburg in south Germany. Its fortunes were founded on the cloth trade but in the fifteenth century the scope of its activities was much enlarged by Jacob Fugger the Rich (1459–1525). He added silks and velvets, spices, metals and jewels to the linens and fustians which had been the firm's original commodities. To sell these goods he set up a chain of counting houses and merchandise depots in all the great cities of central and western Europe. At the same time he went into the metal trade, gaining control of the output of silver, copper and iron in central Europe and of silver and mercury in Spain. Jacob Fugger then bought or financed mines to extend his monopoly.

By the sixteenth century the firm of Fugger had become the leading banking house in Europe. Its wealth was so great that it was even able to come to the rescue of impecunious princes. In return for mining concessions it would do almost anything for the Habsburgs and it was largely owing to its financial assistance that Charles V was elected emperor in 1519. When he delayed over the repayment of his debt Jacob Fugger lost no time in bluntly reminding him: 'it is well known that your Majesty without me might not have acquired the imperial crown'.

The development of banking was closely bound up with the trade boom of the sixteenth century. Few merchants ever paid cash in Antwerp: they bought and sold their goods by means of bills of exchange provided by the bankers. They relied on advances and settled their accounts by instalments. The complex transactions that took place offered incomparable opportunities for speculation. At first, interest rates were high and erratic but they settled down by the 1540s to between twelve and fifteen percent. Henry VIII of England borrowed about a million pounds on the Antwerp market during the last four years of his reign.

The sixteenth century was an age of feverish speculation. The stock exchanges of Antwerp and Lyons were permanent establishments, unlike the old medieval fairs which had been held only from time to time. Merchants setting off on long voyages at sea began to insure their lives. State lotteries and loans made their appearance. An innovation deserving special notice was the creation of the *rentes sur l' Hôtel de Ville* in 1522. The French king, Francis I, obtained a loan from the general public against the security not of the state but of the municipal government of Paris. In return the lenders were promised an annual *rente* representing an interest of about eight percent. In 1555 Henry II launched the *Grand Parti* (Great Deal) of Lyons which started a great rush of investors.

The decline of Antwerp

The golden age of Antwerp was short-lived. In 1549 the Portuguese, finding that they could get silver more easily and cheaply from Spain and that the Germans were willing to trade directly with Lisbon, withdrew their spice staple. This blow was followed by the collapse of the English cloth trade. As a result of the English government's devaluation of silver in 1550, the Merchant Adventurers were able to export a record amount of cloth to Antwerp, causing a temporary glut. When sterling was revalued in the following year the price of cloth shot up and the trade suffered a setback from which it never fully recovered during the rest of the century.

All this coincided with a slump in the Spanish-American trade, a renewal of war between the King of France and the emperor, two successive harvest failures and a round of national bankruptcies. The Spanish government transformed all its debts into state bonds or *juros*. Its example was soon followed by the Netherlands, French and Portuguese governments. As a result the Antwerp bankers defaulted on their obligations and the small investors who had financed the government loans were severely hit. The final blows were struck after the outbreak of the Dutch revolt. In 1576 Antwerp was sacked by Spanish troops, and in 1585 the Scheldt was closed by the Dutch.

Above, a view of Antwerp; in the sixteenth century this city became the trading centre of northern Europe, for wool, cloth, wheat and banking, as well as being the centre of the trade in diamonds. National Scheepvaartmuseum, Antwerp.

Left, The Fight between Carnival and Lent *by Pieter Brueghel; the pagan festival of Carnival still flourished, especially in the Mediterranean countries, and was greatly opposed by the Reformation.*

Opposite top left, cartographers at work in the sixteenth century. The development of navigational skills led to many scientific advances, in astronomy, physics and geography, and special schools were founded to teach these new sciences to the seamen.

Opposite bottom left, an agricultural scene from a book of 1502. The population of western Europe rose in the next century, and a reorganization of agriculture was necessary, both to feed the towns and to provide for industries such as cloth.

Opposite right, this painting of a banker and his wife, by Quentin Massys, shows the spirit of early sixteenth-century capitalism of the Low Countries in action – frugality, devotion to work and relative equality between the sexes. Musée du Louvre, Paris.

Protestantism and capitalism

How far was the rise of capitalism connected with the Reformation? In 1904 the German sociologist, Max Weber, argued that the Protestant concept of the 'calling'—the interpretation of worldly avocations as divinely appointed and capable of fulfilment in a spirit of worship—enabled the Protestant to pursue his daily life energetically and profitably. The Roman Church, he alleged, had condemned the world and opposed economic development, particularly the taking of interest. The Protestant ethic was thus seen as the essential prerequisite for the growth of modern capitalism. Finally, Weber argued, capitalism had developed to a greater extent in Protestant than in Catholic countries, while the Reformation had found its most enthusiastic followers among traders and industrialists.

Attractive as the Weber thesis may seem, it does not stand up well to investigation. Capitalism existed before the Reformation and the late medieval Church was not totally opposed to the taking of interest. In the late fifteenth century the Franciscans established benevolent funds for loans to the poor and charged interest on them to cover administrative costs. The Lateran Council of 1515 recognized the impossibility of interest-free loans. Thus Calvin was not being revolutionary when he grudgingly defended usury at five percent in certain carefully guarded circumstances. Protestant preaching consistently denounced acquisitiveness as sinful. The concept of the calling certainly implied that a man could serve God in the world, but it did not suggest that profit should be his main object in life.

It is also not true to say that capitalism reached its fullest expression in Protestant as distinct from Catholic countries. It was strong in the Netherlands long before Calvinism reached there and it hardly existed in Calvin's own stronghold of Geneva. Jacob Fugger, who once declared his intention to continue enlarging his fortune as long as he could, was not a Protestant. In short, no good reason exists for linking Protestantism and capitalism in any significant way.

Chapter 21

The Reformation

The Reformation was far more than a movement directed against abuses in the Roman Church; it was the culmination of a complex situation with roots deeply buried in the medieval past.

Serious abuses did exist, of course, in the Church on the eve of the Reformation. One of the most widespread was pluralism, the accumulation of more than one benefice in the hands of one man. Often this was economically justified. In an age of inflation it was not always possible for a clergyman to live on the income of a single benefice, so he obtained a papal dispensation to hold more than one. Pluralism was spiritually insidious, however, for it necessarily entailed absenteeism and the neglect of pastoral duties.

Another common abuse was clerical ignorance. Few educational opportunities existed even for the clergy outside the universities, and only a relatively small proportion of clergymen were graduates properly equipped to teach the faith. Among the regular clergy there was a fair amount of laxity about the observance of monastic rules: the choral office was neglected, the refectory abandoned, fasting neglected, silence at meals ignored and the teaching of novices was inadequate. At the highest level of the Church nepotism was a serious problem. One of the worst offenders in this respect was Pope Sixtus IV, who created his nephews cardinals or made them lords of cities. The Renaissance popes generally were much more concerned with their temporal interests in Italy than with their responsibilites as spiritual leaders.

Clerical abuses were a cause of anticlericalism in the late Middle Ages, but they had always existed and churchmen realized the need to remedy them. Decline and renewal were normal processes in the evolution of the Church, which had been largely built up by successive generations of reformers. The Reformation was not primarily a movement of the laity against the clergy. It was largely a movement of the clergy against the growth of centralization in the Church.

The crisis in the Church was constitutional as well as moral. The papacy had become an absolute monarchy: it controlled ecclesiastical appointments through the system of 'reservations' and 'nominations' and it taxed the clergy by means of annates (payments claimed by the pope from the first year's revenue of a new benefice) and tenths (ten percent on all clerical incomes). This caused much discontent among the clergy and the demand arose for a reform of the Church in its head as well as its members. But who was to carry out this reform? Could the papacy be trusted to reform itself?

In the fourteenth century the theory was advanced that the responsibility of reforming the Church lay with a general council of the Church, not with the pope. A disputed election to the papacy in 1378 enabled the conciliarists to put their ideas into practice. If the Council of Constance (1414–18) succeeded in healing the Great Schism, it failed to curb papal authority, and the Council of Basle (1431–49) was equally unsuccessful. By their radicalism the conciliarists had unconsciously harmed the cause of reform, for the popes were thereafter reluctant to call another council, fearing that their authority would be challenged. As a result reform was left to the initiative of individuals whose activities were necessarily limited to particular religious houses or dioceses.

Church versus state

The constitutional conflict within the Church was paralleled by another crisis caused by the emergence of powerful secular forces. The kings and princes of Europe wanted complete mastery of their own states. They aimed at controlling the lives, thoughts and pockets of their subjects. The Church, with its own legal and fiscal organization cutting across national boundaries, was an obstacle in the path of the royal efforts to achieve a centralized administration. Friction between Church and state had always existed, but it now reached a dangerous intensity. The Reformation often took the form of a movement by national lay rulers to achieve their independence from an international Church which had outlived its day.

Finally the Reformation was a reaction againsy the doctrinal teaching of the Church which had ceased to satisfy large sections of the clergy and laity. Throughout Europe the late fifteenth century was marked by a profound spiritual restlessness. People were no longer content to accept the truth, they wanted to understand it. As the Renaissance helped to sharpen their minds they began to re-examine the sources of Christianity, particularly the writings of St Paul.

It is undeniable that a connection existed between the Renaissance and the Reformation but, as the quarrel between Erasmus and Luther over the question of free will was to demonstrate, a deep ideological gulf divided the two movements. Whereas Renaissance scholars believed in man's ability to better himself by his own efforts, the leaders of the Reformation saw him as utterly incapable of achieving salvation without God's grace.

Above, a drawing of Erasmus by Albrecht Dürer; Erasmus' criticisms of the abuses of the Catholic church have led him to be called 'the foster-father of the Reformation', although he disagreed with Luther on many points. Musée du Louvre, Paris.

Opposite top, a printing press at Nuremburg in the fifteenth century. Printing with movable type had been invented in the 1450s and very quickly spread throughout Europe. Many printers were supporters of the New Learning and the Reformation.

Opposite bottom, Amsterdam in the sixteenth century. The city grew rapidly to become the main trading centre of northern Europe, especially as its rival Antwerp suffered during the Dutch War of Independence in the 1570s.

Luther

Martin Luther was born on 10 November 1483 at Eisleben, on the edge of the Thuringian Forest. Though a miner, his father, Hans, was not poor and soon after Martin's birth he moved to Mansfeld where he became part owner of six shafts and two foundries and a town councillor. He was thus able to give Martin a good education.

Luther's childhood appears to have been perfectly normal. His parents were serious, hard-working and devout but not unduly strict or cruel. As a schoolboy Luther mastered Latin and became a good musician. In 1501 he was sent to the University of Erfurt, where he gained the reputation of being cheerful, witty, hard-working and devout.

Religion already meant so much to Luther that he decided not to become a lawyer, as his father had intended, but to enter the Order of Augustinian Hermits in Erfurt. It is often said that he reached this decision after he had narrowly escaped death in a thunderstorm, but he really made up his mind after a long search for God.

From an early age Luther was deeply preoccupied with the question of his own salvation. As a monk and a priest he did all the customary acts of penance: he deliberately inflicted pain upon himself by beating his own body, and spent hours confessing his sins, but peace of mind continued to elude him. In 1510 he was sent to Rome but he returned disillusioned. 'Like a fool', he said later, 'I took onions to Rome and brought back garlic.'

In 1511 Luther was transferred to Wittenberg where he was persuaded to take his doctorate and become a preacher. But he was still groping for the truth. God appeared to him as a demanding and angry judge, not as a gracious and merciful father. His vision of God was at times so terrifying that he once compared it with seeing the Devil.

Then came the light. In 1513 as he was preparing his lectures on the Psalms he began to question the traditional meaning given to the biblical term 'righteousness'. He turned to the text in the first chapter of St Paul's *Epistle to the Romans*: 'For therein is the righteousness of God revealed from faith to faith: as it is written, The just shall live by faith'. Gradually Luther began to see righteousness in a new light: as a forgiving righteousness, not as a punitive one, whereby God reconciled sinful man to Himself. 'When I had realized this', he wrote, 'I felt myself absolutely born again. The gates of Paradise had been flung open and I had entered. There and then the whole of Scripture took on another look to me.'

From this time onwards Luther devoted himself to the task of revealing the truth to his fellow men by liberating Scripture from the false interpretation of the schoolmen. He did not become widely known, however, until November 1517, when he protested against the sale of indulgences by posting up his famous ninety-five theses on the door of the castle church at Wittenberg.

Indulgences were papal certificates releasing men from some of the penalties of sin, and a famous case of their misuse occurred when Albert of Hohenzollern declared that he wished to become Archbishop of Mainz. He already held the sees of Magdeburg and Halberstadt, although he was not old enough to be a bishop at all. The pope was prepared to overlook these impediments in return for the enormous fee of ten thousand ducats. As Albert did not have the money he borrowed it from the Fuggers. The pope assisted him to repay the loan by authorizing a sale of indulgences on condition that half the proceeds would go to the Fuggers and half to the rebuilding of St Peter's in Rome.

Although the certificates of indulgence were carefully worded to exclude the notion that divine forgiveness could be purchased and sold, John Tetzel, who hawked them around in Saxony, indulged in unscrupulous salesmanship. He pointed to the dead souls languishing in the torments of purgatory crying out for relief. 'As soon as the coin in the coffer rings', he explained, 'the soul from purgatory springs.'

When Luther was told about Tetzel's activities he remarked: 'I'll knock a hole into his drum', yet his indignation was not provoked by the sale of indulgences so much as the doctrine upon which it was based, which was incompatible with his own belief in justification by faith. He was deeply concerned about the way in which people assumed that an indulgence was a remission not merely of penalty but also of guilt.

The ninety-five theses were not extreme. They were simply intended to start an academic debate. Within a few weeks, however, they were printed and widely circulated in Switzerland and Germany. The Dominicans in Saxony espoused Tetzel's cause and pressed charges against Luther in Rome. But because of the political situation the papacy failed to act swiftly.

Although the Emperor Maximilian was still alive, it was clear that his days were numbered and that a successor would soon have to be elected. From the papacy's point of view the safest candidate was Frederick the Wise, Elector of Saxony, who happened to be Luther's lord. Frederick did not sympathize with his attack on indulgences but was determined that he should be given a fair hearing on German soil.

In 1518 Luther was ordered to appear before Cardinal Cajetan at Augsburg. The cardinal urged him to revoke his doctrines without preliminary discussion but Luther refused. In June 1519 he was drawn into a debate at Leipzig with the redoubtable Dominican, John Eck. It began as a harmless metaphysical exchange but soon shifted on to the much more dangerous question of papal authority. Eck was prompted to accuse Luther of Hussitism by his contention that Scripture, not the papacy, was the ultimate authority in religious matters.

After the Leipzig debate Luther published several works in which he elaborated his view of the sacraments. They did not in his view function automatically but through faith in the promises of Christ. He doubted if they numbered more than three: baptism, communion, penance. By 1520 he had rejected the Catholic doctrine of transubstantiation according to which, when the priest pronounces the words 'this is my body', the substance of the bread and wine on the altar is changed into the flesh and blood of Christ while continuing to look, taste and feel as before. Luther accepted that the bread and wine are the body of Christ but denied that their substance was changed. God, he argued, is everywhere and in everything, and in administering the sacrament the priest merely serves as an agent in the self-disclosure of God. To this extent Luther continued to believe that God was actually present in the sacrament, so that Catholics and Lutherans shared the doctrine of God's Real Presence.

Meanwhile many people rallied to Luther's side without always understanding the fundamental reasons of his protest. Ulrich von Hutten wished to draw him into a national revolt against Rome. Another humanist, Philip Melanchthon (1497–1560), became his right-hand man and did much to systematize his theology. The great painter, Albrecht Dürer, belonged to a circle of Lutheran intellectuals at Nuremberg. The Imperial Knights, whose unique constitutional position was being threatened by the territorial princes, also came out in support of Luther.

In June 1520 the pope at last condemned Luther in the Bull *Exsurge domine* while allowing him sixty days in which to retract.

Luther's retort was to throw into a bonfire the Bull along with the whole body of canon law before a gathering of university teachers and students. As a result of this incident he was excommunicated in January 1521.

In the meantime, Luther published three pamphlets of great significance. *The Address to the Christian Nobility of the German Nation,* which was written in German, called on the German rulers to reform the papacy and the entire ecclesiastical hierarchy. In *The Babylonian Captivity of the Church* Luther outlined his theology and condemned the papacy for depriving Christians of direct access to God through faith. Yet he had not given up hope of making his peace with the Church. In *The Freedom of a Christian Man* he expounded in a conciliatory tone, for the pope's attention, his idea of the evangelical life, albeit without retracting his views.

The newly elected emperor, Charles V, though not opposed to Church reform or even to a curbing of papal authority, intended to defend the old faith. He feared that rebellion against the Church would easily lead to rebellion against the state. Yet he could not ignore the wishes of the German people and those of the electors, so he agreed to summon Luther to explain himself at the Diet of Worms. Many of the reformer's friends warned him of the dangers of accepting the invitation, even with a safe-conduct in his pocket. But Luther, confident in the power of the Gospel, announced that he would go to Worms even if there were 'as many devils in it as there were tiles on the roofs of the houses'.

When he appeared before the emperor and the Estates he was asked to retract his views, but he refused. He boldly declared,

> Unless I am convinced of error by the testmony of Scripture or by clear reason I cannot and will not recant anything, for it is neither safe not honest to act against one's conscience. God help me. Amen.

As no compromise seemed feasible Luther was given permission to return to Wittenberg. On his way through the Thuringian forest, however, he was spirited off by his friends to the Wartburg castle where he remained for almost a year. In May 1521 he was placed under the imperial ban, but Charles V could not enforce the edict, so that Luther continued his activities without interruption.

In addition to works condemning priestly confession and absolution, monastic vows and clerical celibacy, he produced in the incredibly short time of eleven weeks a translation into German of the New Testament, five thousand copies of which were sold in two months. Meanwhile, his followers, including many members of the regular clergy, preached his doctrine in the towns. They were joined by all kinds of agitators with views far more extreme than Luther's. At Wittenberg, Carlstadt and Zwilling set out to destroy all that remained of the old religious order. The arrival of the Zwickau 'prophets' coincided with riots in which religious images were destroyed and Luther, who strongly disapproved of violence, had to come out of hiding to restore order. He and his friends then began to construct a Church in accordance with the teaching of the gospel.

With the assistance of printing the Reformation spread rapidly to many parts of the empire. By 1528 Brandenburg, Brunswick-Lüneburg, Schleswig-Holstein, Mansfeld and Silesia had become Lutheran. The most popular form of Reformation literature was the pamphlet illustrated by woodcuts. Some of these were designed by Lucas Cranach the Elder (1472–1553), to whom we are indebted for the best portraits of Luther. Hymns and religious plays also helped to popularize the Reformation. Luther himself composed hymns, the best known being *Ein' Feste Burg* (*God is our refuge*). The poet Heine called it 'the Marseillaise of the Reformation'.

The Peasants' War

Popular as it was, the Lutheran movement could not satisfy the social aspirations of the lower orders of German society. The peasants in particular were dissatisfied with their status, which was being depressed by the reception of Roman Law, and wanted to be relieved of many feudal obligations and fiscal burdens. For a time they translated Luther's doctrines into social terms and looked to him as a leader, but if he sympathized with their complaints he was

Above, a painting of the four evangelists stoning the pope for his worldliness and corruption; this work by Girolamo da Treviso illustrates that opposition to the abuses of the Church was not confined to north of the Alps. Royal Collection.

Below, Knight, Death and Devil *(1513) by Albrecht Dürer; the idea of the resolute combating the real distractions of the devil was one that Luther felt personally. British Museum, London.*

Opposite, Martin Luther (1483–1546) painted by Lucas Cranach; Luther had a curiously ambivalent attitude towards authority, demanding freedom from the rules of the Church but insisting on the absolute subjection of the individual to God.

consistently opposed to violent action on their part. However, his *Admonition to Peace* came too late. In June 1524 the Peasants' War had broken out in the Black Forest and it quickly spread to many parts of Germany.

In Saxony and Thuringia Thomas Münzer, a former disciple of Luther, exploited the upheaval to fulfil a mystical vision. Denouncing the princes as 'godless rascals', he issued bloodcurdling orders of the day, signed 'the Sword of Gideon'. Luther was appalled by the turn of events. In *Against the Murdering Hordes of Peasants* he encouraged the princes to 'strike, throttle, thrust, each man who can, secretly or openly and bear in mind that nothing is more poisonous, harmful or devilish than a rebellious man'. Luther feared that the revolt would compromise his own movement, but his attitude was consistent with his theology: civil government and the existing social order were divinely instituted; to rebel against them was an offence against God.

The Peasants' War ended bloodily. When the princes offered terms to the rebels assembled at Frankenhausen, Münzer told them that God had promised them victory and that he would catch the princes' cannon balls in the folds of his cloak. Without cavalry or guns, however, the peasants could do nothing. As the first cannon balls fell upon them they fled in panic and were cut down by the princes' cavalry. Münzer, who was found hiding in a cellar, was tortured and beheaded. As a result of Luther's role in the Peasants' War his movement lost much of its popular appeal. Many peasants and townsmen, feeling that he had let them down, turned to Anabaptism, a more radical form of Protestantism.

After 1525 the religious situation in Germany crystallized. The Catholic princes formed the League of Dessau while the Lutherans banded together at Torgau. Because of the Lutheran majority at the Diet of Speyer in 1526 a law was passed making each prince responsible for his own religious policy. This was revoked three years later by a Catholic majority in the Diet. The Lutherans protested against this decision—hence the term 'Protestant'. But the reformers lacked unity.

In 1529 a conference was called at Marburg to settle differences between the Lutherans and the Zwinglians of Switzerland and south Germany. It failed because Luther and Zwingli could not agree on the interpretation of the communion service or Eucharist. This disunity occurred at the worst possible time, for in 1530 Charles V was able to turn his attention to Germany. At the Diet of Augsburg the Protestants produced not one confession of faith but three, while the Catholics refused to make any doctrinal concessions.

Zwingli

Huldreych Zwingli (1484–1531) departed from Catholic doctrine in 1519 and more radically than Luther. Whereas the latter adhered to the doctrine of Christ's Real Presence in the Eucharist, Zwingli considered the communion service to be simply commemorative. The two reformers also disagreed about baptism, justification by faith and other doctrinal questions.

Fundamentally they differed in their view of human nature. Zwingli was closer to the humanist in his belief that man could acquire faith by studying the Word of God. He was als more of a fundamentalist in that he would accept only practices enjoined by Scripture. Thus, he rejected fasting, clerical celibacy, religious images and church music. His attachment to the Bible was shown by his activities as a preacher and church organizer in Zürich after the bishop's authority had been removed. The Bible was translated and published in Zürich in 1530, four years before the appearance of Luther's German Bible.

Perhaps Zwingli's most important contribution was the stress he placed on discipline. Under his influence matrimonial and moral questions were submitted to a special court made up of clergymen and city magistrates. This identified Church and state in a way that Luther had never envisaged. Zwingli was the most politically minded of the leading reformers. Having taken part in the Italian wars, he was strongly opposed to the mercenary system and persuaded Zürich to give it up. But the poorer Catholic cantons in the Swiss Confederation depended on it for their livelihood. A war developed between them and Zürich and Zwingli was killed at the Battle of Kappel (October 1531). Thereafter Swiss Protestantism lost it belligerency. Under Heinrich Bullinger (1504–75) it concentrated on its spiritual work.

Anabaptism

From the start of the Reformation various reformers showed more radical tendencies than Luther or Zwingli. Because they were generally opposed to infant baptism they became known as Anabaptists (from the Greek word for 'baptising again'). However, their views differed widely, ranging from a passive attitude towards life with devotional contemplation (quietism) to the active promotion of Christ's reign on earth (chiliasm). They sprang up in different places more or less simultaneously and lacked any cohesion.

The first known case of an adult baptism was administered in Zürich in 1525 by Conrad Grebel, who argued that a man was not born into a Church but accepted on profession of faith and the promise to lead a holy life. Because they believed that the professed believers were separate from the world, most Anabaptists refused to serve the state in any capacity. As a result they became regarded as a disruptive influence in society and were fiercely persecuted by the civil authorities and by Catholics and Protestants. After their expulsion from Zürich in 1525 they carried their ideas to southern Germany, Upper Austria, Moravia, Hungary, the Netherlands and elsewhere.

One of the Anabaptist leaders in the Netherlands, David Joris, saw himself as the prophet of the coming millennium, but the quietism of his *Book of Wonders* (1542) was not reflected in the careers of Jan Matthys of Haarlem and Jan Beuckelsz of Leyden. They sent out a call to arms against all unbelievers and in February 1534 led a revolution in the episcopal city of Münster in Westphalia. Common ownership of all things on the basis of the Bible was introduced.

When Matthys died in April, Beuckelsz assumed the title of king under the name of Jan van Leyden. His introduction of polygamy and his unbridled brutality caused considerable resentment, facilitating the city's recapture by Philip of Hesse and the local bishop in June 1535. The Anabaptist leaders were tortured to death and their bodies placed in iron cages and hung in the tower of the Lambert church. Vigorous action was taken at the same time against Anabaptists everywhere in Europe. Their movement became respectable only when it was purged of its radical elements under Menno Simons (1496–1561). From East Friesland his congregation spread to many parts of Europe and America.

John Calvin

Whereas Lutheranism remained largely confined to Germany and Scandinavia and soon lost much of its dynamic force, Calvinism spread from France and Geneva to many parts of Europe, seriously threatening the survival of Catholicism in the second half of the sixteenth century.

John Calvin was born at Noyon in Picardy on 10 July 1509. His father, Gérard Cauvin (Calvin being derived from the Latin form of the name), was a lawyer employed by the cathedral chapter. He obtained two benefices for his son and in 1523 sent him to Paris for his education. At the Collège de la Marche he was taught by Mathurin Cordier, an excellent Latin scholar. Then he was moved to the Collège de Montaigu where Erasmus and Rabelais had studied. The damp walls, disgusting food and harsh discipline nearly ruined his health.

In 1528 his father decided to change the direction of his eduction from theology to law. He was sent to Orléans and to Bourges. Here he also learned Greek and possibly some Hebrew from Melchior Wolmar, a Lutheran scholar. In 1531 Calvin was released by his father's death from the obligation to continue his legal studies. He returned to Paris and devoted his attention to humanism. In April 1532 he published his first work, a commentary on Seneca's *De Clementia*.

No one knows exactly when Calvin first embraced Protestant ideas, but it was probably in about 1533, when he became associated with Gérard Roussel and other evangelicals. His conversion soon brought him into trouble with the authorities. In November 1533 his friend, Nicholas Cop, rector of the University of Paris, delivered an inaugural address betraying Lutheran sympathies. This provoked a strong reaction and Calvin, who was suspected of having written the address, escaped to Saintonge, where he may have started work on his *Institutes* in a fine library placed at his disposal by Louis du Tillet. He called on Jacques Lefèvre d'Ètaples, the founder of French evangelicalism, who was living in retirement at Nérac.

After resigning his ecclesiastical benefices Calvin visited Poitiers and Orléans where he preached and administered the Lord's Supper in a Protestant form. In October 1534 a campaign of persecution was unleashed against Protestants after they had affixed posters attacking the Mass in a number of French towns. Calvin fled to Strasbourg and Basle, where the first edition of his *Institutes of the Christian Religion* was published in March 1536.

Although the *Institutes* was subsequently altered and enlarged, the first edition contained the basic elements of the Calvinistic doctrine. It emphasized the majesty and absolute sovereignty of God and the hopeless corruption of man as a consequence of the Fall. Though predestination was implied in this doctrine, Calvin did not lay stress upon it until later.

Another important aspect of his doctrine was the authority which he gave to scripture, but he made clear that it was not sufficient to read the Bible; it had to be understood, and this required the help of the Holy Spirit. He had no time for a purely mystical approach to religion. Finally, while Calvin believed that the true Church was invisible and made up of the elect of God, he also believed in the necessity of a visible Church, independent of, yet related to, the state.

In later years Calvin devoted much of his time to the elaboration, clarification and enlargement of the *Institutes*. The sixth and last edition on 1559 was five times bigger than the first and was arranged differently. The first French translation was published in 1541. This was an important event not only for the popularization of the Reformation but also for the development of French vernacular literature.

In 1536, after a journey to Italy, Calvin returned to France to deal with some family business. He then planned to go to Strasbourg but, as the direct road was blocked by an imperial army, he made a detour to Geneva, expecting to stop there only one night. The city, however, was in the midst of a religious revolution led by the fiery French Protestant exile, Guillaume Farel, who persuaded Calvin to remain and help him. Calvin described what happened as follows:

Farel strained every nerve to detain me. Having learned that my heart was set on

Below, illustration of 1607 ridiculing the beliefs of the Anabaptists.

Bottom, Adam and Eve *(1504) by Albrecht Dürer; although this work was done before the rise of Protestantism, the themes of the fall of man and original sin figured highly in the preoccupations of the Reformers. Staatliche Museen zu Berlin.*

Opposite, John Calvin (1509–64), who developed a form of Protestantism which gave the individual responsibility for his own spiritual welfare.

devoting myself to private studies he uttered an imprecation that God would curse my retirement and the tranquillity of my studies which I sought if I should withdraw and refuse to give assistance when the need was so pressing. I felt as if God from heaven had laid His mighty hand to arrest me. . . . I was so stricken with terror that I desisted from the journey I had undertaken.

Because of the strange circumstances which had combined to bring him to Geneva, Calvin believed that he had been commissioned by God to build there a truly Christian community. The task did not prove easy, for the leading citizens of Geneva were motivated by political rather than religious considerations. Having overthrown the authority of the bishop, they undertook 'to live in this holy evangelical law and word of God' and to abandon 'all masses and other papal ceremonies and abuses, images and idols'. When, however, Calvin and Farel tried to enforce discipline among them by means of excommunication they resisted and, following a number of incidents, asked the reformers to leave.

Calvin retired to Strasbourg where he became pastor to the congregation of French exiles and married Idelette of Buren. Although his basic ideas did not change, he developed his views on predestination and church organization under Bucer's influence.

In Calvin's absence the political and religious situation in Geneva became so chaotic that he was soon invited to return. At the insistence of his friends he decided to follow God's will and reappeared in the city in June 1541. The authorities gave him a beautiful house and garden near the lake and a salary. Helped by six council members he promptly drew up a new constitution for the Genevan Church called the Ecclesiastical Ordinances.

The Genevan Church was allowed more independence than those of Luther or Zwingli. The chief innovation of the ordinances was the recognition of the four offices of pastor, teacher, elder and deacon. The pastors, numbering five at first, constituted the venerable company. They were responsible for preaching the Gospel, administering the sacraments and admonishing members. New pastors were elected by the venerable company with the approval of the city council.

Frequent services were provided in Geneva's three parishes. The teachers who had the duty of instructing the young in 'sound doctrine' were examined by a two-man committee. The twelve elders were laymen responsible for the enforcement of discipline. Each supervised one of Geneva's twelve districts and was expected to visit each family at least once a year. The deacons assisted the pastors in supervising poor relief, visiting the sick and needy and administering the city hospital.

The central part of the constitution of the Genevan Church was the consistory made up of the twelve elders and five pastors. It gathered once a week to admonish, reprimand and correct citizens who had opposed the official doctrine, stayed away from church or behaved in an un-Christian way. The consistory, which could also excommunicate, undertook its work with more enthusiasm than tact. Citizens were summoned before it for the most trivial deviations from the straight and narrow path, while more serious offences were punished with great severity. Between 1542 and 1546 seventy-six persons were banished from Geneva and fifty-eight executed for heresy, adultery, blasphemy or witchcraft.

For the first five years after his return to Geneva Calvin got along relatively well with the city authorities. He helped to recodify the city's laws and to revise the constitution and his advice was sought on many matters ranging from defence to fire prevention. Yet his leadership was seriously challenged after 1545 when a number of prominent citizens strongly objected to the consistory's activities. In the end, however, he managed to assert his authority.

Calvin's hold on Geneva depended on the faithful exercise of his duties as preacher and teacher. He was therefore very zealous in maintaining 'the pure doctrine' and in rooting out heresy. Sebastian Castellio was banished for denying the inspiration of the Song of Solomon, while Jerome Bolsec suffered the same fate after he had argued that the doctrine of predestination implied that God was the cause of all sin.

In August 1553 Michael Servetus, who had published books repudiating the doctrine of the Holy Trinity, was foolhardy enough to visit Geneva. He was at once arrested, tried and burnt. Calvin justified the execution in *A Defense of the Orthodox Faith,* but Castellio protested against this use of force. In *Concerning Heretics, Whether they are to be Persecuted* he argued that to burn heretics was contrary to Christ's merciful teaching. Most Protestant leaders, however, sided with Calvin. After the Servetus affair his authority in Geneva was unchallenged and in 1559 he was made a citizen.

An event of prime significance for the development of Calvinism was the founding of the Genevan Academy in June 1559. Its first rector was the French humanist, Theodore Beza (1519–1605), who eventually succeeded Calvin as leader of his movement. The academy was divided into a primary or 'private' school, in which the young were taught French, Latin, Greek and the elements of logic, and a secondary or 'public' school, in which Greek, Hebrew, theology and philosophy were taught. Tuition in both was free and the student received a certificate of attendance, not a degree, at the end of his course. At Calvin's death in 1564 the 'private school' numbered 1200 students and the 'public school' 300. The latter were mostly foreigners who, after they had finished their studies, carried Calvin's doctrine back to their own countries.

Calvin went further than Luther in encouraging the Christian to serve God through as well as in his calling. His followers participated actively in political, economic and social life. Success in business came to be regarded as evidence of self-denial and hard work to the glory of God. But if Calvin's example encouraged the bourgeois virtues, it is important to remember that he constantly stressed the traditional Christian virtues of self-sacrifice, humility and joy in God's salvation. Contrary to common belief, Calvin did not initiate a law permitting the taking of interest; he simply gave his approval to an existing law protecting the poor from exorbitant rates. The idea that Calvin was responsible for the rise of capitalism is absurd. His chief concern was moral and religious.

When the final edition of the *Institutes* appeared in 1559 Calvin's doctrine was complete and predestination had become central to it. This was not Calvin's invention; it was rooted in Augustinian and scholastic theology and was shared by the other reformers. Calvin simply made its implications clearer.

Predestination means that before the beginning of the world God chose some men (the elect) for eternal salvation, regardless of their merits in life, and left others to suffer eternal damnation, the fate which all men deserve. This doctrine did not lead to fatalism among Calvin's followers; on the contrary, they were confident that God had chosen them for salvation. The elect, according to Calvin, were those who publicly professed their faith and covenant with God, walked in the ways of God and participated in the sacraments. The clarity of these criteria goes far to explain Calvinistic activism. Certainty of election was accompanied by confidence in the future and hope of establishing a Christian commonwealth on earth.

The spread of Calvinism

The Calvinists were only able to carry out their aims on a large scale in Scotland and in New England; elsewhere they formed an active minority which tried to overcome all obstacles.

From the beginning Calvin was deeply concerned with the progress of the Reformation in his native land. The Huguenots, as the French Calvinists were called (the origin of the word is uncertain), formed themselves into small compact groups. They met in heavily curtained rooms or secluded spots in the countryside to worship or read the Bible. As they grew in size pastors trained in Geneva were sent out secretly to attend to their spiritual needs. Despite fierce persecution under Henry II (1547–59) Calvinism continued to gain strength. It was adopted by many nobles and even by some members of the royal family.

In 1555 the first French Calvinist church with a formal church service, regular preaching and administration of the sacraments and a consistory of elders was set up in Paris, and in the next few years similar congregations appeared all over France. They sent their pastors and elders to the first national synod in Paris in 1559, at which a confession of faith was adopted. A centralized organization was established, consisting of local consistories, regional colloquies, provincial synods and a national synod. By 1561 the national synod represented more than 2000 congregations.

Persecution soon obliged the Huguenots to take up arms against the state. Many were implicated in the Conspiracy of Amboise (March 1560), an unsuccessful attempt to seize the young king, Francis II, and to get rid of his Catholic advisers. Calvin, however, refused to condone rebellion. 'Better', he wrote in 1561, 'that we should all perish one hundred times than that the cause of the Gospel and Christianity should be exposed to such opprobrium'. He sent Beza to take part in a religious debate with the Catholics sponsored by the regent, Catherine de' Medici. Although the Colloquy of Poissy was a failure, a certain measure of toleration was granted to the Huguenots by the edict of January 1562. The result was a strong Catholic reaction led by the Duke of Guise and his supporters. In March 1562 some Huguenots were slaughtered in a barn at Vassy. This was followed by other bloody deeds which precipitated the outbreak of the religious wars.

Calvinism penetrated the Low Countries mainly after the peace of Cateau-Cambrésis (1559). It became a strong motive behind the resistance to Spanish rule which culminated in the outbreak of the Dutch revolt in 1566.

Englishmen first made serious contact with Calvinism when many of them went into exile on the continent under Mary Tudor (1553–58). They hoped that Elizabeth would accede to their wishes on their return and were bitterly disappointed by her religious settlement. Neither wholly Protestant nor unashamedly Catholic but uniting elements of both, it threw Protestant enthusiasts into confusion. As a London priest remarked it was 'halflie forward and more than halflie backward'.

John Knox, who had been to Geneva, carried Calvinism to Scotland. The Lords of the Congregation, who opposed Mary Stuart and the French alliance, formed the Scottish covenant in 1557. Following the Treaty of Edinburgh in 1560 the Scottish Parliament adopted a confession of faith drawn up by Knox.

Within the empire Calvinism took root mainly in the Palatinate, but it also made deep inroads in eastern Europe, notably in Poland and Bohemia.

Wherever it established itself it was characterized by a heroic certainty which the Wars of Religion were to bring into the open.

Above, Calvinist publication of 1584 attacking the Catholic belief in relics. The Reformation led to a large number of satirical pamphlets and woodcuts, as the religious debates took place as much on a popular level as among theologians and politicians.

Opposite, the Calvinist church in Lyon, France, in 1564; its decoration was minimal and the focus of attention was the pulpit rather than the altar. Bibliothèque Publique et Universitaire, Geneva.

Chapter 22

Habsburg-Valois Rivalry

The European political scene in the first half of the sixteenth century was dominated by three young monarchs, Francis I of France (1515–47), Henry VIII of England (1509–47) and the Holy Roman emperor, Charles V (1519–56).

The accession of Francis I to the French throne on I January 1515 was largely fortuitous. Although he was descended from King Charles V, he was only the cousin and son-in-law of his predecessor and would not have become king if Louis XII had been blessed with a son. At the age of twenty-one Francis seemed the very embodiment of ideal kingship. He was intelligent, lively and quite well educated, eloquent, affable and dignified, brave, proud and ambitious. According to an English chronicler, Edward Hall, he was 'a goodly Prince, stately of countenance, mery of chere, broune coloured, great iyes, high nosed, bigge lipped, Faire brested and shoulders, small legges, and long fete.'

On the debit side Francis was extravagant, impetuous and wilful. He made lavish gifts to his mother, Louise of Savoy, and to his friends and showed a strong inclination to authoritarianism, which brought him into collision more than once with the *parlement* of Paris, the supreme court of justice, whose duty it was to uphold the so-called 'fundamental laws' of the kingdom.

Policy, which was determined by the king and his councillors along, was consistently directed towards strengthening royal power at the expense of surviving feudal liberties. The territorial unification of France was taken a stage further by the formal annexation of Brittany in 1532 and by the confiscation of the Bourbonnais following the treason of its duke in 1523. Some attempt was also made to streamline the machinery of government, notably by the establishment of a central treasury.

Francis I was also an outstanding patron of scholarship and the arts. Leonardo da Vinci, Andrea del Sarto, Benvenuto Cellini, Il Rosso and Francesco Primaticcio were among the great Italian artists who visited his court. He built magnificent *châteaux* or palaces in the valley of the Loire in and around Paris, including the Louvre, Chambord and Fontainebleau. With the encouragement of the humanist, Budé, he established public lectureships in the classics which eventually developed into the Collège de France.

From the start of his reign Francis was determined to avenge the series of disasters that had befallen French arms in 1513. Like every other prince of his time he had been educated for war and had already gained some experience of fighting in Guienne and Gascony. As the descendant of Valentina Visconti, he too had a claim to the Duchy of Milan, constituting an honorable pretext for aggression. His accession, therefore, did not mark any new departure in French foreign policy; the Italian wars were to continue.

Emperor Charles V

France's most important neighbour was Charles, Duke of Burgundy, the future emperor Charles V, a shy and unprepossessing youth of fifteen. He was the son of Philip the Fair and Joanna of Castile and the grandson of Emperor Maximilian and of Ferdinand of Aragon. When his father died in 1506 he inherited all the Burgundian territories (Franche-Comté, Luxembourg, Brabant, Flanders, Holland, Zeeland, Hainaut and Artois) except the Duchy of Burgundy itself, which had been annexed by France in 1477.

Though Charles was cosmopolitan by blood, he was a Burgundian by birth and upbringing. His favourite author as a child had been Olivier de la Marche, the panegyrist of Charles the Bold, under whom Burgundy had become one of the most powerful states in Europe. As he grew up his heart and mind were bent on one purpose: to rebuild his mutilated inheritance. In 1515, however, the effective head of his government was Guillaume de Croy, lord of Chièvres, who, as a Walloon, wanted peace with France. So Francis was able to neutralize Charles for the time being without difficulty.

Henry VIII of England

The young king of England was anything but shy and unprepossessing. Tall and well-built, he had auburn hair 'combed straight and short in the French fashion, and a round face so very beautiful that it would become a pretty woman'. An observer thought him 'much handsomer than any sovereign in Christendom, a great deal handsomer than the King of France'. Henry was one of the best sportsmen of his day, excelling in archery, wrestling, jousting and tennis. He was also a good linguist, an accomplished musician and a reasonably competent amateur theologian.

Vanity, jealousy and cruelty were Henry VIII's principal faults. In particular he was anxious that his physical attainments should not be surpassed by those of his young rival across the Channel. An Italian envoy wrote,

> His Majesty came into our arbour and addressing me in French, said 'Talk with me awhile. The King of France, is he as tall as I am?' I told him there was but little difference. He continued, 'Is he as stout?' I said he was not; and he then enquired, 'What sort of legs has he?' I replied 'Spare'. Whereupon he opened the front of his doublet, and placing his hand on his thigh, said, 'Look here; and I have also a good calf to my leg'.

Yet, suspicious and envious as he was, Henry was not inclined to pick a quarrel with Francis at this stage. Having already had a taste of war he was content for the time being to enjoy himself and to leave policy making in the capable hands of his almoner, Wolsey, who wanted peace in Christendom.

Francis I lost no time completing the military preparations begun by his predecessor. By the summer of 1515 he had assembled an army about forty thousand strong at Lyons. The Swiss, on their part, were keeping a close watch on the main Alpine passes. The king, faced with the choice of either fighting his way through them or bypassing them, chose to do the latter. The French army threaded its way through the difficult Col d'Argentière and suddenly appeared in Piedmont, forcing the Swiss to fall back rapidly towards Milan. Some of the cantons began to negotiate peace terms, but the rest launched a surprise attack on the French camp at Marignano 13 September.

The battle which ensued was one of the fiercest of the Italian Wars. It lasted for the best part of two days and its outcome was decided only at the eleventh hour when the Venetians intervened on the French side. Losses were heavy; the gravediggers counted 16,500 bodies. Marshal Trivulzio, who had fought in eighteen battles, called Marignano 'a battle of giants'.

It certainly marked the end of an epoch. The Swiss ceased to be an independent factor in Italian politics. The myth of their invincibility had been exploded and, by the Eternal Peace of Fribourg (1516), they bound themselves to the service of France. Henceforth their role in European wars was simply that of mercenaries.

In Italy the effects of Marignano were important. Francis I became Duke of Milan and Massimiliano Sforza retired to France on a pension. Pope Leo X yielded Parma and Piacenza to the king in return for a guarantee that the Medici would remain in Florence. In December 1515 the pope and the king met in Bologna and put their signatures to a mutually advantageous concordat.

On 23 January 1516 the balance of power in Europe was badly shaken when Ferdinand of Aragon died. He was succeeded by his grandson, Charles of Burgundy, who had so far tried to keep on good terms with Francis I. His inheritance comprised not only Aragon and Castile but also Naples and Navarre. As Duke of Burgundy, Charles had implicitly recognized the Albret claim to Navarre, but he could hardly be expected to do so now. Equally ominous was the search instituted by Francis in the archives of Provence for evidence supporting his own claim to Naples. For a time the *status quo* was maintained by the Treaty of Noyon, but, if Erasmus hoped for a new era of peace, the elements of discord were only thinly veiled.

Above, meeting between Henry VIII and the Holy Roman Emperor Maximilian I (ruled 1493–1519). The emperor's patronizing attitude towards the foreign ambitions of the young English king led Henry into several expensive and abortive attempts to invade France. Royal Collection.

Left, Francis I of France (ruled 1515–47), painted by Jean Clouet. Like his life-long rival Henry VIII, Francis was a typically ostentatious Renaissance prince, concerned primarily with glory.

Below left, Charles V; King of Spain, Holy Roman Emperor, Duke of Burgundy, Duke of Austria, King of the Romans, were just a few of his many titles. Wallace Collection, London.

Opposite, Henry VIII (ruled 1509–47) sailing to meet Francis I in 1520. Henry put a lot of effort into rebuilding and modernizing the English navy, which was essential for his effective participation in European politics.

The imperial election

In 1517 the Emperor Maximilian fell gravely ill. The Holy Roman Empire was elective, not hereditary. Its ruler was chosen by seven electors: the archbishops of Mainz, Cologne and Trier, the King of Bohemia, the Count-palatine, the Duke of Saxony and the Margrave of Brandenburg. Nothing obliged them to choose a member of the house of Habsburg or even a German. Theoretically, they were supposed to put imperial interests first but in practice their own personal advantage had precedence. Though they solemnly promised to vote 'without the least intrigue, reward, salary or promise of any kind' the majority were willing to take bribes.

As early as 1516 four of the electors invited the French king, Francis I, to stand for the empire. He accepted if only to prevent Maximilian's grandson, Charles, from becoming preponderant in Europe by adding the German territories to his already extensive dominions. Charles was immediately advised to win the electors over by bribery. At the Diet of Augsburg in 1518 Maximilian persuaded five electors to vote for Charles. But when the emperor died in January 1519 they indicated their readiness to take new bids from the candidates.

Germany soon became a vast auction room. By scattering gold in all directions French agents tried to create the impression that their master had inexhaustible means. In fact, his credit was poor. To scrape enough money together for the electors Francis had to borrow from his subjects and to sell offices and parts of his demesne. Pope Leo X agreed to support the king as the lesser of two evils, for it was a principle of papal policy to prevent the empire and the kingdom of Naples from falling into the same hands. As for Henry VIII of England, he secretly offered himself as a third candidate.

Public opinion was very important in the election. Using sermons and broadsheets, Habsburg agents stirred up hatred of everything French. The King of France was also hampered by the fact that the German bankers denied him exchange facilities. While his rival was able to use bills of exchange, Francis had to send ready cash, at his own risk. Once it had to be put into bags and dragged along the bottom of the Rhine by boats.

In June 1519 the electors assembled in Frankfurt and all foreigners were ordered to leave the city. The heat was intense, plague raged in the outskirts and the army of the Swabian League stood menacingly by. On 28 June, after several days of feverish lobbying, Charles was unanimously elected. As the Germans rejoiced wildly at the news, the French agents hastened back to France, narrowly escaping molestation.

War with the emperor

In 1521 war broke out between Francis I and Charles V. It was provoked by the King of France who wanted to prevent Charles from going to Italy to be crowned emperor by the pope. Not wishing to go to war himself at this stage, Francis made use of Robert de la Marck, lord of Sedan, and Henri d' Albret, King of Navarre. But he misjudged the emperor's ability to strike back. An imperial army under the count of Nassau overran de la Marck's territories and advanced to within a few miles of the French border. In June a French army that had invaded Spanish Navarre was decisively defeated at Esquiros. In Italy, Pope Leo X overthrew his alliance with France and bestowed the investiture of Naples on Charles V.

By the summer Francis was anxious to stop the war and accepted an offer of mediation from Henry VIII. A conference was held at Calais under the presidency of Cardinal Wolsey. In August the cardinal went to Bruges and signed a secret treaty with the emperor, promising him English help if the war did not end by November. The Calais conference soon became a farce.

Meanwhile the war continued. For three weeks Massau besieged Mézières which Bayard defended heroically. Eventually the imperialists retreated leaving a trail of destruction behind them. In the south, the French captured Fuenterrabia, the key to Spain, and in Italy they relieved Parma. In November, the Calais conference ended unsuccessfully. Wolsey returned home complaining that he was 'sore tempestyd in mind by the outwardness of the chauncelers and oratours on every side'. The improvement in Francis's fortunes proved short lived. The expulsion of the French from Milan in November was quickly followed by the capitulation of Tournai in the north.

Following the death of Leo X in December 1521, Adrian of Utrecht, Charles V's old tutor and regent in Spain, was elected pope. This caused much resentment in France, but Adrian VI turned out to be a humble and devout man who approached his duties in a truly Christian spirit. He hoped to pacify Christendom so that its princes might unite against the Turks.

In April 1522 the French suffered a major setback in Italy when Marshal Lautrec was defeated at La Bicocca near Milan. England chose this moment to declare war on France and in September an expeditionary force under the Earl of Surrey invaded Picardy. Meanwhile the Turkish sultan, Süleyman the Magnificent, captured Rhodes which the knights of St John of Jerusalem had held since 1309. On learning of this the pope exclaimed 'Alas, for Christendom! I should have died happy if I had united the Christian princes to withstand our enemy.' As Francis I prepared to cross the Alps again, Adrian joined the emperor and his allies in a league for the defence of Italy.

The treason of Charles of Bourbon

In 1515 Charles of Bourbon was a handsome young man with a distinguished war record. As constable of France he was responsible for military administration in peacetime and was entitled by custom, if not by right, to command the vanguard under the king in wartime. The first clear sign of discord between him and the king occurred in October 1521 when he was not given command of the vanguard during the campaign in northern France.

Angered by the king's efforts to cheat him of his inheritance, Bourbon entered into secret negotiations with the emperor. In July he signed a treaty promising to lead a rebellion in return for the hand of one of Charles V's sisters. His plan was to wait until Francis had gone to Italy with his army before revealing himself. But the plot was soon discovered.

Meanwhile Francis's patience ran out. He ordered the arrest of the duke's chief accomplices and deferred his own journey to Italy. Finding himself almost trapped, Bourbon fled into the mountains of Auvergne and eventually made his way to imperial territory while the allies tried unsuccessfully to invade France from three directions. Although Bourbon's revolt had failed ignominiously, it had obliged the King of France to alter his plans.

Possessions of Charles V
Holy Roman Empire
ATLANTIC OCEAN
BAY OF BISCAY
FRANCE
HOLY ROMAN EMPIRE
AUSTRIA
OTTOMAN EMPIRE
KINGDOM OF CASTILE
KINGDOM OF ARAGON
MEDITERRANEAN SEA
ADRIATIC SEA
Danube
Frankfurt
Ghent
Calais
Brussels
Luxembourg
Prague
Paris
Metz
Dijon
Augsburg
Vienna
Buda
Besançon
Lyons
Milan
Venice
Florence
Valladolid
Perpignan
Marseilles
Madrid
Toledo
Lisbon
Rome
Naples
Seville
Palermo
Tunis

Above, Francis I and Henry VIII meeting near Calais in 1520 at a great diplomatic showpiece known as the Field of the Cloth of Gold. Despite days of feasting and jousting, no alliance was agreed, and Henry allied with Charles V shortly afterwards.

Top, the empire of Charles V at its height.

Left, the siege train of Maximilian I, the Holy Roman emperor (ruled 1493–1519); artillery played an increasingly important role in the wars of the sixteenth century and led to a new style of siege warfare and defensive planning. Nevertheless such a siege train was costly and ponderous. Graphische Sammlung Albertina, Vienna.

Opposite, Henry VIII arriving at the Field of the Cloth of Gold in 1520.

In July 1524 the imperial army, now commanded by Bourbon, followed up its victory in Italy by invading Provence. The duke hoped that his former vassals in central France would rally to his standard and help him on his way to Lyons and Paris, but they remained quiet. The duke was also let down by his allies and Marseilles proved an insuperable obstacle. While the garrison bravely endured heavy bombardments, Francis I rebuilt an army and marched to Avignon. Seeing that his communications were threatened, Bourbon had to beat a hasty retreat along the coast and the king reoccupied Provence.

Bourbon's retreat from Provence enabled Francis to put into effect his long-deferred plan of leading another invasion of Italy himself and besieged Pavia, the second largest city in the duchy of Milan.

In January 1525 an imperial army marched from Lodi to relieve Pavia. For three weeks the two armies faced each other without making a move. But an acute shortage of supplies obliged the imperialists to take the offensive.

On 23 February a team of sappers, using only rams and picks, breached the wall in three places and the imperial troops poured into the park, taking the French completely by surprise. Francis managed to rally his cavalry and charged through the enemy centre but his infantry lagged behind and suffered heavy losses, Meanwhile the Pavia garrison came into the open, obliging the French to fight on two fronts. Francis tried desperately to rally his men but, after his horse had been killed under him, he was surrounded and captured.

At the end of the battle some eight thousand Frenchmen lay dead on the field, including Admiral Bonnivet and other close friends of the king. Pavia was the biggest massacre of French nobles since Agincourt. The imperialists claimed the loss of only seven hundred men. Charles V received the news of his victory in Madrid on 10 March. Characteristically, he forbade noisy rejoicings, arranged services of thanksgiving and retired to his private oratory. On his instructions the King of France, who spent the first three months of his captivity at Pizzighettone in Lombardy, was treated with all the consideration due to his rank.

For a long time the King of France expected to be released on generous terms, but the emperor was not prepared to be magnanimous at the expense of his own political interest. In March he was urged by his ally, Henry VIII, to join him in the conquest and dismemberment of France. The King of England argued that there had never been so good an opportunity 'utterly to extinct the regiment of the French king and his line, or any other Frenchmen, from the crown of France'. Without waiting for Charles' reply, Henry asked his subjects for an 'Amicable Grant' and prepared to invade France.

But the emperor needed to think carefully before continuing the war. Despite his resounding victory, he was still faced by many problems: in Italy his army was unpaid and mutinous, in Germany the Peasants' War had broken out, and in the east the Turkish threat remained. His chandellor, Gattinara, who believed that a continuation of the war would only benefit England, advised him to show 'the magnanimity of the lion and the mercy of God the Father'. Charles consequently opened negotiations with Francis.

Although the emperor's sentiments were

Left, the Imperial troops quartered in Rome in 1527, where they looted and drove the pope to seek safety in the Castel' San Angelo. Charles V did not order his armies to Rome himself, although they were expressing imperial frustration with the pope's policies.

Below left, Charles V with Pope Clement VII (ruled 1523–34); despite the common front they seem to be adopting here, Clement was slow to realize the danger of Lutheranism, and his opposition to Charles' policies in Italy led the imperial troops to sack Rome in 1527.

Opposite right, the Turkish camp during the abortive siege of Vienna in 1529. The garrison managed to hamper the Turks by a series of sorties from the city, and the siege was lifted after less than three weeks. Österreichische Nationalbibliothek, Vienna.

Opposite left, the Battle of Pavia (1525), at which the French armies were routed by Charles V, and Francis I taken prisoner. Kunsthistorisches Museum, Vienna.

generous, his peace terms were harsh. Francis was to cede Burgundy and all the other territories that Charles the Bold had held at his death; Bourbon was to be reinstated and given Provence as an independent kingdom; and Henry VIII's French claims were to be satisfied. The King of France rejected these terms at the end of April. He was prepared to make substantial concessions but refused to cede an inch of French territory. Early in May the imperial authorities decided to move him to Naples, but he persuaded the viceroy, Lannoy, to take him to Spain instead. Meanwhile, his mother, Louise of Savoy, who ruled France in his absence, sent an appeal for help to the Turkish sultan, Süleyman the Magnificent, and in August 1525 signed the Peace of Moore with England.

When Margaret of Angoulême visited Spain to offer a ransom for her brother, Charles V insisted on the surrender of Burgundy. In the end Francis saw that he would never regain his freedom unless he gave way. By the Treaty of Madrid he abandoned the duchy and all his Italian claims and agreed to hand over his two sons as hostages.

As soon as he had been released, however, Francis declared that he was not bound to keep promises extorted from him under duress. His repudiation of the Treaty of Madrid was immediately followed by the formation of a new coalition against the emperor, called the Holy League of Cognac. It comprised France, the papacy, Venice, Florence and the Milan of Francesco

Sforza. The imperialists in Italy, who were commanded by Bourbon, were vulnerable, being penniless, numerically weak and hated by the population. Yet they were able to hold their own, for the Duke of Urbino, who commanded the league's army, was excessively cautious and Francis failed to send the military help expected of him. As a result Sforza, who had been besieged in Milan castle, had to capitulate and Bourbon's army left the Lombard plain.

The sack of Rome

As the imperial army, now reinforced by a powerful contingent of German mercenaries, marched on Rome, Pope Clement VII tried desperately to avert a disaster. He signed a truce with the emperor, but Bourbon's men refused to be deflected from their course. They were cold, hungry and short of money; only the expectation of booty kept them together. Clement offered to buy them off, but he could not meet their exorbitant demands. On the 6 May 1527 they launched an assault on the virtually defenceless city.

Among the first to fall was the Duke of Bourbon, who was struck by a cannon ball or bullet as he scaled the city's ramparts. His death had the effect of inflaming his already wild and uncontrollable men. They broke into the city and swept across it like a mountian torrent in flood, killing, burning and looting. The pope, some cardinals and about three thousand people took refuge in the castle of Sant' Angelo. The sack continued for more than a week. Indescribable atrocities were committed. People were tortured for money without respect for age, sex or status. The Lutheran troops attacked anything ecclesiastical with special relish. 'From every side'. wrote an eye-witness, 'came cries, the clash of arms, the shrieks of women and children, the crackling of flames, the crash of falling roofs.'

It is impossible to be precise about the number of people who died in the sack of Rome. In two districts alone 2,000 bodies were cast into the Tiber and 9,800 buried. The booty of the soldiers was incalculable; Clement VII estimated the damage at ten million gold ducats. The Sistine Chapel was used as stables and the Vatican Library was saved only because Philibert, Prince of

Orange, who replaced Bourbon, had his headquarters in the palace.

A month after the sack a Spaniard described the Holy City as follows:

No bells ring, no churches are open, no masses are said, Sundays and feastdays have ceased. The rich shops of the merchants are turned into stables, the most splendid palaces are stripped bare; many houses are burnt to the ground; in others the doors and windows are broken and carried away; the streets are changed into dunghills. The stench of dead bodies is terrible; men and beasts have a common grave and in the churches I have seen corpses that dogs have gnawn. In the public places tables are set close together at which piles of ducats are gambled for. The air rings with blasphemies fit to make good men, if such there be, wish that they were deaf. I know nothing wherewith I can compare it, except it be the destruction of Jerusalem.

The sack of Rome shook Francis I out of his lethargy and precipitated another French invasion of Italy, this time under Marshal Lautrec. He recaptured Lombardy, except Milan, and early in 1528 laid siege to Naples. The city was saved by the defection to the imperial side of the Genoese admiral, Andrea Doria, and by an epidemic of typhus or cholera which carried off Lautrec and thousands of his men. In June 1529 another French army, under the Count of Saint Pol, was defeated at Landriano in north Italy.

These events convinced the pope that he had nothing to gain by remaining neutral. 'I have quite made up my mind', he declared, 'to become an imperialist, and to live and die as such.' Clement VII wanted Charles V to help to restore the Medici to power in Florence. On 29 June, therefore, his nuncio signed the Treaty of Barcelona with the emperor. In return for Charles' military assistance, the pope promised to crown him emperor and to absolve all who had taken part in the sack of Rome. The pope's nephew, Alessandro de' Medici, married the emperor's illegitimate daughter, Margaret.

By now Francis I also wished for a respite. A meeting was arranged at Cambrai between his mother, Louise of Savoy, and the emperor's aunt, Margaret of Austria, who ruled the Netherlands. Despite the many differences which existed between the two sides, a settlement was reached known as the Peace of Cambrai or Peace of the Ladies on the third of August.

The Turkish threat to Christendom

In July 1529 Charles V sailed from Barcelona to Genoa. His purpose was to pacify Italy in order to attend to more pressing problems elsewhere. In Germany, the Lutheran heresy was rapidly gaining ground and in central Europe the Ottoman Turks were once again on the move.

Since the fourteenth century the Ottomans had been expanding steadily westward. Under Mehmed II they had captured Constantinople, penetrated far into the Balkans and expelled the Venetians from Euboea; under Selim 'the Terrible' (1512–20) they had conquered Syria, Palestine and Egypt.

The West heaved a sigh of relief when Selim the Terrible died. His twenty-six-year-old son, Süleyman, was reputed to be 'a gentle lamb', but he soon showed himself no less bellicose than his predecessors. In 1521 he captured Belgrade and in 1522 attacked Rhodes. The Knights of St John, who held the island, had long harassed

Above, miniature taken from a life of Süleyman, written in 1579. The Ottoman Turks posed a very real threat to Europe in the sixteenth century; Süleyman the Magnificent (ruled 1520–66) expanded Turkish power in the Balkans and defeated the Hungarians at Mohacs in 1526. Chester Beatty Library, Dublin.

Opposite top, map of Genoa drawn up in about 1540 for Barbarossa, the Turkish pirate and admiral. Turkish raids made the Mediterranean unsafe for western shipping until the defeat of the Turkish fleet at Lepanto in 1571.

Opposite bottom, Süleyman I, seeing Charles V as his main enemy, he was prepared to ally himself with France in 1536 and join the political turmoil of western Europe.

Muslim trade and plundered ships taking pilgrims to Mecca. The siege lasted 145 days and the Turks lost heavily in men and material, but eventually the garrison capitulated.

For three years Süleyman was content to rest on his laurels, but in 1526 he again marched on Hungary at the head of an enormous army. The Hungarians were hopelessly divided between a 'court' party, led by the young king, Louis II, and a 'national' party, led by John Zápolyai, Prince of Transylvania. On 29 August they came up against the Turks on the plain of Mohacs. With insane overconfidence their cavalry charged into the jaws of the sultan's guns only to be shattered to pieces. King Louis and most of his nobles were left dead on the field. Ten days later the victors entered Buda.

Because of Mohacs the defence of Christendom devolved on the Habsburgs, more especially on Charles V's brother, Ferdinand, who now became king of Bohemia and of Hungary. His rival, Zápolyai, turned to the sultan, who recognized him as vassal and king. When Ferdinand called on Süleyman to withdraw from some of the fortresses he had conquered, the sultan declared that he would come to Vienna to satisfy him.

A major offensive on the Danube was a severe test of Ottoman military resourcefulness. Although the campaign season lasted from mid-April to the end of October, the sultan's army could not expect to cross the Sava before July. Rivers had to be spanned by pontoon bridges, roads had to be made over difficult ground, and bad weather frequently impeded progress. Some guns and munitions were carried by boats on the Danube, but most had to be loaded on waggons, carts or beasts of burden. Abundant food was necessary as the retreat might lie through devastated areas.

These difficulties and the premature onset of winter explain why Süleyman failed to capture Vienna in 1529. Incessant rain and flooded rivers prevented him reaching the city before September. Thus Ferdinand had enough time to give it a strong garrison. The Turks had to succeed quickly as their food was running low, but all their assaults were repulsed, so on 14 October Süleyman gave the order to retreat. In 1532 he again marched against the Habsburgs but was held up by the heroic resistance of the small town of Güns. Having lost three precious weeks, he gave up his plan, signed a truce with Ferdinand and became involved in a war with the Persians.

Because of the Turkish threat Charles V was unable to visit Rome in 1529. He asked Clement VII to meet him at Bologna instead. In the course of the four months which they spent together a mutually satisfactory settlement of the Italian situation was reached. Francesco Sforza was restored to power in Milan, Venice promised to give back Ravenna and Cervia to the pope, and an imperial army under the Prince of Orange was sent to besiege Florence in aid of the Medici. In February 1530 Charles V received the crowns of Lombardy and of the Holy Roman Empire amid all the traditional pomp and ceremony. He then moved on to Germany to preside over the doctrinal bickerings of the Diet of Augsburg.

Charles V and the German Lutherans

Although the emperor stood by the pope and his own Edict of Worms, he was anxious to achieve a religious settlement in Germany and treated the Lutherans with courtesy. At his invitation they drew up a confession of faith which was read in the Diet on 25 June. It was mainly Melanchthon's work and was so remarkably conciliatory that it was described by the Bishop of Augsburg as 'the pure truth'. Yet the Catholic theologians would have nothing to do with it. A committee of theologians from both sides failed to break the deadlock. In September, Charles issued a recess in which he promised a General Council within a year and forbade Lutheran innovations in the meantime. The Lutherans rejected the recess and in December formed a defensive alliance, called the Schmalkaldic League.

In 1532, however, a temporary political unity was achieved when the Turks again threatened Christendom. A truce was signed at Nuremberg which enabled Charles to raise a powerful army. After the Turkish retreat he returned to Bologna where he spent the winter trying in vain to persuade Clement VII to call a General Council. In April he returned to Spain.

In the emperor's absence the Lutheran princes again looked to France for support. Early in 1534 Philip of Hesse met Francis I secretly at Bar-le-Duc and obtained a subsidy which he used to restore Duke Ulrich of Württemberg, who had been dispossessed by the Habsburgs in 1520. Charles V was warned that Germany was full of French agents. In 1535 the Schmalkaldic League was renewed for another ten years. Yet the German princes were not yet prepared to ally with Francis against Charles, being still afraid of the Turkish menace and distrustful of the French king because of his persecution of Protestants in his own country.

The conquest of Tunis

The struggle between Christendom and the Infidel was fought not only in the Danube valley but also in the Mediterranean. Even before the fall of Rhodes pirates operating from North African ports had harassed shipping and terrorized the coastal villages of Spain and Italy. The most dreaded of them was Khayr ad-Dīn Barbarossa, who controlled Algiers as a vassal of the Turkish sultan. In 1532 he was appointed grand admiral of the Ottoman fleet and in 1534 he ravaged the coasts of south Italy with more than a hundred ships and expelled Muley Hasan, Charles V's ally, from Tunis.

The emperor could not allow the Turks to dominate the central Mediterranean and to threaten his kingdoms of Sicily and Naples. In 1535, therefore, he assembled a large fleet at Barcelona and an army at Cagliari in Sardinia. Then, on 10 June, the entire expedition sailed for Africa.

Its first objective was the fortress of La Goletta, guarding the narrow entrance to the Bay of Tunis. Although Charles was suffering acutely from gout, nothing would keep him from the front lines. The siege lasted nearly three weeks and the emperor's men suffered severely from the intense heat and shortage of water, but on 14 July they launched an assault from several directions and the defenders fled. Many French guns with the fleur-de-lys embossed on their barrels were among the rich booty found in the fortress and Barbarossa's fleet of eighty-two galleys was captured in the harbour. Charles then seized Tunis while Barbarossa made his escape to Algiers.

The conquest of Tunis was undoubtedly Charles V's greatest personal triumph. The whole world marvelled at his might. When Charles visited Sicily in the autumn of 1535 his triumph seemed complete. As he rode beneath magnificent arches, trophies and inscriptions, the crowds shouted 'Long live our victorious emperor, father of the fatherland, conqueror of Africa, peace-maker of Italy!'

The Castilian empire in the New World

By 1535 Charles V was also master of the New World. The *conquistadores* had gone to America at their own expense and looked forward to living on slave labour, but the Spanish government did not intend a new feudalism to take root overseas, while the Church was concerned that the natives should be treated fairly. An influential advocate of their rights was the Dominican friar, Bartolomé de Las Casas. By about 1550 an official policy had emerged. The Indies were treated as dependencies of the crown of Castile, administered through a distinct royal council. The Indians were free men and direct subjects of the crown.

The Castilians (the Aragonese were deliberately excluded) in the New World comprised soldiers, missionaries and administrators. The good behaviour of the soldiers had to be bought with grants of land (*encomiendas*) and minor salaried offices. They expressed themselves through town councils which were really oligarchies exercising wide administrative powers. Alongside the soldiers were friars from the missionary orders, especially the Franciscans, who undertook the education and peaceful conversion of the natives. Finally, there were the lawyers who kept a close watch on the activities of the provincial governors and viceroys through the *audiencias* or courts of appeal. All important decisions, however, were taken in Spain, which did not make for efficiency.

Stock farming was the typical occupation of the New World Spaniard, arable farming being mainly in Indian hands. Horses, cattle and sheep were imported in large numbers and great estates grew up around ranch houses. In the tropical coast lands sugar was produced. African negroes, who

Above, a seventeenth-century allegorical painting of Charles V; as well as ruling one of the largest empires in history, he aimed to be the defender of Christendom itself, against its enemies within and without. Rijksmuseum, Amsterdam.

Top, Charles V hunting with John Frederick, Duke of Saxony and a leader of the Lutherans, at Torgau, according to a painting by Lucas Cranach. John Frederick was eventually defeated at Mühlberg in 1547.

Opposite left, Flemish engraving of Charles V. Rijksmuseum, Amsterdam.

Opposite right, the siege of Tunis of 1535, one of Charles V's greatest triumphs. His army included Muslim cavalry, even though Tunis was an Ottoman garrison. Kunstsammlungen, Coburg.

could be enslaved as they were not Castilian subjects, were imported to work the plantations.

Spain also imported gold and silver from the New World. To begin with mining was a relatively simple matter of prospecting and washing in streams, but very productive silver mines were discovered at Potosí in 1545 and Zacatecas in 1548. Extensive plant was set up to extract silver from the ore, usually by a mercury amalgamation process. The crown claimed a fifth of all the metal produced and employed a large number of agents to weigh, test and stamp the silver ingots as they issued from the mines and to prevent smuggling. In about the middle of the century a convoy system was devised to protect the bullion cargoes crossing the Atlantic.

Charles V's empire

Personal government and particularism (the desire of certain countries to govern themselves) were the essential characteristics of Charles V's vast empire.

The grand chancellor, Mercurino de Gattinara (1518–30), believed that the imperial title gave Charles authority over the whole world for it was 'ordained by God himself . . . and approved by the birth, life and death of our Redeemer Christ.' Like his compatriot Dante he saw the empire as a unified whole centred on Italy and the emperor as legislator for the whole world 'following the path of the good emperor Justinian'.

But this vision died with Gattinara. In practice the empire was unified only in the emperor's person: otherwise it had no common institutions. To deal with the vast amount of paper work Charles was assisted by two secretaries, one for Spain, Italy and the Mediterranean, the other for territories north of the Alps. The two secretaries, Francisco de los Cobos and Nicholas Perrenot, Lord of Granvelle, were men of considerable ability, but they were not as significant as Gattinara had been before 1530.

Charles V also employed members of his family as governors-general, regents or even kings in his dominions. The Netherlands, the empire itself and Spain were always entrusted to a Habsburg or his consort after 1529. Non-royal viceroys were appointed only in the Italian territories. The emperor was ably served by his relatives, notably by the two regents of the Netherlands, his aunt, Margaret of Austria (1518–30), and his sister, Mary of Hungary (1531–5).

Yet Charles reserved to himself ultimate control over policy and administration. Despite the enormous distances which messengers had to cover, he insisted on taking all important decisions himself in consultation with those advisers who accompanied him on his constant travels. This did not make for efficient administration especially as Charles was unable to take decisions

quickly. He also kept a firm control over public appointments and all forms of patronage. Hence the passionate longing of his subjects that he should reside with them.

The emperor's failure to develop a centralized organization for his empire outside his own person was not, however, solely because of the view he took of his office. It was a result of the intense particularism existing in the different countries making up the empire. The Sicilians, the Spaniards, the Germans and, above all, the Netherlanders were intensely devoted to their own laws, customs, privileges and institutions, and would not have tolerated any diminution of them in the interest of a more unified empire. In 1534, for example, the Estates-General rejected a proposal for a defensive union in the Netherlands because they felt it would undermine provincial liberties.

Charles preferred to comply with vested interests, local traditions and his own immediate financial needs rather than attempt to impose some kind of economic unity on the empire. It was for this reason that the Aragonese were not allowed to participate in the Spanish colonial trade, despite Castile's inability to supply the colonists with all the manufactured goods they needed.

Nowhere was this pervasive particularism more evident than in the Netherlands. Charles wanted them to contribute their share of the imperial expenditure and he was successful up to a point, but the Estates insisted that the redress of grievances must precede any discussion of new taxes and that they should control the collection and expenditure of revenues.

As taxation became heavier after 1530 there was a growing volume of discontent which culminated in Ghent's refusal in 1539 to pay its share of taxes voted by the Estates-General. The rebellion had to be quelled by force and the punishment inflicted on the citizens was severe. Ghent forfeited all its rights and privileges, its public treasure was confiscated and its arms were taken away.

Religion was another source of serious trouble in the Netherlands. Lutheranism reached Antwerp in 1519 and made many converts. It was followed by Anabaptism with its apocalyptic vision of the Kingdom of God on earth and its revolutionary appeal to the socially oppressed. Charles V dealt with heresy much more vigorously in the Netherlands than in Germany where he was less powerful. About 1600 heretics, including the Englishman, William Tyndale, were put to death in the Netherlands during his reign.

Yet Charles never had to face a general revolt in the Netherlands. This was because the provinces did not always see eye to eye

Above, the Holy Roman Empire in the sixteenth century, made up of many semi-independent states ruled over by an emperor, who was elected by the seven chief princes but who was by this time traditionally an Austrian Habsburg.

Opposite, window from Brussels Cathedral made in 1537 showing the Emperor Charles V with his wife; Charles was always popular in the Netherlands but his decision to make the Low Countries part of the Spanish Empire in 1555 was widely resented.

and also because the emperor was sometimes prepared to compromise. Thus he allowed certain provinces to exclude the Inquisition and mitigated the harshness of his anti-heresy laws in their application to Antwerp. But the fact remains that the situation in the Netherlands was not calm under Charles V. The general revolt which broke out under Philip II in 1564 was the result of a financial, religious and political crisis that had been developing for some time. In fact, the Habsburg system in the Netherlands was on the verge of dissolution by 1555.

During the last decade of his reign Charles V was concerned mainly with three questions: his rivalry with France, the Turkish threat and heresy in Germany. They overlapped to some extent, since Francis I continued to intrigue with the Turks and the German Protestants.

In November 1535 the Milanese question was reopened by the death of Francesco Sforza without issue. Francis claimed his duchy for the Duke of Orléans and in February 1536 a French army overran Savoy and occupied Turin. Charles strongly denounced this action in a speech before the new pope, Paul III, and his court. He even challenged Francis to a duel. In order to relieve the pressure on Milan he invaded Provence but the scorched-earth tactics of Anne de Montmorency, constable of France, exhausted his men. Finding that Marseilles was impregnable, he retreated to Italy and signed the Truce of Nice (June 1538). Soon afterwards he met Francis at Aiguesmortes and in 1539 passed through France on his way to quell the Ghent revolt. No peace treaty was signed, however, and in 1542 the war flared up again. Charles made an alliance with Henry VIII and visited Germany to obtain aid. Then, in July 1544, he invaded France and even threatened Paris, while Henry VIII besieged Boulogne. But as Charles wanted a respite to deal with the German situation he signed the Peace of Crépy in September.

The Turks meanwhile continued their aggression in the Mediterranean. Doria's defeat at Prevesa in 1538 destroyed the emperor's hopes of carrying the war into the eastern Mediterranean. Thereafter he had to be content with limited objectives.

In October 1541 he planned to strike hard at Algiers. An impressive armada sailed from the Balearics but it was so severely damaged by a storm off the African coast that the expedition was abandoned. In 1543 Khayr ad-Dīn captured Nice and his fleet was allowed to winter at Toulon. It was described as a second Constantinople with a lively slave market where Christians were offered for sale. When the old corsair died in 1546 his work was carried on by the equally formidable Dragut, who conquered Tripoli in 1551. The western Mediterranean was not freed from the Turkish menace until Don John of Austria's great victory at Lepanto in 1571.

The Peace of Crépy enabled Charles to attend the German question. Behind a smokescreen of doctrinal discussions he proceeded to detach Maurice of Saxony and others from the Schmalkaldic League. He was also reconciled with the Catholic Duke of Bavaria. The Diet of Regensburg (June 1546) showed that a conflict was inevitable. While the Catholics called on the reformers to attend the Council of Trent on the pope's terms, the Protestants demanded a reform of the Church by a diet. Charles meanwhile made an alliance with the pope against the Protestants.

The war between the emperor and the Protestant princes began with a long series of skirmishes. A decision, however, was reached at Mühlberg 24 April 1547 when Charles suddenly fell upon the flank of John Frederick's army. The fighting was soon over and the emperor claimed that he had lost less than ten men killed and wounded. When John Frederick was led into the emperor's presence he exclaimed: 'Most mighty and gracious emperor, I am your captive'. 'Ah!', rejoined Charles, 'you call me emperor now, do you? You lately gave me another style.' (The princes had distributed broadsheets calling him 'Charles of Ghent, who thinks he is emperor'.)

Charles hoped to use his victory to establish an imperial league on the lines of the Swabian League, a confederation of south German towns formed in 1487. The pope's decision to move the council from Trent to Bologna helped to bring him closer to the German Protestants. At the Diet of Augsburg (September 1547) he stated his determination to bring the council back to Trent. He expected the Lutherans to attend it there and in the meantime to live in peace with the Catholics.

On 30 June 1548 he issued the Augsburg *Interim* which aimed at keeping the possibilities of conciliation open. Its underlying assumption was that a council would some day reach a settlement which both sides were held to have accepted in principle. In practice the *Interim* worked out as *cuius regio, eius religio,* i.e., subjects must follow the faith of their ruler.

In September 1551 King Henry II of France declared war on the emperor and soon afterwards entered into negotiations with Maurice of Saxony and other German Protestants. In exchange for a subsidy they recognized Henry as vicar in the empire and allowed him to occupy the 'three bishoprics' of Metz, Toul and Verdun, as well as Cambrai and other imperial cities whose language was not German. Charles V found himself trapped in Germany without any money to raise an army. He thought of making a dash to the Netherlands but was advised not to do so by his sister, Mary of Hungary. She claimed, moreover, that she had no money or means of raising any.

During May 1552 Maurice of Saxony tried to capture the emperor at Innsbruck, but Charles gave him the slip across the Brenner pass and down the Drave valley to Villach in Carinthia. Some years later he recalled how two Lutheran emissaries had met him on a mountain track and made him an offer: if he would only listen to the Protestant princes they would not pursue him but would go with him against the Turk and set him on the throne of Constantinople. But Charles had told them that he wanted no more realms, only Christ crucified, and had spurred on his horse and left them.

Having failed in his attempt to seize the emperor, Maurice of Saxony came to terms with his brother, Ferdinand, at Passau in August 1552 and joined him in a campaign against the Turks in the course of which he was killed. Meanwhile, Charles determined to oust the French from Metz in spite of his sister's advice that he should desist from so dangerous an enterprise. He could not allow Henry II to threaten the Netherlands and the route connecting them with Franche-Comté. The siege of Metz was begun in November 1552 but the city was well fortified and ably defended by the Duke of Guise. Bombardments, mining operations and assaults all failed. Early in January Charles decided to withdraw.

Ferdinand was now left in sole charge of German affairs and at the Diet of Augsburg in September 1555 constitutional form was given to the concessions made three years before to the late Maurice of Saxony. Lutheranism was given equal legal status with Catholicism within the empire, though explicit provision was made to continue the endeavours to restore unity.

Charles V's attempt to re-establish the medieval concept of a united Christendom under the joint leadership of emperor and pope had foundered. Having already relinquished the government of his German dominions, he now decided to hand over the rest of his responsibilities, though not the imperial title itself, to his son, Philip. In

Above, Pope Pius V (ruled 1566–72), a leader of the Counter-Reformation who excommunicated Elizabeth I of England and inspired the alliance that led to the defeat of the Turks at Lepanto in 1571.

Left, the truce of Nice, made in 1538 between Francis I and Charles V. According to its terms, there would be peace for ten years between the two; but only four years later Francis attacked Charles in alliance with Süleyman.

Opposite, Charles V at the Battle of Mühlberg (1547), according to the famous portrait by Titian. This victory paved the way to the religious compromise of the Peace of Augsburg of 1555. Prado, Madrid.

October 1555 he laid down the sovereignty of the Netherlands and in January 1556 divested himself of the Spanish crowns and their dependencies. He then retired to a country palace adjoining the monastery of Yuste in Spain, where he held court and continued, amid his devotions, to take a keen interest in the fortunes of his empire until his death in 1558.

Henceforth the nature of his empire changed radically. Instead of being a universal, Christian empire with a Burgundian soul, it became a Spanish, Catholic empire with a Castilian soul. As the flow of American silver to Spain increased during the second half of the century, the Netherlands ceased to be economically the most advanced and wealthiest part of the empire. The wars in Italy and Germany demonstrated the superiority of Spanish troops over all others. The emperor's council shed its international character and became dominated by Spaniards or Hispano-Italians. In Spain itself Erastianism was superseded by an uncompromising orthodoxy reflected in the activities of the Inquisition. Under its new king, Philip II, Spain became the spearhead of the Counter-Reformation.

Part of Philip's inheritance was the age-old conflict with the Valois kings. His accession was followed by a renewal of war with France, but weariness on both sides led to the Treaty of Cateau-Cambrésis (3 April 1559). France kept Metz, Toul and Verdun as well as Calais which it had recently taken from England, but it abandoned claims in Italy and restored Savoy and Piedmont to Duke Emmanuel-Philibert. Despite its gains France emerged from the Italian wars in debilitated condition. Its financial resources were exhausted and the peace freed large numbers of soldiers for the civil wars which were about to devastate the country.

Chapter 23

The Tudors

The accession of Henry VII in 1485 was for long regarded as a watershed in English history. It was seen as the beginning of a 'new monarchy' able to impose its will on the turbulent nobles who had torn the country apart in the Wars of the Roses. The first Tudor, it was alleged, had infused new life into the dormant machinery of government and by careful management had built up the royal revenues to such an extent that he was able to bequeath more than a million pounds in gold and silver to his son. However, it has recently been shown that some of the administrative reforms attributed to Henry, notably his use of the Chamber as a department of national finance, were initiated by his predecessors. His financial achievement was generally less spectacular than was once supposed. It cannot be proved that he died a millionaire. Nor did 1485 mark the end of civil unrest, which flared up during Henry VII's reign in the revolts of Lambert Simnel and Perkin Warbeck.

Yet Henry VII's achievement was not negligible. Legally he had a very poor claim to the throne. On his father's side he had no claim at all. His mother belonged to the Beaufort family, which traced its illegitimate descent from John of Gaunt. Richard II had legitimized the family but Henry IV had debarred it from the throne. Many people had a better claim than Henry Tudor, notably the young Earl of Warwick, the son of Edward IV's brother, Clarence.

Henry's method of overcoming these disadvantages was forceful and direct. He proclaimed himself king by the grace of God, seeing that the Almighty had given him the victory at Bosworth and made Parliament register his accession and the right of his heirs to succeed to the throne. As for Warwick, he was beheaded. By marrying his children into some of the royal families of Europe Henry VII succeeded in establishing his dynasty on a firm and internationally respectable footing. This was his greatest achievement.

The Henrician Reformation

Another obstacle which the Tudors had to overcome was the survival of independent jurisdictions within the kingdom. The most important was the Church, which had its own law courts and owed allegiance to the pope. As long as it remained independent, the king could not call himself master in his own house. Henry VIII solved this problem by severing the traditional connection with Rome and setting himself up as Supreme Head of the English Church. By so doing he immeasurably enhanced the prestige of kingship; having fixed the crown firmly on his head, he added a halo.

The Henrician Reformation was not just 'an act of state', however, it was also a popular movement. Lollardy (the heretical movement founded by John Wycliffe in the fourteenth century) was far from extinct by the end of the fifteenth century. The act books of the ecclesiastical tribunals and the bishops' registers show a steady rise in the number of prosecutions, abjurations and punishments for heresy from the 1480s onwards.

Dissent was concentrated in Buckinghamshire, London, Essex and Kent, but there were Lollards also at Coventry and in the large diocese of York. Although Lollardy lacked a central administration its wandering missionaries kept scattered congregations in touch with each other. Most Lollards belonged to the common people, though skilled workers outnumbered labourers and husbandmen. They also included some lesser clergymen, London merchants and many women.

It has been claimed that Lollardy provided 'a spring-board of critical dissent from which the Protestant Reformation could overleap the walls of orthodoxy'. Lollards certainly helped to disseminate Lutheran literature, notably Tyndale's *New Testament*. It is arguable, though, that Lollardy was a hindrance to the spread of Lutheranism, for it provided an alternative form of dissent at the popular level and provoked a rigorous campaign of persecution which was well under way by the time Lutheranism first appeared in England.

Luther's name became known in London soon after he had posted up his ninety-five theses. Copies of his works were sent to England by John Froben, the Basle printer, as early as 1519 and they continued to circulate despite censorship measures taken by the government. They were smuggled in by merchants trading with Antwerp or Germany and distributed by the Society of Christian Brethren, which has been aptly described as a kind of 'forbidden book of the month club'. Yet Lutheranism made relatively few converts in England. It was avidly taken up by some young intellectuals at Cambridge, who used to gather at the White Horse Tavern, and it found support among German merchants of the London Steelyard. Otherwise its impact on the English public at large seems to have been small.

Henry VIII's government was opposed to Luther from the start. In May 1521 Wolsey presided over a solemn book-burning at St Paul's Cross, at which John Fisher, Bishop of Rochester, preached a sermon against the new doctrine. Sir Thomas More, who was equally hostile to it, conducted a visitation of the London Steelyard and was empowered by the bishop of London to read Lutheran books so as to reply to them in English. Henry VIII himself attacked Luther in a book called *Assertio Septem Sacramentorum,* for which he was given the title of 'Defender of the Faith' by the pope. Yet only a few years later Henry cast aside his allegiance to Rome.

The royal 'divorce' and the break with Rome

As an act of state the Henrician Reformation was anything but doctrinal. It stemmed directly from the king's determination to obtain an annulment of his first marriage to Catherine of Aragon so as to be free to marry Anne Boleyn. The 'king's great matter' was closely bound up with the succession problem. All Catherine's children had died, except Mary, and the absence of a male heir threatened the survival of the Tudor dynasty.

The prospect of a woman ruler, for which there was no satisfactory precedent in English history, was viewed with apprehension. If she were to marry a foreigner, England would become tied to the destinies of another country. This had to be avoided and Henry was confident that the pope would allow him to remarry, for Catherine had been the wife of his deceased brother, Arthur, and the Bible said: 'And if a man shall take his brother's wife, it is an unclean thing . . . they shall be childless.'

If Clement VII had been a different person Henry would probably have got what he wanted, but the pope was a timid and shifty character, mainly interested in the political situation in Italy. The moral issues raised by Henry's demand for an annulment did not worry him. He even suggested that the king might be allowed to have two wives at once. What really concerned him was that Catherine was the emperor's aunt and that if he gave way to Henry he would lose Charles V's military assistance on which depended the restoration of the Medici to power in Florence. He authorized Wolsey and Campeggio (the Italian papal legate) to try the king's divorce suit in England in 1529 but secretly instructed his legate to procrastinate. Eventually he revoked the case to Rome after he had given a verbal promise not to do so.

An immediate consequence of the pope's action was the fall of Cardinal Wolsey in October 1529. For three years thereafter Henry VIII ruled without a chief minister. It has been suggested that royal policy during these years was 'unimaginative, bombastic and sterile' and that it only became 'direct, simple and successful' after Thomas Cromwell's ascendancy in 1532. Henry VIII did not wish to break with Rome, however, until every approach had been

tried. What a triumph he would have scored if the pope had given way!

The aim of the king's policy was to put pressure on the pope by a campaign of intimidation against the Church of England. In 1531 he extorted a subsidy from the clergy after he had accused them of offending the law of the realm by exercising their independent jurisdiction. As the pope failed to react the campaign was intensified. In 1532 the English Church gave up its legislative independence in a document called the *Surrender of the Clergy*. The death of Archbishop Warham in the same year enabled Henry to appoint his own creature, Thomas Cranmer, as primate. In May 1533 he declared the king's marriage null and void at a special court held in Dunstable. The decree came none too soon for Henry was already secretly married to Anne Boleyn. She was crowned in June and in September Elizabeth was born.

In the meantime a frontal attack was mounted by Thomas Cromwell on papal authority in England. This was done by means of statute law. Never before had Parliament been called upon to participate so actively in policy-making. The Reformation Parliament lasted on and off from 1529 to 1536. It has been called the first modern Parliament because its members were at last given a chance to know each other and to form groups, though nothing comparable with the modern party system as yet existed. Henry did not need to bully its members; a fundamental harmony of interests existed between them.

The most important act passed in 1533 was the Act of Appeals. Its resounding preamble to the effect 'that this realm of England is an Empire' implied that England was a country independent of any external authority, temporal or spiritual. Under the Act of Supremacy Henry VIII became Supreme Head of the English Church.

Anti-clericalism was strong in England in the early sixteenth century, yet it could not be taken as certain that Henry's religious policy would not be resisted. A campaign of anti-papal propaganda was therefore mounted by the government and an example made of Sir Thomas More and John Fisher, Bishop of Rochester, after they had refused to take the Succession Oath imposed on all the king's subjects. This declared that the succession to the throne was vested in the children of Henry's second marriage. Fisher had supported Queen Catherine and More had shown his disapproval of royal policy by resigning the chancellorship in 1532. They were found guilty of high treason and beheaded on Tower Green in 1535.

In 1536 an act was passed dissolving the smaller monasteries, which were alleged to be centres of 'manifest sin, vicious, carnal and abominable living'. This charge was largely unfounded; the government's real motive was the confiscation of monastic wealth. Although the larger monasteries were described as 'great, honourable and solemn' in 1536, they were not spared three years later.

The dissolution of the monasteries was one of the most spectacular revolutions in English history. Within four years landed property worth nearly twenty million pounds passed from one set of owners to another. It was put on the market at a time when land was much in demand and a vested interest in the Reformation was thus established.

From the doctrinal standpoint no radical

Reformation came about as a result of the Henrician. The Ten Articles which Convocation adopted in 1536 made no concessions to the Lutherans despite a conciliatory phraseology. *The Bishops' Book of* 1537 was a conservative statement of belief. Two years later the Act of Six Articles laid down heavy penalties for those who denied the doctrine of transubstantiation and other fundamental Catholic beliefs. Even if Henry himself did incline towards a less orthodox position towards the end of his reign, England did not become a Protestant country till the reign of Edward VI.

Edward VI

The first major crisis which the Tudor monarchy had to face was the minority of Edward VI, who was only nine at his accession in January 1547. His father, Henry VIII, had provided for a council of regency of equal members but its first act was to appoint one of its members, Edward Seymour, Earl of Hertford, as Protector and Duke of Somerset.

Being a man of liberal views, Somerset began by sweeping away Henry VIII's stringent treason laws and the old laws against heresy. People were suddenly able to debate freely and openly about religion, and the situation soon got out of hand. Preachers stormed in their pulpits; printing presses produced a flood of libels and satires; Protestant divines flocked to England from the continent.

Though sympathetic to the Protestant cause, Somerset did not wish to provoke the mass of the people, who continued to worship as they had always done. He therefore embarked on a policy of piecemeal religious change aimed at causing the least offence to anyone. Cranmer's Order of Communion of 1548 contained nothing flagrantly hostile to Catholic beliefs, and the first Prayer Book of 1549 was 'an ingenious essay in ambiguity'. It left much of the old order as it was, though religious services were henceforth to be held in English instead of Latin.

In general the Prayer Book was accepted without resistance, but in Devon and Cornwall it provoked a serious popular rising known as the Western Rebellion. This was ruthlessly crushed by John Russell, Earl of Bedford.

Somerset's social policy also ended in catastrophe and bloodshed. By 1547 the economic situation had become critical:

Above, Thomas Wolsey (c. 1473–1530), who administered England during the first twenty years of Henry VIII's reign. As well as being a fine organizer, Wolsey was a cardinal who hoped to use his position to bring peace to Europe and a supporter of the humanists.

Above left, an engraving of the island of Utopia, the frontispiece to Thomas More's book of the same name published in 1516. A friend of Erasmus, More became Lord Chancellor in 1529 but was executed in 1535 when he refused to accept the Henrician Reformation.

Opposite top, Hampton Court Palace, outside London, first built by Henry VIII's minister Thomas Wolsey but taken over and enlarged by the king as a palace for his second wife Anne Boleyn.

Opposite bottom, John Foxe, an English Protestant, published a Book of Martyrs in 1559; it contained a number of accounts of the suffering of English Protestants at the hands of the Catholics. This illustration shows the exhumation of Wycliffe's bones in 1425.

On page 275, the royal coat of arms adopted by the Tudor dynasty, incorporating both the red and the white rose, the symbols of the opposing factions in the Wars of the Roses; heraldic symbolism had genuine political importance at this time. Victoria and Albert Museum, London.

prices were rising steadily and landowners tried to keep abreast of inflation by resorting to expedients which caused social hardship and unrest. They enclosed arable land, turning it into pasture so as to take advantage of the cloth boom, encroached on common land and went in for rack-renting. At first the government merely made the situation worse by selling off the lands of the dissolved chantries to speculators and continuing the debasement of the coinage begun by Henry VIII.

In 1548, however, Somerset tried to put into effect some of the reforms advocated by a group of enlightened theorists called the Commonwealth Men. He introduced a Subsidy Act to restrict enclosure by taxing sheep and cloth and set up a special commission to enforce existing anti-enclosure statutes. The upshot of this well-intentioned policy was another revolt.

During the summer of 1549 the common people of Norfolk rose under Robert Ket's leadership. Unlike the western rebels, they were not concerned with religion. Their enemies were the gentry, who were refusing to comply with the government's economic measures. Since they regarded the Protector as their friend, they did not march on London but simply staged a kind of sit-down strike outside Norwich. Even so, their movement constituted a threat to the security of the state and was mercilessly put down by Somerset's rival in the council, John Dudley, Earl of Warwick.

Somerset's rule could not survive two major rebellions in one year. He was overthrown in October 1549 and subsequently beheaded, his place being taken by Dudley, who assumed the title of Duke of Northumberland. After siding with the Catholics, Northumberland now joined the extreme Protestants in order to despoil the Church. He ordered the destruction of service books, religious statues and paintings and went far towards depriving bishops of their secular power and property. The second Prayer Book of 1552 altered the communion service and simplified ceremonial so as to get away from the Catholic idea of the mass as a sacrifice. Henceforth the communion was to be celebrated on a table instead of an altar, ordinary bread was to be used and the celebrant was not to wear special vestments or make devotional gestures. The doctrine of the Real Presence was repudiated by Cranmer's Forty-two Articles in 1553.

If Northumberland's religious policy was radical, his economic and social policy was thoroughly reactionary. The Subsidy Act of 1548 was repealed and the Enclosure Commission allowed to lapse. To prevent social unrest the scope of treason was again enlarged, certain gentlemen were allowed to raise cavalry units at the public expense and the sheriff's military powers were transferred to a new official, the lord-lieutenant. Yet Northumberland did did try to reverse the debasement of the coinage and encouraged English overseas enterprise.

Northumberland's power depended on the survival of the young king, whose health was precarious. If Mary Tudor, who was the duke's enemy and a Catholic, came to the throne he and his policy were doomed. So Northumberland bullied the king and his council into altering the succession in favour of his own daughter-in-law, Lady Jane Grey. But when Edward died, on 6 July 1553, Mary managed to give Northumberland the slip and the whole nation, including the royal council, rallied to her side. In a desperate bid to save his skin the duke proclaimed her himself but his volte-face deceived no one. He was arrested and executed, while the unfortunate Lady Jane Grey, her husband and Cranmer were imprisoned in the Tower of London.

Mary Tudor

In 1553 Tudor England entered upon a second crisis. Having survived a minority it now had to overcome the predicament of being ruled by a thirty-seven-year-old Catholic spinster. The accession of Mary Tudor, Henry VIII's daughter by Catherine of Aragon, threatened the survival of both the Tudor dynasty and the English Reformation.

Mary was sincere, devout, kind and cultured but she lacked administrative and political skill. 'I know the queen', wrote the imperial ambassador, 'to be good, easily influenced, inexpert in worldly matters, and

a novice all round. . . . To tell you between ourselves, I believe if God does not preserve her she will be lost.' In fact, Mary turned out to be a pathetic failure.

PARVVLE PATRISSA, PATRIÆ VIRTVTIS ET HÆRES
ESTO, NIHIL MAIVS MAXIMVS ORBIS HABET.
GNATVM VIX POSSVNT COELVM ET NATVRA DEDISSE,
HVIVS QVEM PATRIS, VICTVS HONORET HONOS.
ÆQVATO TANTVM, TANTI TV FACTA PARENTIS,
VOTA HOMINVM, VIX QVO PROGREDIANTVR, HABENT
VINCITO, VICISTI. QVOT REGES PRISCVS ADORAT
ORBIS, NEC TE QVI VINCERE POSSIT, ERIT.

The queen aimed at restoring the old religion, but first she had to secure her succession, for if she remained single the throne would eventually pass to her Protestant half-sister, Elizabeth, who would surely undo her work. The choice of a husband, however, was not easy. The chancellor, Stephen Gardiner, would have liked Mary to marry an English nobleman, but she accepted instead the future Philip II of Spain, thereby bringing her kingdom into the Habsburg orbit.

Mary's decision caused the Kentish rebellion of Sir Thomas Wyatt in 1554. Though he pretended to champion the Prayer Book, he was really opposed to the Spanish marriage. His revolt failed because the Londoners would not join it, and its chief result was the unjust execution of Lady Jane Grey and her husband.

The royal marriage was celebrated at Winchester on 25 July 1554. Philip tactfully agreed to stand down should Mary predecease him without leaving an heir and promised not to appoint Spaniards to important posts in England. Yet the marriage was unpopular, for Englishmen were no longer economically dependent on trade with the Spanish Netherlands and feared that the Spanish Inquisition might be introduced into their country.

Originally Mary asked for nothing more than toleration for Catholics, but she soon began to revert to the religious position that had existed before the schism and Protestant extremists went into temporary exile on the continent. Edward VI's religious legislation was annulled by Parliament and the title of 'Supreme Head' in the royal style was replaced by a convenient 'etc.'.

In November 1554 Cardinal Reginald Pole returned to England as papal legate. He absolved the nation of the spiritual penalties it had incurred by its schism and heresy and wisely refrained from demanding the restoration of Church lands that had been secularized. But the reversion to Catholicism was marred by a campaign of persecution without parallel in English history. Altogether some 300 people were burnt for their beliefs, mainly in southeast England. Most of them were humble folk, though Cranmer was among the victims.

In 1557 Mary allowed herself to be dragged into a war with France which resulted in the loss of Calais, England's last continental foothold. Such was the price of the Spanish marriage which had in any case proved barren. Sterility was the keynote of Mary's reign. She died, execrated by her subjects, on 17 November 1558.

Elizabeth I

Little is known about Queen Elizabeth's religious convictions. She disapproved of

Above, the future King Edward VI of England (ruled 1547–53), painted by Hans Holbein. Edward died before he was able to impress his will on the policies of his advisers. National Maritime Museum, London.

Above left, Thomas Cromwell (c. 1485–1540), England's chief minister from 1531 to 1540. He masterminded the English Reformation, reorganized the administrative system and oversaw the dissolution of the monasteries. He was executed in 1540. Frick Collection New York.

Opposite left, Henry VIII of England (ruled 1509–47), painted by Hans Holbein. Henry became increasingly tyrannical in his later years, and his expensive foreign policies produced no tangible results.

Opposite right, Anne Boleyn (1507–36); Henry's love for her and his frustration with Catharine of Aragon's inability to bear him a son was sufficient to cause England's break with the Church of Rome. National Gallery of Art, Washington.

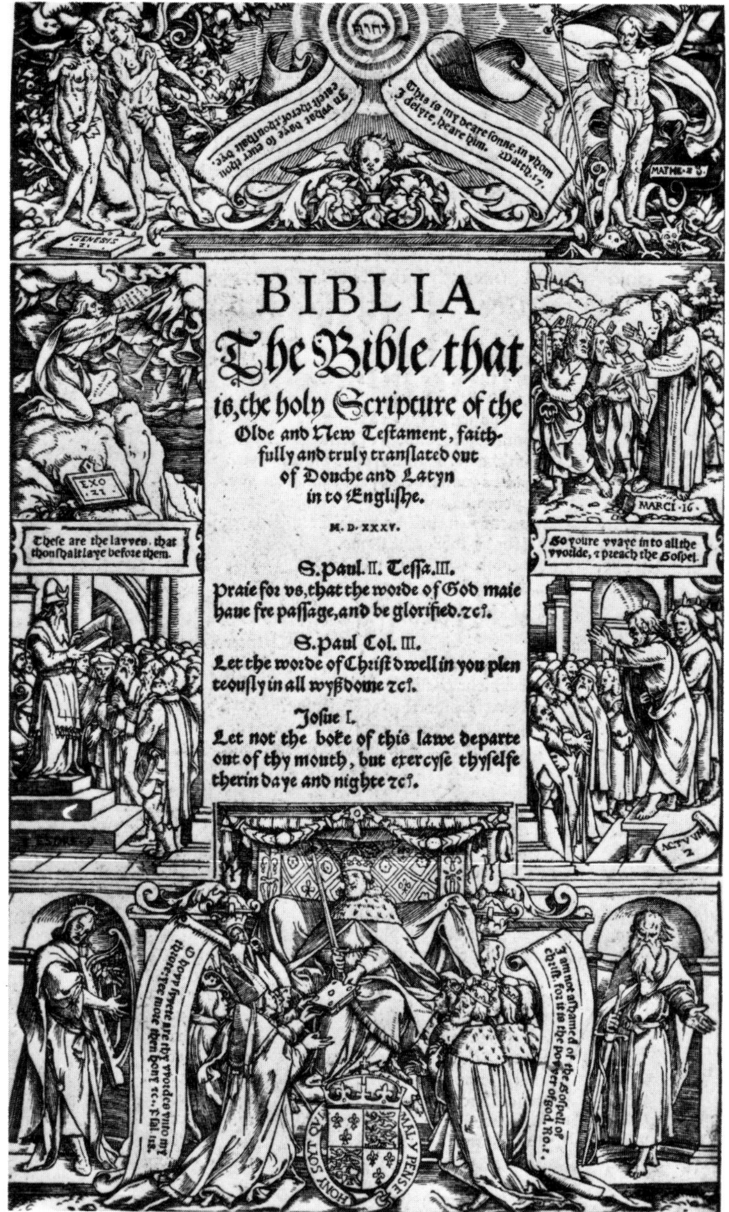
BIBLIA
The Bible/that is, the holy Scripture of the Olde and New Testament, faithfully and truly translated out of Douche and Latyn in to Englishe.

M.D.XXXV.

S.paul.II. Tessa.III.
Praie for vs, that the worde of God maie haue fre passage, and be glorified. &c.

S.paul Col.III.
Let the worde of Christ dwell in you plenteously in all wysdome &c.

Josue I.
Let not the boke of this lawe departe out of thy mouth, but exercyse thyselfe therin daye and nighte &c.

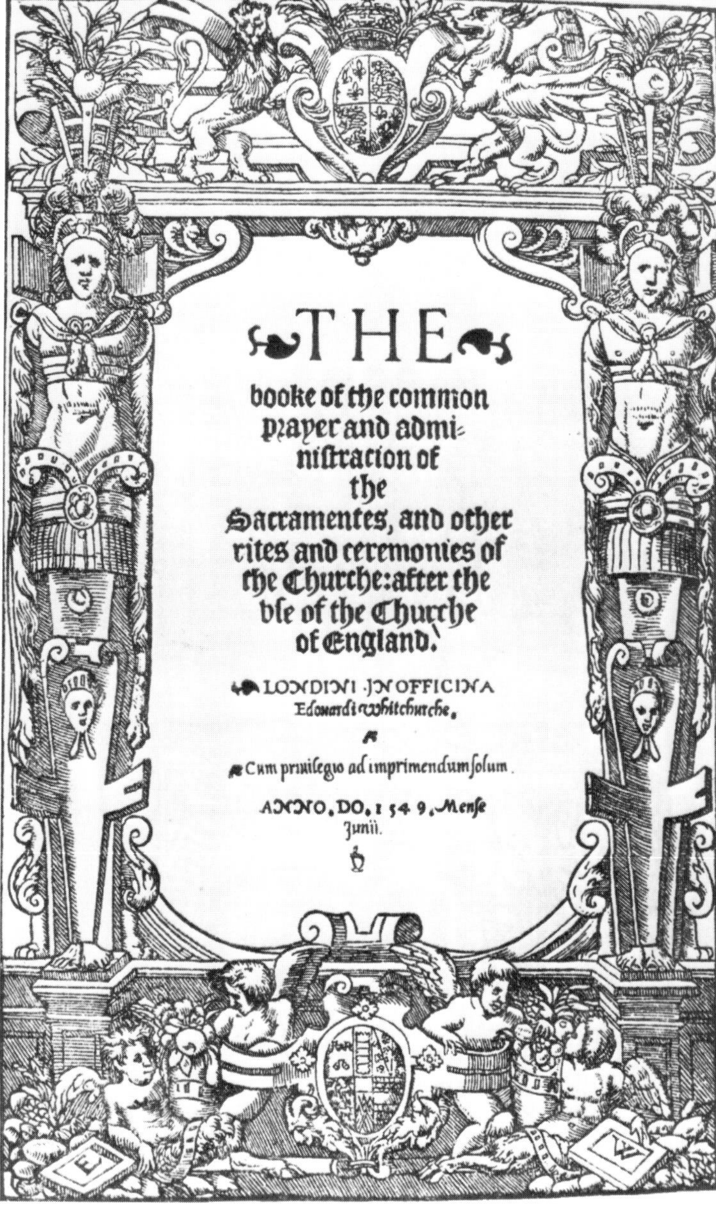
THE
booke of the common prayer and administracion of the Sacramentes, and other rites and ceremonies of the Churche: after the vse of the Churche of England.

LONDINI IN OFFICINA Edouardi Whitchurche.

Cum priuilegio ad imprimendum solum.

ANNO. DO. 1549. Mense Junii.

theological pedantry and clerical marriage; otherwise she kept her beliefs very much to herself. As the daughter of Henry VIII and Anne Boleyn she could hardly be expected to retain the papal supremacy, yet she had no wish to provoke her more conservative subjects by adopting extreme Protestantism. Her original intention was probably to win the Marian bishops over before proceeding to any change of doctrine, but this was not acceptable to certain Protestant hotheads in Parliament. They tried to force a complete Protestant programme on her and the result was a more extreme compromise than the queen had originally envisaged.

The Act of Supremacy of April 1559 restored the royal supremacy, while the Act of Uniformity, passed in the same month, imposed a new Prayer Book. The queen, because of her sex, was described as 'supreme governor' of the English Church, not as supreme head. The new doctrine stood roughly halfway between the Prayer Books of 1549 and 1552. All the Marian bishops except one refused to take the Oath of Supremacy and were accordingly deprived, but a majority of the lesser clergy submitted. The settlement was rounded off by the adoption of the Thirty-nine Articles by Convocation in 1563. Like all compromises it failed to satisfy the extremists on both sides. The Puritan, John Field, described it as, 'a certain kind of religion, framed out of man's own brain and fantasy, far worse than that of popery (if worse may be), patched and pieced out of theirs and ours together'.

Elizabeth was probably wise not to throw in her lot with either the Catholics or the Protestants. By steering a middle course she united all moderate-minded Englishmen and avoided becoming intimately associated with the big religious power blocks on the continent.

In the first decade of Elizabeth's reign the Catholics were not troublesome. Many conformed outwardly to the settlement while continuing to worship in their own way. Philip II persuaded the pope not to excommunicate the queen as he needed England's friendship against France, the traditional enemy of Spain. But the Rebellion of the Northern Earls in 1569 created a false impression abroad that only a signal from Rome was needed to overthrow Elizabeth. Pius V therefore excommunicated her and all who continued to obey her. The Catholics were thus forced to choose between loyalty to the state and allegiance to their faith.

A number of young English Catholics went abroad where they were trained in special colleges at Douai, Valladolid, Rome and elsewhere as missionaries to rescue their homeland from heresy. They began to return in 1574 and operated secretly from country houses up and down the country. The first Jesuit mission led by Edmund Campion and Robert Persons arrived in 1580. The government reacted by means of penal legislation. The fine for recusancy was raised to twenty pounds a month and an intensive drive was launched against missionary priests. Campion was among those martyred. Yet Catholicism was able to make headway, for local officials were sometimes unwilling to enforce the penal laws. After 1588 Catholics were persecuted less, for they had remained quiet during the Armada

Left, Thomas Cranmer (1489–1556), the Archbishop of Canterbury under Henry VIII and Edward VI, being burned at the stake under Mary for his guiding role in the introduction of Protestantism to England.

Below, Mary I of England (ruled 1553–58), painted by the Spaniard Antonio Moro. Despite her nickname Bloody Mary, her persecution of the Protestants was not unduly severe for the times; many of the people she forced into exile went to Geneva where they learnt a far more radical form of Protestantism than England had previously known.

Opposite left, the title page of the Coverdale Bible of 1535, a new English translation by Miles Coverdale. Despite such efforts of the Protestants, Henry VIII was reluctant to accept a Lutheran liturgy in England, and it was not until Edward VI's accession that Protestantism was firmly established.

Opposite right, the title page to the Book of Common Prayer *of 1549, written by the Archbishop of Canterbury Thomas Cranmer. The book represented an attempt to impose a uniform religion on the whole of England; but it was amended in 1552 and again in 1559.*

The extreme Protestants or Puritans were also a serious problem to Elizabeth. The Presbyterians hoped to rebuild the Church on the Geneva model by getting rid of bishops and the royal supremacy, while the Separatists wanted freedom to worship outside the framework of a national Church.

Trouble began in 1559 when the Puritans objected to the survival of certain 'popish' practices, notably the use of vestments. Archbishop Parker campaigned vigorously against nonconformity among the clergy and emerged victorious from the Vestiarian controversy. Meanwhile Puritan members of Parliament put forward bills to reform the Church but were each time foiled by the queen.

About 1569 Puritanism assumed a more revolutionary aspect. By attacking the bishops Thomas Cartwright and John Field, to mention only two of the leaders, were indirectly threatening the queen's quasi-episcopal authority. In 1583 Archbishop Whitgift required all the clergy to subscribe to the royal supremacy, the Prayer Book and the Thirty-nine Articles under pain of deprivation. Largely as a result of his efforts, Puritanism declined and was driven underground where it remained until its revival under James I.

An important feature of Elizabeth's reign was the growing importance of the House of Commons where the country gentry were preponderantly represented. Even boroughs were represented by country gentlemen who usually owed their seats to the patronage of some great nobleman. Parliament enabled young gentlemen to go to London, which was fast becoming the social centre of the kingdom.

The Tudor period saw an extension of parliamentary privilege, but as late as 1558 freedom of speech was not well defined. Some members claimed the right to discuss religion, the succession and foreign affairs, but the queen believed such matters should be raised only with her prior consent. In 1566 Paul Wentworth put three questions to the House which suggested that the queen's ban on any discussion of the succession amounted to a breach of privilege. Ten years later his brother, Peter, resumed the attack. He declared,

In this house which is termed a place of free speech, there is nothing so necessary for the preservation of the prince and the state as free speech, and without, it is a scorn and mockery to call it a Parliament House, for in truth it is none, but a very school of flattery, and so a fit place to serve the devil and his angels in, and not to glorify God and the Commonwealth.

Parliamentary opposition to the crown, then, did not begin with the Stuarts, but under Elizabeth it was fundamentally loyal. What the members feared above all was that they would lose her and all that she stood for. The queen's feelings for her Commons were also tempered by affection. 'I think they speak out of zeal to their countries', she declared, 'and not out of spleen or malevolent affection.'

The age of Drake

To many people the reign of Elizabeth I is above all the age of Drake.

Until the 1550s England showed little interest in exploration. The reasons for this apathy were economic and political. It exported its cloth to Antwerp and did not need to look for markets elsewhere; Spain controlled Antwerp and was England's natural ally against France. In the second half of the century this situation changed

completely. The Antwerp market crashed and Englishmen had to find other outlets for their goods; France was crippled by its civil wars. Thus England was left free to encroach upon the Spanish colonial sphere which it had hitherto respected.

The primary motive of English overseas enterprise was commercial. Englishmen hoped to trade with Cathay (China), which was reputedly rich in gold and spices, but all the known routes to the Far East were closed to them. Their only course was to find a new route to the Far East in the northern hemisphere. The attempt made by Hugh Willoughby and Richard Chancellor to find a northeast passage in 1553 failed, but it did lead to the establishment of commercial relations with Russia. In 1576 Martin Frobisher claimed that he had found the northwest passage. He brought back an Eskimo and pieces of black ore said to contain gold. In fact he had only found a Canadian cul-de-sac and the ore turned out to be worthless. Yet the search for a northwest passage continued.

Privateering became important in the 1560s. With the deterioration of Anglo-Spanish relations, English captains began to see possibilities of gain by penetrating the Carribbean. John Hawkins at first hoped to trade legally with the Spanish colonies but the disaster that befell him at San Juan de Ulua, when his fleet was almost destroyed by the Spaniards as it was refitting in the harbour, convinced him otherwise. Francis Drake then set out to inflict as much damage as possible on the Spaniards and in the course of his circumnavigation of the world (1577–80) he seized a considerable quantity of treasure.

Until the late 1560s Englishmen gave little thought to colonization. It was suggested by Humphrey Gilbert in his *Discourse* (1556), and in 1585 the first English colony was founded at Roanoke, a low-lying island off the coast of modern North Carolina. Though it proved a failure, the experience gained paved the way for the foundation of Jamestown in the next century.

Above, Elizabeth I of England presiding over a meeting of parliament, Elizabeth was unable to prevent the House of Commons from discussing topics that she considered the royal prerogative, including religion, foreign politics and monopolies.

Above left, Francis Drake (c. 1540–96) in a miniature by Nicholas Hilliard. Explorer, pirate and harasser of the Spaniards, Drake was the archetypal Elizabethan seaman who created the legend of English sea power in a space of twenty or thirty years. National Portrait Gallery, London.

Opposite, the Ermine Portrait of Elizabeth I of England (ruled 1558–1603), one of many official portraits of the queen intended to link her image with suitable mythical or literary concepts. In this case, the ermine represents purity and chastity.

Chapter 24

Sixteenth-Century Spain

'If death came from Madrid', said the Spanish viceroy at Naples, 'we should all live a long time.' The chronic delays of the Madrid administration were notorious and at the centre of them was the lonely and conscientious Philip II. During his reign, Spain became the first European power to operate on a global scale. The country which launched the great Armada of invasion against England in 1588 was without exaggeration the most powerful nation in the whole world.

In Europe itself the King of Spain was also after 1580, the King of Portugal, King of Naples and Sicily, Duke of Milan and Lord of the Netherlands. Outside Europe he was ruler of territories stretching from Macao to Lima. As may be imagined so extensive and impressive a facade had many flaws and by the end of the century fissures were beginning to split the structure. But if it is true that neither the financial nor the administrative resources of any sixteenth-century European state were sufficient to meet the demands of such global possibilities, it is also true that the Spanish Empire was no figment of the imagination. To the men of the time it was quite simply the greatest power on earth.

The basis of this power was the formidable strength of the Spanish army, based in turn on its excellent infantry; the fleets of the two greatest maritime powers of the time; the immense physical wealth which flowed in from the American empires, and a sense of national purpose and justification in the eyes of God.

The king had an unshakable, indeed almost fanatical belief in his own divine mission as the champion of the Catholic Church in its struggle with the forces of the new Protestant states and wedded to this was the parallel conviction that it was the destiny of Spain to lead the forces of light. 'I do not propose to be the ruler of heretics', he said and he not only effectively crushed all signs of heresy in his own kingdoms but also kept the southern provinces of the Netherlands Catholic. Besides this he scored a notable victory over the Turk, arch-enemy of Christendom, and indirectly was responsible for preventing the accession of a Protestant monarch to the throne of France.

Philip II

For more than eighty years of the sixteenth century, Spain was ruled by two men, father and son. The father, Charles V, was brought up at the cosmopolitan court of Burgundy and was constantly about his business throughout the length and breadth of Europe. On the other hand, his solitary and introverted son, Philip II, apart from brief visits to France and England, where he married Mary Tudor and was for a while co-ruler of England, retired to Spain when he was only thirty-two and thereafter never left the Iberian peninsula.

Before he was forty, Philip had commissioned the architect for his huge new palace complex, El Escorial, some thirty miles outside Madrid and, as the years went by, he spent more and more time in the dark and labyrinthine interior of this austere building. At the centre stood the royal chapel and within the palace were also to be found not only the administrative offices of state but the state rooms of the court, the mausoleum of the royal family and a monastic community. Such was the environment in which Philip, by choice, conducted the business of the world's mightiest empire.

Philip's composure and reserve were legendary and undoubtedly remarkable, but to picture him as a neurotic recluse would be to exaggerate. He was certainly slow in coming to decisions but prudence was usually justified. Since Philip was the sole coordinator in his administration and took on himself an immense amount of paper work, literally directing an empire from a desk, business was delayed still further; and while he was thoroughly professional, he had a fatal inability to distinguish high policy from trivia.

When Charles V finally resigned the kingship in 1556 his son, Philip II, inherited as his most immediate problem the sixty-year-old conflict with France over the claims of the rival dynasties in Italy. There was also a dispute about the frontiers of the Burgundian Netherlands which had to be settled. Philip, involving his wife, Mary of England, in the struggle, and even waging war on the pope for his support of the French, fought the war to a satisfactory conclusion. He settled his differences with the French king by the important treaty of Cateau-Cambrésis, returning numerous towns and villages on the northern and eastern frontiers of France in return for the French recognition of his position in Milan. The French also surrendered Corsica, a vital post on the Spanish sea route to Naples, but they recovered Calais from the English. The treaty was signed in 1559 and in the same year Philip went back to Spain.

Once he had returned to his country he established his new capital at Madrid. It had the advantage of being an administrative capital without history which was at the geographical centre of the peninsula. In addition, since it was neutral in the eyes of the various regional populations in the country, it did not invite the political jealousy which would have been focused on any of the old capitals which might have been chosen. From Madrid, and later from El Escorial, Philip administered the daily affairs of his kingdom, rarely leaving his capital city and using the councils at the capital and the viceroys in the non-Castilian parts of his empire. Philip's reliance on Castilian officials and his fixed residence in Castile created problems. The fact that of the many languages spoken throughout his dominions Castilian was the only one which he could speak at all fluently also contributed to the unrest in Flanders and Aragon. In both cases this was to flare up into open revolt.

The revolt in Flanders

The highly urbanized area of the Low Countries, whose livelihood was commerce and whose neighbour was Protestant Germany, was a fertile ground for the doctrines of the reformers. In the earlier decades of the century the dangerously liberal views of the great Dutch reformer Erasmus had won a considerable following in Spain itself. The trend had been stopped by the leaders of the Counter-Reformation in Spain and the rigours of the Holy Office of the Inquisition.

Philip, whose religious conviction verged on fanaticism, began to enforce the existing laws with rigour and appointed new bishops himself. This offended even Catholic opinion as unwarranted royal intervention in the affairs of the Church. The Protestant cause grew in natural opposition to the aggressive actions of the alien administration. It was also fostered by the immigration of Calvinists in the 1560s, the representatives of an organized anti-authoritarian and international movement. The situation progressively deteriorated and in 1566 the explosion occurred with wide-scale rioting. The efficiency of Calvinist agitation was a new threat to the regime which tightened up its measures.

The following year Philip sent in the Duke of Alba, one of his top ranking generals, with orders to restore 'law and order' and to suppress heresy. Alba's religious fervour was equal to that of his master and there ensued a reign of terror in which thousands lost their lives.

The Netherlands had been subjected to crippling levels of taxation from the time of the Habsburg accession to the crown of Spain, since they were the richest European provinces in the Spanish Empire. The position was exacerbated still further when Alba imposed new levies in 1572, which not only raised the rate but also denied the estates general the right to assess the distribution of the burden and thus infringed the privileges of its powerful members. But this year marked a new and serious setback for the Spaniards. Although they were impregnable from the land they were highly vulnerable to seaborne attack and for some years this attack had been pressed by privateers from the northern provinces who had their bases in England. In 1572 they were expelled from England and descended in force on the shores of the Low Countries; in the same year these 'Sea Beggars' took the ports of Brill and Flushing and most of Zeeland and Holland. Philip replaced Alba with a new governor, Requesens, but his attempts at a more moderate policy failed and he had to resort to force.

The Spanish army was an uncertain amalgam of various nationalities and its instability was increased by long arrears of pay. In 1576, the year of Requesens' death, the army got completely out of hand and in November, after a skirmish with rebel troops, ran amok in the streets of Antwerp and subjected the great city to a brutal and horrible sack. As a result the rebels, that is the predominantly Catholic movement in the south and the 'Sea Beggars' in the north, formed an alliance against the foreign invader, the Pacification of Ghent. Yet the unity was more apparent than real and the divisions between the Calvinist burghers and the southern Catholic nobles were still there waiting only to be exploited.

As his next governor Philip appointed his half brother Don John of Austria, the hero of the Battle of Lepanto, who seems to have hoped that the Netherlands could be used as a base for an attack on England. He was not the last Spanish general to think so, but he was never given the opportunity to explore the practicalities of the project. Before he was even admitted as governor by the estates general, he had to promise to observe the traditional liberties of the territories and to withdraw Spanish troops, and although he later recalled them before his death in 1578 he did not succeed in establishing his authority against the power of the rebels.

In the same year (1578) the rift widened between the Catholics and the Calvinist townsfolk who were led by William the Silent, the Prince of Orange. The problem was further exacerbated when Philip appointed as governor general Alexander Farnese, Duke of Parma, one of the greatest soldiers of the age and one of Spain's most brilliant statesmen. Farnese quickly came to terms with the Catholic nobility in the south. He promised to withdraw Spanish troops and guarantee the privileges of the aristocrats against the growing power of the bourgeoisie if they withdrew their provinces from the rebels. But the final issue was decided on the battlefield.

Parma had all the ideal qualities of a great commander, courage, vigour and the willingness and ability to share the full rigours of campaigning with his men. In addition he displayed a brilliant sense of timing and a previously unequalled feeling for the terrain of the Low Countries themselves. In him

Above, the Spanish infantry regiments, known as tercios, *formed the finest army in sixteenth-century Europe. They were armed with pikes and muskets. Here they are seen relaxing after capturing Valenciennes in 1567.*

Left, Miguel de Cervantes (1547–1616), the greatest writer of the Spanish Renaissance, publishing his novel Don Quixote *in 1605–15. He spent five years in the 1570s as a slave of the Barbary pirates and the viceroy of Algiers.*

Opposite, the Spanish Armada of 1588, the first great European naval battle in which both sides relied on cannonades and broadsides rather than the medieval tactic of boarding the enemy vessel and fighting hand to hand.

SIXTEENTH-CENTURY SPAIN

1500
- Charles V becomes emperor (1519)

1525
- Birth of Philip II (1527)

1550
- Abdication of Charles V and the accession of Philip II (1556)
- Building of El Escorial (1563–84)
- Alba sent to restore order in Netherlands (1567)
- Death of Don Carlos (1568)
- Battle of Lepanto (1571)
- 'Sea Beggars' seize Brill, Flushing and most of Zealand and Holland (1572)

1575
- Sack of Antwerp (1576)
- Alexander Farnese becomes Governor of the Netherlands (1578)
- Philip II elected King of Portugal (1580)
- William the Silent assassinated (1584)
- Defeat of the Spanish Armada (1588)
- Revolt in the Aragon (1590)
- Death of Philip II (1598)

1600

even William the Silent found his equal, and thanks to the tenacity and effectiveness of his great general's conduct of the war Philip of Spain could claim to have saved at least the southern provinces of the Low Countries for Catholicism.

In an indirect sense Alexander Farnese was the founder of the modern state of Belgium. In a far more direct sense he was author of the continuing reputation of Spanish arms in the later sixteenth century, welding the diverse nationalities and military traditions of his troops into a precise and deadly instrument of military power.

The revolt of the Netherlands, which began in the 1560s, continued for a further twenty years after the formal declaration of independence of the northern provinces in 1581 by William the Silent, who was assassinated three years later. However Spain did not recognize the independence of the new state until the Treaty of Westphalia of 1648.

It is clear that a struggle of such intensity and duration must have had its origins in something deeper than the policy of one man, Some of the factors leading to the break have already been outlined, but it must also be realized that during the later years of the sixteenth century and the beginning of the seventeenth the Dutch had matured as a sea power. They were thus building the foundations of their maritime empire and were gaining an unquenchable sense of national identity and patriotic pride.

As has been noticed elsewhere, one of the busiest trade routes of early modern Europe was that between the Iberian peninsula and the Low Countries, since wool was transported from the north coast Spanish ports to Flanders so that it could be manufactured into cloth. Trading in luxuries also developed later as the Portuguese capital of Lisbon became the European entrepot for the spices, silks and other treasures brought back from the Indies. When therefore in 1594 Philip closed Lisbon to the Protestant merchants of the Low Countries because he was pursuing economic sanctions against them, the response was direct Dutch sailings to the Indies and, in 1602, the founding of the Dutch East India Company.

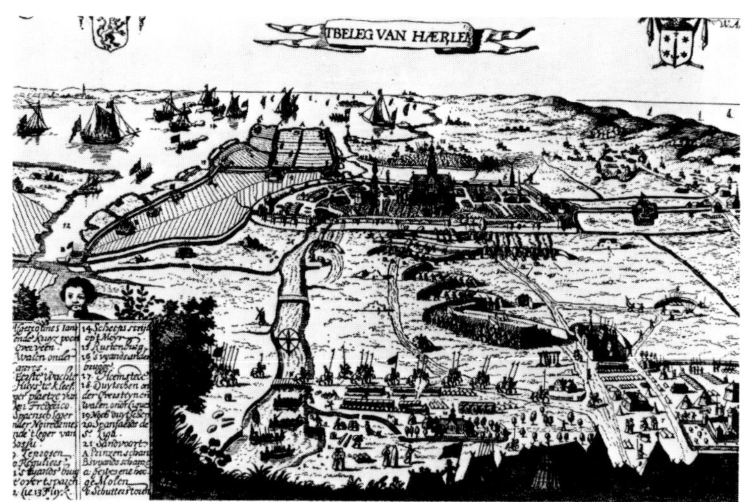

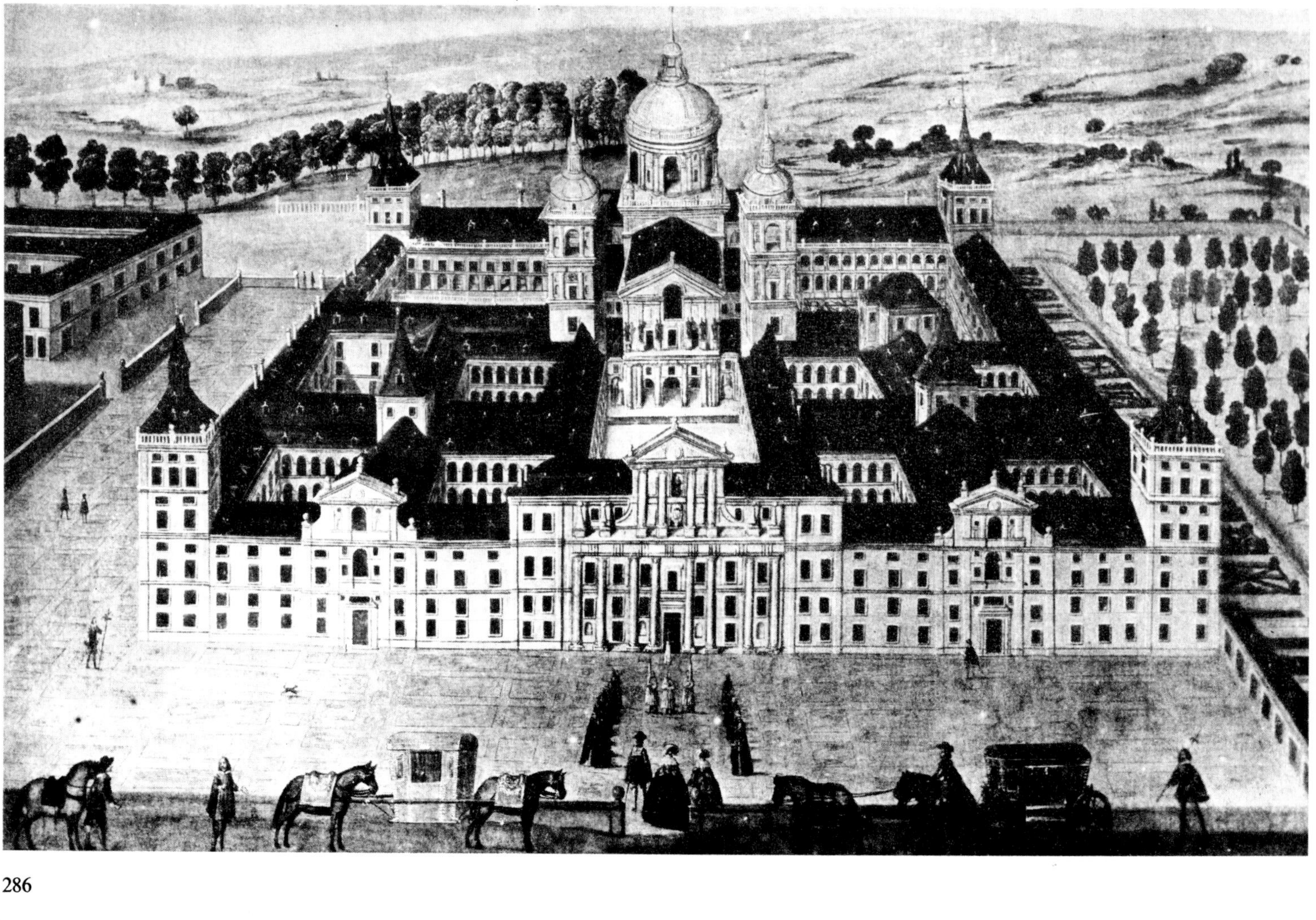

The annexation of Portugal

For the sixty years between 1580 and 1640, the dream of generations of Spanish kings seemed to have been realised: with the accession of Philip II of Spain to the throne of Portugal in 1580, the Iberian peninsula became a single political as well as a geographical unit. The name of 'Spain' had been used since the Middle Ages, but to describe the whole of the peninsula; indeed when Pope Alexander VI granted Ferdinand of Aragon the title of king of Spain, Manuel of Portugal lodged a complaint against the misuse of the term. But throughout the century the two states, which together controlled the only colonial empires of their century, had been growing closer together by a series of dynastic marriages. When therefore in 1578 the disastrous reign of Sebastian of Portugal came to an end on the fateful field of Alcazar-Kebir in Morocco Spain had not only virtually unanswerable arguments in terms of military power but

Below, Philip II of Spain (ruled 1556–98) in a portrait by Titian. Philip saw himself as the ever-vigilant guardian of the interests of the Catholic church as well as the defender of a vastly wealthy empire in the New World. Prado, Madrid.

Opposite top left, the siege of Haarlem in 1572–73 by the Spanish troops. This was a turning point in the revolt of the Netherlands against the Spaniards. The town defended heroically but eventually 2,000 of its citizens were killed. As a result, the Netherlands became far more united in the revolt.

Opposite top right, Lisbon in the late sixteenth century, after Portugal had been joined to the kingdom of Spain. Lisbon was no longer the great port of earlier in the century.

Opposite bottom, the Escorial, a combination of monastery and palace built by Philip II of Spain near Madrid in 1563–84. Its grid-iron layout was intended to symbolize the grill on which St Lawrence was martyred.

also the best claims to the throne by the laws of succession.

A caretaker monarchy was set up under the aged Cardinal Henry who was crowned king and even announced his willingness to marry in the hope of a legitimate Portuguese heir. But no papal dispensation was forthcoming and this last sturdy representative of the great house of Avis died a few months later without having had the opportunity of performing this final service for his country.

His death left the field clear for Philip who, as both nephew and son-in-law of the late king's father, John, was convinced of the superiority of his claim to that of his only rival, Anthony Prior of Crato, who was the illegitimate nephew of King John. But despite his successful diplomacy and bribery among the Portuguese aristocracy, Philip found himself obliged to put on a show of force in view of the militant popular support which Anthony, as the only hope of an independent Portugal, attracted. The campaign swept Anthony and his supporters before it and in 1580 the Cortes was obliged to elect Philip II King of Portugal.

In the eighty years preceding Philip's takeover, Portugal had been consolidating the work of her explorers and merchants so as to produce one of the world's great maritime empires. At home the costs of such an empire to such a small metropolitan country did fatal damage to the economy. This was weakened still further by the huge dowries which John III (1521–57) bestowed on his daughters and, most crippling of all, by the expenses of Sebastian's absurd enterprise against the sultan of Morocco. Quite apart from the terrible loss in manpower and the costs of the expedition itself, the ransoms of the numerous noble prisoners came to well over a million *cruzados*.

The century had opened with the reign of Manuel I, the Fortunate (1495–1521), who continued John II's forceful disciplining of the nobility. Also, learning from the example of Ferdinand of Aragon, Manuel prepared the way for the crown's takeover of the mastership of the military Order of Christ. In other respects the kings of Portugal followed the example of their neighbour. Indeed in some cases they had no choice. As a condition of his wedding to a Spanish princess, Manuel had reluctantly agreed to the forcible expulsion of all unconverted Jews in 1496. The Portuguese officials did their utmost to arrange the conversion of these valuable citizens and any who did become *conversos* (that is converts) were assured that their beliefs would be free from investigation for the following twenty years.

A major problem for Portugal was the drain on her resources of manpower—the riches of the east which had given King Manuel his sobriquet were hard to win and the cost in both men and ships was terrible. The lure of quick riches from seafaring attracted not only the merchants as entrepreneurs but also the labourers as seamen and by the middle of the century Portugal was not only an importer of food stuffs but also had a huge black slave population. By the time of the Spanish conquest then, Portugal was too exhausted to offer any serious resistance.

The Spanish Inquisition

The most sinister of the institutions which were brought into Portugal under the pressure of her powerful neighbour was undoubtedly the Inquisition. It had been set up in Spain in the time of the Catholic Kings. From the beginning it was free from papal control, even being granted, in 1559, independent jurisdiction over bishops. In the reign of Charles V it became a department of state, developing in the fourth and fifth decade of the sixteenth century into the large and oppressive apparatus of thought control which became notorious.

The barbarities of torture and execution employed by the Inquisition were the commonplaces of interrogation and justice of the time; the particular objections to the Inquisition lay in its encouragement of public corruption and private betrayal. The condemned heretic lost not only his life and his honour but also stood to lose his lands. His trial might have been the result of denunciation by an unnamed informer, possibly a relation, and he might be held in prison for years before his case came to trial and then longer still while awaiting a verdict.

The apparatus of informers, denunciations, forced confessions and a public habit of watchfulness are unfortunately all too common in the twentieth century, but although the ritual of the show trial is still familiar the ceremony of the *auto-de-fé* (loosely to be translated as Act of Faith) is fortunately no longer practised. Even in an age of public executions it was outstanding. Crowds would assemble on specially constructed stands in the main squares of towns to watch the mass burning of the condemned heretics, while those who had recanted would process in penitence through the streets. King Philip's first public act in Spain was a personal attendance at an *auto-da-fé* in Valladolid.

Engrav'd for Englands Bloody Tribunal.
The Place & manner of Execution of Persons condemn'd by the Inquisition.

Above, an auto-da-fé, or the burning of heretics by the Spanish Inquisition; the Inquisition's surreptitious methods and its insistence on prosecuting every deviation from the orthodox Catholic line made it hated and feared throughout Europe.

Opposite, Alessandro Farnese, the Duke of Parma (1545–92), one of Philip II's greatest generals; as well as fighting at Lepanto in 1571, he won permanent control of the southern Netherlands for Spain and assisted the Catholic cause in the French Wars of Religion. Musées Royaux des Beaus Arts de Belgique, Brussels.

In the view of Philip's commitment to the re-establishment of orthodox Catholicism throughout Europe the Inquisition was obviously fundamental to his policy. If it was sometimes the vehicle of corrupt practices it was an important factor in the destruction of Protestantism in the Peninsula. During his father's reign action against Jewish *conversos*, too, had become even more severe with the passing of laws to enforce *Limpieza*, that is, the exclusion from public office those not of pure Old Christian descent: no candidate would be admitted to public office who could not prove the purity of his gentile blood. Under Philip the activities of the Inquisition were extended to the field of censorship, while in 1559 students were forbidden to travel abroad.

War against the infidel

In the 1560s Philip saw that the laws against the Moriscos of Granada were more rigorously enforced, in the same way that he had striven to establish orthodoxy amongst his Christian subjects. After their forcible conversion to Christianity in 1502, the Moors of this ancient Muslim kingdom had been able to buy the tolerance of the Christian kings. They were thus able to continue their former customs, dress, language and even, in some cases, religious observances. However, in the sixteenth century social and religious non-conformity were often closely associated and the Moors of Granada were often suspected, with some justice, of conspiracy, supported by their fellow Muslims in North Africa.

In 1568, the year after Philip had introduced his new measures against Muslim practices, the Moriscos of Granada rose in a revolt. This threatened the security of Christians and Spain and had it been vigorously supported by the Islamic powers might seriously have subverted the state of the Catholic Monarch. But the sultan took the opportunity of Philip's diversion in Granada to attack Cyprus, and Algiers reconquered Tunis.

Philip called in his half-brother, Don John of Austria, who had to summon troops from Italy. The Moriscos, who had already suffered the full rigours of the police methods of the Inquisition and who had in their turn massacred hundreds of their Christian oppressors, were now cruelly put down. They fled for refuge to the mountains of Alpujarras, the campaign of terror taking Don John two years to complete. When

the revolt was finally broken the Moriscos were forcibly deported and scattered throughout the length and breadth of Spain and their place was taken by 12,000 peasant families from the Christian north.

No sooner had the internal threat been eliminated than Philip received a call for aid from the Christian powers of the eastern Mediterranean against the Turkish force besieging Cyprus. Mindful of his self-imposed task as defender of the faith, Philip answered the call and despatched a fleet of some 200 galleys to help Venice and the papacy. Again Don John had the command, but he arrived too late to relieve the siege of Cyprus so he sought out the enemy in the bay of Lepanto, on the north coast of the Peloponnese. In the epic fight which followed the Christian fleet utterly destroyed its infidel enemy and the fame of the victory spread thoughout Europe. However the fruits of victory were meagre.

When the news of the defeat reached Constantinople the sultan, although furious with his dead Admiral, Ali Pasha, was not dismayed. 'The beard is singed,' he observed, 'it will grow again.' The observation, famous in another context in which the exultant compatriots of Sir Francis Drake may have missed its full import, was very just. Despite the loss of 210 ships the Turks were not long in repairing their shattered navy. The King of Spain, distracted by the continuing rebellion of his Christian yet heretic subjects in the Netherlands, only gained the recapture of Tunis as the fruits of victory.

The Holy League of allies which had defeated the Turk broke up on the death of the pope in the following year and Venice had to resign herself to the loss of Cyprus. Meanwhile the victorious admiral who had urged that the victory should be followed up by an attack on Constantinople and the destruction of Ottoman power, was despatched to the more prosaic task of putting down rebellion in the Low Countries.

Revolt in Aragon

In the sheer extent of the territories which he controlled and the forces which he could command, Philip of Spain excelled all the world's rulers except possibly the emperor of China. Yet so grandoise were his aims that they exceeded even the huge revenues which flowed annually into the Spanish treasury. In the early years of his reign he himself reckoned that the crown was in debt to the tune of seven times its national income, and some years later he was paying more interest than his combined total revenues. It is estimated that the Armada alone cost the Spanish exchequer ten million ducats and the yearly drain of the revolt in the Netherlands was a seemingly interminable wastage. Yet to Philip it must have seemed that such expenditure was unavoidable if his aims of a reunited Christendom and a united Spain were to be achieved. He did not intend to be the ruler of heretics and he was determined to be the sole ruler of Spain.

In this second aim his policy was in direct conflict with the intentions and ambitions of the once great partner in the Spanish dual monarchy, the kingdom of Aragon. The Catholic monarchs, Ferdinand and Isabella had carefully defined and separated the interests and autonomies of their two kingdoms thereby faithfully reflecting the wishes of their peoples. At that time it was the Castilians who at first feared the domination of the King of Aragon, but by the end of the sixteenth century the roles had been reversed. The administration of the joint kingdom was dominated by Castilians, the merchants of Barcelona had been excluded from the new world of the Indies, and the oppressive scrutiny of the Holy Office was an ever present reminder of the authority of the Castilian-speaking king.

The main cause of Aragonese discontent was the *fueros*, the ancient liberties of the kingdom which were invoked by the nobility to protect archaic feudal privileges and jurisdiction over the peasantry. The real grudge of the nobles, above all, the lesser nobility who lacked the influence and oppotunity open to the magnates, was their effective exclusion from the high offices of state in favour of Castilians. By and large Philip respected the Aragonese constitution, but he was impatient with the second kingdom's insubordination, and so he decided, in 1588, to impose a non-Aragonese viceroy on the country. The justiciar's court refused to acknowledge the validity of the title and regionalist opposition mounted. It broke out into rebellion two years later around the

person of Antonio Perez, the king's once powerful and ambitious secretary.

Perez had been under arrest for some years for his initiation of the murder of Don John of Austria's secretary. Philip, who had at first been inclined to believe Perez's fabrications of treason against his half brother, was implicated but was now determined to eliminate his deceitful adviser. When, therefore, Perez escaped and fled to Aragon and the justiciar, urged on by members of the lesser nobility, refused to surrender him to the king, Philip fell back on the Inquisition, the only body whose powers overrode the *fueros*.

The arrest of Perez on a trumped up charge of heresy led to rioting in Saragossa, but most of the other towns of the kingdom as well as the leading magnates declared themselves for Philip against the 'knights of liberty' (minor nobility and gentry) who had released Perez. Philip's forces marched on the capital, put down the rebels and executed the justiciar. Two years later an invading force under Perez was easily defeated, with the aid of Aragonese contingents, and at the *cortes* of June 1592 the constitution of Aragon was modified though not suppressed.

The Invincible Armada

'You are engaging upon the most important undertaking by God's church for many hundreds of years, with every conceivable pretext for a just and holy war.' The words are taken from one of the many sermons preached in the pulpits of Lisbon during the spring of 1588 to encourage the soldiers and crews of the great Armada which was assembling there.

Philip had maintained a pacific if not exactly amicable policy towards Elizabeth of England since her accession, even at one stage offering to marry her as he had done her Catholic sister Mary; and from the point of view of Spanish supremacy in Europe there was good reason for his policy. The natural heir to Elizabeth, Mary Queen of Scots, was undoubtedly a good Catholic but, in view of her close ties with the powerful French family of Guise, Philip could hardly have regarded her as the ideal queen of England. To expand Spanish resources on setting a friend of France on the throne of England would be a quixotic way for Spain to further the victory of Catholicism. Not only was Philip not prepared to open the way to Mary, but he was also reluctant to undermine the authority of Elizabeth. This was even though the activities of her seadogs Hawkins and Drake in the Spanish Main had brought him to the brink of supporting the rising of 1569. Yet in the following year, after it had failed, he dramatically opposed the papal excommunication of Elizabeth, forbidding the publication of the Bull in Spain and even trying to prevent its reaching England.

The accession of Pope Sixtus V in 1585 introduced a new factor into Spanish papal relations. Just as Philip would not promote a solution to the English problem which favoured the power of France, so the pope

Above, the great crescent formation of the Spanish Armada of 1588, followed by the much smaller English fleet. The bulk of the Spanish fleet was made up of troop-carrying vessels; only fifty were fighting craft and even these were less manoeuvrable than the English ships. National Maritime Museum, London.

Opposite, the converted Moors, or Moriscos, of southern Spain were forcibly dispersed throughout the country in the 1570s; the episode exacerbated the economic stagnation caused by the lack of a strong urban middle class in Spain.

was fearful of seeing the massive power of Spain gain new influence in the north. In the words of a modern historian, 'The domination of the church by the crown was probably more complete in Spain than in any other part of Europe, including Protestant countries.' So real was the pope's fear of seeing this influence extended to the northern kingdom that Sixtus at first hoped by a diplomacy of concilation to win Elizabeth back to Rome. Philip II could have told him how wrong he was, and the execution of Mary in 1587 finally convinced the pope that there was no way out but alliance with Spain. Yet even now, when the king sought financial aid, it was only to be met with a promise from the wily pontiff that the papal treasury would pay out one million ducats in cash when the first Spanish soldier set foot on English soil. From the first Sixtus was sceptical:

The king and his armada are becoming ridiculous, while Queen Elizabeth knows how to manage her affairs. If that woman were only a Catholic she would be loved by us more than any other sovereign for she has great qualities. . . . That Spanish Armada gives us anxieties. We have strong presentiments that it will not succeed.

Yet, with the annexation of Portugal, Philip's finances had improved and the increase in English aid to the Low Countries reinforced the arguments of those of his advisers who urged that the revolt would only be put down when England had been conquered. In 1586, Elizabeth sent not only money but troops under the command of the Earl of Leicester himself. And then, in February the following year, came the execution of Mary Queen of Scots. Philip, who had shown increasing interest in investigating the enterprise against England, now perhaps saw the great danger of a queen friendly to France removed.

Preparations begin

In March 1587 he ordered the beginning of preparations under the directions of the ageing Santa Cruz, who some years previously had drawn up the first specifications for such an enterprise. Either his enthusiasm had waned or, more likely, the full complexity of mounting the expedition only became apparent when work was started in earnest. Whatever the reason, Santa Cruz was unable to press on with the preparations as quickly as the impatient king demanded.

Matters were not helped when, in May, Cadiz harbour was raided by Drake who destroyed not only several great ships but also the vital seasoned timbers from which the barrels for the fleet's provisions were to have been made. The King of Spain's beard had been well and truly singed and the daring exploit ended in tangible profit when Drake captured the treasure carrack *San Felipe*. This was only the most sensational of the innumerable delays which dogged the fitting out of the Armada so that, despite all the king's urgings, the fleet was still not in a fit condition to sail when in February 1588 Santa Cruz died. His successor, the Duke of Medina Sidonia, was appalled by what he found—rotting provisions, fevered crews, ships in need of repair and, above all, pitifully few large guns.

The Spaniards at the time, and many historians since, have made Medina Sidonia the scapegoat for the failure of the whole expedition. The appointment was indeed inapposite as the poor man himself was painfully aware; he confessed to being totally inexperienced in sea-going command and begged to be spared the responsibility. But King Philip insisted and the duke had no option. However, there was one thing in his favour—none of the proud and contentious officers of the fleet could object to taking orders from a man who outranked them all in social station. And Medina Sidonia used his authority to the best possible effect in procuring a further delay in the sailing date and, as far as was possible, made good the terrible deficiencies which his predecessor had left him. Thus when, on 9 May, the grand fleet finally set sail from Lisbon its equipment and provisions were in as good a state as was possible. Even so it was necessary to put in again at Corunna to take on fresh victuals and water and because of this and the terrible weather conditions it was not until late in July that the great Spanish invasion fleet finally arrived at the mouth of the English Channel.

The epic running fight which followed and the final scattering of the huge Armada by fire-ships in the roads of Calais traditionally belong more to the folk history of Britain, and the names of Drake, Hawkins, Frobisher and Admiral Howard are listed among the heroes. And yet it should be realized that up to the very last moment the English commanders treated the enemy with considerable respect. Indeed they had been unable to inflict any mortal damage on the Spaniards until the dangerous crescent formation was finally shattered and dispersed by the use of fire ships when it was anchored in the roads of Calais.

Despite his inexperience, Medina Sidonia showed immense and justified tenacity in taking his formidable but slow-moving force through the lines of the agile and more powerfully gunned ships which the enemy provided. Both his own presence of mind and the considerable seamanship of his crews ensured that the Spaniards were able to maintain their formation. The fleet itself was carrying troops, but the main invasion force was to be the army which Parma had assembled on the Dutch coast and which was to be ferried across in transport barges.

In so far as the English fleet was still intact Medina Sidonia had failed. Nevertheless, against all the odds, he had brought his escort to the rendezvous point. The fact that his ammunition was now practically exhausted was a result of the failure of the king and Santa Cruz to see that adequate preparation was made for the enterprise. Nor was it the fault of the admiral that his great ships could not get close enough inshore to protect the transports from the Dutch fleet which was patrolling the coast. The king had known the danger from the outset. He had received reports both from Medina Sidonia and Parma stating that since the deep sea ports Brill and Flushing were in rebel hands and there was an insufficient number of shallow draft vessels to combat the Dutch the whole strategy of the invasion was invalid.

Broken in spirit, out of ammunition and desperately short of supplies, the once proud Armada made its terrible way through the icy waters round the north of Scotland and down the murderous shores of Ireland; only half of its one hundred and thirty ships returned to Spain. However, one section of the fleet did complete its voyage, without breaking station or losing a single ship, and that was the guardship squadron of Carrera de Indias. It was by far the most efficient branch of the Spanish navy and had been taken off the trans-Atlantic run for this operation.

Philip did not regard the English enterprise as closed. He took the news of the disaster with his customary calm and is supposed to have commented: 'I sent my ships to fight against men, not the winds and the waves of God.' Indeed he seems to have actually begun roughing out the plans for a second expedition. But, to quote an American historian: 'If any one year marks the division between the triumphant Spain of the first two Habsburgs and the defeatist disillusioned Spain of their successors, that year is 1588.'

Despite the heroic endeavours and considerable achievements of Philip II of Spain, the century which followed his death witnessed the uninterrupted decline of Spanish power and the domination of Europe by his arch-enemy France. The story was complete when in 1702 a Bourbon dynasty was set upon the throne of Spain.

VI
The Ld. Admirall Howard
Knighting Thomas Howard,
the Lord Sheffeild, Rogr. Townsen.
Iohn Hawkins, and Martin
Forbisher for their good service

Left, Charles Howard of Effingham, the English admiral during the Armada, knighting several of his captains including the explorer Martin Frobisher and the privateer John Hawkins. Over the previous fifteen years Hawkins had been comptroller of the navy and had supervised its modernization. Museo del Ejercito, Madrid.

A. Thevet cosmographe du Roy

numero de años . Ll .

2

acacitli

quapan

ocelopa

aguexotl

tezineuh

tenuch

xomimitl

xocoyol

tenochtitlan

xiuhcaqui

atototl

colhuacan. pueblo.

tenayucan. pueblo.

Part VI

THE AGE OF DISCOVERY

Introduction

The Age of Discovery was well named. In the span of about a hundred years, roughly the second half of the fifteenth century and the first half of the sixteenth, Europeans learned, with the confidence of experience and first-hand report, to think of the world as a whole. European explorers and travellers actually visited, during those hundred years, most of the habitable regions of the globe. They discovered that the world was larger by far, and more diverse, than any then accepted authority, ancient or medieval, had taught. They found an ocean bigger than the Atlantic, a continent as big as Europe and Africa combined. They proved that the salt seas of the world, with a few insignificant exceptions, were all connected, so that a seaman, with courage, adequate provisions and a reliable ship, could in time reach any country in the world which possessed a sea coast. Their reports, spread about by the new technique of printing, attracted widespread public attention. Some became 'best-sellers'. The enlargement of geographical knowledge which western Europeans achieved in those hundred years was prodigious in its extent and in its speed. In this respect, no other century in the history of the world is remotely comparable.

The enlargement of geographical knowledge, however, was not the primary purpose of fifteenth- and sixteenth-century exploration. The great discoverers were not Renaissance humanists consumed by intellectual curiosity. They were practical men. Distant unknown continents and islands, unless obviously productive of gold or other precious things, were of little interest to them. They set out to discover not new lands but new routes to old lands. Their main purpose, and that of the rulers and investors who sent them out, was to establish direct contact first with West Africa and subsequently with Asia. More specifically their intention was to link individual centres in western Europe with places in India, the Indonesian islands, China and Japan, places known or believed to exist and reputed to be of high civilization and great commercial importance.

Fifteenth-century Europeans knew very little at first hand about Asia. Their great-grandfathers had been somewhat better informed. For a century or so, between the mid-thirteenth and the mid-fourteenth centuries, the military and administrative unification forced upon much of Asia by Genghis Khan and his successors had made it possible to travel overland across the whole length of the continent in reasonable security. There was a considerable East-West trade, woollens and linens one way, silks and spices the other. A number of European merchants and missionary ambassadors had travelled with the caravans across the Great Khan's dominions. Some, of whom Marco Polo was the most celebrated, wrote accounts of their experiences, which became part of the general stock of European knowledge.

All this coming and going was sharply interrupted in the middle of the fourteenth century. The Black Death, which swept both Asia and Europe, brought most long-distance travel temporarily to a standstill. The incursion from the Steppe of yet another pillaging mounted horde—the Ottoman Turks—created a new militant and hostile Muslim Empire as a barrier between East and West. The Tartar Empire broke up; in 1368 the descendants of Kublai Khan were driven from their Peking throne by a native Chinese dynasty, the Mings, who brought back the traditional official dislike and contempt for western barbarians. The 'safe road to Peking'—so described in an early fourteenth-century merchants' guide—became extremely unsafe. European contact with Asia became confined to hazardous and expensive pilgrimages to the Holy Land; to trade with Arab intermediaries, on their terms, in the harbours of the Levant; and to the purchase of Persian silk at exorbitant prices in the Black Sea ports. Europeans knew nothing of Ming China, nothing of the successive Muslim invasions of India (of which the Mogul invasion was to be the most widespread and most lasting), next to nothing of Safawid Persia. Japan and the Indonesian islands had never been more than names. Almost the only eyewitness information about the far and middle East available to fifteenth-century Europeans came from thirteenth-century accounts, reliable enough when they were written but hopelessly out of date. When Columbus went in search of Cathay (i.e. North China) he carried letters of credence for the Great Khan.

Both rulers and business men in Europe had the strongest possible motives for wishing to restore contact with the East. The European craving for spices supplied an obvious commercial motive. Apart from common salt, and a few minor spices such as saffron, Europe produced none of these preservative and flavouring substances. The best condiment and preservative spices grew in southeast Asia: cinnamon in Ceylon, pepper in Java and Sumatra, nutmeg and its derivative mace in Borneo and Celebes, cloves—most valuable of all—in the Moluccas and the Banda Islands at the eastern end of the Malay archipelago. These details, of course, were unknown to fifteenth-century Europe. Europeans tended to lump together large areas of Asia under the general name of India, and they had heard or read of certain harbours—Calicut in particular—as markets where spices were sold. So far as they knew, these Malabar ports, or their hinterland, were the original sources of supply. Spices intended directly for the Arab and Ottoman areas, or indirectly for sale to Europeans, were carried from Malabar across the Indian Ocean by Arab shippers. They went to Ormuz, up the Persian Gulf to Basra, up the Mesopotamian rivers to Baghdad, to Damascus and to the ports of Syria. Alternatively they went to Aden, up the Red Sea and overland via Cairo to Alexandria, where Venetian traders bought them for transmission to Italy and to western Europe. If Africa could be circumnavigated—contrary to the ancient theories of Ptolemy—and if the Malabar ports could be reached by a continuous sea passage, European traders might buy their spices at the source. Thus they could cut out a series of rapacious middlemen, and make immense and continuing profits.

Religious, political and strategic considerations pointed the same way. European Christendom in the fifteenth century was isolated and confined; its bastions against Islam were falling, its territory shrinking. In 1453 the Turks took Constantinople and began the long advance which was to overrun the Balkans, the Levant and North Africa and momentarily to threaten Italy and Spain. In fact of these dangers the Church—the chief symbol of European unity—was divided within itself. The leaders in the Councils, who planned and negotiated to heal the schisms, looked longingly for reunion not only within the Roman communion but with all the communities of Christians throughout the world. They knew, or had heard, of many such communities. There were Orthodox Greeks, fighting their losing battle against the Turk; Armenians, Syrians and Copts living within the boundaries of Muslim power; Chaldeans on the eastern flank of Islam; and Ethiopians, Indians and even Cathayan Christians. Then there were some Christian lands whose very existence was matter of hearsay—St Brendan's Isle and Antilla of the Seven Cities. Of all these distant lands, India was the most appealing; India, where St Thomas had preached and suffered martyrdom, and where the descendants of his followers—it was believed—still lived. If contact could be made, the Christian kingdoms of Europe might gain sympathy, spiritual reassurance, perhaps even military support.

In the political circumstances of late fifteenth-century Asia, contact overland was out of the question, except for a handful of bold individuals who travelled in disguise. However, western European seamen, especially those of the Atlantic coasts of Spain and Portugal, were well equipped to establish contact by sea. The late fifteenth century was a period of rapid development in the design and construction of ships, in the techniques of navigation and instrument making, in cartography and (not least in importance) in the adaptation of artillery for use at sea. Iberian seamen already possessed a great store of experience in oceanic work. This had been accumulated not only in trading, fishing, sealing and slaving all the way from Iceland to Cape Verde but also in settling and fighting in the Atlantic islands—Madeira, the Canaries and the Azores. These islands were soon to become essential way-stations for the longer oceanic voyages.

In addition, Iberian seamen—the Portuguese especially—enjoyed the advantage of consistent royal backing, which for the first time made possible a systematic, step-by-step approach to the whole business of exploration. Once these conditions were established, success followed success with breath-taking speed. In 1492 Columbus found his false Indies in the Caribbean. Six years later, in 1498, Vasco da Gama reached Calicut and by the middle of the sixteenth century, the sea route to India was in regular commercial use. An alternative but longer and more dangerous route was explored by Magellan into the south Atlantic and westward to southeast Asia; trade was opened with Malaya and some of the Indonesian islands, and South China and Japan had been visited.

Naturally, the reality differed from the dream. The eastern Christians proved few, unimportant and unhelpful. 'Prester John' turned out to be not a major Asian potentate but a hard-pressed African one, the Negus of Abyssinia. The richest parts of Asia were grouped in powerful and civilized empires, compared with which the kingdoms of Europe were disorderly petty states. The inhabitants of these empires had little respect for European religion, European habits and the crude products of European industry. Except in the few harbours where Portuguese had settled and were entrenched, trade, diplomatic relations and proselytizing alike were limited to what Asian rulers would permit.

America, on the other hand—originally a disappointment, an unwelcome barrier between Europe and Cathay—had exceeded expectations. It contained, in some areas at least, populous and productive kingdoms, whose technological limitations made them an easy prey to conquistadores. In those areas, Spaniards had established a territorial empire whose great riches, in the middle of the sixteenth century, were just beginning to appear. The metals of the New World were to make Spain, for a time at least, the envy and terror of Europe. They were to finance the armadas and the armies with which Spaniards tried to drive back the Turks, to uphold the Counter-Reformation and to bend Dutchmen, Englishmen and Frenchmen to their will. They were to flow out from exhausted Spain and in the hands of other Europeans were largely to finance the extension, eventually the predominance, of European commerce in the Old World. In all this, the significant factor was not simply discovery but the determination with which discovery was exploited. The most important discovery made by Europeans was that they had long lived in a backwater. In the process of discovery, they navigated, fought and argued themselves into the main stream.

Above, close-up of one of the sculptures of the Teotihuacan god, the plumed serpent Quetzalcoatl, who had been a legendary ruler of central America in days of great prosperity.

On page 284, the Aztec legend of the foundation of Tenochtitlan, at the place where the eagle was sitting on a cactus. Bodleian Library, Oxford.

Chapter 24

Pre-Columbian America

Civilization developed among the American Indian peoples without any contact with the Old World.

More than 40,000 years ago small groups of Stone Age hunters crossed the land bridge from Siberia—before the existence of the Bering Straits—and entered the New World in search of game. Such small-scale entry continued from time to time over many thousands of years. Gradually these peoples, who were the ancestors of the many different groups of American Indians, spread over the whole double continent.

The early part of the story of American Indian culture rests entirely upon archaeological evidence. There is no written or even traditional verbal history which can take us back before AD 600 in Mexico or AD 1000 in Peru. However careful excavation, aided by such modern resources as pollen analysis and carbon-14 dating, has enabled us to build up a reasonably accurate picture of the development of civilization in the Americas.

The early hunting tribes were probably of much the same Mongoloid physical type as most of the later people. They developed great skill in making stone tools, and from the differences in style we can detect a sequence of cultures which existed between 5,000 and 15,000 years ago. This was the time when animals such as mastodons, giant buffaloes and the American horse were the main source of food. However these creatures became extinct and the progress of civilization was continued by a few tribes who were developing the beginnings of agriculture.

The main crop was maize and present evidence suggests that this was developed from a primitive ancestral plant with only two seeds. By 5,000 BC a few tribes in northern Mexico lived by a combination of hunting and maize cultivation and this idea was to spread.

The beginnings of civilization

The development of civilization depended upon people being able to settle in permanent villages. In Peru this had happened by 2000 BC and life was based on coastal fishing and the encouragement of crops such as quinoa and the potato. By 1500 BC there were large villages in Mexico, mostly on the grasslands of the high plateau, where the maize crops were supplemented with tomatoes, squash and probably domesticated turkeys.

The village houses were built from blocks of clay and surrounded by cultivated garden plots. The women were responsible for making pottery vessels, which they did with great skill by coiling clay, a primitive method which had to be employed since no potter's wheel was ever invented by the American Indian peoples. They also made small figurines which represented females, possibly fertility goddesses. The few clothes which the women wore were woven fabric made on the simple back-strap loom, the only apparatus used for weaving in any part of pre-Columbian America. They possessed attractive jewellery.

Despite their apparent primitiveness it is important to realize that human discoveries of basic importance were made by the American Indian peoples. Although the wheel was an Old World discovery, native Americans had discovered pottery and developed their agriculture quite independently of other civilizations.

As far as religion was concerned, the Mexican farming tribes worshipped gods placed in small houses on earthen mounds. At Cuicuilo one of these mounds was faced with rough blocks of stone and in it was found a stone figure of the old fire god of later Mexican religion. Here we reach the beginnings of civilization.

In the highland villages a new type of figurine was developed, which had a body similar to that of a baby and a peculiar jaguar-like mouth. This type of figure appeared again in about 900 BC in the first high civilization of Mexico. It represented one of the gods of the Olmecs, a people who built temple mounds and ceremonial courtyards in the sites of La Venta and Tres Zapotes, near the southern coast of the Gulf of Mexico. These Olmecs were artists of great ability and their work in jade and basalt is outstanding. Huge stone heads were carved by them to stand in sacred places.

Incised symbols show us that these people had a knowledge of writing, although it bears no relation to any other type which was used in the world of that time. They were also creative individuals and Olmec art spread widely over Mexico, being particularly strong in the western state of Oaxaca. Here it was a precursor of the Zapotec culture which existed from 200 BC to AD 1500.

Why Olmec culture disappeared in the last centuries BC is not known. In the south it was succeeded by the beginnings of Maya culture, while on the highland plateau of Mexico a new civilization was developing around Teotihuacan, where work began on the gigantic Pyramid of the Sun in the first century BC.

Teotihuacan is the name given to the ruined city by the Aztecs. It means 'the Place where the Gods were Made'. In its heyday, the huge city may have contained nearly a million inhabitants, at its centre was a group of pyramidal temples clustered around a processional way leading to the temples of the sun and moon.

Wall paintings and numerous pottery figurines show us that the Teotihuacanos dressed in fine clothes and that their nobles decorated themselves with magnificent ornaments of tropical feathers. A simple system of writing in pictorial symbols was known to them.

PRE-COLUMBIAN CIVILIZATIONS

Date	Mexico	Maya area	Peru
2000 BC	Tlatilco village Cuicuilco temple		Coastal villages Chavin de Huantar
1000 BC	Olmec culture Olmec 900 BC– 400 BC	Highland villages	
500 BC	Last of Olmec style Monte Alban Teotihuacan (100 BC)		Paraccas Nasca
0	Teotihuacano expansion	First inscriptions	Rise of Tiahuanaco
AD 500	Fall of Teotihuacan (AD 600) Rise of the Toltecs (750)	Height of classical Maya period Fall of Palenque End of classical period	Tiahuanaco expansion End of Tiahuanaco Rise of the Chimu
AD 1000	Fall of the Toltecs (1000) Beginnings of Aztec power Aztec expansion	Yucatec Maya Toltecs at Chich'en Itzá League of Mayapan Maya Independent cities	Rise of the Incas Conquest of the Chimu Inca expansion
AD 1500	Height of Aztec power Spanish Conquest (1521)	Maya weak and disunited Spanish Conquest (1547)	Conquest of Quito Spanish Conquest (1533)

The gods worshipped at Teotihuacan were the powers of nature, and several of them can be recognized as deities worshipped as late as the sixteenth century AD. They include Tlaloc the god of rain and all sources of water.

Teotihuacano pottery and sculpture is found all over the southern half of Mexico. At Kaminaljuyu, in Guatemala, there was a great Teotihuacano centre in the first century AD before the Maya civilization developed there.

In about AD 550 Teotihuacan was burnt and destroyed. The inhabitants built a new city, Azcapotzalco, nearby but apparently it had no great political power and declined within another century. The cause of the decline of Teotihuacan remains unknown. However, it may possibly be related to the fact that at the same time the tribes from the Pacific coast of Guatemala, and others from northern Mexico, were introducing a new system of writing and languages into Mexico which brought about cultural disintegration.

The Toltecs

Mexico enters history with the settlement of the Toltec kings in the city of Tollan (Tula) a little north of Mexico City. A list of them, with short accounts of their reigns, forms part of the fourteenth-century painted book, *Codex Vindobonesis Mexic.I,* now preserved in Vienna.

The Toltecs worshipped many gods who were personifications of the forces of nature. Important amongst them were the sun, rain, wind, the powerful demon Tezcatlipoca (Smoking Mirror) and the Toltec patron god, Quetzalcoatl, Lord of the Winds and the Breath of Life, after whom the Toltec kings took their titles.

The first Toltec chief began his rule in about AD 750. There were nine high chiefs who gradually extended Toltec influence over the whole of civilized Mexico. In the tenth century there was a bitter civil war and the Toltec empire collapsed. This was described in later times as a battle of magic between the god Quetzalcoatl and the demonic Tezcatlipoca, patron of warriors.

After the débâcle, a number of smaller city states arose in Mexico, but the leaders of the Toltecs escaped to Yucatan, where they erected a city among the Maya which is known to us as Chichen Itzá. Here the Itzá clan ruled for another two centuries before being overthrown by the mixed Maya-Toltec rulers of Mayapan.

The ancient Maya

In the far south of Mexico and parts of Guatemala, the Maya people built up a civilization of their own. Their art and religion, while related to the other Mexican cultures, had great individuality of style, They used a system of writing, probably developed from the Olmec glyphs, which was unique in America because it was phonetic. By using some 650 pictorial symbols for syllables the Maya were able to communicate ideas with accuracy. Their hieroglyphic inscriptions can be partially understood. They contain much mythological and calendrical material, but there is no sign of any historical record.

It appears that the Maya civilization was separatist in character. Great cities were

Above, central and south American civilizations before the arrival of the Europeans. The Mayan civilizations had declined before the rise of the Aztecs and Incas.

built, but the only evidence of confederation occurs during a short period from the fourth to the seventh centuries AD. The cities were mostly religious centres which were surrounded by scattered groups of farms. At Tikal, in Guatemala, however, there are indications that the high pyramidal temples were the centre of an enormous city covering several square miles.

The older phase of the civilization was centred in Guatemala and the Chiapas region of Mexico. Cities were built from the second century AD and were inhabited until the end of the ninth. Temples and free-standing stelae were also erected and covered with elaborate designs, many of which incorporated long inscriptions.

The most important factor in religious life was the calendar, which was used for predicting all kinds of future events. A study of it shows that the Maya were conversant with the movements of all the visible planets and had divided the zodiac into a series of constellations not unlike our own. For mythological purposes they were able to deal with periods of time extending to millions of years.

Basically they used a calendrical year of 360 days divided into eighteen periods, each of twenty days. The 360 day period was known as a Tun, and this was the basis of a count of time which was continually adjusted to bring calendars into line with the true solar year. Its purpose was not scientific from our point of view, for it was mainly concerned with a remarkable system of prognostication. The Maya expended vast intellectual energy on finding 'lucky days' for any activity in which they were interested and thought that their magical calendar expressed the will of their gods. As a matter of fact it was of great value to the farmers for it gave accurate dates for sowing and reaping.

The fine cities and high civilization of the Maya were equalled by their craft work in pottery and wood carving. From their monuments we can deduce that they also made the most remarkable woven garments. They were great painters too and wall frescoes, notably at Bonampak, show the early development of realism in the treatment of the human figure.

This great civilization broke up at the end of the ninth century. No more monuments were erected and the cities were totally abandoned to the encroachment of the forest. Nevertheless Maya tradition revived amongst the cities of Yucatan and from about AD 1000 to 1250 it was dominated by the intrusive Toltecs at Chichen Itzá. Later the country separated into a number of more truly independent Maya cities in which the old arts were revived. However the Spanish conquest of Yucatan in the middle of the sixteenth century and the final fall of the last

Above, Mayan female figure from the Huaxtec culture, which flourished in the modern Veracruz province of Mexico.

Above left, relief from a Mayan building showing a man mutilating himself by passing a cord with thorns through his tongue.

Opposite left, two starkly sculpted gods on the steps of a pyramid at Teotihuacan, the rain god Tlaloc and the plumed serpent Quetzalcoatl. Although at its height (AD 300–900) Teotihuacan was primarily a religious centre, evidence of a long-distance trade has also been found there.

Opposite right, one of a number of stone warriors on the top of the pyramid at Tula, the Toltec capital, dating from shortly before that civilization was taken over by the Aztecs in the thirteenth century.

Maya forest town of Peten Itzá in 1697 removed the Maya from history as an independent people.

The Aztec advance

After the fall of the Toltec Empire, Mexico broke up into a number of warring city states, each one seeking to control its neighbours. In the southwest the Zapotecs were heavily defeated by the Mixtec people under their great war leader Eight Deer Lord of Tilantongo (AD 1009–61) but, on his death, the Zapotecs regained their territory and the Mixtecs split up into their constituent town-states.

In central Mexico a few families of Toltec descent survived the civil war and plague to become ancestors of various local dynasties, but all were eventually absorbed into the Aztec dominion.

The Aztec story began in 1168 when the small and rather primitive tribe was settled at Aztlan, a village on the plateau. Their ancestors are thought to have come from the far northern plains of the American middle west. They were inspired by a magical image of their war god, Huitzilopochtli, to set out on a long pilgrimage to seek a promised land from which they could conquer all Mexico. Because they had committed sacrilege, they were condemned to remain unsettled until such time as they should receive a sign of forgiveness, and for over a century they wandered about the country, always subject to the domination of the more civilized towns.

Eventually they were exiled by the king of Colhuacan to a rocky islet in the Lake of Mexico. There they saw the promised sign of the white eagle on a cactus plant which was to indicate the land pledged to them and they immediately built a small temple to their god.

The earlier Aztecs elected their chiefs and established something like a tribal democracy. However they understood local feeling and made sure that the leading warriors should marry into families which could claim descent from the Toltec rulers. Eventually the range of popular election was restricted so that chieftains could only be elected from one specially important family. This change followed the rescue of the nation in a time of military danger by the war leader Itzcoatl. Under his leadership the Aztecs obtained control of the Valley of Mexico through an alliance with their neighbours in the cities of Tlaltelolco and Tezcuco and, before his death in 1440, the armies of Itzcoatl had fought their way to the coasts of both the Atlantic and the Pacific Oceans.

Itzcoatl was succeeded by Moctecuzoma I who assumed the title of *Uetlatoani*, an approximate equivalent of emperor. Under this ruler, and his son Axayacatl, the Aztec armies gained control of most of the Pacific coast of Mexico. Axayacatl was also responsible for the last and greatest rebuilding of the temples in Mexico City, but it was left to his successor, the Emperor Ahuitzotl, to complete the work. Sacrifice necessarily played an important part in the dedication ceremony and during a two year period proceeding it, Ahuitzotl accumulated the whole manpower of a number of the Mixtec tribes

which he had defeated, some 20,000 men, and sacrificed them to the god of war. This horrified the neighbouring kingdoms and helped to prepare the way for the revolt of subject tribes which assisted Cortes in the destruction of the Aztec power.

On the death of Ahuitzotl in 1502, the power of the Aztecs was given to Montezuma. Despite the fact that his reign was marked by many changes of fortune, the Aztec dominion expanded to the size of the ancient Toltec empire. Montezuma tried to make his capital as glorious and beautiful as ancient Tollan had been, and the surviving works of Aztec sculpture, gold work and feather covered shields show that the height of Aztec culture was reached during his reign.

As in Toltec times, the emperor was the chairman of the council of four, which included the High Priest, the Chief Justice and the Guardian of the Markets. The nobility were warrior chieftains and owed allegiance to the emperor. They were regarded as overlords of the towns in their territory and collected tribute in return for protection. Usually the nobles inherited their position, but a particularly brave warrior might win promotion on the battlefield and become a nobleman.

The mass of the people were small farmers whose intensive agriculture earned them enough to pay taxes to the emperor and tribute to gods and overlords. They added to their resources by barter at the markets, where all manner of goods could be found for exchange. There was no coined currency, but a suitable substitute was found in quills of gold dust, beads of jade, and bunches of tropical feathers. Cocoa beans were also used as a universally acceptable form of currency.

Once in every twenty days a great market was held in Tenochtitlan (Mexico City). On these occasions there were festivals in honour of the gods, often accompanied by human sacrifice. The priests enacted mythological dramas and the people participated

Left, the pyramid of the Inscriptions at Palenque, in southern Mexico, one of the best surviving Mayan monuments. The pyramid is surmounted with a temple.

Opposite, turquoise mask deriving from the Aztec civilization of Mexico; it probably represents Quetzalcoatl, the god of learning and priesthood.

in the dances and signing and in throwing flowers. In some festivals, girls thronged the streets tossing flowers made of coloured popcorn in honour of the maize spirits. And all this activity was set off by the gleaming white walls of the plastered houses, the frescoed pyramids and the glittering water of the canals which intersected the city.

Tenochtitlan was not only one of the largest towns in the world at this time, it was also one of the most beautiful. It was set on an island in the midst of a mountain lake, while in the distance was to be seen a range of mountains with snow-capped volcanoes. Bernal Diaz, who saw it in all its glory in 1519, compared it to a vision from a romance of Amadis of Gaul.

The Aztecs believed that the universe was but a green seed in the hands of the Divine Duality (Ometecuhtli), who had created everything. The earth was a great flat area lying between thirteen heavenly hemispheres and nine underworlds. It was nourished by the rain god Tlaloc and his beautiful consort Chalchihuitlicue, Lady Precious Green. The sun gave life and light and was the fourth sun in a series, each of which represented a new creation of mankind. To become the sun, a god had jumped into a great fire so that his heart had leapt into the sky to give light to mankind. In return, man was compelled to keep the sun moving through the heavens by offering human hearts at regular intervals. Hence the famous and horrible scenes of bloody heart sacrifice at the temples.

All the forces of nature were worshipped as gods, and many of them were also regarded as living in the skies in the form of planets and stars. The Lord of this World was a god called Tezcatlipoca. He was a demonic character and was patron of warriors, magicians and Lord of Fate. Many other gods existed, since each useful plant, especially the maize, had its patron deity. There were goddesses of witchcraft, of healing and of childbirth; also one goddess, Mayauel, was responsible for strong drink.

Magical books were used which gave details of individual fate in varying circumstances and many people consulted the soothsayers about their future.

The sequence of time had a very special relationship to history, since not only the planets but also the gods associated with them were believed to rise and fall. Over a long period it had been believed that the god Tezcatlipoca had triumphed by turning out Quetzalcoatl and causing the ruin of the Toltecs. It was thought that in the year Two Reed (1518 in this case) the god of the Aztecs, who was a form of Tezcatlipoca, would once again be replaced by the reappearance of Quetzalcoatl. Since the Emperor Montezuma had been a priest he was well versed in this calendrical magic. He was already aware of impending doom

for he had seen bad omens in the form of comets in the sky.

In 1508 and 1509 two strange ships had passed along the coast of Mexico. To the Aztecs, who had never seen a European vessel before, they appeared to be birds with huge white wings, carrying men dressed in hard grey stone (armour). These were the ships of Solis and Pinzon seeking trading posts. Montezuma had strange visions of impending catastrophe and of the return of Quetzalcoatl who would demand the seat of power once more. Then, on the precise day, a ship arrived on the coast and a stranger, dressed in black and wearing the hat and breast jewel of Quetzalcoatl, stepped ashore. However, it was not the return of the God. It was the Spaniard, Hernando Cortes. The conquest of Mexico had begun.

Before the Incas

Southwards from Mexico there used to be many smaller civilized areas. In Panama there were groups of villages which produced beautiful pottery and fine gold work which was traded as far as Mexico. In Colombia the Muisca culture was to be found where the tribes speaking Chibcha were adventurous conquerors and their chief was the originator of the El Dorado legend. In the western Colombian river valleys lived many tribal groups, who were amongst the most remarkable gold workers of their day. In Ecuador there was a powerful kingdom ruled by the Scyri of Quito. But all these peoples can only be investigated by the archaeologist. They left no written history.

On the other hand, from about AD 1100 onwards the past were recorded by the people who lived southwards in Peru. Before that we must rely on legends illuminated by the archaeologists. In the early villages of the first two thousand years BC civilization developed gradually. In about 1500 BC maize was introduced from the north, because it could be so easily stored adding greatly to the possibilities of developing a higher civilization.

By 1000 BC a high culture was achieved on the central coast and in the highland valley of the Marañon. Fine textiles, increasingly elegant pottery, great stone carvings and the first working of gold are associated with this Chavin culture.

On the southern coast, where Chavin art was associated with the culture of Paraccas, a further development produced the Nazca civilization which lasted until the early centuries AD. It was contemporary with a different civilization in the northern half of the Peruvian coast known to us as the Mochica culture. Here bronze was used for tools and weapons and great pyramidal temples were built of mud bricks.

Both Mochica and Nazca civilizations were to be dominated by the mountain cities of Tiahuanaco and Huari. There can be little doubt that these represented an empire, but it has neither history nor name for us. After the collapse of this imperium in the ninth century AD the only surviving high culture was on the northern coast, which was now dominated by the Chimu kings. The highland country was so divided that no unified civilization was able to develop until the Incas rose to power.

Inca power

The Incas said that their ancestors came from the east. The first Inca, Manco, who claimed to be the offspring of the sun god, Inti, came with his sister carrying a piece of gold. Where this sank into the ground was to be their home, which would be called Cuzco (a Quechua word meaning 'navel') When this eventually happened they knew that they had arrived at their appointed place, and they found themselves in a small town nestling among mountains. It was inhabited by ordinary Indians, similar to themselves in appearance, but Manco was able to persuade these people of his divine origins and by degrees gained the ascendency. By the fourth generation the Incas

ruled all Cuzco and the mountain valley around it. Then the other mountain tribes threatened them, and a great battle ensued in which the Inca, Viracocha, defeated the enemy and gave his family, and the tribes they ruled, control of the Andean plateau region.

In the middle of the fifteenth century the great Inca, Tupac Yupanqui, captured the Peruvian coast lands and reorganized the Inca State. The resources of the country were harnessed for the benefit of all the people. Ancient roads were extended and new ones were built. The system of records kept on knotted cords called *quipus* was made compulsory in all Inca towns. Through these records the Inca organization knew exactly how much of any commodity was produced in any district. One third was kept locally and used by the people. One third was kept for the sun, to support the temples and schools and also to act as a national reserve in case of natural disaster. One third belonged to the Inca and was used for feeding the army and relieving local distress.

Sometimes the Incas took over parts of the country by force. They kept an army equipped with spears and clubs headed with bronze and their warriors wore quilted cotton armour and helmets of bronze sheets fixed on leather. The army also had an expert corps of slingers to cover assaults on fortresses. Engineers marched with them in order to prepare roads and make suspension bridges over the ravines, and everywhere the Inca armies went the roads were improved, first for the army and later for commerce. Such were the benefits which the Incas brought that many tribes invited them to take over their own territories since they saw that the people in the Inca empire always had enough food and clothing, even in the years of drought. This came about because of the Inca's system of storehouses all over the country.

Eventually the Inca Empire comprised all Peru, Bolivia, half Chile and part of Ecuador, all dependent on the Supreme Inca, who was almost a god because he was thought to be descended from the sun.

Beneath the Supreme Inca was the Inca clan, many thousands of cousins of the

Above, Peruvian figure, probably deriving from the Nazca people of southern Peru. This civilization developed in the first millennium AD but survived into the Inca period. British Museum, London.

Above left, jade figure of Xolotl, one of the chieftains of the Chichimecs, who flourished in the Valley of Mexico between the Toltec and Aztec civilizations, in the eleventh to the fourteenth centuries. Landesmuseum, Stuttgart.

Opposite top, Aztec mask of Xipe Totec, the god of spring and of the rain. His priests dressed in the skins of people sacrificed to him, to symbolize the new skin that the earth grows in springtime.

Opposite bottom, an Aztec human sacrifice. Four priests hold the victim on the sacrifice stone while the high priest cuts out the heart and offers it to the god of the sun and war, Huitzilopochtli. Human sacrifices were carried out in great numbers by the Aztecs.

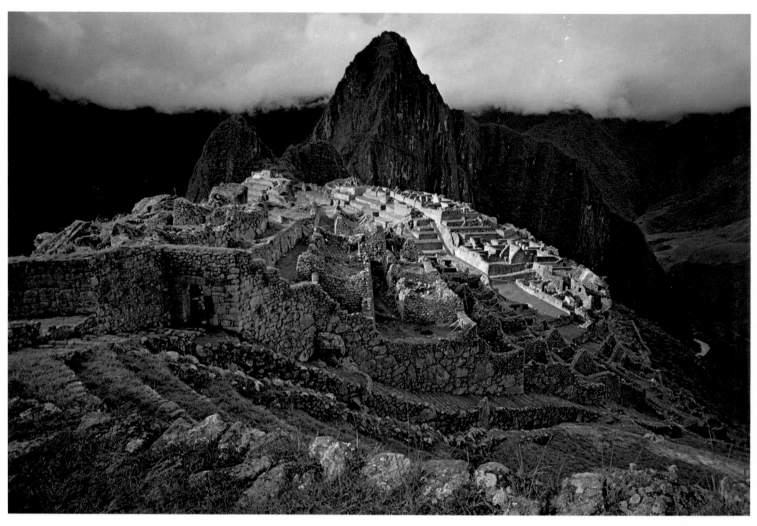

Royal Family who administered the army and civil service. Sometimes brave warriors of ordinary families were made army generals and married Inca princesses.

As for brilliant children, they were educated to hold high official posts, such as the *quipucamayocs*, who were record-keepers and historians. Girls might be chosen and educated as virgins of the sun and could spend their lives like nuns, doing religious work for the temples. On the other hand, many were given as wives to visiting chiefs whom the Inca wished to honour. All social life was regulated, but on the whole it was a fair system under which people found a peaceful existence and enough food for all.

The Incas worshipped a supreme deity, Viracocha, who had no images and only one temple. He was the mysterious power behind the universe, and under him were the sun, moon, rainbow and thunder. Every town had temples to these lesser natural deities. There were also numerous strange objects or places, *huacas*, such as rocks, pools, plants and unusual animals which were full of magical power. Before these and their gods the Incas occasionally sacrificed maize beer (chica) and food. In times of great trouble, and only as a last resort, human beings were thrown over cliffs to placate the gods.

The bodies of dead Incas were specially holy *huacas* and every November were brought out in procession. Every Peruvian was mummified by being dried in the sun either in the hot sands of the coast or in the dry winds of the high plateau. The dead and the living seemed very close to each other, and the aim of custom was to keep to essentially the same way of life as one's grandparents. All had gone well, and so there was little reason for change.

Potatoes and the millet-like grain, quinoa, were the native Peruvian foodstuffs, but they also had maize, pumpkins, chillies and many green vegetables. Llama meat was plentiful, and llamas also provided skins, leather and hard bone for tools. Each town kept great herds numbering thousands grazing on the hill pastures.

All Inca civilization was threatened when a half-brother of the Inca seized the country after a civil war. The true Inca, the Child of the Sun, was imprisoned and the people awaited the wrath of the gods. Their fears were realized by the arrival of the Spanish invaders.

Chapter 26

The Conquistadores

Left, portrait of Christopher Columbus; despite the accolades which greeted him on his return from the New World for the first time, in 1493, he soon lost favour as other navigators proved more successful than he in exploring the coasts of South America. Civico Museo Archelogico, Grosseto.

Opposite top, Macchu Picchu, the most spectacular of all the Inca sites, about 50 miles from the capital Cuzco. It was never taken by the Spanish and was virtually intact when excavated in the early twentieth century.

Opposite bottom, an Inca ceremonial knife; the Inca civilization of Peru flourished in the century before its destruction by the Spanish conquistadors in the 1530s. It had vast supplies of gold and silver, which was used for artefacts such as this knife, which probably represents a god.

Until the middle of the fifteenth century, European voyages had been mostly concerned with coastal trade. It is true that the Scandinavian nations had maintained regular sailings to the Greenland settlements, but these had ceased before the end of the thirteenth century. Thereafter contact was intermittent and in the fifteenth century very occasional. Otherwise there seem to have been only a few fortuitous voyages out into the Atlantic.

The stimulus to new adventure came partly from the desire for commerce, partly from a desire to circumvent Turkish control of all the trade routes to the rich lands which had been discovered by Marco Polo two centuries earlier. The first successful journeys along the coasts of Africa were a result of the energetic policies of the Portuguese prince, Henry the Navigator. From these came the great improvements in ship design, first for carrying more cargo and then for withstanding the rough seas of the great ocean.

As we shall see, the Portuguese navigators had already found the Cape of Good Hope before Spain commenced her transatlantic voyages. The reason lies in the freedom of Portugal from the struggles which occupied the Spanish monarchs—the war with the Moorish kingdom of Granada. In the year when victory was achieved and Granada fell to Spanish arms, a middle-aged Genoese navigator set sail from Palos on a voyage financed, with some difficulty, by the Queen of Spain. He was Christopher Columbus.

Christopher Columbus

Columbus is believed to have been born in Genoa, although several other towns claim him. Similarly, the exact year of his birth is unknown, but 1450 seems a likely date. He was the son of a weaver who became sufficiently important later on in his life to send his son on commercial voyages.

The travels of Columbus extended from the Mediterranean to the Atlantic ports; he acquired a reputation as a navigator and was able to travel with unusual freedom for the period. He had a thorough knowledge of the coasts of western Europe and it is almost certain that he had been in Danish ships as far as Iceland.

After a journey from England, coasting southwards past France and Portugal, Columbus came to Lisbon, where he married a young lady of Italian descent, Felipa Moniz de Perestrello, whose father had been governor of Porto Santo. Columbus then settled for a time on this island near Madeira and during his stay learned of many strange plants and objects which had been found at sea or washed ashore. He also heard of a canoe containing the bodies of two brown-skinned 'Indians' which had been blown from some distant shore across the Atlantic by the westerlies. Such information led Columbus to speculate on the possibilities of further discovery.

He found further clues in Lisbon where there was a letter and a map from the Florentine geographer Toscanelli, which had been sent to Father Martinez, Confessor to King João II of Portugal. Using the map to illustrate his arguments, Toscanelli contended that if the theoretical studies of the Alexandrian geographer Ptolemy were followed then there was every reason to suppose that Asia could be reached by sailing west. This was based on the assumption that the world was round and that the earth's size had been underestimated. It was thus possible that the Atlantic Ocean linked the mainland of Europe with the shores of China, which had been seen by Marco Polo.

Through his acquaintance with Father Martinez, Columbus asked for an audience from King João in Lisbon, seeking support for a voyage of discovery to the west. His reception was polite but cool, and since he was known only as a competent navigator his request was rejected. The quest for support was further pursued, and its scope broadened, with Bartholomew Columbus

of another monarch. Isabella capitulated; Columbus had at last the support he needed.

Money poured in from the royal treasury (although there is no truth in the story that Queen Isabella pawned her jewels) and even more money was supplied by Pinzon. Three ships were provided, the *Niña*, the *Pinta* and the *Santa Maria,* which was Columbus's flagship. The queen also released a number of convicts on condition that they became sailors on the expedition.

The departure from Palos of the expedition in its three small ships, half an hour before sunrise on Friday 3 August 1492, was a drab occasion, for few people expected to see the voyagers return.

At first, Columbus sailed south to the Canary Islands, from which he calculated they would have to traverse about 2,000 miles of ocean to reach the lands of the Great Khan of China. They voyaged into the unknown seas on 6 September and, keeping a little south of west, the ships sailed through waters filled with remarkable creatures such as flying fish. Slowly the food supplies began to dwindle and the crew became apprehensive about their safety. They had no stake in the voyage and did not wish to continue on towards what they regarded as certain destruction. On 10 October they reached breaking point and Columbus was forced to promise them to return if no land was sighted in three days.

Fortunately, on the morning of the next day they sighted some floating twigs—some bearing leaves—masses of weed and a piece of wood which had obviously been broken from a carved figure. A look-out was posted. Then, that night, Columbus himself saw a light. By its rhythmic movement he concluded that it was being carried by a man on a shore. At dawn, a boy on the *Niña*, Juan Rodriguez de Triana, sighted land. A reward had been promised by the king and queen for the first sighting and Columbus claimed this for himself, because of the torch light which he had seen on the previous night. Nevertheless he rewarded the boy with a silk doublet. As for the island, Columbus decided to name it San Salvador.

For the next three months the explorers sailed from island to island. Columbus had only the account of Marco Polo's travels in Asia to guide him, and although his 'Indians' were appropriately light brown with slanting eyes and straight hair he found no advanced civilization. When they reached Haiti, and later Cuba, he hoped that they had found Japan (Cipango), but here again the inhabitants were not what he had expected. They wore little clothing, used tools of stone and lived in thatched huts in large villages. Though they produced elaborate wood carvings and possessed quantities of placer-washed gold, they were obviously not subjects of the Great Khan. Neither were there any elephants or lions to be found. Columbus concluded that he had discovered some hitherto unknown Indian archipelago.

acting as agent for his brother to the kings of France and Britain. But it was still unsuccessful.

Christopher, a widower by this time, left Portugal with his young son in 1484 and went to Spain. He was given advice and shelter by the prior of the monastery of La Rabida and introduced to Queen Isabella's treasurer, Alonso de Quintanilla. Columbus requested aid to finance a voyage across the Atlantic and a commission was set up to investigate its viability. Columbus was so secretive and bad at explaining his intentions that it took four years to reach a decision. It was hardly surprising that the commission's report was unfavourable.

Columbus was soon to return to the attack, this time enlisting the help of the shipowner Martin Pinzón, who agreed to join the scheme as a partner. Somehow Columbus managed to secure another audience at court—which at this point, the latter part of 1491, was at the siege of Granada. The city fell in 1492, and the Spanish monarchs were then able to give their full attention to the Genoese navigator.

He astonished them with his audacious demands—aid to finance the voyage, a guarantee of one-tenth of all the profits made on the journey, the rank of nobleman and the title 'Grand Admiral of the Ocean Sea'. This time he was given a flat refusal—but the king's treasurer, it is said, changed the monarch's minds by making them understand what the country would lose if the expedition succeeded with the support

There was no possibility of any real understanding between the native peoples of the Indies and the sailors, but the usual exchanges of trinkets and tools for food and girls took place. From the native view point these great white strangers, whose powers belonged to the realms of magic, had probably floated down from the skies in their canoes with the white wing-like sails. To the visitors the natives were simple savages.

Columbus gathered a cargo of local curios, strange birds, food plants, carvings, golden ornaments and some of the native peoples, mostly of Tainan stock. By January he was planning the return voyage, but his departure was hastened when he discovered that Martin Pinzón had sailed on ahead, presumably with the intention of claiming the discovery for himself. However, Columbus was the better navigator and even though the *Santa Maria* had to be abandoned when she ran aground he escaped with his men, the Indians and a greater part of the novelties which had been collected and finally reached Palos in the *Niña* on 15 March 1493.

A few hours later the apologetic Pinzón who had planned to be first with the news of the discovery, arrived in the *Pinta*. After a stop at Seville, where he wrote a long letter to Ferdinand and Isabella, Columbus went around the coast and landed the crews of the two ships and the Indians at Barcelona for the ceremonial presentation to the king and queen.

The occasion was a great personal triumph for Christopher Columbus. He was given a patent of nobility which enabled him to display a coat of arms emblazoned with a lion and a castle. His title of 'Grand Admiral of the Ocean Sea' was allowed, and he was given a state pension. However, to his great disgust, he was not permitted to become viceroy over the newly discovered lands.

Trouble with Portugal

The discoveries in the west brought about political difficulties with neighbouring Portugal. The Portuguese had assumed that their discoveries on the coast of Africa and the tip of an Atlantic 'Island' of Brazil, gave them an undisputed claim to all newly discovered lands in the Atlantic. The Spaniards could not accept this, and since they were Catholics asked the pope, who was a Spaniard, to intervene on their behalf.

A decision was eventually reached at Tordesillas, when a plan to define spheres of influence was agreed. This followed in principle the Bull of Pope Alexander VI of 4 May 1493 over which there had been

Above, North American Indians sowing maize, which along with potatoes formed their main crop. The illustration is by Theodore de Bry, a Flemish engraver who, in association with the English writer Richard Hakkluyt, sought to popularize the achievements of the explorers.

Top, Christopher Columbus and his crew say goodbye to their families at Palos at the start of their first journey in 1492. On this expedition he reached the Bahamas, Cuba and Hispaniola. Mariners' Museum, Newport News, Virginia.

Opposite, Martin Pinzon (died 1493), the Spanish sailor who encouraged Columbus and commanded one of the ships, the Pinta, *on Columbus' first voyage in 1492. Museo Navale, Madrid.*

continual disagreement as the new discoveries extended. It was, therefore, thought wiser to keep the contending powers apart by establishing a dividing line running from north to south, 370 leagues west of the Cape Verde Islands. The territory to the east of this line was apportioned to Portugal (this effectively gave her a claim to Brazil), and the territory to the west was assigned to Spain. However, this was to cause problems in less than thirty years, after Magellan's ships had circumnavigated the globe; for where, it was argued, should the territorial rights of discovery end on the other side of the world?

The matter was finally settled by the Treaty of Saragossa in 1529, when the two countries agreed on a new line down the Pacific. Spain renounced her claims to Africa and Asia, while Portugal accepted that all the Americas should be a Spanish sphere of influence. This treaty had far reaching historical consequences, though at the time it seemed to be somewhat academic since other nations were not bound by it.

In 1493, Columbus had been sent out again with a fleet of seventeen caravels and Spain had decided on a course of exploitation of the lands across the Atlantic.

Columbus' later voyages

Columbus' second voyage was not a success politically, even though it enabled him to declare that Cuba, Jamaica and Haiti (Hispaniola) were possessions of Spain. The expedition in spite of its size was unable to find a safe and permanent settlement since there were constant troubles with native *caciques* (chieftains) who attacked the well-armed Spaniards with Stone Age weapons. On other occasions, though, more peaceful exchanges yielded much gold. No mines were discovered however, although Columbus did see a few Indians engaged in washing gold from river sands. Nowhere did he find a single building of stone and nowhere did the people wear more than little aprons of beads. The temples were thatched huts and the wooden idols were served by strange ecstatic medicine-men. A number of captured Indians were taken aboard for the return voyage. They were the major treasure of the expedition.

When Columbus returned to Spain with such a poor report of his failure to reach either Japan or China he lost the confidence of the court and it was two years before he was permitted to sail again. By 1498 he was back in favour and he put to sea once more, this time sailing farther south, his official intention being to find the Straits of Malacca and the sea road to India.

In fact he made a landfall at Trinidad. After this he pushed southwards, passing the mouth of the Orinoca. The current from this river was so powerful that fresh water was still found ten leagues out in the ocean

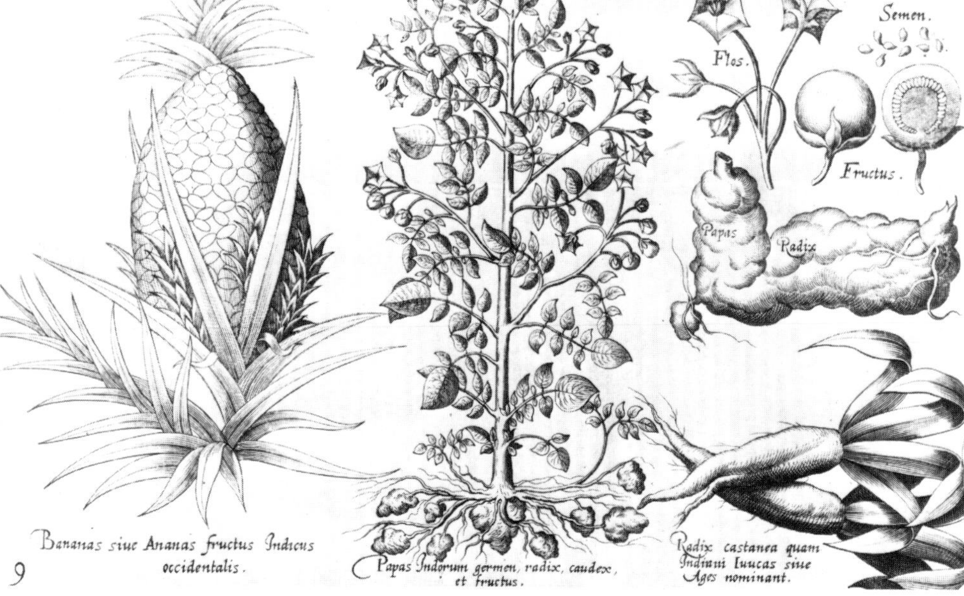

9

Above, mining town in Peru, exploited by the Spaniards to bring enormous wealth back to sixteenth-century Europe. The largest such mine was at Potosì; the silver was dug by Indian slaves, many of whom died underground. This drawing was done in 1613 by the Indian Poma de Ayala. Royal Library of Copenhagen.

Above left, battle between Columbus and Francisco Poraz, the leader of a band rebelling against his authority on Jamaica. Columbus suffered from continual opposition from the colonists he took to the New World.

Opposite top, one of the tiny ships, known as caravelles, used by Christopher Columbus in his four voyages across the Atlantic to the New World.

Opposite bottom, contemporary illustration showing several of the many new plants found by the explorers in the New World. They included tobacco, potatoes, maize, pineapple and manioc. Conversely, the Spanish introduced sugar, and the horse, to the New World. British Museum, London.

and, as a result, Columbus decided that this must be one of the rivers of Paradise. He soon found that he was unable to proceed further so he turned west along the coasts of Venezuela. Then with his battered ships he set sail for Santo Domingo.

The small Spanish settlement which his brother had founded was now a town, and the colony was governed by Francisco de Bobadilla, lately arrived from Spain with powers to investigate complaints of maladministration. The meeting was less than friendly. Columbus still considered that he should have been made viceroy of the Indies, but everything was against him. In the end the great discoverer was arrested and sent back to Spain in chains. The charge against him was illicit trading in gold with the native peoples.

In Spain he was treated with more consideration and in 1502 was allowed to undertake a further voyage. On this last journey he passed Cuba and in the Gulf of Honduras encountered a great trading canoe. The Indians on board described the golden lands to the south and thus sent him towards Costa Rica, whilst preserving their own cities in Yucatan from the mysterious strangers.

Columbus coasted Panama and the Isthmus of Darien, but his ships were now unseaworthy and his own health had deteriorated. He returned to Jamaica as best he could and then travelled to Spain to petition help from the king, for his patron, Queen Isabella, had already died. He received little help and his last months were spent in sickness and heartbreak with only a few loyal friends gathered about him. On 20 May 1506 he died at Valladolid. His petition had not even been discussed.

To the Pacific

It is almost certain that Columbus was not the first visitor to the Caribbean and South America; his great distinction was his understanding of the winds of the Atlantic so that he made it possible for translantic voyages to be undertaken at will. The Norse settlers in Greenland navigated the Atlantic coasts, possibly as far south as Delaware Bay, but they had no permanent settlements apart from the Greenland villages. In one account we are told that in 1492 they appealed to the pope asking him to send them help. However, they died out, probably in the years when the West Indies were opened up for permanent colonization.

The Spanish government was very careful about the royal monopoly of power. Colonial governors were not independent and they were accompanied by accountants, justices and inspectors who made regular reports to Spain. There was a spirit of competition between the various settlers. If they made new discoveries they were likely to be given small financial rewards and fine-sounding titles, but they also gained prestige towards the day when they might be appointed to high office and have control over their fellows. This system encouraged ambition although it led to many personal tragedies, such as the murder of Balboa. In the main, though, the government at home managed to keep a paternalistic control over affairs.

The settlers exploited the Indians with great cruelty and excused themselves by pleading that the natives were animals in human form without true souls. To this the Church replied with an affirmation of the human dignity of other races, but the

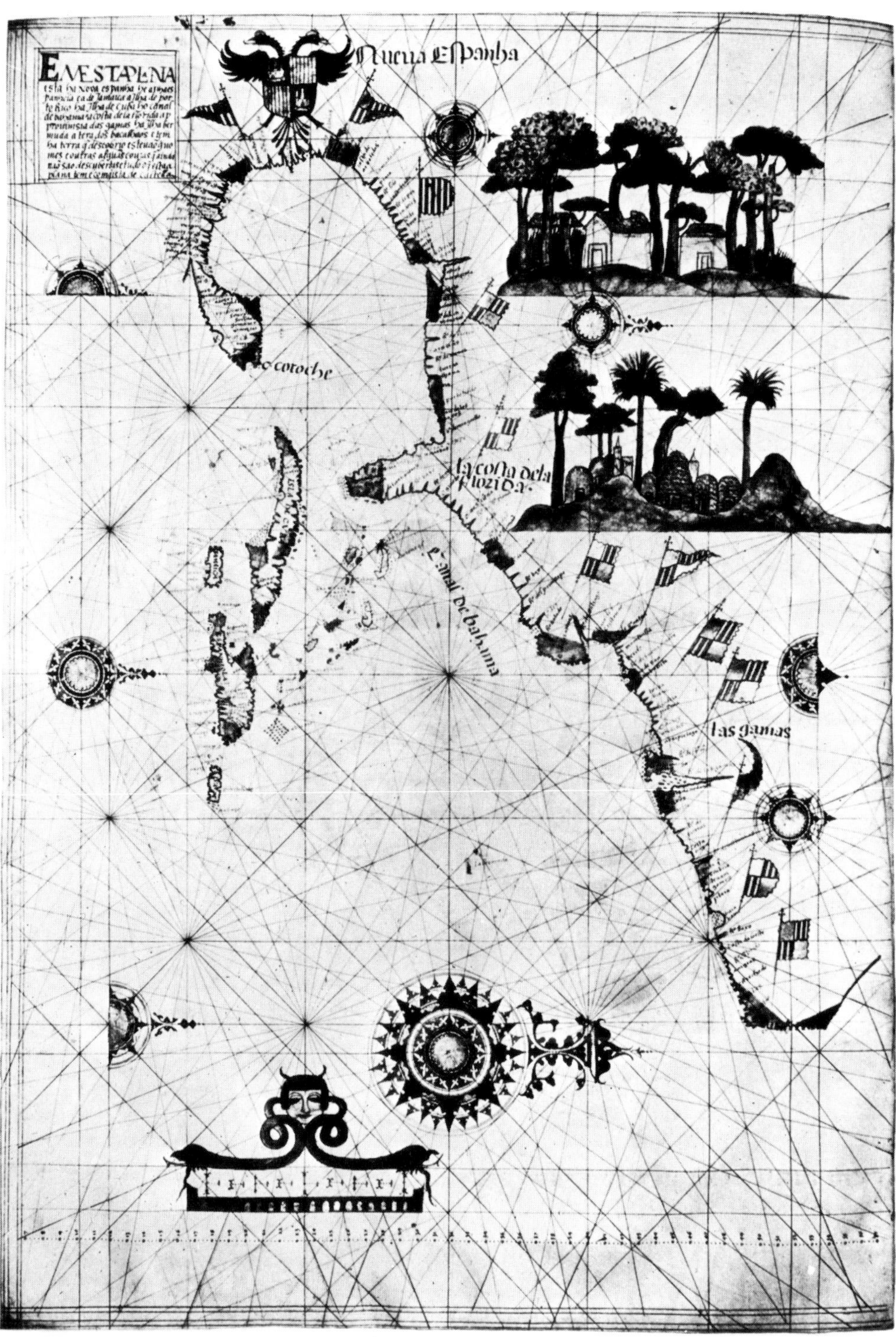

isolation of the colonies made it very difficult for the more humane intentions of the crown to become really effective. Basically the government intended the Indians to become wards of the Spaniards. The term *ecomienda* really meant that the landowner was given total control of the natives in his area with the duty of caring for their welfare and education in the Christian faith. Few of the owners seem to have felt that this implied something different from the brutal exploitation of labour.

The New World gets its name

After the death of Columbus, the number of exploring voyages continued to increase. It soon became clear from these that the New World was not a part of Asia. Among the travellers was Amerigo Vespucci, a Florentine merchant who wrote a description of the land he saw in the south. An incorrect date, given by him or his printer to his description, inspired Martin Waldseemüller, a cartographer of the period, to inscribe the name 'America' on a map of the partially discovered new continent. The name was accepted and has remained to this day without ever being seriously questioned by anybody.

In 1511 the interior of Cuba was 'pacified' by military forces among whom Hernando Cortes took a distinguished part. In the previous year, 1510, Vasco Nuñez de Balboa had landed in Darien as a member of an expedition headed by Martin de Enciso. Balboa was a born leader, and Enciso proved incompetent; soon Balboa was in command and Enciso sent back to Spain as a prisoner. Balboa then conquered the surrounding country in a series of expeditions and soon won the friendship of the natives. It was while he was on one of these expeditions that he heard, for the first time, of the gold in Peru and the great ocean on the other side of the mountains.

Soon after his return to Darien, Balboa received news that Enciso had reached Spain and had complained about his deposition to King Ferdinand who had condemned Balboa's action. Balboa therefore resolved to try to placate his sovereign by some spectacular enterprise. On 1 September 1513 he set out with 190 Spaniards and 1,000 natives, and towards the end of the month he reached the Pacific Ocean. However, his triumph was short-lived for the king gave orders in 1513 that he should be replaced by Pedro Arias de Avila, who wanted none of the natives' goodwill, since he despised them. Balboa himself fell foul of the new governor, who in 1519 had the great leader arrested for treason. Balboa was beheaded on his orders in the same year.

The discovery of Mexico

The first contact between Europeans and the highly civilized Maya people of southern Mexico was probably in about 1512 or 1514. Solis and Pinzón (who had been a companion of Columbus in the first voyage of 1492) went on a trading venture. They gave sufficient details for a map to be drawn and published by Peter Martyr de Angleria, the historiographer of the Indies, before Mexico was officially discovered. They sailed round the coast of the Yucatan peninsula and the Gulf of Mexico, but in their written report they reversed all the sailing directions. However, they set down the Maya town names correctly and there can be no doubt that they were the precursors of Hernandez de Cordoba who was sent from Cuba in 1517 to investigate stories of a new land to the west.

The reports of stone-built cities, gold and jade, as well as a native race clothed in fine cotton garments, roused the interest of the governor of Cuba. He sent his nephew, Grijalva, on another expedition. In the fleet was a young Castillian gentleman, Bernal Diaz del Castillo, who was later to write the best history of the conquest of Mexico. Grijalva's expedition reached the Gulf of Mexico and engaged in trade on a small scale. Enough was learned about the rich and powerful empire to encourage the governor of Cuba to plan an expedition to conquer this land which apparently contained treasures rivalling the gold of India.

Among the adventurers whom Velazquez planned to send on the expedition to Mexico was Hernando Cortes. Cortes came from a noble but impoverished family in Estremadura. He was anxious to go to the New

Above, Aztec lookout watching Cortes' ship arriving at the coast of Mexico in 1518, from the contemporary account of the expedition.

Left, Hernando Cortes (1485–1547), the Spanish soldier who became the archetypal conquistador, conquering Brazil by his combination of boldness, luck and arrogance. Like Columbus, however, Cortes died friendless in Spain.

Opposite, map of the coast of Florida, Cuba and Hispaniola, made by Lazaro Luis in 1563. Most of the islands of the Caribbean were still not known in detail, and in the 1570s Francis Drake was able to find many places in which to hide his ships from the Spaniards.

World to seek his fortune and in 1504, when he was nineteen, arrived in Santo Domingo. He played an active part in the conquest of Cuba, and then settled down to become a farmer as well as a soldier. He married a Spanish lady in Cuba and became quite important in social affairs in the colony. Velazquez was later to regret his choice of leader and sought to rescind the appointment, but Cortes anticipated this and slipped out of Cuba with his force before this could be done.

The fleet sailing with Hernando Cortes took five hundred soldiers, ten small cannon and forty-eight hand guns. There were also sixteen horses. This force was expected to conquer an empire of which the capital city housed nearly a million inhabitants. Cortes knew nothing of the Aztecs at this time. He was merely intent on taking his force beyond the reach of Governor Velazquez.

The pilot Alaminos, who had sailed with Columbus, guided them to a landfall on a small island off the tip of Yucatan. There they found their first stone-built temple which contained strange images of naked women and, lying on the steps, groups of human bodies. They had been sacrificed by having their hearts ripped out.

After leaving this ill-omened island the fleet coasted Yucatan, calling at several cities of the Maya people. One of the more friendly of the Maya *caciques* made a present to Cortes of turkeys and maize for food, jade for good fortune and twenty pretty girls. Shortly after this a curious incident occurred; for one of these girls had been sold to Maya merchants by her mother in order to save her life. She had been born on a day which was so unlucky that she was destined to destroy the god of the Aztecs. Now at eighteen the Princess Ce Malinalli of Painalla, whom the Spaniards called Doña Marina, became a member of the party of strange black-bearded men.

At another town Cortes rescued a shipwrecked Spaniard who had been a slave among the Maya. His name was Aguilar and he had learned to speak the Maya language. He spoke in this to Marina, and she in turn was able to translate this into Nahuatl, the Aztec language. Thus before he reached Mexico Cortes already had an interpreter.

In April 1519 the ships approached the Mexican shores near the city of Cempoalla. The local Totonac people were frightened at the sight of the giant canoes with white wings which, they said, spoke with thunder when a cannon was fired. They feared what might happen on the next day, for this was a magical occasion which occurred only once every fifty-two years. It might be the time when the god Quetzalcoatl, the Lord of the Winds and the Breath of Life, would return to Mexico to combat and destroy the terrible war god of the Aztecs.

Doña Marina knew this, delayed Cortes for a day and sent him ashore in his best black velvet gloves and hose and with a very fashionable flat-topped hat. On his breast was a large shining jewel. He was unaware that in this dress he really resembled the god Quetzalcoatl who wore red face paint, a flat Huaxtec hat and had the black painted limbs of a priest. Similarly the jewel was reminiscent of the sacred wind-jewel of Quetzalcoatl. So from the beginning Cortes was expected to conquer the Aztecs.

The Totonacs welcomed Cortes with politeness and raised no objection to his erecting a camp near their city of Cempoalla. However, Cortes noticed the arrival of a stranger with a retinue of servants. This was a nobleman from Tenochtitlan (Mexico City), who was collecting taxes from the Totonacs who had been conquered some years before by the Aztecs. The stranger had scribes with him who made pictures of the Spaniards and their ships. These were immediately sent by runners to the great ruler Montezuma in the capital. The Totonacs continued to help the Spaniards, for it is possible that they already saw a chance of throwing off the yoke of the hated Aztec conquerors.

Cortes improved his camp and named the little town Villa Rica de Vera Cruz. He sent his first dispatch to the emperor Charles V in Spain, making good the Spaniards' claim to the country and sending presents of gold, featherwork and painted books to the emperor. One of these painted books can be seen in Vienna today. It describes the history of the god Quetzalcoatl, for whom the Mexicans mistook Hernando Cortes.

Cortes' army stayed at Vera Cruz until August 1519, and then Cortes set out on the road to Mexico City. He took 400 foot soldiers, 15 mounted cavalier and some thousands of Totonac porters who carried seven cannons as well as all the military baggage. They had learned by now that the horses were not the same creatures as the riders and so were not afraid of them.

The army marched northwestwards into the mountains. From Mexico, Montezuma sent a messenger saying that it was unnecessary for the Spaniards to visit him in the city. He was aware that they had overwhelming power and feared that they were gods sent to destroy the Aztecs and their war god. Cortes however marched on to meet a mountain people who were at war with the Aztecs. These Tlaxcalan people tested the Spaniards in a battle, accepted defeat and then joined in the plan to advance on Mexico City.

On the journey Cortes, probably inspired by Doña Marina, visited the city of Cholula, which was famous as the holy place of Quetzalcoatl. Here Montezuma sent a group of magicians to destroy Cortes. Having failed they planned to start an insurrection. With the aid of information supplied by Doña Marina the Spaniards attacked and massacred many of the people in the city. Then they continued and eventually crossed the mountains into the Valley of Mexico. They were astonished by their first sight of the great city; it was larger than any town in Europe at that time, built on islands in a lake and surrounded by mountains and volcanoes.

They were welcomed by Montezuma and given a palace in which to stay. It seemed that all was going well and that the Aztecs might be induced to accept Spanish rule.

Meanwhile Velazquez in Cuba showed his envy by sending an expedition to Vera Cruz with instructions to capture Cortes and punish him for disobedience. Cortes left Mexico under a small garrison and marched with most of his troops to deal with the new threat. In a single short battle the Cuban commander was captured, and most of his men voted to join Cortes.

On their return to Mexico the Spaniards encountered an ominous silence. The garrison they had left behind had become alarmed by a great dance before the god of war which was attended by most of the Aztec nobles. They therefore attacked and many Mexicans were killed. After that there could be no peace. The Emperor Montezuma tried to stem a riot but was killed by a stone thrown by his own people.

After a short pause, while they were besieged in the palace by the Aztec people, the Spaniards marched out on a moonless night. They had begun to cross the causeways out of the city when the Aztecs attacked from canoes. The plan was not to confront the Spaniards but to seize them and drag them down to drown in the mud of the shallow lake. Bernal Diaz tells us that many of the newcomers to Mexico were drowned because they were weighed down by the gold they were carrying. The losses were heavy.

After the remnants of the army were marshalled on the shore, Cortes wept to see how many of his companions were missing. Strangely enough the Aztecs did not attack at once, so the army regrouped and began to march towards Tlaxcala. At Otumba the Mexican army was seen: thousands of feathered warriors massed in front of the banners of the war chiefs. Cortes, with his few remaining horsemen, attacked with a

single aim, that of capturing the banner of the army commander. Unexpectedly, they succeeded and the Aztecs suddenly retreated. They never had a real chance to defeat the armoured Spaniards on the field of battle.

After a rest in Tlaxcala, Cortes, with many thousands of Tlaxcalans and other Indians in revolt against the Aztecs, surrounded the lake, cut off all supplies to Mexico city and then invaded it. He had to destroy nearly every building before the last of the Aztec war chiefs, the heroic young Cuauhtemoc, was captured and Mexico became a Spanish possession.

The world encompassed

While the Spanish conquest of Middle America was still incomplete a Portuguese gentleman, Ferdinand Magellan, became a navigator in the service of Charles V, the Hapsburg emperor who now ruled Spain as well as the Austrian dominions. Charles V, a very able man, wished to find the route

Above, cochineal production in Mexico; in Teotihuacan days it was discovered that cochineals, insects that live on a Mexican cactus, formed a valuable dye. Large amounts were exported to Spain in the sixteenth century.

Above left, sixteenth-century Spanish drawing of Cortes on his way through Mexico; the native Aztec civilization had little idea how to cope with his confident aggression.

Opposite, Hernando Cortes with the Tlaxcalec Indians, whom he first defeated and then accepted as allies against the Aztecs. The Tlaxcalecs had defended their independence from Aztec rule for many years.

PORTUGUESE VOYAGES OF EXPLORATION AND CONQUESTS

1400	Conquest of Ceuta (1415) Cabral discovers the Azores (1432)
1450	Cape Verde reached (1456) Death of Henry the Navigator (1460) Gulf of Guinea reached (1471) Diego Cam discovers the mouth of the River Congo (1484) Bartholomeu Dias rounds the Cape of Good Hope (1487) Treaty of Tordesillas (1494) First voyage of Vasco da Gama (1497–9)
1500	Cabral in Brazil (1500) Vasco da Gama's second voyage (1502–3) Albuquerque in the East Indies (1503) Capture of Malacca (1511) Vasco da Gama's third voyage (1521)
1600	

SPANISH AMERICA: DISCOVERY AND CONQUEST

1475	First voyage of Columbus (1492) Last three voyages of Columbus (1493, 1498, 1502)
1500	Cabral in Brazil (1500) Creation of the first *Audiencia* Balboa discovers the Pacific (1513) Hernando Cortes lands in Mexico (1519) Magellan sets off on his voyage Cortes takes Mexico (1521) Pizarro's first expedition among the Incas (1524)
1525	Pizarro's second expedition among the Incas (1526) Cuzco captured by Pizarro (1533) Peru rises against Pizarro Silver mines opened at Potosi in Peru (1544)
1550	

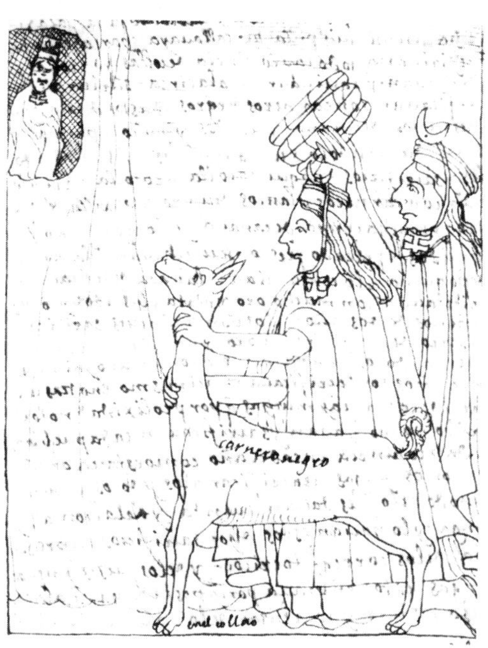

westwards which would lead across the Pacific Ocean to the Spice Islands (Indonesia). His Portuguese rivals were already importing highly profitable cargoes of spice, fine cloth and jewels and Magellan was instructed to coast the American continent and then proceed across the South Sea, so called since it was south of the Isthmus of Panama when Balboa first sighted it.

Magellan left Spain in September 1519, and after a long coastal voyage of discovery beyond Brazil and the estuary of the Rio de la Plata he found the entrance to the Rocky and dangerous straits. After a difficult passage through this cruel region in November 1520, he found the great Pacific Ocean open before him. Had he sailed northwards he would have discovered the Inca empire, but his instructions were to find the Spice Islands. He knew the approximate direction so he set out on the long journey across the Pacific Ocean, during which he missed the Polynesian archipelagoes, except for one small group of islands where the natives stole everything they could carry away.

On 16 March 1521, he made landfall in the Philippine Islands, which were named in honour of Prince Philip who was soon to become King Philip II of Spain. On 27 April 1521, Magellan was killed in a bitter fight with the people of the island of Cebu and his command was taken over by Sebastian del Cano. When he reached the Moluccas one of his ships, the *Trinidad*, was in a dilapidated condition, but the captain decided to try to cross the Pacific to Mexico. However, the ship was captured by the Portuguese and the Spanish soldiers were imprisoned and died, the first to suffer from the commercial rivalry of the two great naval powers.

Similar incidents were to occur in the following years and these eventually led to the Treaty of Saragossa in 1529, which brought the rule of law into the relationships between Spain and Portugal in the tropical seas.

Meanwhile del Cano with his surviving ship left the Moluccas and set off across the Indian Ocean. Reaching the coast of Mozambique he turned south to round the Cape of Good Hope and sailed homewards past west Africa. He reached the port of San Lucar on 6 September 1522 after spending just twelve days less than three years in the first circumnavigation of the globe. It was only thirty years after the first voyage of Columbus who had sought the fabulous treasures of the Indies.

To golden Peru

After the capture of the Isthmus of Darien, Pedro Arias de Avila was made governor. He had heard rumours from the Indians of a distant southern empire where there was a great king who possessed immense quantities of gold. He therefore encouraged Francisco Pizarro, who had served with him in Panama, to discuss the possibility of a voyage to the mysterious southern empire. Pizarro, like Cortes, had been born in a poor family in the province of Estremadura, but unlike his great contemporary he was illegitimate and illiterate. However, he was able to join with two friends, the priest Hernando de Luque, who helped to finance the expedition, and the grim old soldier, Diego de Almagro.

His first expedition brought back definite information about the rich civilization in the mountains of the southern continent. On the second voyage, Almagro and a company of soldiers were landed on an island within reach of the Peruvian port of Tumbez but it was clear that the Peruvians were so powerful that reinforcements were necessary.

Pizarro returned to Spain, was seized and imprisoned for debt, but was rescued on the orders of Charles V who was interested in the story of the golden land. The emperor invested Pizarro with the title of Governor and Captain-General of New Castile. Pizarro returned to Panama and recruited a further 180 men and 27 horses and they sailed for Tumbez to rejoin Almagro.

At that time Peru was recovering from a civil war in which the true Inca, Huascar, had been defeated and imprisoned by his half-brother Atahuallpa. The country was paralysed by the discovery that a true-born

Inca was not omnipotent; the Inca was the son of the sun—he must be divine and therefore omnipotent. The Spaniards landed near Tumbez, occupied the city without any serious fighting and slowly advanced from city to city along the coast of Peru. They learned of the great empire of the Incas and of the civil war. Yet for some time nothing whatsoever happened. Pizarro was soon joined by a small force commanded by Hernando de Soto, who later discovered the Mississippi. They decided to march towards the mountains in an attempt to meet the false Inca, Atahuallpa, who had in the meantime preserved unity by murdering his half-brother and becoming sole leader.

The Spanish army advanced into the mountains and at last heard that Atahuallpa was moving forward to meet them at Caxamarca. At length they saw the camp of the Inca forces and the surrounding hills covered by a million men. Although he had small hope of survival, Pizarro decided to enter the stone-built town, knowing that its massive walls would at least enable him to hold out for some time if attacked. The year was 1532.

The Inca advanced with his nobles, and Pizarro placed his men in strategic positions on the walls and around the town square. As the great king came forward to meet the strangers Pizarro gave an order. Immediately soldiers poured forth and arquebusiers on the walls shot down the Peruvian nobles. Atahuallpa was seized and made prisoner. Eagerly the Inca offered a ransom in order to try to preserve his life, since he realized that these strangers were not gods sent by the sun to revenge the murder of his brother. They were simply greedy for gold. So he gave orders that the royal treasures were to be sent to him. He even had the great gold cornice stripped from the Temple of the Sun in Cuzco, the capital city. But a room full of gold was not enough for the invaders. They decided that Atahuallpa must die. He was offered a choice, to remain a sun-worshipper and be burnt alive or to be baptized and swiftly killed by the garotte. He accepted the easier death.

As they marched inland through the busy cities and along the stone-paved roads of Peru they found more and more evidence of true civilization. There was almost no resistance. The Indians wept for the lost Son of the Sun, Huascar Inca, but they accepted the rule of their new masters. The great Temple of the Sun in Cuzco was desecrated,

Above, map of the world, made by Ortelius in 1570. The much searched-for northwest and northeast passages are still included, but knowledge of the size of the north American continent makes these increasingly unattractive.

Opposite top left, Ferdinand Magellan (c. 1480–1521), the Portuguese sailor who accepted the support of the King of Spain to command the first voyage around the world. Magellan himself was killed in the Philippines, and only eighteen members of his crew actually completed the journey. National Maritime Museum, London.

Opposite bottom left, a llama, depicted in an early sixteenth-century Peruvian manuscript.

Opposite right, illustration from a diary of Magellan's voyage around the world in 1519–22 depicting two of the Portuguese sailors trying out a local sailing boat, probably in Guam. Accounts of voyages of exploration were highly popular throughout the sixteenth century.

and the mummies of the deceased Incas were burned. However, it was to be another year before the Inca revolt occurred. It lasted a few months and then collapsed because all the peasant soldiers deserted.

War continued in Peru, since the conquistadores could not agree on who was to hold power. Almagro was executed in 1538 on the orders of Hernando Pizarro, whose elder brother, Francisco, was in turn murdered by Almagro's former followers. The civil wars lasted from the death of Atahuallpa in 1533 until the Spanish government sent the Licentiate Gasca to restore order to Peru in 1548 and Gonzalo Pizarro was executed. By then all the original leaders of the conquest had died by violence.

The Spanish Empire

In Peru the Indian peoples were neglected when the Inca system collapsed. They took little part in the civil wars but suffered because the old system of transport, food storage and mutual assistance had fallen into disuse. The Spanish government introduced a totally different system, based on European social custom. The descendants of the Incas became grandees after the Spanish style and the mass of the population became poor peasants, most of whom worked in near slavery for the well-born landowners. Later a new and rich version of the culture of Europe in the Baroque period was to develop.

In Mexico there had been an enlightened plan, initiated by Cortes, to assimilate the two cultures. Unfortunately, it foundered through the virtual depopulation of the countryside in three terrible epidemics. The Indians, who at first had been wards of the state, and many of whom had been sufficiently educated to be admitted to the priesthood, were treated more harshly because they were needed as labourers. They became an under-privileged group of workers, often more free than the Indians of Peru, but found it hard to keep any tribal identity in the new culture.

In the West Indies there was virtual genocide. So few of the primitive Indians survived that soon after the middle of the sixteenth century slaves were being brought from merchants who transported them from west Africa.

In the Isthmus there was an area of wild forest and lonely coast and here bands of Indians survived away from the trade roads and *ecomiendas*, the vast estates of the white men.

The process of discovery and conquest continued. Expeditions through the valleys of Colombia and Ecuador linked Peru with the middle American ports. The gold-working cannibals, the Quimbaya, yielded up their treasures of emeralds and platinum as well as gold. The Chibcha warriors were defeated on the high plateau around Bogotá, and the Golden Chieftain was removed from power. Even the dense forests were explored as far as possible. The most notable adventure was Orellana's journey down the Amazon from Peru to the Atlantic in 1542. To the south the Pampas were visited but remained undeveloped. On the other hand the estuary of the La Plata was an excellent place to careen ships and to take on provisions. However, this area was only really put to use a century later with the coming of Jesuit missions.

To the north of Mexico other exploration took place. The ships of Cortes visited the coasts of Baja California and soon after other Spanish sailors sailed as far as the Straits of Juan de Fuca. The city of San Augustin was founded in Florida in 1565. Overland exploration took Spanish captains in search of the Seven Cities of Cibola. These turned out to be the lands of the Pueblo Indians, who were then subjected to the gentle persistence of the early missionaries. De Soto investigated the Mississippi and parts of Florida; the heroic Cabeza de Vaca starved among primitive Indians in Texas and eventually made his way on foot to Mexico. But another high civilization was never found, no more golden treasures were discovered, no more stone cities or great kings. The conquest of America was over within two generations of the discoveries of Columbus.

The effect of the Spanish conquest of America upon European affairs was tremendous. The plunder of the Incas and Aztecs was now poured into Spain, to match the riches of Golconda which the Portuguese had gained. The profits of distant trade caused a great outburst of naval activity in all the western nations. Britain and France vied in discoveries in North America and in the 'piracy' of Portuguese and Spanish overseas colonial areas. Suddenly the whole tenor of the world had altered.

The Portuguese conquests

During the fifteenth century two major events affected the future history of Europe and Asia. These were the advance of the Ottoman Turks, which sealed the eastern Mediterranean against western traders; and the beginnings of the Portuguese enterprises, which opened a sea route to Asia by way of the Cape of Good Hope. These great changes in world affairs marked the beginning of world wide trade. The social changes which were initiated by these events have not, even today, been fully calculated. It was during this period that the Portuguese made a vital contribution to world history. In 1385, after the Battle of Aljubarrota, Portugal was assured of independence from the small but vigorous kingdom of Castille. The victory encouraged expansion at home and a vigorous trade in wheat and wine developed. This trade was largely borne by Portuguese ships and much of it was directed to England and the Low Countries.

King John I of Portugal, who founded the Avis dynasty, had five sons of whom the third was Prince Henry. The princes, who were seeking honour in battle against the infidels, persuaded their father to allow them to take a naval force and assault the Moorish city of Ceuta. Their enterprise succeeded and treasure as well as honour were won. Prince Henry decided that this sea-based victory provided a good opportunity to explore the lands farther south along the coast of Africa. It might also be possible to turn the flank of Islamic power and perhaps find a route to more distant lands such as those described by Marco Polo.

In the beginning Prince Henry had to contend with the popular fallacy that the lands

Above, Henry the Navigator (1394–1460); he financed many of the explorers' expeditions with funds derived from his position as Grand Master of the Order of Christ, the Portuguese branch of the Knights Templar.

Left, Fort Jesus in Kenya, established to defend Portuguese trading routes in the late sixteenth century.

Opposite, the Europeans in the New World in the early sixteenth century. Brazil was allocated to the Portuguese by the Papal Bull of 1494.

nearest the sun were a burning desert waste and that the equatorial seas were filled with strange monsters living in a boiling ocean. The first steps were taken to colonize the Atlantic islands off the African coast. Porto Santo was sighted in 1420, but four years later Perestrello, who was later father-in-law to Christopher Columbus, discovered Madeira. Mariners already knew the Canaries, but they were usually afraid to venture beyond Cape Bojador because of the legendary boiling seas.

Perhaps these legends were the result of theorizing, perhaps somebody had witnessed the effect of an undersea eruption, but these stories were only discredited in 1434. Gil Eannes de Lagos reached the dreaded Cape and then assumed his voyage southwards to cross the Tropic of Cancer. He discovered the beautiful and extensive gulf of the Rio de Oro. More important he proved that the Tropic was not a point of danger. The seas beyond were no more lethal than the ocean to the north. Prince Henry in his castle at Sagres had reason to rejoice at the news, for now the navigators and geographers who stayed with him were encouraged to make further explorations.

It was not until the fifteenth century that the construction of ships became as efficient as the instruments and navigational aids which guided them. For ascertaining the correct position of the sun, navigators used astrolabes which they had developed from traditional Arab instruments. Their excellent quadrants allowed latitude to be determined from observation of the Pole Star and direction was governed by the mariners' compass. Speed at sea was simply estimated by seamen who by long practice had achieved an approximation to accuracy.

Other aids were very good charts; those used by sea captains were made up as *portolans*, that is portable atlases. These maps contained drawings of compass cards with lines radiating from them; these were intended to indicate compass bearings from known points and were not merely for decoration. Such maps were made by internationally known specialists and often a cartographer was employed by various governments as a secret agent who would reveal the first news of overseas discoveries.

Basic knowledge of navigation and cartography was international in western Europe. Similarly the art of shipbuilding was standardized so that all developments were quickly repeated over the whole of the region. The main feature in design was the steady enlargement of the round hulled ship instead of the long Mediterranean galley. At first it was tiny and inefficient, but it became capable of taking two or three hundred people by the end of the fifteenth century.

The Portuguese voyagers sent by Prince Henry the Navigator led the way in an area of international competition. It was his interest in discovery and development which provided the impetus and encouragement for his sea captains. Their exploring boats, coasting the hot shores of Morocco, were not different from those which sailed on more prosaic trading missions to Britain and Denmark. Through the interest of the Prince in bringing navigational experts to regular conferences, a body of knowledge was built up and it was this which was to give Portugal the eventual lead in the race for new commercial outlets for the developing civilization of Europe.

In 1433 King John of Portugal died and the new king, Dom Pedro, urged his brother Henry to press on with the work of discovery. In 1441 Captain Nuño Tristao discovered Cap Blanc and sent home the first negro slaves; two years later he discovered the Bay of Arguin and brought back more.

Slavery was condoned by the Portuguese because it had been a Roman custom apparently accepted by the early Christian church. The idea of the new slavery was to repay the African by giving home care and education. Several of these slaves were eventually returned to their homelands to spread Christianity and new technical knowledge in Africa. However, in 1446 Nuño Tristao and his crew were massacred at a native village just south of Cape Verde. Resistance had been stirred up by the cruelties of the invaders.

Slow progress continued along the coasts of west Africa and Senegal, Gambia and Guinea, were reached. In 1454 Pope Nicholas V confirmed the right of Portugal to rule over all territories discovered between Cape Bojador and the East Indies. He also authorized a just and reasonable commerce in slaves.

In 1456 Sierra Leone was discovered and named after the shape of the great mountain which dominates the site of Freetown. This was the last discovery to be reported to Prince Henry, who died in 1460. It confirmed

Left, map of the African coast in about 1500; little was known about the interior of the country, and all trading contacts, even for slaves, were with the peoples inhabiting coastal regions. Internal African trade was mainly in the hands of Arabs. British Museum, London.

Below, map of the Atlantic by Bartolomeo Pareto, made in 1455. With instruments that could only indicate latitude and longitude approximately, and with no general map projections available, maps at that date were little more than charts of the coastlines. British Museum, London.

Opposite, astrolabe of about 1588; these were used to measure the height of the planets and sun in the sky and could be used to determine both the latitude and longitude. Invented by the Greeks or the Arabs, they were invaluable to explorers sailing in unknown waters. National Maritime Museum, London.

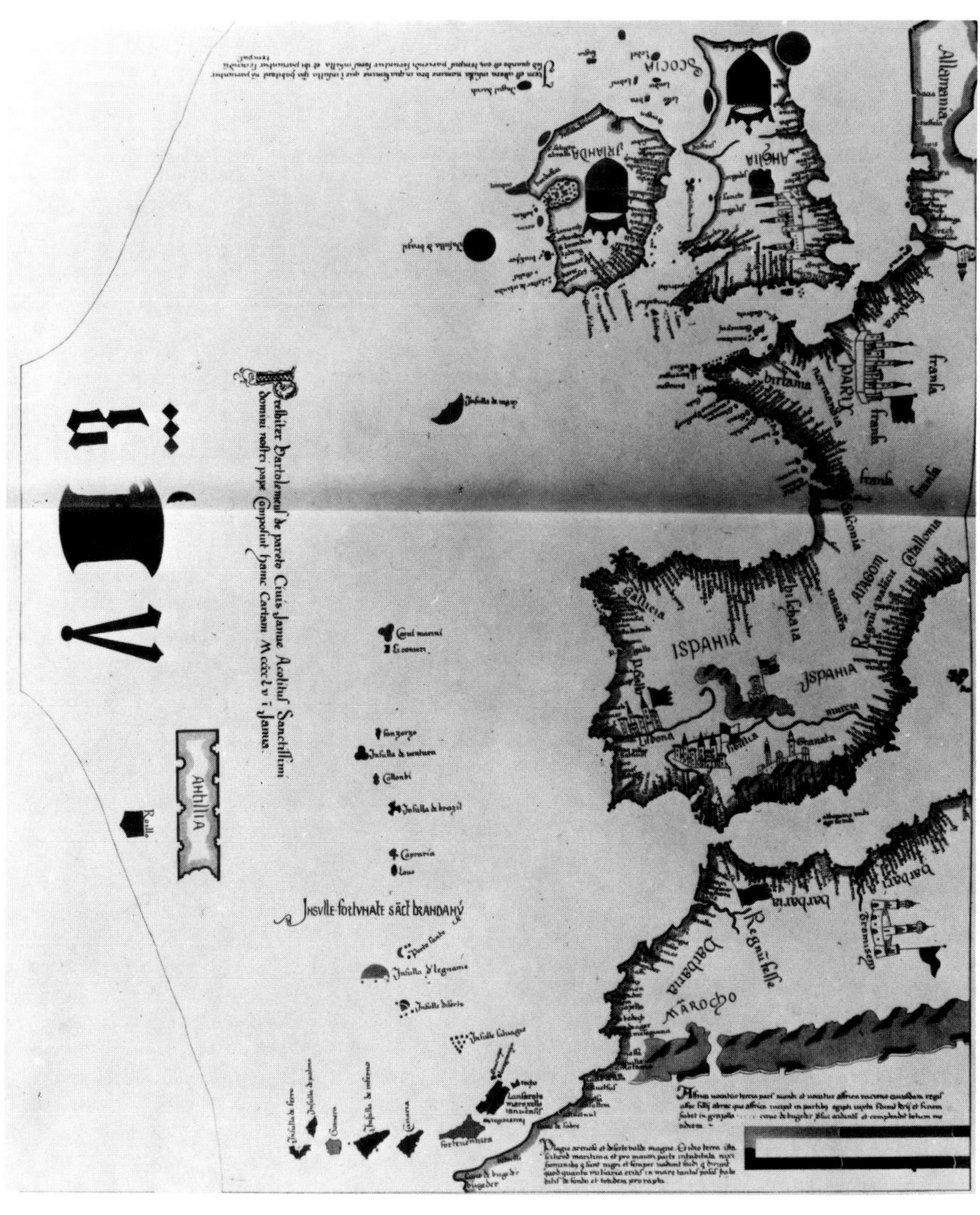

his hope that the coast would trend eastwards.

After his death exploration continued, though on a lesser scale, so it was not until 1481, when King John II ascended the throne, that really vigorous direction aided further explorations. In 1482 Diogo Cao discovered the mouth of the Congo; in west Africa, kingdoms from Ashanti to Benin, whose kind was visited in 1485, were found.

In 1487 Bartholomeu Dias, adventuring still farther south, was caught in a storm which drove him out into the ocean. He knew that he was well to the south of earlier discoveries in Africa; he was to discover later that he was also well to the east. Lack of supplies obliged him to make for home, and he turned westwards only to encounter another storm, in which he discovered the *Cabo Tormentoso* (Cape of Tempests) where the African coast turned eastwards. He had missed it on the stormy outward journey. Later this Cape was to be called the Cape of Good Hope. The sea route to the east had at last been found.

In the same year, 1487, two Portuguese travellers who had been permitted to follow the Nile through Egypt reached the Christian kingdom of Abyssinia, which they described as the realm of Prester John. They heard of the trade of Arab ships along the east African coast. Everything was now ready, a generation after his death, for the final realization of the plans of Prince Henry the Navigator.

The year 1494 was an important one in Portuguese history. It was two years after Columbus reached the West Indies, and the Treaty of Tordesillas made the first rough division of the unexplored regions of the world between Spain and Portugal. In the same year Dom Vasco da Gama was called to a conference with the new King of Portugal, Manuel the Fortunate. The object of the conference was to plan with all speed a voyage to India before the Spanish venturers to the West discovered the way.

The voyage of Vasco da Gama

It was not until July 1497 that all was ready and Dom Vasco da Gama's ships, a caravel and three smaller naus, left the estuary of the Tagus with great ceremony. Nothing had been spared to make the voyage a success and the ships were loaded with provisions and trade goods. They were also armed with cannon fore and aft and were well provided with ammunition. The crews numbered 160 men, and these included a proportion of volunteers released from prison on condition that they took part in the dangerous adventure.

Vasco da Gama's voyage was a far less hazardous undertaking than the one Columbus had faced. The stories of Marco Polo had made it quite clear that there was widespread trade in the Indian Ocean, and that Arab vessels had ventured far to the south along the coast of Africa, as well as eastwards towards China. Now that the end of Africa had been found in the Tormented Cape, there was good reason for renaming it *Cabo de Bona Esperanza* or Cape of Good Hope.

The expedition left Lisbon in April and reached the Cape in December. It then sailed east and north and on Christmas Day sighted a beautiful hilly coastline, which they named Natal in honour of the Nativity. On 11 January 1498 they reached the mouth of the Zambesi. They were now near the lands of the Monomotapa who traded gold and ivory with the Arabs in exchange for fine pottery. However, da Gama continued northwards to Malindi and was welcomed by its Arab ruler. He gave the Portuguese the services of an Arab pilot, and they set off under his direction into the vast spaces of the Indian Ocean. On 20 May 1498 they approached the west coast of India and made landfall at the port of Calicut. The search for the sea route to India was complete.

When the Portuguese arrived, India was in a state of political confusion. In the north, following the invasion of Tamerlane and his Tartar armies, an Afghan dynasty ruled the Islamic state. Babur had not yet conquered this Lodi dynasty to found the Mogul Empire. In central India there were Muslim kingdoms as well as Hindu realms. The south was Hindu, forming the empire of Vijayanagar. The Portuguese were acceptable visitors not only for trade but because local rulers knew that they might be employed as useful allies in their wars of territorial aggrandizement.

The Zamorin (Rajah) of Calicut was a Hindu, but the traders who reached his port were entirely controlled by the Arab merchants and ship-owners. They brought silks from China, spices from the Moluccas, gems from Ceylon, strange drugs and medicines from Indonesia and ivory and gold from Africa. They were well aware that Vasco da Gama was a threat to their commerce. It was no doubt because of their influence that the Rajah received his Portuguese visitors with scant courtesy and disdained their gifts. However after long and difficult negotiations the Rajah gave permission for the ships to be loaded with spices in return for their merchandise, especially good quality iron. This result, though, was only obtained after da Gama had forcibly taken hostages to secure a safe hearing.

In order to express friendship after da Gama had released the hostages, the Rajah gave the navigator a letter for the King of Portugal. He greeted his royal brother, thanked him for sending Vasco da Gama and stated that he was sending a gift of cinnamon, ginger, cloves and precious stones. In return he asked for silver, coral and scarlet cloth from Portugal.

Having thus agreed to commence trade, Vasco da Gama set sail for Portugal.

The voyage home was a disaster. The Portuguese had insufficient knowledge of the winds of the Indian Ocean and because of a succession of calms they took three months to reach the coast of Africa. There was no fresh food or fruit available, and scurvy broke out. This terrible disease, caused by vitamin deficiencies, played havoc among the sailors and there were only sufficient fit men to sail two of the ships, the *Sao Gabriel* and the *Berrio*. After reaching Africa they pursued their slow voyage around its coasts keeping close inshore, for as yet the wind systems of the Atlantic remained unknown.

On 19 July 1499, the remainder of the expedition reached Lisbon. The voyage had taken two years and two days and of the 160 sailors only 55 returned. However, Vasco da Gama had opened the road to the East and had broken the monopoly in spices which had belonged to Genoa and Venice. He was created Admiral of the Indian Ocean as a recognition of his distinguished services.

Left, Vasco da Gama (c. 1469–1524), the Portuguese explorer who in 1497–99 was the first to sail to India around the south of Africa. He later helped to establish a permanent Portuguese power in the west of India.

Opposite, a map of the gulf of China made by Portuguese explorers in 1519.

The Cabral expedition

The second Portuguese expedition to India was led by Pedro Alvarez Cabral. The occasion of the sailing was witnessed by enormous crowds of citizens and was blessed by the church. It is likely that the mission had two objectives. The first was to confirm the existence of a land across the Atlantic within the Portuguese area of influence as defined in the Treaty of Tordesillas. The second was formally to commence a regular trade in spices from India. The Portuguese were by now well aware of the importance of overseas discoveries and the possibilities of improved commercial wealth for their country.

Cabral sailed with ten ships and the journey across the Atlantic took a month. On Easter Day 1500 they sighted a mountain to the west. A landing was made and they expected to meet dark skinned peoples like those in Africa, but to their surprise they met a yellowish skinned race with long black hair, wearing coronets of coloured feathers. These were the Tupinamba, a race of canoe-using villagers of American Indian stock. Two condemned felons who had obtained a remission of sentence by volunteering to be put ashore in the newly discovered lands were left behind. They rendered a good service to Portugal by learning the Tupi language and opening the possibilities of settlement and commerce.

The name of Brazil was not given to the country at once. It had long been a name for some mysterious island in the western Atlantic, but when the brazil-wood used by dyers to obtain a permanent red colour was found to be plentiful the name was applied to the country. However the discovery of Brazil was not an immediate advantage to Portugal. The Tupinamba, though enterprising, had few sources of wealth, and inland the primitive tribes of the Botocudo gave no indication that hidden riches existed.

The departure from the Brazilian coast was tragic. A hurricane broke up the squadron and four ships were lost. Among the mariners drowned was the great navigator Bartholomeu Dias.

Only six ships sailed across the South Atlantic to round the Cape and call at Mozambique and Malindi. However, Cabral had shown the feasibility of using the wind systems of the Atlantic for a safe oceanic route towards India. It was an advance which would last for another three centuries while ships were dependent upon the winds for their propulsion. The value of the discovery is shown by the date of Cabral's arrival off Calicut in December 1500, nine months after leaving Lisbon.

At Calicut there was more trouble with the Arab merchants, who had realized that the foreigners might well be dangerous commercial competitors. They attacked the stores and trading booths of the Portuguese, killing forty-eight of the traders and some of the Indians who were working there. Cabral replied with a naval bombardment of the city. He then sailed southwards and began trading in spices with the rival city of Cochin. This southerly move was important because it brought nearer the expansion of the Portuguese market towards the Indonesian archipelago, which was to become the real focus of the spice trade.

The return of the expedition to Portugal in July 1501 showed the solid advantages of the Atlantic route pioneered by da Gama on his first voyage around Africa. In spite of the losses in the hurricane, the voyages had been a great success. The territory of Brazil was given to the Portuguese king, a real trading venture had succeeded in India, and the fracas with the traders of Calicut had shown the contingencies which must be met.

There was still an urgency in the development of this new trade with Asia. As yet no one knew whether the Spanish colonies far to the west were really island territories off the east coast of Asia. It was still twelve years before Balboa was to sight the Pacific from Darien. King Manuel decided to send another and stronger expedition to the Indies to follow up the discoveries of Cabral and to consolidate the new trading stations. The command was entrusted to Vasco da Gama.

Vasco da Gama's return

In February 1502 the armada set sail. There were 15 ships, 800 soldiers and a battalion of artillery, intended to show the terrible power of the Portuguese kingdom in defence of trading rights.

The port of Quiloa (Kilwa), where da Gama had received a hostile reception on his first voyage, was attacked and after the bombardment the Portuguese issued a proclamation stating that the sultan would be hunted down and paraded in an iron collar to show what happened to those who defied the crown of Portugal. After this exploit the vengeful expedition sailed to India. Off the coast they came across hundreds of pilgrims in a ship on the way to Mecca. Da Gama ordered some children to be seized and forcibly baptized. Then he systematically bombarded the ship for three days, leaving it a burning hulk.

In October the squadron was well received by the Rajah of Cannanore. The stay was short because the hostility experienced by Cabral at Calicut had to be revenged. First fifty local fishermen were captured. Their hands and feet were cut off, and then were sent ashore on a raft with a message to the Zamorin of Calicut that this present was a return for the murder of Portuguese sailors. For the goods which had been pillaged the inhabitants of Calicut must pay a hundredfold. The town was then bombarded and part of it was set on fire, after which da Gama sailed to Cannanore, having left six armed caravels there to mount a blockade.

The rulers of Cochin and Cannanore were pleased that their rival port was subdued, but for their own safety they made fine presents to the Portuguese and gave land on which forts could be erected. The first Portuguese colonial garrisons were settled there and trade was good. Da Gama returned to Portugal with a fantastic cargo of 1,500 tons of spices and all the gold and other plunder from captured ships. He had left behind him not only a memory of terror but solidly based trading posts backed by fortresses manned by Portuguese soldiers.

Before long Vasco da Gama approached the king and demanded that a lordship formerly confiscated by King João II should be returned to his family. The king was angered at the presumption of the great navigator and exiled him to his private estates, where he spent twenty years of unhappy old age.

Affonso de Albuquerque

Affonso de Albuquerque was the next commander of Portuguese India. He was descended from a noble family, and his earlier exploits had included service in North Africa against the Muslim kingdoms. King

Left, the great Portuguese fort at Aguada in Goa, on the west coast of India, epitomized the determination with which the Europeans intended to protect their new trading contacts from interference. Goa became the headquarters of Portuguese trade in India.

Opposite, the ships comprising Vasco da Gama's fleet on his voyage to India in 1497–99. The introduction of multi-masted vessels was important in extending the range and size of these European ships. Science Museum, London.

Manuel had hitherto ignored this former friend of João II but now recalled him to command some of the African outposts. After the dismissal of Vasco da Gama, Albuquerque was given a mission to relieve a Portuguese garrison besieged by the Zamorin of Calicut. The army of Calicut had attacked and burnt Cochin, and the Rajah of Cochin was forced to take refuge with the Portuguese garrison on a rocky islet. In 1503 Albuquerque arrived with ten caravels, liberated Cochin and effectively terrorized the Zamorin.

The victory was an occasion for rejoicing in Portugal and Albuquerque was given a royal audience in which he presented a plan for the control of the spice trade of the Indian Ocean. This was a daring scheme to set up fortresses after attacking each important Arab port in turn. To the admiral this was a crusade. His ferocity in opposition to Islam was more than could be expected if this were just war for trading rights; however, the daring enterprise received royal approval. It was a planned step towards imperial power.

The policy of Albuquerque was certain to bring Portugal into conflict with Egypt, Turkey, Arabia and Persia. Although the Caliphate was now divided there was still a powerful sense of unity in the Islamic world. In 1505 the Portuguese king gave his admiral a new title of Viceroy of Cochin, Cannamore and Quiloa. He then sent him out to the Indies in command of a fleet of 22 ships, with 1,500 highly trained soldiers. The expedition reinforced the garrison in east Africa. Then they set out across the ocean to Ceylon. They were well received, and a present of an elephant was sent to Portugal.

The Venetians much worried about the great losses incurred by their failing spice trade, sent envoys to Egypt. As a result the Egyptians sent a message to the pope warning him that if this illicit Portuguese occupation of trading ports in India continued they would destroy all the Christian shrines in the Holy Land and remove the clergy who tended them. To this the Portuguese king had an answer. He took care that all involved should be warned that the Portuguese wielded sufficient power to capture Mecca and to take the remains of the Prophet and scatter them to the four winds. Such challenges and threats made a war in the Indian Ocean inevitable.

Albuquerque returned to Europe, but after two years he led another heavily armed squadron, this time carrying instructions to supersede the Viceroy of India, Francisco de Almeida. The expedition was captained by Tristao da Cunha and, although the two commanders differed between themselves, they had considerable success in the beginning. The east African ports were attacked, and Arab trade almost ceased on that side of the Indian Ocean. Then Socotra was seized as a base for controlling the exit and entrance to the Red Sea. The Arab garrison was slaughtered and the great mosque stripped and turned into a Christian church.

After this important victory the commanders parted company Tristao da Cunha returned to Portugal, discovering on his way the south Atlantic island which still bears his name. Albuquerque continued eastwards along the coast of Arabia, bombarding and burning the towns of Curiate and Muscat. Then, greatly daring, he entered the Strait of Hormuz in 1507 and attacked the great city of gold where all the merchants of the east had trading stations, the ancient island port of Hormuz. However, he was unable to do more than burn a few streets before he heard of the naval disaster which had overtaken

the Portuguese ships in the battle with the Egyptian flotilla at Chaul, where the Viceroy of India's son had been killed.

Albuquerque sailed as rapidly as he could to India, which he reached in 1508. He was promptly arrested on arrival by Governor Almeida who refused to give way and allow himself to be replaced. Almeida then sought revenge for the death of his son and sailed along the Indian coast, burning and wrecking many ports, including Goa and Chaul. He eventually reached Diu where he encountered the Egyptians whom he overwhelmed by sheer fire power. His more notable prisoners were blasted to pieces by being tied to cannons which were fired through their bodies.

Meanwhile a new Portuguese fleet arrived at Cochin bearing full instructions from the king to Albuquerque and Almeida. It was quite clear that Albuquerque was closely in touch with the court at home and Almeida retired immediately and decided to leave India. However, when he landed in southern Africa, he and 150 of his men were slain by the spears of a group of Bantu warriors, perhaps soldiers of the powerful Monomotapa who ruled many tribes from his great stone kraal at Zimbabwe.

Albuquerque was now free from all opposition and, for political reasons, decided to foster the illusion that he was the defender of the Hindu kingdoms against the Moslem states. To effect this he formed an alliance with the Rajah Narasingha of Vijayanagar. They attacked Calicut but their assault was ill planned and the city remained unconquered.

In February 1511 Albuquerque set sail again and arrived at Goa where he intervened in the disputes between Hindus and Muslims and secured the port for Portugal without much trouble. It was obviously a most advantageous site for a really permanent headquarters for the Portuguese. However, it was soon reconquered by the Sultan of Bijapur who used 50,000 soldiers to assault the town. The Portuguese retreated in some disorder and returned to Cannanore. It was at this time that Albuquerque and Magellan quarrelled so badly that Magellan deserted the Portuguese cause.

In 1510 Albuquerque reversed his defeats. He assaulted Goa and captured it. The horrible massacre which ensued was deliberate policy; but it was characteristic of war in that time and place. The victorious viceroy claimed that no Muslim tomb or mosque had been preserved and that all captured Muslims had been killed or roasted alive. He vowed, in the spirit of some ancient crusader, that no living Muslim should enter the city again. Surprisingly the town flourished; after a while peace returned and a great commercial port developed, a truly colonial centre for Portugal in India. Its effectiveness was soon diminished by the new unity of most of India under the rule of the advancing Mogul rulers, who established a liberal Muslim empire at Delhi. By this time the trade with the east had become much more important to Portugal than matters of religion and Albuquerque himself was dead by then.

The settlement of Malacca

Albuquerque envisaged a further assault on the Islamic countries by way of the Red Sea, but because of supply problems the base at Socotra had been abandoned. The expedition therefore had to be organized from India, and Albuquerque gathered a fleet of nineteen ships for the attack.

Meanwhile, at the other end of the Indian Ocean, there had been trouble at Malacca. This great city was a centre of Far Eastern trade, for there Indonesian, Chinese and Indian merchants met with Arabs to exchange vast treasures of spices and jewels. Permission had also been given for the establishment of a Portuguese trading post in 1509 but the Arabs, not unnaturally, objected. They attacked the post, burnt the building and imprisoned and tortured the Portuguese traders. The news reached Portugal next year and King Manuel sent Mendes de Vasconcellos with four ships to punish the Arab merchants.

Naturally, the squadron called in at Goa, where they were received with scant courtesy by Albuquerque, whose fleet of nineteen ships set sail for the Red Sea in April 1511. It was delayed by storms, and the monsoon blew up with such fury that the viceroy decided to reverse his plans and sail before the wind to join in the reprisals against Malacca. In July the fleet arrived quite unexpectedly. The Portuguese seized the great city and hastily erected a fortress. They then took possession of the tin mines in order to have some economic control. Meanwhile, they had sent messages of friendship to the embassies of China, Siam and Java, to make sure that the town would not be deserted by the traders now that control was in Portuguese hands. One may judge the complete success of the plan by the fact that the Portuguese needed a garrison of only 300 men to control a population of over, 100,000.

The Portuguese government at home fully realized the importance of the seizure of Malacca. When the first merchant ship from that port reached Lisbon in 1513 it was welcomed with a state procession and a display of trade goods. A Venetian spy reported home to the Council of Ten that the procession included a horse from Hormuz, a panther from Persia and an elephant from India. Portugal was displaying symbols of the conquest of the Indian Ocean.

The monsoon which had destroyed the original plans of Albuquerque had led to the founding of commercial prosperity for Portugal on a base much more secure than she had known hitherto. From Malacca the Portuguese gradually extended control of the Moluccas and the Spice Islands of Indonesia. Trade in spice and jewels was assured in almost unlimited quantities.

The way was now open for Portuguese merchants to visit Indo-China and commence trade with the Chinese mainland and the islands of Japan. The warning that Portugal was not alone came in 1521 when Magellan, sailing under the orders of Spain, reached the Philippines, where he was killed in a local disturbance. But with Spanish ships on the Pacific coast of Mexico there was soon bound to be a series of clashes. Eventually they were quietened by the Treaty of Saragossa in 1529 which guaranteed that the Philippines should be the boundary of Spanish territory in the East Indies.

Later, when Portuguese power declined at home, English, French and Dutch merchants arrived under naval protection. The Portuguese monopoly was broken, but the honour of discovery and settlement went to Portugal together with some centuries of very profitable commercial and political influence. The capture of Malacca had altered the course of history in the Far East.

Below, San Salvador in Brazil, founded by the Portuguese in 1549 as a centre for sugar plantations. It became the capital of Portuguese Brazil; this illustration depicts its temporary capture by the Dutch in the 1620s. Despite Dutch aggression, the Portuguese managed to hold on to most of their American possessions. British Museum, London.

Opposite, a Portuguese officer in the East Indies being carried in a litter; many Portuguese made their fortunes trading in the Far East in the early sixteenth century.

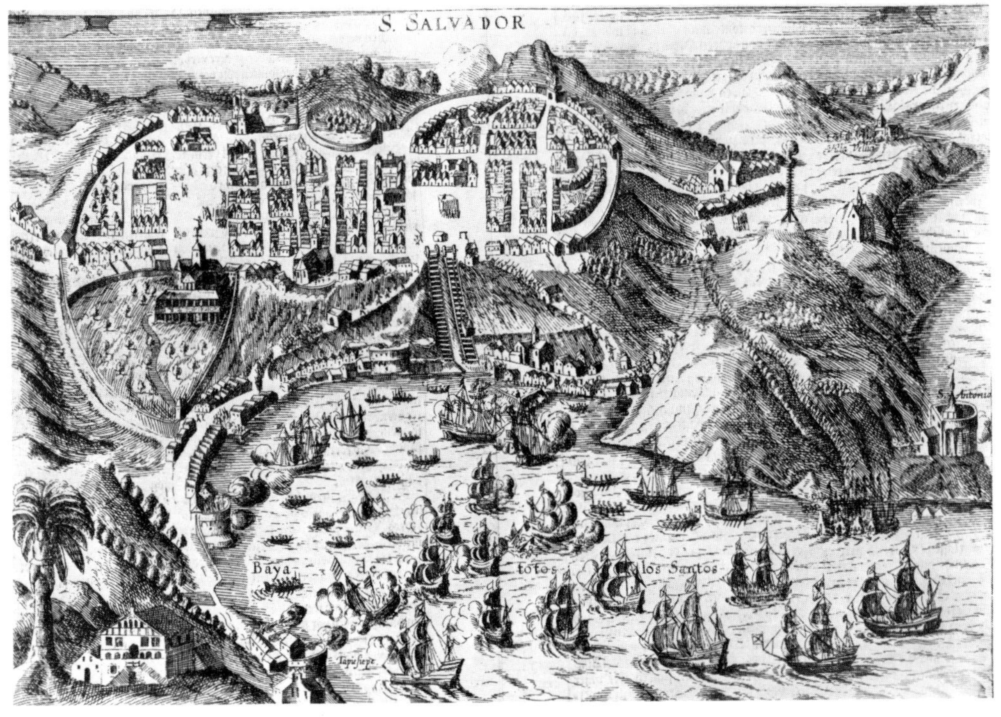

Part VII

THE EASTERN WORLD

Introduction

To the European, Asia was fabulously wealthy but infinitely dangerous, a mysterious amalgam of the splendours of Cathay, the heathen Saracens, who had deprived Christendom of its rightful centre in Jerusalem, and the destructive and devilishly cruel Mongol hordes. Occasional travellers, men such as Marco Polo, ventured to the East and brought back accounts of what they found there; but this small source of factual knowledge was worked up with a mountain of innuendo and imagination which left the average educated European entirely ignorant of the real conditions of the East.

In the same way, the East showed very little curiosity about the West. It was absorbed with the spread and intermingling of its own cultures; and one of the features of the age was the growth of the two Eastern religions that were to achieve an influence beyond the cultural borders in which they developed—Islam and Buddhism. The former spread throughout the Near East, and in alliance with the ancient culture of Persia, spread in central Asia as far as India; the latter moved into China, South-East Asia and Japan. Unlike medieval Christianity, these two religions were assimilated into their new cultural homes, with benefit to both the religion and the older civilization in which it now flourished. These new religions often brought in their wake a dramatic assertion of cultural confidence in the form of huge building projects; the temple of Angkor Wat in Cambodia was only the most spectacular of many such enterprises.

The age saw the consolidation of the main spheres of cultural influence in Asia—China, South-East Asia, India—but it also saw the astonishing Mongol Empire which, as well as being the largest land empire in history, dramatically changed the history of the continent. To the Europeans, as has been noted, Genghis Khan, Timur and the lesser Mongol rulers were nothing more than rabid destroyers, scourges sent from God leaving a trail of smoking ruins and mutilated bodies in their wake. This picture was true, and yet the Mongols brought more to Asia than Christendom was aware: they brought a peace and unity that lasted for more than a century and enabled safe long-distance trade for the first time.

To China, the Mongols brought a great catharsis. The effete Sung dynasty was swept away, and the new Yüan dynasty, ruled by the legendary Kublai Khan, founded the imperial City of Peking as a mark of the glory of its rule, a glory that was to grow ever more brilliant under the Ming. To other civilizations, the struggle against Mongol rule brought a new cultural identity, or helped to arouse a more certain idea of it—Japan and Muscovy prospered in the defence of their lands against Mongol domination. India, too, survived without effective Mongol penetration, and yet eventually it fell to another conqueror from outside claiming descent from Timur—the Mogul dynasty. By introducing a strong Persian influence to India, and consolidating the still weak Islamic culture there, the Moguls brought India to one of the most glorious periods in its history, and created the most unified state in the subcontinent since the days of Ashoka. In doing so, the Mogul Empire demonstrated all the best features of Asian rule at this date—religious toleration, assimilation, diversity and mutual benefit—and it was not until the first of these was replaced by an Islamic fanaticism that the Empire was seen to rest on mere shadows.

The Asia that the Europeans set out to explore in the fifteenth century was close to the peak of its splendour; it needed nothing from Europe, and wanted less. Nor was the East yet decadent and passive when faced with the energetic Europeans, as was to become true in the following centuries—Christian missionaries were expected to justify their beliefs in terms comprehensible to scholarly followers of Mohammed, the Buddha or Confucius, and were accepted according to the quality of their philosophies and the morality of their followers. Traders at Agra or Peking had to offer a worthwhile exchange, or leave empty-handed. Asia was confident, by 1500; the complexity and hierarchy of its societies provided stability and an incredible richness which could offer a full life without seeking beyond its frontiers. Yet this self-sufficiency would, eventually, lead to its demise in the face of European assertion and confident energy.

Opposite, Babur giving instructions to his gardeners. As well as being a great general, Babur was a poet and a lover of gardens; his gardens at Kabul can still be seen. British Museum, London.

On page 328, the thirteenth-century Persian poet Faridun with his family. His work was mystical and explored the perceptions of the Sufi form of Islam. Chester Beatty Library, Dulbin.

Chapter 27

Muslim India

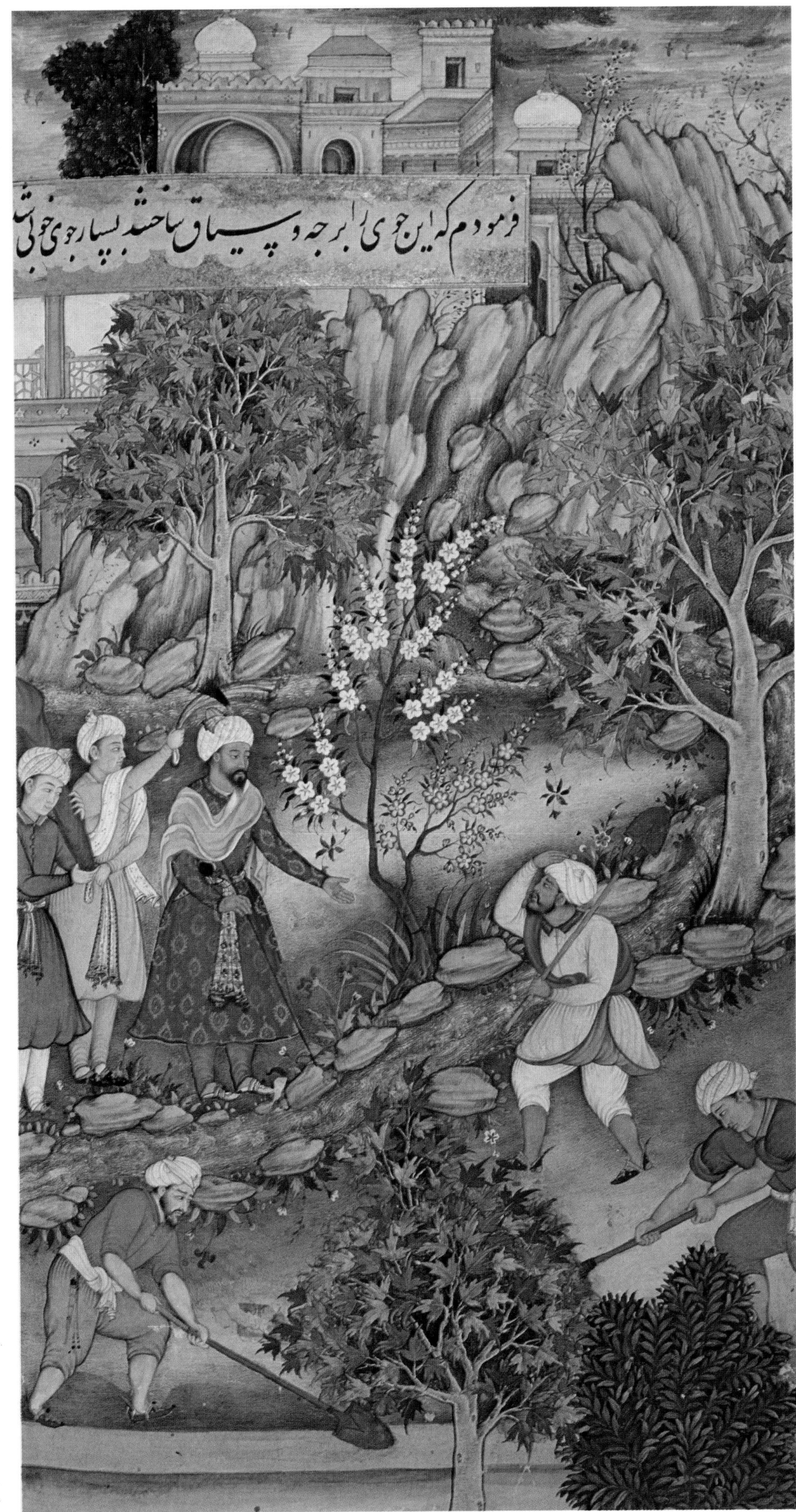

India did not succumb to the Muslim invaders all at once, nor did community of religion mean that the various invaders who appeared were of one nation and of one mind. The Gurjara-Pratihara kings successfully contained the Arab kingdom of Sind, founded in 712, and the raids of Mahmud of Ghazni, carried out at the expense of the kings of northern India, resulted only in the annexation of the Punjab and the north-west. It was not until the beginning of the thirteenth century that a dynasty of Ghurid Turks captured the frail kingdoms of northern India and established the first sultans of Delhi.

India once again had to face a murderous central Asian cavalry; but now for the first time it was confronted with rulers who would not be Hinduized. The old Indo-European-speaking peoples had been tolerant of the gods of other peoples and places: Rome had offered the gods of its enemies more sumptuous temples and more devoted attendants if they would favour the Roman soldiers in battle. The tolerance of Asoka for all religious sects matched the tolerance Cyrus the Great had shown to the Jews and the homage he paid to the gods of Babylonia and Egypt.

In the ancient Middle East it was otherwise: the gods of enemies defeated in battle were enslaved or destroyed. The iconoclasm of their Middle Eastern religion suited only too well the native temper of the Turkish dynasties of central Asia.

But, in spite of the pillage and destruction which the early representatives of Islam in India carried out, and the oppressive rule of the later Muslims, ancient India did not entirely die. The same Indian classes which staffed the bureaucracy, from village headman to the secretariat, before the Muslims appeared often continued to do so while kings rose and fell. Indian life, especially in the Deccan and the south, was not on the whole radically disturbed.

The decisive difference was the permanent presence of Islam itself and of Islamic, and in particular Persian, culture. In the past only the missionary zeal of Asoka and the Buddhist monks and the allure of the Roman and Far Eastern trade had aroused Indians to an interest in foreign parts. Now India had perforce broken its shell of isolation. Under the Moguls music, painting and religious poetry flourished as never before. A new Indian culture was being born.

The Delhi sultanate

The Muslim conquest of India was undertaken by Turks who had initially settled in the area now known as Turkestan, bordering on Persia, from which they absorbed both Iranian and Islamic cultural influences. In the eleventh century they expanded westwards, defeated the Byzantine emperor Romanus at the Battle of Manzikert (1071), and captured Jerusalem five years later. Increasing Turkish pressure on India, which continued during the next 100 years, reaching a climax at the end of the twelfth century with the campaigns of Muhammad Ghuri.

This brillant Turkish leader moved into northern India from his base in Ghazni. At the first battle of Tarain in 1191 he was successfully opposed by a coalition of Rajput chiefs under Prithvi Raj, but he returned to the same battlefield in the following year with a mixed force of 120,000 Afghans, Turks and Persians. On this occasion the Rajput chiefs were overcome by the mobile armoured cavalry of the Turks. Prithvi Raj fled but was later killed. Delhi was captured and the surrounding territories of northern India were absorbed by the Muslim invaders. During the next three centuries northern India was under Turkish rule.

From Delhi in the thirteenth century successive rulers pushed by stages southwest to Gujarat and east to Bihar and Bengal. In the fourteenth century they moved across the tangled Vindhya mountains into southern India, and by 1327 conquest was so advanced that Sultan Muhammad bin Tughluq founded a second capital in the Deccan. The moment formed one of two peaks of Muslim rule in India: not until the heyday of Mogul rule would a Delhi empire spread so widely again.

The might of empire was made visible at Delhi. Here, seven miles from the old Rajput capital, on a rise above the river Jumna, stood Tughluqabad, a new city four miles in circuit, which contained a great palace precinct and a massive citadel. This city proclaimed the foreignness of the dynasty with battlements on the circling walls, pointed arches and the domes and minarets of mosques, colleges and royal tombs. All these features had come from western Asia. The Turki or Persian blood and speech of the ruling class, their horses, armour and weapons, wine and musk-melons were equally alien. The stiff and splendid ceremonial of the court and the titles of the nobles were Persian in style, while the sultan himself was legitimized in the eyes of Muslims by a robe of honour from the caliph, the religious head of the Muslims.

In mosque and Muslim college were to be found the *ulema* who were leaders in communal prayer, expounders of the holy Koran and the sayings of the Prophet and his Companions. In addition they upheld one or other of the four great schools of Muslim law, were masters of Arabic grammar and lexicography and poets and historians in the Persian tradition. These men also looked outside India for the origin and renewal of their faith, learning and culture.

This note of foreign domination and culture sounded across all north India, from the Indus to the Brahmaputra. It was heard in every garrison town, army encampment and provincial centre and wherever a mosque was built or the *ulema* set their new orthodoxy against the old orthodoxy of Hinduism. Even in the countryside the new influence was felt, for newly arrived Sufi orders of Muslim mystics were preaching Islam to the people in a form which stressed personal devotion rather than formal ritual as the best approach to God. Because of their message, a process of mass conversion to Islam took place in what are now Pakistan and Bangla Desh.

The Slave dynasty

The first Muslim dynasty established at Delhi was under Qutb-ud-Din Aybak, a slave of Muhammad Ghuri. The use of slaves in high positions was a common practice in the early Turkish dynasties. Many of these slaves were the educated sons of captured chiefs who achieved distinction through ability and loyal service. In the first century of Turkish rule in India each of the rulers at Delhi was either a slave or the descendant of a slave, thus giving the dynasty its name.

It was mainly through Aybak's efforts that Benares, Gwalior, Gujarat and Kalinjar were occupied and Muslim control extended over northern India. As a reward for his services, he was given the viceroyalty at Delhi in 1206, where his administration was harsh but just to Hindus and Muslims alike. He died in 1210 after falling from a horse while playing polo, and the throne passed to a slave of Aybak's named Iltutmish.

Iltutmish (1211–36) may be regarded as the real founder of the Slave dynasty, which ruled at Delhi throughout the thirteenth century. He consolidated the Turkish hold over northern India and established the military system of government which maintained the position of the Muslim minority. He also continued the rebuilding of the old city of Delhi, begun by Aybak.

At the same time Persian cultural influences were encouraged. Persian men of letters, who fled to Delhi after the rise of the Mongols under Genghis Khan, were employed as scribes and officials. Although Hindi was tolerated, the delicate Sanskrit language was used in administration, and alongside it there developed a new language which reflected the cross-fertilization of cultural ideas during the Muslim period in India. This was Urdu, the 'language of the camp', a mixture of Sanskrit, Arabic and Turki, used only by the common people at first, but accepted as a medium of literary expression by the seventeenth century.

After Iltutmish's death in 1236 the dissolute behaviour of his son seriously undermined the stability of the sultanate at Delhi. His daughter Raziyya, whom Iltutmish had wished to succeed, attempted to take over the government, but the proud Turkish nobles could not tolerate the rule of a woman, and rebellion broke out. The dynasty was saved by the rise of another slave, Balban.

Ghiyas-ud-Din Balban was undoubtedly the most capable of the slave kings who ruled at Delhi in the thirteenth century. In his youth he had persuaded Iltutmish to purchase him, and he had served Iltutmish successfully as water-carrier, chief huntsman, commander of the cavalry and lord chamberlain. He then continued as chief minister to the sultan Nasir-ad-Din and succeeded to the throne himself on the sultan's death in 1266.

During his rule Balban ruthlessly subdued internal unrest and strengthened the northern frontiers against the Mongols. He also reorganized the administration and enhanced the royal status by introducing Persian concepts of kingship and by insisting on the strict observance of an elaborate court etiquette. He believed that the royal dignity should be based on respect, and he always appeared correctly dressed before his courtiers, who were not permitted to appear lighthearted in his presence.

The Mongol threat

To the medieval observer, the expansion of the Mongols in the thirteenth century seemed to be checked at the borders of civilization only by the decline of its own momentum. In record time the implacable nomadic horsemen of Genghis Khan and his successors, who had ridden out of central Asia, swept everything before them and created an empire which stretched across Europe and Asia from Germany in the west to Japan in the east. In China the disciplined hordes of Kublai Khan brought an end to the Sung dynasty and established Mongol rule.

In the northeast the Khanate of the Golden Horde imposed itself on the emerging Russian state and menaced the position of the Slavs. In the Middle East the empire of Hulagu Khan transformed the Muslim world. Mongol pressure in this area steadily increased from the time of Genghis Khan's invasion of Transoxiana in 1219 to Hulagu Khan's sack of Baghdad in 1258, which brought the Abbasid caliphate to an end.

Signs of this Mongol eruption appeared in India when Jalal-ad-Din, the courageous shah of Khwarizin was driven into the Sind by Genghis Khan in 1221. Thereafter for several decades the Mongols pressed southwards, attracted by the wealth of the Indian

Left, the Mongol leader Hulagu, grandson of Genghis Kahn, on a campaign to put down a rebellion in Persia in 1256. He virtually destroyed the Ishamaili or Assassin sect which had won great power in Persia. British Museum, London.

states. Lahore was destroyed in 1241 and the Sind and the Punjab were harried.

For the greater part of the thirteenth century the defence of India's northern borders preoccupied successive sultans who ruled at Delhi. By successfully opposing the spread of the Mongols the Delhi sultans performed a signal service to India, which more than justified the harsh nature of Turkish military control.

The death of Balban in 1287 brought an end to the Slave dynasty which had ruled at Delhi throughout the thirteenth century. The weakness of Kaigubad, who succeeded him, opened the way for the Khaljis, a clan of Afghan origin. They established a dynasty which ruled at Delhi for thirty years.

The first of the Khalji sultans, the aged and peace-loving Jalal-ud-Din Firuz Shah, was soon replaced by his nephew, 'Ala' ad-Din. 'Ala'ad-Din, the most capable of the Khalji rulers, proved a worthy successor to Balban. He was extremely ambitious, although somewhat unrealistic in his aims and visionary in outlook. He had wild dreams of emulating Alexander the Great's achievement and of conquering the world, and even had coins struck which depicted him as Alexander the Second.

These dreams came to nothing, but during his twenty-year reign 'Ala'ad-Din did achieve two things. He successfully opposed a Mongol threat across the northern borders between 1295 and 1306, when Mongol armies repeatedly penetrated into northern India, devastating the countryside around Delhi. 'Ala'ad-Din who showed himself a brilliant soldier, slowly forced them back and even took the offensive in Mongol territory. Second, he extended his rule into central India and then set out to conquer the south, an area which had remained largely independent of Turkish rule during the period of the Slave dynasty.

The move into south India was largely the work of Malik Kafur, a Hindu convert who had become 'Ala'ad-Din's chief general. In a series of brilliant military moves Kafur advanced into the Deccan, occupied Devagiri, sacked the fort of Warangal and plundered innumerable Hindu temples. He returned to Delhi with hundreds of elephants, thousands of horses and countless chests of gold and precious stones, amongst which was reputedly the famous Koh-i-noor diamond.

Hindus and Muslims

The Muslim conquest of northern India had a profound effect on Hindu society. The Ilbari Turks who established the first dynasty carefully maintained themselves as a distinct group. They acted as conquerors, ruled by the sword, and made little effort to convert their Indian subjects to Islam. The Muslim nobles kept themselves aloof and looked outward across the northern borders for their marriage connections and their administrative officials.

Numerous accounts can be found in the early chronicles of the harsh treatment which was meted out to the Hindus, who were frequently persecuted because of their religious beliefs. Slavery was common and even high-born Hindu women were forced to become dancing girls. Slaves were often given as gifts. This was a favourite practice of Muhammad Tughluq, who bestowed them freely on relations and friends. On one occasion he sent as a present to the Chinese emperor '100 male slaves and 100 slave songstresses and dancers from among the Indian infidels'.

In time a considerable number of Hindus were converted to the Muslim religion. The followers of Islam formed a brotherhood in which everyone was equal in the sight of

God. This concept of equality appealed to large numbers of the poorer classes of the people, who were traditionally kept down by the rigid Indian caste system.

The work of conversion was largely carried out by the Sufis, mystics who migrated to India from Persia and moved into the rural areas where they attracted followers by their example. Consequently, although during the early sultanate the Muslim minority maintained its position by the sword, the work of conversion was carried out peacefully and was generally more successful in those areas where Turkish military control was less obvious.

These Indian converts to Islam were known as Hindustanis. At first restrictions were placed on them as on the Hindus and they were discouraged from raising themselves socially or from gaining political eminence. However, with the decline of the Ilbari dynasty after the death of Balban, a more tolerant attitude emerged. Some of the Hindustanis achieved high positions, notably Malik Kafur, the favourite of 'Ala'ad-Din Khalji.

In time Muslim society was influenced by Hindu customs. The sultans and the nobles adopted ornate Indian costumes and wore rings and jewelled necklaces, which were forbidden to the faithful by Islamic law. Richly-spiced Indian food was sought after by the Muslim nobility and the Indian custom of chewing betel leaf became very popular.

Nevertheless, although there was some merging of social customs during the three centuries of Muslim domination, Hinduism and Islam remained clearly distinct. The irreconcilable antagonism of the two religious groups which emerged during the early sultanate was to remain an aspect of Indian history during the next six centuries.

Beyond the immediate area of Muslim control life for the Hindu peasant went on much as it had done before the Turkish conquest. In the rural areas Hindu landowners retained much of their power, and Hindu merchants were largely in control of trade and commerce. Agricultural products, textiles, herbs and scents were sent to nearby countries and to southeast Asia. The textile industry, in particular, developed during the Muslim period. Different and improved varieties of cloth were introduced by the Muslims from Persia and Arabia and large factories, some of which employed several thousand weavers, were set up.

One of the more pleasant aspects of Muslim rule in India was the cultural development which took place during this period. Throughout the thirteenth century, and particularly after the sack of Baghdad in 1258, there was a steady influx of artists and learned men who fled to India to escape from the Mongols. At Delhi the various sultans patronized the arts and encouraged the emergence of schools where religious studies, literature and scientific subjects were taught. Although 'Ala'ad-Din Khalji was almost illiterate, he supported literary activity as much as any of the other sultans. and during his reign Delhi became the centre of the Muslim cultural world.

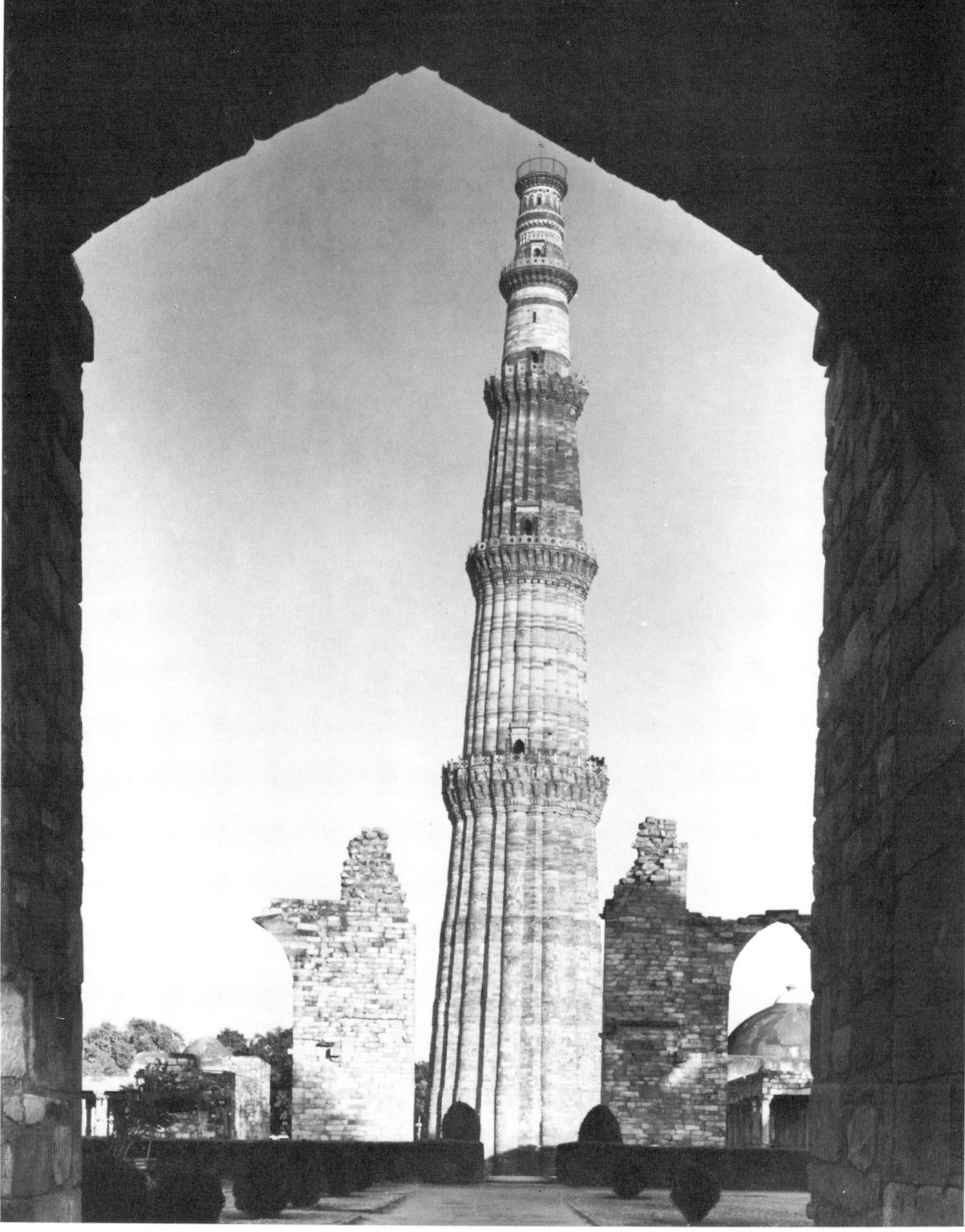

The foremost literary figure in this period was the writer and poet Amir Khusrau (1253–1325). He enjoyed the patronage of seven successive sultans and produced his greatest works during 'Ala'ad-Din's reign. Khusrau, who is regarded as the greatest Persian poet of India, represented the new cultural outlook which began to emerge after it became clear that the Muslim conquerors were to stay in India permanently. He was the son of an immigrant Turk and an Indian Muslim woman of Turkish origin. He wrote in Persian, knew Arabic, studied Sufi philosophy and was one of the first to use Hindi as a literary medium.

The fusion of Indo-Muslim artistic trends can most readily be seen in the architectural forms which appeared during the sultanate. The Turkish rulers of the early dynasty zealously destroyed many of the Hindu temples and used the material to build mosques. Islamic craftsmen from Persia as well as Hindu builders were used in this work. As a result the two architectural traditions merged to form a new Indo-Islamic style, which is represented in many of the mosques and other buildings in and around Delhi.

The Tughluqs

The third of the Turkish dynasties in India was formed by Ghiyas-ud-Din Tughluq, the son of a slave of Balban who, as warden of the frontier marshes, seized power after the death of 'Ala'ad-Din. The Tughluqs ruled from 1320 to 1398, and their most outstanding figure was Muhammad bin Tughluq (1325–51). He was a man of brilliant ideas, a keen student of Persian poetry and a philosopher trained in Greek metaphysics. He worked hard to carry out administrative and economic reforms. His reign was, however, a tragic one. Many of the measures which he tried to introduce were too advanced for his age. Consequently his good intentions were misunderstood and the people resented his rule.

One of the schemes which he put forward was a reform of the currency. He tried to introduce a standard copper unit of money which would replace the silver *tanka*. In a short while Hindus all over the country had begun to mint money in their own homes and, with the economy about to collapse, Muhammad had to call in all his copper tokens. These were piled in mountainous heaps outside the royal treasury, where they remained for over a century.

However, it was in his expansionist plans that Muhammad Tughluq's visionary aims and practical failings can be most clearly seen. The shift of Muslim power southwards which had been begun by 'Ala'ad-Din Khalji was continued by Tughluq. In an attempt to place himself in a central position in order to draw on the sources of revenue from the Deccan, he conceived the plan of transferring the capital 700 miles southwards to Deogir, which was re-named Daulatabad. The whole of the population of Delhi was forcibly shifted, and in the resulting chaos thousands of displaced people died. Muhammad realized his mistake and the people were ordered back, but this did little for his reputation.

Muhammad Tughluq had even more grandiose plans for subjugating the territories beyond India. He dreamt of conquering Persia and even of invading China. To this end, he gathered at his court any foreigners who could give him information about these distant regions, granting them high office and paying them lavishly. Among them was Ibn Battuta (*c.* 1304–78), the Moorish traveller, whose *Book of Travels* contains a fascinating account of Islamic society in India in the fourteenth century.

After Tughluq's death India returned to quieter conditions. His cousin, Firoz Shah, who succeeded him was a gentle man, without Muhammad's far-reaching ambition and impetuous tendency to innovate reforms which aroused popular opposition. He reduced taxation, reformed abuses and resettled the displaced communities. Firoz Shah's rule provided a long period of peace which proved a welcome change for his subjects.

When the Tughluqs thrust deep into the Deccan, toppling one Hindu ruler after another, organizing new provinces and setting up a new capital, it seemed as though all India was to be subject to Muslim power. Yet Muslim authority and influence, though so extensive was not complete and areas of Hindu rule survived in Rajputana, the far south and in much of the countryside.

The sultanate drew its revenues from the land, from millions of peasant cultivators in scattered villages. A few thousand royal officials, even when supported by the cavalry of the Muslim provincial governors, could not themselves ensure due payment of a share in the harvest from so many villagers. Some local authority was required to prevent fraud and intimidate the villagers, who stood armed behind their mud walls or bamboo stockades awaiting the arrival of the tax collector. Such intermediaries, whether rajas of petty states, warrior clans, or professional revenue collectors, had to be allowed sufficient local strength to force the peasants to pay but not enough to defy the state whose overlordship they had been compelled to recognize.

The balance was a delicate one, and any conflict within the foreign Muslim ruling group, any weakness at the centre, might allow the intermediaries to deny the revenues to the sultan and divert them to their own use. Such a breakdown might invite new conquerors from outside India, usurpation by local Muslim governors or, since the intermediaries were Hindu, a re-emergence of Hindu rule.

Just such a breakdown occurred soon after 1327 when Muhammad bin Tughluq was called north from his new Deccan capital to deal with revolts in Sind and Bengal. In his absence various Hindu princes and intermediaries in the south declared their independence. More serious, two royal officers, princes captured by the sultan and converted to Islam who were sent to the Deccan to enforce obedience to Delhi, chose to renounce their new religion and allegience. They proceeded to found what became the Hindu empire of Vijayanagar and by 1387 the brothers had re-established Hindu rule everywhere south of the Tungabhadra river. However, the whole peninsula did not fall to them because in 1347 an independent Muslim kingdom was established in the northern Deccan by a rebel governor, the founder of the Bahmani dynasty. Delhi itself took no counter measures and for over two hundred years it played no further part in Deccan affairs, which became the story of the conflict between Vijayanagar and the Bahmanis and their successors.

This conflict can be seen as a religious struggle and Muslim chroniclers delighted in describing the desecration of temples, whilst Sanscrit court poetry depicted the Vijayanagar rulers as defenders of Hinduism. An element of religious and cultural antagonism existed, but the Deccan wars were waged mainly for practical considerations and secular ends. There were the usual objectives such as the fertile lands between the Tungabhadra and the Krishna, the diamond mines of Golconda and the splendid ports of Goa, through which the cavalry horses which could not be bred in the Deccan were brought from South Arabia. Until 1511 the conflict was over possession of Goa but thereafter it was for an alliance with the Portuguese who had seized it. Vijayanagar did not hesitate to destroy its Hindu neighbours or to use Muslim aid against Hindu Orissa. The Bahmanis likewise fought as savagely against Muslim

Opposite, the Qutb Minar in Delhi, an example of early Islamic architecture in India built in about 1230. It probably celebrates a victory of the Delhi Sultanate: the stone for it was taken from a Hindu temple nearby.

Malwa as against Vijayanagar. All along the western coast the Hindu princes of the pepper ports welcomed the Arab and Persian merchants who linked them to the Persian Gulf, the Red Sea and the trade of the Levant and gave them freedom to build mosques and to worship. In the Vijayanagar armies Muslim troops were employed, in the administration of the Bahmanis Hindu clerks and revenue officials.

Institutionally the Bahmani and Vijayanagar kingdoms had much in common. Both relied heavily on land revenues collected either by farming them out to the highest bidder—which could mean that the peasantry were charged excessive rents—or through the great provincial governors, which was dangerous if the ruler were not vigorous and vigilant. But both also drew larger revenues than were usual in north India from an active trade, westwards to the Near East and Africa, eastwards to Malacca, the Spice Islands and even China, to which Vijayanagar sent at least one embassy. South India formed a natural entrepot, in days of monsoon sailing, between the Indian Ocean and China Sea trading areas, and she provided valuable products of her own for international trade: pepper, cinnamon and ginger and fine hand-printed cottons in great variety.

Portuguese travellers in both Vijayanagar and the Muslim sultanates marvelled at the great armies put into the field. They admired the splendour of the cities adorned with floridly ornate temples and spectacular domed mausoleums and noted the luxury of the ruling classes, with their trains of servants, closely guarded harems and their horses and elephants clad in ornate armour. The travellers also noticed, though, that this display of strength and luxury was achieved at the expense of a peasantry living in hovels and clad in rags.

The Bahmani and Vijayanagar kingdoms arose when Muhammad bin Tughluq was drawn north to deal with revolts. Both he and his successor had to wage bitter, fruitless campaigns as far apart as Sind, Gujarat and Bengal, and when these were followed by savage wars of succession disaster overcame the dynasty.

Timur

At the end of the fourteenth century the Muslim position in India was shaken by the sudden appearance of Timur. Born in 1336 he was the most ferocious of the nomadic adventurers who came out of central Asia to conquer the world. In one of his early battles he was wounded by an arrow in the leg which left him with a limp. Because of this he became known as Timur-i-lang, Timur the lame, or Tamerlane.

Timur built up his power in central Asia on the remnants of the empire of Genghis Khan. In quick succession he conquered

ASIA BEFORE THE EUROPEAN CONQUESTS

Date	India	China	Japan	Mongol conquests
1000	Mahmud of Ghazni invades India	Reforms of Wang An Shih	Gosanjo emperor (1068)	
	Rajendra Chola (1014–35)		Power of Fujiwara broken	
		Hui Tsung (1101–35)		Mongol expansion under Genghis Khan
	The Ghaznevids in the Punjab	Division of China between the Chin and the Sung	Struggle between the Taira and the Minamoto	
	Invasion of India by Muhammad Ghuri		Yorimoto establishes shogunate at Kamakura (1192)	
1200	Delhi sultanate	Peking taken by Genghis Khan (1215)	Hojo regency	Conquest of central Mongolia, China and Turkestan
	The Slave dynasty (1206–90)		Failure of Mongol expeditions (1274–81)	
	Iltutmish (1211–36)			
	Balban (1266–87)		Revival of Buddhism	Mongols in Persia, Caucasia and southern Russia
	Khalji dynasty (1290–1320)			
1300	Expansion of Delhi sultanate into south India		Overthrow of Hojo regency	
		Mongol or Yüan dynasty (1279–1368)		Mongols expelled from southern China
	Tughluq dynasty (1320–1413)	Kublai attacks Japan and Indo-China	Civil war between the Southern and Northern dynasties	
	Muhammad Tughluq (1325–51)	Ming dynasty founded by Hung wu (1368)		
	Timur's raid on India (1398)			Timur invades Persia, Russia and India
1400	Sayyid dynasty (1414–51)	Yung-lo emperor (1403–24): moves capital to Peking		
	Lodi dynasty (1451–1526)		Muromachi period	Death of Timur (1405)
	Portuguese reach India (1498): take Goa in 1511	Chinese fleets sail west to India and Africa (1405–33)		
1500	Babur overthrows Lodis (1526); First Mogul empire	Portuguese settle at Macao (1556)	St Francis Xavier first preaches Christianity in Japan (1549)	
	Afghans retake north India (1539–55)	Wan-li emperor (1573–1620): growth of eunuch power	Portuguese merchants at Nagasaki (1569)	
	Akbar refounds and organizes Mogul empire in India (1556–1605)		Oda Nobunaga builds up a central power (1560–82)	
			Hideyoshi consolidates and organizes (1582–98)	
1600	Jahangir succeeds Akbar (1605)	Manchus take Peking (1644)	Ieyasu founds the Tokugawa shogunate (1603) lasting to 1868	
1650				

Transoxiana, Persia, Syria, Turkistan and most of Asia Minor. He was then attracted by the wealth of India. In 1398, he proclaimed a holy war against the infidels and descended on India with a vast army. Before his first battle he ordered his troops to kill all the men, to make prisoners of the women and children and to plunder and lay waste all their property. This instruction became the general pattern of behaviour during the year that Timur's army was in India. At the siege of the fort of Kator 10,000 Hindus were killed in an hour and Timur adopted his usual practice of heaping their skulls in a pile in the shape of a minaret.

Thereafter the demoralized Indians offered only ineffectual resistance to Timur as he moved on Delhi. Eventually Sultan Mahmud gathered an army to oppose him and the two forces met on the field of Panipat outside Delhi. A grim event occurred before the battle which showed Timur's callous disregard for human life. By this time his troops had gathered more than 100,000 Hindu prisoners. As it was felt that they could neither be left in the camp nor released orders were given that they be massacred.

Timur subsequently defeated Sultan Mahmud and sacked Delhi. His undisciplined hordes then pushed through northern India, displaying ferocious cruelty towards the people, who were killed or carried off into slavery in their thousands. The devastation and disruption allowed the warlike Rajput clans to reassert themselves in Rajputana, Gwalior and the lands between the Ganges and the Jumna, withholding both tribute and obedience. Beyond this Hindu barrier provinces such as Gujarat, Malwa or Bengal emerged as independent Muslim kingdoms.

Gujarat remained independent for a century and a half under sultans famous for their judgement and valour—or for their enormous appetite and immunity to poison. The beauty of the Sarkhej palace complex and of the Ahmedabad mosques, with their delicately carved minarets, the great output of fine cottons, silks and indigo, the wealth of shipping, and the technical skill of the army, the first in India to use firearms, gave lustre to the dynasty.

Bengal remained isolated from main currents even longer, notable for agricultural plenty and for its Muslim rulers' tolerance and patronage of Hindu literature and culture. Both played a considerable part in the spread of Islam through the Indonesian archipelago.

The long independence of these old provinces of Delhi makes it clear that the rulers

Opposite, the great Portuguese fort at Aguada in Goa, on the west coast of India, epitomized the determination with which the Europeans intended to protect their new trading contacts from interference. Goa became the headquarters of Portuguese trade in India.

Below left, Timur's armies descending a mountain on their way to invade India in 1398.

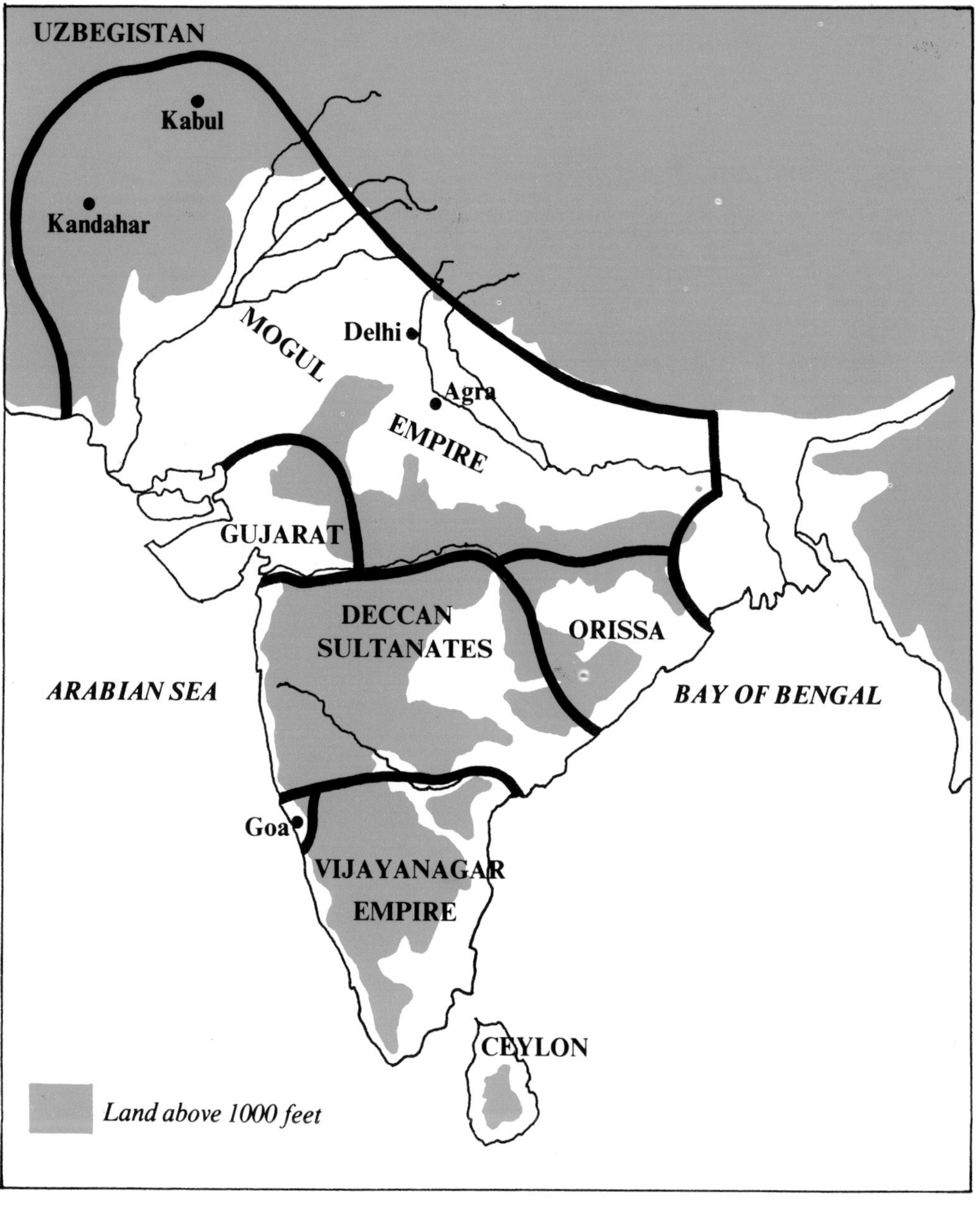

who took over the capital after Timur's holocaust had been unable to impose unity even upon northern India. In fact not until 1451, when an Afghan governor of the Punjab overthrew his master and proclaimed himself sultan at Delhi, was the rebuilding of an empire begun. The following century is the story of Afghan efforts to weld north India into a whole again.

The kings of the Lodi tribe

The pressure of poverty and of the Mongols sweeping across Central Asia had for many years driven the Afghan clans down from their hills to seek their fortune in India. In the fourteenth century, as their numbers grew, they had made abortive bids for power in Multan, Gujarat and the Deccan. Now in 1451 the incompetence of the Sayyid rulers installed by Timur had delivered Delhi into the hands of Bahlul Khan Lodi. He hastened to call yet more Afghans to hold what he had seized: 'Come to this country. The name of sovereignty will remain with me, but the lands I have taken and may conquer shall be shared among us as brothers.' Men of his own Lodi and of other clans, Farmuli, Lohani, Niyazi and Sur, responded. As he pushed east conquering Jaunpur in the middle Ganges valley and then Bihar, Bahlul assigned large fiefs (feudal estates held on condition of service) to the leaders of the clans. They in turn sent for other leaders among their fellow tribesmen, assigning to them the revenues from districts or villages within their fiefs, in return for the maintenance of a set number of mailed horsemen ready for service. The Afghan clan structure proved an admirable recruiting agency, while the tribal settlements around the leading nobles, bound together by ties of kinship, were apt instruments for holding down the countryside.

Bahlul Lodi reigned for thirty years and successively reduced the turbulent Mewatis between the Ganges and Jumna and the Rajputs to their south and then overthrew the kingdom of Jaunpur, a rival to Delhi ever since its sack by Timur. His successor Sikandar Shah, from a forward base at Agra, seized a ring of great Rajput fortresses, Kalpi, Chanderi and Ranthambhor, to guard the southern passes into Malwa. In 1517, after Sikandar's death, his son Ibrahim completed the arc by taking Gwalior. Once again the Delhi sultanate stretched from the Punjab through Gwalior and Bundelkhand to the borders of Bengal. The consolidation of Afghan power was then interrupted by a Mogul invader, Babur, who killed Ibrahim Shah Lodi at Panipat on the approaches to Delhi in 1526. He followed this up by defeating the great clan leaders in eastern India in 1529.

Sher Khan the Sur

After Babur's death in 1530 the Afghans rallied in Jaunpur and Gujarat to challenge his son Humayun. These first counterstrokes failed. But in Bihar, Sher Khan of the Sur clan was assembling a new Afghan power. His grandfather, a horse dealer in central Afghanistan, had come to the Punjab at Bahlul Lodi's call and secured a small fief. His father had moved to Jaunpur, serving the governor.

Sher Khan going east again had become guardian to the young Lohani governor of Bihar and now by force, fraud and treachery had made himself master of Bihar and Bengal. In 1593 and 1540 he quite outgeneraled Humayun and drove the Moguls headlong out of India. Sher Shah strongly fortified the northwest and then turned to deal with the Rajputs. Under the leadership of Rana Sangram Singh of Mewar they had become very formidable, a Muslim historian mourning that, 'there was not a single ruler of the first rank in all these great countries like Delhi, Gujarat and Mandu who was able to make head against him.' Their power, though checked in a fierce battle by Babur, was still threatening. Sher Shah now drove them back in desperate campaigns, taking Ajmer and the magnificent hill for of Chitor to clear the way for his conquest of Malwa and Raisen to open the way south. From the Punjab, meanwhile, his governor pushed down river to Multan. In 1545, just as Rajput Kalinjar fell, Sher Shah died of wounds, but his son Islam Shah was able to maintain intact the whole Afghan empire, a twelve hundred miles swathe from the Indus to Brahmaputra. Not till 1556, after Islam Shah's death, was Humayun able to retake north India for the Moguls, and not until 1575 did his son the Emperor Akbar annex the last Afghan kingdom of Bihar and Bengal.

Humayun's reconquest, like Babur's earlier victory, had been made possible by Afghan disunity. The tribal structure might aid recruitment and settlement, but clan independence made the maintenance of imperial unity extremely difficult. There was constant tension between sultan and nobles.

Initially Bahlul could rely on Lodi strength in the Punjab, on Afghan awareness of the threats to their infant kingdom and on the rewards he could offer during

Above, Mogul miniature of a battle, inside and outside a town's walls. Miniature painting, of realistic scenes of court life, legends and recent history, was the finest achievement of Mogul art.

Left, the three great founders of the Mogul empire, with their attendants. To the left is Babur (1483–1530), who founded the empire, with its capital at Kabul in Afghanistan; in the centre is Timur, from whom Babur claimed to be descended, and on the right is Babur's son Humayun (ruled 1530–56).

Opposite, India in the sixteenth century; the Mogul Empire gradually won control of the south, exploiting the conflicts between Muslim sultanates and the Hindu Vijayanagar empire.

years of constant success. Even so he always treated the great clan chiefs with deference —as confederates rather than servants. Sikandar adopted the older Turkish royal style, issuing his commands from the throne and demanding that his missives be respectfully received. But since the kingdom was growing, assignments of land revenue could still be freely made and the chiefs not held to strict account for the monies they collected. But as external threats seemed to fade and as expansion ceased, royal control weakened.

Bahlul had set aside only modest areas for the crown, while assigning the revenues of large tracts to his supporters. By his grandson's day the great chiefs looked on their grants as hereditary and resented any transfers or control by the sultan. Moreover, since it was the clan leaders rather than the sultan who enlisted tribesmen and assigned them fiefs or shares in village revenues, it was to these leaders, often kinsmen, that the soldiers' loyalty was given. Ibrahim Lodi fell because of this structural weakness in the Afghan sultanate.

Sher Shah rose to power by exploiting Afghan divisions astutely switching sides in a triangular clan struggle for Oudh and Bihar. However once he had climbed to kingship by conquering rich Bengal and routing the Moguls he was careful to strengthen central control. He pretended to be humble when dealing with the chiefs but at the same time took care to enlarge the standing army. He also posted royal garrisons in the great fortresses from Rohtas in the Punjab to Rajmahal in Bengal, including many Hindu musketeers from Bihar, the centre of his personal power. There were still great frontier commands, such as that of Haibat Khan Niyazi in Multan, carrying

large revenue assignments, but care was taken to prevent the chiefs underpaying their troops, while royal branding of their horses prevented fraud at muster. The nobles were recalled at intervals for service under Sher Shah's eye, while a system of trunk roads and posting stations and an efficient spy network made surveillance possible even at a distance.

At Islam Shah's accession some of the nobles attempted to reassert themselves and oppose him. He became more autocratic in consequence, dispersing some clans and driving the Niyazis from Multan into exile. When he could he substituted cash payments from the treasury for the assignment of revenues which gave nobles too much independence. The branding regulations were rigidly enforced, newswriters were attached to every army, and Islam Shah made increasing use of Hindu officers. There were, for example, the talented Todar Mal, later finance minister of the Mogul emperor Akbar, and Hemu, who proved a brilliant general, and many others in the revenue department.

Both Sher Shah and Islam Shah also strengthened their rule by their care for justice and their encouragement of trade. The acquisition of Bengal opened the whole Ganges valley to overseas trade, while the construction of roads provided with caravansarais (inns for travellers) fostered inland trade. Still more important was reform of the land revenue system, mainstay of all Indian kingdoms. The perennial problem was to know how much the country would yield and how to ensure collection of what was due. The Lodis had relied on the *qanungos*, hereditary recorders of village payments, and upon inspection of the ripening crops in assessing revenues, and if grants yielded more to the chiefs than intended little could be done.

Over his wider empire Sher Shah imposed a tighter, bureaucratic control. His hierarchy of officials down to village level regularly measured the area which each peasant put under crop. They laid down an imperial schedule of average yields for every crop, and with the acreage known a demand equivalent to one-third of the expected harvest could be made upon the cultivator in advance. Such a system removed much of the guesswork from financial administration and prevented the chiefs drawing more from their assignments than the cost of their military contingents entitled them to. Crown revenues increased, those of chiefs and intermediaries declined. The display of royal dignity which the Sur sultans made thus rested on solid foundations.

Islam Shah died in 1553 and his son, a boy of twelve, was put upon the throne. The restive nobles, chafing under Islam Shah's autocracy, leapt at the opportunity. Within three days the lad had been murdered by his uncle, Mohammed Adil Shah. Within a month several rival claimants to the throne were in the field. For a while, Sultan Adil's Hindu general Hemu prevented collapse, but in 1554 Humayun led his Mogul troops from Kabul to seize Lahore and by July 1555 he was master of Delhi. Humayun's early death momentarily revived Afghan hopes. However, with the Sur empire now divided among three claimants, the young Akbar was able to destroy one army at

Panipat later in 1556 and defeat all the other leading Afghans the following year.

The Mogul conquerors

The divisions within Afghan tribal society may explain the Lodi and Sur collapses—but why did the Moguls succeed? Babur, a Turk, had been driven in defeat from his Central Asian kingdom to the strongholds of Afghanistan when, with a mere twelve thousand mailed horsemen, he clattered down the passes to victory in the Punjab plains. In 1555 an elderly Humayun, a sometime penniless exile in Persia, led the Moguls back into India, only to die by feckless accident six months later, leaving a boy as heir.

Babur's own *Memoirs*, a classic autobiography, an adventure story vibrant with life, provide one answer as to how the Moguls succeeded, for they reveal how thoroughly he believed in his right to rule. He and his descendants were very conscious of their descent from Timur and Genghis Khan and were proud of their ancestors. In 1494, at the age of eleven, Babur succeeded to mountainous Farghana in modern Uzbegistan. When fourteen he wrested the oasis city of Samarkand from his cousin, at eighteen he lost it. At twenty-one he conquered once-Timurid Kabul and from this new base, with Persian help, again took Samarkand. When he could not hold it, he turned to India instead, defeated Ibrahim Lodi and carved out a new empire.

Babur inherited a position in a ruling family, and once he had shown that he could hold his own among half-brothers and uncles who took his youth or misfortune as an invitation to overthrow rather than to protect him he also inherited a following. He could usually rely on support from some Timurids and Turks and even from the unreliable Mongols. But their loyalty had constantly to be earned by the exercise of leadership—as when he led his nobles and followers over the snow-covered passes from Khorasan, beating a track himself through the breast-deep snow and refusing the comfort of a cave while his men slept in the open.

Above, the Emperor Humayun (ruled 1530–56) in his court. His failure to prevent the rising of Sher Khan in the 1530s cost him his empire until 1555 when he won back control of northern India with Persian help. Royal Academy of Arts, London.

Above left, the Mogul Emperor Akbar (ruled 1556–1605) receiving a Persian ambassador at his court in Agra in 1565. Persian influence was strong at the Mogul court, and it is particularly evident in the miniature painting of the period. Victoria and Albert Museum, London.

Opposite left, Babur receiving a state visitor.

Opposite right, the Emperor Akbar receiving gifts. Despite the splendour of his court his authority resided in the acceptance of his rule by his subjects. During the seventeenth century Mogul power evaporated as their intolerance of Hinduism made them unpopular. Victoria and Albert Museum, London.

Birth, leadership, success were essential and even these at times might barely suffice. Thus, following the victory at Panipat, his nobles clamoured to return to Kabul when the Indian hot weather set in, even though they had been rewarded with great riches. Babur with difficulty restrained them, commenting bitterly, 'When I set out from Kabul this last time I had raised many of low rank to the dignity of nobles, in the expectation that had I chosen to pass through fire and water they would have followed me.' Again only stirring speeches and dramatic gestures from Babur held his men steady for the decisive battle against the Rajputs. Although there was no fierce clan loyalty or refusal to recognize the royal prerogative such as had weakened the Afghans, Babur found that the empire he had assembled between Kabul and the middle Ganges was almost as precarious a structure as the Lodi kingdom. It was still a personal construction, no more solid than the loose and shifting loyalties of the motley handful of Timurids, Mongols, Uzbegs and client Afghans on which it was based. If proof were needed, Humayun's reign provided it.

Humayun inherited a kingdom and in dashing campaigns in Gujarat and Bihar enlarged it and displayed great personal valour. But thereafter he showed himself indolent and indecisive, and when disaster overtook him at Sher Shah's hands his brothers, nobles and troops quickly deserted. While Humayun went into exile, his more competent if faithless brother Kamran took over his followers and built a kingdom in Afghanistan. It was not until 1553 that Humayun was able to turn the tables on Kamran, and even then it was two years before he could return to Delhi.

If personality betrayed Humayun, it triumphed in Akbar. In 1556, as a young boy, he succeeded to a makeshift and precarious kingdom. For four years a most able, loyal Persian, his guardian Bairam Khan, threw back Afghan counterstrokes and prevented disaffection weakening the Mogul kingdom from within. Thereafter Akbar took command, showing all the personal magnetism, generalship, judgement and imagination of his grandfather Babur. Typical was his nine-day, six hundred-mile ride with 3,000 horsemen to crush a rebellious army in Gujarat 20,000 strong.

Such leadership and driving energy created in one lifetime an empire as extensive as that earlier built up by Khaljis and Tughluqs. First the Malwa plateau, then the Rajput territories on the western flank and in 1573 the province of Gujarat fell before him. Delhi was thus linked with the western ocean and given control of India's richest manufacturing province. In 1573 the young Afghan ruler of Bengal refused to recognize Mogul suzerainty. Akbar, ignoring the torrential monsoon rains, drove him back into Bengal, which was annexed in 1576. Delhi thus gained another outlet to the sea, and the foodstuffs, silks, fine muslins and saltpetre of a most profitable province. In

1586 Kashmir, in 1592 Orissa and in 1595 Sind were added, completing the re-unification of the whole north.

Not content, Akbar then turned upon the Deccan. Here the Bahmani Empire had disintegrated early in the sixteenth century into five successor sultanates. This had come about because of the conflict between its foreign-born nobility, Persian, Arab and Mogul, often Shia Muslims, with the Decanni Muslims and Hindu converts who were orthodox Sunni Muslims. Their rivalries had permitted a great increase in the power of Vijayanagar, especially under Ramaraja, who was to ally himself with Ahmadnagar and Golconda against Bijapur and then with Bijapur against Ahmadnagar, inflicting great losses on all the sultanates.

In 1565 the Muslim sultans united their whole force at Talikota, overwhelmed the vast Vijayanagar host, slew Ramaraja and destroyed his capital. Then, having eliminated this danger from the south, the sultans found themselves threatened from the Mogul north. Before his death in 1605 Akbar had made deep inroads into the most northerly Deccan sultanates, Berar and Ahmadnagar.

Had Akbar's empire remained a merely personal structure it might have vanished with its creator. But the Mogul empire endured—in strength until 1712, as a still potent name until the last emperor was deposed at Delhi in 1857. Such longevity implies the existence of efficient institutions, a broad measure of popular acceptance, some special aura round the dynasty. These, too, were Akbar's gifts.

When Babur invaded India his nobles and troops were mainly Turki or Mogul, with some Persian and a few Afghans. In his *Memoirs* he sees himself as a foreigner in India, faced by hostility and treachery from both Muslim and Hindu. Akbar also began by depending on nobles who were three-quarters foreign born, chiefly central Asian. His successes attracted many able men to India, including more Persians, and this enabled him to rely less heavily on his own Timurid stock. But more important and imaginative was his employment of Rajput nobles.

In 1562 the Rajput ruler of Amber (Jaipur) sought Akbar's protection and gave him his daughter in marriage. The political marriage was not new in Muslim India, but the result of this was. For the happiness brought by his wife, mother of his first son Jahangir, and the fine service rendered by her relatives led Akbar to entrust Rajputs with the highest offices and most responsible commands. Some clans rejected imperial service and fought for their independence. Many more became loyal, trusted servants of the state, linked by marriage with the imperial family itself. By according them equal status with his Turki or Persian nobles, and by abolishing such general symbols of Hindu inferiority as the *jizya* or poll-tax on non-Muslims Akbar made the Rajputs partners in the Mogul empire for the next two centuries. A few other Hindus, such as the *khatri* Todar Mal, Islam Shah's officer, who now became a Mogul finance minister and general, reached high positions. Many more were employed as clerks or intermediaries. The Moguls who were once aliens became an Indian dynasty which was accepted by most of the people.

The change was aided by the fact that Akbar, like others of his family, was not very orthodox in religion. As a child he had been much with Persians, Muslims of the Shia sect. He was also attracted to Sufi mysticism. By now several Sufi orders were at work in India, and, equally important, devotional mysticism within Hinduism had spread across north India from the Tamil south. Whether stressing loving self-surrender to God or a more sin-conscious hope in His mercy, this *Bhakti* movement rejected the ritualism and reasoning of older Hinduism. Preachers like Kabir or Nanak, the founder of the Sikh religion, speaking directly to all classes of men rejected the rigidities of caste and the pretentions of the Brahmins.

Akbar's questioning mind therefore found it easy to step from court debates about Muslim tenets to wider discussions about Hinduism, Jainism, Zoroastrianism and, after 1580, when Portuguese Jesuits reached court, Christianity. As a result, in 1582 Muslim orthodoxy and the older nobility, both jealous of newcomers, joined in rebellion. This Akbar crushed and thereupon ended his religious discussions by promulgating his own *Din i Ilahi* or Divine Faith, which drew ideas from many religions and was a cult formed round the emperor himself. This religious Order emphasized his semi-divine status—pictorially indicated by the halo round the emperor's head—and raised him above rulers, Muslims or Hindu, as overlord of all.

The institutions of the Mogul state

Continued success, cultivated splendour divine right, the good fortune of four long reigns in succession, these lifted the Mogul throne above its supporters. Akbar who recruited widely into his service aristocracy was not compelled, as Bahlul Lodi or Sher Shah had been, to rely only on clan or tribal support. By his death an imperial bureaucracy had been created with regular procedures, inter-ministerial checks which prevented undue concentration of power and patterns of promotion which favoured talent as well as birth. The administration was sufficiently self-regulating, impersonal and secure to subordinate even the greatest official to the rulers, while permitting all to speak frankly.

The empire was no longer divided, sultanate fashion, into semi-hereditary military fiefs and marcher lordships. Instead

Opposite left, the Emperor Akbar supervising the building of the Red Fort at Agra in 1566. The Mogul Empire in India was initially based on forts established on the major trade routes of northern India.

Opposite right, Akbar's siege train prepares to attack Ranthambor, in Rajastan, in 1568. Akbar greatly increased the extent of the Mogul Empire, especially in northwestern India and the Indus valley.

there were regular provinces, districts and village circles, each with executive and revenue officers reporting weekly or monthly according to departmental codes to their ministries at the capital. In the towns a commissioner was responsible for police, market regulations, public order and morals, while even the larger villages had a *qazi* to administer canon law to the Muslim population. Honest administration was further encouraged by the appointment to all provincial headquarters and armies of imperial newswriters reporting independently, by the tours of the emperor and by the use of an intelligence service.

At the capital, the *wazir* or chief minister, who under the sultanate had often been all powerful while he survived, now had to share authority with a paymaster-general, high steward and revenue minister. All important actions required the countersignature of one or other of these ministers, though each of course had specific departmental duties and a separate secretariat and large body of specialist clerks. The bureaucracy so formed was both loyal and efficient. This can be seen in the work of the revenue ministry, with its four departments in charge respectively of crown lands, salaries, accounts and audit.

Sher Shah and Islam Shah had already tightened up revenue assessment and collection by introducing measurement of the area sown and a single, pre-calculated scale of payments per crop. Akbar's officials went on to make due allowance for variations first in market prices from province to province and then in regional crop yields. Finally they collected detailed statistics of the average yields and prices for each district of the empire, for both spring and autumn harvest for each of some forty crops during the last ten years. These they averaged out in complete tables from which any district official could readily decide the cash revenue payment per acre which the local cultivators would have to pay on whatever crops they sowed. A continuous recalculation of the moving average ensured that variations in harvest yields and long-term price changes would be allowed for.

When Akbar died in 1605 his empire stretched from Kandahar to Calcutta, from the Himalayas to the Deccan plateau. His administration, both strong and efficient, attracted and made room for the talents of Turk, Uzbeg, Persian, Indian Muslim and Rajput alike. He had ignored or softened the religious differences between his subjects. His court provided the unifying experience of common imperial services and fostered a common culture, Persian in language and style, but enriched by Indian contributions in music, art and architecture. Jahangir, his half-Rajput son, inherited a throne exalted above all others.

Above, the Mogul city of Fatehpur Sikri, in north India, which was founded by the Emperor Akbar in 1569 to be his capital and now survives almost intact.

Left, a market scene in Delhi during Babur's reign in the 1520s. Mogul power was asserted by control of the major trade routes of northern India: as foreigners to India, the Moguls had to rule by a combination of force and compromise with the existing authorities.

Below left, a sixteenth-century garden in Kashmir, high up in the Himalayas. The fruits include melons, grapes, asparagus and aubergines. Royal Commonwealth Society Library, London.

Opposite left, a Mogul prince on horseback, carrying a lance. Royal Academy of Arts, London.

Opposite right, the Mogul Emperor Babur saluting the standards by throwing kumin on them. British Museum, London.

Chapter 28

The Ancient Kingdoms of Southeast Asia

From early times Southeast Asia lay at the crossroads of the maritime trade route between east and west. Several ancient kingdoms emerged in this area, where foreign influences joined with indigenous cultures to form societies which reflected the diverse ethnic origins of the various peoples.

One of the earliest of the states was Funan, which developed in the valley of the Mekong. It was apparently founded by an Indian merchant who married a Cambodian princess, thus establishing a Hindu kingdom in the East Indies. Funan is the Chinese form of the Khmer *phnom*, meaning 'mountain', a name which probably derived from the practice of the early rulers, who built their temples on high ground and called themselves 'the kings of the mountain'. The importance of Funan in this early period was that it provided a convenient landfall in the east for the numerous small trading vessels which made the journey across the Erythraean Sea, as the Indian Ocean was then known.

From the first century AD there was a growing interest in the west in the maritime trade of southeast Asia. In western literature it figures as a golden land where precious metals were to be obtained. The Latin geographer Pomponius Mela, writing in AD 43, referred to the islands of Chryse and Argyre. Pliny in his *Natural History* wrote of the promontory of Chryse. A fuller account was then given by a Greco-Egyptian sea captain in a remarkable work called the *Periplus of the Erythraean Sea*. In it the inhabitants of southeast Asia are described as men with short bodies, broad, flat faces and of a peaceful disposition.

Ptolemy thought of the place as a gold-producing island populated by cannibals with tails. The small vessels which engaged in this trade were forced to make the journey in stages. Funan, which stretched across the southeast Asian mainland to the Bay of Bengal, was the natural landfall for the trans-shipment of goods.

To the east of Funan lived the warrior Cham people who formed the kingdom of Champa in the second century AD. The Chams established a religious centre near Hue, accepted Hinduism and Buddhism and adopted Indian customs.

However, from the beginning the political stability of Champa was menaced by the growth of Chinese influence in the north. As early as the seventh century BC the feudal state of Ch'u displayed an interest in the southern tropical regions. By the third century BC the armies of the Ch'in Empire had penetrated southwards and had briefly occupied the Nam-Viet.

The Ch'in sent a military official named Chao T'o to administer the area. He married a Viet woman, introduced the Chinese language and declared the region independent after the fall of Ch'in, taking the title 'Martial King of Vietnam'. The Han rulers made several attempts to re-establish Chinese control over the area, but they were too preoccupied with the barbarian incursions in the north.

Over the succeeding centuries there were frequent clashes between the Chinese and the Chams. Eventually, in AD 679, the powerful armies of the T'ang swept south and established the protectorate of Annam.

The rise of Chenla

By this time a new power had risen in the Mekong valley to subdue the ancient kingdom of Funan. This was the state of Chenla, whose people were the Khmers or Cambodians. After conquering Funan the Cambodians were weakened by internal dissension and were dominated by the piratical Sailendra kings of Java. However, in the ninth century the Khmers were reunited under King Jayavarman II, who laid the foundations of the great Khmer Empire.

The most enduring achievement of King Jayavarman II and his successors was their extensive and costly building programme. Angkor, their capital, was filled with a profusion of edifices in wood, brick and stone, elaborately carved with Buddhist and Hindu motifs. Outstanding amongst these was Angkor Wat, the sanctuary to Vishnu built by Suryavarman II (1113–50). This complex of buildings, whose ruins still remain, extended over a square mile and is thought to be the largest religious monument in the world.

Between the ninth and the thirteenth centuries the Khmer people maintained their supremacy on the southeast Asia mainland against the Chams, Laos, Burmese and Thais. Periodically the Chinese attempted to extend their control from the north, and on three occasions during the thirteenth century the region was invaded by the Mongols of Kublai Khan.

The island empires

Long before this time the main centre of political and economic activity had moved south, where the insular empires of Java, Sumatra and Borneo had grown in importance. Foremost among these was Srivijaya, which developed from Indian trading settlements in southern Sumatra. After the fourth and fifth centuries, as Funan began to decline, the maritime trade from India moved past Sumatra around the tip of the Malay peninsula, leading to a natural development of the trading settlements scattered along these coasts.

In the fifth century the Chinese pilgrim, Fa-hsien, who had travelled to India by the overland silk route, returned this way by sea. At one stage of his journey (which lasted five months) he was forced to wait at the trading settlement of Yeh-o'O-ti on the northern coast of Borneo for the monsoon winds which would carry him to Canton. He noted then with disapproval that Brahmanism was flourishing in the region while the Buddhist faith was in decline.

By the end of the seventh century the position of Buddhism had greatly improved in southeast Asia. The Chinese monk, I-ching, who travelled to India by the maritime route, stayed for a number of years in Srivijaya where he translated Sanskrit scriptures and contributed to the spread of Mahayana Buddhism.

Throughout the eight and ninth centuries Srivijaya grew in strength. The capital Palembang became a regular port of call for the ships which carried the products from east Africa, Arabia, Persia and the Coromandel coast of India. As its importance grew it attracted trade from the area of the Straits of Malacca and from China. In

Above, a carving from one of the temples at Borobudur in Java, one of the largest and most complex Buddhist shrines in the world. It was built in the ninth century AD.

Left, a relief from the thirteenth-century Khmer temple of Bayon, built when the Khmer Empire was at the height of its glory.

Opposite, a statue of a woman, taken from a relief showing details of the life of Buddha from the temple of Borobudur; its style is influenced by the earlier art of India, in its tranquil, rounded forms.

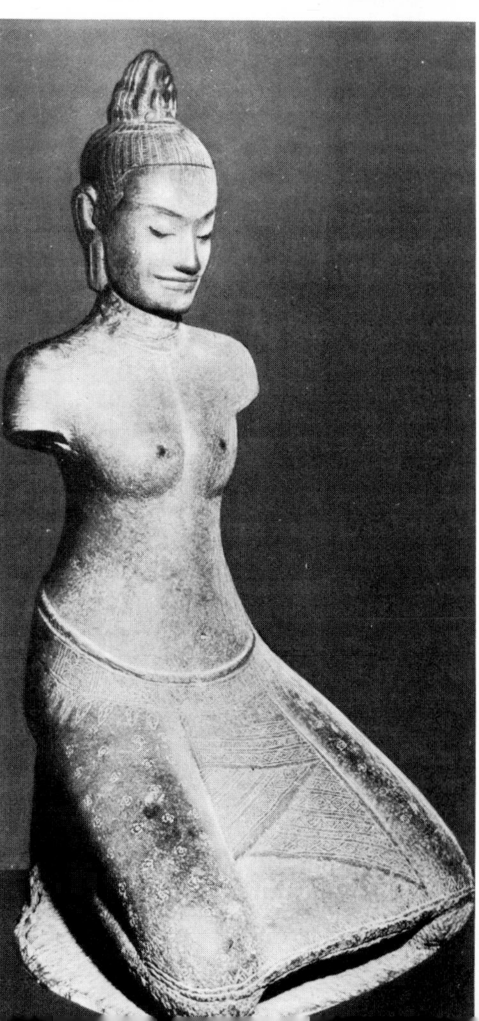

fact, in time the vigorous activity of the Persian and Arab traders was extended up the coastline to Canton, which in T'ang times assumed a cosmopolitan character. After 850 Srivijaya united with the Sailendras kingdom of Java and became the dominant power in southeast Asia. By the twelfth century its influence reached as far as Formosa in the north.

However, from the thirteenth century Srivijaya began to decline. An increasing demand for the natural products of the area (gold, tin, ivory, ebony, camphorwood), and, above all, the spices so invaluable to the medieval world (pepper, nutmeg and cloves) encouraged the growth of the states where these products were to be found. In turn, the Java states of Kediri, Singosari, Malayu and Majapahit began to dominate the politics of the area and to absorb the all-important spice trade.

For over a century Majapahit, the greatest and also the last of these Hindu-Javanese states, claimed domination over the islands as well as the mainland as far north as Annam. The spread of Islam eastwards in the fourteenth century then brought about the commercial supremacy of the Muslim centre of Malacca, which was itself eclipsed a century later when the Portuguese arrived to usher in a new age.

Opposite top, the front view of the huge temple of Angkor Wat, dedicated to Vishnu in the early twelfth century. At its centre was housed the royal phallus, symbol of the emperor's authority.

Opposite bottom left, one of the reliefs that cover the walls of the Angkor Wat temple. It has been suggested that the cost of these building projects contributed to the ruin of the Khmer Empire.

Opposite bottom right, a twelfth-century Khmer statue depicting the goddess Tara; freestanding sculpture was far more static and reserved than the bas-reliefs of the same date. Musée Guimet, Paris.

Below, a head of the god Lokeshvara, commissioned by the Khmer king Jayavarman VII, who expanded the Empire in Cambodia.

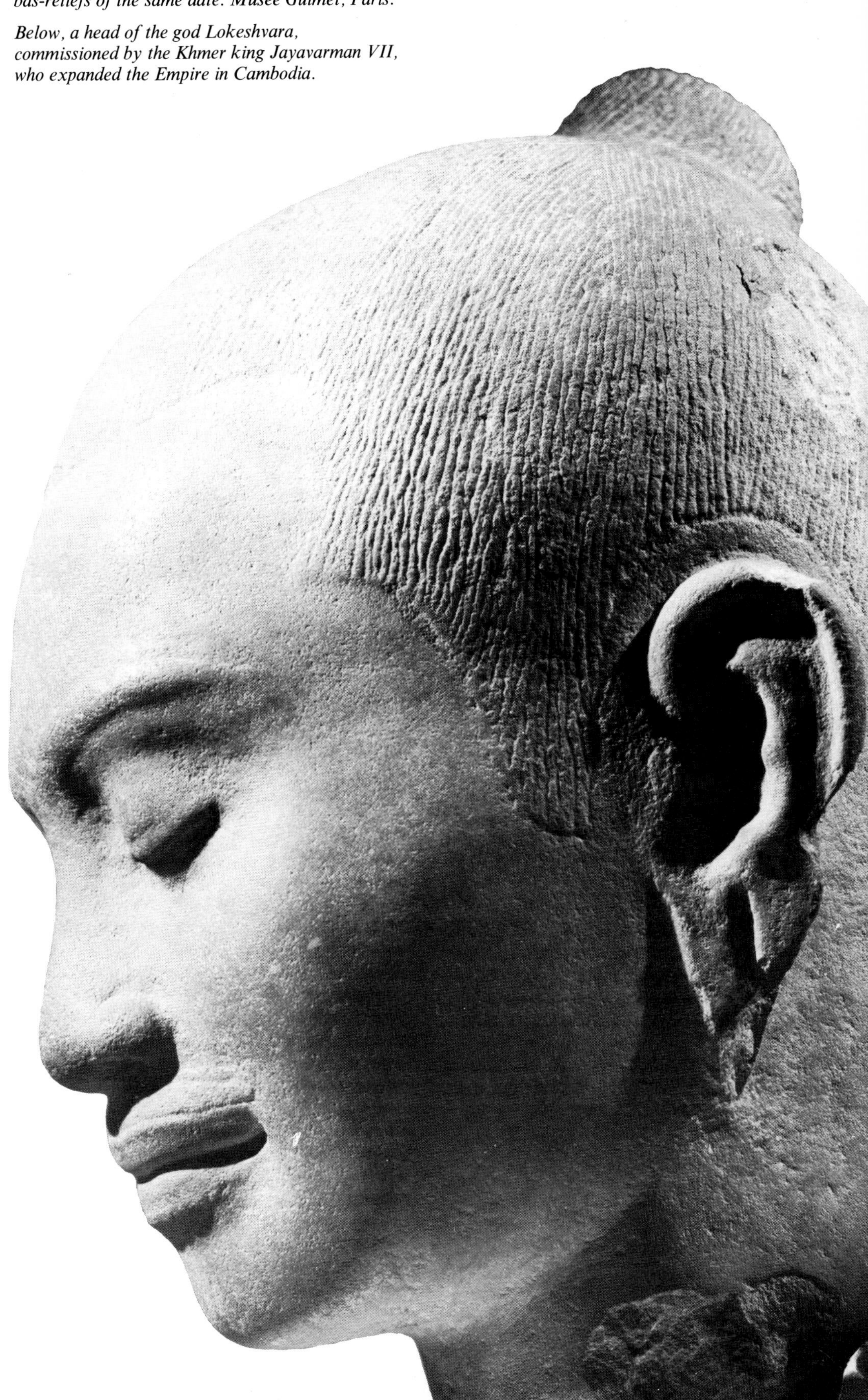

Chapter 29

The Chinese Experience

The period of political disunity which had emerged in China after the fall of the T'ang was brought to an end in 960 by the Sung. The Sung emperors, who ruled from 960 to 1297, established the third of the great dynasties in Chinese history. Both in character and achievements this period contrasted sharply with those of the Han and the T'ang.

For 1,000 years, from the time when the Ch'in had first united the country, the Chinese had been outward-looking and expansionist, displaying a confident and aggressive attitude in foreign affairs which had enabled them to extend Chinese influence far into central Asia, Korea and Annam. In the mid-T'ang period this expansive phase came to an end.

The steady pressure of barbarian tribes along the northern and western land frontiers created a critical problem for the Chinese during the tenth and eleventh centuries. Militarily much weaker and increasingly forced to rely on mercenaries, the pacifically inclined Sung people slowly yielded to the barbarian pressure from the north. From the beginning they had to come to terms with the powerful Liao kingdom of the Tartars, which dominated Manchuria, Mongolia and a substantial part of northern China. To keep them pacified the Sung abandoned China's traditional policy of demanding tribute in recognition of Chinese suzerainty. Instead, an annual tribute of gold and silk was sent to the Liao.

In the twelfth century, during the reign of Hui Tsung, the Juchen tribes to the north of the Liao arose in revolt. The Sung rather unwisely formed an alliance with them, with the intention of bringing the Liao more under control. It was a disastrous move. The Juchen swept south, completely defeated the Liao in 1125 and set up the Chin dynasty.

The Sung made desperate efforts to come to terms with their new and belligerent neighbours, but within a few years a Chin army had raided the Sung capital at K'ai-feng, capturing the emperor and most of his court. The remnants of the Sung government then fled to the south where they regrouped themselves under a son of Hui Tsung, who formed the Southern Sung dynasty with his capital at Hangchow.

In this new political setting the dynasty made a surprizing recovery and developed new activities, leaving an impressive record of achievement over the next 150 years, when it was finally conquered by the Mongols of Kublai Khan.

The move to the south did not interrupt the steady development of technical knowledge which is characteristic of the Sung period. Significant advances were made in the fields of medicine, biology, architecture, mathematics as well as military techniques. References in Chinese writings around 1000 show that the explosive qualities of gunpowder, known in China from early times, were effectively applied with catapults against the Chin. Also, after their move to the south, the Sung used their increased technical knowledge in water irrigation and conservancy measures, thereby improving the food supply for the large numbers of people who fled to the area from the north.

Sung activity in maritime commerce, in particular, was stimulated by the southern move. From Han times Chinese vessels had traded along the coast and down into southeast Asia, but the greater part of China's foreign trade had been carried overland. The decline of Chinese influence in central Asia during the later T'ang period then encouraged the pattern to change, leading to a steady growth in the importance of maritime traffic between the eighth and the thirteenth centuries. Improved methods of navigation and the construction of larger and more seaworthy ships aided this development.

At the same time, Arab and Persian merchants operating in southeast Asian waters displayed a growing interest in Chinese goods, which were abundantly available after the long period of T'ang prosperity. As a result there was a significant expansion of oceanic trade during the Sung period. This trade was initially under Arab and Persian control and sizeable foreign communities were to be found at various posts along the China coast. However, under the southern Sung the traffic passed into the hands of Chinese merchants who rapidly came to dominate the trade in precious silks, fine Chinese handicrafts and porcelains which were in demand in southeast Asia and further afield.

To a large extent, the growth in this overseas luxury trade reflected the expanding Chinese economy. Despite their recurrent political difficulties, the Sung people lived in a period of rich technical and cultural achievement, which saw the full flowering of centuries of creative development. The artistic perfection of Sung porcelain, particularly the delicately tinted green celadon ware, was even at that time justly prized. The Sung genius also expressed itself in painting. With the decline of Buddhism, artists turned from religious themes and began to experiment in impressionistic landscape and nature paintings.

A vigorous intellectual activity matched these cultural achievements. Literature, which had broken new ground in the T'ang period, flourished and took on new forms. There was a rapid increase in the number of schools and academies. The popular pursuits of urban life, with its theatres, teashops and restaurants, generally reflected the high literacy of the people.

To a large extent, the intellectual renaissance of the Sung is to be explained by the

advances made in printing and book production in this period. From Han times the Chinese had followed the practice of carving classical texts on stone and seals in wood or metal for official and private use.

This led to the development of wood-block printing, which was used extensively during the Buddhist centuries for the production of religious texts. When the blocks were printed in series and then folded the Chinese form of the book appeared. A Buddhist *sutra* was printed in this way in 868. During the following century the whole of the ancient classics were similarly produced. Printing was extensively developed during the Sung period, mostly in block form but with some experimentation in movable type.

Above, a seventeenth-century illustration of the legend of the Emperor Kao-Tsong. He searched the country for the man with whom, he once dreamed, he should share his rule. Eventually he discovered a poor peasant of the right description, whom he made into a minister of state.

Opposite top, the three-storeyed theatre in the grounds of the imperial summer palace, outside Peking.

As in the West at the time of the Renaissance, when the printed book became available, the discovery led to significant advances in scholarship. Vast compilations were made of the classics, early historical records and encyclopedias. This habit, which had developed in late T'ang times, was pursued by the Sung and continued by the succeeding dynasties, turning the Chinese into the most assiduous compilers of documents in the world.

Inevitably, this literary activity aroused a critical spirit and a closer awareness of the classical works so carefully collected. It occurred as well at a time when Buddhism was beginning to lose its hold and when there was a revival of interest in Confucianism and in early Chinese philosophical and political ideals.

Through the efforts of a number of scholars the basic tenets of Confucianism were reinterpreted, reaching a high point of synthesis in the work of Chu Hsi (1130–1200), who established the orthodox view which was to dominate the Chinese outlook until the nineteenth century.

The Chinese outlook

From the beginning the Chinese were intensely naturalistic and rational in their view of the world. In early Chinese thought there was very little speculation on the origin of creation. The emergence of civilization was attributed not to a divine will, but to the intelligence of the ancient sages. Similarly, the evolution of a well-ordered society was regarded essentially as the work of human endeavour.

Human efforts and the welfare of society were likely to be successful if they were in harmony with nature, or rather, with the natural and appointed order of things. Social disorder indicated a violation of the cosmic order, and the instinctive reaction was to restore that balance of forces which would place man in harmony with nature.

This belief lay at the root of the Chinese philosophical outlook. In its broadest terms, there was the concept of the interaction of *yang* and *yin*, the male and female elements, from which all things and relationships flowed.

The inter-relationships of nature, to which man's behaviour should accord, were also represented in the qualities of the five elements, wood, metal, fire, water and earth, each of which acted on the other in a predetermined way. The early naturalists of the Chou period dwelt on the mystical force of these connections and, in time, their theories were written into the content of Taoist and even Confucian thought.

This passion for order and for tabulation dominated the Chinese view of the structure of society. Ideally, this was formed around a well-defined social hierarchy in which everyone knew his place. A predominantly agricultural population was expected to remain content under an educated bureaucracy which looked for guidance to a humane and solicitous emperor.

The cultured man was one who recognized his place in the scheme of things and who lived out his life and made his contribution to the common good without violating the established world order. His conduct was regulated by an ingrained feeling for correct

Left, a Japanese illustration of a Chinese silk loom; the earliest silk woven in China is said to date back to 2460 BC. Chinese silk was profitably imported to Japan.

behaviour, which he knew instinctively without being told. It was firmly believed that man was by nature good and that a government based on virtue could win the hearts of men. These concepts form a substantial part of Chinese philosophical terminology.

The accepted norm was the principle of social righteousness, *yi*, to which people were expected to conform through correct ways of behaviour, *li*, and by maintaining good faith, *hsin*. The *chuntzu* or superior man was one who demonstrated his mastery of *li* by presenting people with examples of his benevolence, *jen*.

Although this code of conduct was applied more rigorously to the upper classes it pervaded all levels of Chinese society and dictated the pattern of the five major relationships of Confucianism: father and son, ruler and subject, husband and wife, elder and younger brother, and friend and friend.

This emphasis on correct relationships greatly strengthened the family system and, through the family, the clan and the guild. Furthermore, by Han times it had been built up into a political creed. Confucianism, which made conformity a virtue, gave successive emperors the willing allegiance of their countless subjects as they pursued the imperial ideal.

Throughout imperial times, the role of the emperor and the state in this structure was not clearly defined. Theoretically, while the emperor was supreme he was also expected to conform to the accepted code of moral conduct. A ruler who acted in an arbitrary manner and destroyed the natural balance could commit the country to a period of calamity. In the popular mind natural catastrophes such as flood or famine were often taken as portents of the failure of the ruler, who could only rightfully expect to enjoy the mandate of heaven if his actions remained in harmony with nature. In his writings the philosopher Mencius even implied that the people had the legal right to rebel if the natural balance was wilfully destroyed.

As the state extended its control it was not always ready to accept this restriction on its behaviour. Ch'in Shih Huang Ti's support of the legalists and his attempt at thought control, as seen in his burning of the books in 213 BC, was an early example of the way in which the ruler sought to apply a different code of values. In time, the concept of *chung* or loyalty to one's superior was given greater prominence. In practice, as in the experience of the early Greeks, there was often a clash between different loyalties, leading to a tragic conflict of right against right.

These beliefs, first formulated at the time of the Han, were overshadowed during the succeeding centuries of foreign invasion and political change. Between the Han and the T'ang dynasties, there was a more ready response to the teachings of Taoism, with its greater appeal to the mystical side of the human spirit, and to Buddhism, with its promise of personal salvation.

By the tenth century the ebb and flow of Chinese expansionism had come to an end. The Sung, menaced by hostile neighbours and thrown back on themselves, developed an awareness of the need to reaffirm and to preserve the essential elements of their own cultural traditions. Thus, at a time when Chinese civilization had reached a level of maturity unparalleled elsewhere in the world, neo-Confucianism was born. Henceforth, the Chinese scholars who controlled the policies of the Confucian state enshrined their cultural achievement and looked back on an idealized past.

The Mongol conquest of China

The Chinese world, which encompased both the densely settled lands of the tropical south and the harsh empty pastures of the Central Asian steppes, was ruled alternately by men from one or other of these regions. In the thirteenth century it was the turn of the northern nomads, the Mongols. Their brilliant, savage leader Genghis Khan began the attack on Sung China in 1211 and his grandson Kublai completed the conquest in 1279, establishing a new dynasty, the Yüan. It was a very foreign dynasty, brutal in conquest, powerfully centralizing, ready to use Muslims, Nestorian Christians and other alien officials from the Mongol conquests in western Asia to supervise the Chinese provincial administration. Kublai and his successors carried out their ceremonial duties as rulers, acknowledged the

Opposite left, Ming painting of a Taoist priest. Taoism developed an elaborated ritual and gave rise to many monasteries.

Opposite right, Ming-period painting of the old philosopher Lao Tsu and his disciples. Lao Tsu's emphasis on power never to be defined by action, his idea of transcendence through passivity and his emphasis on mysticism were all appealing in the stratified structure of Chinese society.

Below, white-glazed porcelain ewer, its shape reflecting a Buddhist influence. It dates from the Sung period (960–1279), when a widespread demand for ceramics in China led to the development of this functional but highly elegant style.

officially accepted moral code of the philosopher Confucius and revived some use of examinations for the recruitment of officials.

But neither these gestures, nor their considerable practical successes, such as refurbishing the eleven-hundred mile canal system between Hangchow and Peking or in extending the use of a standardized paper currency from China to Central Asia and Korea, won acceptance for the dynasty. Mongol patronage of popular Buddhism irritated Confucian scholars—and the meagre allocation of state appointments to the mistrusted Sung south annoyed them even more. When after 1307 a series of short reigns culminated in a civil war in 1328, when inflation undermined the revenue system and a breakdown occurred in the flood control of the Yellow River, revolts against the Mongols began in southern China. In 1368 a new dynasty emerged from the heartlands of the Yangtse valley. After the violence of the Yüan, this new native dynasty, the Ming, ushered in over two hundred and fifty years of stable and comparatively prosperous rule.

The rise of the Ming dynasty

The warlord who founded the dynasty was Hung-wu, an orphan who had secured an education as a Buddhist monk and military experience in the White Lotus secret society. In 1356 his war-band seized Nanking, key to the rice of the Yangtse delta, and from that base he first drove rivals from the southern provinces and then in 1368 expelled the Mongols from their capital Peking. The Mongols were thereafter pursued through the northwest as far as their original centre Karakorum, and by 1382, with the conquest of Szechuan and Yunnan, all China was in Hung-wu's hands. His envoys had already been despatched to announce the establishment of the Ming to China's neighbours and tribute missions had dutifully arrived from southern India, Malaysia, Indonesia, Japan and Korea.

Hung-wu was succeeded by a grandson, but after four years of war the boy was overthrown by his uncle, the commander on the northern frontier. In 1402 this uncle captured Nanking and ascended the throne as Yung-lo. He maintained Nanking's metropolitan status but made Peking the real capital, building there a magnificent nest of cities, with the Forbidden City or palace complex at its heart as a proper setting for the Son of Heaven. From this advance-post of agrarian China he personally led expeditions deep into Outer Mongolia against the nomads and built up the three regional commands which guarded the exposed frontier. Behind Peking was also created the military labour force required to move some twelve million bushels of tax rice a year along the rebuilt Grand Canal system to feed the capital and its army.

At the same time, such was the vigour of the dynasty, a regular administration was newly introduced into the western provinces, while Chinese armies repeated the earlier Mongol invasion of Vietnam, though with no permanent result. More unexpectedly there was a burst of maritime activity. Between 1405 and 1433 the Muslim eunuch Cheng-ho led seven successive fleets, which might mean up to 28,000 men in sixty or more great junks, as far as east Africa, the Red Sea and Persian Gulf. By sacking recalcitrant ports such as Calicut in south India or by carrying off prisoner rulers from Ceylon and Sumatra, and eliciting everywhere tribute and embassies to the Ming, he forced people to acknowledge Chinese power. For a moment landward

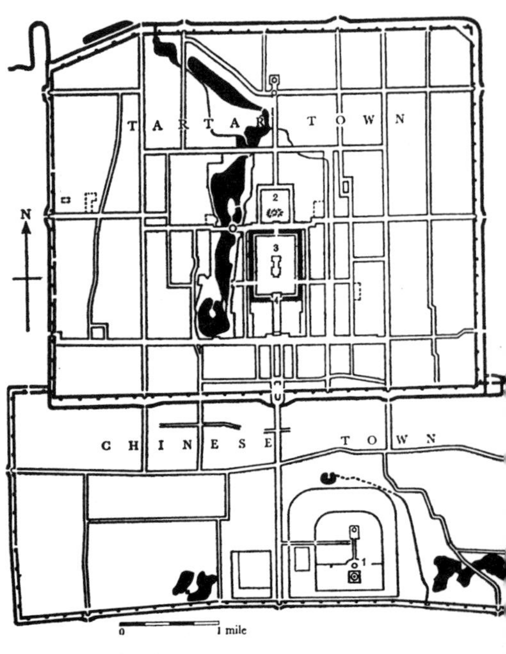

expansion was matched by a stupendous deployment of naval power.

Expansion was made possible by internal reconstruction. The traditional structure of fifteen provinces, subdivided into prefectures, sub-prefectures and nearly twelve hundred districts, was restored, and new registers of land and population were prepared. Thereafter the heavy land revenue demand on the spring and autumn harvests and the grievous burden of labour services imposed by the Mongols could be lightened and more fairly reallocated. Some land was redistributed to the poor and the swollen holdings of the Buddhist temples were reduced. There was also considerable internal migration, with an opening up of the southwest and a return also to the northern provinces.

Cotton cultivation was notably expanded, often under government advice or pressure, while in the later years of the dynasty maize, sweet potatoes and peanuts—the last two probably from the Spanish Philippines—also spread, adding usefully to the crops which could be grown on inferior soils. Large-scale production of porcelain, some of it for export, an increased handicraft production of silk and later of cotton cloth and a growing output of tea, led to an intensification of trade, which was facilitated by the flow of silver from the Philippines and Japan. The state also aided by paving highways, building bridges, refurbishing irrigation works and the system of state granaries and by enlarging of the canal system which by-passed the dangerous Shantung coast.

Physical reconstruction was matched by institutional renewal. A new code of administration and criminal law, freed of Mongol elements, was promulgated in 1397, and the collected statutes of the dynasty, setting out imperial purposes, in 1511. Though Hung-wu had been a Buddhist monk, he restored the traditional patronage of orthodox state Confucianism, and the emperors, fulfilling their ceremonial function as mediators between man and nature, duly sacrificed at the great public altars of Earth and Heaven at the time of each solstice. They likewise resumed an active sponsorship of letters, notably in the great manuscript encyclopedia completed in 1407, which gathered up all past Chinese intellectual achievement, and also in the official histories of the preceding dynasties. The meticulous compilations of official documents produced by the board of historians, and the numerous district gazetteers, botanical and medical works written by individual scholars, reasserted Confucian concern with society and politics and re-established continuity with the civilized tradition of earlier dynasties.

Perhaps the most obvious sign of a return to the orthodox Chinese pattern was the full restoration of state examinations for recruitment to the bureaucracy. Like the Mogul imperial officials, the mandarins were not an hereditary, feudal aristocracy. Those who wished to enter the state service had to prepare for the examinations, as young children by learning the *Three-Character Classic*, a rhymed repository of basic maxims, thereafter by the study with a tutor or at a private or state academy of neo-Confucian texts. Having first qualified in district examinations, candidates could proceed to take the bachelors degree which conferred scholar-official status, together with freedom from labour services and degrading corporal punishment. From such degree holders the lower levels of the imperial services were selected. The more ambitious could later go forward to the masters and doctorate examinations, the latter held at the imperial capital, to qualify themselves for superior posts in the bureaucracy.

The conduct of the examinations, which preserved uniformity and impartiality, made service genuinely open to talent. Their form, a study of the teachings of the Confucian classics about the nature of man and the right ordering of society, ensured that all candidates acquired a common attitude of mind, a public spirit or morality, and a loyalty to the system whose values they shared and from which they derived their prestige. This was important for both the cultural unity and the administrative efficiency of the vast Ming empire, particularly as many lower degree holders, though qualified, would never enter the bureaucracy

Below, bronze lion guarding the Gate of Heavenly Purity in the Peking Imperial Palace.

Opposite top, an imperial dragon, from the Forbidden City, Peking.

Opposite bottom left, view of Peking in 1671, at the time of an embassy from the Dutch East India Company to the emperor. The Europeans were unable to obtain anything more than limited trading concessions in China until the nineteenth century.

Opposite bottom right, the plan of Peking as laid out by the Ming Dynasty in the fifteenth century. It was partly on the site of the old Mongol or Tartar town. At the centre was the Imperial Palace, intended to be the very hub of the civilized world.

but would be expected nonetheless to use their influence in the countryside and also to undertake unpaid public duties on behalf of the government.

The system was not without weaknesses. If the examinations were to test intelligence rather than memory they needed to be open-ended, hence the move towards the general essay question. But if these were to be marked uniformly and fairly throughout China, it was necessary to prescribe an approved approach—that of the Chu Hsi school—to the Confucian classics which were the basis of study. A long series of examinations all limited and stereotyped in this way, might narrow rather than cultivate the mind, as critics within Ming officialdom were later to argue. Again, preparing for the various examinations was a lengthy and expensive task. Many officials entered service in debt and were consequently tempted to reimburse their families by corruption and misuse of power. Office was often found associated with landownership in Ming China—but usually office came first.

Entry to the civil service was not open to all on equal terms. A would-be scholar-official did well to be born in the south-eastern provinces, where kinship organizations among the scholars who had fled before the Mongols were strong, rather than in the northwest. Likewise more scholars came from the towns where schools and libraries were plentiful than from the countryside, and more from the families of officials or merchants with money to pay for their long training than from peasant homes. It was possible indeed to purchase a degree, though not to buy office, under an honours system which enabled government to widen its support at some sacrifice of principle. Nevertheless it is clear that under the Ming recruitment by examination did secure the services of many men of ability within the bureaucracy and outside it. The spread of printing from Sung times had widened the circle of the literate. And the records show that even after the initial influx of Ming supporters at the foundation of the dynasty, nearly half of all officials with a doctorate continued to come from new non-mandarin families. Conversely, of course, they show that officials were less able than in Europe to entrench their families in office and power. It seems certain that a boy from a working class family had a better chance of entering the higher civil service in sixteenth-century Ming China than he had in twentieth-century Britain.

The degree-holder who was selected for the civil service, like the Mogul imperial official, was a generalist, expected to tackle any administrative task to which he was assigned and to change jobs at regular intervals. He might be posted to a court department—ceremonial sacrifices or imperial stud; or to the national university which prepared locally recommended students for their examinations; or to the judicial service. But he was most likely to enter the general service as a district magistrate, the most junior but omni-competent representative of the emperor. Thence, through eighteen grades, each with an appropriate salary, he might rise to one of the 159 prefectures, to a provincial administrative commissionership, or finally to one of the Six Ministries—Personnel, Revenue, Rites, War, Justice and Works. He was unlikely to be concerned with the army, however, except at a senior supervisory level, for both the officers and the several million troops were normally drawn from designated military families, which supplied one son in each generation for permanent services as their tax contribution. Officers were selected from such families by inheritance or on merit, the qualifications being both in practical skills and the theory of war. Only after 1478 did open competition begin to be used to supplement such direct recruitment.

Outside these various branches stood the surveillance and censorial officials, a link between the bureaucracy and the imperial court. The Jesuit Matteo Ricci, the first missionary to gain access to Peking, was amazed by their courage and frankness in voicing public grievances and exposing officials who broke the law, declaring them 'a source of wonder to strangers and a good example for imitation'. Under the Mongols they had been mainly state instruments of repressive control, such as Legalist philosophers had recommended. Under the Ming, their role as critics and reformers within the system was restored, on the Confucian maxim that 'for one near the throne not to remonstrate is to hold office merely for mercenary motives'.

The Ming system had various regulatory devices: imperial officials might not serve in their home provinces nor hold any office for more than nine years. They were also subject to constant report and review by their superiors, being called to Peking every nine years for a grand accounting, followed by appropriate punishment or reward. These checks, however, were made from within and so were subject to departmental esprit de corps, cliquism or favour. The censors and surveillance officers provided a check administered from outside by men selected for character and attainment who, being still fairly junior, were anxious to make their mark. They worked as individuals, never more than four hundred of them for all China, and reported directly to the emperor.

They functioned firstly by attendance at all imperial audiences and ministerial councils and at sittings of the high courts, regional military commissions and provincial councils. Then censors were always on tour, inspecting schools, supervising examinations, overseeing recruitment from military families. Others on special duty would investigate famine areas, the movement of tax grain on the Grand Canal or the state of government granaries. Most redoubtable of all, as regional inspectors they reviewed prison and trial records, checked office files to ensure that all government edicts had been complied with inside the time limit prescribed in the document, audited local accounts, received popular complaints and petitions and interrogated officials. Some censors were corrupt or compliant, others vindictively partisan, but many were dedicated men, and if need be martyrs to principle. As a result for some two and a half centuries Ming China was probably as orderly and prosperous as any part of the globe.

The arts in Ming China

Economic security and prosperity encouraged a flowering of the arts—bronzes of great purity, splendid blue on white porcelain and later polychrome glazed and enamelled ware from the imperial kilns, rich silk brocades and a variety of sumptuous lacquer work. In architecture, after an initial reversion to Sung traditions, a Ming style emerged, simple, monumental but making effective use of colour, as in the Peking palaces. The emperors, notably Hsüan-te (1426–35), who was himself a very fair artist, also patronized painting and calligraphy, encouraging particularly the rather conservative but splendidly decorative tradition of bird and flower painting.

Outside the court, the Ming was an era of private connoisseurship when great collections were formed, early scroll paintings being sought out, restored and documented, and rare books reprinted. Printing, indeed, reached a very high standard, both from wood blocks and movable type, while books were frequently embellished with woodcuts, in later years often in colour. The individual's interest in the arts was active as well as passive—if an Elizabethan was expected to contribute voice or instrument to a madrigal, a Ming gentleman would pride himself on his calligraphy and painting, on his ability to turn a poem or plan a garden. Many scholar-officials had moved south during Mongol rule, withdrawing from office to live on their lands. Such men cultivated the arts as a means of personal expression and symbol of their civilized taste. As men accustomed to writing with a brush, they appreciated fine brushwork in ink and wash painting, and in a period of eager collection of old masters they were able to study and practice the techniques of the past.

From this flowed not only much personal painting of various quality but also much theorizing. Some of this took the form of manuals on how and what to paint. But in the sixteenth century the Wu school, from the Soochow region of the Yangtse delta, produced a positive philosophy of the amateur artist. Painting—especially landscape painting—was a spiritual exercise, they argued, through which men expressed their understanding of the inner harmonies and principles of nature. The professional was concerned with surface experience only the cultivated man, attuned to the natural order, could express the inner reality. As for

Above, sixteenth-century illustration of rice planting in southern China. Rice had been the staple crop of China since at least 2000 BC.

Opposite left, the Thousand Autumns Pavilion in the gardens of the Peking Imperial Palace.

Opposite right, sixteenth-century Chinese ship, with sails made of reed. The Chinese were not interested in exploration, and their trading voyages were disrupted by Japanese pirates.

the manner of expression, that required a study of the great masters and a definition of those who truly were such—hence the Ming passion for cataloguing and for classifying artists into schools.

The scholar class naturally stressed this amateur aestheticism, but there was also much popular art turned out by craftsmen for sale over the counter—though then the subject was horses after the style of Chai Meng-fu rather than sunflowers after Van Gogh. Popular taste in literature and drama was still more important in creating new or reshaping old forms: the Ming period introduces the fully-fledged Chinese opera and novel. The process began under the Mongols, who used the written vernacular rather than the purely literary classical Chinese. They also scattered court circles, denied office and patronage to scholars, and so forced such men to find a more popular audience and employ their talents in new ways. The scholars turned to the stage and then to the novel, giving a more complete form to existing arts.

Operas had long been popular, written in verse upon well known themes, with parts

Above, landscape painting, done in ink on paper, by the Ming artist T'ang Yin (1479–1523).

Left, detail from silk screen painting entitled By the River at the Spring Festival*: it shows the gate of Kaifeng city, in Honan province, an important centre during the five Dynasties in the tenth century and the capital of the northern Sung until 1127.*

Opposite, seventeenth-century Chinese painting of the ancient emperor Yang-Ti, famous for his fine palaces and gardens, riding with his concubines.

both sung and danced, accompanied by an orchestra which had a major role in the performance. They were given without scenery, though with an elaborate repertoire of conventional dress, make up and gesture —as in the Indian dance—to indicate action or character. But whereas operas hitherto had been composed of short scenes, they now became longer four act productions, their limited range of stock characters—like those of pantomime—was extended, the plots became more varied, while their libretti were often printed. Under the later Ming even greater freedom was given, the four act convention in its turn was abandoned, and others besides the lead characters were given singing roles. Writing for the theatre never became respectable, acting certainly not, but opera became a most vigorous and widely popular art form.

The opera had the court masque as one source, the popular miracle play as another. In the same way the Ming novel could look back to T'ang short stories written in the classical style but also to the lively art of the street corner storyteller. From Sung times the growing urban population had been entertained by storytellers, who had recognized pitches and even specialist themes—religious, historical, love or adventure. Their stories incorporated well-known episodes, but endlessly elaborated, so that prompt-books came to be printed, setting out the main points for the teller.

Some of this material was further developed in opera, some was used by scholars to create the Chinese novel. Language became more correct, style more polished, character more fully developed, but the new novel could still be enjoyed by anyone who could read at all.

Just as there had been several types of story, so there were many kinds of novel. The early works were mainly historical novels, such as the still popular *Romance of the Three Kingdoms* which deals with the fall of the Han dynasty. Another novel, *Monkey*, is an allegorical and satirical tale in the style of the Buddhist miracle story, while the *Golden Lotus*, written by a late sixteenth-century official who rose to be Minister of Rites, take up the love story and transforms it into a very complete study of middle class domestic life. In the same way, from the story-teller's adventure yarn, yet another scholar creates *All Men are Brothers*, an episodic story of a bandit and his companions which is also a bitter, subversive attack upon the corruption and injustice of the Ming court and its officials.

The decline of the Ming

A growing trade, an effective examination system and the vitality of the arts might suggest that all was well with Ming China. Peasant risings, failure on the frontiers, corruption and conflict within the administration, the urgent memorials of reformers and the savage denunciations of the novelists show that this was not so.

The founder of the Ming had begun as leader of a peasant revolt against oppressive demands from Mongol officials and local landholders. His first acts had been to curb abuses and lighten burdens. But the problem remained that the imperial higher officials, perhaps 15,000 in all, were necessarily dependent upon the village headman and influential landholders for information and assistance in governing the countryside. As in India, such local leaders unless firmly controlled usually pursued private interest rather than the public good. This was the easier because the tax system was complicated, including as it did land revenue from the two harvests, salt and tea monopolies, levies of silk and silver, and a system of forced labour, elaborately graded, from all adult males. (This unpaid labour was used in the postal service, on flood works, in moving tax grain, in the local militia and on other state tasks.) Moreover these taxes and labour services were not taken directly from each individual by government collectors. Instead, one leading family in a section of eleven families—ten sections made a 'village'—was made responsible for tax collecting and organizing labour services. State registers of land and households were intended to ensure that families paid according to their size and land holdings. But the powerful and wealthy, charged with responsibility for administering the very complex revenue system, were able gradually to falsify the registers and push the burden on the weak. Degree-holders were exempt from labour services and might use their prestige and connections to dodge taxation. As a result there was increasing pressure on the peasantry, flight from the land, and from the early sixteenth century, revolt.

In the second half of the century these evils were reduced by a drastic simplification of the tax and household classification structure and by changing grain and labour dues into cash payments. This was made possible because of the great inflow of silver from Japan and from Spanish American mines by way of Portuguese Macao or the Spanish Philippines. Cash payments, made direct, cut out the village head, and permitted labour to be hired instead of conscripted. However, imperial officials, who might be posted to provinces whose language, customs and economy were entirely strange, remained very dependent on local officials, a dangerous invitation to the latter to abuse their power.

Whether control and reform or weakness and corruption would triumph depended in large measure upon the imperial centre. The Ming took over from a most authoritarian regime and initially tightened rather than relaxed central control. Theoretically the power of decision had always lain with the emperors, the earthly legates of Heaven. But in practice they required the co-operation of the bureaucracy, particularly the

Chancellery, which co-ordinated the work of the Six Ministries, the chiefs-of-staff and the censorate, under a Grand Councillor or prime minister. He had enjoyed considerable powers of action and could check the absolutism or make good the deficiencies of the emperors. But in 1380 a conspiracy involving a Grand Councillor led Hung-wu to abolish the Chancellery and undertake himself the coordination of ministries, the reviewing of the daily flood of memorials to the throne and the final decision making.

In time, however, an unofficial body of secretaries, mainly drawn from the superior scholars of the Hanlin Academy who expounded the classics and worded imperial edicts, was assembled by the emperor. They considered all incoming documents and submitted proposals for action, the most senior of them assuming many of the old Grand Councillor's functions. But these secretaries belonged to the court rather than the bureaucracy, they were junior in service to the ministers and generals whose work they controlled, and they were consequently disliked and distrusted. Some were men of great ability, like Chang Chü-ching who served Wan-li in the late sixteenth century, but all of them depended upon the emperor's favour, and the anomaly of their position led to constant friction and often to personal corruption. Such corruption was the more likely since they had to seek imperial support through the eunuchs, the only males allowed within the inner palace.

Hung-wu had strictly limited the number and rank of the eunuchs, had kept them illiterate and barred from official business on pain of death. But as successive emperors became palace recluses rather than leaders of armies they were thrown into even closer contact with the eunuchs, whom they knew from childhood. By the middle of the fifteenth century there were thousands of eunuchs, with a palace school and a palace army. As trusted confidants they managed a secret police designed to check and if necessary to act against the bureaucracy and filled many lucrative and important positions. They were socially despised and being mainly northerners were further disliked by the bulk of the officials who were from the south. Nevertheless early in the sixteenth century the eunuchs achieved great power, dividing or terrorizing officials, selling offices and extorting bribes. The notorious Liu Chen amassed 250,000,000 ounces of silver before his fall. A check was then imposed but the violence of some emperors, the irresponsibility of Wan-li between 1582 and 1620 and the feeble-mindedness of his successor allowed a rapid renewal of eunuch power in the seventeenth century. Greed and corruption triumphed, court officials were set against the regular bureaucracy, which was skilfully split into factions by the eunuchs or purged with terror if any reform were attempted. And while eunuchs acted like gangsters, enemies gathered on the frontiers.

The fall of the Ming

Ever since Yung-lo's last expedition to overawe the northern nomads China's inner frontier had been under pressure. One rash emperor was captured with his army, others purchased relief by making rich gifts of silks and tea to 'tribute-missions' from the tribes, or as in 1570 by hopefully granting honours to an 'Obedient and Righteous Prince' of the eastern Mongols who had raided Peking's suburbs. In the south, after an

Below, Dutch ships in the harbour of Canton in the mid-seventeenth century. This was the main port used by European traders until the nineteenth century.

Below left, salt production in China; salt was a government monopoly in Ming times, as were other basic commodities.

Opposite, painting by Wang Chen from the Sung dynasty depicting the legendary Island of the Immortals, where people never died and the houses were made of gold and silver.

initial burst of maritime energy, the Ming had abandoned the coast to devastating raids from the Wako, bodies of Japanese trader-buccaneers and freebooting Chinese operating from the offshore islands. The Ming response was to end trade with Japan, ban overseas voyages and evacuate the coastal districts. Ming weakness and the arrival of Portuguese middlemen at Macao in the 1550s permitted a gradual growth of trade again, fostered by the growth of stronger regulatory forces in Japan. But then in 1592 and 1597 Japanese unification led to the launching of two invasions of Korea which the Ming felt bound to repel. Korea was saved by Ming armies—a naval counterstroke against Japan being judged impossible—but at crippling cost. Thereafter military adventure in Indo-China, a major peasant rising in western China and famine in the north fatally weakened the country, while official factions and eunuch bosses struggled over the centre, raising tax levels and leaving armies unpaid.

The empire might nevertheless have recovered had not the emperors been mostly effeminate weaklings who were very much the puppets of ambitious eunuch ministers. These secured undue political influence by leading the rulers into vicious courses and so making themselves the arbiters of policy. They were greedy for power and wealth and no one could obtain office or any other imperial favour except by paying heavy bribes. Those who bought appointments in this manner endeavoured to recoup themselves by extortion from the people they governed, which fostered discontent and eventual rebellion. Officials who protested against these evils were deprived of their posts, exiled and sometimes executed.

The rise of the Manchu

Meanwhile in Manchuria a Juchen chief, Nurchachi, was busy uniting by marriage, diplomacy or force the tribes which the Ming had long sought to keep divided. As a tribal commander and tribute-trader under the Ming he fortified his position and with the help of Chinese advisers created a sound administration for his infant state, complete with the traditional examination system and six board central government. Then in 1618 he overran the Ming province of Liaotung, making Mukden his capital. His and his successor's victories and their success in adopting a traditional Confucian style of government won over more and more Chinese who despaired of the Ming. So when a Chinese rebel, Li Tsü-ch'eng, exploiting factional paralysis in the court, hatred of the eunuchs and misery among the peasants, seized north China and in 1644 took Peking, the Ming commander of the north did not surrender to him. Instead he called the Manchu ruler to join him against the rebel and went on to help him to take all north China. The Ming who had once been the restorers of native rule had so alienated the scholar-officials and army and so oppressed their people that a nomad dynasty could now be welcomed as upholders of Confucian ideals.

Chapter 30

The Emergence of Japan

The fact that the early Chinese were not a seafaring people explains the relatively late development of a distinct civilization in Japan. During the centuries from the Shang to the Han dynasties, while a rich and complex civilization was emerging in China, the Japanese islands remained isolated from events on the mainland. The people there, closely knit in tight clan organizations and continually at war with the surrounding aborigines, lived their lives by hunting and fishing, without having developed the practice of agriculture. A type of Stone Age culture existed, traced back to the third millenium BC, to which the name *Jomon* is given, from the straw rope patterns impressed on the handworked pottery of the period.

From the third century BC it was displaced by the more sophisticated Yayoi culture, a name derived from one of the archaeological sites near Tokyo. During the Yayoi period which lasted until the third century AD, increasing cultural and technological influences from China transformed the Japanese way of life. Archaeological evidence shows that at this time bronze and iron were introduced simultaneously into Japan, most probably from the mainland by way of Korea.

Equally important was the introduction of rice, which led to the development of an agricultural economy. The close communion with nature to be found in an agricultural community, with its collective responses to changes in the weather, encouraged Shinto beliefs. The simple respect and homage rendered to the forces of good and evil in wind and rain, mountains and sea was built up into a religious outlook in which human behaviour was subordinated to Shinto—'the way of the gods'.

These Shinto beliefs, which were later to be associated with emperor worship, had a significant effect on modern Japanese nationalism and influenced conceptions of government from early times.

In the second century AD a struggle for supremacy between the various tribes resulted in a confederation of states under Queen Himiko of the Yamato tribe. She apparently lived in seclusion in a fine palace and was a religious leader who transmitted the words of the gods.

A distinctive practice which emerged in the late Yayoi period was the custom of burying rulers and nobles in large mounds, or *kofun*. Some of these *kofun* were of a considerable size. The largest, that of the emperor Nintoku, is about 1,500 feet long and 120 feet high and is said to be the largest tomb in the world. In these tombs mirrors, swords, armour and gold and silver objects have been found buried. It was during this period of the tomb culture of the fourth and fifth centuries that Japan began to emerge as a unified state from the conglomeration of tribes on the Yamato plain.

Between the fifth and the seventh centuries the Yamato court established its position and continued the process of unifying the country. The surrounding areas were pacified, irrigation projects were carried out and the influence of the independent clan leaders was gradually suppressed. Very little is known of this early development because it was not until the fifth century that a written language emerged in Japan. Such records as exist are preserved in the Chinese annals and, to the Chinese, Japan was known as *Wa*—'the land of the barbarians'.

However, Chinese cultural influences soon flowed into the country. During this and the succeeding Nara period the influx of Chinese ideas transformed every facet of Japanese life. The Japanese rulers, dazzled by the achievement of the Han and then the T'ang dynasties, modelled the government on Chinese patterns. Chinese conceptions of law, institutional procedures and means of political control were eagerly adopted and used to break down the power of the independent nobles. It is also true that Chinese artistic and literary trends enjoyed great popularity.

In fact, the acceptance of Chinese philosophical patterns did much to bring about the development of a conscious Japanese literary tradition. The *Kojiki* and the *Nihon Shoki*, which form the basis of the historical chronicles of Japan, made their appearance at this time.

Buddhism and feudalism

Between the eight and the twelfth centuries these formative influences were absorbed and a distinctive Japanese culture emerged. The impact of Buddhism in particular transformed the country. Initially, there had been some fear of offending the old gods and the religion was resisted. A violent struggle over this issue had taken place between two clans, the Soga and the Mononobe. After Soga's victory in 587 a Buddhist temple, the Asuka monastery, was erected at the Yamato court. The influence of Buddhism then spread rapidly and the period is sometimes called the Asuka age.

At the end of the century Prince Shotoku, who was renowned for his piety, gave a further impulse to the spread of the religion. He wrote commentaries on the *Lotus Sutra*,

Above, pagoda in Nara, in south Honshu, Japan. Nara was the imperial capital in the eighth century AD and was built on the Chinese model.

Opposite, Buddhist fresco of the genius of war from south China. Although this work dates from the Ming period, that dynasty tried to restore the philosophy of Confucianism.

built impressive temples and made it the official creed. As a result, in Japan as elsewhere the seventh and eight centuries were the golden age of Buddhist activity. A permanent capital, closely modelled on Chang-an, the capital of T'ang China, was established at Nara, from which this period is named.

However, Buddhism in Japan developed characteristics which did not emerge in China. As the monasteries grew in strength they built up private armies of monks and meddled in politics. In 764 this activity came to a climax when the monk Dokyo seized power, became the grand minister of state, and aspired to the throne. Only with great difficulty was his power broken by the aristocracy and Dokyo banished.

This usurpation had far-reaching effects. In 794 the Emperor Kammu, who was determined to break free of the grip of the monasteries, decided to leave Nara and to set up a new capital at Heiankyo, the site of present-day Kyoto. However, in the Heian period (794–1185) the Yamato court was increasingly involved in the complexities of Japanese politics. It became impossible for the throne to control the nobles who built up private forces and supported the rise of a warrior class.

From early times the warrior tradition had been strong in Japan. The constant struggles between the warring clans, the forcible suppression of the aboriginal tribes and the stirring accounts of the unification of the country preserved in the Japanese tradition, gave rise to the supremacy of the warrior.

In Heian times, the fiercely loyal bands of armed retainers built up a rigorous code of conduct and emerged as a distinctive class. the *bushi.* By the tenth century each noble was surrounded by a band of devoted followers. The term samurai, which comes from the verb *samurau*, 'to stand by the side of', vividly illustrates their status and function.

One of the first of the families to rise to prominence in this struggle of the aristocracy was the Fujiwara. For over a century they exercised dictatoral control over the court. until their strength was broken by the Emperor Gosanjo when he ascended the throne in 1068.

To raise the prestige of the imperial court, the Emperor Gosanjo introduced a measure which was to have far-reaching consequences in Japanese politics during the succeeding century. This was the *insei* system, by which the emperor left the throne to a puppet and retired to a monastery, while in reality maintaining control of affairs. The aim was to free the emperor from politics, but the result was otherwise.

In a short while a growing number of cloistered emperors added to the difficulties of the situation, matching themselves against one another and depending on the nobility for support. In this *insei* period the dynamic feudal tendencies of the powerful aristocratic families, supported by their samurai followers, carried Japan into one of the most dramatic phases of its development.

The military struggle was decided between the houses of Minamoto, or Genji, who had risen to prominence as vassals of the Fujiwara and the Heike, also called Taira, who were favoured by the court. The bitter and protracted wars between the Taira and Minamoto dominated twelfth-century politics. At first triumphant, the Taira were then isolated and defeated by Minamoto-no Yoritomo, to whom the court gave administrative control of the eastern half of the country. From this centre, Yoritomo

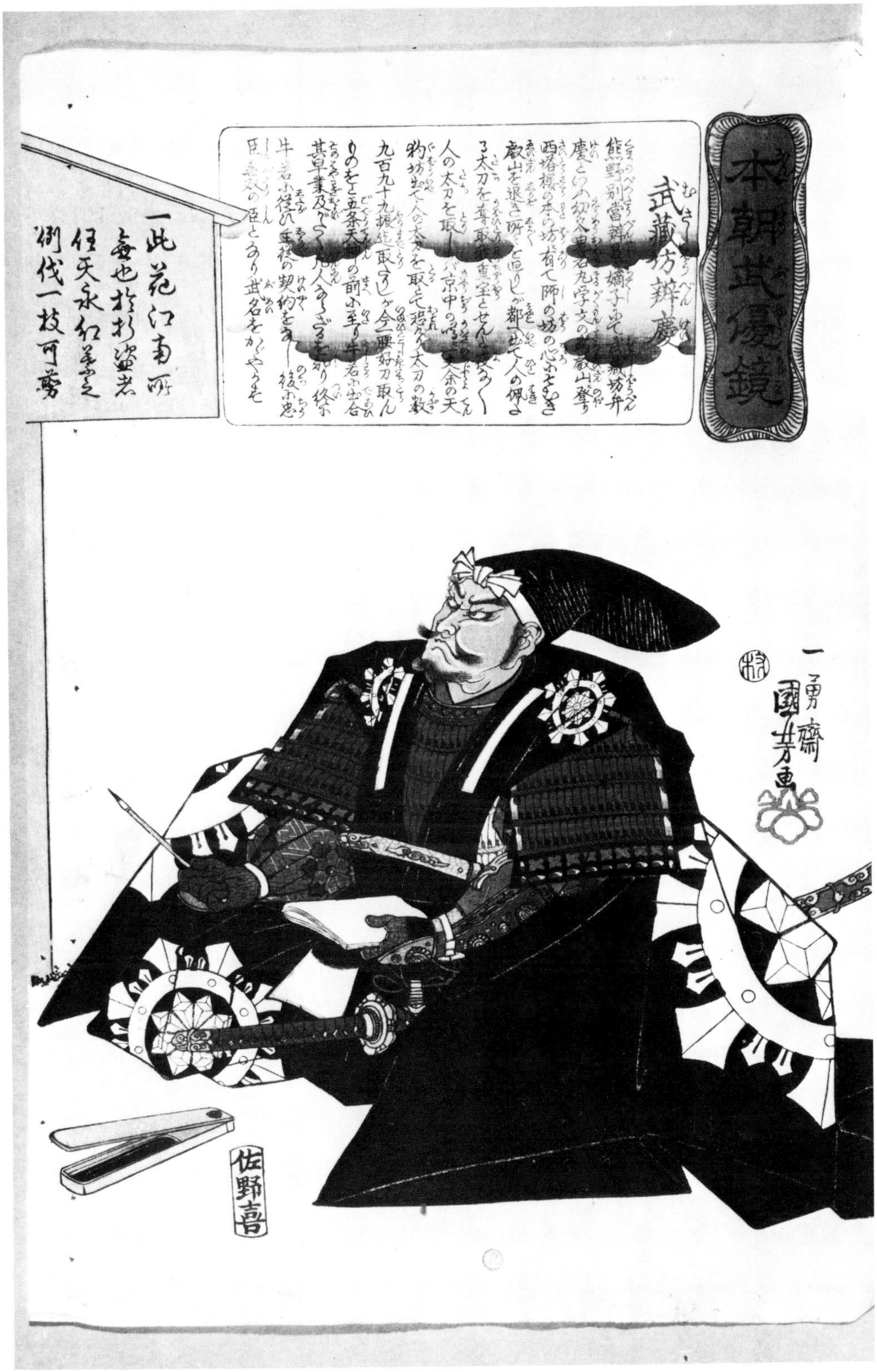

Above, Saito Musashi-bo Berkei, a follower of Minamoto Yoskitsune, shortly before the final destruction of the Taira family.

Left, a fourteenth-century illustration of a battle between two Japanese families. Warfare between the clans was endemic in Japan, where society was organized on a system similar to the feudalism of western Europe. Victoria and Albert Museum, London.

Opposite left, samurai warrior of the thirteenth or fourteenth century. The samurai class arose in the feudal wars of the twelfth century, and their chivalric traditions dominated Japan until the nineteenth century. Museum of Fine Arts, Boston.

Opposite right, a samurai youth practising archery with a wooden horse, used as a training mount, in the background. A samurai was skilled in all the martial arts and was permitted to wear two swords. Victoria and Albert Museum, London.

built up his power with the help of his younger brother, Yoshitsune. In 1185 he annihilated the Taira at the great naval battle of Dan-no-ura'.

Literature

During the Nara period a growing awareness of a distinctive cultural identity led to an interest in literary activity in Japan. However, free expression was restricted by the lack of a Japanese script, which did not emerge until after the fifth century. Writings were expressed in Chinese or rendered phonetically in Chinese characters. The early Japanese historical chronicles, the *Kojiki* (712) and the *Nihon shoki* (720), are presented in these forms. Despite this difficulty, the urge to poetic expression overcame the absence of a written language. In the Nara era an anthology was compiled of more than 4,000 poems. This was the *Man'yoshu* or the 'Collection of Myriad Leaves', which preserved the rough songs of peasants as well as lilting poems to nature by aristocratic court ladies.

In the Heian period the spoken language broke free of the rigid Chinese characters.

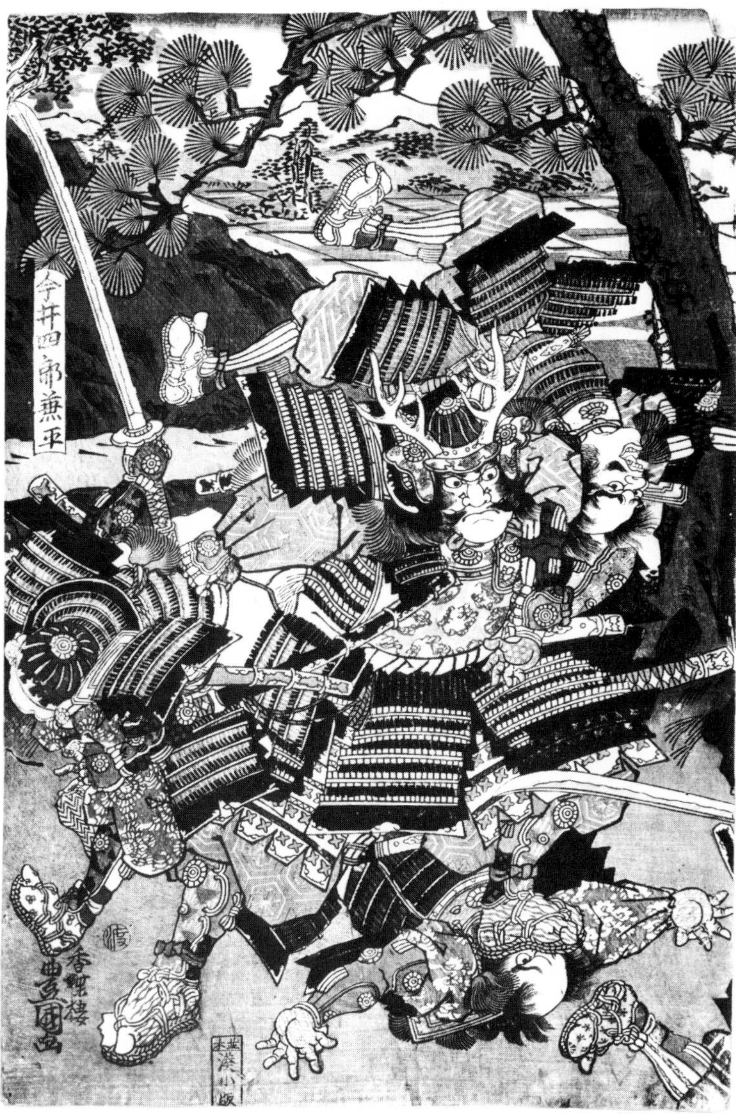

A simplified form of them was adopted, the *katakana* and the cursive *hiragana* thus creating a distinctive Japanese script. With this impulse, a rich body of poetry had emerged by the mid-ninth century, introspective in character and revealing a supreme awareness of man's closeness to, and dependence on, nature.

During the following century there were rapid developments in a wide variety of literary forms. The lead in this activity was taken by the leisured aristocracy at the imperial court, who for their subject matter turned frequently to their own social situation and to the delicate and complicated relationships of their class.

In this way a number of outstanding *monogatari* or prose narratives appeared, many of which were written by gifted and cultured court ladies. One of the most famous of these works was the *Tale of Genji* by the Lady Murasaki. This lengthy novel recreated the life and exploits of Prince Genji with a wealth of intimate detail and affectionate sympathy. An equally unforgettable work, also by a woman, was the *Pillow Book of Sei Shonagon,* which appeared in about AD 1000.

Legends, folktales and travel diaries also date from this period. These traveller's accounts provide valuable descriptive information on conditions in the country. They had their origin in the requirement placed on the nobility to attend at the various administrative centres of feudal Japan.

One of the most popular themes in early Japanese literature was the tragedy and triumph of the country's history. Tales of battles, which recalled the heroic exploits and the relentless struggles of the warring clans, were told and retold by successive writers, creating a tradition of dedication and personal self-sacrifice which added to the prestige of the warrior class.

These tales reached their greatest output during the feudal period of the Kamakura shogunate. In time stories were produced which recounted with a wealth of imaginative detail the series of events and wars which had led to the triumph of the Minamoto over the Taira. They had an immense popular appeal, and were often chanted, with lute accompaniments to groups of listeners.

By the fourteenth century dramatists such as Kanami Kiyotsuga (1333–84) and his son, Zeami Motokiyo (1363–1443), had fused the Japanese genius for poetic expression with dramatic representations of these time-honoured epics and had created the repertoire of *No* plays.

The Kamakura Shogunate

The triumph of the Minamoto over the Taira marked the end of the formative period in Japanese history and ushered in a new era which looked forward to the modern age.

For centuries, as the centralized state had slowly emerged, the clans had struggled for political control, both among themselves and against the emperor who represented the imperial government. Minamoto Yoritomo's victory over the Taira resolved both these issues.

Yorimoto was aware that he owed his success to the eastern barons. Consequently after his victory he did not try to take over the court at Kyoto. Instead, he remained in the east where he set up an independent government at Kamakura. He carried out military and economic reforms, established a means of keeping the unruly vassals under control and took over the administration of civilian justice. A new type of government emerged, which was apparently of a temporary nature because of the military

demands of the moment. It was given the name *bakufu* or 'tent headquarters'.

However, Yoritomo soon consolidated his position in the east in a decisive way. He crushed a rebellion headed by his younger brother Yoshitune, who had been encouraged to revolt by the ex-emperor, Go-Shirakawa. He also insisted on establishing stewards in the provincial administrative systems. As these were drawn from his own followers the measure extended his personal control over the country. Against the objections of the ex-emperor, he then claimed the title of *taishogun* or 'barbarian-subduing Generalissimo'.

The Kamakura shogunate, which evolved in this way, had at the end of the twelfth century established a system of government which persisted in Japan until the nineteenth century. The emperor and his court were allowed to continue as the titular government at Kyoto, but the real power was maintained by the Bakufu at Kamakura. The title of shogun, which Yoritomo had forced from the court, ensured that this military power was not arbitrary but delegated by the emperor, on whose behalf all decisions were technically made.

The first test of the shogunate came in 1199 when Yoritomo died. His two capable brothers and his uncle had earlier been put to death. His inexperienced young son, Yoriie, succeeded, but political power at Kamakura soon passed to the Hojo family of Yoritomo's wife. At the same time, the vigorous and capable ex-emperor, Go-Toba, made an unsuccessful attempt to regain control of the country in the Jokyu war of 1221. The Hojo resisted this challenge and maintained the Kamakura system for over a century.

The strength of the system lay in the high sense of personal loyalty which was characteristic of feudal Japan. This was the age of the warrior whose life centred on his rigid code of conduct and concept of loyalty to his feudal lord. *Hara-kiri*, suicide by disembowelment, appears as a practice at this time.

The Mongol invasions

The emphasis on military efficiency which dominated the outlook of the Japanese during the thirteenth century was to prove their salvation. In 1259 the Mongol armies of Genghis Kahn, under his grandson Kublai, swept over China and established the Yuan dynasty. Kublai Khan then sent

Above, painting depicting the burning of the Sanjo Palace in 1160. The eleventh and twelfth centuries saw growing conflict between the rival feudal clans of Japan, until the Minamoto won permanent control in 1184. Museum of Fine Arts, Boston.

Opposite left, painted paper screen from Kyoto, possibly the work of the artist Kano Motonobu (1476–1569). The period of Ashikaya rule in Japan (1333–1573) saw many fine artistic achievements. British Museum, London.

Opposite right, battle of the feudal wars of eleventh-century Japan; the headdresses and armour were highly decorated, partly in order to frighten the enemy. Victoria and Albert Museum, London.

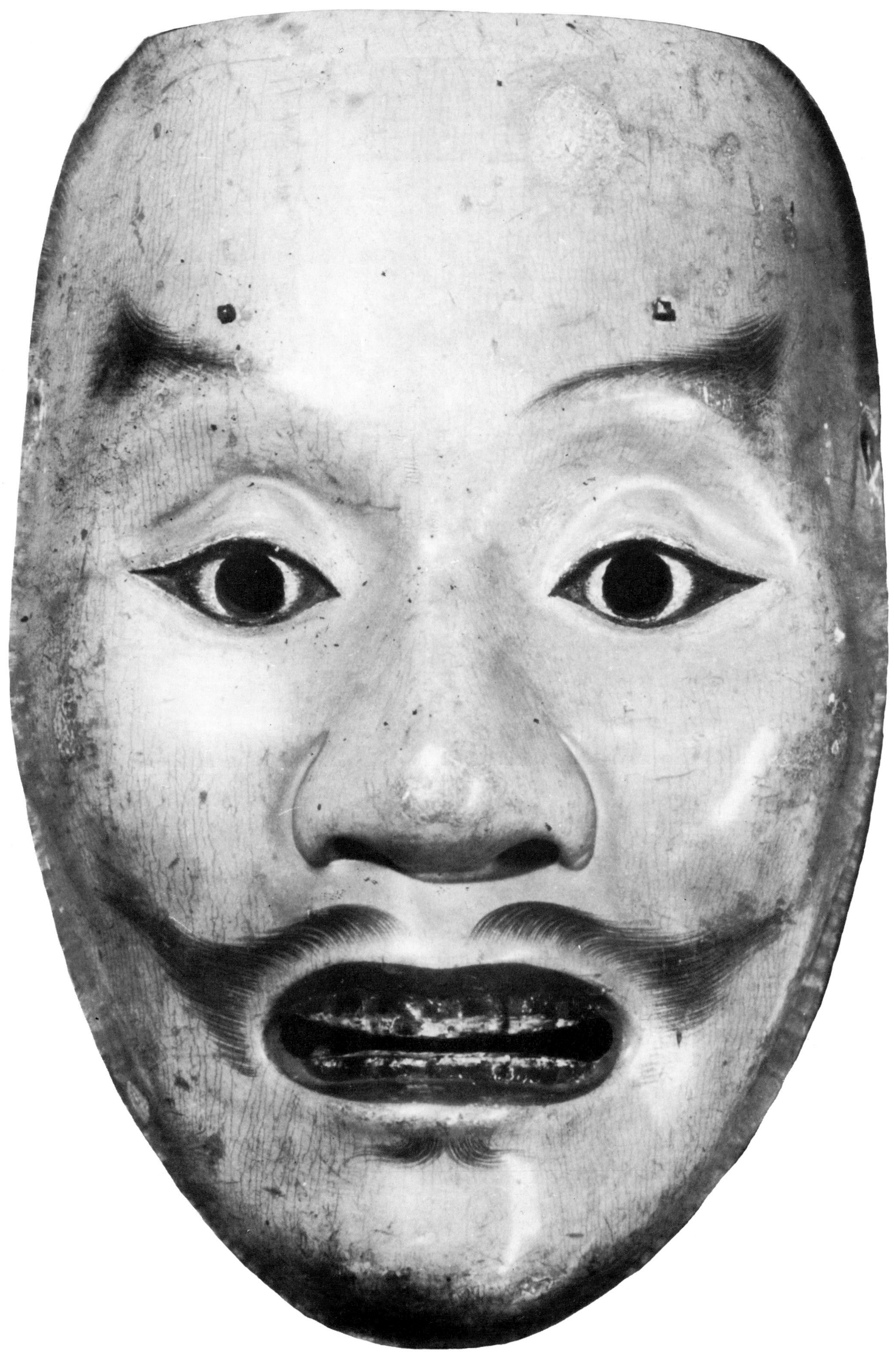

envoys to the surrounding states with peremptory demands that they should submit to his rule. The Japanese rejected him and Kublai twice attempted to invade the country.

In the first invasion of 1274 the Mongols sent an armada of 900 Korean ships carrying over 25,000 warriors to attempt a landing at Kakata bay in Kyushu. A fierce battle followed between the Japanese warriors and the Mongol troops, which ended when a storm arose causing the battered invaders to re-embark and flee to Korea.

A second and larger expedition was sent in 1281. This time the Mongols massed a huge army of about 140,000 men, which was carried over in Korean and Sung ships. The Japanese meanwhile had feverishly put up a protective stone wall around Hakata bay. When the Mongols arrived there was a desperate battle over the wall which lasted for two months. For a second time, the Japanese were saved by a typhoon, which destroyed the enemy fleet.

The revival of Buddhism

An extensive revival of Buddhism occurred during the early Kamakura period. This was partly a result of the disturbed political situation of the country. A general feeling of insecurity encouraged speculation on the transience of life. It also drew its support from the simple faith and religious fervour of the samurai warriors.

In the feudal period of the twelfth and thirteenth centuries Buddhism became less a philosophical creed and more the religion of the emerging lower classes. To an increasing extent the faith was practised and taught by the common people.

Above, a twelfth-century Japanese battle between two of the warring clans.

Left, painting of an incident in the war between the Minamoto and Taira clans in the twelfth century; the Minamoto ride down a cliff to attack the Taira camp. Victoria and Albert Museum, London.

Opposite, mask used in the Japanese No plays, a form of stylized tragic drama developed in the fourteenth century. Each character wore a mask displaying his or her emotions. This mask depicts a samurai. No Theatre of the Kongo School, Kyoto.

A number of sects emerged, and each in turn attempted to achieve a simpler and more direct message. One such was the *Jodo* or 'Pure Land' sect, taught by the monk Honen. Honen's teaching described paradise as the pure land which could be attained merely by rejecting the Buddha's name. His disciple Shinran (1173–1262) simplified the teaching even further. He believed that a single sincere appeal to Buddha was sufficient to ensure salvation. On the other hand, the monk Ippen (1239–89) practised his faith and gained a following by singing and dancing around the countryside. In his view a man could be sure of salvation only by continually reciting Buddha's name.

Another group led by the monk Nichiren (1222–82) placed their faith in the Lotus Sutra, and devotees were taught to chant the phrase 'Hail to the Sutra of the Lotus of the Wonderful Law'. The simplicity of these teachings and the promise of direct salvation appealed to the common people, and many of these sects have persisted to the present day.

The most significant branch of Buddhist teaching to develop in the Kamakura period was the Zen or meditation school. The sect, which had first developed in Sung China, stressed the importance of personal discipline and control through calm meditation. Its emphasis on the importance of personal character and spiritual self-searching gave it a widespread appeal among the warrior class. When Zen Buddhism was introduced into Japan by the monk Eisai in 1191, he settled at Kamakura, where he rapidly obtained the support of the shogunate. Zen Buddhism subsequently reached the peak of its achievements in Japan between the fourteenth and sixteenth centuries.

The medieval period

In the early Middle Ages the Japanese emperors tried to introduce a Chinese style of government, with a trained bureaucracy paid and appointed by the state and taxes and labour services collected according to elaborate registers of lands and families. Simultaneously Chinese writing and other arts, together with Buddhism, made their way into Japan.

But Japanese clan and family feeling made it impossible to select civil servants purely on merit and their payment with land grants instead of money undermined the centralized empire. In the countryside owners and managers of land grants encroached upon the state revenues and used them to build up bodies of armed knights. Such fighting groups grew until, in the twelfth century, one feudal family from the rich rice plains Japan. At Kyoto, the emperor, his court aristocracy and the great Buddhist monasteries survived, but they had to recognize the power of the new supreme commander or shogun.

This first military government fell in the fourteenth century, as original loyalties weakened and invasions from China by the Mongol emperor Kublai strained the shogun's finances. However, after years of war, complicated by the emperor's attempt to re-establish his authority, a new shogunal family, the Ashikaga, emerged in 1336; they were to survive until 1573. Their power, however, was limited to their own lands east of the Inland Sea, for there were few aristocratic estates to distribute to their followers and many local war-lords or *daimyo* who were too firmly established to be dispossessed. The Ashikaga wielded authority, therefore, not directly over individual warriors or samurai but through their leaders the *daimyo*, manipulated by diplomatic alliances. The future lay with these ambitious *daimyo*. They mopped up what remained of imperial taxes and estates. They

Above, seventeenth-century screen recording an early trading mission in Japan: the Portuguese were the first Europeans to trade with Japan, which they reached in 1542. The Europeans were mainly concerned to win control of Japan's existing trade in the Far East. Musée Guimet, Paris.

consolidated their demesnes, encouraging trade and industry. They recruited armies of pikemen from their peasantry, who replaced the costly bodies of knights. After fighting throughout the 'age of warring states' a handful of *daimyo* families emerged triumphant in the sixteenth century, one of which, the Tokugawa, became feudal masters of all Japan in 1603. The shadowy emperors remained, but the Tokugawa shoguns really ruled until 1867.

The Ashikaga period was one of political disorder but great cultural achievement. The early shoguns sought profit and prestige from tribute missions to Ming China, and this trade renewed Chinese influence. Zen Buddhist monks, coming or drawing inspiration from China, became leading scholars, writers and artists at the shogun's court and in provincial centres. Many examples of Chinese art were imported, but the Japanese soon equalled them, whether as painters in the Sung landscape tradition, as architects of the Golden and Silver Pavilions at Kyoto or creators of the great monastic and palace landscape gardens.

Zen stress upon contemplation and understanding of nature's harmonies led to a love of the simple, natural and intimate. This is clearly seen in the plain but harmoniously proportioned houses, with rush mat floors and natural wood surfaces, or in the dignified tea-taking ceremony. The feeling for beauty also appears in the practice of having an alcove where a vase, scroll-painting or flower arrangement was placed for contemplation. Again the linking of short poems into sequences which now became popular challenged the aesthetic judgement of the poet.

Under Chinese influence short stories developed from Buddhist miracle stories while history acquired a new importance. This interest in the past led to a revival of Japanese Shintoism. Great Shinto shrines like that at Ise came to be supported by associations of devotees in the same way as the popular Buddhist devotional sects. The rise of *daimyo* power and wealth ensured that these new outside influences were carried from the court to the provinces.

The growing importance of the *daimyo* also strengthened feudal elements in Japanese culture. There was stress upon bravery, honour and loyalty to one's lord, a cult of the magnificent Japanese sword. Bardic poetry recounted the rise and fall of great feudal houses, scroll paintings depicted scenes of war, architects built magnificent new castles. Even Zen Buddhism served the warrior class by teaching individual self-discipline and devotion. And just as the Confucian imperial law code had been superseded by the Ashikaga shoguns' code, so now that too was replaced by the House Laws of the greater *daimyo*.

These laws inculcated the general virtues of loyalty and frugality. They also laid down practical rules for guarding against spies, by keeping their families in the lord's castle town—redressing grievances, and imposing punishments upon the guilty and their relatives and servants. Every effort was made to enlarge and consolidate the *daimyo's* domains so as to encourage large-scale production and trade. Irrigation was undertaken and double cropping with improved rice varieties increased yields. New copper and silver mines were opened and better methods of smelting introduced. Roads were built and harbours improved and the *daimyo* sought to establish markets and attract artisans and traders to their castle towns. In western Kyushu they took part in trade or piracy in China and when the Portuguese arrived in the mid-sixteenth century there was keen competition to secure their commerce. Acceptance of Christianity, taught by Jesuit fathers, may initially have been fostered by the wish to attract Portuguese to their ports, though of course many of the 30,000 converts in Japan were truly religious in their attitude.

Efficient *daimyo* management required the consolidation of estates previously in scattered ownership—and as the estates disappeared the village became the economic unit. In the same way, as the influence of the clans declined, so the individual family became the social unit. Individuals became freemen instead of serfs, while villages enjoyed self-government so long as they paid their taxes. As infantrymen superseded cavalry, armed villagers leagued under local leaders could resist *daimyo* demands. And as towns and trade grew, individuals used their freer status to produce varied crops for market.

Left, illustration of the adventures of Kibi in China, dating from the eleventh or twelfth century; many stories of the court date from this period, including Pillow Book of Sei Shonagon *and* The Tale of Genji. *Museum of Fine Arts, Boston.*

Below, popular play and dance enacted at Shijo-Gawa at Kyoto. The realistic, action-filled Kabuki theatre derived from such performances. Seikado Library, Japan.

Opposite, copper smelting in Japan; Japanese society was strictly agricultural and military, and craftsmen and industrialists were granted only a lowly status.

Similarly in the towns and ports rising near *daimyo* castles, Buddhist or Shinto shrines, and on the busy highways—like the Tokaido running east from Kyoto—craftsmen and traders threw off their slave status and won their independence. They formed guilds to protect themselves against *daimyo* exactions, often linked with a Buddhist sect whose armed followers could defend them. Such guilds could also secure local monopolies, and as money came into general use and trade prospered wholesalers of great wealth and influence appeared. The provision of funds and supplies for *daimyo* armies and the despatch of offerings from all over Japan to important shrines also led to the appearance of important groups of bankers and brokers. In a major port city like Sakai, modern Osaka, a middle-class society developed, with its own life, fostering new arts such as the colour print and the popular novel.

The unification of Japan

The sixteenth century in Japan saw rapid change and advance and it was long uncertain where this would lead. Japanese merchants became increasingly adventurous, trading to China, Indonesia, the Philippines and even reaching South America, to the consternation of the Spanish authorities. The development of roads and coastal shipping and the spread of a common culture gave Japan a new cohesion. And then three most able men gave political unity also.

First a minor *daimyo*, Nobunaga, by cunning and ruthless fighting between 1560 and 1582 enlarged his small but strategic fief on the gulf of Owari into a dominant central block of territories. Then his general, Hideyoshi, from 1582 to 1598 used force and alliances to extend control west and north. Finally Ieyasu Tokugawa, general and ally, seized the inheritance, defeated all rivals and emerged as master, the founder of the Tokugawa line of shoguns.

The power thus assembled might have been used for overseas expansion—Hideyoshi did twice invade Korea—or for the creation of a new form of centralized nation-state. Instead it was used to consolidate military feudalism, built upon personal loyalties and obligations. Tokugawa control was ensured by dispersing the hostile lords and placing loyalists in key positions. Official reporters in the chief cities, check points on the roads, a ban on the movement of samurai from the service of one *daimyo* to another, supervision of *daimyo* marriage alliances—all made sure there would be no rebellion. At the same time the military power of the Buddhist sects was broken and the peasantry were disarmed in a great 'Sword Hunt'. When Christian missionary activity seemed too much linked with European military ambitions, persecution destroyed the Church. New laws rigidly defined the role of lords, warriors and peasants. Finally all links with the outside world were ended. Stability and unity were maintained, but at the cost of two centuries of isolation.

Above, Tokugawa Ieyasu (1543–1616) established the shogunate in his family until 1868, keeping a strict control over the activities of the other families and encouraging agriculture and Confucianism. Science Museum, London.

Left, Japanese painting of seven divinities.

Below left, Japanese court sword, decorated with pearl shell, copper gilt and enamel. The art of swordmaking was highly developed in Japan, and the swordsmith had a semi-priestly status.

Opposite, a Japanese Buddhist scroll-painting. Religionskundliche Sammlung der Universität, Marburg.

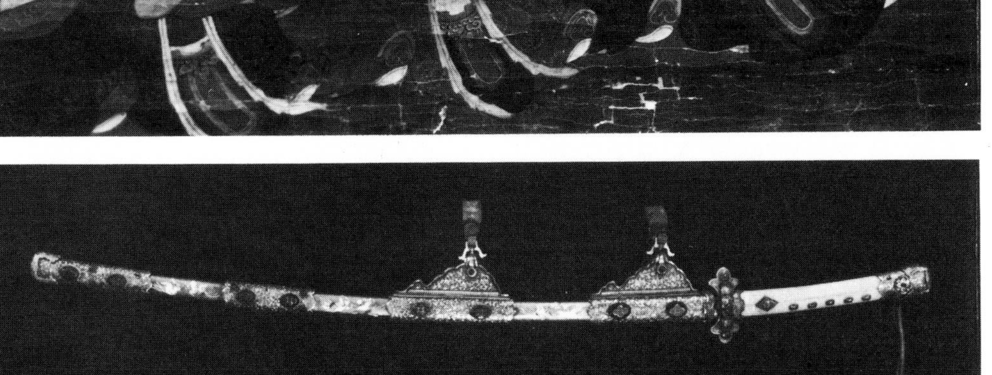

Further reading

The best introduction to the period from the fall of the Roman Empire to the end of the tenth century is to be found in J. M. Wallace-Hadrill, *The Barbarian West, 400–1000* (Hutchinson, London, 3rd edition, 1967; Harper and Row, New York, 1967). For Charlemagne there is D. Bullough, *The Age of Charlemagne* (Elek, London, 2nd edition, 1973). G. Barraclough, *The Crucible of Europe* (Thames and Hudson, London, 1976; University of California Press, Berkeley, 1976) covers the ninth and tenth centuries. On the Vikings, G. Jones, *A History of the Vikings* (Oxford University Press, London and New York, 1968) is most informative and very readable. For the society and economy of the early and central Middle Ages in western Europe, G. Duby, *The Early Growth of the European Economy* (Weidenfeld and Nicholson, London, 1974; Cornell University Press, Ithaca, 1974) covers the seventh to twelfth centuries. R. W. Southern, *The Making of the Middle Ages* (Hutchinson, London, 1953; Yale University Press, New Haven, 1953) concentrates on the major developments in society in the period *c.* 970 to *c.* 1215, and M. Bloch, *Feudal Society* (Routledge and Keegan Paul, London, 1961; University of Chicago Press, 1961) studies the basic form of social organization in this period. For an economic history of the whole of the Middle Ages there is C. Cipolla (ed.), *The Fontana Economic History of Europe*, volume I, *The Middle Ages* (Fontana, London, 1972) and for a broad perspective on medieval society, especially in the later Middle Ages, see D. Hay, *The Medieval Centuries* (Methuen, London, 1964; Barnes and Noble, New York, 1964; Methuen University Paperbacks, 1977). The best introduction to the history of the Church is R. W. Southern, *Western Society and the Church in the Middle Ages* (Penguin Books, Harmondsworth, 1970). On the Papacy throughout this period there is G. Barraclough, *The Medieval Papacy* (Thames and Hudson, London, 1968; Harcourt Brace Jovanovich, New York, 1968) and for a more theoretical treatment, W. Ullmann, *A Short History of the Papacy in the Middle Ages* (Methuen, London, 1972; Barnes and Noble, New York, 1972). C. H. Haskins, *The Renaissance of the Twelfth Century* (Harvard University Press, Boston Mass., 1976) is the most comprehensive study of the greatest century of intellectual activity in the Middle Ages proper, and A. B. Cobban, *The Medieval Universities: their development and organisation* (Methuen, London, 1975; Barnes and Noble, New York, 1975) deals with the rise of a great medieval institution.

For the history of England and France in the Middle Ages, there is a great deal more literature available on the former than on the latter. F. M. Stenton, *Anglo-Saxon England* (Oxford University Press, London and New York, 3rd edition, 1975) is the most comprehensive account of its subject, while H. R. Loyn, *Anglo-Saxon England and the Norman Conquest* (Longman, London, 1962; St Martin's Press, New York, 1963) concentrates on society and economy. Two volumes in the *Pelican History of England* series, volume 3, D. M. Stenton, *English Society in the Early Middle Ages* (Penguin Books, Harmondsworth, 4th edition, 1965) and volume 4, A. R. Myers, *England in the Late Middle Ages* (Penguin Books, Harmondsworth, 2nd edition, 1963) provide the best coverage of English society and politics from the Norman Conquest to the late fifteenth century. A number of the most important English kings have been fortunate in receiving excellent biographical treatment, especially in: F. Barlow, *Edward the Confessor* (Eyre and Spottiswoode, London, 1970; University of California Press, Berkeley, 1970), D. Douglas, *William the Conqueror* (Eyre and Spottiswoode, London, 1964; University of California Press, 1964), W. L. Warren, *Henry II* (Eyre and Spottiswoode, London, 1973), W. L. Warren, *King John* (Eyre and Spottiswoode, London, 1961; Norton, New York, 1961) and C. Ross, *Edward IV* (Eyre and Spottiswoode, London, 1974; University of California Press, Berkeley, 1974). The best introduction to the French monarchy is R. Fawtier, *The Capetian Kings* (Macmillan, London, 1960; St Martin's Press, New York, 1960) and for the fullest account of the great Anglo-French struggle of the fourteenth and fifteenth centuries there is E. Perroy, *The Hundred Years' War* (Eyre and Spottiswoode, London, 1965; G. P. Putnam's Sons, New York, 1965). Good accounts of fifteenth-century France are to be found in the biographies: M. G. A. Vale, *Charles VII* (Eyre-Methuen, London, 1974; University of California Press, Berkeley, 1974) and P. M. Kendall, *Louis XI* (George Allen and Unwin, London, 1971; Norton, New York, 1971). On Louis's unlucky Burgundian contemporary there is R. Vaughan, *Charles the Bold* (Longman, London, 1973; Barnes and Noble, New York, 1973). R. H. Hilton, *Bond Men Made Free* (Maurice Temple Smith, London, 1973; Viking, New York, 1973; Methuen University Paperbacks, 1977) studies the English Peasants' Revolt of 1381, against the background of peasant movements in later medieval Europe as a whole.

The most authoritative short history of the Crusades is to be found in H. E. Mayer, *The Crusades* (Oxford University Press, Oxford and New York, 1973) and for a longer account there is S. Runciman, *A History of the Crusades*, 3 volumes (Cambridge University Press, Cambridge, 1951–54; Penguin Books, Harmondsworth, 1965). The standard history of the Byzantine Empire is G. Ostrogorsky, *A History of the Byzantine State* (Blackwells, Oxford, 2nd edition, 1968; Rutgers University Press, 1969) and on Eastern Europe in the Middle Ages, D. Obolensky, *The Byzantine Commonwealth* (Weidenfeld and Nicholson, London, 1971; Praeger, New York, 1971) provides a detailed coverage. The best introductions to the history and culture of the Muslim world may be found in A. Guillaume, *Islam* (Penguin Books, Harmondsworth, 1954) and, for the Middle Ages in particular, in D. M. Dunlop, *Arab Civilisation to 1500* (Longman/Librairie du Liban, London and Beirut, 1971; Praeger, New York, 1971). For relations between Islam and the West in this period see N. Daniel, *The Arabs and Medieval Europe* (Longman/Librairie du Liban, London and Beirut, 1975; Longman, New York, 1974). The rise and expansion of the Ottoman Empire is most conveniently treated in S. J. Shaw, *A History of the Ottoman Empire and Modern Turkey*, volume 1 (Cambridge University Press, Cambridge, 1976).

The history of Spain in the later Middle Ages is given an excellent treatment in A. MacKay, *Spain in the Middle Ages, from Frontier to Empire, 1000–1500* (Macmillan, London, 1977; St Martin's Press, New York, 1977) and also in J. N. Hillgarth, *The Spanish Kingdoms, 1250–1516*, 2 volumes (Oxford University Press, London and New York, 1976 and 1978). D. W. Lomax, *The Reconquest of Spain* (Longman, London, 1978) studies the whole history of relations between Christians and Muslims in the peninsula. For a treatment of Spanish expansion to the Americas, there is J. H. Parry, *The Spanish Seaborne Empire* (Hutchinson, London, 1966; Knopf, New York, 1966; Penguin Books, Harmondsworth, 1973). G. C. Vaillant, *The Aztecs of Mexico* (Doubleday, New York, 2nd edition, 1962; Penguin Books, Harmondsworth, 1965) and J. Alden Mason, *The Ancient Civilisations of Peru* (Penguin Books, Harmondsworth, 2nd edition, 1969; Peter Smith, New York, 1969) investigate the civilisations with which the Spaniards came into contact in the Americas. J. Hemming, *The Conquest of the Incas* (Macmillan, London, 1970; Harcourt Brace Jovanovich, New York, 1970) describes the effects of that contact. A life of the most famous of Spanish kings is found in P. Pierson, *Philip II of Spain* (Thames and Hudson, London, 1975; Transatlantic 1976).

Italy up to the time of Dante is best covered in J. K. Hyde, *Society and Politics in Medieval Italy* (Macmillan, London, 1973; St Martin's Press, New York, 1973), whilst good accounts of the early Renaissance period are to be found in D. Hay, *The Italian Renaissance in its Historical Background* (Cambridge University Press, Cambridge, 2nd edition, 1977) and B. Pullan, *A History of Early Renaissance Italy* (Allen Lane/Penguin Press, Harmondsworth, 1973; St Martin's Press, New York, 1973). For a wider perspective there is M. Aston, *The Fifteenth Century: The Prospect of Europe* (Thames and Hudson, London, 1968; Harcourt Brace Jovanovich, New York, 1968). On the sixteenth century useful introductions will be found in G. R. Elton, *Reformation Europe* (Fontana, London, 1969; Harper and Row, New York, 1968) and A. G. Dickens, *Reformation and Society in Sixteenth Century Europe* (Thames and Hudson, London, 1966; Harcourt Brace Jovanovich, New York, 1966), to be followed by A. G. Dickens, *The Counter-Reformation* (Thames and Hudson, London, 1968; Harcourt Brace Jovanovich, New York, 1968). A good biography of one of the leading Reformers is to be found in T. H. L. Parker, *John Calvin* (Dent, London, 1975; Westminster, Philadelphia, 1976). On the history of England in this period there is G. R. Elton, *England under the Tudors* (Methuen, London, 2nd edition, 1974; Barnes and Noble, New York, 1974), and A. G. Dickens, *The English Reformation* (Batsford, London, 1964; Schocken, New York, 1968) provides an account of the religious changes. The best biographies of the most important English monarchs are S. B. Chrimes, *Henry VII* (Eyre and Spottiswoode, London, 1972; University of California Press, Berkeley, 1973), J. J. Scarisbrick,

Acknowledgements

Henry VIII (Eyre and Spottiswoode, London, 1968; University of California, Berkeley, 1968) and J. E. Neale, *Elizabeth I* (Jonathan Cape, London, 1938).

For the history of the Far East during the European medieval centuries useful introductions will be found in R. Dawson, *Imperial China* (Hutchinson, London 1972; Oxford University Press, New York, 1972; Penguin Books, Harmondsworth, 1976) and R. Storry, *A History of Modern Japan* (Penguin Books, Harmondsworth, revised edition, 1972).

The following illustrations were reproduced by gracious permission of Her Majesty the Queen 138 right, 255 top, 260, 262.

The following illustration was reproduced by permission of the Archbishop of Canterbury and the Trustees of Lambeth Palace Library 171.

The following illustration was reproduced by permission of the Dean and Chapter of Canterbury Cathedral 191 top.

Colour

Bibliothèque Nationale, Paris 18; Bisonte 42, 99, 154 right; Bodleian Library, Oxford 95 top, 143 top; British Library, London 95 bottom, 155; British Museum, London 62–63, 95 bottom, 339 left; Chester Beatty Library, Dublin 267; Entwistle Photo Services, Canterbury 191 top; Werner Forman Archive, London 367; Fotomas Index, London 138 right, 174; Photographie Giraudon, Paris 127 top, 131 top, 199, 218, 362; Graphische Sammlung Albertina, Vienna 263 bottom left, Susan Griggs Agency, London 55 top left; Studio Hachette, Paris 310 top; Sonia Halliday, Weston Turville 54, 82, 86, 266 top, 270, 275; Hamlyn Group Picture Library 67 right, 102, 331; Robert Harding Associates, London 75 left, 347 top; John Hillelson, London 306 top; John Hillelson/Magnum—Georg Gerster 354 top; Michael Holford, London 302, 306 bottom, 315 left, 339 left, 342 left, 342 right, 370–371; Henry Huntingdon Library, San Marino, California 135 right; Mansell Collection, London 22, 115 right, 190; Metropolitan Museum of Art, New York 247 top; Nationalmuseet, Copenhagen 211 right; National Scheepvaartmuseum, Antwerp 251 top; Novosti Press Agency, London 207 top; Picturepoint, London 34 top, 38 left, 62 left, 90, 123 left, 158, 166, 170 left, 183, 186, 198; Royal Library, The Hague 102; Marquis of Salisbury 282; Scala, Florence 58, 219, 231, 235 top, 238–239, 242, 243 left, 287; Snark International, Paris 250 right, 351, 358; Staatsbibliothek, Munich 27.

Black and white

Alinari, Florence 43 right, 53 left, 127 bottom, 220, 225, 233 top, 235 bottom, 236 left, 239 bottom, 243 bottom right; ATA, Stockholm 203 top; P. Almasy, Paris 201; Biblioteca Nacional, Madrid 313 top; Bibliothèque Albert I, Brussels 248 top right; Bibliothèque Nationale, Paris 23 left, 56 right, 79 left, 85 bottom, 93 top, 240 left, 241 left, 241 centre top, 241 centre bottom, 241 right, 243 top right, 247 bottom; Bibliothèque Publique et Universitaire, Geneva 258; Bisonte 35 right, 46 left, 73 top left, 93 bottom left, 94 top right, 101, 103 bottom right, 105 left, 134 left, 138 left, 151 left, 185 top, 203 bottom; Bodleian Library, Oxford 19 bottom, 105 top right, 294; Boston Museum of Fine Arts 373 top; J. Bottin, Paris 297; E. Boudot-Lamotte, Paris 20 bottom, 195, 210; British Library, London 28 top, 28 bottom, 36, 38 right, 74 top right, 97 top, 115 bottom left, 134 centre, 135 left, 145 top, 145 bottom, 147, 149 top right, 152 right, 156 top, 156 bottom left, 168 left, 180 top, 185 bottom, 197 top right, 200 top right; British Museum, London 10–11, 137 top left, 197 bottom, 236 bottom right, 238 bottom, 255 bottom, 281 top, 305 right, 310 bottom, 321 top, 321 bottom, 333, 344 right; Burgerbibliothek, Berne 94 centre bottom, 97 bottom, 117 bottom left; Camera Press, London 62 centre top; Chester Beatty Library, Dublin 328; Christie Manson and Woods, London 229 left; Civico Museo Archeologico, Grosseto 307; Cleveland Museum of Art 57 top right; Corpus Christi College, Cambridge 94 centre top; Courtauld Institute of Art, London 21; John Donat Photography, London 56 left, 64 left; Elsevier, Amsterdam 314; Mary Evans Picture Library, London 233 centre, 276 top; Fitzroy Creative Services, London 117 top left, 117 bottom right, 133 right, 153 centre, 221 bottom; Fitzwilliam Museum, Cambridge 128, 162; Fogg Art Museum, Cambridge, Massachusetts 79 right; Werner Forman Archive, London 62 top right, 62 bottom right, 65 left, 67 left, 68 right, 72 centre, 72 right, 319 bottom, 359 bottom, 364 left, 365 right, 368, 373 bottom, 375 bottom; Forschungsbibliothek, Gotha 105 bottom right; Freer Gallery of Art, Washington 57 top left; Frick Collection, New York 279 left; Leonard and Mary Gayton, London 189; Photographie Giraudon, Paris 29 bottom left, 35 top left, 39 left, 41 left, 44 bottom, 80–81, 88 left, 107 bottom, 110, 113, 114–115, 125 top, 139 top, 139 bottom, 141 bottom, 143 bottom, 146 bottom left, 146 right, 163, 164 bottom, 173, 176 right, 177 left, 177 right, 178 left, 179 left, 180 bottom, 181 right, 182, 184 left, 184 right, 213, 246 bottom, 252 top, 254, 261 centre, 304 top; Sonia Halliday, Weston Turville 64 right, 79 centre, 80 left, 80 centre, 85 top, 88 top right, 88 bottom right, 249 bottom, 350, 355, 356 left; Hamlyn Group Picture Library 16, 26 centre, 29 bottom right, 51, 53 top right, 59 bottom, 75 right, 87 bottom right, 94 bottom right, 118, 151 bottom right, 178 right, 179 right, 181 left, 207 bottom, 209 top left, 216, 221 top, 226, 230 bottom, 234, 236 top right, 284, 311 left, 315 right, 340 left, 348 bottom right, 356 right, 359 top, 365 left, 366 left, 375 top left, 375 right; Robert Harding Associates, London 353 right; John Hillelson Agency, London 77, 81 right; John Hillelson/Magnum—Bruno Barbey 325, 345 top left; Michael Holford, London 53 bottom right, 300 right, 301 left, 301 right, 303, 312, 316 right, 317, 319 right, 336, 339 right, 341 left, 345 top right; George Howard 278 left; Ikon, London 304 bottom; Luc Ionesco, Paris 347 bottom, 349; A. F. Kersting, London 76, 334; Paolo Koch, Zollikon 348 bottom left, 348 top; Kunsthistorisches Museum, Vienna 251 bottom, 264 left; Kunstsammlungen, Coburg 268 right; Kupferstichkabinett, Berlin-Dahlem 249 top right; Landesmuseum, Stuttgart 305 left; Larousse, Paris 13 left, 26 centre, 47, 68 left, 327; Mansell Collection, London 11 bottom, 12, 15 left, 23 right, 26 top, 26 bottom, 29 top, 30, 32, 33, 34 bottom, 35 bottom left, 37, 41 right, 43 left, 69, 70, 73 top right, 89, 93 bottom right, 94 left, 103 left, 103 top right, 107, 109 top, 109 bottom, 117 top right, 120, 123 right, 125 bottom, 129 top, 129 bottom, 130, 133 top left, 133 bottom left, 134 right, 135 centre, 137 bottom left, 141 top, 141 centre, 144, 146 top left, 148 top left, 148 bottom left, 148 right, 149 top left, 149 bottom left, 153 top, 153 bottom, 154 left, 157, 160, 164 top, 168 right, 169, 187 top left, 200 left, 200 bottom right, 205 top, 217 left, 217 right, 222 left, 222 right, 223, 240 right, 245 top, 249 top left, 250 top left, 250 bottom left, 252 bottom, 256, 263 bottom right, 265 bottom, 266 bottom, 269 top, 276 bottom, 277 right, 280 left, 280 right, 283 right, 289, 309 bottom, 323, 326, 354 bottom left, 361 right; Bildarchiv Foto Marburg 8, 13 right, 15 right, 25, 40, 132, 205 bottom, 208, 352 left, 374; Mariners' Museum, Newport News, Virginia 309 top; Mas, Barcelona 196–197, 286 top right, 313 top, 313 bottom; Francis Mayer 65 right; Metropolitan Museum of Art, New York 48, 55 top right, 57 bottom; Musées Royaux des Beaux Arts de Belgique, Brussels 288; Museo del Ejército, Madrid 376; Museo Navale, Madrid 308; National Gallery of Art, Washington 233 bottom, 279 right; National Maritime Museum, London 87 left, 245 bottom, 246 top, 248 bottom, 273 right, 286 bottom, 291, 293, 316 top left, 320; National Palace Museum, Taiwan 352 right, 360; National Portrait Gallery, London 137 bottom right, 170 right, 187 bottom left, 187 right, 191 bottom, 193, 277 left, 278 right, 283 left; Marquis of Northampton 281 bottom; Novosti Press Agency, London 209 top right, 211 left; Österreichische Nationalbibliothek, Vienna 106, 209 bottom, 264 right; Picturepoint, London 61, 63 bottom; Prado Museum, Madrid 272; Public Record Office, London 137 centre left, 152 left; Rijksmuseum, Amsterdam 268 left; H. Roger-Viollet, Paris 44 top, 346; Jean Roubier, Paris 24, 237 left; Royal Academy of Art, London 341 right, 344 left; Royal Commonwealth Society Library, London 345 bottom; Royal Library of Copenhagen 311 right, 316 bottom left; Scala, Florence 230 top, 232; Science Museum, London 324, 375; Staatliche Museen zu Berlin 229 bottom right, 257 bottom; Staatsgemäldesammlungen, Munich 229 top right, 265 top; Wim Swaan, New York 363; Thames & Hudson, London 353 left; Üniversitäts-Bibliothek, Basel 151 top right; Vatican Library, Rome 20 top; Victoria and Albert Museum, London 121 top, 156 bottom right, 165, 340 right, 364 right, 366 right, 369 top, 369 bottom; Wallace Collection, London 261 bottom; Walters Art Gallery, Baltimore 131 bottom; Weidenfeld & Nicolson, London 71 bottom, 72 left, 73 bottom, 74 left, 74 bottom right, 337.

Index

Figures in italics refer to illustrations

上総七兵衛景清
一寿斎芳員画
土肥四郎